SIX SIGMA FOR GREEN BELTS AND CHAMPIONS

SIX SIGMA FOR GREEN BELTS AND CHAMPIONS

FOUNDATIONS, DMAIC, TOOLS, CASES, AND CERTIFICATION

Howard S. Gitlow, Ph.D.

*Department of Management Science
School of Business Administration,
University of Miami*

David M. Levine, Ph.D.

*Department of Statistics and Computer Information Systems
Zicklin School of Business,
Bernard M. Baruch College (CUNY)*

An Imprint of PEARSON EDUCATION
Upper Saddle River, NJ • New York • London • San Francisco • Toronto • Sydney
Tokyo • Singapore • Hong Kong • Cape Town • Madrid
Paris • Milan • Munich • Amsterdam

www.ftpress.com

Library of Congress Cataloging-in-Publication Number: 2004105828

Editorial/production supervision: *Kerry Reardon*
Cover design director: *Sandra Schroeder*
Cover designer: *Nina Scuderi*
Manufacturing buyer: *Dan Uhrig*
Executive editor: *Jim Boyd*
Editorial assistant: *Richard Winkler*
Marketing manager: *Martin Litkowski*
Managing editor: *Gina Kanouse*
Senior project editor: *Sarah Kearns*

© 2005 Pearson Education, Inc.
Publishing as FT Press
Upper Saddle River, NJ 07458

FT Press offers excellent discounts on this book when ordered in quantity for bulk purchases or special sales. For more information, please contact: U.S. Corporate and Government Sales, 1-800-382-3419, corpsales@pearsontechgroup.com. For sales outside of the U.S., please contact: International Sales, 1-317-581-3793, international@pearsontechgroup.com

"Six Sigma" is a trademark of the Motorola Corporation.

Printed in the United States of America

Fourth printing

ISBN 0-13-117262-X

Pearson Education LTD.
Pearson Education Australia PTY, Limited
Pearson Education South Asia, Pte. Ltd.
Pearson Education Asia Ltd.
Pearson Education Canada, Ltd.
Pearson Educación de Mexico, S.A. de C.V.
Pearson Education–Japan
Pearson Malaysia S.D.N. B.H.D.

Dedicated to our families:

Ali Gitlow

Sharyn Levine Rosenberg

Daniel Rosenberg

Shelly Gitlow

Marilyn Levine

Beatrice Gitlow (in loving memory)

Abraham Gitlow

Lee Levine (in loving memory)

Reuben Levine (in loving memory)

CONTENTS

2   Six Sigma Roles, Responsibilities, and Terminology   25

PART II: SIX SIGMA MODEL   43

3   Macro Model of Six Sigma Management (Dashboards)   45

PART III: SIX SIGMA TOOLS
AND METHODS   227

14   Control Charts for Six Sigma Management   417

15   Additional Tools and Methods   463

PART IV: SIX SIGMA CASE STUDIES   487

16 PAPER ORGANIZERS INTERNATIONAL: A FICTITIOUS SIX
     SIGMA GREEN BELT CASE STUDY   489

17   A PAPER HELICOPTER CASE STUDY   539

PREFACE

UNIQUE ASPECTS OF THE BOOK

Six Sigma for Green Belts and Champions: Foundations, DMAIC, Tools, Cases, and Certification, has numerous features that make this book unique.

- **Contains coverage of the foundations of management necessary for professional Six Sigma management.** This includes how to deploy an organization's mission statement throughout an organization through a cascading and interlocking system of key objectives and key indicators, called a *dashboard.* It is illustrated with many practical and relevant examples.

- **Presents a thorough and detailed anatomy of the Six Sigma improvement model, called the *DMAIC model.*** DMAIC is an acronym for Define–Measure–Analyze–Improve-Control. The DMAIC model is a well-tested vehicle for guiding an improvement team through the maze of a complex process improvement project.

- **Integrates coverage of Six Sigma management with detailed coverage of those statistical methods that are appropriate for Green Belt and Champion certification.** Each statistical method is explained and applied to an example involving actual data in a quality improvement context. Coverage of statistics begins with an introduction and basic definitions, along with graphs and descriptive statistical measures; provides critical insights into probability and probability distributions; and covers the essential topics of confidence intervals, hypothesis testing, design of experiments, and control charts, all from an applied quality improvement perspective. Output from the Minitab statistical software package, widely used in Six Sigma management, is illustrated.

- **Includes chapter ending appendixes that provide step-by-step instructions for using Minitab Version 14 for the statistical methods covered in each chapter.**

- **Includes two case studies in Six Sigma management.** Each case study provides a detailed examination of all the steps involved in using the DMAIC Six Sigma approach. One case is from a service industry, and the other relates to manufacturing.
- **Includes information on Champion and Green Belt certification exams, along with sample test questions.**

ACKNOWLEDGMENTS AND THANKS

We are grateful to the organizations that allowed us to use their data in developing examples in this book. We would like to thank the American Society for Quality, the American Society for Testing and Materials, the American Statistical Association, and Marcel Dekker, Inc. We would also like to thank Tim Krehbiel, Miami University; Edward Popovich, Boca Raton Community Hospital; and Rip Stauffer, BlueFire Partners for their comments that have made this a better book. We would especially like to thank Jim Boyd, of Financial Times Prentice Hall. We would also like to thank Marti Jones for her copyediting, Lynne Michaud for her proofreading, and Kerry Reardon of Laurel Road Publishing Services for her work in the production of this book.

CONTACTING THE AUTHORS

We have gone to great lengths to make this book both pedagogically sound and error-free. If you have any suggestions or require clarification about any of the material, or if you find any errors, please contact us at HGITLOW@MIAMI.EDU or DAVIDMLEVINE@MSN.COM.

Howard S. Gitlow
David M. Levine

ABOUT THE AUTHORS

**Dr. Howard S. Gitlow** is Executive Director of the University of Miami Institute for the Study of Quality in Manufacturing and Service and a Professor of Management Science, University of Miami, Coral Gables, Florida. He was a Visiting Professor at the Science University of Tokyo in 1990 where he studied Quality Management with Dr. Noriaki Kano. He received his Ph.D. in Statistics (1974), M.B.A. (1972), and B.S. in Statistics (1969) from New York University. His areas of specialization are Six Sigma Management, Dr. Deming's theory of management, Japanese Total Quality Control, and statistical quality control.

Dr. Gitlow is a Six Sigma Master Black Belt, a senior member of the American Society for Quality Control and a member of the American Statistical Association. He has consulted on quality, productivity, and related matters with many organizations, including several Fortune 500 companies.

Dr. Gitlow has co-authored several books. These include: *Quality Management: Tools and Methods for Improvement*, Richard D. Irwin Publishers (2005), third edition; *Quality Management Systems*, CRC Press (2000), *Total Quality Management in Action,* Prentice-Hall, (1994); *The Deming Guide to Quality and Competitive Position,* Prentice-Hall, (1987), fifteenth printing; *Planning for Quality, Productivity,* and *Competitive Position,* Dow Jones-Irwin Publishers (1990); and *Stat City: Understanding Statistics Through Realistic Applications,* Richard D. Irwin Publishers (1987), second edition. He has published over 45 academic articles in the areas of quality, statistics, management, and marketing.

While at the University of Miami, Dr. Gitlow has received awards for Outstanding Teaching, Outstanding Writing, and Outstanding Published Research Articles.

 **David M. Levine** is Professor Emeritus of Statistics and Computer Information Systems at Bernard M. Baruch College (City University of New York). He received B.B.A. and M.B.A. degrees in Statistics from City College of New York and a Ph.D. degree from New York University in Industrial Engineering and Operations Research. He is nationally recognized as a leading innovator in business statistics education and is the co-author of such best-selling statistics textbooks as *Statistics for Managers Using Microsoft Excel, Basic Business Statistics: Concepts and Applications, Business Statistics: A First Course,* and *Applied Statistics for Engineers and Scientists using Microsoft Excel and Minitab,* He has published articles in various journals including *Psychometrika, The American Statistician, Communications in Statistics, Multivariate Behavioral Research, Journal of Systems Management, Quality Progress,* and *The American Anthropologist.*

Six Sigma Basics

OVERVIEW OF SIX SIGMA MANAGEMENT

CHAPTER OUTLINE

LEARNING OBJECTIVES

After reading this chapter, you will be able to:

- Understand that Six Sigma is an excellent style of management
- Appreciate the history of Six Sigma management
- Understand the key ingredient for success with Six Sigma management
- Appreciate the benefits of Six Sigma management
- Define a process and understand common and special causes of variation
- Define quality
- Define the Voice of the Customer (VoC)
- Define the Voice of the Process (VoP)
- Define Six Sigma management
- Understand what is new about Six Sigma management

INTRODUCTION

This chapter is all about getting you comfortable with Six Sigma management. We accomplish this objective by: (1) providing you with strong anecdotal evidence that Six Sigma is a very successful style of management, (2) explaining how Six Sigma must be emphatically led from the top of the organization, and finally, (3) introducing you to the definitions and jargon unique to Six Sigma management. This chapter could serve as a brief introduction to Six Sigma management for any stakeholder of your organization.

1.1 SUCCESSFUL APPLICATIONS OF SIX SIGMA MANAGEMENT

Manufacturing organizations have experienced great success with Six Sigma management. A partial list of the manufacturing organizations using Six Sigma management includes:

- Asea-Brown-Boveri
- AT&T
- Bombardier
- Eli Lilly
- Foxboro
- General Electric
- Honeywell/Allied Signal
- IBM-UK
- Lockheed Martin
- Motorola
- Raytheon
- Seagate
- Texas Instruments

Additionally, service organizations have had excellent results with Six Sigma management. A partial list of service organizations using Six Sigma management includes:

- Allstate Insurance
- Amazon.com

- American Express
- Bank of America
- Bankers Life Insurance
- Capital One Services
- J. P. Morgan Chase
- Merill Lynch
- Microsoft
- United Health Group

Jack Welch, Chairman emeritus and CEO of General Electric, was so committed to and impressed with Six Sigma that he stated:

Six Sigma GE Quality 2000 will be the biggest, the most personally rewarding, and, in the end, the most profitable undertaking in our history.

... we plunged into Six Sigma with a company-consuming vengeance just over three years ago. We have invested more than a billion dollars in the effort and the financial returns have now entered the exponential phase. GE's letter to shareowners (February 12, 1999)

1.2 TIMELINE FOR SIX SIGMA MANAGEMENT[*]

1978   At a Motorola officer's meeting, Art Sundry, Motorola VP, stood up and stated that Motorola's quality "stunk." Motorola's key products included car radios and TVs. Both of these products were later abandoned or sold by Motorola to other corporations. In fact, the TV manufacturing plant became a Quasar TV production facility by the late 1970s. Moreover, the TVs produced were of higher quality than those produced when Motorola ran the facility, even though essentially the same workers were producing the TVs. Apparently, it was management that made a big difference.

1981   Motorola's chairman, Bob Galvin, decided after meeting with customers and studying Motorola's quality effort that the company would now be focused on reducing manufacturing defects by tenfold within a 5-year period. Also, reducing total cycle time was a key component of the effort.

---

[*]The authors would like to thank Dr. Edward Popovich of Boca Raton Community Hospital for contributing the timeline of Six Sigma management. The authors take complete responsibility for the accuracy of this section.

1987	Motorola met its goal of a tenfold reduction in defects. Unfortunately, some major competitors had improved faster in that time period. The goal of tenfold improvement was a good goal but 5 years was not fast enough.
1987	Motorola top management raised the "bar" to a tenfold improvement every 2 years, 100-fold every 4 years, and a target of 3.4 defects per million was set for 5 years. The name *Six Sigma* was given to this target and Sigma became a metric that was equated to defects per million opportunities (DPMO). In addition, the total cycle time reduction goal of 50% was mandated as a synergistic part of Six Sigma.
Late 1980s	Motorola top management realized that reducing defects and cycle time in their internal processes would reduce "concept to market cycle time," thus reducing cost and reaction time to changing markets and technology, and would reduce failures in the field, resulting in increased customer satisfaction and decreased warranty costs.
1988	Motorola is awarded the Malcolm Baldrige National Quality Award in its inaugural year. One of the duties of an award recipient is to share its quality story and approach with others throughout the United States.
1989–93	Texas Instruments, ABB, and Kodak join Motorola to support the Six Sigma Institute.
Mid-1990s	General Electric and Allied Signal popularized the Six Sigma approach by attributing their increase in market capitalization to the results attained by their drive for Six Sigma quality.

1.3 KEY INGREDIENTS FOR SUCCESS WITH SIX SIGMA MANAGEMENT

The key ingredient for a successful Six Sigma management process is the commitment (not only support) of top management. Executives must have a burning desire to transform their organizations into Six Sigma enterprises. This means total commitment from the top to the bottom of the organization. An executive's commitment is shown by how she or he allocates time and resources and by the questions she or he asks of others. Many Six Sigma executives spend at least 25% of their time on Six Sigma matters and allocate major organizational resources to promote the Six Sigma style of management. An executive who asks: "What was yesterday's production volume?" is saying, "I care about quantity, not quality." An executive who asks: "What is happening with the Production Department's Six Sigma projects?" is saying, "I care about quality *and* quantity."

1.4 BENEFITS OF SIX SIGMA MANAGEMENT

There are two types of benefits from Six Sigma management—benefits to the organization and benefits to stakeholders. Benefits to an organization are gained through the continuous reduction of variation and centering of processes on their nominal levels. The benefits are:

- Improved process flows
- Reduced total defects
- Improved communication (provides a common language)
- Reduced cycle times
- Enhanced knowledge (and enhanced ability to manage that knowledge)
- Higher levels of customer and employee satisfaction
- Increased productivity
- Decreased work in progress (WIP)
- Decreased inventory
- Improved capacity and output
- Increased quality and reliability
- Decreased unit costs
- Increased price flexibility
- Decreased time to market
- Faster delivery time
- Conversion of improvements into hard currency

Benefits to stakeholders are a by-product of the organizational benefits. The benefits to stakeholders include:

- Stockholders receive more profit due to decreased costs and increased revenues.
- Customers are delighted with products and services.
- Employees experience higher morale and more satisfaction from joy in work.
- Suppliers enjoy a secure source of business.

1.5 PROCESS BASICS (VOICE OF THE PROCESS)

Definition of a Process

A **process** is a collection of interacting components that transform inputs into outputs toward a common aim, called a *mission statement*. It is the job of management to optimize the entire process toward its aim. This may require the suboptimization of selected components of the

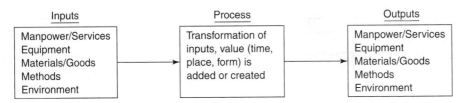

FIGURE 1.1 Basic Process

process. For example, a particular department in an organization may have to give up resources in the short run to another department to maximize profit for the overall organization.

The transformation, as shown in Figure 1.1, involves the addition or creation of value in one of three aspects: time, place, or form. An output has "time value" if it is available when needed by a user. For example, you have food when you are hungry, or material inputs are ready on schedule. An output has "place value" if it is available where needed by a user. For example, gas is in your tank (not in an oil field), or wood chips are in a paper mill (not in a truck). An output has "form value" if it is available in the form needed by a user. For example, bread is sliced so it can fit in a toaster, or paper has three holes so it can be placed in a binder.

Processes exist in all facets of organizations, and our understanding of them is crucial. Many people mistakenly think only of production processes. However, administration, sales, service, human resources, training, maintenance, paper flows, interdepartmental communication, and vendor relations are all processes. Importantly, relationships between people are processes. Most processes can be studied, documented, defined, improved, and innovated.

An example of a generic assembly process is shown in Figure 1.2. The inputs (component parts, machines, and operators) are transformed in the process to make the outputs (assembled product).

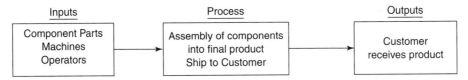

FIGURE 1.2 Production Process

An organization is a multiplicity of micro subprocesses, all synergistically building to the macro process of that firm. All processes have customers and suppliers; these customers and suppliers can be internal or external to the organization. A customer can be an end user or the next operation downstream. The customer does not even have to be a human; it could be a machine. A supplier could be another firm supplying subassemblies or services, or the prior operation upstream.

Variation in a Process

The outputs from all processes and their component parts may be measured; the measurements invariably vary over time and create a distribution of measurements. The distribution of measurements of the outputs from a process over time is called the **Voice of the Process (VoP)**. Consider a process such as getting ready for work or class in the morning. Some days you are busier than usual, and on other days you have less to do than usual. Your process varies from day to day to some degree. This is **common variation**. However, if a construction project begins on the highway you take to work or school, you might drastically alter your morning routine. This would be **special variation** because it would have been caused by a change external to your driving to work or school process. If the traffic patterns had remained as they were, your process would have continued on its former path of common variation.

Common causes of variation are due to the process itself. **Process capability** is determined by inherent common causes of variation, such as hiring, training, or supervisory practices, inadequate lighting, stress, management style, policies and procedures, or design of products or services. Employees cannot control a common cause of variation and should not be held accountable or penalized for its outcomes. Managers must realize that unless a change is made in the process (which only they can make), the process's capability will remain the same. Special causes of variation are due to events external to the usual functioning of the process. New raw materials, a drunken employee, or a new operator can be examples of special causes of variation. Identifying the occurrence of special and common causes of variation is discussed extensively in Chapter 14.

Because unit-to-unit variation decreases the customer's ability to rely on the dependability and uniformity of the outputs of a process, managers must understand how to identify and reduce variation. Employees use statistical methods so that common and special causes of variation can be differentiated, special variation can be resolved, and common variation can be removed by management action, resulting in improvement and/or innovation of the outputs of a process.

The following fictionalized case history demonstrates the need for management to understand the difference between common and special causes of variation to take appropriate action. In this case history, an employee comes to work intoxicated. His behavior causes productivity, safety, and morale problems. You, as the supervisor, speak to the employee privately, try to resolve the situation, and send the employee home with pay in a taxi. After a second instance of intoxication, you speak to the employee privately, try to resolve the problem again, and send the employee home without pay in a taxi. A third instance causes you to refer the employee to an employee assistance program. A fourth offense results in your terminating the employee. As a good manager, you document the employee's history to create a paper trail in case of legal action. All the above is necessary and is considered to be good management practice.

It is interesting to note that the thought process behind the above managerial actions is that the employee is the problem. In other words, the employee's behavior is viewed as the special cause of variation from the desired sober state. However, this is true only if there is a statistically significant difference between the employee in question and all other employees. If the employee's behavior is in fact part of a process that allows such behavior to exist, then the problem is not a special cause but rather a common cause and requires a different solution. In the latter case, the employee must be dealt with as before, but additionally, organizational policies and procedures (processes) must be changed to prevent future incidents of intoxication. This new view requires a shift in thought. With the new thought process, if existing organizational policies and procedures allow employees with drinking problems to be present in the workplace, an intoxicated employee must be dealt with according to the original solution, and policies and procedures must be improved to prevent future incidents of such behavior on the job.

Feedback Loops

An important aspect of any process is a **feedback loop**. A feedback loop relates information about outputs from any stage or stages back to another stage or stages to make an analysis of the process. Figure 1.3 depicts the feedback loop in relation to a basic process.

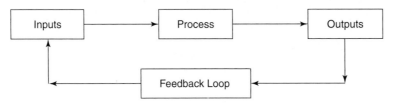

FIGURE 1.3 Feedback Loop

The tools and methods discussed in this book provide vehicles for relating information about outputs to other stage(s) in the process. Decision making about processes is aided by the transmission of this information. A major purpose of Six Sigma management is to provide the information (flowing through a feedback loop) needed to take action with respect to a process.

There are three feedback loop situations: no feedback loop, special cause only feedback loop, and special and common cause feedback loop. A process that does not have a feedback loop is probably doomed to deterioration and decay, due to the inability of its stakeholders to rejuvenate and improve it based on data from its outputs. An example of a process without a feedback loop is a relationship between two people (manager and subordinate, husband and wife, or buyer and seller) that contains no vehicle (feedback loop) to discuss issues and problems with the intention of establishing a better relationship in the future. A process in which all feedback information is treated as a special cause will exhibit enormous variation in its output. An example of a process with a special cause-only feedback loop can again be seen in a relationship between two people, but in this case, the relationship deteriorates through a cycle of successive overreactions to problems that are perceived as special by both members of the relationship. In fact, the problems are probably repetitive in nature, due to the structure of the relationship itself and common causes of variation. Finally, a process in which feedback information is separated into common and special causes, special causes are resolved, and common cause are removed will exhibit continuous improvement of its output. For example, the relationship problems between a superior and a subordinate can be classified as due to either special or common causes; statistical methods are used to resolve special causes and to remove common causes, thereby improving the relationship in the future.

Consider the following example. Paul is a 40-year-old midlevel manager who is unhappy because he wants his boss to give him a promotion. He thinks about his relationship with his boss and wonders what went wrong. He determines that over a period of 10 years, he has had about 40 disagreements with his boss, one per quarter.

Paul thinks about what caused each disagreement. Initially, he thought each disagreement had its own special reason. After studying the pattern of the number of disagreements per year,

Paul discovers that it was a stable and predictable process of common causes of variation. Subsequently, he writes down the reason for as many of the disagreements as he can remember (about 30). However, after thinking about his relationship with his boss from the perspective of common causes, he realizes his disagreements with his boss were not unique events (special causes); rather, they were a repetitive process, and the reasons for the disagreements can be classified into common cause categories. He is surprised to see that the 30 reasons collapse down to four basic reasons (poor communication of a work issue, a process failure causing work not to be completed on schedule, unexcused absence, and pay-related issues), with one reason—poor communication of a work issue—accounting for 75% of all disagreements. Armed with this insight, he schedules a discussion with his boss to find a solution to their communication problems. His boss explains that he hates the e-mails that Paul is always sending him and wishes he would just talk to him and say what is on his mind. They resolve their problem, their relationship is greatly improved, and eventually, Paul receives his promotion.

1.6 DEFINITION OF QUALITY (VOICE OF THE CUSTOMER)

Goalpost View of Quality

Quality is a concept whose definition has changed over time. In the past, *quality* meant "conformance to valid customer requirements." That is, as long as an output fell within acceptable limits, called **specification limits**, around a desired value, called the **nominal value** (denoted by *m*), or target value, it was deemed conforming, good, or acceptable. We refer to this as the "goalpost" definition of quality. The nominal value and specification limits are set based on the perceived needs and wants of customers. Specification limits are called the **Voice of the Customer (VoC)**. Figure 1.4 shows the goalpost view of losses arising from deviations from the

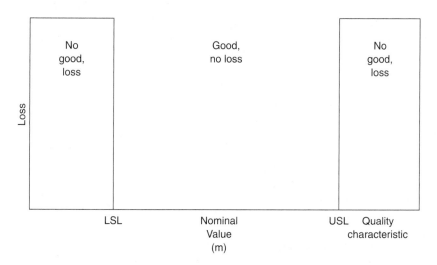

FIGURE 1.4 Goalpost View of Losses Arising from Deviations from Nominal

nominal value. That is, losses are minimum until the **lower specification limit (LSL)** or **upper specification limit (USL)** is reached. Then suddenly, they increase and remain constant, regardless of the magnitude of the deviation from the nominal value.

An individual unit of product or service is considered to conform to a specification if it is at or inside the boundary (USL or LSL) or boundaries (USL and LSL).

Individual unit specifications are made up of a nominal value and an acceptable tolerance from nominal. The nominal value is the desired value for process performance mandated by the customer's needs and/or wants. The tolerance is an allowable departure from a nominal value established by designers that is deemed nonharmful to the desired functioning of the product or service. Specification limits are the boundaries created by adding and/or subtracting tolerances from a nominal value:

USL = upper specification limit = nominal + tolerance and

LSL = lower specification limit = nominal − tolerance.

A service example of the goalpost view of quality and specification limits can be seen in a monthly accounting report that must be completed in 7 days (nominal) but no earlier than 4 days (LSL—not all the necessary data will be available) and no later than 10 days (USL—the due date for the report in the board meeting). Therefore, the "Voice of the Customer" is that the report must be completed ideally in 7 days but no sooner than 4 days and no later than 10 days.

A manufacturing example of the goalpost view of quality and specification limits is to produce stainless steel ball bearings 25 mm in diameter (the nominal value). A tolerance of 5 mm above or below 25 mm is acceptable to purchasers. Thus, if a ball bearing diameter measures between 20 mm and 30 mm (inclusive), it is deemed conforming to specifications. It does not matter whether the diameter of a ball bearing is 21 mm or 29 mm; they are both conforming units. If a ball bearing diameter measures less than 20 mm or more than 30 mm, it is deemed not conforming to specifications and is scrapped at a cost of $1.00 per ball bearing. Therefore, the "Voice of the Customer" states that the diameters of the ball bearings must be between 20 mm and 30 mm, inclusive, with an ideal diameter of 25 mm.

Continuous Improvement View of Quality

A more modern definition of *quality* states that: "**Quality** is a predictable degree of uniformity and dependability, at low cost and suited to the market." [see Reference 1, p. 229.] Figure 1.5 shows a more realistic loss curve in which losses begin to accrue as soon as a quality characteristic of a product or service deviates from the nominal value. As with the goalpost view of quality, once the specification limits are reached, the loss suddenly becomes positive and constant, regardless of the deviation from the nominal value beyond the specification limits.

The continuous improvement view of quality was developed by Genichi Taguchi [see Reference 7, pp. 7–11.] The **Taguchi Loss Function**, called the *Loss curve* in Figure 1.5, expresses the loss of deviating from nominal within specifications: the left hand vertical axis

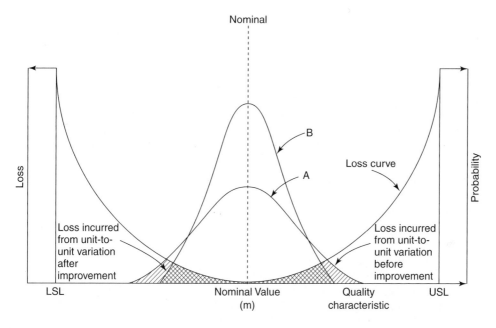

FIGURE 1.5 Continuous Improvement View of Losses of Deviations from Nominal

is "loss," and the horizontal axis is the measure, y, of a quality characteristic. The loss associated with deviating $(y - m)$ units from the nominal value m, is:

$$L(y) = k(y - m)^2 = \text{Taguchi Loss Function}$$

where

y = the value of the quality characteristic for a particular item of product or service,

m = the nominal value for the quality characteristic, and

k = a constant, A/d^2

A = the loss (cost) of exceeding specification limits (e.g., the cost to scrap a unit of output), and

d = the allowable tolerance from the nominal value that is used to determine specification limits.

Under this Taguchi Loss Function, or the Loss curve in Figure 1.5, the continuous reduction of unit-to-unit variation around the nominal value is the most economical course of action, absent capital investment (more on this later). In Figure 1.5, the right-hand vertical axis is probability, and the horizontal axis is the measure, *y*, of a quality characteristic. The distribution of output from a process before improvement is shown in curve A, and the distribution of output after improvement is shown in curve B. The losses incurred from unit-to-unit variation before process improvement (the lined area under the loss curve for distribution A) is greater than the losses incurred from unit-to-unit variation after process improvement (the hatched area under the loss curve for distribution B). This definition of quality promotes continual reduction of unit-to-unit variation (uniformity) of output around the nominal value, absent capital investment. If capital investment is required, an analysis must be conducted to determine whether the benefit of the reduction in variation in the VoP justifies the cost. The capital investment for a process improvement should not exceed the single lined area under the Taguchi Loss Function in curve A but not under curve B, in Figure 1.5. Note that this modern definition of quality implies that specifications should be surpassed, rather than merely met, because there is a loss associated with products that deviate from the nominal value, even when they conform to specifications.

To illustrate the continuous definition of quality, return to the example of the production of stainless steel ball bearings. Every millimeter higher or lower than 25 mm causes a loss that can be expressed by the following Taguchi Loss Function:

$$L(y) = k(y - m)^2 = (A/d^2)(y - m)^2 = (\$1.00/[5^2])(y - 25 \text{ mm})^2$$
$$= (0.04)(y - 25 \text{ mm})^2$$
$$if \ 20 \leq y \leq 30$$
$$L(y) = \$1.00 \qquad if \ y < 20 \ or \ y > 30$$

Table 1.1 shows the values of L(y) for the quality characteristic (diameter of ball bearings).

Under the loss curve shown in Table 1.1, it is always economical to continuously reduce the unit-to-unit variation in the diameter of stainless steel ball bearings, absent capital investment. This will minimize losses in production of stainless steel ball bearings.

1.7 DEFINITIONS OF SIX SIGMA MANAGEMENT (RELATIONSHIP BETWEEN VoC AND VoP)

Nontechnical Definitions of Six Sigma

Six Sigma management is the relentless and rigorous pursuit of the reduction of variation in all critical processes to achieve continuous and breakthrough improvements that impact the bottom line and/or top line of the organization and increase customer satisfaction.[*] Another common definition of Six Sigma management is that it is an organizational initiative designed to

---

[*] Private conversation with Dr. Edward Popovich (Boca Raton Community Hospital, Boca Raton, FL) in 1999.

TABLE 1.1 Loss Arising from Deviations in Diameters of Ball Bearings

Diameter of ball bearing (y)	Value of Taguchi Loss Function (L[y])
18	1.00
19	1.00
20	1.00
21	0.64
22	0.36
23	0.16
24	0.04
25	0.00
26	0.04
27	0.16
28	0.36
29	0.64
30	1.00
31	1.00
32	1.00

create manufacturing, service, and administrative processes that produce a high rate of sustained improvement in both defect reduction and cycle time (e.g., when Motorola began its effort, the rate chosen was a tenfold reduction in defects in 2 years, along with a 50% reduction in cycle). For example, a bank takes 60 days on average to process a loan with a 10% rework rate in 2000. In a Six Sigma organization, the bank should take no longer than 30 days on average to process a loan with a 1% error rate in 2002 and no more than 15 days on average to process a loan with a 0.10% error rate by 2004. Clearly, this requires a dramatically improved/innovated loan process.

Technical Definition of Six Sigma Management

The Normal Distribution. The term *Six Sigma* is derived from the normal distribution used in statistics. Many observable phenomena can be graphically represented as a bell-shaped curve or a normal distribution (see Section 10.6) as illustrated in Figure 1.6.

When measuring any process, it can be shown that its outputs (services or products) vary in size, shape, look, feel, or any other measurable characteristic. The typical value of the output of a process is measured by a statistic called the *mean* or *average*. The variability of the output of a process is measured by a statistic called the *standard deviation*. In a normal distribution (see Section 10.6), the interval created by the mean plus or minus 2 standard deviations contains 95.44% of the data points, or 45,600 data points per million (sometimes called *parts per million*, denoted ppm) are outside of the area created by the mean plus or minus 2 standard deviations [$(1.00 - 0.9544 = 0.0456) \times 1,000,000 = 45,600$]. In a normal distribution, the interval

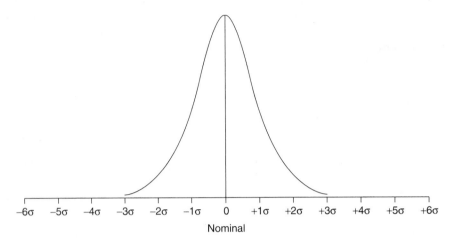

$$-6\sigma \quad -5\sigma \quad -4\sigma \quad -3\sigma \quad -2\sigma \quad -1\sigma \quad 0 \quad +1\sigma \quad +2\sigma \quad +3\sigma \quad +4\sigma \quad +5\sigma \quad +6\sigma$$

Nominal

FIGURE 1.6 Normal Distribution with Mean ($\mu = 0$) and Standard Deviation ($\sigma = 1$)

created by the mean plus or minus 3 standard deviations contains 99.73% of the data, or 2,700 ppm are outside of the area created by the mean plus or minus 3 standard deviations [$(1.00 - 0.9973 = 0.0027) \times 1,000,000 = 2,700$]. In a normal distribution, the interval created by the mean plus or minus 6 standard deviations contains 99.9999998% of the data, or 2 data points per billion data points (ppb) outside of the area created by the mean plus or minus 6 standard deviations.

Relationship Between VoP and VoC. Six Sigma promotes the idea that the distribution of output for a stable normally distributed process (Voice of the Process) should be designed to take up no more than half of the tolerance allowed by the specification limits (Voice of the Customer). Although processes may be designed to be at their best, it is assumed that over time, the processes may increase in variation. This increase in variation may be due to small variation with process inputs, the way the process is monitored, changing conditions, etc. The increase in process variation is often assumed for sake of descriptive simplicity to be similar to temporary shifts in the underlying process mean. The increase in process variation has been shown in practice to be equivalent to an average shift of 1.5 standard deviations in the mean of the originally designed and monitored process. If a process is originally designed to be twice as good as a customer demands (i.e., the specifications representing the customer requirements are 6 standard deviations from the process target), then even with a shift, the customer demands are likely to be met. In fact, even if the process shifted off target by 1.5 standard deviations, there are 4.5 standard deviations between the process mean ($\mu + 1.5\sigma$) and closest specification ($\mu + 6.0\sigma$), which results in at worst 3.4 ppm at the time the process has shifted or the variation has increased to have similar impact as a 1.5 standard deviation shift. In the 1980s, Motorola demonstrated that a 1.5 standard deviation shift was in practice what was observed as the equivalent increase in process variation for many processes that were benchmarked. Figure 1.7 shows the "Voice of the

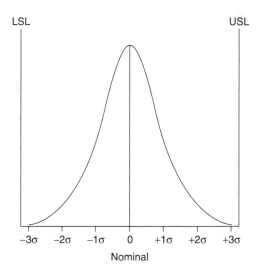

FIGURE 1.7 Three Sigma Process with 0.0 Shift in the Mean

Process" for an accounting function with an average of 7 days, a standard deviation of 1 day, and a stable normal distribution. It also shows a nominal value of 7 days, a lower specification limit of 4 days, and an upper specification limit of 10 days. The accounting function is referred to as a Three Sigma process because the process mean plus or minus 3 standard deviations is equal to the specification limits; in other terms, USL $= \mu + 3\sigma$ and LSL $= \mu - 3\sigma$. This scenario will yield 1,350 defects per million opportunities at either specification limit or one early or late monthly report in 61.73 years [(1/0.00135)/12].

Figure 1.8 shows the same scenario as in Figure 1.7, but the process mean shifts by 1.5 standard deviations (the process average is shifted down or up by 1.5 standard deviations [or 1.5 days] from 7.0 days to 5.5 days or 8.5 days) over time. This is not an uncommon phenomenon. The 1.5 standard deviation shift in the mean results in 66,807 defects per million opportunities at the nearest specification limit or one early or late monthly report in 1.25 years ([1/0.066807]/12).

Figure 1.9 shows the same scenario as Figure 1.7 except the VoP takes up only half the distance between the specification limits. The process mean remains the same as in Figure 1.7, but the process standard deviation has been reduced to a half-day through application of process improvement. In this case, the resulting output will exhibit 1 defect per billion opportunities at either specification limit or one early or late monthly report in 83,333,333 years ([1/0.000000001]/12).

Figure 1.10 shows the same scenario as Figure 1.9, but the process average shifts by 1.5 standard deviations (the process average is shifted down or up by 1.5 standard deviations [or 0.75 days = 1.5 × 0.5 days] from 7.0 days to 6.25 days or 7.75 days) over time. The 1.5 standard deviation shift in the mean results in 3.4 defects per million at the nearest specification limit or one early or late monthly report in 24,510 years [(1/.0000034/12]. This is the definition of Six Sigma level of quality.

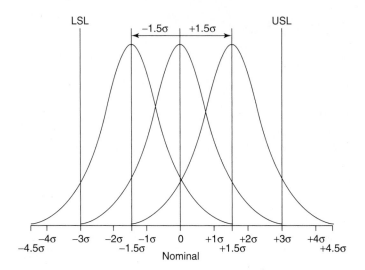

FIGURE 1.8 Three Sigma Process with a 1.5 Sigma Shift in the Mean

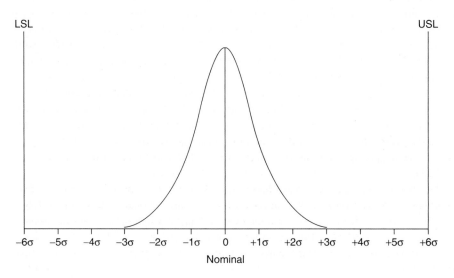

FIGURE 1.9 Six Sigma Process with a 0.0 Shift in the Mean

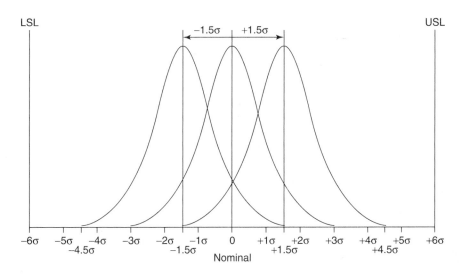

FIGURE 1.10 Six Sigma Process with 1.5 Sigma Shift in the Mean

Another Look at the 1.5 Sigma Shift in the Mean.[*] The engineer responsible for creating the concept of Six Sigma at Motorola was Bill Smith. Bill Smith indicated that product failures in the field were shown to be statistically related to the number of product reworks and defect rates observed in production. Therefore, the thought was that the more "defect and rework free" a product was during production, the more likely there would be fewer field failures and customer complaints. Additionally, Motorola had a very strong emphasis on total cycle time reduction. The more steps a business process takes to complete its cycle, the more chance there is for changes and unforeseen events, and the more opportunity for defects. Therefore, reducing cycle time is best accomplished by streamlining the process, removing non–value-added effort, and as a result, reducing the opportunities for mistakes (defects). What a concept! Reducing cycle time by simplifying a process will result in fewer defects, lower remediation/warranty/service costs, and ultimately, increased customer satisfaction with the results.

Some proof of this was gained in the period from 1981 to 1986 when Bob Galvin (CEO) set a goal of tenfold improvement in defect rates over those 5 years. As stated earlier in the chapter, during those 5 years, positive results were demonstrated in field failures and warranty costs. However, some of Motorola's key competitors improved at a faster rate. In 1987, Motorola indicated it would increase the rate of improvement to tenfold improvement every 2 years, rather than 5 years. What was the target? The target was called *Six Sigma* quality (which was defined to be 3.4 ppm) by 1992.

---

[*]The authors would like to thank Dr. Edward Popovich of Boca Raton Community Hospital (Boca Raton, FL) for contributing this explanation of the 1.5 Sigma shift in the mean. The authors take complete responsibility for the accuracy of this section.

Of course, it was asked whether there was a trade-off between reducing defect rates and implementation cost. Bill Smith and others were not advocating increasing costs by increasing inspection, but rather that engineers design products and production processes so that there would be little chance for mistakes/defects during production and customer usage. The focus was on the upstream variables (Xs) that are the indicators of future performance and process outputs (Ys). The Y variables were the observed and measured downstream defect rates, rework rates, and field failures.

Motorola's strict focus on the rate of improvement challenged engineering, supply management, and production to develop materials, production equipment, and products that were more robust to variation and, as a result, less sensitive to processing variation. Hence, the focus was on understanding the upstream X variables.

What is interesting about all that is often the focus of statistical process control (SPC) and many other tools associated with organizations preaching total quality management (TQM) is that the initial focus was often limited to the use of tools to monitor Y variables or average/target values of processing variables. The Six Sigma effort did not really change the tools but instead focused the tools on their usage upstream on X variables (in particular on understanding the relationship of the variation in the X variables on the variation of the Y variables) and on using the tools in such a sequence as to uncover the relationships and be able to improve and control the results.

Studies did show that Bill Smith's insights were valid. The parts per million (ppm) and defects per unit (DPU) measures calculated in the production facilities did predict field performance, customer complaints, and warranty costs. Therefore, ppm and DPU became metrics of emphasis at Motorola.

Around the same time that these studies were done, Motorola also gathered empirical evidence that even when ppm and DPU were in statistical control (these are Y variables), the process itself could have uncontrolled X variables. Also, statistical process control as practiced in many operations was more of a monitoring method on the Y variables, and the only "out-of-control" indicator that was tracked was how often observations would be beyond the control limits. Frequently, runs tests[*] were not used as indicators of out-of-control variation within the control limits. Empirical evidence indicated that the process could shift within the Three Sigma control limits as much as 2 standard deviations and stay there for some run of points before a point outside 3 standard deviations was observed. In fact, if a process with stable variation shifts 1.5 standard deviations, there is an average run of 16 points that would be observed before one was beyond the 3 standard deviation control limits. Keep this in mind because it will be used in the following paragraphs.

In addition to ppm and DPU measures, Motorola was concerned about variables that could be measured on a continuous scale (i.e., measurement data rather than classification or count attribute data—see Section 9.4), especially the upstream X variables. A focus on means and

---

[*]A run is a consecutive series of similar items that are preceded or followed by items of a different type. For example, in tossing a coin sixteen times, the sequence, HHHHHHHHHTTTTTTTT contains two runs, a run of eight heads followed by a run of eight tails. A runs test is a statistical test that determines whether a particular sequence has a random pattern.

spreads (i.e., standard deviations) was needed to control measurement data. If the VoP is equal to the VoC, the process's mean output plus or minus 3 standard deviations equals the specification limits, about 0.27% of the process output is "defective," given a normal distribution. If SPC were utilized to track that variable and the mean shifted halfway to the control limits (i.e., this assumes an individual, moving-range type of SPC chart, discussed in Chapter 14), there could be an average run of 16 observations before a "traditional" out-of-control condition would be noted. That implies that there would be a run of 16 observations, although the VoP is half the VoC during that period of time! Another way of saying this is there could be an increase in ppm from 2,700 to 66,807 during the period of time the process had shifted, but no out-of-control condition was observed. If various runs tests were conducted, the shift in the mean would be detected, but in practice, production personnel rarely shut down a process for failure of a runs test if no points were outside the control limits.

So why does Six Sigma often reference a 1.5 standard deviation shift in the mean of a process? Studies of various production lines at Motorola showed that even in a state of control, where the only out of control condition to be checked was observations outside of 3 standard deviation control limits, there often would be uncontrolled shifts of between 1 and 2 standard deviations. For example, for some manual assembly processes, the shift was noted to average between 1.2 and 1.8 standard deviations at the time an out-of-control observation was recorded. Of course, for automated processes, this degree of shift is frequently not allowed.

A statistical purist would argue that the genesis of the sigma metric is flawed because it is based on a shift factor. The engineers viewed the metric as a worst case ppm for a process because it was assumed that any shift factor significantly larger than 1.5 would be caught by the common usage of SPC (a point beyond a Three Sigma control limit). If there is a shift less than 1.5 sigma, that is all to the good, because the ppm is less.

From a practical standpoint, Six Sigma seems to be an effective form of management. Moreover, the argument against the 1.5 sigma shift in the mean seems similar to claiming that a yard is not really 3 feet. Some say a yard was based on the distance from the tip of the nose to the tip of the middle finger on an outstretched arm for an average male. What is an "average" male? Is that similar to knowing an "average" shift? It turns out that eventually everyone accepted the definition that a yard is equal to 3 feet, and few remember the original derivation. At Motorola, the story is similar in that only a few folks remember the original reason for definition of the sigma levels, and it is accepted that the ppm levels can be equated with sigma levels.

Interestingly, many of those who continue to argue about the derivation of sigma levels are those who have learned about Six Sigma in the last 4 years. It seems that they are trying to understand the "legend" of Six Sigma, rather than seeing the up side and benefit. We can continue to argue about this, but it seems that practitioners are getting on with improving their organizations, regardless of any technical flaws in the derivations of the methods.

Does Six Sigma Matter? The difference between a Three Sigma process (66,807 defects per million opportunities) and a Six Sigma process (3.4 defects per million opportunities) can be seen in a service with 20 component steps. If each of the 20 component steps has a quality level of 66,807 defects per million opportunities, assuming each step does not allow rework, then the likelihood of a defect at each step is 0.066807 (66,807/1,000,000). By subtraction, the likelihood of a defect-free step is 0.933193 ($1.0 - 0.066807$). Consequently, the likelihood of delivering a defect-free final service is 25.08%. This is computed by multiplying 0.933193 by itself 20 times ($[1.0 - 0.066807]^{20} = 0.2508 = 25.08\%$). However, if each of the 20 component parts has a quality level of 3.4 DPMO (0.0000034), the likelihood of delivering a defect-free final service is 99.99932% ($[1.0 - 0.0000034]^{20} = 0.99999966^{20} = 0.9999932 = 99.99932\%$). A Three Sigma process generates 25.08% defect-free services, whereas a Six Sigma process generates 99.99932% defect-free services. The difference between the Three Sigma process and the Six Sigma process is dramatic enough to believe certainly that Six Sigma level of performance matters, especially with more complex processes having a greater number of steps or activities

1.8 WHAT IS NEW ABOUT SIX SIGMA MANAGEMENT?

Many people think that Six Sigma management is an "old wine in a new bottle." This notion is both false and true. It is false for several reasons:

- It is false because Six Sigma projects are far more structured and formatted than projects in most previous quality management processes.

- It is false because Six Sigma management provides metrics for discussing the quality of processes that can transcend ownership of the processes (i.e., finance, human resources, engineering, and service processes can be compared). It creates "apples-to-apples" metrics for understanding process improvements. Other quality management approaches do not have such metrics.

- It is false because Six Sigma is very focused on impacting the bottom line or top line of an organization, and it has a specific method for accomplishing this objective. Most other quality management approaches do not have such a clear financial focus. The cost of poor quality and other similar concepts have been investigated by the quality profession, but they have not been well utilized outside the quality profession until Six Sigma management.

- It is false because Six Sigma is focused on ongoing rapid improvement of the enterprise. Most other quality management processes are focused on incremental continuous improvement, whereas Six Sigma demands breakthrough improvement.

- It is false because past quality management efforts were initially spurred on by quality professionals, consultants, or academics, while Six Sigma is being promoted by executive managers such as George Fisher (Motorola) and Jack Welch and Jeffrey Immelt (General Electric).

- It is false because Six Sigma is facilitated by an infrastructure of Six Sigma experts overlaying the current organizational structure. Other quality management approaches use supervisors, managers, or workers to facilitate teams. Expert facilitation of teams is a big step forward in rapid process improvement that impacts the bottom line of an organization.

On the other hand, it is true because most of the tools, methods, and theories were borrowed from the quality management predecessors of Six Sigma. The authors believe that Six Sigma is more an example of evolutionary management than revolutionary management. The founders of Six Sigma management stood on the shoulders of the giants who preceded them in the quality movement, such as Walter Shewhart, W. Edwards Deming, Joseph Juran, Kaoru Ishikawa, and Genichi Taguchi.

SUMMARY

A process is a collection of interacting components that transform inputs into outputs toward a common aim, called a *mission statement*. Two kinds of variation exist in a process, special variation and common variation. Common causes of variation are due to the process itself, and are the responsibility of management. Special causes of variation are due to events external to the usual functioning of the process and are usually the responsibility of workers and engineers on the line. A feedback loop relates information about outputs from any stage or stages back to another stage or stages so that an analysis of the process can be made.

The goalpost view of quality states that as long as a unit of output falls within acceptable limits, called *specification limits*, around a desired value, called the *nominal* or *target value*, it is deemed conforming, and there is minimum cost. The continuous improvement view of quality states that quality is a predictable degree of uniformity and dependability at low cost and suited to the market. This is a more realistic view in that losses begin to accrue as soon as a quality characteristic of a product or service deviates from the nominal value, even within specification limits. The pursuit of quality requires that organizations globally optimize their process of interdependent stakeholders.

Six Sigma management is the relentless and rigorous pursuit of the reduction of variation in all critical processes to achieve continuous and breakthrough improvements that impact the bottom line and top line of the organization and increase customer satisfaction. Another common definition of Six Sigma management is that it is an organizational initiative designed to create an order of magnitude change in processes by reducing defects tenfold while simultaneously reducing processing time by 50% every 2 years. Finally, it is the objective of Six Sigma management to create processes that are twice as good as the customer demands so that if the process variation does increase, it will not generate more than 3.4 defects per million opportunities.

The methodology or improvement roadmap utilized in Six Sigma management to lead to breakthrough improvement in current existing processes is the DMAIC model. DMAIC is an acronym for Define-Measure-Analyze-Improve-Control. DMAIC is introduced in Chapter 2 and discussed in detail in Chapters 4–8. The methodology used to create new processes, products, or services or to innovate existing processes, products or services is **Design for Six Sigma** (DFSS). The key ingredient for a successful Six Sigma management process is the commitment of top management to the Six Sigma style of management.

REFERENCES

1. Deming, W.E., *Quality, Productivity, and Competitive Position* (Cambridge, Mass.: Massachusetts Institute of Technology Center for Advanced Engineering Study, 1982).

2. Gitlow, H., Oppenheim, A., Oppenheim, R. and Levine, D., *Quality Management: Tools and Methods for Improvement*, 3rd ed. (New York: McGraw-Hill-Irwin, 2005).

3. Gitlow, H., *Quality Management Systems: A Practical Guide* (Boca Raton, FL: St. Lucie Press, 2000).

4. Hahn, G. J., N. Dogannaksoy, and R. Hoerl, "The Evolution of Six Sigma," *Quality Engineering*, 2000, 12, 317–326.

5. Ishikawa, K. and Lu, D. , *What Is Total Quality Control? The Japanese Way* (Englewood Cliffs, NJ: Prentice Hall, 1985).

6. Snee, R. D., "The Impact of Six Sigma on Quality," *Quality Engineering*, 2000, 12, ix–xiv.

7. Taguchi, G. and Wu, Y., *Introduction to Off-Line Quality Control* (Nagoya, Japan: Central Japan Quality Control Association, 1980).

Six Sigma Roles, Responsibilities, and Terminology

CHAPTER OUTLINE

2.1 Roles and Responsibilities in Six Sigma Management
2.2 Technical Terminology of Six Sigma Management
2.3 Beginning Six Sigma Management
2.4 Nonmanufacturing Industries

LEARNING OBJECTIVES

After reading this chapter, you will be able to:

- Understand the roles and responsibilities of Six Sigma management
- Understand the technical terminology of Six Sigma management
- Understand how to begin Six Sigma management
- Know the relevance of Six Sigma in nonmanufacturing industries

INTRODUCTION

Six Sigma management is replete with jargon. One would think that the sheer volume of jargon in Six Sigma management would kill it, but that doesn't seem to be the case. In any event, if you want to discuss Six Sigma management, you have to know the terminology. The aim of this chapter is to get you familiar and comfortable with the terms specific to Six Sigma management. If you decide to begin a Six Sigma journey, you will need a roadmap for getting started. This chapter presents such a roadmap. The journey is difficult but worth the effort. People in all sectors of the economy can use this roadmap, for example, people in manufacturing and services industries, as well as people in government and education. If you decide to take this journey, it begins with learning the language of the land. Here we go!

2.1 ROLES AND RESPONSIBILITIES IN SIX SIGMA MANAGEMENT

There are several jobs that are critical to the Six Sigma management: senior executive (CEO or president), executive committee member, champion, master black belt, black belt, green belt, and process owner. The roles and responsibilities of each of the above jobs are described as follows.

Senior Executive

The **senior executive** provides the impetus, direction, and alignment necessary for Six Sigma's ultimate success. The senior executive should:

- Study Six Sigma management.
- Lead the executive committee in linking objectives to Six Sigma projects.
- Participate on appropriate Six Sigma project teams.
- Maintain an overview of the system to avoid suboptimization.
- Maintain a long-term view.
- Act as a liaison to Wall Street, explaining the long-term advantages of Six Sigma management, if appropriate.
- Constantly and consistently, publicly and privately champion Six Sigma management.
- Conduct presidential tollgate reviews of Six Sigma projects.

The most successful, highly publicized Six Sigma efforts have had one thing in common—unwavering, clear, and committed leadership from top management. There is no doubt in anyone's mind that Six Sigma is "the way we do business." Although it may be possible to initiate Six Sigma concepts and processes at lower levels, dramatic success will not be possible until the senior executive becomes engaged and takes a leadership role.

Executive Committee Member

The members of the **executive committee** are the top management of an organization. They should operate at the same level of commitment for Six Sigma management as the senior executive. The members of the executive committee should:

- Study Six Sigma management.
- Deploy Six Sigma throughout the organization.
- Prioritize and manage the Six Sigma project portfolio.
- Assign champions, black belts, and green belts to Six Sigma projects.
- Conduct reviews of Six Sigma projects with the senior executive and within their own areas of control.

- Improve the Six Sigma process.
- Remove barriers to Six Sigma management.
- Provide resources for Six Sigma management.

Champion

Champions take a very active sponsorship and leadership role in conducting and implementing Six Sigma projects. A champion should be a member of the executive committee, or at least a trusted direct report of a member of the executive committee. She or he should have enough influence to remove obstacles or provide resources without having to go higher in the organization. Champions work closely with the executive committee, project leaders (called *black belts*) assigned to their projects, and the master black belts (supervisors of black belts) overseeing their projects. A champion has the following responsibilities:

- Identify the project on the organizational dashboard (see Chapter 3).
- Develop and negotiate the project objective with the executive committee.
- Select a black belt (or a green belt for a simple project) to lead the project team.
- Remove any political barriers or resource constraints to the Six Sigma project (run interference).
- Provide an ongoing communication link between the project team(s) and the executive committee.
- Help team members manage their resources and stay within the budget.
- Review the progress of the project with respect to the project's timetable.
- Keep the team focused on the project by providing direction and guidance.
- Assure that Six Sigma methods and tools are being used in the project.
- Participate in the tollgate review process for their Six Sigma projects.

Master Black Belt

A **master black belt** takes a leadership role as keeper of the Six Sigma process and advisor to executives or business unit managers, leveraging his/her skills with projects that are led by black belts and green belts. Frequently, a master black belt reports directly to a senior executive or a business unit manager. A master black belt has successfully led many teams through complex Six Sigma projects. He or she is a proven change agent, leader, facilitator, and technical expert in Six Sigma management. Master black belt is a career path. It is always best for an organization to grow its own master black belts. Unfortunately, sometimes it is impossible for an organization to grow its own master black belts due to the lead time required to become a master black belt. It takes years of study, practice, tutelage under a master, and project work. Ideally, master black belts are selected from the black belts within an organization; however, sometimes circumstances require hiring master black belts external to the organization.

Master black belts have the following responsibilities:

- Counsel senior executives and business unit managers on Six Sigma management.
- Identify, prioritize and coordinate Six Sigma projects on a dashboard (see Chapter 3).
- Continually improve and innovate the organization's Six Sigma process.
- Apply Six Sigma across both operations and transactions-based processes, such as sales, human resources, information technology, facility management, call centers, finance, etc.
- Teach black belts and green belts Six Sigma theory, tools, and methods.
- Mentor black belts and green belts.

Senior master black belts have 10 years of ongoing leadership experience and have worked extensively with mentoring the organizational leaders on Six Sigma management.

Black Belt

A **black belt** is a full-time change agent and improvement leader who may not be an expert in the process under study [Reference 3]. The ideal candidate for a black belt is an individual who possesses the following characteristics:

- Has technical and managerial process improvement/innovation skills.
- Has a passion for statistics and systems theory.
- Understands the psychology of individuals and teams.
- Understands the Plan-Do-Study-Act (PDSA) cycle and learning.
- Has excellent communication and writing skills.
- Works well in a team format.
- Can manage meetings.
- Has a pleasant personality and is fun to work with.
- Communicates in the language of the client and does not use technical jargon.
- Is not intimidated by upper management.
- Has a customer focus.

The responsibilities of a black belt include:

- Help to prepare a project objective.
- Communicate with the champion and process owner about progress of the project.
- Lead the Six Sigma project team.

- Schedule meetings and coordinate logistics.
- Help team members design and analyze experiments.
- Provide training in tools and team functions to project team members.
- Help team members prepare for reviews by the champion and executive committee.
- Recommend additional Six Sigma projects from the dashboard.
- Coach green belts leading projects limited in scope.

A black belt is a full-time, quality professional who is mentored by a master black belt, but may report to a manager for his or her tour of duty as a black belt.

An appropriate time frame for a tour of duty as a full-time black belt is 2 years. Black belt skills and project work are critical to the development of leaders and high-potential people within the organization.

Green Belt

A **green belt** is an individual who works on projects part time (25%), either as a team member for complex projects or as a project leader for simpler projects. Green belts are the "work horses" of Six Sigma projects. Most managers in a mature Six Sigma organization are green belts. Green belt certification is a critical prerequisite for advancement into upper management in a Six Sigma organization because it is the accepted best practice style of management.

Green belts leading simpler projects have the following responsibilities:

- Define the project objective.
- Review the project objective with the project's champion.
- Select the team members for the project.
- Communicate with the champion, master black belt, black belt, and process owner throughout all stages of the project.
- Facilitate the team through all phases of the project.
- Schedule meetings and coordinate logistics.
- Analyze data through all phases of the project.
- Train team members in the use of Six Sigma tools and methods through all phases of the project.

In complicated Six Sigma projects, green belts work closely with the team leader (black belt) to keep the team functioning and progressing through the various stages of the Six Sigma project.

Green Belt versus Black Belt Projects. Black belt and green belt Six Sigma projects differ on the basis of five criteria. Green belt projects tend to be less involved (e.g., they have one Y and few Xs), do not deal with political issues, do not require many organizational resources, do not require significant capital investment to realize the gains identified during the project, and utilize only basic statistical methods. On the other hand, black belt projects tend to deal with more complex situations (for example, substantial political issues or are cross-functional in nature), require substantial organizational resources, may need substantial capital investment to realize the gains made during the project, and utilize sophisticated statistical methods. One exception is in organizations where executives act as green belt team leaders because they control large budgets and are responsible for major systems and issues. In these cases, the executives get assistance from black belts or master black belts. Another exception is where a process owner with great area expertise takes on the mantle of team leader. This occurs if area expertise is more critical than Six Sigma expertise in the conduct of a project. In this situation, the black belt takes more of a nonvoting, facilitator role, and the process owner/team leader is a voting member who is more involved in the content. Black belts take more of a formal leadership role early in the project, when the team is forming and storming and needs a lot of direction and support. As the team becomes more self-directed and comfortable with the tools and methods of Six Sigma and as they begin to implement changes, the process knowledge of the team leader becomes more important to success, and the black belt can become more of an observer, coach, and mentor to the team.

Supervision Ratios Between the Different Levels of Six Sigma Certification. Table 2.1 shows the percentage of an organization needing each level of Six Sigma certification. Additionally, the table shows the supervision ratios between the different levels of belts. For a small organization (e.g., 100 people), an organization would need 1 master black belt, between 6 and 12 black

TABLE 2.1 Supervision Ratios for Six Sigma Belts

Certification level	Percentage of organization needing certification level (Approximations depend on level of general knowledge in the organization and expertise of those individuals who are certified)	Supervision ratios
Master Black Belt (MBB)	1% of organization	An MBB can mentor about 10 BB at a time, but if the MBB is skilled and several skilled BBs are available, there can be 1 senior MBB managing many BBs.
Black Belt (BB)	6–12% of organization	A BB can mentor about 4–8 GBs at a time
Green Belt (GB)	25–50% of organization (includes executives as GBs)	

belts, and between 25 and 50 green belts. For a large organization (e.g., 100,000 people), an organization would need 1,000 master black belts, between 6,000 and 12,000 black belts, and between 25,000 and 50,000 green belts. These supervision ratios demonstrate that Six Sigma must be a strategic initiative in an organization and must represent a critical key to advancement up the organization hierarchy.

Process Owner

A **process owner** is the manager of a process. She or he has responsibility for the process and has the authority to change the process on his or her signature. The process owner should be identified and involved immediately in all Six Sigma projects relating to his or her area.

A process owner has the following responsibilities:

- Be accountable for the best practice methods and output of his or her process.
- Empower his or her employees to follow and improve best practice methods.
- Focus the project team on the project objectives.
- Assist the project team in remaining on schedule.
- Allocate the resources necessary for the project (people, space, etc.).
- Accept and manage the improved process after completion of the Six Sigma project.
- Turn the PDSA cycle for the revised process.
- Ensure that process objectives and indicators are linked to the organization's mission through the dashboard (see Chapter 3).
- Understand how the process works, the capability of the process, and the relationship of the process to other processes in the organization.
- Participate in the tollgate review process for their Six Sigma project.

2.2 TECHNICAL TERMINOLOGY OF SIX SIGMA MANAGEMENT

Six Sigma practitioners use a lot of jargon. You must know the language of Six Sigma management if you want to use it.

Unit   A unit is the item (e.g., product or component, service or service step, or time period) to be studied with a Six Sigma project.

CTQ   CTQ is an acronym for critical-to-quality characteristic for a product, service, or process. A CTQ is a measure of what is important to a customer, for example, average and variation in waiting time in a physician's office for a sample of four patients by day, percentage of errors with ATM transactions for a bank's customers per month, or number of car accidents per month on a particular stretch of highway for a department of traffic might all be CTQs. Six Sigma projects are designed to improve CTQs.

Defect   A defect is a nonconformance on one of many possible quality characteristics of a unit that causes customer dissatisfaction. For a given unit, each quality characteristic is defined by translating customer desires into specifications. It is important to operationally define each defect for a unit. For example, if a word in a document is misspelled, that word may be considered a defect. A defect does not necessarily make a unit defective. For example, a water bottle can have a scratch on the outside (defect) and still be used to hold water (not defective). However, if a customer wants a scratch-free water bottle, that scratched bottle could be considered defective.

Defective   A nonconforming unit is a defective unit.

Defect Opportunity   A defect opportunity is each circumstance in which a CTQ can fail to be met. There may be many opportunities for defects within a defined unit. For instance, a service may have four component parts. If each component part contains three opportunities for a defect, the service has 12 defect opportunities in which a CTQ can fail to be met. The number of defect opportunities generally is related to the complexity of the unit under study. Complex units have more opportunities for defects to occur than simple units.

Defects per Unit (DPU)   Defects per unit refers to the average of all the defects for a given number of units, that is, the total number of defects for n units divided by n, the number of units. If you are producing a 50-page document, the unit is a page. If there are 150 spelling errors, DPU is 150/50, or 3.0. If you are producing ten 50-page documents, the unit is a 50-page document. If there are 75 spelling errors in all 10 documents, DPU is 75/10, or 7.5.

Defects per Opportunity (DPO)   Defects per opportunity refers to the number of defects divided by the number of defect opportunities. If there are 20 errors in 100 services with one defect opportunity per service, the DPU is 0.20 (20/100). However, if there are 12 defect opportunities per service, there would be 1,200 opportunities in 100 services. In this case, DPO would be 0.0167 (20/1,200). (The DPO may also be calculated by dividing DPU by the total number of opportunities.)

Defects per Million Opportunities (DPMO)   DPMO equals DPO multiplied by 1 million. Hence, for the above example the DPMO is $(0.0167) \times (1,000,000)$, or 16,700 DPMO.

Process Sigma   Process sigma is a measure of the process performance determined by using DPMO and a stable normal distribution. Process sigma is a metric that allows for process performance comparisons across processes, departments, divisions, companies, and countries, assuming all comparisons are made from stable processes whose output follows the normal distribution. In Six Sigma terminology, the sigma value of a process is a metric used to indicate the number of DPMO, or how well the process is performing with respect to customer needs and wants.

Yield   Yield is the proportion of units within specification divided by the total number of units, that is, if 25 units are produced and 20 are good, the yield is 0.80 (20/25).

Rolled Throughput Yield (RTY)   Rolled throughput yield is the product of the yields from each step in a process. It is the probability of a unit passing through all k independent steps of a process and incurring no defects. RTY $= Y_1 * Y_2 \ldots Y_K$, where $k =$ number of independent steps in a process, or the number of independent component parts or steps in a product or service. Each yield Y for each step or component must be calculated to compute the RTY. For those steps in which the number of opportunities is equal to the number of units, $Y = 1 - $ DPU. For those steps in which a large number of defects are possible but only a few are

TABLE 2.2: Values of $Y = e^{-DPU}$

DPU	$Y = e^{-DPU}$
1	0.367879
2	0.135335
3	0.049787
4	0.018316
5	0.006738
6	0.002479
7	0.000912
8	0.000335
9	0.000123
10	0.000045

observed (e.g., number of typographical, grammatical, spelling errors in a document), the yield Y (the probability of no defects in a unit) can be found by $Y = e^{-DPU}$, for the step. The values for $Y = e^{-DPU}$ for values of DPU from 1 through 10 are shown in Table 2.2.

For example, if a process has three steps and the yield from the first step (Y_1) is 99.7%, the yield from the second step (Y_2) is 99.5%, and the yield from the third step (Y_3) is 89.7%, the RTY is 88.98% $(0.997 \times 0.995 \times 0.897)$.

The left side of Table 2.3 is used to translate DPMO statistics for a stable, normally distributed process with no shift in its mean (0.0 shift in mean) over time into a process sigma metric, assuming that defects occur at only one of the specifications if there are lower and upper specifications. The right side of Table 2.3 is used to translate DPMO statistics for a stable, normally distributed process that has experienced a 1.5 sigma shift in its mean over time into a process sigma metric.

For example, suppose a process has three independent steps, each with a 95% yield. The RTY for the process is 85.74% $(0.95 \times 0.95 \times 0.95)$ and the DPO is 0.1426 (DPO = 1.0 − RTY = 1.0 − 0.8574), assuming each step has only one opportunity so that DPU and DPO are the same. The DPMO for the process is 142,600 (DPMO = DPO × 1,000,000). The process sigma metric is obtained, assuming a 1.5 sigma shift in the process mean over time, by looking down the DPMO column to the two numbers bracketing to 142,600. The actual process sigma metric lies between the corresponding two bracketing process sigma metrics. In this example, 142,600 is bracketed by a DPMO of 135,661 and a DPMO of 158,655. The corresponding bracketing process sigma metrics are 2.60 and 2.50. Hence, the actual process sigma metric is approximately 2.55.

SDSA Model.   The **SDSA (Standardize-Do-Study-Act) model** is a method or roadmap that helps employees standardize a process [Reference 1]. It includes four steps:

1. **Standardize**: Employees study the process and develop "best practice" methods with key indicators of process performance.

TABLE 2.3 Process Sigma DPMO Table

Assume 0.0 sigma shift in mean				Assume 1.5 sigma shift in mean			
Process σ level	Process DPMO	Process σ level	Process DPMO	Process σ level	Process DPMO	Process σ level	Process DPMO
0.10	460,172.1	3.30	483.5	0.10	919,243.3	3.10	54,799.3
0.20	420,740.3	3.40	337.0	0.20	903,199.5	3.20	44,565.4
0.30	382,088.6	3.50	232.7	0.30	884,930.3	3.30	35,930.3
0.40	344,578.3	3.60	159.1	0.40	864,333.9	3.40	28,716.5
0.50	308,537.5	3.70	107.8	0.50	841,344.7	3.50	22,750.1
0.60	274,253.1	3.80	72.4	0.60	815,939.9	3.60	17,864.4
0.70	241,963.6	3.90	48.1	0.70	788,144.7	3.70	13,903.4
0.80	211,855.3	4.00	31.7	0.80	758,036.4	3.80	10,724.1
0.90	184,060.1	4.10	20.7	0.90	725,746.9	3.90	8,197.5
1.00	158,655.3	4.20	13.4	1.00	691,462.5	4.00	6,209.7
1.10	135,666.1	4.30	8.5	1.10	655,421.7	4.10	4,661.2
1.20	115,069.7	4.40	5.4	1.20	617,911.4	4.20	3,467.0
1.30	96,800.5	4.50	3.4	1.30	579,259.7	4.30	2,555.2
1.40	80,756.7	4.60	2.1	1.40	539,827.9	4.40	1,865.9
1.50	66,807.2	4.70	1.3	1.50	500,000.0	4.50	1,350.0
1.60	54,799.3			1.60	460,172.1	4.60	967.7
1.70	44,565.4	Process	Defect per	1.70	420,740.3	4.70	687.2
1.80	35,930.3	σ level	billion	1.80	382,088.6	4.80	483.5
1.90	28,716.5		opportunities	1.90	344,578.3	4.90	337.0
2.00	22,750.1	4.80	794.4	2.00	308,537.5	5.00	232.7
2.10	17,864.4	4.90	479.9	2.10	274,253.1	5.10	159.1
2.20	13,903.4	5.00	287.1	2.20	241,963.6	5.20	107.8
2.30	10,724.1	5.10	170.1	2.30	211,855.3	5.30	72.4
2.40	8,197.5	5.20	99.8	2.40	184,060.1	5.40	48.1
2.50	6,209.7	5.30	58.0	2.50	158,655.3	5.50	31.7
2.60	4,661.2	5.40	33.4	2.60	135,666.1	5.60	20.7
2.70	3,467.0	5.50	19.0	2.70	115,069.7	5.70	13.4
2.80	2,555.2	5.60	10.7	2.80	96,800.5	5.80	8.5
2.90	1,865.9	5.70	6.0	2.90	80,756.7	5.90	5.4
3.00	1,350.0	5.80	3.3	3.00	66,807.2	6.00	3.4
3.10	967.7	5.90	1.8				
3.20	687.2	6.00	1.0				

2. **Do**: Employees conduct planned experiments using the best practice methods on a trial basis.

3. **Study**: Employees collect and analyze data on the key indicators to determine the effectiveness of the best practice methods.

4. **Act**: Managers establish standardized best practice methods and formalize them through training.

PDSA Model.   The **PDSA** model is a method or roadmap that helps employees improve and innovate a process by reducing the difference between customers' needs and process performance [Reference 1]. It consists of four stages: Plan, Do, Study, and Act. Initially, a revised flowchart is developed to improve or innovate a standardized best practice method (**Plan**). The revised flowchart (Plan) is tested using an experiment on a small scale or trial basis (**Do**). The effects of the revised flowchart are studied using measurements from key indicators (**Study**). Finally, if the study phase generated positive results, the revised flowchart is inserted into training manuals, and all relevant personnel are trained in the revised method (**Act**). If the study phase generated negative results, the revised flowchart is abandoned, and a new Plan is developed by employees. The PDSA cycle continues forever in an uphill progression of never-ending improvement.

DMAIC Model.   The **DMAIC** model has five phases: Define, Measure, Analyze, Improve, and Control. It is an alternative to the PDSA model. The relationship between the VoC (nominal value and specification limits), the VOP (distribution of output), and the DMAIC model is illustrated in Figure 2.1. The left side of Figure 2.1 shows the flowchart for the existing process with its three Sigma output distribution, assuming no shift in the process mean. The right side of Figure 2.1 shows the flowchart for a revised process with its Six Sigma output distribution, assuming no shift in the process mean. The DMAIC model is utilized in Six Sigma management to move from the existing process to the revised process.

To demonstrate the DMAIC model, return to the accounting report example discussed on page 12.

1. **Define phase**: The define phase involves preparing a project charter (rationale for the project), understanding the relationships between Suppliers-Inputs-Process-Outputs-Customers (called *SIPOC* analysis), analyzing VoC data to identify the CTQs important to customers, and developing a project objective.

   For example, a Six Sigma team was assigned by top management to review the production of a monthly report by the accounting department as a potential Six Sigma project. This involved identifying the need for the project (relative to other potential projects), the costs and benefits of the project, the resources required for the project, and the timeframe of the project. As a consequence of doing a SIPOC analysis (see Section 4.4) and a VoC analysis, the team determined that management wants a monthly accounting report to be completed in 7 days (the normal time to complete is 7 days with a standard deviation of one day). They also determined that the report should never be completed in less than 4 days (the relevant information is not available before then) and never later than 10 days. Team members identified the project objective as follows:

   > Reduce (direction) the variability in the cycle time (measure) to produce an error-free accounting report (system) from the current level of 7 days plus or minus 3 days to 7 days plus or minus 1½ days (target) by January 10, 2004 (deadline).

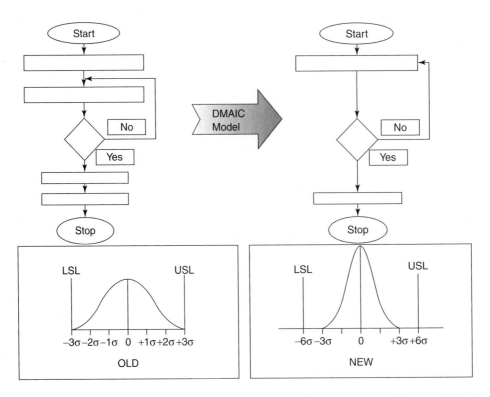

FIGURE 2.1 Relationship Between the VoC, the Voice of the Process, and the DMAIC Model

2. **Measure phase:** The measure phase involves developing operational definitions for each CTQ variable, determining the validity of the measurement system for each CTQ, and establishing baseline capabilities for each CTQ.

   For the accounting report example, the team members created an operational definition of variability in cycle time such that all relevant personnel agreed on the definition (for example, they clearly identified the start and stop points needed to compute cycle time). Next, they performed a statistical study to determine the validity of the measurement system for variability in cycle time. Finally, team members collected baseline data about variability in cycle time and statistically analyzed it to get a clear picture of the current situation.

3. **Analyze phase:** The analyze phase involves identifying the upstream variables (Xs) for each CTQ, using a flowchart. Upstream variables are the factors that affect the performance of a CTQ. To restate this quantitatively:

$$CTQ = f(X_1, X_2, X_3, \ldots, X_k),$$

where CTQ = the critical-to-quality characteristic important to customers identified in the define phase and clarified in the measure phase of the DMAIC model and

X_i = upstream i^{th} variable that is hypothesized to have an impact of the performance of the CTQ.

Additionally, the analyze phase involves operationally defining each X, collecting baseline data for each X, performing studies to determine the validity of the measurement system for each X, establishing baseline capabilities for each X, and understanding the effect of each X on each CTQ.

Referring to the example of the accounting report, team members identify all input and system variables, called the Xs, that impact the CTQ ("variability in cycle time") using a flowchart (see Section 15.1 in Chapter 15). They are:

X_1 = number of days from request to receipt for line item A data,

X_2 = number of days from request to receipt for line item B data,

X_3 = number of days from request to receipt for line item C data,

X_4 = number of days from request to receipt for line item D data,

X_5 = number of days to reformat the line item data to prepare the report,

X_6 = number of days to prepare the report,

X_7 = accounting clerk preparing the report (Mary or Joe),

X_8 = number of errors in the report,

X_9 = number of days to correct the report,

X_{10} = accounting supervisor performing the corrections to the report (Harry or Sue), and

X_{11} = number of signatures required before the report is released.

For example, the number of signatures required before releasing the report (X_{11}) may affect the average time to produce the report, or the accounting clerk preparing the report (X_7) may dramatically affect the variability in cycle time to produce the report. Next, team members operationally define the Xs and perform statistical studies to determine the validity of their measurement systems. Then, team members collect baseline data to determine the current status of each X using control charts (see Chapter 14). Finally, team members study the data and develop hypotheses about the relationships between the Xs and the CTQ. In this case, separate histograms (see Section 9.8) of the CTQ for each level of each X indicated that: X_1 (number of days from request to receipt for line item A data), X_3 (number of days from request to receipt for line item C data), X_7 (accounting clerk preparing the report [Mary or Joe]), and X_{10} (accounting supervisor performing the corrections to the report [Harry or Sue]) may be important to the reduction of variability in the cycle time (CTQ). The other Xs did not substantially affect the CTQ.

Many practitioners include the identification, operational definition, and measurement systems analyses of the Xs in the measure phase, especially for well-monitored systems where these variables have been studied, such as in previous DMAIC projects.

4. **Improve phase**: The improve phase involves designing experiments to understand the relationships between the CTQs and the Xs, determining the levels of the critical Xs that optimize the CTQs, developing action plans to formalize the level of the Xs that optimize the CTQs, and conducting a pilot test of the revised process.

   Team members conducted an experiment to identify the levels of the critical Xs identified in the analyze phase to minimize variation in the time to produce the accounting report. The experiment revealed that team members had to work with the personnel responsible for line items A and C to decrease the average and standard deviation of days to forward the line items to the department preparing the report. Further, the experiment revealed that there is an interaction between the clerk preparing the report and the supervisor correcting the report. The analysis showed that if Mary prepared the report, it was best for Sue to correct the report, or if Joe prepared the report, it was best for Harry to correct the report. A pilot run of the revised system to produce the accounting report showed it to generate a stable normal distribution of days to produce the report with a mean of 7 days and a standard deviation of one-half day.

5. **Control phase**: The control phase involves avoiding potential problems with the Xs with risk management and mistake proofing, standardizing successful process revisions, controlling the critical Xs, documenting each control plan, and turning the revised process over to the system owner. Risk management involves developing a plan to minimize the risk of increasing variation in cycle time. Mistake proofing involves installing systems/methods that have a low probability of producing errors in the production of the accounting report, from incoming data to submitted report.

   Team members identify potential problems and methods to avoid them with X_1, X_3, X_7, and X_{10} using risk management and mistake-proofing techniques. For example, they establish procedures to ensure the coupling of clerks and supervisors and data collection methods to identify and resolve future problems in the reporting system. The new system is standardized and fully documented in training manuals. At this point, team members turn the revised process over to the process owner and celebrate their success. The process owner continues to work toward improvement of the revised process beyond its current level of output. The distribution of days to produce the report has been improved to have an average of 7 days with a standard deviation of one-half day and is a stable and predictable normal distribution. This translates to a report being early or late about once every 24,500 years! The team chose not to wait around for an error to occur.

2.3 BEGINNING SIX SIGMA MANAGEMENT

Starting Six Sigma Management

Six Sigma management begins the moment the senior executive and the executive committee begin to manage using the Six Sigma theory and methods [Reference 2]. The time required to obtain the benefits from Six Sigma management is a function of the resources allocated to the Six Sigma effort in an organization. Lack of top management commitment will stop a Six Sigma process before it can begin.

Responding to a Crisis

Top management creates and directs the energy necessary for Six Sigma management. There are only two known sources for this energy, a **crisis** or a **vision** [Reference 4]. Many companies begin a program of Six Sigma management as a reaction to crises discovered by top management. Top management can uncover and bring to the forefront the real or potential crises that face an organization in at least two ways. First, management can highlight a crisis by asking a probing question, such as What are the characteristics of our products and/or services that are most important to our customers? This question was stated by Dr. Noriaki Kano of the Science University of Tokyo in 1989. Frequently, top managers are not able to answer this question. This may create a crisis because top managers realize that they are out of touch with their customers. This can create a burning desire for transformation of an organization to Six Sigma management. Second, management can highlight a crisis by conducting a brainstorming session on the crises facing the organization and analyzing the data [Reference 4]. This can also create a burning desire for transformation of an organization to Six Sigma management.

On the other hand, top management can initiate action for Six Sigma management through a provocative vision. A vision can stimulate top management to expend the energy needed to transform an organization. This idea is critical for organizations not facing a crisis. A vision can replace a crisis as a rallying point for Six Sigma Management.

An example of a vision that drove top management to transform an organization is a situation that occurred in a social service agency. The agency, a group home program for troubled teenagers, was achieving its mission, adequately providing temporary shelter and basic care for adolescents separated from their families. However, the top management of the agency knew, through surveys of clients and referral agents, what the program needed to change to provide other services. These services included individual, group, and family therapy; academic counseling; and an overall plan coordinated for the clients that includes appropriate social workers, psychologists, house parents, teachers, and other involved staff members.

Top management had a vision of transforming the agency to one in which the needs of the clients were met in a more professional manner, utilizing a team to carry out an integrated plan. There was no crisis that stimulated this transformation. Top management saw a need to change the organization to exceed the clients' needs, which were not being addressed by the program in its current state.

One technique that can be used to create a vision is to imagine the following scenario in which the developer(s) of the vision personify the organization; that is, they pretend the organization is a person.

> Imagine that it is 100 years in the future, and your organization has just died. All the stakeholders of the organization are standing around the coffin, and the clergyman reads the eulogy. The eulogy ends with these words: "Here lies *insert the name of your organization*; it was known and loved for *insert the reason*."

The reason inserted above is the vision of your organization. A vision should be a noble statement of long-term purpose. It should inspire people to take action to transform their organization. It should be very short and easy to remember. Anecdotally, in the experience of the authors, organizations that are vision driven stay with Six Sigma over the long haul, whereas organizations that are crisis driven may revert back to preexisting behaviors once the crisis passes.

Initiating Action for Six Sigma Management

As stated above, top management initiates action for Six Sigma management through a crisis and/or a vision. Top management synthesizes, studies, and digests the crises facing the organization, as well as formulates and articulates the vision of the organization. If they feel it is warranted, they communicate the information about the crises and/or vision to relevant stakeholders. This process promotes commitment to Six Sigma management among top management and stakeholders.

Retaining Outside Counsel

After management has communicated the crises and/or vision, they need to retain a master black belt. A master black belt is necessary for two reasons. First, expertise in the Six Sigma management is not likely to be found within an organization. Second, organizations frequently cannot recognize their own deficiencies with respect to Six Sigma management; that is, they don't know what they don't know.

Window of Opportunity Opens

Once a master black belt has been retained, a **window of opportunity** for Six Sigma management opens. The window of opportunity has an unspecified time limit that varies from organization to organization. If signs of Six Sigma management do not become obvious to the stakeholders of an organization, they will not believe that top management is serious, and the window of opportunity will begin to close. This is a common reason for the failure of Six Sigma management in organizations. Another reason Six Sigma is not effective in some organizations is the failure to engage middle management. True, you cannot usually engage middle management without commitment at the top, but if all you get is commitment at the top and a lot of black belts running projects, the resulting middle management revolt will be a wall that cannot be breached from below or above.

Develop a Six Sigma Transformation Plan

An important role of the master black belt is to help the executive committee assess the current status and predict the future condition of relevant stakeholders with respect to their desire to transform the organization into a Six Sigma organization. The master black belt conducts a study to determine the **barriers against** and the **aids for** a fruitful **transformation** to Six Sigma management at all levels within an organization and throughout the organization's interdependent system of stakeholders. The executive committee and the master black belt develop a plan to transform the organization to a Six Sigma organization, with a training plan, budget, and implementation schedule.

Window of Opportunity Begins to Close

Once initial Six Sigma training of top management is complete, the window of opportunity for Six Sigma management begins to close unless the members of the executive committee take two actions. First, they must promote the transformation plan to transform the organization from its current style of management to a Six Sigma management style. Second, they need to diffuse Six Sigma management theory and practice within the organization (employees) and outside the organization to relevant stakeholders, such as the board of directors, stockholders, suppliers, customers, regulators, and the community.

2.4 NONMANUFACTURING INDUSTRIES

Six Sigma management is equally applicable in manufacturing and service industries, education, and government. Most people in manufacturing organizations are employed in service functions, for example, human resources, payroll, food services, risk management, to name a few areas. General Electric has been very successful utilizing Six Sigma theory and methods in its nonmanufacturing functions, for example, GE Capital. Additionally, service organizations such as American Express and the University of Miami have experienced great success with Six Sigma management.

Granted, service transactions are frequently "one-of-a-kind" transactions that take place on demand (zero inventory) in the presence of the customer (zero time between production and use of service) with subjective service quality characteristics. Still, Six Sigma is appropriate in this type of environment. For example, a subjective quality characteristic in a restaurant is how patrons feel about the taste of the green peas served with the filet mignon dinner. One way to measure this is to ask patrons how they feel about the taste of the peas on a 1–5 Likert scale, where 1 = very dissatisfied, 3 = neutral, and 5 = very satisfied. This type of measurement is very subject to inaccuracies caused by factors such as embarrassment at telling the "truth." Another way to determine how a patron feels about the taste of peas is to instruct one busboy to collect the first steak and peas dinner eaten by a patron each of the six evening hours each day and to weigh the peas left on the plate. All dinners go out with 4 ounces of peas, so 4 ounces minus the weight of peas returned is the weight of peas eaten by the patron. With the above information, the chef can estimate the average and range (maximum–minimum) of ounces of peas eaten by patrons each day. Consequently, the chef can modify the recipe for preparing peas and see from the statistics whether the patrons eat more peas (higher average) with less variation (smaller range) per day. If they do, the chef assumes that the patrons like the taste of the peas better with the new recipe than with the old recipe.

SUMMARY

The senior executive provides the impetus, the direction, and the alignment necessary for Six Sigma's ultimate success. The members of the executive committee are the top management of an organization and actively promote Six Sigma management throughout the organization. Champions take a very active sponsorship role with Six Sigma projects. A champion should be a member of the executive committee or at least a trusted direct report of a member of the executive committee. A black belt is a full-time change agent and improvement leader who may not be an expert in the process under study. A green belt is a part-time (25%) team member for complex projects and acts as a team leader for simple projects. Green belts are the "work horses" of Six Sigma projects. Most managers should seek to attain green belt level skills. A master black belt is a partner with the executive team in the success of Six Sigma process. It is a staff job whose purpose is to teach, promote, and advise the members of an organization on Six Sigma management. A process owner is the manager of a process.

The following technical terminology is important to Six Sigma management. A unit is the item (e.g., product or component, service or service step, or time period) to be studied with a Six Sigma project. A nonconforming unit is a defective unit. A defect is a nonconformance on one of many possible quality characteristics of a unit that causes customer dissatisfaction. A defect opportunity is each circumstance in which a CTQ can fail to be met. There may be many opportunities for defects within a defined unit. Defects per unit (DPU) refers to the total number of defects for n units divided by n, the number of units. Defects per opportunity (DPO) refers to the number of defects divided by the number of defect opportunities. Defects per Million Opportunities (DPMO) equals the DPO multiplied by 1 million. Yield is the proportion of units within specification divided by the total number of units. Rolled Throughput Yield (RTY) is the product of the yields from each step in a process. It is the probability of a unit passing through all steps of a process correctly the first time with no rework and incurring no defects. Process sigma is a metric that allows for process performance comparisons across processes. The SDSA cycle is an acronym for Standardize-Do-Study-Act. It is the quality management model for standardizing a process. The PDSA cycle is an acronym for Plan-Do-Study-Act. It is the quality management model for improving a process. The DMAIC model is an acronym for Define-Measure-Analyze-Improve-Control. It is the Six Sigma method for improving a process, service, or product. It is used as an alternative to the PDSA cycles.

Six Sigma management begins in an organization the moment top management realizes that it is the management style they will use to resolve crises or to promote a vision. Once Six Sigma has begun, top management retains a master black belt to develop a plan to transform the organization from its current style of management to a Six Sigma style of management. Next, top management is trained, and a window of opportunity to diffuse Six Sigma throughout the organizations opens. Six Sigma management is equally applicable in manufacturing and service industries, education, and government.

REFERENCES

1. Gitlow, H., Oppenheim, A., Oppenheim, R. and Levine, D., *Quality Management: Tools and Methods for Improvement*, 3rd ed. (New York: McGraw-Hill-Irwin, 2005)

2. Gitlow, H., *Quality Management Systems: A Practical Guide*, (Boca Raton, FL: St. Lucie Press, 2000).

3. Hoerl, R., "Six Sigma Black Belts: What Do They Need to Know?," *Journal of Quality Technology*, 33, 4, October 2001, pp. 391–406.

4. Kano, N., "A Perspective on Quality Activities in American Firms," *California Management Review*, Spring 1993, pp. 14–15.

Six Sigma Model

Macro Model of Six Sigma Management (Dashboards)

CHAPTER OUTLINE

3.1 Structure of a Dashboard
3.2 Components of a Dashboard
3.3 Example of a Dashboard
3.4 Managing with a Dashboard
3.5 Prioritization of Six Sigma Projects
3.6 Management Decides Whether a Project Team Is Necessary

LEARNING OBJECTIVES

After reading this chapter, you will be able to:

- Use a dashboard to manage an organization
- Develop different types of key objectives
- Use different types of key indicators
- Prioritize Six Sigma projects

INTRODUCTION

A **dashboard** is a tool used by management to clarify and assign accountability for the "critical few" key objectives, key indicators, and projects/tasks needed to steer an organization toward its mission statement. Dashboards have both strategic and tactical benefits.

The **strategic benefits** of dashboards include:

- Monitoring deployment of the mission statement throughout an organization using a cascading and interlocking system of key objectives and indicators.

- Balancing management's attention between customer, process, employee, and financial key objectives.

- Increasing communication between and within the levels of an organization.

The **tactical benefits** of a dashboard include:

- Linking all processes (jobs) to the mission statement.

- Eliminating overreaction to random noise in organizational processes; that is, not treating common causes of variation as special causes of variation, as discussed in Chapter 1.

- Developing and testing hypotheses about the effectiveness of potential process improvements.

3.1 STRUCTURE OF A DASHBOARD

The president's key objectives and indicators emanate from the mission statement (see row 1 and columns 1 and 2 of Table 3.1). Direct reports identify their key objectives and indicators by studying the president's key indicators (column 2 of Table 3.1) that relate to their area of responsibility. The outcome of these studies is to identify the key objectives and indicators (see columns 3 and 4 of Table 3.1) required to improve the president's key indicator(s) (see column 2 of Table 3.1) to achieve a desirable state for presidential key objective(s) (see column 1 of Table 3.1). This process is cascaded throughout the entire organization until processes are identified that must be improved or innovated with Six Sigma projects or tasks (see column 5 of Table 3.1).

TABLE 3.1 Generic Dashboard

Mission statement:

President		Direct reports		
Key objectives	**Key indicators**	**Key objectives**	**Key indicators**	**Potential Six Sigma projects**
Key objectives must be achieved to attain the mission statement.	One or more key indicators show progress toward each key objective.	Key objectives are established to move president's key indicator in the proper direction.	One or more key indicators show progress toward each key objective.	Six Sigma projects are used to improve or innovate processes to move indicators in the proper direction.

3.2 COMPONENTS OF A DASHBOARD

Mission Statement

A **mission statement** is a declaration of the reason for the existence of an organization. It should be short and memorable, as well as noble and motivational. It should be easily remembered by all stakeholders of the organization and should be used in decision making at all levels within the organization. State Farm Insurance Company has an excellent mission statement: "To help people manage the risks of everyday life, recover from the unexpected and realize their dreams." Or, to restate this mission in terms of the State Farm philosophy statement: "Like a good neighbor, State Farm is there." This is a noble and memorable statement.

Mission statements are constructed using several methods. One method is for the president to develop a mission statement in the privacy of his or her own mind. Another method is for top management to go off on a retreat and come back with a mission statement. Yet another method is for top management, in conjunction with the organization's stakeholders, to use quality management tools to develop a mission statement. In the opinion of the authors, all three methods are correct in the right circumstances.

The third method for constructing a mission statement involves having a meeting of organizational stakeholders in which brainstorming is conducted around the question, What should be the elements of the mission statement? Once brainstorming is ended, the people at the meeting study the data (using an affinity diagram, which is discussed in Section 15.1) to identify the underlying structure of the key elements of the mission statement for the organization. Next, a subgroup of the people attending the meeting develop a draft mission statement and circulate it for comment. This process is repeated until consensus is achieved for the mission statement.

Key Objectives

There are two kinds of **key objectives**, business objectives and strategic objectives [Reference 5, p. 69]. **Business objectives** are the goals that must routinely be pursued within an organization if it is to function. Producing paper in a paper mill, answering customer inquiries in a call center, preparing paychecks in a payroll department, or doing return on investment (ROI) calculations in a finance department are examples of business objectives. **Strategic objectives** are the goals that must be accomplished to pursue the presidential strategy of an organization. For example, one of the strategic objectives of the University of Miami is to "gerontologize" the entire university. *Gerontologize* is a term used at the University of Miami to describe the strategic objective of creating a focus on human aging in all relevant processes and functions. Any objective at any level within the university that promotes gerontologizing the university is a strategic objective. Any other objective (provided that it doesn't support another of the president's strategies) is not a strategic objective; it is a business objective. Another example of a strategic objective is the implementation of Six Sigma management as the method for conducting business at General Electric. Any General Electric objective at any level that promotes Six Sigma management is a strategic objective. Any other objective (provided that it doesn't support another of the president's strategies) is not a strategic objective; it is a business objective.

There are four basic categories of key objectives: financial, process improvement and innovation, customer satisfaction, and employee growth and development [see Reference 5, p. 69]. Examples of each key objective category are shown below.

Financial Key Objectives. Examples of **financial key objectives** include management and stockholders' desire for more profit, market share, dominance and growth, and the desire for less waste, turnover, financial loss, and customer defection.

Process Improvement Key Objectives. Examples of **process improvement key objectives** include:

1. Management's desire for consistency and uniformity of output
2. High productivity
3. Products, services, and processes that exceed the needs and wants of current and future stakeholders
4. Products, services, and processes that are easy to create and low cost to provide
5. Products and services that meet technical specifications
6. Products and services that do not incur warranty costs
7. Products that are easy to distribute throughout the channels of distribution.

Customer Satisfaction Key Objectives. There are four types of **customer satisfaction key objectives:**

1. Customers' desired outcomes,
2. Customers' undesired outcomes,
3. Customers' desired product and service attributes, and
4. Customers' desired process characteristics.

Examples of customer desired key objectives include joy, security, personal time, belonging, and health, and customer's undesired outcomes such as avoidance or elimination of death, taxes, discomfort, wasted time, and frustration. Examples of customers' desired product and service attribute key objectives include ease-of-use, accessibility, low cost of ownership, durability, and appeal. Examples of customers' desired process characteristic key objectives include timely arrival of product, no waiting time, and ease of acquisition.

Employee Growth and Development Key Objectives. Examples of **employee growth and development key objectives** include:

- Improving leadership skills,
- Providing training opportunities,

- Providing educational opportunities
- Creating the opportunity to work on stimulating special assignments

Leading and Lagging Indicators. It is interesting to consider that financial objectives are a result of customer satisfaction objectives, that customer satisfaction objectives are a result of process improvement objectives, and that process improvement objectives are a function of employee growth and development objectives.

Key Indicators

A **key indicator** is a measurement that monitors the status of a key objective. There are five types of key indicators:

1. Attribute indicators
2. Measurement indicators
3. Binary indicators
4. List by time period indicators
5. Gantt chart indicators

Attribute Key Indicators. Attribute indicators are used when a key objective is being monitored using attribute data (classification or count data, see Section 9.4) over time. Some examples of attribute-type classification indicators are the percentage of defective products produced by week, the percentage of customers complaining per month, and the percentage of accounts receivables over 90 days by quarter. Some examples of attribute type count indicators are the number of industrial accidents per week, the number of customer complaints per month, and the number of thefts per quarter.

Measurement Key Indicators. Measurement indicators are used when a key indicator is being monitored using measurement type data (see Section 9.4). Measurement data can be displayed over time in a run chart, by average and range by time period, by average and standard deviation by time period, or by a distribution by time period. Examples of measurement-type indicators are cycle time to file a report, waiting times in a bank, and diameter of a ball bearing.

Binary Key Indicators. Binary indicators (Yes/No by date) are used to monitor whether an action has been accomplished by a given date. An example of a binary key indicator is "Computer system operational by July 12, 2004? (Yes or No)."

List Key Indicators. List indicators are used to monitor a group of people or items for compliance to some deadline or standard. Two examples of list key indicators are "List of employees not trained in the new safety standards by December 31, 2004" and "List of laboratories not up to federal code standards as of June 15, 2004."

Gantt Chart Key Indicators. Gantt chart indicators (see Section 15.10) are used as a record-keeping device for following the progression in time of the tasks required to complete a project. A Gantt chart indicates which tasks are on or behind schedule. An example of a generic Gantt chart key indicator is shown in Table 3.2.

Table 3.2 shows that task 3 is planned to begin in May and end in September, and task 4 begins in September and ends in December.

TABLE 3.2 Generic Gantt Chart

Tasks	Resp.	J	F	M	A	M	J	J	A	S	O	N	D	J	F	Comments
Task 1	HG	B		E												
Task 2	HG				B		E									
Task 3	DL					B				E						
Task 4	DL									B			E			
Task 5	DL											B	E			
Task 6	HG													B	E	

HG = Howard Gitlow, DL = David Levine, B = begin, E = end.

Flag Diagrams. A tool used to track the contributions of subordinate key indicators to the pursuit of superior key indicators is called a **flag diagram** [see Reference 3, pp. 3 and 34]. There are two types of flag diagrams, additive flag diagrams and nonadditive flag diagrams.

If corporate indicators are the summation of departmental indicators, then it is appropriate to use an **additive flag diagram**. An example of an additive flag diagram in which the corporate indicator (Y) is a linear combination of the departmental indicators $(X_1 + X_2 + X_3 + X_4)$ can be seen in the case of burglaries on a university campus as a function of the buildings where the burglaries occurred.

Y_i = total burglaries on campus in month i

X_{1i} = burglaries in building 1 in month i,

X_{2i} = burglaries in building 2 in month i,

X_{3i} = burglaries in building 3 in month i,

X_{4i} = burglaries in building 4 in month i.

(This assumes that all burglaries are inside one of the four buildings.)

If corporate indicators are not the summation of departmental indicators, it is appropriate to use **nonadditive flag diagrams**. In this case, knowledge, experience, and statistical expertise are required to determine the relationships between corporate and departmental indicators. An example of a nonadditive flag diagram in which the corporate indicator (Y) is not a linear combination of the departmental indicators ($Y = f[X_{11}, X_{12}, X_{21}, X_{22}, X_{31}, X_{32}, X_{41}, X_{42}]$) can be seen in the number of burglaries on a university campus as a function of the number of doors left open (unlocked) in the building where the burglaries occurred.

Y_i = total burglaries on campus in month i

X_{11i} = number of open doors in building 1 in month i,

X_{12i} = number of hours police patrol in building 1 in month i,

X_{21i} = number of open doors in building 2 in month i,

X_{22i} = number of hours of police patrol in building 2 in month i,

X_{31i} = number of open doors in building 3 in month i,

X_{32i} = number of hours of police patrol in building 3 in month i,

X_{41i} = number of open doors in building 4 in month i,

X_{42i} = number of hours of police patrol in building 4 in month i.

Tasks and Projects

A **task** is a process improvement activity in which the necessary process change is known by the process owner, but he or she has not yet had an opportunity to effect the process change. The need for a task is determined by a chronic gap between the real and the ideal value of a key indicator. A **project** is a process improvement activity in which the necessary process change is unknown by the process owner. Generally, the process owner forms a Six Sigma team to identify and test the necessary process change(s). The need for a project is determined by a chronic gap between the real and the ideal values of a key indicator. There are three categories of projects or tasks: zero projects or tasks, increase projects or tasks, and decrease projects or tasks [see Reference 4].

Zero Project or Task. In a **zero project or task**, the ideal value of a key indicator is zero or the optimal difference between the current value and the ideal value of a key indicator is zero. The purposes of a zero project or task are to get the current value of a key indicator to be zero (the ideal value of the key indicator) by a given date or to reduce the gap to zero between the current value of a key indicator and the ideal value of a key indicator by a given date. Examples of zero tasks or projects are to reduce to zero the proportion of defective units by day or to reduce unit-to-unit variation around nominal of gold bar weights.

Increase Project or Task. In an **increase project or task**, the ideal value of the key indicator is X units or Y percentage points higher than the current value of the key indicator. The purposes of an increase task or project are:

1. To get the real value of a key indicator to be X units or Y percentage points higher by a given date
2. To raise the ideal value of the key indicator by a given date
3. To establish or clarify the ideal value for a key indicator by a given date.

Examples of increase projects or tasks are to increase revenue or to increase profit.

Decrease Project or Task. In a **decrease project or task,** the ideal value of the key indicator is X units or Y percentage points lower than the current value of the key indicator. The purposes of a decrease task or project are:

1. To get the current value of a key indicator to be X units or Y percentage points lower by a given date
2. To lower the ideal value of the key indicator by a given date
3. To establish or clarify the ideal value for a key indicator by a given date

Zero is not a rational target for a decrease task or project. Most costs of doing business cannot be zero if the business is still operating. Examples of decrease tasks or projects are to reduce costs or to decrease cycle time.

Models for Managing Projects. There are two popular models for managing projects, the SDSA - PDSA model and the DMAIC model. Both of these models were defined and discussed in Chapter 2. The DMAIC model is discussed in detail in Chapters 4–8.

3.3 EXAMPLE OF A DASHBOARD

The University of Miami has a classic type of organizational structure. It is composed of several divisions, for example, Medical Affairs, Academic Affairs, Business and Finance, Governmental Relations, and Student Affairs. Each division is composed of several departments, for example, the Business and Finance division is composed of Business Services, Facilities Administration, Human Resources, Information Technology, Continuous Improvement, Treasurer, Controller, and Real Estate. Each department is composed of several areas, for example, the Business Services department is composed of Public Safety and Parking, Purchasing, and Safety and Environmental Health, to name a few.

An example of a dashboard between a third- (Vice President of Business Services) and fourth- (Chief of Campus Police) tier manager in Figure 3.1 is shown in Table 3.3.

The mission of the Business Services Department is "Optimum SAS" (security, assets and services). The Vice President of Business Services promotes the Business Services department mission statement through three key objectives:

1. Improve security on campus
2. Protect university assets
3. Improve university services

The first key objective (improve security on campus) is measured through eight key indicators:

1. Number of murders by month (SEC1)
2. Number of rapes by month (SEC2)

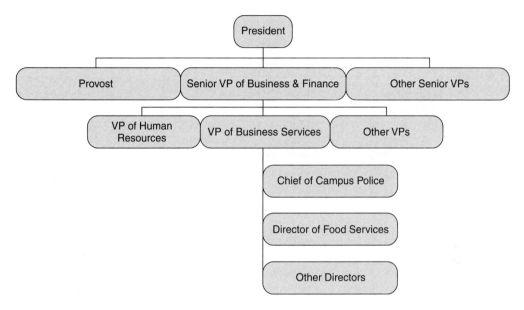

FIGURE 3.1 Partial Organizational Chart of the University of Miami

TABLE 3.3 Portion of a Dashboard from the Above Organizational Chart

Mission statement for Business Services Department of the Business and Finance Division of the University of Miami: *"Optimum SAS."*				
Vice President of Business Services		**Chief of Campus Police**		**Tasks or projects**
Key objectives	**Key indicators**	**Key objectives**	**Key indicators**	
Improve security on campus	SEC1: Number of murders, by month	No murders. No objective other than to continue with current processes	SEC1: List of murders, by month	No murders. No task or project
	SEC2: Number of rapes, by month	Detail not shown		
	SEC3: Number of robberies, by month	Detail not shown		
	SEC4: Number of aggravated as-saults, by month	Detail not shown		*(continued)*

TABLE 3.3 Portion of a Dashboard from the Above Organizational Chart   *(Continued)*

Mission statement for Business Services Department of the Business and Finance Division of the University of Miami: *"Optimum SAS."*				
Vice President of Business Services		**Chief of Campus Police**		**Tasks or projects**
Key objectives	**Key indicators**	**Key objectives**	**Key indicators**	
	SEC5: Number of burglaries, by month	Reduce number of open doors on campus	SEC5A: Number of open doors, by department, by building, overall, by month	The Police Chief established a team to study SEC5. Team members determined that most burglaries occurred when doors were left open (SEC5A).
	SEC6: Number of larcenies, by month	Detail not shown		
	SEC7: Number of auto thefts by month prior to September 1999 (see Figure 3.2)	Optimize deployment of police patrols in parking lots	SEC7: Number of auto thefts by month before and after September 1999 (see Figure 3.3)	The Police Chief established a team to study SEC7. Team members determined that most auto thefts occur in two parking lots between 7:00 a.m. and 7:00 p.m. Consequently, the Police Chief redeployed the police force to heavily patrol the two problematic lots between 7:00 a.m. and 7:00 p.m. during September 1999. SEC7 showed a dramatic reduction after redeployment of the police force (see Figure 3.3).
	SEC8: Number of arsons, by month	Detail not shown		
Protect University assets	Detail not shown			
Improve University services	Detail not shown			

SAS = Security, assets, and services.

3. Number of robberies by month (SEC3)

4. Number of aggravated assaults by month (SEC4)

5. Number of burglaries by month (SEC5)

6. Number of larcenies by month (SEC6)

7. Number of auto thefts by month (SEC7)

8. Number of arsons by month (SEC8)

An example of a key indicator can be seen in Figure 3.2. Figure 3.2 shows the number of auto thefts by month (SEC7) before September 1999. September 1999 is the month that a Six Sigma project team implemented a change to the process for patrolling parking lots.

The Chief of Campus Police promotes the mission statement of the Business Services Department by studying his superior's key indicator data to identify his key objectives. For example, the Police Chief established a daily management team to study the number of auto thefts by month (SEC7), as shown in Figure 3.2. The team members determined that the number of auto thefts per month is a stable process, and most auto thefts occur in two campus parking lots between 7:00 a.m. and 7:00 p.m. The Police Chief redeployed the police force to patrol the two problematic lots heavily between 7:00 a.m. and 7:00 p.m. in September 1999. Subsequently, as shown in the line graph in Figure 3.3, there was a drastic reduction in the number of auto thefts by month (SEC7).

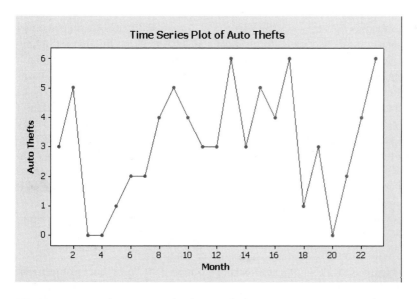

FIGURE 3.2 Minitab Line Graph of Auto Thefts on Campus per Month prior to September 1999

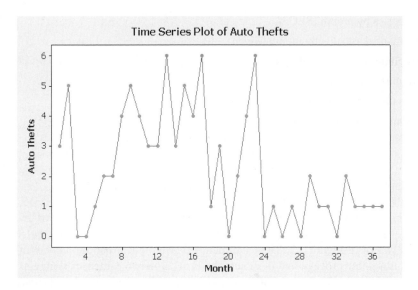

FIGURE 3.3 Minitab Line Graph of Auto Thefts on Campus per Month before and after September 1999

3.4 MANAGING WITH A DASHBOARD

Top management uses a dashboard at monthly operations review meetings for several purposes. First, managers use dashboards to clarify key objectives and accountability among all personnel and areas. Second, managers use dashboards to promote statistical thinking by monitoring key indicators using control charts (see Chapter 14). For example, is the sales volume for last month due to a special or common cause of variation in the selling process? Third, a manager uses dashboards to develop and test hypotheses concerning potential changes to processes. A hypothesis test analyzes the effect of a change concept on a key indicator (e.g., Figure 3.3 for the auto theft example). Fourth, a manger uses dashboards to ensure the routine and regular updating of key indicators. Fifth, a manager uses dashboards to provide a context for crises. For example a hospital experiences a medical error that has dramatic consequences for a patient. The ensuing legal action may focus solely on the one medical error. A dashboard puts the error in context by dividing it by the number of medical interactions in the time frame in question. Further, the dashboard records the "% of medical errors" indicator over time.

Managers can use the following questions when conducting a monthly review meeting to get the most out of their dashboards [see Reference 5].

- Are the key objectives and key indicators on the dashboard the "best" set of objectives and indicators to attain the mission statement?
- Is the dashboard balanced with respect to customer, process, employee, and financial objectives? Do any areas have too much (or too little) representation on the dashboard?

- What products and/or services are most critical to your organization achieving its mission statement? List the top 5 or 10 products and services.

- Are targets being met in a timely fashion for all key objectives? Remember, targets are set to allocate resources to projects.

- What process is used to manage, perform, and improve project work?

- Which key indicators on the dashboard are used to measure customer satisfaction and dissatisfaction? Are these measures operationally defined? Are these measures adequate?

- What process is used to motivate project work? Six Sigma?

- Does your organization have the ability to identify the ROI from its dashboard? How is ROI measured?

Coordinating Projects in a Department or Area

Departments or areas that are assigned multiple projects or tasks coordinated them through a **local steering team (LST)** [see References 1 and 2]. An LST is a departmental or area committee that is responsible for promoting and managing the resources and people necessary to accomplish all of the Six Sigma projects and tasks in their department or area.

3.5 PRIORITIZATION OF SIX SIGMA PROJECTS

Once the Six Sigma projects and tasks required to pursue the presidential key objectives have been identified through the dashboard, the projects are prioritized for receiving resources using a project prioritization matrix. A **project prioritization matrix** (see Table 3.4) is constructed using the following method. First, the Office of the President creates the shell matrix shown in Table 3.4 by listing the actual presidential objectives in the rows and the potential Six Sigma projects in the columns; there may be a lot of columns. Second, the Finance Department weighs the importance of the presidential key objectives to achieving bottom-line results on a 0–1 scale; the weights are called the W_i, where W_i indicates the weight of the ith presidential objective. The sum of the $W_i = 1.0$. Third, a committee is appointed by the Office of the President to document the relationships between potential projects (columns in Table 3.4) and the presidential objectives (rows in Table 3.4). The relationship values are recorded in the appropriate cells of Table 3.4. The relationship values are: 0 = no relationship, 1 = weak relationship, 3 = moderate relationship, and 9 = strong relationship. Cell values are determined by the committee members with the strong guidance of the Finance Department. Fourth, the committee members compute the weighted average relationship scores for each project in the "Weighted average of potential projects (benefits)" row of Table 3.4. Fifth, the committee members estimate the budget for each potential project and record the values in the "Estimated budget for potential project (costs)" row of Table 3.4. Sixth, committee members compute the benefit/cost ratio for each potential project and place the values in the "(Benefit/cost) ratio for potential project" row of Table 3.4. Seventh, the potential projects with the highest benefit/cost ratios are funded by the Office of the President, up to the total budget available for projects. Eighth, project team members create a

TABLE 3.4 Shell Project Prioritization Matrix

Presidential objectives			Potential Six Sigma projects			
			Project 1	**Project 2**	**. . .**	**Project k**
O1	W	W1				
O2	E	W2				
	I					
	G					
Om	H	Wm				
	T					
	S					
Weighted average of potential projects (Benefits)						
Estimated budget for potential project (cost)						
(Benefit/cost) ratio for potential project						
Gantt chart for selected project						

draft Gantt chart (see Section 15.6) for the selected projects and review the timelines with top management. The Gantt charts are pretty rough at this stage of the projects.

A portion of the project prioritization matrix for the University of Miami case study presented earlier is shown in Table 3.5.

Table 3.5 shows that the "open door" project (resulting from analysis of Key Indicator SEC5 in Table 3.3) and the "auto theft" project had the highest benefit/cost) ratios. Further, only $15,000 was available to finance projects, making it possible to support both projects.

Questions for champions to ask each potential project team:

- Why do the project at all?
- Why do the project now?
- Describe the current problem or opportunity. What is the pain or gain?
- Describe the goal (desired state) for the future.
- What are the expected benefits?

TABLE 3.5 Project Prioritization Matrix

Presidential business objectives			Potential projects			
			Project 1: Open Door Project	**Project 2: Auto Theft Project**	. . .	**Project k**
BO1: Improve security	W E I G H T S	W1 = ..33	9	9		
BO2: Protect assets		W2 = ..33	9	3	. . .	
BO3: Provide services		W3 = ..33	9	3		
Weighted average of potential projects (benefits)			9.0	5.0		2.2
Estimated budget for project (cost)			$5,000	$10,000	. . .	$100,000
(Benefit/cost) ratio for Project × 1,000,000			1800	500		22
Gantt chart for project						

3.6 MANAGEMENT DECIDES WHETHER A PROJECT TEAM IS NECESSARY

The process owner and champion decide whether a potential Six Sigma project creates a high-priority opportunity to positively impact customers' needs and wants and key objectives. If the project receives a "no" to the above question, the project is dropped, at least for now. If the project receives a "yes" to the above question, the project continues to the define phase so the process owner and champion can charter the Six Sigma team.

SUMMARY

Dashboards are valuable tools that focus employees' efforts on the mission statement of their organization. This is accomplished by developing a cascading and interlocking system of key objectives and indicators throughout all levels of the organization. Each employee can identify his or her key objectives by studying his or her superior's key indicators. This study identifies the projects and tasks needed to attain key objectives.

REFERENCES

1. Gitlow, H., Oppenheim, A., Oppenheim, R. and Levine, D., *Quality Management: Tools and Methods for Improvement,* 3rd ed. (New York: McGraw-Hill-Irwin, 2005)

2. Gitlow, H., *Quality Management Systems: A Practical Guide,* (Boca Raton, FL: St. Lucie Press, 2000).

3. Kano, Noriaki, Second Report on TQC at Florida Power & Light Company, (Miami, FL), October 1, 1986.

4. Kano, N., Yamaura, M., Toyoshima, M., and Nishinomiya, K., "Study on the Methods for Solving Increase, Reduction, and Zero Problems Encountered in the Promotion of TQC: Pasts I and II," unpublished paper.

5. Lawton, R., "Balance Your Balanced Scorecard," *Quality Progress,* 35, 2002, p. 66–71.

DEFINE PHASE OF THE DMAIC MODEL

CHAPTER OUTLINE

4.1   Activate the Six Sigma Project Team
4.2   Structure of the Define Phase
4.3   Prepare the Project Charter
4.4   Conduct an SIPOC Analysis
4.5   Perform a Voice of the Customer Analysis
4.6   Finalize the Project Objective
4.7   Champion and Process Owner Tollgate Reviews
4.8   Presidential Tollgate Reviews
4.9   Define Phase Tollgate Review Checklist

LEARNING OBJECTIVES

After reading this chapter, you will be able to:

- Activate a Six Sigma project
- Prepare a business case for a Six Sigma project
- Conduct an SIPOC analysis
- Conduct a Voice of the Customer analysis
- Construct a Six Sigma project charter
- Conduct a tollgate review of the Define phase
- Get sign-off for a Six Sigma project from the champion and the process owner

INTRODUCTION

This chapter explains how to perform the define phase of the Six Sigma DMAIC model. The define phase has three main component parts. The first part is the development of a project charter, which includes a project objective for the Six Sigma project. The second part is performing an SIPOC analysis to: identify the **S**uppliers to the process under study, list the **I**nputs provided by those suppliers, flowchart the **P**rocess under study at a very high level of abstraction, list the **O**utputs of the process, and finally, identify the **C**ustomers or market segments for the outputs. The third step is to perform a Voice of the Customer (VoC) analysis to discover the product, service, or process characteristics that are critical to the customer's view of quality, called *critical to quality* (CTQ). Finally, team members go back and revise the entire define phase based on any facts discovered in the SIPOC analysis or the VoC, for example, the project objective.

4.1 ACTIVATING A SIX SIGMA PROJECT TEAM

Recall, a Six Sigma project is identified when a key indicator for a key objective on an organization's dashboard exhibits a problematic difference between its ideal state and its actual state. A difference is considered problematic if it is deemed so by management. A problematic difference could be due to either a special cause or a common cause of variation. For example, a key objective might be "to reduce the number of auto thefts on a college campus" with a key indicator of "number of auto thefts by month." If the ideal number of auto thefts per month is zero and the actual number of auto thefts per month exhibits a stable distribution with an average of nine auto thefts per month (and rarely goes above 18), some managers might consider this to be a problem. In another example, a key objective might be "to arrive on time in the conduct of service calls by week" with a key indicator of "the average and range of minutes early or late from a random sample of five service calls each week for each service representative." If the ideal number of minutes early or late is zero, but the actual number of minutes early or late appears to be stable and predictable with an average of 240 minutes and an average range of 70 minutes for a particular service representative, many managers might consider this to be a problematic difference between the ideal and the actual number of minutes early or late for a service call for that service representative.

If a problematic difference exists for a key indicator attached to a key objective, this creates a potential Six Sigma project. Recall, management prioritizes potential Six Sigma projects for attention by teams using Table 3.4 on page 58. The potential projects with the highest benefit/cost ratios are funded up to the total budget available for projects. Project team members create Gantt charts for the selected projects and review the timelines with top management.

For Six Sigma projects that have been funded, the champion and process owner select a green belt or black belt to be the team leader. Next, the team leader selects the team members. Then the team leader and champion identify the Finance and Information Technology (IT) representatives and obtain all approvals for team activities.

A fictitious case study (see References 6 and 7) is used to illustrate all phases of the DMAIC model. The idea for this case study came from an exercise that was originally developed by Oriel, Inc. (Madison, WI) for Six Sigma materials used in part by Johnson & Johnson, including

Cordis Corporation, a division of Johnson & Johnson. This case study concerns a company called Paper Organizers International (POI). POI offers a full range of filing, organizing, and paper-shuffling services. To accomplish these tasks, POI purchases metallic securing devices (MSDs, or paper clips), staplers, hole punchers, folders, three-ring binders, and a full range of related products to serve its customers' paper-handling needs. The employees, or internal customers, of POI use MSDs to organize piles of paper pending placement into folders or binders.

The Purchasing Department of POI has noticed an increase in complaints from employees in the Paper-Shuffling Department (PSD) about MSDs breaking and failing to keep papers together. This creates opportunities for client papers to be mixed together. The Purchasing Department would like to improve the process for purchasing MSDs to eliminate complaints from employees in the Paper-Shuffling Department.

POI's mission statement is "Put the Right Information in the Right Place," **RIP** it! To accomplish this mission, POI has established a cascading set of business objectives and business indicators, which ultimately result in potential Six Sigma projects; see Table 4.1 below.

TABLE 4.1 POI's Business Objectives and Indicators with Potential Six Sigma Projects

President		Director of PSD		
Business objectives	**Business indicators**	**Area objectives**	**Area indicators**	**Potential Six Sigma projects**
Increase the number of orders	Number of orders/month	Increase the number of orders in PSD	Number of orders in PSD/month	New Customer Promotions Project
Increase the number of POI services (filing, organizing, etc) utilized by each customer	1. Average number of services utilized per customer/quarter 2. Standard deviation of number of services utilized per customer/ quarter	Increase the number of services utilized by each customer in PSD	1. Average number of services utilized per PSD customer/quarter 2. Standard deviation of number of services utilized per PSD customer/quarter	Existing Customer Promotions Project
Minimize production costs	Production costs/ month	Minimize production costs in PSD	Production costs in PSD/ month (see Figure 4.1)	MSD Quality Project
Eliminate employee complaints	Number of employee complaints/month	Eliminate employee complaints from PSD	Number of employee complaints from PSD/ month	Employee Morale Project

The monthly production costs in the PSD are shown on the Individuals and Moving Range control chart in Figure 4.1 below; see the next-to-last row in the fourth column in Table 4.1. Control charts are discussed in Chapter 14 of this book.

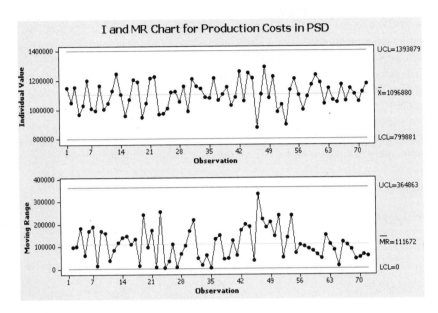

FIGURE 4.1 Individual and Moving Range Chart Obtained from Minitab of Monthly Production Costs in the PSD

Monthly production costs form a stable and predictable system of variation, with an average monthly production cost of $1,096,880 (top panel of Figure 4.1) and an average moving range of $111,672 (bottom panel of Figure 4.1). The distribution of monthly production costs is approximately normally distributed; see Figure 4.2. Team members discovered that PSD management considers monthly production costs to be very high, given the volume of work being processed by the department.

The four potential Six Sigma projects shown in the rightmost column of Table 4.1 are prioritized for attention in Table 4.2. Table 4.2 is a matrix that weighs the importance of each potential Six Sigma project to each of POIs business objectives.

The cell values are assigned by top management and are defined as follows: 0 = no relationship, 1 = weak relationship, 3 = moderate relationship, and 9 = strong relationship. The Finance Department developed the importance weights for each business objective to maximize the impact of Six Sigma projects on the bottom line of the organization. Consequently, the most critical project with respect to the business objectives is the MSD Quality Project. It has a weighted average of 4.95, as shown in the last row of Table 4.2. The champion of the MSD Quality Project and the process owner of the MSD purchasing process activated the MSD quality team.

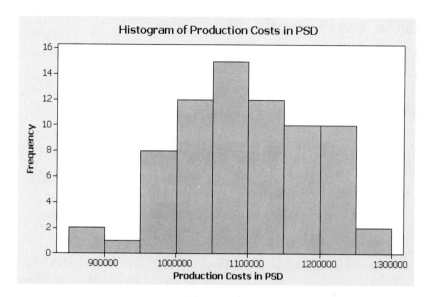

FIGURE 4.2 Histogram Obtained from Minitab of Monthly Production Costs in the PSD

TABLE 4.2 Prioritization of Six Sigma Projects

			Potential Six Sigma projects			
Business objectives			**New Customer Promotions Project**	**Existing Customer Promotions Project**	**MSD Quality Project**	**Employee Morale Project**
Increase the number of orders	W E	0.35	3	3	0	0
Increase the number of POI services utilized by each customer	I G H	0.10	1	3	0	0
Minimize production costs	T S	0.40	0	0	9	3
Eliminate employee complaints		0.15	0	0	9	9
Weighted average of potential Six Sigma projects			1.15 = 0.35 × 3 + 0.1 × 1 + 0.4 × 0 + 0.15 × 0	1.35 = 0.35 × 3 + 0.10 × 3 + 0.40 × 0 + 0.15 × 0	4.95 = 0.35 × 0 + 0.10 × 0 + 0.40 × 9 + 0.15 × 9	2.55 = 0.35 × 0 + 0.10 × 0 + 0.40 × 3 + 0.15 × 9

4.2 STRUCTURE OF THE DEFINE PHASE

The define phase of the DMAIC model has three distinct parts:

1. Prepare an initial project charter.
2. Conduct an SIPOC analysis.
3. Perform a VoC analysis.

4.3 PROJECT CHARTER

Introduction

The background for a project charter consists of a business case, a problem statement, a goal statement, a scope, a schedule with milestones, a list of benefits, a list of roles and responsibilities, and a draft project objective. It provides the basis for a "go-no go" decision on a Six Sigma project and, if it is a "go" decision, documentation for an agreement between management and a Six Sigma project team about deliverables.

Background for the Business Case

The purpose of the **business case** is to get the Six Sigma project team members to answer a set of partially redundant questions on the benefits and costs of a project. The questions are:

- What is the name of the process?
- What is the aim of the process?
- Why do the project at all?
- Why do the project now?
- What are the consequences of not doing the project?
- What other projects have higher or equal priority, if any?
- What presidential objectives on the dashboard are supported by the project?

The above questions are partially redundant to increase the likelihood of team members obtaining all of the information needed for the project charter.

The answers to the above questions are as follows for the MSD purchasing process Six Sigma project.

1. Question: What is the name of the process?

   Answer: MSD purchasing process. The first step in the supply chain for the MSD process is the process for purchasing MSDs; hence, the first operation to be investigated by MSD

Quality Project team members is the process for purchasing MSDs. Team members may study other factors that affect the quality of MSDs, such as method of use or shelf life, at a later time.

2. Question: What is the aim of the process?

Answer: The aim of the purchasing process as it relates to this project is to purchase MSDs that improve the productivity and morale of the employees in the PSD.

3. Question: Why do the MSD project at all?

Answer: According to a judgment sample of three employees and two managers from the PSD, team members determined that MSDs that cannot withstand four or more bends are unacceptable because they are unlikely to remain intact throughout the paper-shuffling processes and will not hold papers tightly. This is called *durability*. Defective MSDs create costs for POI, for example: (a) papers from different clients may get mixed together if not properly bound, requiring additional processing time; (b) employees may have to use multiple MSDs for one project, creating additional material costs; and (c) employees get frustrated and do not perform their jobs efficiently and productively, increasing labor costs. Additionally, team members discovered that a large proportion of the boxes containing MSDs arrive at the PSD with more than five broken MSDs. This is called *functionality*. This creates additional processing costs for POI—for example, increased unit costs and frustrated and nonproductive employees and managers. Team members used the same judgment sample as above and determined that approximately 60% of individual MSDs do not meet durability criteria, and 60% of MSD boxes do not meet functionality criteria, as illustrated in the survey questionnaire in Figure 4.3 and the data matrix in Table 4.3.

Survey
Name: _____

1. Please estimate the percentage of MSDs that cannot withstand 4 or more bends. _____
2. Please estimate the percentage of MSD boxes that contain greater than 5 broken MSDs. ____

FIGURE 4.3 Survey Questionnaire

TABLE 4.3 Survey Data

Survey Number	Response Q1	Response Q2
1—Employee 1	55	70
2—Employee 2	50	55
3—Employee 3	60	65
4—Manager 1	65	60
5—Manager 2	70	50
Average	60	60

4. Question: Why do the MSD project now?

   Answer: The PSD is experiencing very high monthly production costs; see Figures 4.1 and 4.2 on pages 64 and 65. Also, internal customers, including managers and hourly employees, are submitting an increased number of complaints: 14 in the first quarter, 18 in the second quarter, and 32 in the third quarter, as recorded in the PSD's complaint log for the fiscal year 2000. There are 100 hourly workers in the PSD.

5. Question: What business objectives are supported by the MSD Quality Project?

   Answer: The MSD project is most strongly related to the "minimize production costs" and "eliminate employee complaints" business objectives; see Table 4.2.

6. Question: What are the consequences of not doing the project?

   Answer: The consequences of not doing the project are decreased profit margins due to higher production costs and decreased employee motivation due to frustration with materials.

7. What projects have higher or equal priority?

   Answer: At this time, the MSD Quality Project has the highest priority; see Table 4.2 on page 65.

Problem Statement

The purpose of the **problem statement** is to describe the problem, opportunity, or objective in clear, concise, and measurable terms. The problem statement answers the question, What pain is the organization experiencing that this Six Sigma project could reduce or eliminate?

The answer to the above question for the MSD Quality Project is that low-quality MSDs create additional production costs and employee frustration.

Goal Statement

The **goal statement** describes the team's improvement objective. It begins with a verb such as *reduce, eliminate, control,* or *increase.*

The goal statement for the MSD Quality Project, as determined by the champion and process owner of the MSD purchasing process, is initially to create a 100-fold improvement in MSD quality. The concept of a 100-fold improvement is derived from Motorola's 1986 stated improvement rate of tenfold every 2 years or 100-fold every 4 years during the kickoff of the Six Sigma effort. Because 100-fold improvement means that the defects per million opportunities (DPMO) would decrease from 600,000 (60% defect rate $\times$ 1,000,000 from Table 4.3) to 6,000, and a DPMO of 6,210 represents a Four Sigma process, team members decided to use Four Sigma as the goal for the MSD project.

Project Scope

The **project scope** is created by answering the following questions:

1. What are the process boundaries?
2. What, if anything, is out of bounds?
3. What resources are available for the project?
4. Who can approve expenditures?
5. How much can the team spend beyond its budget without authority?
6. What are the obstacles and constraints of the project?
7. What time commitment is expected of team members?
8. What will happen to each team member's regular job during the project?

The answers to the above questions for the MSD Quality Project are as follows:

1. What are the process boundaries?

   Answer: The starting point for the project is when the Purchasing Department receives purchase orders from the PSD. The stopping point for the project is when the PSD places MSDs into inventory.

2. What, if anything, is out of bounds?

   Answer: The project team cannot change the way employees handle or use MSDs.

3. What resources are available for the project?

   Answer: The budget for the MSD project is $30,000. This includes estimated hourly salaries of project participants. Team members Brian Mercurio and Jeremy Pressman are the only project participants who will incur additional job responsibilities as a result of the project. Budget estimates show "opportunity cost" and "hard costs" (see Table 4.4). The expected opportunity cost ($15,540) and the estimated hard cost ($10,500) are both less than the budget of $30,000.

TABLE 4.4 Estimated Labor Costs for the Project

Name	Position	Estimated salary/ hour	Expected number of hours per week	Expected opportunity costs for 21 weeks	Expected hard costs for 21 weeks (direct labor costs)
Howard Gitlow	Champion	$100	2	$4,200	
Dana Rasis	Process owner	$50	2	$2,100	
Bettina Arguelles	Black belt	$50	5	$5,250	
Brian Mercurio	Team member	$25	10	$0	$5,250
Jeremy Pressman	Team member	$25	10	$0	$5,250
Lindsey Barton	Finance rep.	$45	2	$1,890	
Mary Montano	IT rep.	$50	2	$2,100	
Total				$15,540	$10,500

4. Question: Who can approve expenditures?

   Answer: Only the process owner, Dana Rasis, can approve expenditures.

5. How much can the team spend beyond its budget without authority?

   Answer: Nothing.

6. What are the obstacles and constraints of the project?

   Answer: The team must work within a $30,000 budget and a 21-week time constraint.

7. What time commitment is expected of team members?

   Answer: Team members are expected to be present at weekly Friday morning meetings from 8:00 a.m. until 9:00 a.m. Team members are also expected to provide progress of project tasks at each meeting. Completion of project tasks may require additional hours of work per week.

8. What will happen to each team member's regular job during the project?

   Answer: If any, overtime hours will be compensated for team members and support staff. Note: The estimated rate for overtime labor is 1.5 times normal labor. The overtime labor rate is not used in the budget in Table 4.4.

A Schedule with Milestones

A Gantt chart is used to construct a schedule for the project and list out any milestones. It is a bar chart that plots tasks and subtasks against time. Once a list of tasks and subtasks has been created for a project, responsibilities can be assigned for each task or subtask. Next, beginning and finishing dates can be scheduled for each task and subtask. Finally, any milestones relevant to a task or subtask are placed on the Gantt chart. A generic Gantt chart is shown in Table 4.5.

The Gantt chart for the MSD project is shown in Table 4.6. As you can see, the define phase is expected to take 6 weeks, the measure phase 2 weeks, the analyze phase 3 weeks, the improve phase 6 weeks, and the control phase 4 weeks. After each phase, a set of deliverables or milestones is presented to the champion and process owner at a tollgate meeting. For example, the tollgate after the define phase requires an acceptable business case, SIPOC analysis, VoC analysis, and project objective.

Benefits and Costs

Six Sigma projects have both **soft benefits** and **hard benefits.** Examples of soft benefits include improving quality and morale and decreasing cycle time. Examples of hard (financial) benefits include increasing revenues or decreasing costs. Project team members "guesstimate" the dollar impact of the Six Sigma project. This guesstimate will be refined through iterative learning.

There are two taxonomies for classifying the potential cost-related benefits that may be realized from Six Sigma project.

Taxonomy 1: Cost Reduction versus Cost Avoidance. Cost reduction includes costs that fall to the bottom of the profit and loss statement. A cost reduction can be used to offset price or

TABLE 4.5 Generic Gantt Chart

Tasks	Responsibility	Timeline (Month)																		Milestones
		J	F	M	A	M	J	J	A	S	O	N	D	J	F	M	A	M	J	
Task 1																				
Subtask 1a																				
Subtask 1b																				
Task 2																				
Task 3																				
Subtask 3a																				
Subtask 3b																				
Subtask 3c																				

TABLE 4.6 Gantt Chart for the MSD Project

Tasks	Resp.	Week																					Milestones
		1	2	3	4	5	6	7	8	9	10	11	12	13	14	15	16	17	18	19	20	21	
Define	BA	x	x	x	x	x	x																Tollgate
Measure	BA							x	x														Tollgate
Analyze	BA									x	x	x											Tollgate
Improve	BA												x	x	x	x	x	x					Tollgate
Control	BA																		x	x	x	x	Tollgate

BA = Bettina Arguelles.

increase profit, or it can be reinvested elsewhere by management. Cost reductions are calculated by comparing the most recent accounting period's actual costs with the previous accounting period's actual costs. Cost avoidance includes those costs that can be reduced if management chooses to do so but until action is taken, no real costs are saved. An example is reducing labor hours needed to produce some fixed volume of work. Unless the head count that produces this fixed volume is reduced or an increased volume of work is completed with the same head count, there are no real savings realized. The impact of cost avoidance is not visible on the profit and loss statement and is difficult to define but is still important in meeting organizational goals.

Taxonomy 2: Tangible Costs versus Intangible Costs. Tangible costs are easily identified: for example, the costs of rejects, warranty, inspection, scrap, and rework. Intangible costs are costs that are difficult to measure: for example, the costs of long cycle times, many setups, expediting costs, low productivity, engineering change orders, low employee morale, turnover, low customer loyalty, lengthy installations, excess inventory, late delivery, overtime, lost sales, and customer dissatisfaction. It is important to realize that some of the most important benefits are unknown and unknowable. Hence, the guesstimate of benefits in the define phase often identifies a minimum estimate of intangible benefits.

The project team members develop a formula to guesstimate the potential benefits that the organization may realize due to the Six Sigma project. For example, a possible formula appears below:

Cost reductions _____

PLUS Cost Avoidance _____

PLUS Additional Revenue _____

LESS Implementation Costs _____

EQUALS Financial Benefits _____

The soft and hard benefits for the MSD project are shown below. The soft benefits of the project include eliminating complaints from the PSD and increasing employee morale. The hard (financial) benefits of the project are minimizing labor and material costs. The hard cost-related benefits are estimated in Table 4.7.

TABLE 4.7 Labor Costs

---

100 employees in the PSD

  × 40 hours/week/paper-shuffling employee

  × 10% of time devoted to clipping

@ 400 hours/week devoted to clipping in PSD

  × $25/hour/paper-shuffling employee

$10,000/week devoted to clipping

  × 50 weeks/year

$500,000/year devoted to clipping (does not include material costs)

  × 0.60 defective clips (judgment sample estimate of durability of the current system)

$300,000/year on defective clipping for current system

  × 0.0062 defective clips (durability of the proposed system) Again, broken clips are not selected for use on jobs.

$3,100/year on defective clipping for proposed system

Hence, the annual cost reduction on labor costs from improving the MSD purchasing process is $300,000 − $3,100 = $296,900. The PSD can now process its current work volume with six fewer full-time employees (computed by $296,900/$25 hour = 11,876 hours; 11,876/40 hours per week/50 weeks per year = 5.938, or approximately 6 employees). Note: The six employees are transferred to another department (making the same salary) that needs to hire six more workers due to attrition. The material costs of the current system are shown in Table 4.8.

TABLE 4.8 Material Costs

---

100 employees in the PSD
  × 60 projects/week/paper-shuffling employee
  × 50 weeks/year
@ 300,000 projects/year requiring 3,000,000 MSDs (10 clips per project on average)
  × 0.60 defective clips (judgment sample estimate of current system)
7,500,000* clips must be used to complete 300,000 projects
  × 0.01/clip
@ $75,000/year on clips in current system
  × 0.0062 defective clips **(proposed system)**
3,018,000** clips must be used to complete 300,000 projects
  × 0.01/clip
@ $30,180/year on clips in proposed system

---

*1/(1 − 0.6) = 2.5 clips needed to get a good clip. So 3,000,000 × 2.5 = 7,500,000.
**1/(1 − 0.0062) = 1.006 clips needed to get a good clip. So 3,000,000 × 1.006 = 3,018,000.

Hence, the annual savings on material costs from improving the MSD purchasing process is $75,000 − $30,180 = $44,820. This yields an annual total hard benefit savings of $296,900 +$44,820 = $341,720.

Roles and Responsibilities

The roles and responsibilities of team members must be clearly specified and agreed to by appropriate managers and supervisors. The roles and responsibilities of the team members for the MSD project are shown in Table 4.9.

Prepare a Draft Project Objective

A **project objective** is a clear statement of the purpose of a Six Sigma project. It contains five key elements: process, critical-to-quality (CTQ) characteristics measure, CTQ target, CTQ direction, and a deadline. A project objective is **SMART (Specific, Measurable, Attainable, Relevant, Time Bound).** The champion, team leader (green or black belt), process owner, and team members define a draft project objective.

TABLE 4.9 Roles and Responsibilities

Project Name: MSD Purchasing Process

Role	Responsibility	Stakeholder		Supervisor's Signature
		Signature	**Date**	
Champion	Howard Gitlow	HG	9/1/2003	
Process Owner	Dana Rasis	DR	9/1/2003	
Team Leader (Green Belt)	Bettina Arguelles	BA	9/2/2003	DR
Team Member 1	Bryan Mercurio	BM	9/3/2003	DR
Team Member 2	Jeremy Pressmen	JP	9/3/2003	DR
Finance Rep	Lindsey Barton	LB	9/4/2003	JR
IT Rep	Michelle Montano	MM	9/4/2003	LM

Draft Project Objective for the MSD Case Study : To decrease (direction) the percentage of MSDs that cannot withstand four or more bends without breaking (measure) and to decrease (direction) the proportion of boxes of MSDs that contain five or more broken clips (measure) bought by the Purchasing Department (process) to 00.62% (goal) by January 1, 2004 (deadline).

4.4 CONDUCTING AN SIPOC ANALYSIS

The second part of the define phase requires that team members perform an SIPOC analysis. An **SIPOC analysis** is a simple tool for identifying the suppliers and their inputs into a process, the high-level steps of a process, the outputs of the process, and the customer segments interested in the outputs. The format of an SIPOC analysis is shown in Figure 4.4.

Team members identify relevant suppliers by asking the following questions:

- Where does information and material come from?

- Who are the suppliers?

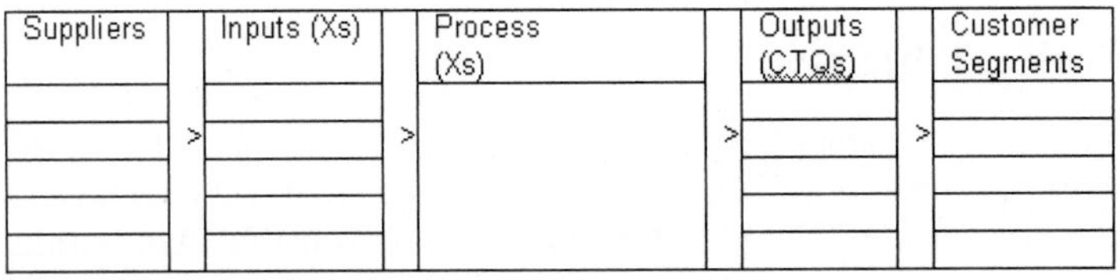

Suppliers	Inputs (Xs)	Process (Xs)	Outputs (CTQs)	Customer Segments
>	>		>	>

FIGURE 4.4 Format for a Generic SIPOC Analysis

Team members identify relevant inputs by asking the following questions:

- What do your suppliers give to you?
- What effect do the inputs or supplies (Xs) have on the process?
- What effect do the inputs or supplies (Xs) have on the CTQs?

Team members create a high-level flowchart of the process, taking particular care to identify the beginning and ending points of the process. A flowchart is a pictorial summary of the flows and decisions that comprise a process. The **American National Standards Institute (ANSI)** has approved a standard set of flowchart symbols, and the information written within the symbols provides information about that particular step or decision in a process. Figure 4.5 shows the basic symbols for **flowcharting** a process.

Figure 4.6 shows the flowchart for the MSD purchasing process.

Team members identify relevant outputs by asking the following questions:

- What products or services does this process make?
- What are the outputs that are critical to the customer's perception of quality? These outputs are the CTQs of the process.

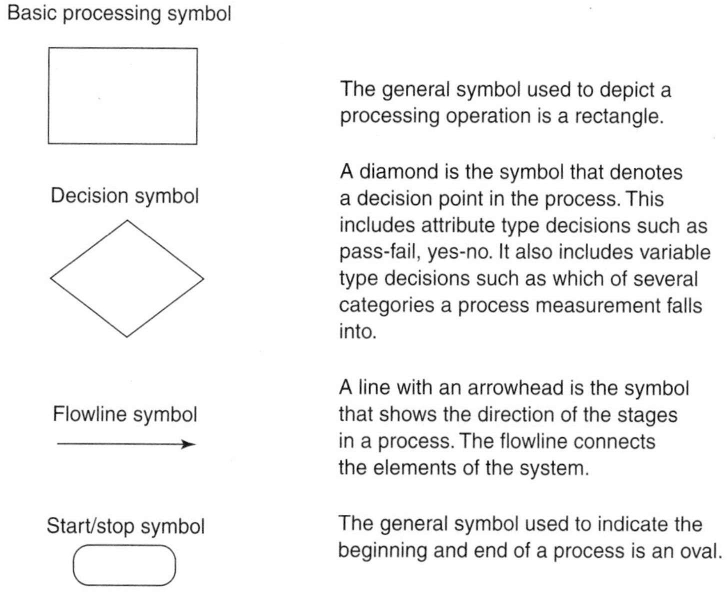

Basic processing symbol

The general symbol used to depict a processing operation is a rectangle.

Decision symbol

A diamond is the symbol that denotes a decision point in the process. This includes attribute type decisions such as pass-fail, yes-no. It also includes variable type decisions such as which of several categories a process measurement falls into.

Flowline symbol

A line with an arrowhead is the symbol that shows the direction of the stages in a process. The flowline connects the elements of the system.

Start/stop symbol

The general symbol used to indicate the beginning and end of a process is an oval.

FIGURE 4.5 Basic Flowcharting Symbols

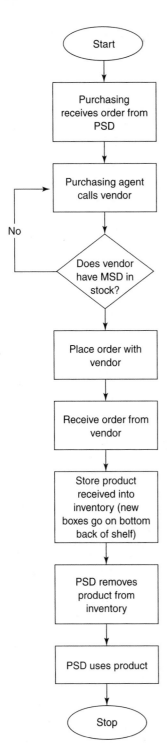

FIGURE 4.6 Flowchart of the MSD Purchasing Process

Team members identify relevant customers (market segments) by asking the following questions:

- Who are the customers or market segments of this process?
- Have we identified the CTQs for each market segment?

An SIPOC analysis of the MSD purchasing process is shown in Figure 4.7.

Suppliers	Inputs (Xs)	Process (Xs)	Outputs (CTQs)	Customers (Market Segments)
Ibix	Size	Insert flowchart of POIs Purchasing Process for MSDs (see Figure 4.6)	Durability	Workers of POI
Office Optimum	Ridges		Color	
	Vendor		Functionality	Managers of POI

FIGURE 4.7 SIPOC Analysis

4.5 VOICE OF THE CUSTOMER ANALYSIS

Background on Market Segmentation

Market segmentation is the dividing of a market into homogeneous subsets of customers, where any subset may conceivably be selected as a target market to be reached with a distinct marketing mix. A marketing mix is a unique combination of a version of the product or service that appeals to the members of the market segment under study (for example, Raisin Bran in 6-ounce or 60-ounce packages); a pricing structure ($4.00 per box or $7.00 for two boxes); a promotional strategy (TV ads on The Simpsons or TV ads on CNN); and a place or distribution strategy (sell via mail or in convenience stores). Market segmentation creates groups of consumers that respond differentially to marketing strategies and tactics (Product-Price-Promotion-Place). Individuals within a market segment respond homogeneously to a marketing strategy and tactics, whereas individuals across market segments respond heterogeneously to marketing strategies and tactics.

The simplest method for segmenting a market is to study the SIPOC analysis and focus attention on the outputs and on the customers by asking:

1. What are the outputs of your process?
2. Who are the customers of those outputs?
3. Are there particular groups of customers whose needs focus on specific outputs?

Once a market segment(s) has been highlighted for attention, a Six Sigma project team conducts a VoC analysis to identify the CTQs for this market segment(s). There are two types of

VoC data, reactive data and proactive data. Reactive VoC data arrives regardless of whether the organization collects it: for example, customer complaints, product returns or credits, contract cancellations, market share changes, customer defections and acquisitions, customer referrals, closure rates of sales calls, Web page hits, technical support calls, and sales. Proactive VoC data arrives only if it is collected by personnel in the organization. It is data obtained through positive action: for example, data gathered through interviews, focus groups, surveys, comment cards, sales calls, market research, customer observations, or benchmarking.

Proactive Voice of the Customer Data

Dr. Noriaki Kano of the Science University of Tokyo developed a method for collecting proactive VoC data in a market segment (see References 4 and 5). The method has four stages.

Stage 1: Collect Voice of the Customer Data

Step 1:

The first step in a VoC analysis is to select a product, service, or process in a given market segment(s) to serve as the subject of the Six Sigma project.

Recall that the example used here is a study of the MSD purchasing process within POI. There are two employee segments of the MSD purchasing process, managers in the PSD and hourly employees in the PSD.

Step 2:

The second step in a VoC analysis is to identify lead users and heavy users. **Lead users** are the consumers of a product, service, or process who are months or years ahead of regular users in their use of the item and will benefit greatly by an improvement or innovation (see Reference 8). For example, a lead user of a hair dryer may attach a portable battery pack and use it as a body warmer at football games played in cold weather. **Heavy users** are consumers who purchase relatively large quantities of a product, service, or process.

Team members identify lead users and heavy users using the following five-step procedure.

First, team members find appropriate people (e.g., managers) in an organization to help them identify experts with the product, service, or process under study.

Second, team members ask the appropriate people to help them identify the experts using the following questions:

* Whom do you regard as the person most expert in the use of this product, service or process?

* Whom do you turn to when facing difficulties with this product, service or process?

Third, team members ask the experts:

- What environment, images, emotions, needs and wants come to mind when you think of lead or heavy users of this product, service or process?
- For what purpose do lead or heavy users use this product, service or process?
- How do lead or heavy users use this product, service or process?
- What are the characteristics of lead or heavy users of this product, service or process?

Fourth, team members construct a "lead and heavy user characteristics by market segment" matrix; see Table 4.10.

TABLE 4.10 Lead and Heavy User Characteristics Matrix for MSDs

List of characteristics of lead and heavy users of MSDs	Market segment A: Managers in the PSD	Market segment B: Hourly employees in the PSD
Very high productivity		(X) Elvira Loredo
Very low area costs	(X) Mary McKenry	

The rows of the matrix list the identifying factors of lead and heavy users obtained from the above questions. The columns list the market segments for regular users. The cells of the matrix are either shaded, blank, or contain an *X*. A shaded cell indicates an impossible characteristic and market segment combination. A blank cell indicates a characteristic and market segment combination in which experts were not able to identify a lead or heavy user. A cell with an *X* indicates a characteristic and market segment combination in which the experts were able to identify one or more lead or heavy users.

Fifth, team members ask experts to insert names of lead users and heavy users in a Lead and Heavy User Characteristics Matrix; see Table 4.10.

Step 3:

The third step in a VoC analysis is to collect proactive data from lead and heavy users about the emotions and circumstances surrounding their use of the product, service, or process under study. This is called **circumstantial data.** Circumstantial data is obtained from lead and heavy users by asking the following questions: What emotions and images come to mind when you think about the product, service, or process? What circumstances arise in your mind when you think about the product, service, or process? It is critical that team members keep circumstantial data in the language of the customer. Team members also collect reactive VoC data from lead and heavy users by analyzing data such as: customer complaints, product returns or credits, contract cancellations, market share changes, customer defections and acquisitions, customer referrals, closure rates of sales calls, Web page hits, technical support calls, and sales.

Proactive VoC data is verbal or written information collected from a sample of lead and heavy users in a selected market segment. The questionnaire used to collect data from lead and heavy users of MSDs in the PSD is shown in Table 4.11.

TABLE 4.11 Voice of the Customer Questionnaire

Questions
What circumstances come to mind when you think about MSDs? What emotions and/or images come to mind when you think about MSDs?

Stage Two: Analyze Voice of the Customer Data

Step 4:

Classify the VoC data as circumstantial data or **product-related data.** Circumstantial data provides insight into the context in which a product, service, or process is used by a lead or heavy user. Product related data identifies the current expectations and perceptions of lead and heavy users. Product-related data is useful for improving existing products, services, or processes. Circumstantial data is useful for identifying major new features of existing products, services, or processes, or in creating entirely new products, services, or processes.

Team members classify the VoC data obtained from lead and heavy users into circumstantial data or product-related data by market segment using a classification matrix; see Table 4.12. Team members select only circumstantial VoC data by market segment. Table 4.13 on page 82 shows part of the circumstantial VoC data for the MSD case study.

Step 5:

Team members survey regular users to identify the critical circumstantial data for the product, service, or process under study. If a large amount of circumstantial data was obtained in steps 3 and 4, team members create a questionnaire listing all circumstantial data points (statements) with the instruction to respondents to indicate whether a circumstantial data statement is important to their needs or wants with respect to the product, service, or process under study. The results of the study yield a reduced set of key circumstantial data points. Step 5 was not performed for the MSD case study.

Stage Three: Develop New Features

Step 6:

Focus points are the underlying themes for one or more circumstantial data points. Team members determine the focus point for each key circumstantial data point or group of key

TABLE 4.12 Circumstantial or Product-Related Data Classification Matrix

Selected market segment(s)	Raw VoC data	Data classification (product-related or circumstantial)
Segment A		
High-priority customer A1	Comment A11	Product-related data
	Comment A12	Product-related data
	Comment A13	Circumstantial data
Lead user A2	Comment A21	Circumstantial data
	Comment A22	Product-related data
Segment B		
Lead user B1	Comment B11	Circumstantial data
	Comment B21	Circumstantial data
High-priority customer B2	Comment B21	Circumstantial data
	Comment B22	Product-related data
Lead user B3	Comment B31	Circumstantial data
	Comment B32	Circumstantial data
Segment C		
High-priority customer C1	Comment C11	Circumstantial data
	Comment C12	Product-related data
	Comment C13	Product-related data

circumstantial data points using an affinity diagram. **An affinity diagram** (see Section 15.2) is a tool used to identify the critical themes—called *focus points*—underlying circumstantial data points. The highlights of affinity diagrams are presented here, with minor modification for VoC analysis, for your convenience.

A team should take the following steps to construct an affinity diagram:

1. The team leader (green belt or black belt) transfers all the key circumstantial data collected from lead and heavy users (from Table 4.13) to 3 × 5 cards; one idea per 3 × 5 card.

2. The team leader spreads all the 3 × 5 cards on a large surface (table) in no particular order, but all cards face the same direction.

3. In silence, all team members simultaneously move the 3 × 5 cards into clusters so that the 3 × 5 cards in a cluster seem to be related; that is, they have an unspoken underlying theme.

4. After the team members agree that the clusters are complete, they discuss all the cards in each cluster and prepare a header card that sums up the theme for each cluster. The themes on the header cards are called *focus points*. Focus points are the initial statements of the CTQs.

TABLE 4.13 Analysis Table for Circumstantial Voice of the Customer Data

1	2
Selected market Segment	**Raw circumstantial VoC data**
Managers	"My employees are frustrated about the MSDs. They complain that they break too fast."
	"My employees are complaining that the MSDs are not holding up during the organizing process."
	"The employees are also complaining that the color of the MSDs change from one day to the next. It seems to be confusing them."
	"My employees are very unhappy with the purple and blue MSDs. They would prefer that only one color of MSDs be used consistently"
	"My employees say that more than five MSDs per box arrive broken."
	"I've heard from numerous employees that the MSDs coming straight from inventory are already broken."
	.
	.
	.
Hourly employees	"The MSDs are falling apart before we are ready to file the papers into binders. An MSD should be able to take at least four bends."
	"The MSDs aren't helping us to do our work efficiently."
	"I would prefer if we used only one color of MSDs."
	"I don't understand why we use different colors of MSDs."
	"The MSDs just break when trying to bend them over the paper stacks. They should take at least four bends."
	"It is very frustrating when you open a brand new box of MSDs and find that more than five of the clips are already broken."
	"It is very time-consuming to sift out the broken MSDs from a brand new box coming straight from inventory."

Step 7: Develop cognitive images for each focus point.

This step actually creates potential improvements and innovations by translating focus point (users' underlying and unexpressed needs and wants) into detailed, unambiguous, qualitative statements of needs and wants in the language of design engineers. These statements are **cognitive images.**

The pathways available to translate focus points into cognitive images include:

1. Team members restate each focus point into one or more operationally definable CTQs.

2. Design engineers use technical knowledge to restate each focus point into one or more operationally definable CTQs.

3. Experts in the field under study use their product knowledge to restate each focus point into one or more operationally definable CTQs.

Team members use the key circumstantial VoC data by market segment (see columns 1 and 2 of Table 4.14) to create affinity diagram themes, called *focus points* (see boldface numbers linking columns 2 and 3 in column 3 of Table 4.14). Next, team members identify the engineering issue underlying each focus point, called *cognitive issues* (see column 4 in Table 4.14). Then team members convert each cognitive issue into one or more characteristics (features or products or services) that an engineer or designer can "sink his or her teeth into," called *CTQ variables* (see column 5 in Table 4.14). Finally, team members develop **technical specifications** for each CTQ (see column 6 of Table 4.14).

Stage Four: Evolve Strategies for Features

Step 8: Team members classify cognitive images

Kano (References 4 and 5) developed a questionnaire that can be used by team members to classify cognitive images into strategic categories. The strategic categories help team members understand the significance of each cognitive image to regular users of a product, service, or process and assists team members in determining the optimal tactics to use when offering the cognitive images to regular users in the form of improvements or innovations to existing products, services, or processes, or entirely new products, services, or processes. Additionally, a Kano questionnaire helps team members set a pricing structure for an improved, innovated, or new product, service or process.

A **Kano questionnaire** (see Table 4.15 on page 86) is a tool used by team members to classify a set of cognitive images (see column 1 in Table 4.15) into an appropriate **Kano quality category** (see columns 2 and 3 in Table 4.15) from a large nonprobability sample of regular users of a product, service, or process.

There are six common Kano categories:

1. **One-Way** (O)—User satisfaction is proportional to the performance of the feature: the less performance, the less user satisfaction, and the more performance, the more user satisfaction (see Figure 4.8 on page 87).

2. **Must-Be** (M)—User satisfaction is not proportional to the performance of the feature: the less performance, the less user satisfaction, but high performance creates feelings of indifference to the feature (see Figure 4.8).

3. **Attractive** (A)—Again, user satisfaction is not proportional to the performance of the feature: low levels of performance create feelings of indifference to the feature, but high levels of performance create feelings of delight to the feature; see Figure 4.8.

TABLE 4.14 Analysis Table for Voice of the Customer Data

1	2	3	4	5	6
Selected market segment	Raw VoC data	Affinity diagram theme (focus point)	Driving issue (cognitive issue)	CTQ	Tech specs
Paper organizing managers	"My employees are frustrated about the MSDs. They complain that they break too fast." 1 & 2	Variation in durability 1	Durability	Ability to withstand bending	≥ 4 bends without breaking
		Variation in color 2	Color	The number of different MSD colors	= 1 color of MSDs
	"My employees are complaining that the MSDs are not holding up during the organizing process." 1	Variation in functionality 3	Functionality	The number of broken MSDs in a box	≤ 5 broken MSDs in a box
	"The employees are also complaining that the color of the MSDs change from one day to the next. It seems to be confusing them." 2				
	"My employees are very unhappy with the purple and blue MSDs. They would prefer only one color of MSDs be used consistently" 2				
	"My employees say that more than five MSDs per box arrive broken." 3				
	"I've heard from numerous employees that the MSDs coming straight from inventory are already broken." 3				

Hourly employees

"The MSDs are falling apart before we are ready to file the papers into binders. An MSD should be able to take at least four bends." **1**

"The MSDs aren't helping us to do our work efficiently." **1 & 2**

"I would prefer if we used only one color of MSDs." **2**

"I don't understand why we use different colors of MSDs." **2**

"The MSDs just break when trying to bend them over the paper stacks. They should take at least four bends." **1**

"It is very frustrating when you open a brand new box of MSDs and find that more than five of the clips are already broken." **3**

"It is very time consuming to sift out the broken MSDs from a brand new box coming straight from inventory." **3**

TABLE 4.15 Kano Questionnaire for MSDs

Column 1	Column 2	Column 3	Column 4
Cognitive images	How would you feel if the following CTQ were **present** in the product?	How would you feel if the CTQ were **not present** in the product?	What percentage cost increase over current costs would you be willing to pay for this CTQ?
Ability to withstand ≥ 4 bends	Delighted [ ] Expect it and like it [ ] No feeling [ ] Live with it [ ] Do not like it [ ] Other [ ]	Delighted [ ] Except it and like it [ ] No feeling [ ] Live with it [ ] Do not like it [ ] Other	0% [ ] 10% [ ] 20% [ ] 30% [ ] 40% or more [ ]
$= 1$ color of MSDs	Delighted [ ] Expect it and like it [ ] No feeling [ ] Live with it [ ] Do not like it [ ] Other [ ]	Delighted [ ] Except it and like it [ ] No feeling [ ] Live with it [ ] Do not like it [ ] Other	0% [ ] 10% [ ] 20% [ ] 30% [ ] 40% or more [ ]
≤ 5 broken MSDs in a box	Delighted [ ] Expect it and like it [ ] No feeling [ ] Live with it [ ] Do not like it [ ] Other [ ]	Delighted [ ] Except it and like it [ ] No feeling [ ] Live with it [ ] Do not like it [ ] Other	0% [ ] 10% [ ] 20% [ ] 30% [ ] 40% or more [ ]

4. **Indifferent** (I)—User does not care about the feature.

5. **Questionable** (Q)—User's response does not make sense (e.g., delighted if feature is present and delighted if feature is absent).

6. **Reverse** (R)—User offers responses opposite the responses expected by individuals conducting the Kano survey (e.g., "do not like it" if feature is present and "delighted" if feature is absent)

Team members use Table 4.16 to classify Kano questionnaire responses into their Kano categories.

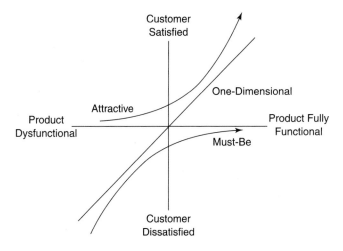

FIGURE 4.8 Pictorial View of Kano Quality Categories

The questionnaire in Table 4.15 was given to the 100 paper shufflers in the PSD. Table 4.16 was used to classify the survey responses from each of the 100 paper shufflers for each of the CTQs into their Kano categories.

The analysis of data from a Kano questionnaire for the purpose of determining the Kano category of a cognitive image is dependent on the level of detail of the study that identified the cognitive image. If the study is conducted at a very general level (for example, a study in the supermarket industry), data from respondents will provide an excellent vehicle to determine the

TABLE 4.16 Classification Table for Responses to a Kano Questionnaire

			Not present question response (see column 3 in Table 4.17)				
			Expect it				
P	Q	R		Delighted	and like it	No feeling	Live with it	Do not like it
r	u	e	Delighted	Q	A	A	A	O
e	e	s	Expect it	R	I	I	I	M
s	s	p	and like it					
e	t	o	No feeling	R	I	I	I	M
n	i	n	Live with it	R	I	I	I	M
t	o	s	Do not like it	R	R	R	R	Q
	n	e						
(see column							
2 in Table 4.17)							

Kano category of a cognitive image. In this case, the Kano category that occurs most often is used to determine the Kano category for the cognitive image, in other words:

$$\text{Kano category} = \text{maximum } (A, O, M, I, Q, R).$$

On the other hand, if the study is conducted at a very specific level (for example, a study in the fruit and vegetable department of a supermarket), data from respondents will contain much noise in the form of indifferent "I" responses and will not provide a sound vehicle to determine the Kano category for a cognitive image. In this case, there are two steps for reducing noise and determining the Kano category for a cognitive image. The first step is to segment the data by market segments. The second step is to determine the Kano category for a cognitive image in a particular market segment (or overall) as follows:

$$\text{If } (A + O + M) > (I + R + Q), \text{ then Kano category} = \text{maximum } (A, O, M),$$

however,

$$\text{If } (A + O + M) < (I + R + Q), \text{ then Kano category} = \text{maximum } (I, R, Q)$$

[see Reference 1].

For example, if one of the paper shufflers answered the Kano survey about durability as is shown in Table 4.17, the CTQ would be classified as "Attractive" for that paper shuffler; see Table 4.16 for classification table.

Additionally, Kano developed a technique to determine how much regular users desire a cognitive image by asking them what percentage increase in costs over current costs they would be willing to accept to have the new feature; see column 4 in Table 4.15. There are three "tolerable cost increase" distributions in practice—uniform, triangular, and J-shaped.

TABLE 4.17 Kano Questionnaire for MSDs

CTQs	How would you feel if the following CTQ were PRESENT in the product?	How would you feel if the CTQ were NOT PRESENT in the product?
Durability: Ability to withstand ≥ 4 bends	Delighted [X] Expect it and like it [ ] No feeling [ ] Live with it [ ] Do not like it [ ] Other [ ]	Delighted [ ] Expect it and like it [ ] No feeling [X] Live with it [ ] Do not like it [ ] Other [ ]

The **uniform cost distribution** shows that 80% of a market segment will pay at least a 10% cost increase to obtain the feature described by the cognitive image under study; see Figure 4.9.

Cognitive images exhibiting the uniform cost distribution can be used to develop ideas for completely new products.

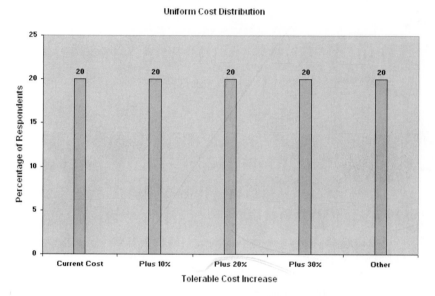

FIGURE 4.9 Uniform Cost Distribution

The **triangular cost distribution** shows that 60% of a market segment will pay at least a 10% cost increase to obtain the product feature described by the cognitive image under study; see Figure 4.10.

Cognitive images exhibiting the triangular cost distribution can be used to develop major new features of existing products, services, or processes.

The **J-shaped cost distribution** shows that 10% of a market segment will pay only a 10% cost increase to obtain the product feature described by the cognitive image under study; see Figure 4.11.

Cognitive images exhibiting the J-shaped cost distribution can be used to improve existing products, services, or processes.

The Kano cost distribution for a particular cognitive image is determined using the following formula: Kano Cost Category = max (Uniform, Triangular, J-shaped).

Occasionally, a cognitive image will appear on a Kano questionnaire that asks about price. The cost increase question does not seem to make sense for this type of question. In this case, explain to the respondent that the cost increase question is being used to get an indication of how he or she feels about the price-related cognitive image.

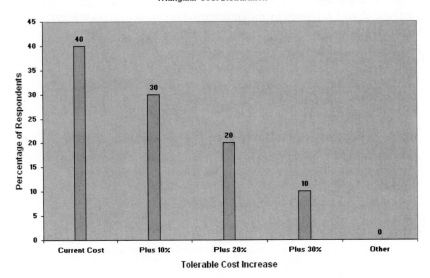

FIGURE 4.10 Triangular Cost Distribution

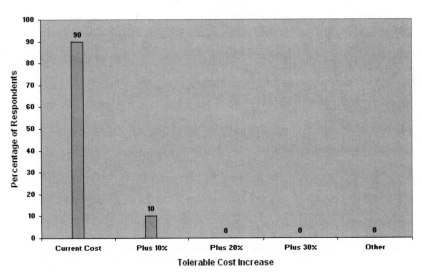

FIGURE 4.11 J-Shaped Cost Distribution

Occasionally, a respondent will ask: "If I check off that I can tolerate a 10% price increase for two cognitive images, does that mean that the price of the entire product will go up 20%?" The answer is: "No, the costs of the cognitive images are not additive; they just are being used to get a feel for how strongly you feel about product features."

Next, team members draw a judgment sample of regular users and tabulate their responses by market segment. The responses for the 100 paper shufflers in the PSD of POI are shown in Table 4.18.

TABLE 4.18 Tabulated Responses to Kano Questionnaire

Cognitive images	Kano quality Category	Kano cost Category
Durability: ability to withstand four or more bends	$M = 80$ $O = 20$	$0\% = 100$
Color: only one color per box	$M = 35$ $O = 15$ $I = 50$	$0\% = 100$
Functionality: less than or equal to five broken MSDs in a box	$M = 10$ $O = 90$	$0\% = 100$

Durability is a must-be quality characteristic, and its presence is required to achieve employee indifference. Its absence creates employee dissatisfaction. The PSD is not willing to pay more for durable MSDs. Functionality is a one-way quality characteristic. Its absence is related to employee dissatisfaction, and its presence is related to employee satisfaction. The PSD is not willing to pay more for functional MSDs. Color is an indifferent quality characteristic. PSD employees do not care about it and are not willing to pay more for MSDs that are uniform in color.

Step 9: Develop CTQs for each cognitive image by market segment.

The cognitive images that are selected in step 8 are called *CTQs*. An assessment of the effectiveness of the CTQs is done by visiting one or more experts with the product, service, or process under study and asking for their opinion of the CTQs. The CTQs for the MSD purchasing process are shown in Table 4.19.

4.6 FINALIZE PROJECT OBJECTIVE

Returning to the first part of the define phase, team members can now finalize the project's objectives.

Project Objective 1: To decrease (direction) the percentage of MSDs that cannot withstand 4 or more bends without breaking (measure) bought by the Purchasing Department (process) to 00.62% (goal) by January 1, 2004 (deadline). Go for Four Sigma!

TABLE 4.19 Definition of CTQs

CTQ	Definition of unit	Definition of opportunity for defect	Definition of defect	Kano category
Durability: ability to withstand bending	MSD	MSD	Break < 4 bends	Must-Be: fundamental to the delivery of the most basic level of customer satisfaction.
Color: number of different MSD colors	1 box of MSDs	MSD	MSD Colors in one box > 1	Indifferent: far less critical than durability to paper shufflers.
Functionality: number of broken MSDs in a box	1 box of MSDs	MSD	Broken MSDs in one box > 5	One-Way: improving the number of functional MSDs in a box will improve employee satisfaction in a linear fashion.

Project Objective 2: To decrease (direction) the percentage of boxes of MSDs with more than five broken clips (measure) bought by the Purchasing Department (process) to 00.62% (goal) by January 1, 2004 (deadline). Go for Four Sigma!

A correlation exists between the two project objectives. A broken MSD cannot withstand four or more bends because it is already broken. Improving the percentage of functional MSDs per box will increase the percentage of MSDs that can withstand four or more bends.

4.7 CHAMPION AND PROCESS OWNER TOLLGATE REVIEWS

The team leader (black belt or green belt) enters the information from the Define Phase of the Six Sigma project into the organizational **Quality Project Tracking (QPT)** system. Once the project has been entered into the QPT system, a Master Black Belt critiques the Six Sigma theory and method aspects of the project, a member of the Finance Department critiques the financial impact of the project on the bottom-line, a member of the Information Technology department critiques the computer/information related aspects of the project, the Process Owner critiques the process knowledge aspect of the project, and the Champion critiques the political/resource aspects of the project. Finally, if all of the elements are acceptable, the champion, team leader, and process owner pass the project through the define phase tollgate.

A Six Sigma team presents its project to their Champion and the Process Owner for approval in a series of **tollgate** reviews. Tollgate reviews involve a questioning process by the Champion and Process Owner of the Six Sigma team members after each phase of the DMAIC model.

Tollgate Style Questions

A tollgate review includes a questioning process that asks questions "one inch wide and one mile deep," as opposed to questions that are "one mile wide and one inch deep." This means that the review probes root causes to a high level of detail. A technique that helps people probe for root causes in the above manner is the 5W1H process. The 5W1H process is used to ask "Why" a problem occurs five times and then "How" the problem can be resolved, as opposed to just asking "How" the problem can be resolved. Historically, a person asks a question like, "Why didn't the lawn get mowed this week?" and gets an answer like, "The mower broke." This usually leads to the person responsible for mowing the lawn being blamed and no improvement in the lawn-mowing process. What the 5W1H process is suggesting is something like the following:

Sample "5W1H" Process

Question 1: "Why didn't the lawn get mowed this week?"

Answer 1: "The mower broke."

Question 2: "Why did the mower break?"

Answer 2: "The bearing burned out."

Question 3: "Why did the bearing burn out?"

Answer 3: "The bearing burned out because it wasn't oiled properly."

Question 4: "Why wasn't the bearing oiled properly?"

Answer 4: "The bearing wasn't oiled properly because the oil line was clogged."

Question 5: "Why was the oil line clogged?"

Answer 5: "The oil like was clogged because there is no routine and proactive maintenance program to examine the oil line."

Question 6: "How can we resolve this problem so it doesn't happen again?"

Answer 6: "Develop and follow a policy of routine and proactive maintenance for the oil line."

As you can see, questions 1 through 5 focus attention on the root cause ("Why") of the problem, while the last question focuses on "How" to improve a process or "How" to overcome a deficiency in one or more steps of a tollgate review; the procedure promotes asking questions that are "one inch wide and one mile deep."

Tollgate Situations

Tollgate reviews focuses on whether a Six Sigma team properly completed each step of a given phase of the DMAIC model. Table 4.20 shows the relationship between a team properly following a particular phase of the DMAIC model and obtaining a sign-off by the Champion and Process Owner.

TABLE 4.20 Relationship between Following a Particular Phase of the DMAIC model and Achieving Sign-Off by the Champion and Process Owner

	Sign-off by Champion and Process Owner	Failure to achieve sign-off by Champion and Process Owner
Team properly follows a particular phase of the DMAIC model	1	2
Team does not follow a particular phase of the DMAIC model	3	4

Cell 1 shows the outcome of a Six Sigma project team properly following a particular phase of the DMAIC model *is* achieving a sign-off by the Champion and Process Owner. No remedial action is warranted by the Champion and Process Owner in this case.

Cell 4 shows the outcome of a Six Sigma project team not following a particular phase of the DMAIC model *is* not achieving sign-off by the Champion and Process Owner. To reverse this failure, the Champion and Process Owner instruct team members to follow all of the steps of the phase of the DMAIC model under tollgate review. A future tollgate review is scheduled in which the team members show their revised project efforts. The following tollgate review questions may assist the Champion and Process Owner in diagnosing the source of the case 4 deficiencies in the tollgate review.

1. What step was not followed?
2. Who failed to follow a particular step? Note: The focus is on system problems, not on the individual. This will help promote joy in work and pride in the outcome.
3. Why did the employee not follow the step? Was it due to ignorance, misunderstanding, lack of training, negligence, problems with experimentation?
4. Should the step be changed to resolve problems due to ignorance, misunderstanding, lack of training, negligence, problems with a machine, or problems with an experiment?

Cell 2 shows the outcome of a Six Sigma team properly following a particular phase of the DMAIC model *is* not achieving sign-off by the Champion and Process Owner. In this case, the Champion and Process Owner study the difficulties of the project under investigation. The following questions may be helpful to the Champion and Process Owner in diagnosing the source of case 2 deficiencies in a tollgate review.

1. Does the project have political implications that are impeding its progress?
2. Does the project require capital investment that is impeding its progress?
3. Does the project have IT issues that are impeding its progress?
4. Do we (Champion and/or Process Owner) exhibit some problematic behavior that prevents progress in the project?

Cell 3 shows the outcome of a Six Sigma team not properly following a particular phase of the DMAIC model *is* achieving sign-off by the Champion and Process Owner. In this case, a Master Black Belt may find the following questions helpful:

1. What step was missed in the tollgate review?
2. Who missed the step in the tollgate review? Champion? Process Owner? Both?
3. Why was the step missed? Was it missed due to ignorance, lack of training, problems with experimentation?

Once these questions are answered, the necessary information may be available for improvement or innovation of the tollgate review process. These questions focus on improvement and innovation of the best practice method, not on blaming the individual.

4.8 PRESIDENTIAL TOLLGATE REVIEWS

Introduction

The President conducts tollgate reviews of selected Six Sigma projects after the Champion and Process Owner tollgate review of the Control phase. The purpose of presidential tollgate reviews is to determine the state of the organization and to develop a plan of action for the promotion of corporate policy (for example, Six Sigma management).[1]

Departmental managers explain to the President the status of their Six Sigma projects emanating from the organizational dashboard during presidential tollgate reviews. Normally, this information is conveyed through presentations. Much attention is devoted to the linkage between corporate and departmental objectives. Problems in achieving objectives are discussed and attempts are made to identify the causes of these problems. The President is able to evaluate the state of Six Sigma management in the organization through Presidential Review.

Reasons for Conducting Presidential Reviews

Presidential Reviews are conducted for several reasons. First, Presidential Reviews are conducted to determine the extent of achievement of the organizational mission through key objectives. Second, Presidential Reviews are conducted to determine the cost to the organization of achieving its key objectives. Third, Presidential Reviews are conducted to prevent deterioration in those processes which have not been highlighted for attention with Six Sigma projects, due to the reallocation of resources to processes which have been highlighted for attention. Finally, Presidential Reviews identify the major problems facing the organization. The President tries to discover those problems that affect functional performance, but cannot be solved at the functional level. Generally, these problems must be addressed at the company level since the causes

---

[1]The authors would like to thank Francisco Avello of Florida Power & Light Company (Miami, FL) for contributing heavily to this section of the book.

cross many organizational boundaries. In this situation, no single function has the authority to promote solutions. Most major company problems are cross-functional and thus difficult to identify. The Presidential Review, because of its cross-functional nature, provides a significant opportunity to identify such problems. Once identified, these problems are turned over to appropriate Six Sigma cross-functional teams.

Benefits of Presidential Reviews

One benefit of Presidential Reviews is that they create a dialogue between the President and mid-level management, encouraging an atmosphere of trust that helps bring out information about problems. The information provides an opportunity for the President to promote joy in work and pride in the outcome for all employees.

Another benefit is the insight they give to the President about the operations and culture of the organization. Frequently, this information is not available through normal channels of communication. Examples of information that can be gleaned by the President include the skill level of the managers and supervisors, the attitudes of employees toward improvement of methods, and employee morale. This information is necessary to promote the organization's key objectives.

The President will have a good understanding of the major problems facing the organization after a full round of Presidential Reviews. So, to a certain extent, the president should have good ideas about the possible causes of problems. The President knows the areas that should be involved with Six Sigma projects and should know the attitudes and skills of employees in carrying out the Six Sigma projects. Finally, the president knows the level of training that will be needed throughout the organization to work on the Six Sigma projects.

Barriers to the Presidential Review

Initially, the President may resist conducting Presidential Reviews due to time demands. All too often, there is a desire to obtain information from an Executive Summary; however, the Executive Summary does not provide sufficient information to establish or change the direction of the company. One company President tells the story of how he went from opposing Presidential Reviews to so thoroughly embracing them that he began to conduct half-day reviews on a quarterly basis with each of his departments.

Selecting the Departments and Topics to Review

Departments and projects are selected for Presidential Review by identifying problematic indicators on the organizational dashboard. It is important that the President does not assign fault for problems: blame-fixing makes people defensive and unwilling to identify problems. It creates fear in the work place. The President must take responsibility for problems in the system.

Informing the Departments to be Reviewed

Once the topics and functions have been identified, the next step is to announce the reviews. This is done through a meeting of senior managers, where the purpose of the reviews is explained, the names of the departments that will participate in the reviews are announced, and the format of the reviews is discussed. If necessary, the President should offer staff members help in further clarifying the objectives, guidelines, and manner of the reviews. This is also a good time to define the ground rules to follow during the reviews.

Ground Rules for the Presidential Review

Probably the most important ground rule for Presidential Review is that the presenter submits his department's Six Sigma project at least one week prior to the review. This rule is usually resisted, since most presenters will make changes to their presentation until the last minute. However, as will become apparent in the next section, it is important to enforce this rule.

The presenting department may bring and use as many presenters as needed to fully explain the principal issues or to answer questions. The President usually invites managers from related departments to the review, not only to make them aware of the important issues of that department, but also for them to get a glimpse of the review procedures and thus help them prepare for their own reviews. The atmosphere of the review should be informal but serious.

Preparing for the Review

Proper preparation for a Presidential Review is important. Many reviews fail before they begin because of poor preparation by the President. Good reviews are the result of careful prior study of the department's Six Sigma project, allowing the President to establish a focus for the review, identify issues needing clarification, and formulate questions.

It is critical to have a Senior Master Black Belt help the President prepare for the reviews. The Senior Master Black Belt assists the President in fully understanding the present situation of the presenting department and in developing a list of topics or broad questions to ask the presenters. More specific questions will normally follow from the answers given by the presenters. The President conducts the review and should become knowledgeable enough to conduct future reviews without extensive help; therefore, a key task of the Senior Master Black Belt assisting the President is to instruct and coach the President so that he or she can become a competent reviewer.

Conducting the Review

Usually, the review begins with a presentation by the management of a department, rather than by the team members who performed the work in the department. This structure is critical because it places management "in the line of fire" for Six Sigma efforts. Management must be involved with, and learn about, Six Sigma management to effectively perform its responsibilities in a presidential review. The presentation is followed by a question and answer period that is led by the President. It is customary to allow the presenter to finish the presentation without interruption, except for clarifying questions.

When the presenter has concluded, the President begins the question and answer period. It is an opportunity for the President to probe deeply into issues surrounding a Six Sigma project. Often, the President will be persistent and ask the same question several times to get the appropriate answer.

The attitude of the President during the review is critical. Often, the President has to be persistent to obtain the answers needed to make decisions. In some cases, the President pushes the presenters to obtain a desired performance level or behavior; this may be seen as judgmental or harsh by the presenters. The President's job is to establish an atmosphere of teamwork, providing constructive criticism, examples of ideas for improvement, and/or guidance on where to go for help.

The Senior Master Black Belt helping the President during the review should assume a low profile. She or he should ask questions only at the request of the President, after the President has finished the questioning process.

After the reviews, the Senior Master Black Belt meets with the President to identify the President's successful and unsuccessful actions and behaviors during the review. The purpose of this meeting is to improve the reviewing skills of the President.

Keys to Successful Reviews

The most important determinant in a successful Presidential Review is whether the President can gain the trust of management. It is critical that presenters feel they will not be punished in any way if they disclose problems in their departments.

Another key to a successful review is the quality of the preparation by the President. If the President learns about the project being reviewed and focuses on the steps of the DMAIC model that offer opportunities for improvement, it is more likely to create a positive review process.

Another important factor in a successful review is the assignment of action items to presenters when a Six Sigma project does not go as planned. Failure to assign action items due at a later review may communicate to the organization that mediocrity is acceptable.

4.9 DEFINE PHASE TOLLGATE CHECKLIST

A checklist of items that can form the basis of a define phase tollgate review by the Champion and Process Owner of a Six Sigma team is shown in Table 4.21. The outcome of a tollgate review is either "satisfactory . . . needs improvement," "yes or no," "assigned . . . not assigned," or "normal or other," with critique on how to overcome the specific deficiency.

TABLE 4.21 Define Phase Tollgate Review Checklist

1. Project selection	(Satisfactory . . .	Needs Improvement)
• Relevant dashboard	(Satisfactory . . .	Needs Improvement)
• Prioritization matrix	(Satisfactory . . .	Needs Improvement)
• Weighted averages	(Satisfactory . . .	Needs Improvement)
• Selection of highest priority project(s)	(Satisfactory . . .	Needs Improvement)
2. Activation of Six Sigma team	(Yes . . .	No)

(continued)

TABLE 4.21 Pre-Define Phase Tollgate Review Checklist (*Continued*)

3. Project charter	(Satisfactory	. . .	Needs Improvement)
• Business Case	(Satisfactory	. . .	Needs Improvement)
◦ Name of the process	(Satisfactory	. . .	Needs Improvement)
◦ Aim of the process	(Satisfactory	. . .	Needs Improvement)
◦ Reason to do project at all	(Satisfactory	. . .	Needs Improvement)
◦ Reason to do project now	(Satisfactory	. . .	Needs Improvement)
◦ Consequences of not doing project	(Satisfactory	. . .	Needs Improvement)
◦ Projects with higher or equal priority	(Yes	. . .	No)
◦ Bus. objectives supported by project	(Yes	. . .	No)
• Problem statement	(Satisfactory	. . .	Needs Improvement)
• Goal statement	(Satisfactory	. . .	Needs Improvement)
• Scope	(Satisfactory	. . .	Needs Improvement)
◦ Process boundaries identified	(Yes	. . .	No)
◦ Out of boundaries listed	(Yes	. . .	No)
◦ Adequate resources available	(Yes	. . .	No)
◦ Expenditure sign-off clear	(Yes	. . .	No)
◦ Expenditures w/o approval clear	(Yes	. . .	No)
◦ Obstacles and constraints listed	(Satisfactory	. . .	Needs Improvement)
◦ Team's time commitments ok	(Yes	. . .	No)
• Milestones and schedule	(Satisfactory	. . .	Needs Improvement)
• Benefits	(Satisfactory	. . .	Needs Improvement)
◦ Hard benefits and costs	(Satisfactory	. . .	Needs Improvement)
◦ Soft benefits and costs	(Satisfactory	. . .	Needs Improvement)
• Roles	(Satisfactory	. . .	Needs Improvement)
◦ Members	(Assigned	. . .	Not Assigned)
◦ BB/GB	(Assigned	. . .	Not Assigned)
◦ IT representative	(Assigned	. . .	Not Assigned)
◦ Finance representative	(Assigned	. . .	Not Assigned)
◦ Champion	(Assigned	. . .	Not Assigned)
◦ Process Owner	(Assigned	. . .	Not Assigned)
• Resources (Budget)	(Adequate	. . .	Insufficient)
• Draft project objective	(Satisfactory	. . .	Needs Improvement)
4. SIPOC analysis	(Satisfactory	. . .	Needs Improvement)
• List of suppliers	(Satisfactory	. . .	Needs Improvement)
• List of inputs	(Satisfactory	. . .	Needs Improvement)
• Flowchart of process	(Satisfactory	. . .	Needs Improvement)
• List of outputs	(Satisfactory	. . .	Needs Improvement)
• List of stakeholder segments	(Satisfactory	. . .	Needs Improvement)

(*continued*)

TABLE 4.21 Pre-Define Phase Tollgate Review Checklist (*Continued*)

5. Voice of the Customer analysis	(Satisfactory . . .	Needs Improvement)
• Identify and prioritize stakeholder segments	(Satisfactory . . .	Needs Improvement)
• Collect VoC data by segment	(Satisfactory . . .	Needs Improvement)
• Develop CTQs	(Satisfactory . . .	Needs Improvement)
○ Nominal value	(Satisfactory . . .	Needs Improvement)
○ Specification limit(s)	(Satisfactory . . .	Needs Improvement)
6. Finalized project objective	(Satisfactory . . .	Needs Improvement)
7. Input from the Finance department	(Satisfactory . . .	Needs Improvement)
8. Input from IT department	(Satisfactory . . .	Needs Improvement)
9. Input from Legal department, if necessary	(Satisfactory . . .	Needs Improvement)
10. Schedule for regular team meetings	(Satisfactory . . .	Needs Improvement)
11. Sign-off from Champion	(Satisfactory . . .	Needs Improvement)
12. Sign-off from Process Owner	(Satisfactory . . .	Needs Improvement)

Summary

A Six Sigma project is identified when a key indicator for a key objective on an organization's dashboard exhibits a problematic difference between its ideal state and its actual state. For selected Six Sigma projects, the champion and process owner select a green belt or black belt to be team leader. Next, the team leader selects the team members. Then, the team leader and champion identify the Finance and IT representatives and obtain all approvals for team activities.

The define phase of the DMAIC model has three distinct parts:

1. Prepare project charter (business case, problem statement, goal statement, scope, milestones and schedule, benefits, roles, and project objective).
2. Conduct an SIPOC analysis.
3. Perform a VOC analysis.

The team leader enters the information from the define phase of the Six Sigma project into the organizational QPT system. Once the project has been entered into the QPT system, a master black belt critiques the Six Sigma theory and method aspects of the project, a member of the Finance Department critiques the financial impact of the project on the bottom line, a member of the IT department critiques the computer-information-related aspects of the project, the process owner critiques the process knowledge aspect of the project, and the champion critiques the political/resource aspects of the project. Finally, if all of the elements are acceptable, the master black belt approves the define phase of the project and green lights the measure phase of the project.

REFERENCES

1. Center for Quality Management, "A Special Issue on Kano's Methods for Understanding Customer-Defined Quality, *The Center for Quality Management Journal,* 2, 4, Fall 1993 (Cambridge, MA), p. 13.

2. Gitlow, H., Oppenheim, A., Oppenheim, R., and Levine, D., *Quality Management: Tools and Methods for Improvement,* 3rd ed., (New York: McGraw-Hill-Irwin, 2005)

3. Gitlow, H., "Innovation on Demand," *Quality Engineering,* 11, 1, 1998–1999, pp. 79–89.

4. Kano, N. and Takahashi, F., "The Motivator Hygiene Factor in Quality," JSQC, 9(th) Annual Presentation Meeting, Abstracts, pp. 21–26, 1979.

5. Kano, N., Seraku, N., Takahashi, F., and Tsuji, S., "Attractive Quality and Must-Be Quality," *Hinshitsu (Quality)* 14, 2, 1984 pp. 147–156 (in Japanese).

6. Rasis, D., Gitlow, H. and Popovich, E., "Paper Organizers International: A Fictitious Six Sigma Green Belt Case Study—Part 2," *Quality Engineering,* 15, 2, 2003, pp. 259–274.

7. Rasis, D., Gitlow, H. and Popovich, E., "Paper Organizers International: A Fictitious Six Sigma Green Belt Case Study—Part 1," *Quality Engineering,* 15, 1, 2003, pp. 127–145.

8. Von Hoppel, E., "Lead Users: A Source of Novel Product Concepts," *Management Science,* 32, 7, 1986, pp. 791–805.

CHAPTER 5

MEASURE PHASE
OF THE DMAIC MODEL

CHAPTER OUTLINE

LEARNING OBJECTIVES

After reading this chapter, you will be able to:

- Construct an operational definition for a CTQ
- Determine the validity of the measurement system for a CTQ
- Collect baseline data for a CTQ
- Establish the baseline capability of a CTQ
- Estimate the process sigma for a CTQ
- Prepare for a measure phase tollgate review (if team member)
- Conduct a measure phase tollgate review (if champion or process owner)

INTRODUCTION

The **measure phase** of the DMAIC model is about team members concretely understanding the operational definition, measurement system, and current capability of each critical-to-quality (CTQ) characteristic. Team members must clearly understand the behavior of each CTQ to improve them in the future.

5.1 Constructing Operational Definitions for CTQs

Background

An **operational definition** promotes understanding between people by putting communicable meaning into words. Operational definitions are required to give communicable meaning to terms such as *late, clean, good, red, round, 15 minutes,* or *3:00 p.m.*

An operational definition contains three parts: a criterion to be applied to an object or group, a test of the object or group, and a decision as to whether the object or group met the criterion.

1. **Criteria**—Operational definitions establish "Voice of the Process" (VoP) language for each CTQ and "Voice of the Customer" (VoC) specifications for each CTQ.
2. **Test**—A test involves comparing VoP data with VoC specifications for each CTQ for a given unit of output.
3. **Decision**—A decision involves making a determination whether a given unit of output meets VoC specifications.

Problems such as endless bickering and ill will can arise from the lack of an operational definition. A definition is operational if all relevant users of the definition agree on it.

Effect of No Operational Definition

The supervisor in charge of the deburring operation in a factory producing medical devices was asked for a definition of a burr. He stated that a burr is a bump or protrusion on a surface. He also said, "The Deburring Department has five inspectors. Each one has more than 15 years of experience on the job. They know a burr when they see one."

A test was conducted to determine whether the definition of a burr was consistent among all five inspectors. In the test, 10 parts were drawn from the production line and placed into a tray so that each part could be identified by a number. Each of the inspectors was shown the tray and asked to determine which parts had burrs; see Table 5.1.

Although inspectors B and C always agree, they always disagree with inspector E. Inspector A agrees with inspectors B and C 40% of the time, with inspector E 60% of the time, and with inspector D 50% of the time. Inspector D agrees with inspectors, B, C, and E 50% of the time.

The preceding example shows that the absence of an operational definition can create problems and confusion. The manager of the Deburring Department (process owner) and inspectors have no consistent concept of their jobs.

Examples of an Operational Definition

Mary lends Susan her coat for a vacation. Mary requests that the coat be returned clean. Clean is the CTQ. In Mary's opinion, Susan returns it dirty. Is there a problem? Yes! What is it? The problem is failing to define clean operationally. Mary and Susan have different definitions of clean. Failing to define terms operationally can lead to problems.

TABLE 5.1 Identification of Burrs on 10 Parts

Part Number	Inspector				
	A	B	C	D	E
1	0	1	1	1	0
2	0	1	1	0	0
3	1	1	1	1	0
4	1	1	1	0	0
5	0	1	1	1	0
6	0	1	1	0	0
7	1	1	1	1	0
8	1	1	1	0	0
9	0	1	1	1	0
10	0	1	1	0	0

0 = No burr on part, 1 = burr on part.

A possible operational definition of a clean coat is that Susan will get the coat dry cleaned before returning it to Mary. This is an acceptable definition if both parties agree on the definition. This operational definition is shown below.

Criteria: The coat is dry cleaned and returned to Mary.

Test: Mary determines whether the coat was dry cleaned.

Decision: If the coat was dry cleaned, Mary accepts the coat. If the coat was not dry cleaned, Mary does not accept the coat.

From past experience, Mary knows that coats get stained on vacation and that dry cleaning may not be able to remove a stain. Consequently, the above operational definition is not acceptable to Mary. Susan thinks dry cleaning is sufficient to clean a coat and feels the above operational definition is acceptable. Because Mary and Susan cannot agree on the meaning of clean, Mary should not lend Susan the coat.

An operational definition of clean that is acceptable to Mary is shown below.

Criteria: The coat is returned. The dry cleaned coat is clean to Mary's satisfaction or Susan must replace the coat, no questions asked.

Test: Mary examines the dry cleaned coat.

Decision: Mary states the coat is clean and accepts the coat. Or Mary states the coat is not clean and that Susan must replace the coat.

Susan doesn't find this definition of clean acceptable. The moral is: Don't lend things to people who don't accept your standards.

Another example of an operational definition concerns a firm that produces washers. One of the CTQs is roundness. The following procedure is one possible procedure to use to arrive at an operational definition of roundness, as long as a buyer and seller agree on it.

Step 1: Criterion for roundness.

Buyer: "Use calipers that are in reasonably good order." (You perceive at once the need to question every word.)

Seller: "What is 'reasonably good order'?" (We settle the question by letting you use your calipers.)

Seller: "But how should I use them?"

Buyer: "We will be satisfied if you just use them in the regular way."

Seller: "At what temperature?"

Buyer: "The temperature of this room."

Buyer: "Take six measures of the diameter about 30 degrees apart. Record the results."

Seller: "But what is 'about 30 degrees apart'? Don't you mean exactly 30 degrees?"

Buyer: "No, there's no such thing as exactly 30 degrees in the physical world. So try for 30 degrees. We'll be satisfied."

Buyer: "If the range between the six diameters doesn't exceed 0.007 centimeters, we will declare the washer to be round." (They have determined the criterion for roundness.)

Step 2: Test of roundness.

a. Select a particular washer.

b. Take the six measurements and record the results in centimeters: 3.365, 3.363, 3.368, 3.366, 3.366, and 3.369.

c. The range is 3.363–3.369, or a 0.006 difference. They test for conformance by comparing the range of 0.006 with the criterion range of less than or equal to 0.007 (step 1).

Step 3: Decision on roundness.

Because the washer passed the prescribed test for roundness, it is declared to be round.

Operational Definitions of the CTQs in the MSD Case Study

Recall that there are two CTQs in the MSD case study: durability and functionality. Durability relates to the number of bends that an MSD can withstand before it breaks into two parts. Functionality refers to the number of broken MSDs in a box of MSDs.

Operational Definition for CTQ_1: Durability

Criteria for a selected MSD: An MSD is durable if it can withstand four or more bends. The procedure for counting bends is shown in Figure 5.1.

1. Bend Zero: Closed clip

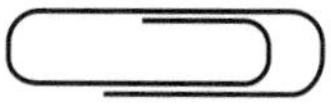

2. Bend One: Open clip

3. Bend Two: Closed clip

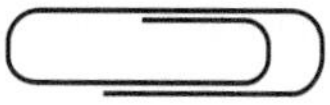

4. Bend Three: repeat bend One
5. Bend Four: repeat bend Two
6. Bend n: repeat until break
7. Count number of successful bends. Do not count the bend the break occurs on.

FIGURE 5.1 Procedure for Counting Bends

Test for a selected MSD:

1. Select the "top front" box of MSDs on the shelf in the inventory room.
2. Close your eyes, then open the box of MSDs, then haphazardly select one intact MSD. No switching is allowed.
3. Utilize the criteria for the selected MSD.
4. Count the number of bends until breaking.

Decision for a selected MSD:

If the number of bends is ≥ 4, then the MSD is conforming.

If the number of bends is < 4, then the MSD is defective.

Operational Definition for CTQ₂: Functionality

Criteria for a box of MSDs: Count the number of "broken" clips. A clip is "broken" if it is in two pieces, regardless of the relative sizes of the pieces. Note to the reader: Assume that clips can be broken only into two pieces.

Test for a box of MSDs:

1. Select the "top front" box of MSDs on the shelf in the inventory room.
2. Count the number of "broken" clips.

Decision for a box of MSDs:

If the number of MSDs that are broken ≤ 5, then the box of MSDs is conforming.
If the number of MSDs that are broken > 5, then the box of MSDs is defective.

The same box of MSDs is used for both operational definitions.

5.2 ESTABLISHING THE VALIDITY OF THE MEASUREMENT SYSTEM FOR EACH CTQ

Questions to Ask about a Measurement System

Process owners should ask themselves the following questions to better understand the capability of the measurement system for a particular CTQ to deliver the information needed for making process improvement decisions.

- Is the measurement system capturing the correct data? Does the data reflect what is happening in the system?
- How big is the measurement error?
- Can we detect process changes when they occur?
- What are the sources of measurement error (e.g., inspectors, gages)?
- Is the measurement system stable over time?
- Is the measurement system capable of generating the data needed for making decisions for this study?
- Can the measurement system be improved in the future?

The statistical tools needed to determine the validity of a measurement system are illustrated in this chapter using Minitab 14 statistical software. These tools are discussed in depth in Part 3 of this book (Chapters 9–14). Readers may wish to refer to the pertinent sections of those chapters for a detailed presentation of each statistical tool. Appendices at the end of Chapters 9–14 illustrate how to use Minitab with each of these statistical tools. The appendix at the end of this chapter shows how to use Minitab for Gage R&R studies, a topic that is not discussed in Chapters 9–14.

Terminology

There are several terms and concepts that must be defined to discuss variation in a product, service, or process due to the measurement system; see Figure 5.2.

1. **Part-to-part variation** is the variability created by the measurement of multiple parts under identical conditions (same operator, same lab). The ideal measurement system has 100% of variability due to part-to-part variation.
2. **Reproducibility** (variation due to operators) is the variability created by multiple conditions, such as multiple operators or labs.
3. **Variation due to gages** is the variability created by repeatability, calibration, stability, and linearity.
   a. **Repeatability** (or precision) is the variability created by multiple measurements of the same unit under identical conditions (same operator, same lab). This is called *within-group variation* or *common variation*.

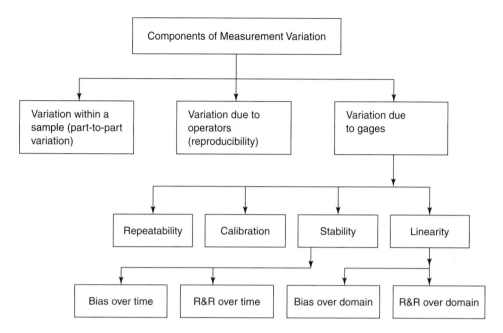

FIGURE 5.2 Components of Measurement Variation

b. **Calibration** is the adjustment of a measurement instrument to eliminate bias. It is important that adjustment of a measurement instrument is not overreactive to noise in the system. For example, if a marksman adjusts his rifle site every time he shoots by how far he is off target, as opposed to shooting six shots and adjusting the sites by how far the average of the six points is off the target, he will increase the variation of the shots on the target.

c. **Stability** (or drift) is a change in the accuracy (bias), repeatability (precision), or reproducibility of a measurement system when measuring the same part for a single characteristic over time. **Bias over time** (accuracy) is the difference between the observed process average and a reference value over time.

d. **Linearity** is the difference (bias) between the part reference value and the part average over the different values of the domain of the gage. **Bias over domain** (accuracy) is the difference between the observed process average and a reference value over the domain of a gage. An example of a linearity issue occurs when reading an automobile speedometer. If the speedometer has a 10% error rate, then the error of measurement in a school zone (20 mph with an error rate of 2 mph) is different than the error of measurement at highway speeds (70 mph with an error rate of 7 mph). If a constant error rate over the domain of a measurement system is desired, then different measurement instruments should be used at different speeds.

4. **Percent R&R** is the percentage of the process variation due to the repeatability and reproducibility of the measurement system. Percent tolerance is the percentage of the part tolerance due to the repeatability and reproducibility of the measurement system.

5. **Resolution** (discrimination or number of distinct categories) is the fineness of the measurement system (meters, centimeters, millimeters, etc.). At a minimum, the measurement system must be able to distinguish between excellent, good, fair, and poor units (four categories). A gage scale (measurement tool) should be able to divide the tolerance (upper specification limit − lower specification limit [USL − LSL]) into at least 10 parts measurable by significant digits. For example, a 12-inch ruler marked in whole inches yields two significant digits to the left of the decimal point and one doubtful digit to the right of the decimal point (10.7 inches yields two significant digits [1 and 0] and one doubtful digit [7]). If this is a sufficient resolution, you can continue. If it is not the gage (measurement tool) is inadequate, and it must be replaced or fixed.

A sign of inadequate discrimination for a measurement system of a continuous variable is when a range chart (R-chart) exhibits three or fewer values within the control limits or when the R-chart exhibits four values within the control limits and more than 25% of the ranges are zero.

Variation due to the measurement process must be separated from variation due to the actual process to address variation due to the process.

Measurement System Studies

Measurement system studies are used to calculate the capability of a measurement system. There are three component parts to a measurement system study:

1. Measurement System Analysis (MSA) Checklist
2. Test-Retest Study
3. Gage R&R Study

Measurement System Analysis Checklist. A **measurement system analysis checklist** involves determining whether the following tasks have been completed.

1. Description of the ideal measurement system (flowchart the process).
2. Description of the actual measurement system (flowchart the process).
3. Identification of the causes of the differences between the ideal and actual measurement systems.
4. Identification of the accuracy (bias) and precision (repeatability) of the measurement system using a Test-Retest study (see page 111).
5. Estimation of the proportion of observed variation due to unit-to-unit variation and R&R variation using a Gage R&R study (see page 113). R&R variation includes repeatability (e.g., within person variation), reproducibility (e.g., between person variation), and

operator-part interaction (e.g., different people measure different units in different ways). A common rule of practice that has developed over the years is:

- If R&R variation <10% of observed total variation, the measurement system is acceptable. R&R variation is called *Study Variation* in Minitab, but this is a misnomer because R&R variation is based on the standard deviation, not the variance. Because variance is the square of standard deviation, an R&R variation of 10% is equivalent to an R&R variance (called *R&R Contribution* in Minitab) of 1%.

- If 10% ≤ R&R variation <30% of observed total variation, the measurement system is borderline acceptable (acceptability depends on situation). Alternatively, R&R variance is marginal between 1% (0.10^2) and 10% (approximately 0.30^2).

- If R&R variation ≥30% of observed total variation, the measurement system is unacceptable. Alternatively, R&R variance greater than 10% (approximately 0.30^2) is unacceptable.)

Test-Retest Study. **Test-Retest studies** are performed by repeatedly measuring the same item under the same conditions, operator, inspector, gage, location, etc. It is important to remember to completely mount and dismount items before each measurement. A general rule is to collect at least 20 observations and to calculate the mean and standard deviation of the repeated measurements (see Sections 9.9 and 9.10). The resulting statistics are analyzed as follows:

1. If the standard deviation <[1/10] × tolerance, the measurement system has acceptable precision or repeatability. If the standard deviation ≥[1/10] × tolerance, the measurement system has unacceptable precision or repeatability. In the latter case, the measurement system must be improved or replaced before baseline data can be collected for a Six Sigma project.

2. A **standard unit** or reference value is required to determine the bias in a measurement system. Bias = (standard value − mean value). Without a standard unit, it is impossible to determine the accuracy of the measurement system.

A Test-Retest study was conducted on a measuring device used to test the thickness of a unit on a standard unit that is 40 inches thick. The allowable tolerance (USL − LSL) of the measurement system is 10 inches (±5 inches). One hundred repeated measurements (across the rows of Table 5.2) were taken under the same conditions.

An I-MR chart of the 100 measurements using Minitab shown in Figure 5.3 (see Chapter 14 for a discussion of I-MR control charts) revealed a stable system of measurements (no trends or drifts in the measurement system over time).

A basic descriptive statistical analysis (see Sections 9.9 and 9.10 for a discussion of basic statistics) of the 100 measurements on a standard unit using Minitab revealed a mean of 39.8 and a standard deviation of approximately 1.5 ($\overline{R}/d_2 = 1.667/1.128$). (See Chapter 14 for the computation of the process standard deviation.) The following conclusions can be drawn from the Test-Retest study:

TABLE 5.2 100 Repeated Measurements on a Standard Unit

41	38	41	39	40	38	40	40	40	39
38	39	42	40	37	38	37	41	42	41
40	40	37	38	38	40	43	39	41	41
38	42	41	43	40	39	39	40	38	38
39	40	39	43	42	42	40	42	40	40
40	38	40	37	39	41	41	38	39	41
39	41	42	39	38	40	38	39	43	39
41	39	42	38	38	38	43	41	39	39
39	41	40	39	40	41	39	41	41	40
39	42	39	40	41	40	40	39	41	38

THICKNESS

1. The measurement system is stable and predictable into the near future.
2. The standard deviation $>$ [1/10] $\times$ tolerance so 1.5 $>$ [1/10] $\times$ 10, hence, the measurement system exhibits unacceptable precision.
3. The bias of the measurement system (Bias = standard value − mean value) = (40.0 − 39.8) = 0.2. If the bias remains constant over time, 0.2 should be added to all future measurements.

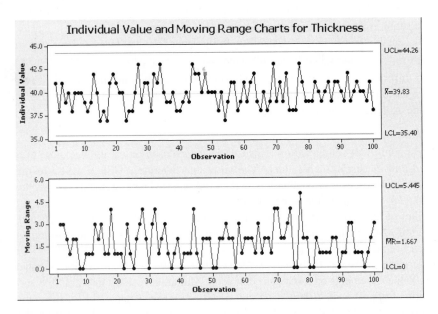

FIGURE 5.3 Minitab I-MR Chart of 100 Measurements on a Standard Unit

Conduct a Gage R&R Study. A **Gage R&R study** is used to estimate the proportion of observed total variation due to unit-to-unit variation and R&R variation. R&R variation includes repeatability, reproducibility, and operator-part interaction (different people measure different units in different ways). If R&R variation is large relative to unit-to-unit variation, the measurement system must be improved before collecting data.

The data required by a Gage R&R study should be collected so that it represents the full range of conditions experienced by the measurement system. For example, the most senior inspector and the most junior inspector should repeatedly measure each item selected in the study. The data should be collected in random order to prevent inspectors from influencing each other.

An example of a Gage R&R study follows. Two inspectors independently use a light gage to measure each of five units four separate times; this results in 40 measurements. The data to be collected by the five inspectors is shown in Table 5.3. Table 5.3 presents the "standard order," or the logical pattern, for the data to be collected by the team members.

Table 5.4 shows the random order used by team members to collect the measurement data required for the measurement study. Random order is important because it removes any problems

TABLE 5.3 Standard Order for Collecting Data for the Gage R&R Study

Row	Unit	Inspector	Measurement	Row	Unit	Inspector	Measurement
1	1	Enya	To be collected	21	3	Lucy	To be collected
2	1	Enya	To be collected	22	3	Lucy	To be collected
3	1	Enya	To be collected	23	3	Lucy	To be collected
4	1	Enya	To be collected	24	3	Lucy	To be collected
5	1	Lucy	To be collected	25	4	Enya	To be collected
6	1	Lucy	To be collected	26	4	Enya	To be collected
7	1	Lucy	To be collected	27	4	Enya	To be collected
8	1	Lucy	To be collected	28	4	Enya	To be collected
9	2	Enya	To be collected	29	4	Lucy	To be collected
10	2	Enya	To be collected	30	4	Lucy	To be collected
11	2	Enya	To be collected	31	4	Lucy	To be collected
12	2	Enya	To be collected	32	4	Lucy	To be collected
13	2	Lucy	To be collected	33	5	Enya	To be collected
14	2	Lucy	To be collected	34	5	Enya	To be collected
15	2	Lucy	To be collected	35	5	Enya	To be collected
16	2	Lucy	To be collected	36	5	Enya	To be collected
17	3	Enya	To be collected	37	5	Lucy	To be collected
18	3	Enya	To be collected	38	5	Lucy	To be collected
19	3	Enya	To be collected	39	5	Lucy	To be collected
20	3	Enya	To be collected	40	5	Lucy	To be collected

TABLE 5.4 Random Order for Collecting Data for the Gage R&R Study

Random Order	Standard Order	Unit	Inspector	Random Order	Standard Order	Unit	Inspector
1	36	5	Enya	21	27	4	Enya
2	5	1	Lucy	22	19	3	Enya
3	30	4	Lucy	23	10	2	Enya
4	29	4	Lucy	24	33	5	Enya
5	26	4	Enya	25	37	5	Lucy
6	28	4	Enya	26	2	1	Enya
7	6	1	Lucy	27	35	5	Enya
8	8	1	Lucy	28	23	3	Lucy
9	4	1	Enya	29	13	2	Lucy
10	3	1	Enya	30	7	1	Lucy
11	18	3	Enya	31	15	2	Lucy
12	20	3	Enya	32	22	3	Lucy
13	40	5	Lucy	33	14	2	Lucy
14	9	2	Enya	34	34	5	Enya
15	31	4	Lucy	35	1	1	Enya
16	24	3	Lucy	36	12	2	Enya
17	38	5	Lucy	37	16	2	Lucy
18	17	3	Enya	38	39	5	Lucy
19	32	4	Lucy	39	21	3	Lucy
20	11	2	Enya	40	25	4	Enya

induced by the structure of the standard order. Table 5.4 is an instruction sheet to the team members actually collecting the data.

Table 5.5 shows the data collected in the Gage R&R study in random order.

A visual analysis of the data in Table 5.5 using a Gage R&R run chart from Minitab revealed the results shown in Figure 5.4 on page 116. In Figure 5.4, each dot represents Enya's measurements, and each square represents Lucy's measurements. Multiple measurements by each inspector are connected with lines. Good repeatability is demonstrated by the low variation in the squares connected by lines and the dots connected by lines for each unit. Figure 5.4 indicates that repeatability (within-group variation) is good. Good reproducibility is demonstrated by the similarity of the squares connected by lines and the dots connected by lines for each unit. Reproducibility (one form of between-group variation) is good. The gage run chart shows that most of the observed total variation in light gage readings is due to differences between units.

A statistical analysis using the two-way analysis of variance (ANOVA) method (see Section 13.2) of the data in Table 5.5 using a Gage R&R study (crossed) from Minitab yielded the results in Figure 5.5.

TABLE 5.5 Data for Gage R&R Study

Random Order	Standard Order	Unit	Inspector	Measure
1	36	5	Enya	21.85
2	5	1	Lucy	21.19
3	30	4	Lucy	23.14
4	29	4	Lucy	23.09
5	26	4	Enya	23.28
6	28	4	Enya	23.23
7	6	1	Lucy	21.29
8	8	1	Lucy	21.24
9	4	1	Enya	21.24
10	3	1	Enya	21.33
11	18	3	Enya	22.28
12	20	3	Enya	22.34
13	40	5	Lucy	21.78
14	9	2	Enya	21.65
15	31	4	Lucy	23.02
16	24	3	Lucy	22.17
17	38	5	Lucy	21.84
18	17	3	Enya	22.31
19	32	4	Lucy	23.19
20	11	2	Enya	21.67
21	27	4	Enya	23.24
22	19	3	Enya	22.31
23	10	2	Enya	21.60
24	33	5	Enya	21.84
25	37	5	Lucy	21.76
26	2	1	Enya	21.29
27	35	5	Enya	21.93
28	23	3	Lucy	22.14
29	13	2	Lucy	21.50
30	7	1	Lucy	21.21
31	15	2	Lucy	21.51
32	22	3	Lucy	22.23
33	14	2	Lucy	21.55
34	34	5	Enya	21.89
35	1	1	Enya	21.34
36	12	2	Enya	21.56
37	16	2	Lucy	21.55
38	39	5	Lucy	21.81
39	21	3	Lucy	22.18
40	25	4	Enya	23.27

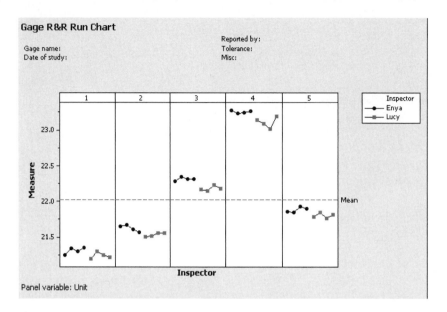

FIGURE 5.4 Gage R&R Run Chart Obtained from Minitab

Two-Way ANOVA Table With Interaction

Source	DF	SS	MS	F	P
Unit	4	17.6209	4.40522	2005.79	0.000
Inspector	1	0.1061	0.10609	48.31	0.002
Unit * Inspector	4	0.0088	0.00220	1.23	0.319
Repeatability	30	0.0536	0.00179		
Total	39	17.7894			

FIGURE 5.5 Minitab Gage R&R Study of the Light-Gage Measurement System

Variation under identical conditions (same gage, inspector, and lab), called *within-group variation, common variation,* or *repeatability,* is used to test for the statistical significance of the part-to-part and reproducibility variance components. If it turns out that the part-to-part variation is small, relative to the repeatability component of variation, the Gage R&R will be high relative to the part-to-part variation, indicating that either the measurement system is poor or that the parts were chosen to be too close in measurement value to each other to distinguish them from each other. If the latter is the case, the design of the measurement study (e.g., selection of the specific parts) is poor.

Figure 5.5 provides the following insights into the "goodness" of the measurement system. First, unit-to-unit variation accounts for most of the observed total variation (*p*-value = 0.000·;

p-values are discussed in Chapter 12). This is a strong indicator of a good measurement system. Second, inspector-to-inspector variation (gage-to-gage or lab-to-lab, called *reproducibility*) is a small but a statistically significant portion of the observed total variation (p-value = 0.002). Third, inspector*unit variation is a small and not a statistically significant portion of the observed total variation (p-value = 0.319). This indicates that inspectors consistently apply inspection methods over different units.

If the measurement system exhibits a low Gage R&R component of variation, it does not necessarily indicate a good measurement system. Why? If the tolerance range of the specifications (USL − LSL) is such that the measurement system cannot distinguish good from bad, then the measurement system is not capable of making decisions.

Figure 5.6 combines repeatability variation and inspector*unit variation because inspector*unit variation is not statistically significant. Again, part-to-part variation and inspector variation are statistically significant.

Two-Way ANOVA Table Without Interaction

Source	DF	SS	MS	F	P
Unit	4	17.6209	4.40522	2400.86	0.000
Inspector	1	0.1061	0.10609	57.82	0.000
Repeatability	34	0.0624	0.00183		
Total	39	17.7894			

FIGURE 5.6 Two-Way ANOVA Table Without Interaction Obtained from Minitab

Figure 5.7 shows that the total effect of repeatability and reproducibility on the measurement system is 11.24% (see Total Gage R&R %Study Var on Figure 5.7). This indicates a marginal measurement system because Gage R&R variation is between 10% and 30% of total variation.

Additional indications of a good measurement system are:

1. Part-to-part variation, as opposed to repeatability variation and reproducibility variation, is a large proportion of the observed total variation. The relative contributions to the observed total variation of the part-to-part variation, repeatability variation, and reproducibility variation are identified on a bar chart.

2. Inspectors assign the same measure to the same unit in repeated measurements of the unit. This is called *reproducibility.* Reproducibility is identified by a stable R-chart (see Section 14.8), where a subgroup contains the repeated measurements for a given unit and inspector.

3. Small ranges in the subgroups based on the repeated measurements for a given unit and inspector yield an $\overline{X}$ chart with extremely narrow control limits. If $\overline{R}$ is small, the control

---

*A p-value is a measure of the statistical significance of a population parameter(s) being studied using a hypothesis test. Smaller p-values are associated with greater statistical significance. Common values for considering a test statistically significant occur when a p-value is less that 0.05 or 0.01.

Gage R&R

Source	VarComp	%Contribution (of VarComp)
Total Gage R&R	0.007048	1.26
Repeatability	0.001835	0.33
Reproducibility	0.005213	0.94
Inspector	0.005213	0.94
Part-To-Part	0.550423	98.74
Total Variation	0.557471	100.00

Source	StdDev (SD)	Study Var (5.15 * SD)	%Study Var (%SV)
Total Gage R&R	0.083950	0.43234	11.24
Repeatability	0.042835	0.22060	5.74
Reproducibility	0.072199	0.37183	9.67
Inspector	0.072199	0.37183	9.67
Part-To-Part	0.741905	3.82081	99.37
Total Variation	0.746640	3.84519	100.00

Number of Distinct Categories = 12

FIGURE 5.7 Gage R&R Contribution to Observed Total Variation Obtained from Minitab

limits will be narrow. Narrow control limits cause the subgroup averages on the $\overline{X}$ chart to be out of control. If the $\overline{X}$s are out of control, this indicates that the major component of observed total variation is part-to part variation, not repeatability variation or reproducibility variation.

4. A run chart in which the subgroups are composed of all of the repeated measurements for all inspectors by unit shows very little variation in the distribution of individual measurements by subgroup. However, the $\overline{X}$ for each subgroup can be very different from each other. This indicates large part-to-part variation.

5. A dot plot (see Section 9.8) of all the repeated measurements for all units by inspector shows similar distributions of measurements for each inspector.

6. Superimposed $\overline{X}$ charts for each inspector show the subgroups, which are composed of all of the repeated measurements by unit for each inspector. If the $\overline{X}$ charts for each inspector show parallel lines over all units, most of the observed total variation is due to part-to-part variation.

Figure 5.8 shows the above additional analysis for the light-gage measurement system. The left side of Figure 5.8 reveals that:

1. Part-to-part variation, as opposed to repeatability variation and reproducibility variation, is a large proportion of the observed total variation, (see the components of variation panel of Figure 5.8). This is an indicator of a good measurement system.

2. Reproducibility exists when inspectors assign the same measurement to the same unit in repeated measurements of the unit. Reproducibility is identified by a stable *R*-chart of the

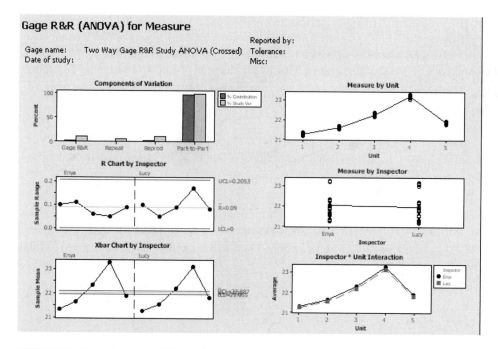

FIGURE 5.8 Minitab Gage R&R Study

range between the repeated measurements for each unit by each inspector (see the R-chart by inspector panel of Figure 5.8). The stable R-chart is an indication of a good measurement system.

3. Part-to-part variation is a large proportion of observed total variation, as opposed to repeatability variation or reproducibility variation, if the $\overline{X}$ chart by unit by inspector indicates many points beyond the control limits (see the $\overline{X}$ chart by inspector panel of Figure 5.8). This is an indicator of a good measurement system because the major source of variation is unit to unit.

The right side of Figure 5.8 shows that:

1. Part-to-part variation is a large proportion of observed total variation, as opposed to repeatability variation or reproducibility variation, if the distribution of light-gage readings by unit is very tight. In other words, most of the variation is due to unit-to-unit variation, not between inspectors (repeatability) or within an inspector (reproducibility), (see the by-unit panel of Figure 5.8). This chart indicates a good measurement system.

2. Repeatability variation is a small proportion of observed total variation, as opposed to part-to-part variation or reproducibility variation, if the distributions of light-gage measurements by inspector are the same. The distributions of light-gage readings are very similar by inspector, (see the by inspector panel of Figure 5.8). This is an indication of a good measurement system.

3. A low interaction between inspectors and units is indicated by parallel lines on the lower right panel. Crossing lines indicate that inspector's ratings are dependent on the unit being inspected. This chart shows parallel lines—hence, no inspector-unit interaction, (see the inspector*unit panel of Figure 5.8). This is an indication of a good measurement system.

In conclusion, the light-gage measurement system is adequate for the collection of baseline data.

Another example of a Gage R&R study is the Gage R&R study for CTQ = functionality from the MSD case study. The measurement system for functionality is studied using the following sampling plan.

1. A shelf in the storage area contains boxes of MSDs purchased throughout the week. There are different types of MSD boxes in the storage area (different vendors, sizes, etc.).

2. The Gage R&R study required two inspectors to sample the same 10 boxes of MSDs twice.

3. The top 10 boxes on the front of the shelf were selected for the Gage R&R study.

4. The study is repeated as is deemed necessary by PSD management.

Two PSD managers have the responsibility of inspecting the MSDs for functionality. They are called *Inspector 1* (Tom) and *Inspector 2* (Jerry). Both Tom and Jerry counted the number of defective MSDs, twice, in random order. The functionality data is shown in Table 5.6, in standard order.

A Gage R&R run chart shows that there is very little variation within inspectors (reproducibility) or between inspectors (repeatability), as seen in Figure 5.9. Most of the variation is between the 10 boxes of MSDs. This is an indicator of a good measurement system.

A statistical analysis using the two-way ANOVA method (see Section 13.2) of the data in Table 5.6 using a Gage R&R study (crossed) from Minitab yielded the results in Figure 5.10 on page 122.

Figure 5.10 provides the following insights into the "goodness" of the measurement system. First, box-to-box (unit-to-unit) variation accounts for most of the observed total variation (p-value $= 0.000$). This is a strong indicator of a good measurement system. Second, inspector-to-inspector variation (gage-to-gage or lab-to-lab, called *reproducibility*) is a statistically insignificant portion of the observed total variation (p-value $= 0.168$). Third, inspector*box variation is a statistically insignificant portion of the observed total variation (p-value $= 0.552$). This indicates that inspectors consistently apply inspection methods over different units.

Figure 5.11 combines repeatability variation and inspector-unit variation because inspector*unit variation is not statistically significant. Again, box-to-box variation is statistically significant (p-value $= 0.000$) and inspector variation is statistically insignificant (p-value $= 0.161$).

Figure 5.12 shows that the effect of repeatability and reproducibility on the measurement system is only 8.93% (see Total Gage R&R %Study Var) of the total variation.

Figure 5.13 shows the "additional analysis" for the functionality measurement system. The left side of Figure 5.13 reveals that:

TABLE 5.6 Gage R&R Data for Functionality

Box	Inspector	Count	Functionality	Box	Inspector	Count	Functionality
1	1	1	11	6	1	1	9
1	1	2	10	6	1	2	9
1	2	1	10	6	2	1	9
1	2	2	10	6	2	2	9
2	1	1	9	7	1	1	6
2	1	2	9	7	1	2	6
2	2	1	9	7	2	1	6
2	2	2	9	7	2	2	6
3	1	1	5	8	1	1	6
3	1	2	5	8	1	2	6
3	2	1	4	8	2	1	6
3	2	2	5	8	2	2	6
4	1	1	4	9	1	1	9
4	1	2	4	9	1	2	9
4	2	1	4	9	2	1	9
4	2	2	4	9	2	2	9
5	1	1	5	10	1	1	11
5	1	2	5	10	1	2	11
5	2	1	5	10	2	1	11
5	2	2	5	10	2	2	11

GAGE R&R-FUNCTIONALITY

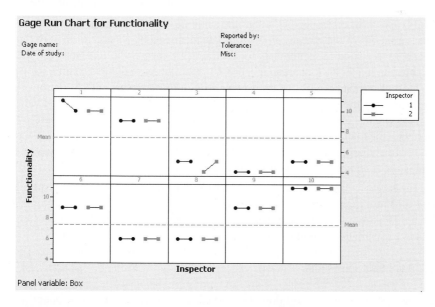

FIGURE 5.9 Gage Run Chart for Functionality Obtained from Minitab

Two-Way ANOVA Table With Interaction

```
Source          DF     SS      MS       F        P
Box              9   228.1   25.3444  570.250  0.000
Inspector        1     0.1    0.1000    2.250  0.168
Box * Inspector  9     0.4    0.0444    0.889  0.552
Repeatability   20     1.0    0.0500
Total           39   229.6
```

FIGURE 5.10 Two-Way ANOVA Table with Interaction Obtained from Minitab

Two-Way ANOVA Table Without Interaction

```
Source         DF     SS      MS       F        P
Box             9   228.1   25.3444  524.992  0.000
Inspector       1     0.1    0.1000    2.071  0.161
Repeatability  29     1.4    0.0483
Total          39   229.6
```

FIGURE 5.11 Two-Way ANOVA Table Without Interaction Obtained from Minitab for Functionality

1. Part-to-part variation is a large proportion of the observed total variation, (see the components of variation panel of Figure 5.13). This is an indicator of a good measurement system.

2. Reproducibility exists when inspectors assign the same measurement to the same unit in repeated measurements of the unit. Reproducibility is identified by a stable R-chart of the range between the repeated measurements for each unit by each inspector. However, the data in this situation makes an R-chart an inappropriate tool because there is so little variation among most of the data points that even a small variation causes an out-of-control situation (see the R-chart by inspector panel of Figure 5.13). The R-chart is not a good indicator of the performance of the measurement system in this case. However, the R-chart can be compared with the tolerance range $(USL - LSL)$. If the range of measurements on the R-chart is a relatively large percentage of the tolerance range, it is likely that the measurement system is not adequate for decision-making purposes.

3. Part-to-part variation is a large proportion of observed total variation if the $\overline{X}$ chart by unit by inspector indicates many points beyond the control limits; see the $\overline{X}$ bar chart by inspector panel of Figure 5.13. This is an indicator of a good measurement system because the major source of variation is unit to unit.

The right side of Figure 5.13 shows that:

4. Part-to-part variation is a large proportion of observed total variation if the distribution of functionality measurements by unit is very tight. In other words, most of the variation is

Gage R&R

Source	VarComp	%Contribution (of VarComp)
Total Gage R&R	0.05086	0.80
Repeatability	0.04828	0.76
Reproducibility	0.00259	0.04
Inspector	0.00259	0.04
Part-To-Part	6.32404	99.20
Total Variation	6.37490	100.00

Source	StdDev (SD)	Study Var (5.15 * SD)	%Study Var (%SV)
Total Gage R&R	0.22553	1.1615	8.93
Repeatability	0.21972	1.1315	8.70
Reproducibility	0.05085	0.2619	2.01
Inspector	0.05085	0.2619	2.01
Part-To-Part	2.51476	12.9510	99.60
Total Variation	2.52486	13.0030	100.00

Number of Distinct Categories = 15

FIGURE 5.12 Gage R&R Contribution to Observed Total Variation Obtained from Minitab for Functionality

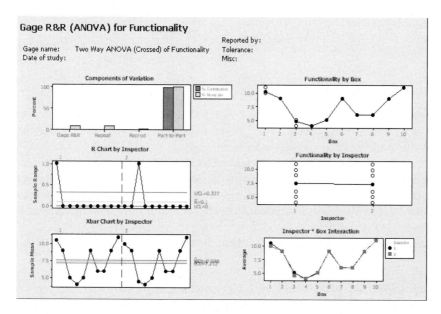

FIGURE 5.13 Gage R&R Study Obtained from Minitab for Functionality

due to unit-to-unit variation, not between inspectors (repeatability) or within an inspector (reproducibility); see the functionality by box panel of Figure 5.13. This chart indicates a good measurement system.

5. Repeatability variation is a small proportion of observed total variation if the distributions of functionality measurements by inspector are the same. The distributions of functionality measurements are very similar by inspector; see the functionality by inspector panel of Figure 5.13. This is an indication of a good measurement system.

6. A low interaction between inspectors and units is indicated by parallel lines on the lower right panel. Crossing lines indicate that inspectors' ratings are dependent on the unit being inspected. This chart mostly shows parallel lines; hence, there is almost no inspector*unit interaction (see the inspector*box interaction panel of Figure 5.13). This is an indication of a good measurement system.

5.3 ESTABLISHING THE BASELINE CAPABILITIES FOR CTQS

Background

Baseline data needs to be collected to determine the stability and capability (see Chapter 14) of each CTQ. If a dashboard is being used in an organization, baseline data already exists for each CTQ (see the key indicators on the dashboard). If a dashboard is not being used in an organization, baseline data must be collected for each CTQ.

The collection of baseline data requires a data collection plan. The elements of a data collection plan include a data collection form, a sampling plan (sample size, sample frequency), and sampling instructions (who, where, when, and how).

Collect and Analyze VoP Data for Each CTQ

Team members collect passive baseline data for each CTQ. Passive baseline data is data that is collected as a direct consequence of doing business. There is no intervention into the process to control the conditions that generate outputs.

For example, waiting times in a bank are measured by a clock that is accurate to the second. A wait time longer than 5 minutes (300 seconds) is deemed unacceptable by customers (VoC). A sample of the last five customer wait times every hour (the bank is open 8 hours per day) is collected for 2 weeks (Monday through Friday). A list of the 400 wait times in sequential order (across the rows) is listed in Table 5.7.

Team members analyze the baseline data to answer the following questions:

- Does the baseline data for the CTQ exhibit any patterns over time? A run chart (see Section 9.8) is used to study raw baseline data over time.

TABLE 5.7 Bank Wait Time Data

81	185	274	232	239	112	148	155	174	166	149	261	172
121	181	114	169	160	183	124	89	23	119	132	172	217
240	190	294	171	200	231	162	218	198	170	207	168	183
132	307	138	246	77	161	221	181	102	154	258	193	23
262	191	223	308	279	198	199	108	238	222	235	229	300
148	185	162	150	192	181	220	256	167	253	153	178	127
95	260	168	166	238	236	121	236	334	90	189	116	258
224	74	302	162	151	224	153	204	67	188	214	251	203
210	120	110	186	108	140	166	175	170	184	117	140	225
140	104	250	176	146	172	112	217	243	226	228	246	124
65	176	118	142	177	188	132	248	162	262	90	155	228
80	180	195	246	75	310	144	125	85	168	264	237	106
226	191	128	83	206	52	217	140	148	20	190	179	105
133	157	226	186	201	211	298	144	133	269	128	157	136
149	123	119	120	283	186	319	155	105	160	151	215	127
111	58	243	52	196	159	160	211	226	214	169	81	188
159	179	136	110	191	230	141	146	187	206	109	142	149
164	255	100	122	32	212	174	163	120	201	184	205	233
249	188	139	129	146	230	127	123	159	352	172	277	254
109	149	139	207	153	250	250	257	124	263	200	147	221
155	167	5	174	231	223	174	196	192	142	215	201	178
129	256	118	129	42	187	67	265	176	240	171	240	187
112	175	255	173	111	225	122	113	238	134	188	147	138
241	173	124	203	155	208	215	164	209	197	320	174	174
267	163	136	146	253	89	188	113	219	100	192	131	133
154	110	201	225	116	69	136	269	178	209	119	217	183
232	166	215	221	259	73	206	199	121	201	163	233	97
78	177	257	201	283	225	193	233	193	190	224	108	157
120	228	180	104	208	143	186	167	203	98	44	162	190
309	162	175	246	218	223	245	140	206	79	118	201	129
84	102	110	77	223	122	171	241	113	112			

 BANK

- Is the baseline data for the CTQ stable? Does it exhibit any special causes of variation? Control charts (see Chapter 14) are used to determine the stability of a process.
- If the CTQ is not stable (exhibits special causes of variation), then where are the special causes of variation so that appropriate corrective actions can be taken by team

members to stabilize the process? Again, a control chart is used to identify where and when special causes of variation occur. However, they are not used to identify the causes of special variations. Tools such as log sheets, brainstorming, and cause-and-effect diagrams are used to identify the causes of special variations (see Chapter 15).

- If the baseline data for the CTQ is stable, then what are the characteristics of its distribution? In other words, what is its spread (variation), shape (distribution), and center (mean, median, and mode)? Basic descriptive statistics are discussed in Sections 9.9–9.11.

The answers to the above questions for the waiting times in a bank baseline data are as follows.

- Does the baseline data for the waiting times in a bank exhibit any patterns over time?

A run chart of the wait times for each subgroup of five customers is shown in Figure 5.14.

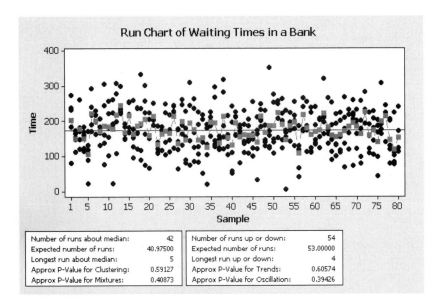

FIGURE 5.14 Run Chart Obtained from Minitab of the Waiting Times in a Bank

Figure 5.14 reveals individual wait times randomly scattered around a mean wait time of about 175 seconds. The variability of wait times seems to be relatively constant over all of the subgroups and fluctuates between 5 seconds and 352 seconds. Additionally, Figure 5.14 shows a connected plot of points that are the subgroup averages computed from the actual data.

- Is the baseline data for the waiting times in a bank stable? Does it exhibit any special causes of variation? If waiting times in a bank are stable, what are their characteristics?

An $\overline{X}$ and R-chart of the subgroups of five customer wait times is shown in Figure 5.15. Figure 5.15 shows that both the R-chart and the $\overline{X}$ chart are stable; that is, neither chart exhibits any special causes of variation in the wait time in a bank. This control chart analysis verifies the findings from the run chart in Figure 5.14.

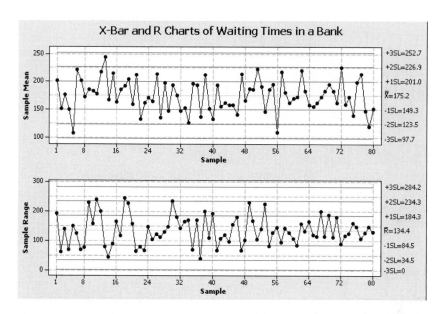

FIGURE 5.15 $\overline{X}$ and R-Charts Obtained from Minitab of Wait Times in a Bank

A basic statistical analysis (see Sections 9.9 and 9.10) of the wait times in a bank data are given in Figure 5.16.

The median and the mean are approximately the same, indicating that the distribution of wait times in a bank is symmetric around the mean of 175 seconds. Further, the standard deviation is approximately 60 seconds. A histogram of the wait times is shown in Figure 5.17.

The histogram shows an approximate bell-shaped normal distribution with a mean of 175 seconds with a standard deviation of 60 seconds.

```
            Total
Variable    Count    Mean   StDev  Minimum      Q1  Median      Q3  Maximum
Time          400  175.18   59.32     5.00  132.00  174.00  218.00   352.00


Variable    Range
Time       347.00
```

FIGURE 5.16 Descriptive Statistics Obtained from Minitab for Wait Times at a Bank

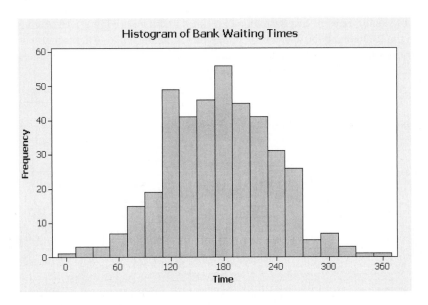

FIGURE 5.17 Histogram of Wait Times Obtained from Minitab

Estimate Process Capability for Each CTQ

Process capability compares the output of a process (VoP) with the customer's specification limits for the outputs (VoC). A process must be stable (as shown in a control chart) to determine its capability. There are two types of process capability studies: attribute process capability studies and variables process capability studies.

Attribute Process Capability. **Attribute process capability studies** determine a process's capability in terms of fraction of defective output or counts of defects for a unit of output. The major tools used in attribute process capability studies are attribute control charts discussed in Chapter 14. The process capability for a stable process that generates classification type attribute data over time is $\bar{p}$ (the average fraction of defective units generated by the process). The process capability for a stable process that generates equal areas of opportunity of count type attribute data over time is $\bar{c}$ (the average number of defects per unit generated by the process for a given area of opportunity). Finally, the process capability for a stable process that generates unequal areas of opportunity of count type attribute data over time is $\bar{u}$ (the average number of defects per unit generated by the process where the area of opportunity varies from subgroup to subgroup).

A shortcoming of this type of study is that it begins with a specification, but it is not specific about the reason for failure to meet that specification. The *p* chart does not indicate whether defective units result from the process being off nominal and too close to the specification limit, or because the process has too much unit-to-unit variation, or because the process is not stable with respect to its mean and/or variance.

Variables Process Capability. **Variables process capability studies** determine a process's ability to meet specifications stated by the customer. The major tools used in variables process capability studies are variables control charts, discussed in Chapter 14. Variables control charts are used to stabilize a process so we can determine meaningful upper and lower natural limits.

Natural limits are computed for stable processes by adding and subtracting three times the process's standard deviation to the process centerline. In general, for any variables control chart, the upper natural limit (UNL) and lower natural limit (LNL) are:

$$UNL = mean + 3(standard\ deviation)$$
$$LNL = mean - 3(standard\ deviation)$$

The standard deviation of the statistic is a function of the average range for subgroups of sizes 2–10 $(\overline{R}/d_2)$ and a function of the average standard deviation for subgroups of size 11 or more $(\overline{S}/c_4)$. d_2 and c_4 are factors developed for a stable and normally distributed process (see Chapter 14). Both factors are a function of the subgroup size. The factors are presented in Table C.4.

If the variable under study is not symmetric (for example, square feet, cycle time with measurements close to or equal to zero, signal-to-noise ratios, Richter scale results, sound pressure in decibels), the natural limits are often not symmetric. If the sample sizes are large for non-symmetric variables and the resulting statistic is an average, it becomes appropriate to use the above formulas for natural limits. But often in control charting, sample sizes are large enough to compensate for nonsymmetric variables.

As a rule, natural limits should not be shown on variables control charts because natural limits apply to individual units of output, and control limits apply to subgroup statistics. One notable exception to this rule is the individuals control chart for variables. In that case, the subgroups consist of individual units, and natural limits and control limits are the same.

Interpretation of the natural limits requires stability of the process under study and knowledge of the shape of the distribution (see Section 9.11 for a discussion of the various shapes of distributions). If the output distribution of a process is stable and normally distributed, then for the UNL and LNL equations, we can say that 99.73% of all process output will be between the natural limits (see Section 10. 6).

For example, if samples of the five wait times in a bank from Table 5.7 on page 125 are stable and normally distributed with an average of 175 seconds and an average range of 134.5 seconds, we can say the following:

1. The process's UNL is:

$$UNL = 175 + 3(134.4/2.326) = 175 + 3(57.8) = 175 + 173.4 = 348.4\ seconds.$$

2. The process's LNL is:

$$LNL = 175 - 3(134.4/2.326) = 175 - 3(57.8) = 175 - 173.4 = 1.6\ seconds.$$

3. 99.73% of the wait times in a bank will last between 1.6 and 348.4 seconds. This is what the waiting time in a bank process is capable of generating; it is the identity of the process.

Natural Limits and Specification Limits. **Natural limits** (VoP) and **specification limits** (VoC) are comparable quantities for stable processes because they are both measured with respect to the individual units of output generated by the process under study. There are four basic relationships between natural limits and specification limits for stable processes. Each relationship is portrayed using a normal distribution.

Relationship 1. The process's natural limits are inside the specification limits, and the process is centered on nominal. This is illustrated in Figure 5.18(a).

Relationship 2. The process's natural limits are inside the specification limits, and the process is not centered on nominal. This is illustrated in Figure 5.18(b).

Relationship 3. The process's natural limits are outside the specification limits, and the process is centered on nominal. This is illustrated in Figure 5.18(c).

Relationship 4. The process's natural limits are outside the specification limits, and the process is not centered on nominal. This is illustrated in Figure 5.18(d).

In the wait times in a bank example, the USL for acceptable wait times in a bank is 300 seconds; that is, USL = 300 seconds. From Table 5.7 and the histogram in Figure 5.17, we see that 7 of the 400 wait times exceed the USL; hence, 1.75% of the wait times in a bank are out of specification from an empirical perspective.

If we assume that the distribution of wait times in a bank are stable and normally distributed with a mean of 175 seconds and a standard deviation of approximately 60 seconds, we can calculate the theoretical proportion of wait times in a bank that are over 300 seconds as follows (see Section 10.6):

$$P(\text{wait time} > 300 \text{ seconds}) = 1.0 - P(\text{wait time} \le 300 \text{ seconds})$$
$$= 1.0 - P\{Z < [(300 - 175)/60]\} = 1.0 - P\{Z < 2.08\} = 1.0 - 0.9812 = 0.0188.$$

Hence, 1.88% of all wait times in a bank will be more than 300 seconds in duration, according to the normal distribution. This translates into about 7.5 of the 400 wait times (0.0188×400). In fact, 7 of the wait times were over 300 seconds. The difference is due to the fact that the distribution of wait times in a bank is only approximately normally distributed.

The theoretical defects per opportunity (DPO) for the waiting times in a bank baseline data is 0.0188, and the actual DPO is 0.0175. Hence, the theoretical yield from the wait time in a bank baseline data is 0.9812 (1.0 − [7.5/400]), and the actual rolled throughput yield (RTY) is 0.9825 (1.0 − [7/400]). The theoretical defects per million opportunities (DPMO) is 18,880 ($0.0188 \times 1,000,000$), and the actual DPMO is 17,500 ($0.0175 \times 1,000,000$).

The short-term process sigma for waiting times in a bank, assuming a 1.5 sigma shift in the process mean over time, is approximately 3.6 from a theoretical viewpoint and 3.5–3.6 from an actual viewpoint. An objective of Six Sigma management is to get long-term process variation that considers both common and special causes of variation to equal short-term process variation, which considers only common causes of variation.

In sum, Table 5.8 on page 132 presents the current and desired conditions, as well as the gap for the waiting time in a bank process.

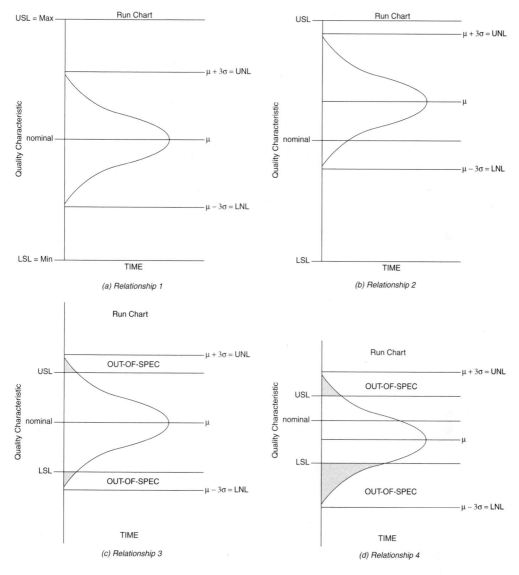

FIGURE 5.18 Relationship Between Natural Limits and Specification Limits

TABLE 5.8 Summary of Waiting Time in a Bank

CTQ	Yield			DPMO			Short-term Process Sigma		
	Current	Desired	Gap	Current	Desired	Gap	Current	Desired	Gap
Wait Times	0.9825	.9999966	.0174966	17,500	3.4	17,496.6	3.6–3.7	6.0	2.3–2.4
CTQ2									
⋯									
⋯									
CTQ8									

Baseline for Durability and Functionality from the MSD Case Study

Team members conduct a study (as part of routine business) to determine the baseline capability for each CTQ. At the beginning of each hour, one box of MSDs is selected from the storage area. The procedure for selecting a box of MSDs is simply to select the top frontmost box on the shelf. The selection process was not altered during a sampling period of two 8-hour shifts. Baseline capability data is shown in Table 5.9.

TABLE 5.9 Baseline Capability Data

Hour	Durability	Functionality
Shift 1 — Hour 1	5	12
Shift 1 — Hour 2	7	4
Shift 1 — Hour 3	3	8
Shift 1 — Hour 4	2	6
Shift 1 — Hour 5	9	1
Shift 1 — Hour 6	2	5
Shift 1 — Hour 7	1	11
Shift 1 — Hour 8	1	9
Shift 2 — Hour 1	12	6
Shift 2 — Hour 2	9	6
Shift 2 — Hour 3	3	9
Shift 2 — Hour 4	1	5
Shift 2 — Hour 5	1	4
Shift 2 — Hour 6	1	5
Shift 2 — Hour 7	1	9
Shift 2 — Hour 8	4	10
Yield	6/16 = 0.375	6/16 = 0.375

BASELINE

Durability. The answers to the questions stated earlier for the durability baseline data are shown below.

- Does the baseline data for the durability exhibit any patterns over time?

    Answer: A run chart of the durability for each box of MSDs is shown in Figure 5.19.

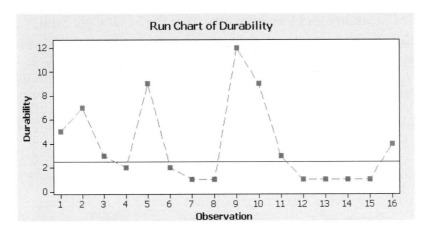

FIGURE 5.19 Run Chart of Durability Obtained from Minitab

The run chart of durability is scattered around a median of 2.5 bends. The variability of durability seems to exhibit a high spike on the ninth MSD. Durability (number of bends) seems to fluctuate between 1 bend and 12 bends.

- Is the baseline data for the durability stable? Does it exhibit any special causes of variation? If it is stable, what are the characteristics of the distribution?

  Answer: An I-MR chart of the number of bends per MSD is shown in Figure 5.20. Figure 5.20 shows a moving range chart is out of control due to the ninth point; that is, there is a special cause of variation in durability. This control chart analysis verifies the findings from the run chart in Figure 5.19.

Durability does exhibit a positive special cause of variation on the moving range chart due to the number of bends of the ninth MSD. A brainstorming session about the cause(s) of the 12 bends on the ninth MSD generated no ideas. Because the baseline data for durability is not stable, a basic statistical analysis does not carry much weight with respect to predicting the near future of the durability of the MSD process. Nonetheless, Figure 5.21 shows the questionable statistics for durability.

The median (2.5) is smaller than the mean (3.875), indicating that if the distribution of durability for MSDs was stable, it might be skewed to the right. Further, the standard deviation is 3.538 bends. The mean minus 3 standard deviations is less than zero, again indicating that the distribution of durability is not normally distributed. This might be true if the data were stable. A dot plot of durability from Table 5.9 is shown in Figure 5.22 on page 136.

The dot plot shows a distribution skewed to the right. This verifies the results of the descriptive statistics that showed that the mean was substantially greater than the median.

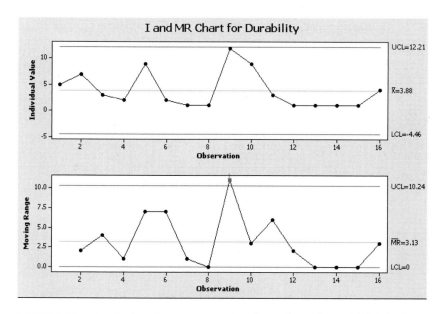

FIGURE 5.20 Individual and Moving Range Chart of Durability Obtained from Minitab

Descriptive Statistics: Durability

Variable	N	N*	Mean	StDev	Minimum	Median	Maximum
Durability	16	0	3.875	3.538	1.000	2.500	12.000

FIGURE 5.21 Descriptive Statistics of Durability Obtained from Minitab

It is not possible to estimate the capability of durability for the MSD process because the process is not stable. Additionally, it is not possible to predict the future DPO, RTY, DPMO, or process sigma for the durability of the MSD process.

Functionality. The answers to the two questions stated earlier for the functionality baseline data are shown below.

- Does the baseline data for the functionality exhibit any patterns over time?

  Answer: A run chart (with one observation per subgroup) of the functionality for each box of MSDs is shown in Figure 5.23.

The run chart of functionality (number of broken MSDs per box) is scattered around a median of 6 broken MSDs per box and fluctuates between 1 and 12 MSDs per box.

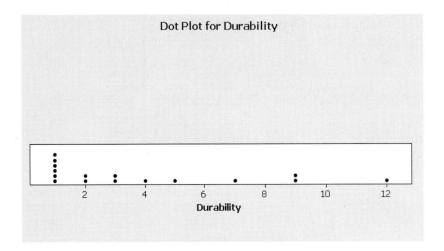

FIGURE 5.22 Dot Plot of Durability Obtained from Minitab

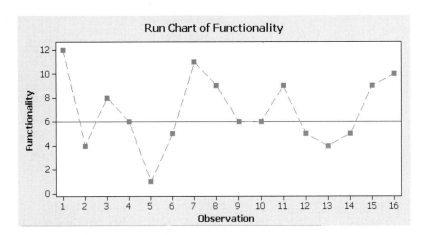

FIGURE 5.23 Run Chart of Functionality Obtained from Minitab

- Is the baseline data for the functionality stable? Does it exhibit any special causes of variation? If it is stable, what are the characteristics of the functionality distribution?

  Answer: A *c*-chart of the number of broken MSDs per box is shown in Figure 5.24. Figure 5.24 shows that the functionality of the MSD process is in statistical control; that is, there are no special causes of variation.

Because the baseline data for functionality is stable, a basic statistical analysis can be useful to predict the near future of the functionality of the MSD process. A basic statistical analysis of the functionality of MSDs process is shown in Figure 5.25.

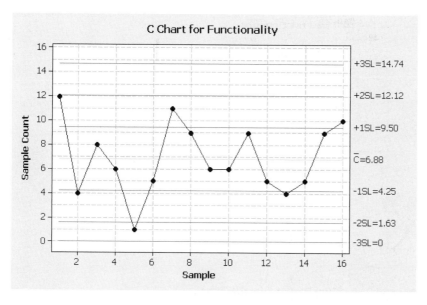

FIGURE 5.24 c-Chart of Functionality Obtained from Minitab

Descriptive Statistics: Functionality

Variable	N	N*	Mean	StDev	Minimum	Median	Maximum
Functionality	16	0	6.875	2.964	1.000	6.000	12.000

FIGURE 5.25 Descriptive Statistics Obtained from Minitab for Functionality

The mean (6.875 broken MSDs per box) and the median (6.0 broken MSDs per box) are reasonably close, indicating possible symmetry of the distribution of functionality. Further, the standard deviation is approximately 3.0 broken MSDs (actually, 2.964 MSDs) per box. A dot plot of functionality is shown in Figure 5.26.

The dot plot seems to show a bimodal distribution. However, a normal probability plot indicates that functionality is approximately normally distributed (see Section 10.7); see Figure 5.27. Although the functionality data is count type attribute data appropriate for a c-chart, the distribution for functionality can be approximated by a normal distribution in this case because the mean (6.875) is greater than or equal to 5.

If the functionality of MSDs forms a stable and approximately normal distribution with an average of approximately 7 and a standard deviation of approximately 3, we can say the following about the functionality of the MSD process:

1. The process's upper natural limit is:

$$UNL = 7 + 3(3) = 16 \text{ broken clips per box.}$$

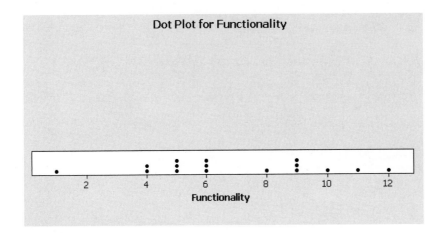

FIGURE 5.26 Dot Plot of Functionality Obtained from Minitab

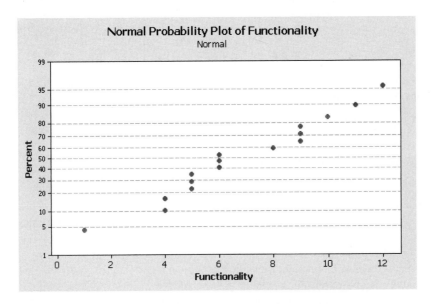

FIGURE 5.27 Normal Probability Plot of Functionality Obtained from Minitab

2. The process's lower natural limit is:

$$\text{LNL} = 7 - 3(3) = -2 \text{ or } 0 \text{ broken clips per box.}$$

3. Approximately 99–100% of the boxes of MSDs will have less than 17 broken clips per box. Note that any substantial deviation from 99% to 100% is caused by the distribution of functionality not being approximately normally distributed.

TABLE 5.10 Summary of Theoretical Functionality of Boxes of MSDs

CTQ	Rolled Throughput Yield			DPMO			Short-term Process Sigma		
	Current	Desired	Gap	Current	Desired	Gap	Current	Desired	Gap
Funct CTQ2	0.25	0.9938	0.7438	750,000	6,210	743,790	0.8–0.9	4.0	3.1–3.2
...									
...									
CTQ8									

The USL for acceptable functionality is 5 broken clips per box; that is, USL = 5 broken clips. From the run chart in Figure 5.23, we see that 10 of the 16 boxes of MSDs exceed the USL; hence, 62.5% of the actual number of boxes of MSD are out of specification.

If we assume that the distribution of functionality is stable and normally distributed with a mean of 7 MSDs per box and a standard deviation of 3 MSDs per box, we can calculate the theoretical proportion of boxes of MSDs that are out of specification as follows:

$$P(\text{functionality} > 5 \text{ broken MSDs per box}) = P[Z > (5 - 7)/3] = P(Z > -0.67)$$
$$0.7486 = \text{approximately } 75\%.$$

Hence, 75% of all boxes of MSDs will have more than 5 broken MSDs per box, according to the normal distribution. This translates into about 12 of the 16 boxes (0.75×16). In fact, 10 of the boxes of MSDs have more than 5 broken MSDS per box. The difference is due to the fact that the distribution of functionality is only approximately normally distributed.

For the functionality baseline data, the theoretical DPO is 0.75, and the actual DPO is 0.625. Hence, the theoretical RTY from the functionality baseline data is 0.25, and the actual RTY is 0.375. The theoretical DPMO is 750,000, and the actual DPMO is 625,000.

The long-term process sigma for functionality (assuming a 1.5 sigma shift in the process mean over time) using the DPMO obtained from the normal distribution (DPMO = 750,000) is between 0.8 and 0.9. The long-term process sigma for functionality (assuming a 1.5 sigma shift in the mean over time) using the DPMO obtained from the raw data (DPMO = 625,000) is between 1.1 and 1.2.

Table 5.10 shows the current and desired conditions, as well as the gap for the functionality of the MSD process.

TABLE 5.11 Measure Phase Tollgate Review Checklist

1. Operational definition for each CTQ	(Satisfactory . . . Needs Improvement)
2. Measurement Systems Analysis by CTQ	(Satisfactory . . . Needs Improvement)
3. Baseline capabilities for each CTQ	(Satisfactory . . . Needs Improvement)
• Data collection plan	(Satisfactory . . . Needs Improvement)
• Baseline data	(Satisfactory . . . Needs Improvement)
• Stability of baseline data	(Yes . . . No)
• Distribution of baseline data	(Normal. . . Other)
4. Process capability statistics for each CTQ	(Satisfactory . . . Needs Improvement)
• DPMO	(Yes . . . No)
• Process Sigma	(Yes . . . No)
5. Input from the Finance department	(Satisfactory . . . Needs Improvement)
6. Input from IT department	(Satisfactory . . . Needs Improvement)
7. Sign-off from Champion	(Satisfactory . . . Needs Improvement)
8. Sign-off from Process Owner	(Satisfactory . . . Needs Improvement)

Notice the desired 100-fold improvement shown in the DPMO columns (current = 625,000 and desired = 6,210). This is consistent with the goals stated in question 5 of the define phase of the DMAIC model (see page 68).

5.4 MEASURE PHASE TOLLGATE REVIEW CHECKLIST

A checklist of items that can form the basis of a measure phase tollgate review is shown in Table 5.11.

SUMMARY

The measure phase of the DMAIC model involves three key tasks for a Six Sigma project. The first task is to develop an operational definition for each CTQ identified in the define phase. The second task is to conduct a Gage R&R study for each CTQ to determine the capability of its measurement system. The third task is to collect passive baseline data for each CTQ to determine whether the CTQ is stable and normally distributed. It is critical to properly complete the define and measure phases of the DMAIC model before proceeding to the analyze phase.

REFERENCES

1. Berenson, M.L., Levine D.M., and Krehbiel T.C., *Basic Business Statistics: Concepts and Applications,* Ninth Ed. (Upper Saddle River, NJ: Prentice Hall, 2004)

2. Gitlow, H., Oppenheim, A. Oppenheim, R., Levine, D.M., *Quality Management: Tools and Methods for Improvement,* New York: McGraw-Hill-Irwin 3rd edition, 2005.

3. Gitlow, H., and Oppenheim, R., *STATCITY: Understanding Statistics Through Realistic Applications,* Homewood, IL: Richard D. Irwin, Inc., 2nd edition, 1986.

APPENDIX 5.1

USING MINITAB FOR GAGE R&R STUDIES

Before using Minitab for the gage studies done in this chapter, refer to the Introduction to Minitab in Appendix 9.1.

OBTAINING A GAGE RUN CHART

To obtain the gage run chart in Figure 5.9 on page 121, open the 🌐 GAGER&R-FUNCTIONALITY worksheet.

Select **Stat → Quality Tools → Gage Study → Gage Run Chart.** Then do the following:

1. In the Gage Run Chart dialog box (see Figure A5.1), enter **Box** or **C1** in the Part numbers: edit box, **Inspector** or **C2** in the

Operators: edit box, and **Functionality** or **C4** in the Measurement data: edit box.

2. Click the **OK** button.

OBTAINING A GAGE R&R STUDY (CROSSED)

To obtain the gage R&R study (crossed) in Figures 5.10–5.13 on pages 122–123, open the 🌐 GAGER&R-FUNCTIONALITY worksheet.

Select **Stat → Quality Tools → Gage Study → Gage R&R Study (Crossed).** Then do the following:

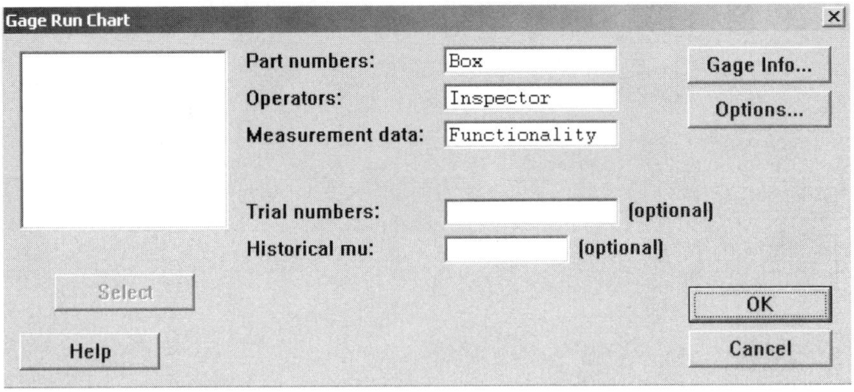

FIGURE A5.1 Gage Run Chart Dialog Box

1. In the Gage R&R Study (Crossed) dialog
   box (see Figure A5.2), enter **Box** or **C1**
   in the Part numbers: edit box, **Inspector**
   or **C2** in the Operators: edit box, and

Functionality or **C4** in the Measurement
data: edit box. Under Method of Analysis,
select the ANOVA option button.

2. Click the **OK** button.

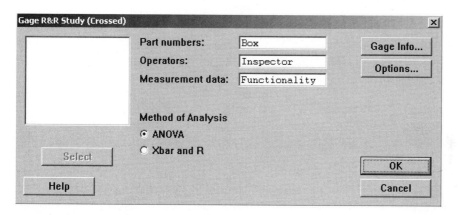

FIGURE A5.2 Gage R&R Study (Crossed) Dialog Box

ANALYZE PHASE
OF THE DMAIC MODEL

CHAPTER OUTLINE

LEARNING OBJECTIVES

After reading this chapter, you will be able to:

- Identify and operationally define the high-risk *X*s for each CTQ
- Establish measurement systems and collect baseline data for the high-risk *X*s
- Stabilize the high-risk *X*s that are out of control
- Identify major nuisance variables
- Reduce the set of *X*s with screening designs
- Develop hypotheses about the effect of the high-risk *X*s on the CTQ
- Prepare for an analyze phase tollgate review (if team member)
- Conduct an analyze phase tollgate review (if Champion or Process Owner)

INTRODUCTION

The analyze phase of the DMAIC model identifies and prioritizes the Xs that impact the spread, center, and shape of each CTQ. *Team members attempt to reduce the number of Xs to a small set of high-risk Xs and identify the relationships between the high-risk Xs and the CTQ.*

6.1 IDENTIFY THE XS FOR THE PROCESS UNDER STUDY

The first step in identifying the Xs in a process that impacts the CTQ is to identify its boundaries, that is, the starting and ending points of the process. The second step in identifying the Xs is to create the actual flowchart of the current process, using the flowcharting symbols discussed in Figure 4.5 on page 75. The third step in identifying the Xs is to highlight the linkages between the current process and "other" processes. The fourth step is to identify the Xs for each step in the process on the flowchart (see Figure 6.1).

The fifth step, if possible at this point, is to hypothesize the relationships between the Xs and each CTQ. This is stated quantitatively as follows:

$$CTQ_a[center, spread, shape] = f(X_{1a}[center, spread, shape], \ldots, X_{na}[center, spread, shape])$$
$$CTQ_b[center, spread, shape] = f(X_{1b}[center, spread, shape], \ldots, X_{nb}[center, spread, shape])$$
$$CTQ_c[center, spread, shape] = f(X_{1c}[center, spread, shape], \ldots, X_{nc}[center, spread, shape])$$
$$CTQ_d[center, spread, shape] = f(X_{1d}[center, spread, shape], \ldots, X_{nd}[center, spread, shape])$$
$$CTQ_e[center, spread, shape] = f(X_{1e}[center, spread, shape], \ldots, X_{ne}[center, spread, shape])$$

In this fifth step, each CTQ along with its central tendency, spread or variation, and shape of its distribution is expressed as a function of a set of X variables, each of which has its own central tendency, spread or variation, and shape. The sixth step is to state the optimization problem for the Six Sigma project. It will involve the global optimization of one or more CTQs. This may require the suboptimization of one or more CTQs in the short term. This is stated quantitatively as follows: Optimize $\{CTQ_a, CTQ_b, CTQ_c, CTQ_d, CTQ_e\}$.

It is helpful if team members visualize the current process as a "lean" process because it provides a starting point for understanding the potential of the current process. "**Lean management**" is useful in eliminating waste in almost any area of an organization, for example

- Supplier relations
- Plant or facility layout
- Procedures for setting up machines

- Procedures for maintaining equipment
- Training programs
- Measurement systems
- Work environment

Lean management promotes decreased cycle times, reduced complexity of processes, and lower costs by reducing the lead time and the resources required between the delivery of a service or product and the start time of the process that requires the delivery [Reference 1].

Team members eliminate waste by reducing complexity and decreasing cycle times. First, complexity frequently increases the incidence of non-value added steps in a process. Non-value added steps include any step that:

1. Customers are not willing to pay for
2. Do not change the product or service
3. Contain errors, defects, or omissions
4. Require preparation or setup

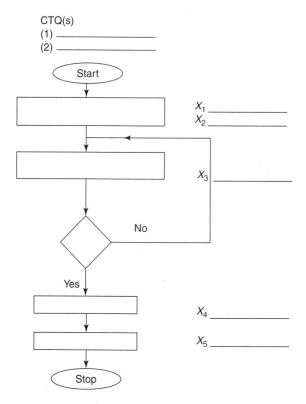

FIGURE 6.1 Flowchart with Xs and CTQ(s)

5. Involve control or inspection

6. Involve overproduction, special processing, and inventory

7. Involve waiting and delays

Value-added steps include steps that customers are willing pay for because they positively change the product or service in the view of the customer. Figure 6.2 shows a generic flowchart constructed to highlight value added (VA) and non-value added (NVA) steps. **VA/NVA flowcharts** are used to identify and modify or eliminate non-value added steps in a process, thereby reducing the complexity of the process.

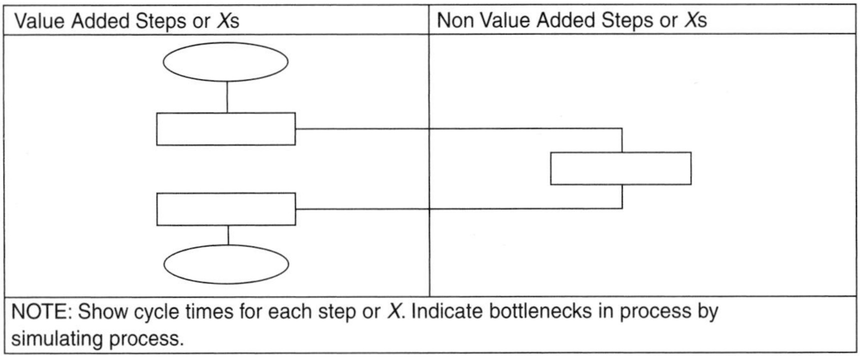

Value Added Steps or *X*s	Non Value Added Steps or *X*s

NOTE: Show cycle times for each step or *X*. Indicate bottlenecks in process by simulating process.

FIGURE 6.2 VA/NVA generic flowchart

Imagine a flowchart for making a photocopy of a document. It might include the following steps: turn on the machine, wait for it to warm up, open the lid, insert the document, close the lid, press the copy button, wait for the copy, open the lid, remove the original document, close the lid, remove the copy, turn off the machine. Imagine how complex the photocopy process gets if the machine runs out of toner, jams, or runs out of paper, to name a few problems. All of the functions in the previous sentence are non-value added functions that add an enormous amount of complexity to the process.

Second, cycle time is a critical *X* for many steps in a process. The cycle time for a step can be described by the mean, standard deviation, and shape of the distribution (see Sections 9.9–9.11) of individual cycle times for the step. One major method for reducing cycle time is to reduce the complexity of a process, as discussed previously. Another method for reducing cycle time is to eliminate bottlenecks in a process. A **bottleneck** is any step in a process whose capacity is lower than the outputs produced by the previous process step and that limits the amount of information or material that flows through a process. For example, consider an assembly line in which each of six serial assembly stations ideally can complete its portion of the final product at a rate of 100 units per hour. Assuming no errors or fatigue, let us examine four possible scenarios for the assembly line, shown in Figure 6.3.

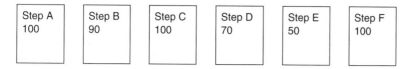

FIGURE 6.3 Assembly line with actual capacity per hour in each step

As you can see, the elimination of bottlenecks can dramatically reduce cycle time per hour. In other words, a process cannot produce outputs faster than its step with the lowest throughput rate.

Returning to the MSD case study [see References 7 and 8], team members prepared a detailed process map to identify the Xs, to determine VA/NVA steps, and to identify the bottlenecks (see Figure 6.4).

6.2 IDENTIFY THE XS RELATED TO EACH CTQ

Team members identify the Xs related to each CTQ using **cause-and-effect (C&E)** analysis (see Section 15.3). The output from C&E analysis is one or more functions, such as $CTQ1 = f(X_1, X_2, X_3, X_4, X_8)$ and $CTQ2 = g(X_3, X_4, X_5, X_6, X_7)$. These functions are interpreted as: CTQ1 is dependent on $X_1, X_2, X_3, X_4,$ and X_8, whereas CTQ2 is dependent on $X_3, X_4, X_5, X_6,$ and X_7. There are two types of cause and effect analyses: **Cause and Effect diagram** and **Cause and Effect matrix.** A cause and effect diagram is used if there is only one CTQ in a Six Sigma project, whereas a cause and effect matrix is used if there are two or more CTQs in a Six Sigma project.

A **Cause and Effect (C&E) diagram** is a tool used to organize the possible sources of variation (Xs) in a CTQ and to assist team members in the identification of the most probable causes (Xs) of the variation. The data for a cause and effect diagram can come from a flowchart. Frequently, the data for a cause and effect diagram comes from a brainstorming session, but for our purposes, we will think of a flowchart as a tool useful in identifying the Xs related to a CTQ. Figure 6.5 on page 151 shows an example of a C&E diagram for errors in producing printed airline tickets (CTQ) with major causes (Xs) and subcauses (Xs). Note that in Figure 6.5, the following notation is used:

$$CTQ = \text{Printed airline ticket errors}$$
$$X_1 = \text{Printing}$$
$$X_{1a} = \text{Quality}$$
$$X_{1b} = \text{Speed}$$
$$X_2 = \text{Ticket stock}$$
$$X_{2a} = \text{Age}$$
$$X_{2b} = \text{Paper}$$
$$X_{2c} = \text{Carbon density}$$

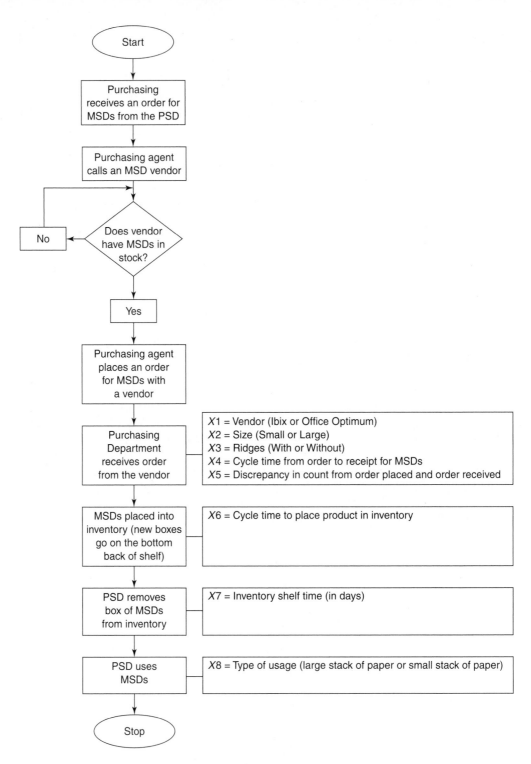

FIGURE 6.4 Process Map Identifying the Xs for the MSD Purchasing Process

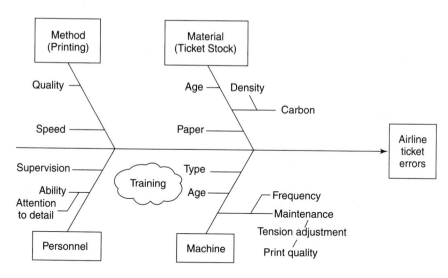

FIGURE 6.5 Causes of Errors in Printing Airline Tickets

A **cause and effect matrix** is a tool used to organize the possible sources of variation (*Xs*) for several CTQs simultaneously and to assist team members in the identification of the most probable causes (*Xs*) for each CTQ. A C&E matrix is a multivariate C&E diagram (see Table 6.1). As with C&E diagrams, the data analyzed by a C&E matrix can come from a flowchart.

The cells in Table 6.1 show the degree of the relationship between each CTQ and each *X*. The degree of relationship measures are developed by team members using the following scale:

TABLE 6.1 Cause and Effect Matrix

		Xs				
		Weights	X_1	X_2	....	X_m
CTQ	CTQ_1	W_1	9	3		
	CTQ_2	W_2		1		
	CTQ_{11}	W_{11}				
Weighted averages						

9 = strong relationship (positive or negative)

3 = moderate relationship (positive or negative)

1 = weak relationship (positive or negative)

0 = no relationship (blank cell)

An internal committee of experts in the process under study is assembled to identify and record the cell values in Table 6.1. It is important for the committee members to document the logic for the cell relationship values. If this is not done, the entire analysis may collapse under the weight of scrutiny by management.

The weights in Table 6.1 are derived from the Voice of the Customer (VoC) analysis in the define phase. Each weight is between 0.0 and 1.0, and the sum of all of the weights equals 1.0. The bottom row of Table 6.1 shows the weighted averages for each column (X) using the weights column (Ws). The Xs with the highest weighted averages are viewed as the vital few Xs for the entire set of CTQs.

Additionally, team members study Table 6.1 for empty rows or columns. An empty row (as in CTQ11) indicates a CTQ that is not being serviced by any Xs or that the relationships between the CTQ and the Xs are unknown. This represents an opportunity to identify unknown relationships and fill an unmet stakeholder need or want (CTQ). An empty column (as in X_m) indicates an X that is not related to any CTQ. This represents an opportunity to eliminate unnecessary complexity—in other words, to eliminate an X or to eliminate the reason for monitoring that X, unless that X has an impact on another CTQ. An empty column also may indicate an X that requires further study about its impact on a CTQ. This represents an opportunity to identify unknown relationships between the X and the CTQ that previously were not considered by team members.

Example of a C&E matrix. Raychem Corporation, a global materials science company, develops and manufactures high-performance industrial products. It serves customers in the electronics, industrial, and telecommunications markets. A product development team (PDT) at Raychem Corporation was charged with the development of a new cable television (CATV) connector for indoor use for its telecommunications market [see Reference 4]. The customers in the telecommunications market for the product, approximately 100 CATV system-operating companies in the United States control about 8,000 cable systems nationwide. Raychem had supplied high-performance exterior connectors to this market for a number of years; the indoor connector addressed a different set of customer needs. The coaxial cable and connector are shown in Figure 6.6.

The cable consists of a protective outer jacket, a layer of aluminum wires (braid) braided around an insulation layer, and a center conductor. In Figure 6.6b, the F port pictured on the left is a standard feature of home video, television, or converter equipment. The CATV connector shown on the right side of Figure 6.6b is installed onto the coaxial cable. The connector consists of three parts: a mandrel, a ring, and a shell. The metal mandrel contacts the braid portion of the coaxial cable and slides over the exterior of the F port. The polymeric ring residing between the

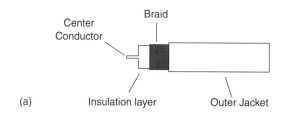

(a)

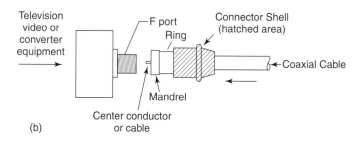

(b)

FIGURE 6.6 Coaxial Cable (6.6a) and Connector (6.6b)

mandrel and the shell has teeth that hold the connector in place on the cable. The connector shell slides over the mandrel and ring, locking the connector to the port.

PDT members set out to develop a new CATV connector for the U.S. telecommunications market. A VoC study led to the creation of a list of CTQs for a C&E matrix (see Figure 6.7).

For example, "Convenient Installation" was subdivided into "Obvious and Simple to Install," and "Easy to Tell When Properly Installed." "Obvious and Simple to Install" was subdivided into "Push-On" and "Pull-Off" type connectors, as well as other categories (not shown in Figure 6.7 due to proprietary information). In this way, the VoC was broken down into primary, secondary, and tertiary CTQs, such that each CTQ provided increasingly specific and operational information to team members.

Table 6.2 on page 155 is an abbreviated C&E matrix showing the primary and secondary CTQs and the weighted averages in its rows (tertiary customer needs are not shown because it is proprietary information) and the list of Xs developed by team members and the weights for the CTQs in its columns.

Team members also used Table 6.2 to detail the degree of relationship between each CTQ and X. This was accomplished by having team assign a strength of relationship value for each CTQ (row) and each X (column) pair (see each cell in Table 6.2). The strength of relationship values were 9 = strong relationship, 3 = moderate relationship, 1 = weak relationship, 0 = no relationship. The relationship between CTQ_1 (function and reliability—clear picture after abuse) and X_3 (RF shielding), X_4 (forces on equip. panel), and X_5 (number of install modes) is stated quantitatively as $CTQ_1 = f_1(X_3, X_4, X_5)$. Also, the relationship between CTQ_2 (function and reliability—customer need) and X_3 (RF shielding) and X_6 (additional technical requirements) is stated quantitatively as $CTQ_2 = f_2(X_3, X_6)$.

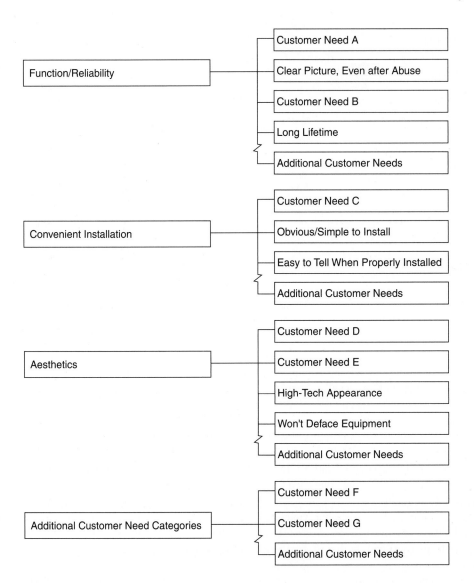

FIGURE 6.7 Partial List of CTQs for a CATV Connector

6.3 IDENTIFY THE HIGH-RISK *X*S FOR EACH CTQ

Team members select the *X*s with the highest weighted averages from the C&E matrix, or the high-risk *X*s identified on a C&E diagram (discussed in the previous section), and input them into a **failure modes and effects analysis (FMEA).** FMEA is a tool used to identify, estimate, prioritize, and reduce the risk of failure in CTQs through the development of actions (process changes) and contingency plans based on *X*s.

TABLE 6.2 Cause and Effect Matrix

		Weights	Xs	Force to Install X_1	Force to Remove X_2	R. F. Shielding X_3	Forces on Equip. Panel X_4	No. of Install Modes X_5	Additional Technical Req X_6	Technical Req X_7
Primary CTQs	Secondary CTQs									
Function and Reliability	Clear Picture after Abuse CTQ1					●	●	●		
	Customer Need CTQ2					●			●	
Convenient Installation	Customer Need CTQ3									
Aesthetics	Customer Need CTQ4									
Other	Customer Need CTQ5						●			
Weighted Averages		1.00								

● = 9 strong relationship

○ = 3 moderate relationship

△ = 1 weak relationship

Note: True relationship values are the proprietary information of Raychem. Values shown are for illustrative purposes only.

Source: Liner, M. E. S. Loredo, H. S. Gitlow, and N. G. Einsprach, "Quality Function Deployment Applied to Electronic Component Design," *Quality Engineering*, 1996, 9, pp. 237–248.

Before we discuss risk, you can determine your attitude toward risk by using the following test:

A million dollars is yours (tax free), but there is a 1 in a _____ chance you will experience a quick and painless death, and your family will not get to keep the money. What risk would you accept for the opportunity to get the million dollars?

1 in a 1,000,000
1 in 100,000
1 in 10,000
1 in 1,000
1 in 100
1 in 10

Some people will not accept the 1 in a million chance, whereas a few actually will accept 1 in 10 chance.

There are 9 steps to conducting a FMEA.

1. Team members identify the critical parameters and their potential failure modes for each X identified in the C&E matrix or diagram through brainstorming or other tools, that is, ways in which the process step (X) might fail (columns 1 and 2 of Table 6.3).

2. Team members identify the potential effect of each failure (consequences of that failure) and rate its severity (columns 3 and 4 of Table 6.3). The definition of the **severity scale** is shown in Table 6.4 on page 158.

3. Team members identify causes of the effects and rate their likelihood of occurrence (columns 5 and 6 of Table 6.3). The definition of the **likelihood of occurrence scale** is shown in Table 6.5 on page 158.

4. Team members identify the current controls for detecting each failure mode and rate the organization's ability to detect each failure mode (columns 7 and 8 of Table 6.3). The definition of the **detection scale** is shown in Table 6.6 on page 159.

5. Team members calculate the **RPN** (**risk priority number**) for each failure mode by multiplying the values in columns 4, 6, and 8 (column 9 of Table 6.3).

6. Team members identify the action(s), contingency plans, persons responsible, and target completion dates for reducing or eliminating the RPN for each failure mode (columns 10 and 11 of Table 6.3). Actions are the process changes needed to reduce the severity and likelihood of occurrence, and increase the likelihood of detection of a potential failure mode. **Contingency plans** are the alternative actions immediately available to a process owner when a failure mode occurs, despite process improvement actions. A contingency plan might include a contact name and phone number in case of a failure mode.

7. Team members identify the date the action was taken to reduce or eliminate each failure mode (column 12 of Table 6.3).

8. Team members rank the severity (column 13 of Table 6.3), occurrence (column 14 of Table 6.3), and detection (column 15 of Table 6.3) of each failure mode after the recommended action (column 10 of Table 6.3) has been put into motion.

9. Team members multiple the values in columns 13, 14, and 15 of Table 6.3 to recalculate the RPN for each failure mode after the recommended action (column 12 of Table 6.3) has been put into motion.

Table 6.8 on page 160 shows a FMEA for a student accounts office process with four steps: student waits for clerk, clerk pulls record, clerk processes record, and clerk files record. X_2 (clerk pulls record) is a critical failure mode because it exhibits such a high-risk priority number (RPN = 700), whereas X_3 (clerk processes record) is not a critical failure mode due to its low-risk priority number (RPN = 42). In a brainstorming session, the clerks determined that the most likely reason for not locating a record is because another clerk was using it. Consequently, the recommended action (column 10) was to "insert a note in a file if it is in use with the user's name." The department manager, Hiram, said that the revised best practice method would take effect no later than 1/30/03 (column 11); in fact, it was in effect on 12/15/02 (column 12). The calculation of the revised RPN number is shown in columns 13–16. The recommended action lowered the RPN number from 700 to 28.

TABLE 6.3 Format for an FMEA

1	2	3	4	5	6	7	8	9	10	11	12	13	14	15	16
Critical parameter	Potential failure mode	Potential failure effect	Severity	Potential causes	Occur-rence	Current controls	Detection	RPN	Recom-mended action	Responsi-bility and target date	Action taken	Severity	Occur-rence	Detection	RPN

Before RPN =   After RPN =

TABLE 6.4 Definition of "Severity" Scale = Likely Impact of Failure

Impact	Rating	Criteria: A Failure Could. . .
Bad	10	Injure a customer or employee
V	9	Be illegal
V	8	Render the unit unfit for use
V	7	Cause extreme customer dissatisfaction
V	6	Result in partial malfunction
V	5	Cause a loss of performance likely to result in a complaint
V	4	Cause minor performance loss
V	3	Cause a minor nuisance; can be overcome with no loss
V	2	Be unnoticed; minor effect on performance
Good	1	Be unnoticed and not affect the performance

TABLE 6.5 Definition of "Occurrence" Scale = Frequency of Failure

Impact	Rating	Time period	Probability of Occurrence
Bad	10	More than once per day	>30%
V	9	Once every 3–4 days	≤ 30%
V	8	Once per week	≤ 5%
V	7	Once per month	≤ 1%
V	6	Once every 3 months	≤ 0.3 per 1,000
V	5	Once every 6 months	≤ 1 per 10,000
V	4	Once per year	≤ 6 per 100,000
V	3	Once every 1–3 years	≤ 6 per million (approx. Six Sigma)
V	2	Once every 3–6 years	≤ 3 per 10 million
Good	1	Once every 6–100 years	≤ 2 per billion

6.4 DEVELOP OPERATIONAL DEFINITIONS FOR HIGH-RISK Xs

Operational definitions were discussed in Section 5.1. As previously stated, an operational definition consists of three parts: criterion, test, and decision. Each X must have an operational definition that is agreeable to relevant personnel.

Example. Returning to the MSD case study [see References 7 and 8], team members develop an operational definition for each X variable identified on the process map. The operational definitions for X_1, X_2, X_3, and X_8 relate to individual MSDs and are shown in Table 6.7.

TABLE 6.6 Definition of "Detection" Scale = Ability to Detect Failure

Impact	Rating	Definition
Bad	10	Defect caused by failure is not detectable
V	9	Occasional units are checked for defects
V	8	Units are systematically sampled and inspected
V	7	All units are manually inspected
V	6	Manual inspection with mistake proofing modifications
V	5	Process is monitored with control charts and manually inspected
V	4	Control charts used with an immediate reaction to out-of-control condition
V	3	Control charts used as above with 100% inspection surrounding out-of-control condition
V	2	All units automatically inspected or control charts used to improve the process
Good	1	Defect is obvious and can be kept from the customer or control charts are used for process improvement to yield a no-inspection system with routine monitoring

TABLE 6.7 Criteria for Selected X's in the MSD Case Study

Criteria: Each *X* conforms to either one or the other of the options.

X_1	Vendor	Ibix	Office Optimum
X_2	Size	Small (stock size)	Large (stock size)
X_3	Ridges	With ridges	Without ridges
X_8	Type of usage	Large stack of paper (# papers is 10 or more)	Small stack of paper (# papers is 9 or less)

Source: Liner, M. E. S. Loredo, H. S. Gitlow, and N. G. Einsprach, "Quality Function Deployment Applied to Electronic Component Design," *Quality Engineering,* 1996, 9, pp. 237–248.

Test: Select MSD.

Decision: Determine X_1, X_2, X_3, and X_8 options for the selected MSD.

The operational definitions for the procedures used to measure X_4, X_5, X_6, and X_7 are as follows.

Criteria: Compute cycle time in days by subtracting the order date from the date on the bill of lading.

X_4	Cycle time from order to receipt for MSDs	In days

Test: Select a box of MSDs upon receipt of shipment from vendor. Compute the cycle time.

TABLE 6.8 Partial FMEA Chart

1	2	3	4	5	6	7	8	9	10	11	12	13	14	15	16
Process step (Xs) or critical parameter	Potential failure mode(s) for each X	Potential failure effect	Severity	Potential causes	Occurrence	Current controls	Detection	RPN	Recommended action	Resp. and target date	Action taken	Severity	Occurrence	Detection	RPN
X_1 Cycle to student waits for clerk															
X_2 Cycle time to pull record	Record cannot be located	Student leaves, frustrated without processing record	7	File misplaced	10	Search for missing file	10	700	Clerks inserts note with his/her name in file when using a record	Hiram 1/30/03	12/15/02	7	4	1	28
X_3 Cycle time to process record	Record cannot be processed	Student leaves, frustrated without processing record	7	Record/clerk is missing information	3	Clerks update best practice method	2	42							
X_4 Cycle time to file record															

Decision: Determine X_4 for the selected box of MSDs.

Criteria: Count the number of boxes of MSDs received for a given order. Subtract the number of boxes ordered from the number of boxes received for the order under study.

X_5	Discrepancy in count of boxes from order placed and order received	In boxes of MSDs by order

Test: Select a particular purchase order for MSDs.

Decision: Compute the value of X_5 in number of boxes for the selected purchase order.

Criteria: Compute cycle time in days to place a shipment of MSDs in inventory by subtracting the date the shipment was received from the date the order was placed in inventory.

X_6	Cycle time to place product in inventory	In days

Test: Select a particular purchase order.

Decision: Compute the value of X_6 in days for the selected purchase order.

Criteria: Compute inventory shelf-time in days for a box of MSDs by subtracting the date the box was placed in inventory from the date the box was removed from inventory.

X_7	Inventory shelf-time	In days

Test: Select a box of MSDs.

Decision: Compute the value of X_7 in days for the selected box of MSDs.

6.5 ESTABLISH MEASUREMENT SYSTEM FOR HIGH-RISK XS

Gage R&R (repeatability and reproducibility) studies were discussed in Section 5.2. Gage R&R studies are used to determine whether the measurement system for each X is repeatable (multiple tests of the same item by the same inspector yield the same values of X) and reproducible (multiple inspectors testing the same item yield the same values of X) over time and conditions. Remember, Gage R&R studies must be completed with satisfactory results prior to collecting baseline data. Recall, often the identification of the high-risk X's and Gage R&R studies are done in the measurement phase for well-documented processes with dashboards.

Example. Returning to the MSD case study [see References 7 and 8], team members decided that the measurement systems for all of the Xs are known to be repeatable and reproducible. Thus, Gage R&R studies were not conducted by team members.

6.6 ESTABLISH BASELINE PROCESS CAPABILITIES FOR Xs

As with CTQs, team members collect baseline data for each X using a **check sheet.** A check sheet is used to collect data in a logical format. The data collected can be analyzed using statistical methods such as control charts (see Chapter 14). There are three major types of check sheets: **attribute check sheets, variables check sheets,** and **defect location check sheets.**

    Attribute Check Sheet. Attribute check sheets can be used to collect baseline data about an X that is count attribute data (see Section 9.4), such as the number of accidents in a factory by month, the number of defects in an automobile by automobile, or the number of errors made in a call center by day. In all of the these examples the number of problems are counted in a given area of opportunity (month, automobile, day) and can be of many different types. (accidents can be strains/sprains to the back, foreign objects in the eye, or contusions to the fingers).

    Table 6.9 shows an attribute check sheet for the causes of defects when organizing papers to be clipped in a bunch.

TABLE 6.9 Attribute Check Sheet Not Considering Time (January 1–15, 2003)

Defects	Frequency	Percentage
Clip too small	3	6
Clip too large	5	10
No clip available	3	6
Clip wrong color	3	6
Clip had ridges	19	38
Clip is broken	17	34
Total	50	100

    This check sheet was created by tallying each type of defect during the period January 1–15, 2003. The data in Table 6.9 ignores the time order of the defects. Another attribute check sheet that considers the time order of the data is shown in Table 6.10.

    Variables Check Sheet. Variables check sheets can be used to collect baseline data about an X that consists of measurement data (see Section 9.4), such as the cycle time to process a travel request, the weight of an ice cream cone, or the length of a piece of glass. In all of these examples, the measurement is on a unit of material or service.

    Table 6.11 shows the cycle time in minutes to process the paperwork of 50 consecutive clients.

TABLE 6.10 Attribute Check Sheet Considering Time (January 1–15, 2003)

Frequency	1	2	3	4	5	6	7	8	9	10	11	12	13	14	15	Total
6																
5							X			X						
4	X		X			X		X			X		X			
3		X		X					X						X	
2					X							X				
1																
0														X		
Total	**4**	**3**	**4**	**3**	**2**	**4**	**5**	**4**	**3**	**5**	**4**	**2**	**4**	**0**	**3**	**50**
Clip too small	0	0	1	1	0	0	0	0	0	1	0	0	0	0	0	3
Clip too large	1	0	2	0	0	0	1	0	0	1	0	0	0	0	0	5
No clip available	0	1	0	0	0	0	1	0	0	1	0	0	0	0	0	3
Clip wrong color	0	1	0	0	0	0	0	0	1	0	1	0	0	0	0	3
Clip had ridges	3	1	0	0	0	1	3	2	1	0	2	1	3	0	2	19
Clip is broken	0	0	1	2	2	3	0	2	1	2	1	1	1	0	1	17

TABLE 6.11 Cycle Time Data (in minutes)

47	3	22	32	21	39	16	22	11	26
13	34	5	15	15	42	21	52	24	3
35	28	12	15	37	15	12	51	22	32
27	42	32	12	8	30	33	23	20	17
31	2	17	21	22	12	22	22	25	24

CYCLETIME

Table 6.12 shows a measurement check sheet for collecting and organizing the 50 measurements.

Defect Location Check Sheet. Defect location check sheets are used to gather attribute data about one or more Xs that are difficult to quantify. Usually, defect location check sheets include a picture of a product or service that allows a respondent to circle the part of the product or service that is causing trouble. Team members then analyze the resulting pictures. Figure 6.8 shows a defect location check sheet concerning defects on the front of a refrigerator door. It

TABLE 6.12 Measurement Check Sheet Not Considering Time

Cycle time to process paperwork	Frequency	Percentage
0 min. to less than 10 min.	5	10
10 min. to less than 20 min.	13	26
20 min. to less than 30 min.	17	34
30 min. to less than 40 min.	10	20
40 min. to less than 50 min.	3	6
50 min. to less than 60 min.	2	4
Total	50	100

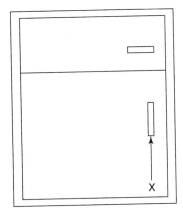

Examiner: Dan Horton	Date:	Serial No. DL 41317
Remarks: *Bolt holding bottom of handle is not tight*		

FIGURE 6.8 Defect Location Check Sheet

shows the location of a defect as being where the handle is attached to the refrigerator door. This could lead to the identification of an X, such that:

$$X_{\text{bolt to door}} = 0 \text{ if handle is properly bolted to the refrigerator door, or}$$
$$= 1 \text{ if handle is not properly bolted to the refrigerator door.}$$

Once baseline data for a given X has been collected using an appropriate check sheet, team members answer the following two questions:

1. Does the baseline data for the X indicate a stable process? (Yes or No)
2. Is the baseline data for the X normally distributed? (Yes or No)

The answers to these two questions result in four possible scenarios, as shown in Table 6.13.

TABLE 6.13 Four Scenarios for Each X

		X is Normally Distributed	
		Yes	No
X is stable	Yes	(1)	(2)
	No	(3)	(4)

Scenario 1 presents a situation where the RTY (rolled throughput yield), DPMO (defects per million opportunities), and process sigma can be estimated using the normal distribution. Scenario 2 presents a situation where the RTY, DPMO, and process sigma can be estimated using the actual distribution of the data, if the distribution is well known (e.g., exponential distribution or Poisson distribution). Scenarios 3 and 4 presents two situations where the RTY, DPMO, and process sigma cannot be estimated for an X due to the lack of stability.

In accordance with Table 6.13, team members estimate the actual process capability statistic for each X in scenarios 1 and 2. Additionally, they determine the desired process capability statistic and the gap between the actual and desired process capability statistic. Table 6.14 shows a scorecard for the Xs in a Six Sigma project that reflects these statistics.

TABLE 6.14 Scorecard for Xs

Xs	**RTY**			**DPMO**			**Short-term process sigma**			**Deadlines**
	Actual	**Desired**	**Gap**	**Actual**	**Desired**	**Gap**	**Actual**	**Desired**	**Gap**	
X_1 X_2										
X_m										

Example. Returning to the MSD case study [see References 7 and 8], team members gathered baseline data on durability (CTQ_1) and functionality (CTQ_2), and the high-risk Xs using the following sampling plan. For a 2-week period, the first box of MSDs brought to the PSD each hour was selected as a sample. For each sampled box, team members determined the durability (CTQ$_1$) and functionality (CTQ$_2$) measurement. Furthermore, they collected information concerning the vendor (X_1), size of the MSD (X_2), whether or not the MSD has ridges (X_3), and inventory shelf-life (X_7). Note that:

$$X_1 = \text{Vendor } (0 = \text{Office Optimum and } 1 = \text{Ibix})$$
$$X_2 = \text{Size } (0 = \text{small and } 1 = \text{large})$$
$$X_3 = \text{Ridges } (0 = \text{without and } 1 = \text{with})$$
$$X_7 = \text{Inventory shelf-life, in days}$$

The purchasing department separately studied cycle time from placing the order to receiving the order (X_4), discrepancy between ordered and received box counts (X_5), and cycle time from receipt of order to placement in inventory (X_6). These three factors may influence the choice of vendor, ordering procedures, and inventory control, but they do not impact durability and functionality. Furthermore, the MSDs are not tested after they are used, so the type of usage (X_8) is not studied here. As was indicated in the define phase, certain variables (e.g., X_4, X_5, X_6, and X_8) can be addressed in subsequent Six Sigma projects.

The baseline data revealed that the yield for durability (CTQ$_1$) is 0.4625 (37/80), and the yield for functionality (CTQ$_2$) is 0.425 (34/80). This indicates very poor levels for the CTQs in the Paper-Shuffling Department (PSD). For comparison purposes, the judgment sample carried out by the team during the define phase showed that the yield was approximately 40% (i.e., the team assumed the failure rate was approximately 60%) for both durability and functionality. The slight increase in yields in this study was probably due to common variation in the process. The baseline data also showed that 56.25% of all MSDs are from Office Optimum (X_1), 42.50% of MSDs are small (X_2), 50.00% of all MSDs are without ridges (X_3), and the average shelf-time for boxes of MSDs (X_7) is 6.5 days, with a standard deviation of 2.5 days.

6.7 STABILIZE HIGH-RISK XS

Team members analyze the baseline data for each X using a control chart (see Chapter 14) to determine whether the X exhibits any special causes of variation (scenarios 3 and 4 in Table 6.13). If an X exhibits one or more special causes of variation, team members determine where and when they occurred to take appropriate corrective action(s). Team members use tools such as log sheets, brainstorming, and C & E diagrams (see Chapter 15) to identify the root cause(s) of the special variation(s).

For example, the student accounts payable process at a major university is comprised of several subprocesses. They are the student arrival/wait process, the clerk pulls record process, the clerk takes appropriate action process, and the clerk files record process. One key objective and indicator of the student accounts payable process is:

Key objective: Reduce "total time" to process student accounts

Key indicator: "total time" (wait time + record-pulling time + process time + record-filing time) in minutes for students involved in the student accounts process by day. An $\overline{X}$

and R-chart (see Chapter 14) is used to study this data. A sample of four students is drawn each day from the student accounts process. Total time is calculated (sum of wait and processing time) for the first student entering the office at 9:00 a.m., 11:00 a.m., 2:00 p.m., and 4:00 p.m.

The subprocesses for the "reduce total time to process student accounts" are broken down into several subobjectives and subindicators, they are:

Key micro-objective: Reduce line wait time.

Key microindicator: Line wait time in minutes for students involved in the student accounts process by day. This data is analyzed using an $\overline{X}$ and R-chart.

Key micro-objective: Reduce record pull time.

Key microindicator: Record-pulling time by day. This data is analyzed using an $\overline{X}$ and R-chart.

Key micro-objective: Reduce process time.

Key microindicator: Process time in minutes for students involved in the student accounts process by day. This data is analyzed using an $\overline{X}$ and R-chart.

Key micro-objective: Reduce record filing time.

Key microindicator: Record filing time by day. This data is analyzed using an $\overline{X}$ and R-chart.

Part of the dashboard for the student accounts process is shown in Table 6.15.

TABLE 6.15 Partial Dashboard for the Student Account Office

Process owner		Process employee		Project or task
Key objective	**Key indicator**	**Key objective**	**Key indicator**	
Decrease total time for processing student accounts	Average and range of total processing time for student accounts in seconds by day ($\overline{X}$ and R-chart)	Reduce line wait time	$\overline{X}$ and R-chart of line wait time	
		Reduce record pull time	$\overline{X}$ and R-chart of record pull time	Record pull time project
		Reduce record process time	$\overline{X}$ and R-chart of record process time	
		Reduce record file time	$\overline{X}$ and R-chart of record file time	

A dot plot (Figure 6.9) and an $\overline{X}$ and R-chart (Figure 6.10) of "total time" for 52 weeks shows a stable and normal process with a mean of 1,223 seconds (20.4 minutes) and a standard deviation of 285 seconds ($587/d_2 = 587/2.059 = 285$), or 4.8 minutes.

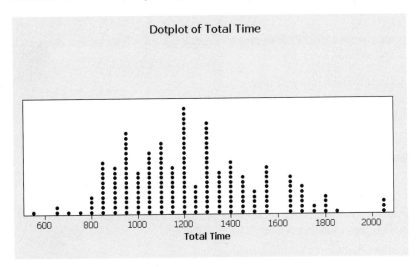

FIGURE 6.9 Minitab Dot Plot of Total Processing Time

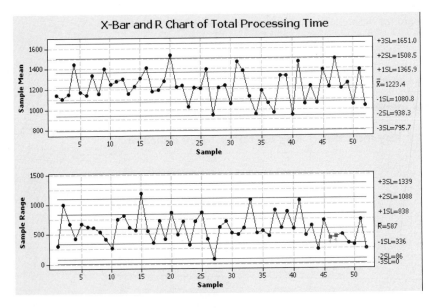

FIGURE 6.10 Minitab $\overline{X}$ and R-charts of Total Processing Time

A dot plot (Figure 6.11) and an $\overline{X}$ and R chart (Figure 6.12) of "record pull time" for 52 weeks shows an unstable, bimodal process with a mean of 360.9 seconds (approximately

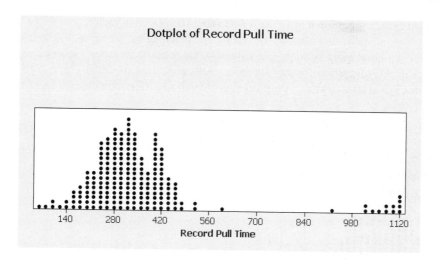

FIGURE 6.11 Minitab Dot Plot of Record Pull Time

6 minutes) and a standard deviation of 169 seconds ($348/d_2 = 348/2.059 = 169$), or 2.8 minutes.

Team members analyzed the out-of-control points on the R-chart (see bottom panel of Figure 6.12) and determined that the out-of-control (large) ranges were caused by misplaced records that could not be located because they were being processed by another clerk. Brainstorming

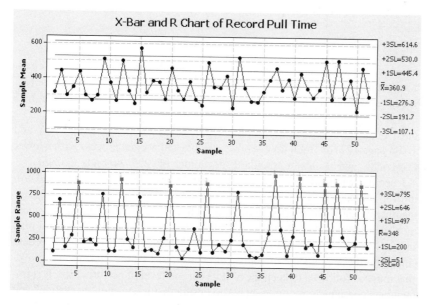

FIGURE 6.12 Minitab $\overline{X}$ and R-chart of Record Pull Time

by team members led to the suggestion that a Post-it note should be placed in each record's location as it is being processed, indicating who has the record, and that the Post-it note should be removed after the file is replaced in its location. Consequently, the "clerk pulls report" subprocess was modified to include this suggestion. Twenty-six more weeks of data are collected. Figure 6.13 shows a before (coded 1) and after (coded 2) dot plot of record pull time. The after data appears to

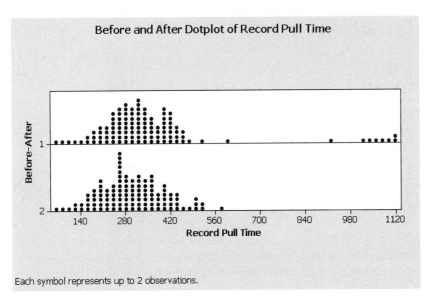

FIGURE 6.13 Minitab Before and After Dot Plot of Record Pull Time

be normally distributed. Figure 6.14 shows a before (coded 1) and after (coded 2) $\overline{X}$ and R-chart. The after data shows a stable and normal process with a mean of 296.9 seconds (approximately 5 minutes) and a standard deviation of 99 seconds ($203/d_2 = 203/2.059 = 99$ seconds), or 1.65 minutes.

A before (coded 1) and after (coded 2) dot plot (Figure 6.15) and before and after $\overline{X}$ and R-chart (Figure 6.16 on page 172) of "total time" shows a stable and normal process with a lower mean of 1,190.8 seconds and a lower standard deviation of 227 seconds ($529/d_2 = 529/2.059 = 227$). It seems that the team was successful in stabilizing a chaotic process and creating a slightly improved process.

Next, team members identify the process owner for each X (column 2 of Table 6.16), specify the data collection plan for each X (column 3 of Table 6.16), and document the control plan for each X (column 4 of Table 6.16). A control plan specifies the tasks required by the process owner of the X to maintain the X in a state of statistical control; that is, the process and procedures (flowchart) that must be followed to keep the X at its current level of performance. It is important that team members continue to monitor each X to ensure that it does not "backslide" and move into a chaotic state.

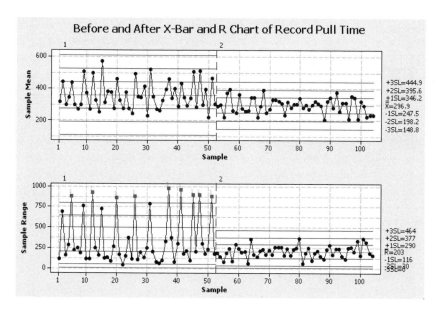

FIGURE 6.14 Minitab Before and After $\overline{X}$ and R-chart of Record Pull Time

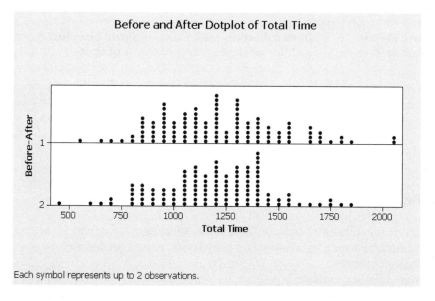

Each symbol represents up to 2 observations.

FIGURE 6.15 Minitab Dot Plot for Before and After Analysis of Total Time

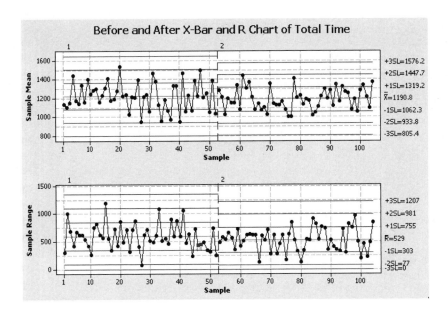

FIGURE 6.16 Minitab Before and After $\bar{X}$ and R-chart for Total Time

TABLE 6.16 Documentation of Control Plan for Each X

1	2	3	4
Xs	**Process owner of each X**	**Data collection plan for each X**	**Control plan for each X**
X_1 X_2 X_m			

6.8 CONSIDER MAJOR NUISANCE VARIABLES

Nuisance variables are often classified as controllable, uncontrollable, or noise factors. They are variables in an experiment that must be accounted for to have valid results, but that may not be of direct interest to the experimenter.

A **controllable nuisance variable** is a factor (X) whose levels can be set by an experimenter. For example, an experimenter can select different days of the week for an experiment.

The principle of blocking is used to deal with controllable nuisance variables. **Blocking** is a method that allows team members to collect experimental data about a CTQ in such a way that it is possible to isolate the effect of a controllable nuisance variable on the CTQ. For example, the day of the week that data is collected may not be an X that is being studied in an experiment, but it may have an effect on the CTQ, so blocking allows team members to estimate the effect of day of the week on the CTQ.

An **uncontrollable nuisance variable** is a factor that can be measured but not controlled in an experiment. Statisticians use a procedure called *analysis of covariance* (see Reference 5) to understand the effect of uncontrollable nuisance variables. For example, the ambient temperature in a factory may affect the results of an experiment. If ambient temperature can be measured but not controlled, it is an uncontrollable nuisance variable.

A **noise variable** is a factor that is not included in an experiment and can affect the center, spread, and shape of a CTQ. A noise variable (also called a **lurking variable**) is an X that may or may not be known to the experimenter and is difficult to control. A lurking variable, say X_3, can make two unrelated variables, say Y and X_2, seem correlated, when in fact they are uncorrelated. For example, until 1947 in the United States, there was almost a perfect correlation between the number of mules born per year (X_3) and the number of new PhDs per year (Y). However, further investigation led to the realization that the population of the United States was growing (X_2) and consequently, the population of new farmers and the population of new PhDs. The correlation between Y and X_3 was a spurious correlation. X_3 is called an *uncontrollable noise* or *lurking variable* if its effect on Y and X_2 was unknown at the time the data was studied. **Randomization** is a major method for averaging out the effects of lurking Xs.

Multivari charts and regression analysis (see Reference 6) are tools that can be used to study passive data to uncover noise variables.

A multivari chart graphically presents data in the form of CTQ $= f(X_1, X_2, X_3, X_4)$, where CTQ is a measurement variable and the Xs are classification attribute variables. These charts provide a preliminary visual display of the effect that a set of factors (Xs) have on the variability in a CTQ (Y). A multivari chart displays the mean of the CTQ (Y) at each level of every factor (X) in a hierarchical format.

A multivari chart shows the effect of nuisance variables on a CTQ because in a passive study, the Xs do not vary much during data gathering, but the nuisance variables do vary, so they will show up on the multivari chart. Therefore, the only real variation that is seen on a multivari is chart related to nuisance variables.

For example, suppose a multivari chart is being constructed for three Xs: factor X_3 has three levels, called $X_3 = 1$, $X_3 = 2$, and $X_3 = 3$; factor X_2 has two levels, called $X_2 = 1$ and $X_2 = 2$ for each level of factor X_3; and factor X_1 has two levels, called $X_1 = 1$ and $X_1 = 2$ for each combination of the levels of factors X_3 and X_2. A generic data matrix for a three-factor multivari chart is shown in Table 6.17. Five observations of Y are collected at each combination of X_3 and X_2 and X_1, called Y_{ijkn}, where $n = 1$ to 5.

A multivari chart requires that observations exist for all combinations of the levels of all factors (i.e., Xs). If certain combinations are not observed, a multivari chart cannot be constructed using the factors in which combinations are not observed.

The structure of the data matrix in Table 6.17 is shown as Minitab 14 output in Table 6.18.

TABLE 6.17 Structure of Data Matrix for Three-Factor Multivari Chart

	$X_3 = 1$			$X_3 = 2$			$X_3 = 3$	
	$X_2 = 1$	$X_2 = 2$		$X_2 = 1$	$X_2 = 2$		$X_2 = 1$	$X_2 = 2$
$X_1 = 1$	38.9,43.3, 40.8,48.6, 43.3	Y_{ijkn}	$X_1 = 1$	Y_{ijkn}	Y_{ijkn}	$X_1 = 1$	Y_{ijkn}	Y_{ijkn}
$X_1 = 2$	Y_{ijkn}	Y_{ijkn}	$X_1 = 2$	Y_{ijkn}	Y_{ijkn}	$X_1 = 2$	Y_{ijkn}	Y_{ijkn}

TABLE 6.18 Data Matrix in Minitab 14 Output

Row	X_1	X_2	X_3	Y	Row	X_1	X_2	X_3	Y	Row	X_1	X_2	X_3	Y
01	1	1	1	38.9	21	2	1	3	59.3	41	1	2	2	44.3
02	1	1	2	43.6	22	2	2	1	44.7	42	1	2	3	44.8
03	1	1	3	52.1	23	2	2	2	43.4	43	2	1	1	41.1
04	1	2	1	48.6	24	2	2	3	49.5	44	2	1	2	47.3
05	1	2	2	46.4	25	1	1	1	40.8	45	2	1	3	59.1
06	1	2	3	43.9	26	1	1	2	41.0	46	2	2	1	39.5
07	2	1	1	41.1	27	1	1	3	60.3	47	2	2	2	43.8
08	2	1	2	47.3	28	1	2	1	43.8	48	2	2	3	42.8
09	2	1	3	59.1	29	1	2	2	44.8	49	1	1	1	43.3
10	2	2	1	39.5	30	1	2	3	45.1	50	1	1	2	41.3
11	2	2	2	43.8	31	2	1	1	46.5	51	1	1	3	60.5
12	2	2	3	42.8	32	2	1	2	46.5	52	1	2	1	43.0
13	1	1	1	43.3	33	2	1	3	58.7	53	1	2	2	44.8
14	1	1	2	41.3	34	2	2	1	45.0	54	1	2	3	46.7
15	1	1	3	60.5	35	2	2	2	48.3	55	2	1	1	44.7
16	1	2	1	43.0	36	2	2	3	38.7	56	2	1	2	47.6
17	1	2	2	44.8	37	1	1	1	48.6	57	2	1	3	59.3
18	1	2	3	46.7	38	1	1	2	43.1	58	2	2	1	44.7
19	2	1	1	44.7	39	1	1	3	60.3	59	2	2	2	43.4
20	2	1	2	47.6	40	1	2	1	51.9	60	2	2	3	49.5

 MULTIVARI

Figure 6.17 is a three-factor multivari chart. Factors X_1 and X_2 have two levels, and factor X_3 has three levels. The multivari chart consists of the following information. First, each panel represents one level of factor X_3. The diamonds represent the means for each factor level. The dashed line connects the factor level means. As you can see, there is a slight increase in the mean of Y over the first two levels of factor X_3 and a large increase in the mean of Y for the third level of factor X_3. Second, each panel is divided into sections (each section is distinguished at the bottom or top of the panel) that correspond to each level of the factor X_2. The squares represent the means for each factor level of X_2 for a given level of factor X_3. The dashed line connects the factor level means. As you can see, there is a small increase in the mean of Y between the first and second levels of factor X_2 but a large decrease in the mean of Y between the first and second levels of X_2 for the third level of X_3. Third, each section of a panel has a set of symbols that correspond to each level mean for factor X_1. The different symbols represent each level of factor X_1 for each combination of the levels of X_2 and X_3. The solid line connects the means for factor X_1 for each combination of the levels of X_2 and X_3. As you can see, the mean of factor X_1 shows a minor increase from level 1 to level 2 for $(X_3 = 1$ and $X_2 = 1)$, $(X_3 = 2$ and $X_2 = 1)$, $(X_3 = 3$ and $X_2 = 1)$, and the mean of factor X_1 shows a minor decrease from level 1 to level 2 for $(X_3 = 1$ and $X_2 = 2)$, $(X_3 = 2$ and $X_2 = 2)$, and $(X_3 = 3$ and $X_2 = 2)$. $(X_3 = 2$ and $X_2 = 1)$ show the biggest difference between the mean of Y for the two levels of X_1, and $(X_3 = 1$ and $X_2 = 2)$ show the next biggest difference between the mean of Y for the two levels of X_1, but these differences are still relatively small. It seems that X_2 and X_3 are significant factors, whereas X_1 is

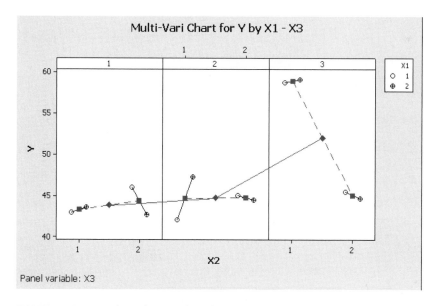

FIGURE 6.17 Minitab Multivari Chart for Y by Factors X_1, X_2, and X_3

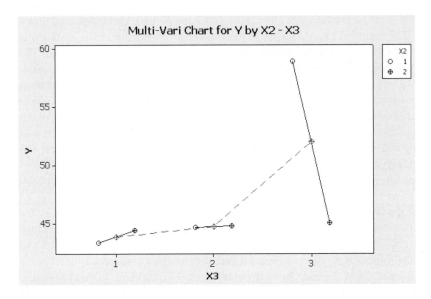

FIGURE 6.18 Minitab Multivari Chart for Y for the Factors X_3 and X_2

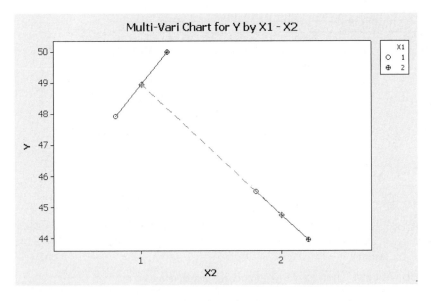

FIGURE 6.19 Minitab Multivari Chart for Y for the Factors X_2 and X_1

not a significant factor. Now, turning our attention to the interactions between the Xs, we see that X_3 and X_2 have a significant interaction. Figure 6.18 shows that the mean of Y is marginally smaller for $X_2 = 1$ than $X_2 = 2$ for $X_3 = 1$ and $X_3 = 2$. Additionally, the mean of Y is significantly larger for $X_2 = 1$ than $X_2 = 2$ for $X_3 = 3$. There is a significant interaction between X_2 and X_1. Figure 6.19 shows that the mean of Y is significantly larger for $X_2 = 1$ than $X_2 = 2$.

6.9 USING SCREENING DESIGNS TO REDUCE THE NUMBER OF HIGH-RISK XS

Screening designs (see Reference 5) are a possible step in proactive experimental design and analysis useful in the analyze phase or improve phase of a Six Sigma project to reduce the number of Xs that may affect a CTQ. They are used when knowledge about the process is very low; that is, process experts do not know which Xs are critical to optimizing a CTQ. Screening designs provide information about which individual Xs impact a CTQ for a low number of experimental runs (low cost) at the expense of understanding the impact of the interactions between the Xs (for example, X_2X_3) on the CTQ (high cost). An experimental run is a test of a process with preset values of the Xs.

6.10 DEVELOP HYPOTHESES ABOUT THE RELATIONSHIPS BETWEEN THE HIGH-RISK XS AND THE CTQS

Team members develop hypotheses that explain the relationships between specific Xs and each CTQ. A **hypothesis** states a premise about a CTQ (for example, the mean value of CTQ $>$ 25 units) or about a relationship between variables (for example, CTQ $= b_0 - b_1X_1 + b_2X_2$). CTQ $= b_0 - b_1X_1 + b_2X_2$ is the hypothetical statement of "If I increase X_1, then CTQ will decrease by b_1, and if I increase X_2, then CTQ will increase by b_2," assuming there is no interaction between X_1 and X_2.

A hypothesis can be developed from several sources: a dashboard, process knowledge, review of the literature (library and Internet), and statistical methods.

Dashboard. A dashboard can be used to develop a hypothesis because it presents the Xs relating to a CTQ or higher level X. In the student accounts payable example discussed earlier, the dashboard facilitates the creation of a hypothesis about the relationship between the CTQ (total processing time for student accounts) and X_1 (line wait time), X_2 (record pull time), X_3 (record process time), and X_4 (record file time). It is: CTQ $= f(X_1, X_2, X_3, X_4)$, or more specifically, CTQ $= b_0 + b_1X_1 + b_2X_2 + b_3X_3 + b_4X_4$. The last statement of the hypothesis indicates that as X_1, X_2, X_3, or X_4 increase, CTQ will also increase. Also, this hypothesis eliminates any interactions between the Xs, for example, $X_2 X_3$, or X_2X_4, as having an effect on CTQ.

Process Knowledge. Team members can use process knowledge to develop a hypothesis. Process knowledge is the result of studying the theory of a process or the result of experience with a process that reinforces the theory of the process. For example, "lean manufacturing" theory explains the direct relationship between batch size and cycle time; if batch size is decreased, then cycle time is decreased.

Review of the Literature. A review of the literature can be used to develop a hypothesis. For example, in the trade journal of the Linen Supply Association of America (LSAA), *The Linen Supply News,* an article reported a study that suggests a statistically significant negative relationship between dryness of sheets after processing and thread count of sheets. In other words, the higher the thread count of a sheet, the dryer it will be after processing, or to state this quantitatively: $CTQ = b_0 + b_1 X$, where

$$CTQ = \text{dryness of sheet after processing, and}$$
$$X = \text{thread count of sheet.}$$

Team members can use this knowledge to generate their own hypotheses.

Once team members develop hypotheses from either a dashboard, process knowledge, or a review of the literature, they collect passive data from the process to test out their hypotheses. This can be done using existing X and CTQ data or by obtaining new X and CTQ data. Either way, the hypotheses must be tested to eliminate the low-risk Xs and to highlight the high-risk Xs before the beginning of the improve phase.

Statistical Methods. Team members can use statistical methods to test a hypothesis between a CTQ and a set of Xs. For example, team members collected passive data from the typical functioning of a process to determine whether either X_1 and/or X_2 are related to the CTQ. Figure 6.20 shows a dot plot of CTQ that reveals a very wide distribution. This led team members to think that one of the Xs might be a contributing factor to such a large variance for CTQ. Dot plots of CTQ by X_1 and X_2 reveal that X_2 does not seem to have an effect of CTQ (Figure 6.21), but X_1 does seem to have an effect on CTQ (Figure 6.22 on page 180). As a result of this analysis, team members decide to drop X_2 and retain X_1 as an explanatory factor of the CTQ.

Example. Returning to the MSD case study [see References 7 and 8], team members develop hypotheses about the relationships between the Xs and the CTQs to identify the Xs that affect the center, spread, and shape of the CTQs. In this case, the baseline data is a passive data set that will be subject to statistical analysis. Dot plots of durability (CTQ_1) and functionality (CTQ_2) stratified by $X_1, X_2, X_3,$ and X_7 can be used to generate some hypotheses about main effects (i.e., the individual effects of each X on CTQ_1 and CTQ_2). **Interaction plots** can be used to generate hypotheses about **interaction effects** (i.e., those effects on CTQ_1 or CTQ_2 for which the influence of one X variable depend on the level or value of another X variable) if all combinations of levels of X variables are studied. If all combinations of levels of X variables are not studied, interaction effects are often not discovered.

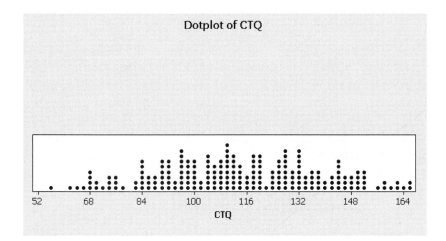

FIGURE 6.20 Minitab Dot Plot of Cycle Time Data

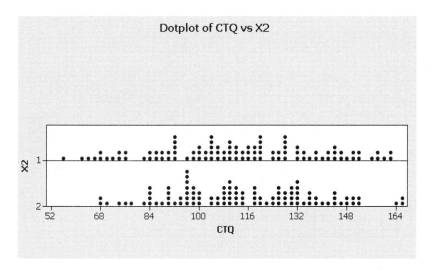

FIGURE 6.21 Minitab Dot Plot of Cycle Time Data by Level of X_2

Team members constructed dot plots from baseline data to check whether any of the Xs (i.e., main effects) impact durability (CTQ_1) and functionality (CTQ_2). The dot plots for durability are shown in Figures 6.23 through 6.26. The dot plots for functionality are shown in Figures 6.27 through 6.30.

The dot plots for durability (CTQ_1) indicate:

1. The values of durability tend to be low or high with a significant gap between 4 and 6 for X_1, X_2, X_3 and X_7,

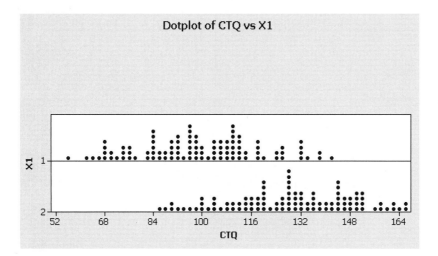

FIGURE 6.22 Minitab Dot Plot of Cycle Time Data by Level of X_1

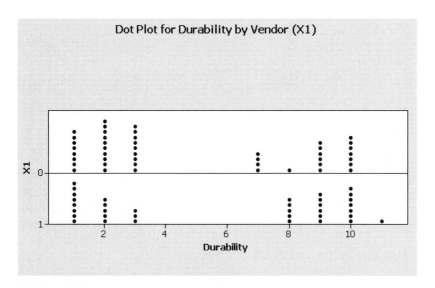

FIGURE 6.23 Minitab Dot Plot for Durability by X_1 (i.e., Vendor)

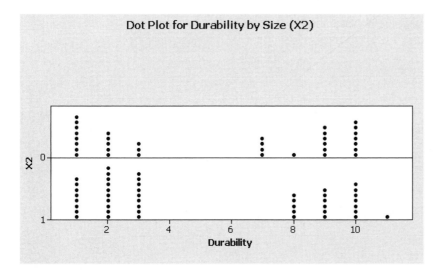

FIGURE 6.24 Minitab Dot Plot for Durability by X_2 (i.e., Size)

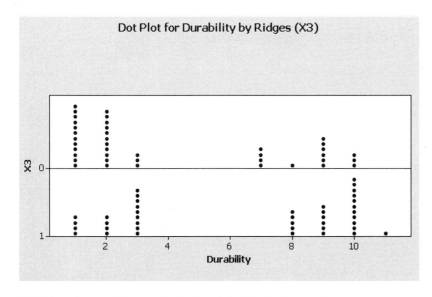

FIGURE 6.25 Minitab Dot Plot for Durability by X_3 (i.e., Ridges)

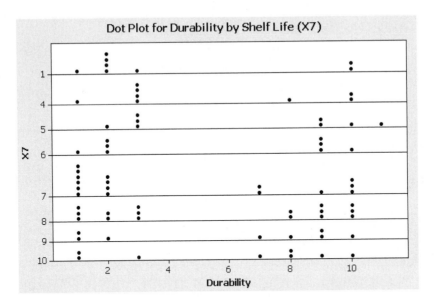

FIGURE 6.26 Minitab Dot Plot for Durability by X_7 (i.e., Shelf-life)

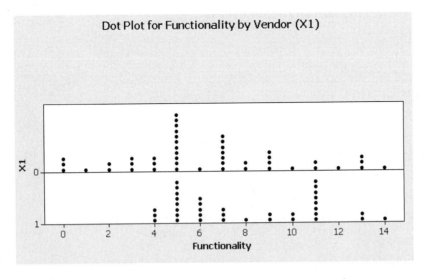

FIGURE 6.27 Minitab Dot Plot for Functionality by X_1 (i.e., Vendor)

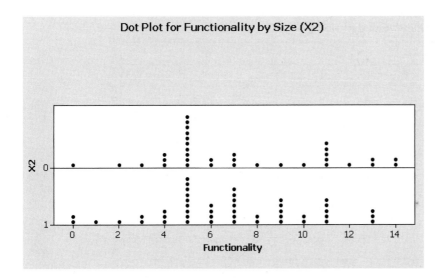

FIGURE 6.28 Minitab Dot Plot for Functionality by X_2 (i.e., Size)

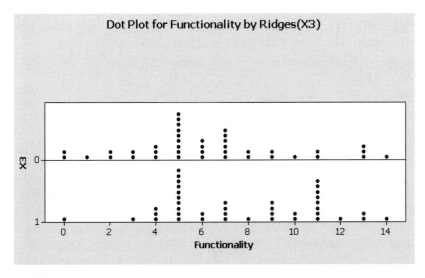

FIGURE 6.29 Minitab Dot Plot for Functionality by X_3 (i.e., Ridges)

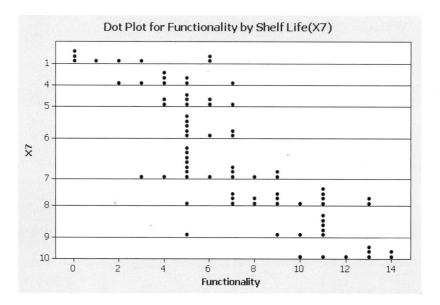

FIGURE 6.30 Minitab Dot Plot for Functionality by X_7 (i.e., Shelf-life)

2. The variation in durability is about the same for all levels of X_1, X_2, X_3 and X_7

The dot plots for functionality (CTQ$_2$) indicate:

1. The values of functionality tend to be lower when $X_1 = 0$ than when $X_1 = 1$,
2. The variation in functionality is about the same for all levels of X_2 and X_3
3. The values of functionality tend to be lower for low values of X_7

Discussion of the Analysis of Durability. Because there are no clear differences in variation (i.e., spread) of durability for each of the levels of X_1, X_2, X_3, and X_7, the team wondered
whether there might be differences in the average (i.e., center) for each level of the individual Xs.
Team members constructed a main effects plot for durability to study differences in averages (see
Figure 6.31).

Figure 6.31 indicates that for the range of shelf-lives ($X_7 = 1$ to 10 days) observed, there
is no clear pattern for the relationship of shelf-life to the average durability (CTQ$_1$). On the other
hand, it appears that ridges (X_3) have a positive relationship to the average durability. At first
glance, it would seem that the better results for the average durability are seen when the vendor
Ibix ($X_1 = 1$) is chosen, using small MSDs ($X_2 = 0$), whereas using large MSDs ($X_2 = 1$)
from Office Optimum ($X_1 = 0$) yield worse results.

While discussing the dot plots and main effects plot, we suggested that it is dangerous to
make any conclusions without knowing whether there are interaction effects. An interaction effect is present when the amount of change in the CTQ introduced by changing one of the Xs

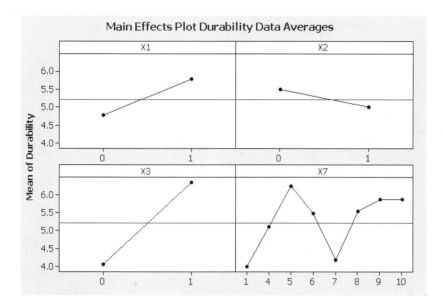

FIGURE 6.31 Minitab Main Effects Plot for Durability by X_1, X_2, X_3, and X_7

depends on the value of another X. In that case, it is misleading to choose the best value of the Xs individually without first considering the interactions between the Xs. Consequently, team members did interaction plots for X_1, X_2, and X_3. X_7 was not included in the interaction plots because the main effects plot indicated no clear pattern or relationship with durability (CTQ_1). All combinations of levels of the X variables must be present to draw an interaction plot. This is often not the case with passive data (i.e., no plan was put in place to insure all combinations were observed in the data-gathering phase). Fortunately, although not all combinations were observed equally often, they were all present. Figure 6.32 is the interaction plot for durability.

Surprise! The interaction plot indicates that there is a possible interaction between X_1 (i.e., vendor) and X_2 (i.e., size). How is this known? When there is no interaction, the lines should be approximately parallel to each other, indicating that the amount of change in average durability when moving from one level of each X variable to another level should be the same for all values of another X variable. Figure 6.32 shows the lines on the graph of X_1 and X_2 are not parallel, but they cross. The average durability is the highest when either large Ibix MSDs (i.e., $X_1 = 1$ and $X_2 = 1$) or small Office Optimum MSDs (i.e., $X_1 = 0$ and $X_2 = 0$) are used. This means the choice of vendor may depend on the size of MSD required. The main effects plot suggests that the best results for average durability would occur when small MSDs from Ibix are used, but the interaction plot suggests this combination would yield a bad average durability. To study all this further, the team decides that during the improve phase, they will run a full factorial design to examine the relationship of X_1, X_2, and X_3 on durability (CTQ_1).

Discussion of the Analysis of Functionality. Figures 6.33 and 6.34 represent the main effects and interaction effects plots, respectively, for functionality (CTQ_2).

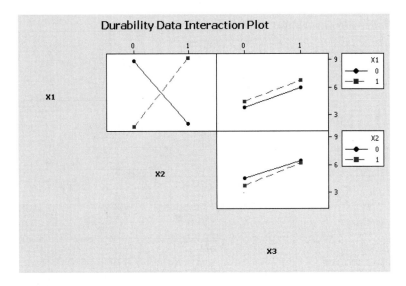

FIGURE 6.32 Minitab Interaction Effects Plot for Durability by X_1, X_2, and X_3

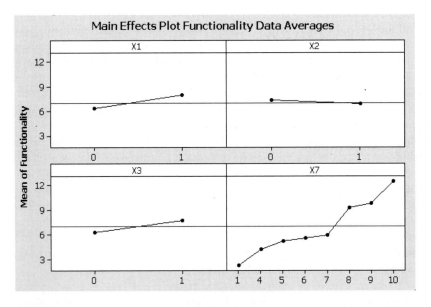

FIGURE 6.33 Minitab Main Effects Plot for Functionality by X_1, X_2, X_3, and X_7

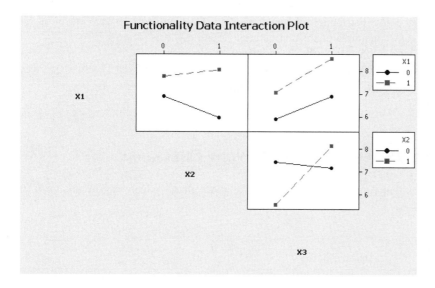

FIGURE 6.34 Minitab Interaction Effects Plot for Functionality by X_1, X_2, and X_3

The main effects plot indicates that higher values of shelf-life (X_7) yield higher values for functionality (CTQ_2). The team surmised that the longer a box of MSDs sits in inventory (i.e., higher values of shelf-life), the higher the count of broken MSDs (i.e., functionality will be high). From a practical standpoint, the team felt comfortable with this conclusion. They decided the purchasing department should put a Six Sigma project in place to investigate whether the potential benefit of either a "just-in-time" MSD ordering process or establishing better inventory handling procedures will solve the problem.

The interaction effect plot indicates a potential interaction between the X_2 (i.e., size) and X_3 (i.e., ridges). The better results for functionality (i.e., low values) were observed for large MSDs without ridges (i.e., $X_2 = 1$ and $X_3 = 0$). Why this may be the case needs to be studied further. Also, there may be an interaction between X_1 (i.e., vendor) and X_2 (i.e., size), but it appears that better results are observed whenever Office Optimum is used (i.e., $X_1 = 0$). In other words, the average count of broken MSDs is lower (i.e., functionality average is lower) whenever Office Optimum is the vendor.

Analyze Phase Summary for the MSD Case Study. The analyze phase resulted in the following hypotheses:

Hypothesis 1: Durability = $f(X_1 =$ vendor, $X_2 =$ size, $X_3 =$ ridges), with a strong interaction effect between X_1 and X_2.

Hypothesis 2: Functionality = $f(X_1 =$ vendor, $X_2 =$ size, $X_3 =$ ridges, $X_7 =$ shelf-life), the primary driver being X_7, with some main effect due to X_1 and an interaction effect between X_2 and X_3.

X_7 is the main driver of the distribution of functionality (CTQ_2) and is under the control of the employees of POI. Hence, team members restructured Hypothesis 2 as follows:

$$Functionality = f(X_1 = vendor, X_2 = size, X_3 = ridges),$$
$$\text{for each fixed level of } X_7(\text{shelf-life}).$$

6.11 ANALYZE PHASE TOLLGATE REVIEW CHECKLIST

A checklist of items that can form the basis of an analyze phase tollgate review is shown in Table 6.19.

TABLE 6.19 Analyze Phase Tollgate Review Checklist

1. Identify Xs for each CTQ	(Satisfactory . . . Needs Improvement)
• Detailed process map or flowchart	(Satisfactory . . . Needs Improvement)
• Detailed VA/NVA process map or flowchart	(Satisfactory . . . Needs Improvement)
• Identify potential Xs	(Satisfactory . . . Needs Improvement)
• Cause and Effects analysis	(Satisfactory . . . Needs Improvement)
• C&E diagram	(Satisfactory . . . Needs Improvement)
• C&E matrix	(Satisfactory . . . Needs Improvement)
• FMEA to identify high risk Xs	(Satisfactory . . . Needs Improvement)
2. Operational definitions for high risk Xs	(Satisfactory . . . Needs Improvement)
3. Measurement Systems Analysis by X	(Satisfactory . . . Needs Improvement)
4. Baseline capabilities for each CTQ	(Satisfactory . . . Needs Improvement)
• Data collection plan	(Satisfactory . . . Needs Improvement)
• Baseline data	(Satisfactory . . . Needs Improvement)
• Stability of baseline data	(Yes . . . No)
• Distribution of baseline data	(Normal . . . Other)
5. Process capability statistics for each X	(Satisfactory . . . Needs Improvement)
• DPMO	(Yes . . . No)
• Process Sigma	(Yes . . . No)
6. Effect of each X on each CTQ	(Satisfactory . . . Needs Improvement)
• Dot plots of CTQs by Xs	(Satisfactory . . . Needs Improvement)
• Interaction plots	(Satisfactory . . . Needs Improvement)
7. Input from the Finance department	(Satisfactory . . . Needs Improvement)
8. Input from IT department	(Satisfactory . . . Needs Improvement)
9. Sign-off from Champion	(Satisfactory . . . Needs Improvement)
10. Sign-off from Process Owner	(Satisfactory . . . Needs Improvement)

6.12 THE ANALYZE PHASE FOR PROCESSES WITH A WELL-ESTABLISHED DASHBOARDS

New processes or processes without dashboards will most likely use the analyze phase as it is discussed in this chapter. However, most of the steps in the analyze phase are included in the measure phase for organizations with well-established dashboards and processes. The steps in the analyze phase that are frequently found in the measure phase for organizations with well-established dashboards are: identifying the Xs for the process under study, identifying the Xs related to each CTQ, identifying the high-risk Xs for each CTQ, developing operational definitions for high-risk Xs, establishing measurement systems for high-risk Xs, establishing baseline process capabilities for Xs, stabilizing the high-risk Xs that are out of control, considering major noise variables, and using screening designs to reduce the number of Xs. As additional Xs are discovered in the analyze phase for organizations with well-established dashboards, practitioners iterate back to the measure phase and incorporate the measure phase tools on these newly discovered Xs.

SUMMARY

The analyze phase has ten steps:

1. Identify the Xs for the process under study
2. Identify the Xs related to each CTQ
3. Identify the high-risk Xs for each CTQ
4. Create operational definitions for each high-risk X
5. Establish measurement systems for Xs
6. Establish baseline data for high-risk Xs
7. Stabilize high-risk Xs that are out of control
8. Identify nuisance variables
9. Reduce set of Xs with screening designs
10. Study the effect of the high-risk Xs on the CTQs

Each step was discussed and illustrated with an integrated example.

Figure 6.35 summarizes the analyze phase of the DMAIC model [Reference 9]. A flow-chart (process map) is used to identify Xs that are studied and screened for importance to each CTQ. A C & E matrix, an FMEA, and Multivari charts are used to identify the high-risk Xs for each CTQ. If there are more than five high-risk Xs, a screening design is performed to reduce the set of high-risk Xs, as much as is reasonable. If there are 2–5 high-risk Xs or the screening design was successful in reducing the set of high-risk Xs to the 2–5 range, hypotheses are developed that explain the relationships between the Xs and their interactions on the center, spread, and shape of each CTQ.

Once team members have stated possible hypotheses, the champion and process owner sign off on the project at the tollgate review.

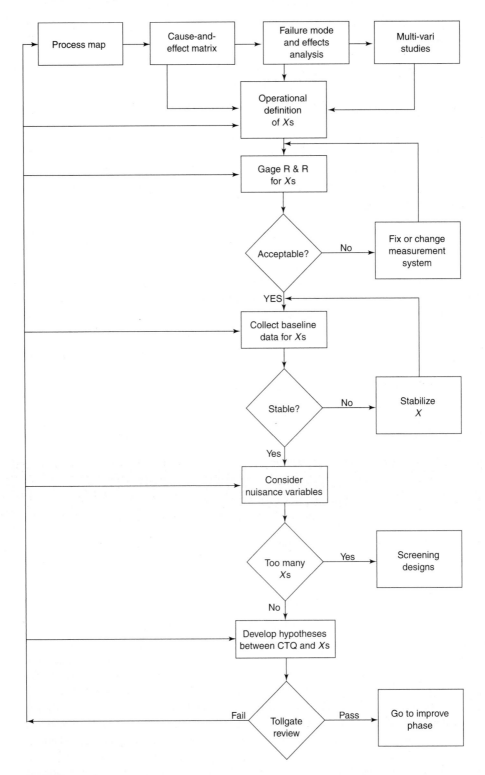

FIGURE 6.35 Steps of the Improve Phase

REFERENCES

1. Alukal, G., "Create a Lean, Mean Machine," *Quality Progress,* April 2003.

2. Gitlow, H., Oppenheim, A. Oppenheim, R., and Levine, D.M. *Quality Management:* (New York: McGraw-Hill-Irwin, 3rd ed., 2005)

3. Gitlow, H., *Quality Management Systems,* (Boca Raton, FL: CRC Press, 2000)

4. Liner, M., Loredo, E., Gitlow, H., and Einspruch, N., "Quality Function Deployment Applied to Electronic Component Design," *Quality Engineering,* 9, 2, 1996–1997, pp. 237–248.

5. Montgomery, D., *Design and Analysis of Experiments* 5th edition, (New York: John Wiley & Sons, 2001)

6. Neter, J., Kutner, M., Nachtsheim, C., and Wasserman, W., *Applied Linear Statistical Models,* 4th edition, (Burr Ridge, IL: McGraw-Hill, 1996).

7. Rasis, D., Gitlow, H., and Popovich, E., "Paper Organizers International: A Fictitious Six Sigma Green Belt Case Study—Part 1," *Quality Engineering,* 15, 1, 2002, pp. 127–145.

8. Rasis, D., Gitlow, H., and Popovich, E., "Paper Organizers International: A Fictitious Six Sigma Green Belt Case Study—Part 2," *Quality Engineering,* 15, 2, 2002, pp. 259–274.

9. Snee, R., "Eight Essential Tools," *Quality Progress,* December 2003, pp. 86–88.

A P P E N D I X   6

USING MINITAB TO OBTAIN A MULTIVARI CHART

Before using Minitab for the Multivari chart done in this chapter, refer to the Introduction to Minitab in Appendix 9.1.

Obtaining a Multivari Chart

To obtain the multivari chart in Figure 6.17 on page 175, open the **MULTIVARI.MTW** worksheet. Select **Stat → Quality Tools → Multi-Vari Chart.** Then do the following:

1. In the Multi-Vari Chart dialog box (see Figure A6.1), enter **Y** or **C5** in the Response: edit box, **X1** or **C2** in the Factor 1: edit box, **X2** or **C3** in the Factor 2: edit box and **X3** or **C4** in the Factor 3: edit box. Click the **Options** button.

2. In the Multi-Vari Chart—Options dialog box (see Figure A6.2), select the

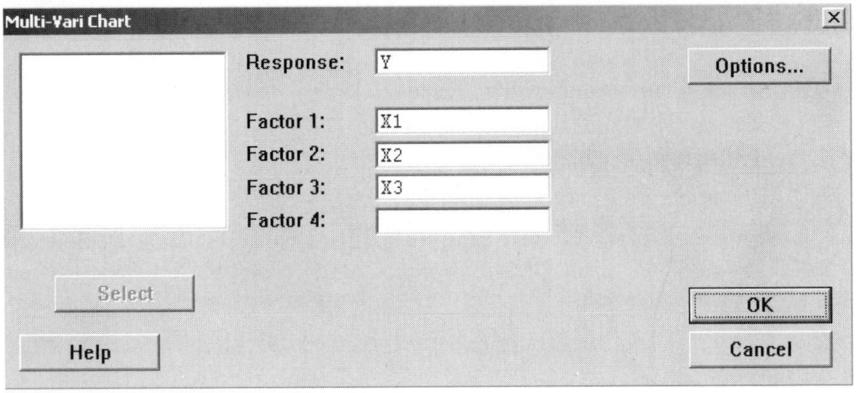

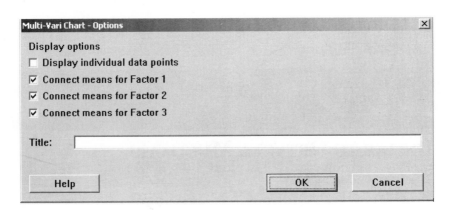

FIGURE A6.1 Minitab Multi-Vari Chart Dialog Box

Connect means for Factor 1, Connect means for Factor 2, and the **Connect means for Factor 3** check boxes. Click

the **OK** button to return to the Multi-Vari Chart dialog box.

3. Click the **OK** button.

FIGURE A6.2 Minitab Multi-Vari Chart—Options Dialog Box

IMPROVE PHASE
OF THE DMAIC MODEL

CHAPTER OUTLINE

LEARNING OBJECTIVES

After reading this chapter, you will be able to:

- Design and analyze a simple experiment on the high-risk Xs to optimize the CTQ(s)
- Avoid potential problems in the Xs
- Conduct a pilot study of the optimized process (i.e., levels of the Xs that optimize the CTQ[s])
- Identify the actions needed to implement the optimal levels of the Xs
- Present the Improve phase in a tollgate review (if team member)
- Conduct an Improve phase tollgate review (if Champion or process owner)

INTRODUCTION

The improve phase is about team members actively intervening in the operation of a process using a designed experiment to determine the settings of the high-risk Xs that optimize the center, spread, and shape of each CTQ. Once the optimal settings of the high-risk Xs are identified, team members identify and mitigate the risks involved with the optimized settings of the Xs. Next, team members run a pilot study of the revised process to determine its capability. Finally, team members identify the actions needed to formalize the optimized process and obtain the support and approval of their champion and the process owner.

7.1 PURPOSE OF DESIGNED EXPERIMENTS

Design of Experiments (DoE) is a collection of statistical methods for studying the relationships between **independent variables or factors,** the Xs (also called *input variables* or *process variables*), and their interactions on a **dependent variable,** the CTQ or Y (also called the *outcome variable* or *response variable*). Refer to Chapter 13 for more information on design of experiments [Reference 7].

The concepts of experimental design discussed in this chapter represent a *proactive* intervention into a process by a Six Sigma team. Process changes on the Xs (Ys or CTQs) are planned and tested by team members and the data caused by those changes are studied to determine the effect of the process change. This kind of experiment actively intervenes in the function of the process while collecting data to determine the impact of the intervention(s).

7.2 LEVEL OF PROCESS KNOWLEDGE

Experimental designs are used to study processes, products, or services. The purpose of an experimental design depends on the level of knowledge available concerning the process, product, or service being studied. **Screening designs** are used when there is a low level of knowledge about the Xs that are critical to optimizing the CTQ or Y. Researchers use these experiments to identify the high-risk Xs needed to optimize each CTQ. Screening designs reduce the number of trials and hence the cost of an experiment, by giving up learning about the interactions between the Xs. **Full factorial designs** are used when researchers have a low level of knowledge of the interactions between the high-risk Xs necessary to optimizing the CTQ or when there are only a few Xs to be studied in the experiment. **Fractional factorial designs** are most often used when the number of Xs to be studied is large or when there is a moderate level of knowledge about the interactions between the key Xs needed to optimize the CTQ. Fractional factorial designs are used to decrease the number of trials—hence the cost of an experiment—by taking advantage of knowledge about interactions. **Response surface methodology designs** are used to determine the settings of the Xs that will optimize a CTQ. Usually, a response surface design is used following the use of factorial design because there will then be a higher level of knowledge about the key Xs and their interactions needed to optimize the CTQ.

7.3 SOME FLAWED EXPERIMENTAL DESIGNS

There are three classic flawed experimental designs:

1. The one-factor-at-a-time strategy,
2. The stick-with-a-winner strategy
3. The change-many-factors-at-once strategy

One-factor-at-a-time experiments are experiments in which the researcher simply changes one X at a time to determine its effect on Y while maintaining the other Xs at some specified, fixed level. They are simple to design and analyze, but they have shortcomings. First, they provide no information on interactions between the Xs (factors). For instance, if the impact of one X depends on the level of another X, it is unlikely that the relationship of this combination of Xs will be uncovered using this type of experiment. Second, experimenters may run out of time and/or money before they have enough information to make an informed decision. Table 7.1 shows eight trials in an experiment. Each column in Table 7.1 (except the first and last columns) represents one of the independent variables, called *factors* or Xs, that are manipulated to optimize the dependent variable (last column), called a *response variable* or Y. Each row in Table 7.1 (except the first row) represents one possible combination of settings for the Xs. Each cell contains either a plus (+) or a minus (−). The − represents the low or current setting for an independ-

TABLE 7.1 One-Factor-at-a-Time Experiments

Description	X_1	X_2	X_3	X_4	X_5	X_6	X_7	Y
Standard	−	−	−	−	−	−	−	
Trial 2	+	−	−	−	−	−	−	
Trial 3	−	+	−	−	−	−	−	
Trial 4	−	−	+	−	−	−	−	
Trial 5	−	−	−	+	−	−	−	
Trial 6	−	−	−	−	+	−	−	
Trial 7	−	−	−	−	−	+	−	
Trial 8	−	−	−	−	−	−	+	

ent variable (X). The + represents the high setting for an independent variable. For example, suppose that X_2 = machine speed. If X_2 = −, it signifies that the machine is set at the low speed. If X_2 = +, it signifies that the machine is set at the high speed. The standard trial, or trial 1 (second row in Table 7.1) sets all of the independent variables at the low level. Trial 2 (third row in Table 7.1) sets X_1 at the high level, but X_2 through X_7 are set at the low or current levels, and so on.

An example of a one-factor-at-a-time experiment would be trying one vitamin (X) at a time to decrease cholesterol (Y). For example, suppose your total cholesterol level is 270. In a one-factor-at-a-time experiment, you would do the following. First, take no-flush niacin for one-month and measure your cholesterol at the end of the one month time period. (suppose it was 220.) Second, stop taking the niacin and begin taking red yeast for 1 month and measure your cholesterol again (suppose it is 240.) Third, stop taking red yeast and begin taking garlic for one month and measure your cholesterol (suppose it is 260.) What would you conclude from this experiment? No-flush niacin lowers your cholesterol? Red yeast lowers or raises your cholesterol? Garlic lowers or raises your cholesterol? Do you know anything about the interactions between niacin and red yeast, niacin and garlic, red yeast and garlic? This experiment assumes that the vitamins have no residual effects; that is, they lose potency as soon as you stop taking them. Is this true? Does the experiment provide any information about residual effects of the vitamins? Some thoughts on the above questions are:

> No-flush niacin lowers your cholesterol. Maybe red yeast lowers your cholesterol, but what about the effect of taking niacin before red yeast? Maybe garlic lowers your cholesterol, but what about the effect of taking niacin and red yeast before garlic? In addition, do you know anything about the interactions between Niacin and red yeast, niacin and garlic, red yeast and garlic? Does the experiment provide any information about residual effects of the vitamins? Because all of these questions are still undetermined after the experiment has been undertaken, this one-factor-at-a-time approach is not a very useful design.

Stick-with-a-winner experiments suffer some of the same shortcomings as one-factor-at-a-time experiments. First, they provide limited and possibly misleading information on interactions between factors. Second, experimenters may run out of time and/or money before they have enough information to make an informed decision. Third, they seem to be scientific, but they are not. Table 7.2 shows a stick-with-a-winner-design. In this design, the first trial sets all of the Xs at their low (or current) levels, yielding Y = 1.2. The second trial sets X_1 = + and X_2 through X_7 = −, yielding Y = 1.8. Because 1.8 > 1.2, the third trial sets X_1 = X_2 = + and X_3 through X_7 = −, yielding Y = 1.6. Because 1.6 < 1.8, the fourth trial sets X_1 = +, reverses X_2 back to the low (−) setting, and sets X_3 = + and X_4 through X_7 = −, yielding Y = 1.7. This process of sticking with a winner continues through all of the trials.

This stick-with-a-winner design, like the previous one-factor-at-a-time design, is a very flawed experimental design.

A **change-many-factors-at-once design** suffers all of the shortcomings as one-factor-at-a-time experiment, plus an additional shortcoming. The additional shortcoming is that you cannot even determine the effects of the individual Xs. Table 7.3 shows a change-many-factors-at-once design.

TABLE 7.2 Stick-with-a-Winner Design

Description	X_1	X_2	X_3	X_4	X_5	X_6	X_7	Y
Standard	−	−	−	−	−	−	−	1.2
Trial 2	+	−	−	−	−	−	−	1.8
Trial 3	+	+	−	−	−	−	−	1.6
Trial 4	+	−	+	−	−	−	−	1.7
Trial 5	+	−	−	+	−	−	−	2.0
Trial 6	+	−	−	+	+	−	−	2.2
Trial 7	+	−	−	+	+	+	−	2.1
Trial 8	+	−	−	+	+	−	+	2.5

TABLE 7.3 Change-Many-Factors-at-Once Design

Description	X_1	X_2	X_3	X_4	X_5	X_6	X_7	Y
Standard	−	−	−	−	−	−	−	1.2
Trial 2	+	+	+	+	+	+	+	1.8

Returning to the cholesterol example, the change-many-factors-at-once design would go from measuring cholesterol after taking no vitamins for 1 month to measuring cholesterol after taking niacin, red yeast, and garlic for 1 month. This is an all-or-nothing experiment. It is a common and flawed form of experimentation.

7.4 TWO-FACTOR FACTORIAL DESIGNS

In this section, we introduce the study of experimental designs in which the effects of two factors (Xs) are studied simultaneously. These experimental designs are called **two-factor factorial designs.** In this section, we will be concerned only with two-factor designs in which there are two levels for both factors and an equal number of **replicates** (that is, the sample size) for each combination of the levels of the factors (Xs). Experimental designs are discussed more fully in Chapter 13 and in References 4 and 7.

In a two-factor factorial design model with equal replication in each cell, the sum of squares total (SST) is subdivided into sum of squares due to factor A (or SSA), sum of squares due to factor B (or SSB), sum of squares due to the interacting effect of A and B (or SSAB), and sum of squares due to inherent random error (or SSE). This partitioning of the total variation (SST) is displayed in Figure 7.1.

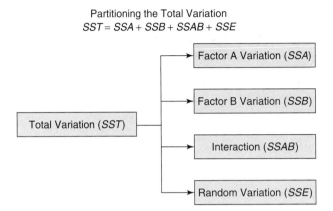

Partitioning the Total Variation
$$SST = SSA + SSB + SSAB + SSE$$

FIGURE 7.1 Partitioning the Total Variation in a Two-factor Factorial Design Model

The **sum of squares total** (**SST**) represents the total squared deviation of all the observations around the grand mean of the CTQ. The **sum of squares** due to **factor A** or X_A (**SSA**) represents the sum of squares of the deviations of the mean levels of factor A with the grand mean of the CTQ. The **sum of squares** due to **factor B** or X_B (**SSB**) represents the sum of squares of the deviations of the mean levels of factor B with the grand mean of the CTQ. The **sum of squares** due to the interaction effect of **A** and **B** (**SSAB**) is used to determine the effect of the joint combination of factor A and factor B on the CTQ. The **sum of squares error** (**SSE**) represents the sum of squares of deviations of the individual observations of the CTQ within each cell (i.e., each specific combination of one level of X_A and one level of X_B) with the corresponding cell mean. If each of the sums of squares is divided by its associated degrees of freedom (see Chapter 13 for a discussion of degrees of freedom), the results are four estimates of variance or mean square terms (*MSA, MSB, MSAB,* and *MSE*), which should be nearly equal if there is no impact due to factor A, factor B, or their interaction. These estimates of variation, mean squares, are needed for analysis of variance (ANOVA) and are obtained as shown in Table 7.4.

If the levels of factor A and factor B have been *specifically selected* for analysis (rather than being *randomly selected* from a population of possible levels), there are three tests of hypotheses in the two-way ANOVA.

1. Test of no difference due to factor A

   H_0: All levels of factor A have the same mean value of the CTQ vs.
   H_1: Not all levels of factor A have the same mean value of the CTQ.

This test of hypothesis consists of an *F* test of *MSA* divided by *MSE* (see Chapter 13). This assumes that the variation of the errors per cell is the same at all levels of *A;* otherwise, a rejection of the null hypothesis may be due to the variation of the results that depends on the level of *A.*

TABLE 7.4 Analysis of variance table for the two-factor model with replication.

Source	Degrees of freedom	Sum of Squares	Mean Square (Variance)	F
A	$r - 1$	SSA	$MSA = \dfrac{SSA}{r - 1}$	$F = \dfrac{MSA}{MSE}$
B	$c - 1$	SSB	$MSB = \dfrac{SSB}{c - 1}$	$F = \dfrac{MSB}{MSE}$
AB	$(r - 1)(c - 1)$	SSAB	$MSAB = \dfrac{SSAB}{(r - 1)(c - 1)}$	$F = \dfrac{MSAB}{MSE}$
Error	$rc(n' - 1)$	SSE	$MSE = \dfrac{SSE}{rc(n' - 1)}$	
Total	$n - 1$	SST		

r = the number of levels of factor A;
c = the number of levels of factor B;
n' = the number of values (replications) for each cell (assumes equal cell sizes);
n = the total number of observations in the experiment.

2. Test of no difference due to factor B

   H_0: All levels of factor B have the same mean value of the CTQ vs.
   H_1: Not all levels of factor B have the same mean value of the CTQ.

This test of hypothesis consists of an F test of MSB divided by MSE (see Chapter 13). This assumes the variation of the errors per cell are the same at all levels of B; otherwise, a rejection of the null hypothesis may be due to the variation of the results that depends on the level of B.

3. Test of no interaction of factors A and B

   H_0: There is no interaction between factors A and B on the CTQ vs.
   H_1: There is an interacting effect between factors A and B on the CTQ.

This test of hypothesis consists of an F test of MSAB divided by MSE (see Table 7.4 and Chapter 13). This assumes that the variation of the errors for each cell (i.e., representing each combination of A and B) are the same. If team members fail to uncover significant interactions, it might undermine all of their efforts and potentially create a disaster. For example, giving a child a chemistry set that has iron filings (X_1), sulfur (X_2), and potassium nitrate (X_3) without understanding the three-way interaction $(X_1 X_2 X_3)$ between the three chemicals could result in a serious accident or death. The above three chemicals are the components of gunpowder. Each chemical by itself is inert, each combination of any two of the chemicals is inert, but the three chemicals in equal portions are explosive.

7.5 EXAMPLE OF A DESIGNED EXPERIMENT

Returning to the MSD case study, team members conducted an experimental design to determine the effect of X_1 (vendor), X_2 (size), and X_3 (ridges) and their interactions on the CTQs, with X_7 = 0 (no shelf-life; MSDs are tested immediately upon arrival to POI before they are placed in inventory). A 2^3 full factorial design with two replications was performed for durability. The 2^3 refers to an experiment with three factors (X_1, X_2, and X_3), each with two possible settings. The treatment levels for vendor (X_1) are Office Optimum (-1) or Ibix (1); the treatment levels for size (X_2) are small (-1) or large (1), and the treatment levels for ridges (X_3) are without ridges (-1) or with ridges (1). The two replications signifies that each combination of the settings of the Xs will be run twice, for example, (X_1 = Ibix) and (X_2 = small) and (X_3 = with ridges) will be run two times in the experiment. The experiment was set up in two **blocks** to increase experimental reliability, with the first eight runs conducted in the morning and the second eight runs conducted in the afternoon. The runs were randomized within each block. The purpose of the blocks and randomization is to help prevent lurking (nuisance) variables that are related to time (e.g., time of day and order in which data is collected) from confusing the results. The design matrix for the 2^3 full factorial design with two replications with the first eight runs constituting the first replicate (block) is shown in Table 7.5.

The structure of Table 7.5 allows the team members to study all possible combinations of every level of every factor with every level of every other factor to understand the effect of each X and its interactions on the CTQ.

TABLE 7.5 2^3 Full Factorial Design with Two Replications in Blocks

Block	Standard order	X_1	X_2	X_3	CTQ$_1$ (durability)
Morning (Block 1)	1	−	−	−	
	2	+	−	−	
	3	−	+	−	
	4	+	+	−	
	5	−	−	+	
	6	+	−	+	
	7	−	+	+	
	8	+	+	+	
Afternoon (Block 2)	1	−	−	−	
	2	+	−	−	
	3	−	+	−	
	4	+	+	−	
	5	−	−	+	
	6	+	−	+	
	7	−	+	+	
	8	+	+	+	

Pareto charts are frequently used to highlight the statistical significance of both main and interaction effects on a CTQ. Minitab 14 plots the effects of the main effects and interaction effects on the CTQ in decreasing order and draws a reference line on the Pareto chart at a specified level of significance (see Chapter 13). Any effect that extends past this reference line is statistically significant.

A Pareto chart showing which of the vital few Xs and the interactions between them have a statistically significant effect on durability (CTQ_1) at the 10% level of significance can be seen in Figure 7.2.

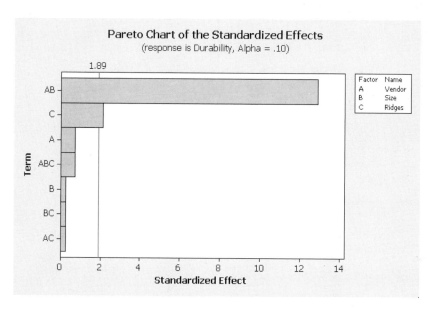

FIGURE 7.2 Minitab Pareto Chart of Effects for Durability

The major effects (i.e., those that have significance level less than 0.10) for durability are the interaction of vendor and size and the main effect due to ridges. The team decided to construct an interaction effect plot for vendor and size. Figure 7.3 on page 202 is the interaction effect plot for vendor and size, relative to durability.

The interaction effect plot between size and vendor shown in Figure 7.3 indicates that the best results for durability are obtained using small MSDs supplied by Office Optimum or large MSDs supplied by Ibix. The reasons for this interaction may be due to factors such as materials used for each size of MSD, differences in supplier processes for each size of MSD, or other supplier-dependent reasons. Team members can ask each vendor why its sizes show significant differences in average durability, if there is a preference to use only one vendor. Otherwise, the Purchasing Department should buy small MSDs from Office Optimum or large MSDs from Ibix to optimize durability (CTQ_1).

The only significant main effect not involved within a significant interaction effect is $X_3 =$ ridges. The main effect for ridges on durability is shown in Figure 7.4 on page 202.

It indicates that the average durability is about $6.5 - 5.4 = 1.1$ more when an MSD with ridges is used rather than an MSD without ridges. Therefore, because ridges is a main effect

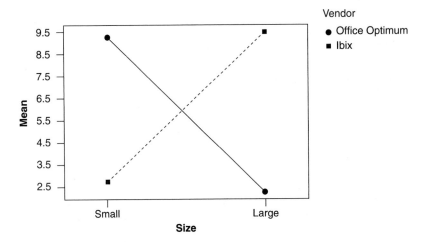

FIGURE 7.3 Minitab Interaction Effect Plot for Vendor and Size for Durability

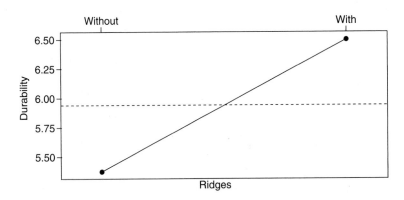

FIGURE 7.4 Minitab Main Effect Plot for Ridges for Durability

independent of any interaction effects, the right selection of MSDs is to use Office Optimum for small MSDs with ridges and Ibix for large MSDs with ridges. As long as the variation (spread) of results is small enough so that no individual durability result is far from these averages, the team is successful with respect to durability. The variation in these results can be monitored using control charts after changing the purchasing process for selecting MSDs.

The team members decided to purchase all MSDs with ridges. In addition, the choice of vendor and size will be as follows: (vendor = Office Optimum) and (size = small) or (vendor =Ibix)and (size = large) to maximize average durability. The revised flowchart for the Purchasing Department incorporating the findings of the Six Sigma project is shown in Figure 7.5.

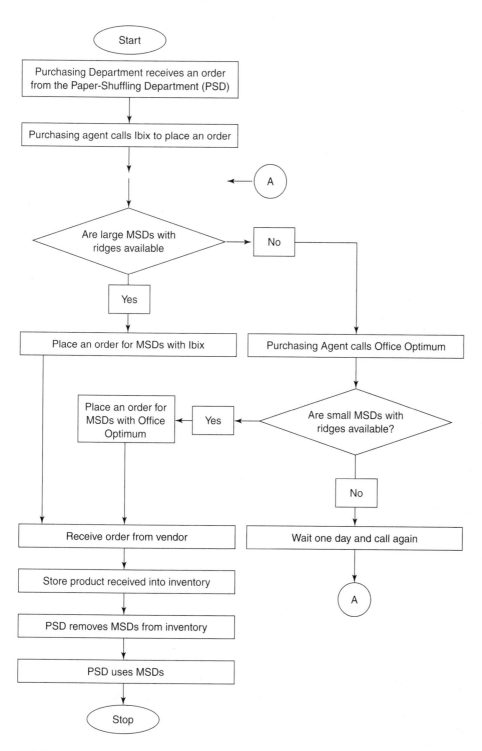

FIGURE 7.5 Revised Flowchart of the Purchasing Department

7.6 AVOID POTENTIAL PROBLEMS IN THE *X*S

Once the settings of the *X*s that optimize the center, spread, and shape of the CTQs are identified using a designed experiment, team members mitigate the risks of using these settings with risk management and mistake proofing. It is important that the settings of the *X*s that team members recommend to the process owner not only optimize the CTQs but also are not associated with a high potential for failure.

Risk Management

Team members use risk management to identify the **risk elements** of the proposed settings of the *X*s. Risk elements include:

- reliability
- safety
- complex functions
- hazardous design elements
- complex interactions with existing processes or products
- unclear requirements or specifications
- available products/services not properly evaluated
- functional capability requirements not appropriate for use
- new or unfamiliar technology
- unstable project team
- project team unfamiliar with business area
- project team skills inadequate for project
- poor project management
- unfavorable economic cycles
- poor project planning
- poor organizational structure
- hostile external factors

Risk management systematically and continuously identifies and quantifies risk elements to prevent them from occurring through risk abatement programs and communicates risks to management.

Team members identify the risk elements of the optimized settings of the *X*s using several techniques, for example

- brainstorming with individuals who possess the appropriate process knowledge
- reviewing lessons learned from past Six Sigma projects
- considering previous experience
- creating checklists
- and prioritizing the risk elements for management.

Risk elements for the optimized settings of the Xs are rated and prioritized using the following method.

Step 1: Team members identify measures of risk for each setting of the optimized Xs.

It is a good idea for team members to refer back to the FMEA analysis conducted in the measure phase. For example, the safety program in a paper mill exhibits the following risk elements:

1. Number of deaths overall, by cause, by location, by year,
2. Number of OSHA-reportable accidents overall, by type of injury, by body part, by cause, by location, by month, and
3. Number of unsafe behaviors overall, by type, by location, by month.

Step 2: Team members identify risk targets for each critical parameter with significant risk elements.

For example:

1. Number of deaths overall, by cause, by location, by year $= 0$,
2. Number of OSHA-reportable accidents overall, by type of injury, by body part, by cause, by location, by month $= 0$, and
3. Number of unsafe behaviors overall, by type, by location, by month $= 0$.

Step 3: Team members assign and prioritize risk ratings to the risk elements.

Each element is rated on its likelihood of occurrence on a 1 (low) to 5 (high) scale and on its impact of occurrence on a 1 (low) to 5 (high) scale. The computed risk element score $=$ likelihood scale $\times$ impact scale. It is a 1–25 scale, such that: (1) a high-risk element has a risk element score of 16–25, a medium-risk element has a risk element score of 9–15, and a low-risk element has a risk element score of 1–8 (see Table 7.6).

TABLE 7.6 Risk Element Scores

Risk element score		Severity		
		Low (1)	**Medium (3)**	**High (5)**
Likelihood	High (5)	5	15	25
	Medium (3)	3	9	15
	Low (1)	1	3	5

Step 4: Team members prioritize the risk elements

Table 7.7 provides a template for prioritizing the risk elements. The Xs are stated in column 1, the risk element(s) (for example, failure modes) for each setting of the Xs are stated in column 2, the potential source(s) of harm (hazards) are listed in column 3, the source(s) or actual injury or damage (harm) are listed in column 4, the likelihood score is shown in column 5, the severity score is shown in column 6, and the risk element score is shown in column 7.

TABLE 7.7 Prioritization of Risk Elements

1	2	3	4	5	6	7
Setting of the Xs	Risk element of the setting of the X	Hazard (potential source of harm)	Harm (physical injury to person and/or damage to property)	Likelihood 1 = low 5 = high	Severity 1 = low 5 = high	Risk element Score 1–8 = low 9–15 = medium 16–25 = high
X_1 = setting						
X_2 = setting						

Fifth, team members construct risk abatement plans for risk elements with high- and medium-risk elements; that is, a risk element score of 9–25. Sixth, team members identify process, product, or service changes to reduce the risk for each high- and medium-risk element. Seventh, team members estimate the risk element scores after the risk abatement plans are set into motion. Eighth, team members identify the risk element owner and set a completion date for the risk abatement plans to become operational. Ninth, team members document the risk abatement plans. A format for a risk abatement plan is shown in Table 7.8.

Tenth, team members carry out all risk abatement plans. Eleventh, the team members document the lessons learned for each risk element and transfer the knowledge to other relevant risk elements. Twelfth, team members incorporate the risk abatement plans into a control plan for the process owner.

TABLE 7.8 Format for a Risk Abatement Plan

Potential risk element	Potential harm	Measure for risk element	Risk element score		Counter-measure	Risk owner	Completion date for counter-measure
			Before	**After**			

In the case of the MSD project that was discussed in Chapters 4–7, the risk elements for the MSD purchasing process were: (1) failing to train new purchasing agents in the revised purchasing process, and (2) Office Optimum and Ibix are out of MSDs with ridges. Team members assigned risk ratings to both risk elements (see Table 7.9).

TABLE 7.9 Risk Elements for Purchasing Process

Risk elements	Risk category	Likelihood of occurrence	Impact of occurrence	Risk element score	
Failing to train new purchasing agents	Performance	5	5	25	High
Vendor out of MSDs with ridges	Materials	2	5	10	Medium

Both risk elements must be dealt with in risk abatement plans. The risk abatement plan for "failing to train new purchasing agents" is to document the revised purchasing process in training manuals. The risk abatement plan for "vendor out of MSDs with ridges" is for POI to request that both Office Optimum and Ibix manufacture only MSDs with ridges, due to their superior durability. This is a reasonable and acceptable suggestion to POI, Office Optimum, and Ibix because the cost structures for manufacturing MSDs with and without ridges are equal, and neither Office Optimum nor Ibix has other customers requesting MSDs without ridges. Office Optimum and Ibix agree to produce only MSDs with ridges after a 6-month trial period in which they check incoming purchase orders for requests for MSDs without ridges. If the trial period reveals no requests for MSDs without ridges, the POI Purchasing Department will revise the appropriate documentation to reflect the possibility of purchasing only MSDs with ridges. Additionally, Office Optimum and Ibix thanked POI for pointing out to them that average durability is higher for MSDs with ridges than for MSDs without ridges. Both vendors claim that they are going to experiment with possible different ridge patterns to increase durability and decrease costs. Both vendors stated that they anticipate decreased costs from producing only MSDs with ridges because of the lower amortized costs of having only one production line.

Mistake Proofing

Mistake proofing is used to create "robustness" for the optimized settings of the Xs; that is, the optimized settings of the Xs are not susceptible to human error. It is used on the optimized settings of the Xs shown in column 1 in Table 7.10 and on the potential failure modes shown in column 2 of Table 7.10. Column 12 in Table 7.10 is used to list a mistake-proofing solution to potential failure modes (column 2). There are many types of mistake-proofing solutions to prevent failure modes, for example, alarms that indicate danger to an operator, color coding medical records by type (green for pediatric and orange for geriatric), or a hand harness for a press to prevent an operator from getting his/her hands crushed in the press. Team members can brainstorm for mistake-proofing solutions to potential failure modes or they can review the literature on mistake-proofing techniques.

In the MSD case study, team members identified two potential failure modes in the PSD purchasing process that could be eliminated with mistake-proofing methods. They were: (1) purchasing agents do not specify "with ridges" on a purchase order, and (2) purchasing agents do not consider that the choice of vendor depends on the size of the MSDs being requested on the purchase order. Team members created solutions that make both errors very unlikely. The solutions are: (1) the purchase order entry system does not process the order unless "with ridges" is specified on the purchase order, and (2) the purchase order entry system does not process an order unless Office Optimum is the selected vendor for small MSDs and Ibix is the selected vendor for large MSDs.

7.7 CONDUCT A PILOT STUDY

The effect of the optimized and risk-proofed settings of the Xs is tested using a pilot study. A **pilot study** is a small-scale test of a revised process. It can be in a limited number of locations for a trial period of time or in all locations for a limited period of time. Whichever type of pilot study is used, its purpose is to validate the results from the newly identified treatment levels of the Xs on the CTQ. Additionally, a pilot study is important to facilitate buy-in by stakeholders of the revised process.

There are seven steps in a pilot study of a revised process.

1. Team members prepare a plan for the pilot study. The plan answers the "5W/1H" questions about the pilot study: Who, What, Where, When, Why, and How.

2. Team members inform all stakeholders of the revised process of the impending pilot study. This communication answers any questions the stakeholders may have about the pilot study.

TABLE 7.10 Format for a FMEA

1	2	3	4	5	6	7	8	9	10	11	12	13	14	15	16
Optimized settings of the Xs	Potential failure mode	Potential failure effect	Severity	Potential causes	Occur-rence	Current controls	Detec-tion	Before RPN	Recom-mended action	Respon-sibility and Target Date	Action taken	Severity	Occur-rence	Detection	After RPN

3. Team members train all relevant employees who will be involved in the conduct of the pilot study.

4. Team members and appropriate employees conduct the pilot study on a small scale and/or for a limited time frame.

5. Team members evaluate the results of pilot study on the distribution of the CTQ.

6. If the results are favorable, team members and appropriate employees increase the scope (locations and timeframe) of the pilot study to include a wider set of conditions.

7. Again, if the results are favorable, team members calculate the new process sigma.

Several tips that may make a pilot study more effective follow.

1. It is important that team members are on hand when the pilot study is performed to uncover and observe problems.

2. Team members should make sure that the test conditions are as similar as possible to actual conditions.

3. Team members and appropriate employees should be sure to record the treatment levels for the Xs to highlight any unanticipated relationships between the Xs and CTQ(s).

4. All involved employees should collect log sheet (diary) data along with the numeric results of the pilot study.

5. Team members and the process owner should not be surprised by problems in the revised process that did not surface during the pilot study.

7.8 EXAMPLE OF A PILOT STUDY

An example of a pilot study can be seen by returning to the MSD case study. Table 7.11 shows the data from a pilot study of the revised process for purchasing MSDs. The data includes both the CTQ (durability) and the critical Xs (vendor, size, and ridges).

Figure 7.6 shows that durability is in control, that is, it exhibits only common causes of variation, with a higher mean number of bends for all MSDs in the pilot study. The test pilot data shown in Table 7.11 includes results for both small MSDs from Office Optimum and large MSDs from Ibix.

Subsequently, team members realized that, with all things being equal, large MSDs from Ibix should have a higher average durability than small MSDs from Office Optimum. Consequently, team members constructed two control charts, one for small MSDs from Office Optimum and another for large MSDs from Ibix (see Figures 7.7 and 7.8, respectively).

Figures 7.6, 7.7, and 7.8 show that durability (CTQ_1) is in control, but it is dangerous to compute any process capability statistics due to the small sample sizes. However, estimates for the mean and standard deviation of small MSDs from Office Optimum are 8.625 and 1.05 (calculated from the data but the calculation is not shown here), respectively. The mean and standard

TABLE 7.11 Data from the Pilot Study

Hour	Vendor	Size	Ridges	Durability
Shift 1 – Hour 1	Office Optimum	Small	With	10
	Ibix	Large	With	11
Shift 1 – Hour 2	Office Optimum	Small	With	7
	Ibix	Large	With	11
Shift 1 – Hour 3	Office Optimum	Small	With	10
	Ibix	Large	With	11
Shift 1 – Hour 4	Office Optimum	Small	With	8
	Ibix	Large	With	11
Shift 1 – Hour 5	Office Optimum	Small	With	9
	Ibix	Large	With	10
Shift 1 – Hour 6	Office Optimum	Small	With	9
	Ibix	Large	With	9
Shift 1 – Hour 7	Office Optimum	Small	With	8
	Ibix	Large	With	11
Shift 1 – Hour 8	Office Optimum	Small	With	9
	Ibix	Large	With	10
Shift 2 – Hour 1	Office Optimum	Small	With	9
	Ibix	Large	With	11
Shift 2 – Hour 2	Office Optimum	Small	With	8
	Ibix	Large	With	10
Shift 2 – Hour 3	Office Optimum	Small	With	10
	Ibix	Large	With	9
Shift 2 – Hour 4	Office Optimum	Small	With	7
	Ibix	Large	With	9
Shift 2 – Hour 5	Office Optimum	Small	With	7
	Ibix	Large	With	10
Shift 2 – Hour 6	Office Optimum	Small	With	9
	Ibix	Large	With	11
Shift 2 – Hour 7	Office Optimum	Small	With	10
	Ibix	Large	With	9
Shift 2 – Hour 8	Office Optimum	Small	With	8
	Ibix	Large	With	11
			RTY	32/32 = 100%

 PILOT

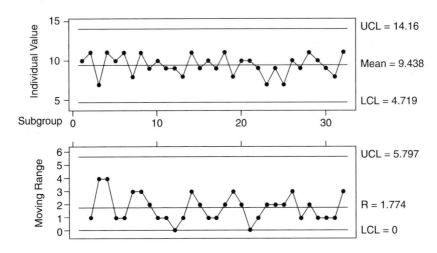

FIGURE 7.6 Minitab $\bar{X}$ and R Charts for Durability

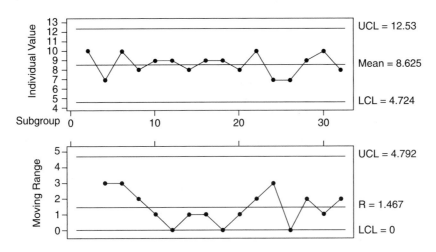

FIGURE 7.7 Minitab $\bar{X}$ and R Charts for Durability for Small MSDs from Office Optimum

deviation for large MSDs from Ibix are 10.25 and 0.83, respectively. Because the CTQ for durability requires the number of bends to be 4 or more, this requirement is 4.4 standard deviations below the mean for small MSDs from Office Optimum and 7.5 standard deviations below the mean for large MSDs from Ibix. Team members all agreed that as long as the process for both small MSDs from Office Optimum with ridges and large MSDs from Ibix with ridges remain in control, it is extremely unlikely that the MSDs will fail the CTQ for durability (CTQ_1).

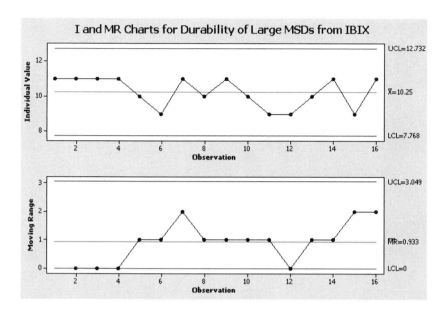

FIGURE 7.8 Minitab Individual Value and Moving Range Charts for Durability for Large MSDs from Ibix

7.9 IDENTIFY ACTIONS NEEDED TO IMPLEMENT OPTIMIZED PROCESS

Once team members have identified the treatment levels of the Xs needed to optimize the distribution of the CTQ, they can brainstorm the actions required to implement the new treatment levels. The data (ideas) from the brainstorming session can be analyzed using an affinity diagram and/or a cause-and-effect (C & E) diagram. The affinity diagram and/or C & E diagram (see Chapter 15) should highlight the actions that team members need to take to implement levels of the Xs to optimize the CTQ.

For example, the MSD case study used a C & E diagram to display the actions necessary to implement the optimized process (see Figure 7.9). As you can see, the purchasing system must be modified to accept only purchase orders that specify either large Ibix MSDs with ridges or small Office Optimum MSDs with ridges.

Team members answer the following questions with respect to each action:

- What is the schedule for the action?
- What is the cost of the action?
- Who will take the action?
- What are the implementation difficulties for the action?

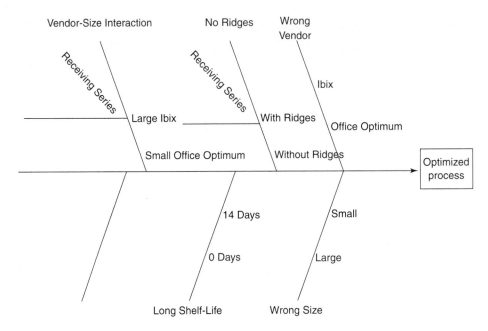

FIGURE 7.9 Minitab C & E Diagram of Actions Necessary to Implement Optimized Process

- Does the action create new problems in the process?
- Does the team have the authority to select the action?
- What communication and training are required for the action to be effective and efficient?
- What benefits are expected from the action?

Answers to the above questions will result in an action plan for each action required to implement the treatment levels of the Xs needed to optimize the CTQ.

7.10 IMPROVE PHASE TOLLGATE REVIEW CHECKLIST

A checklist of items that can form the basis of an improve phase tollgate review is shown in Table 7.12.

SUMMARY

This chapter presented the steps of the improve phase with a detailed example. Note that the example utilized a full factorial experiment with three Xs. A fractional factorial experiment was not utilized because the number of Xs studied is small, and each assumed only one of two values.

TABLE 7.12 Improve Phase Tollgate Review Checklist

1) Design experiment (CTQs = f[Xs])	(Satisfactory ...	Needs Improvement)
• Plan experiment	(Satisfactory ...	Needs Improvement)
• Collect data from trials	(Satisfactory ...	Needs Improvement)
• Analyze data from experiment	(Satisfactory ...	Needs Improvement)
2) Set levels of Xs to optimize CTQ(s)	(Satisfactory ...	Needs Improvement)
3) Pilot test revised process	(Satisfactory ...	Needs Improvement)
4) Compute capability statistics	(Satisfactory ...	Needs Improvement)
• Collect baseline data	(Satisfactory ...	Needs Improvement)
• Stability of process	(Yes ...	No)
• Distribution of process data	(Normal ...	Other)
• DPMO	(Yes ...	No)
• Process Sigma	(Yes ...	No)
5) FMEA of optimized process	(Satisfactory ...	Needs Improvement)
6) Input from the Finance department	(Satisfactory ...	Needs Improvement)
7) Input from IT department	(Satisfactory ...	Needs Improvement)
8) Sign-off from Champion	(Yes ...	No)
9) Sign-off from Process Owner	(Yes ...	No)

Furthermore, a response surface design was not needed because the number of levels for each X is only two, so the factorial design helped to optimize the CTQ results. If any of the Xs were continuous (measurement) variables having levels that can fall along some interval, a response surface design may be useful for optimizing the results. The improve phase is the part of the DMAIC model in which the Xs are manipulated to optimize the distribution of the CTQ(s). It includes a pilot study of the revised configuration of the Xs to ensure that they in fact do optimize the distribution of the CTQ(s). The improve phase concludes with a tollgate review of the Six Sigma project to date by the champion and process owner.

REFERENCES

1. Bisgaard, S., "Industrial Use of Statistically Designed Experiments: Case Study References and Some Historical Anecdotes," *Quality Engineering,* 4, 1992, pp. 547 – 562.

2. Box, J. F., "R. A. Fisher and the Design of Experiments," *American Statistician,* 34, 1980, pp. 1 – 10.

3. Daniel, C., "Use of Half-Normal Plots in Interpreting Factorial Two-Level Experiments," *Technometrics,* 1, 1959, pp. 311 – 341.

4. Hicks, C. R. and K. V. Turner, *Fundamental Concepts in the Design of Experiments,* 5th ed. (New York: Oxford University Press, 1999).

5. Lenth, R. V., "Quick and Easy Analysis of Unreplicated Factorials," *Technometrics,* 31, 1989, pp. 469 – 473.

6. *Minitab for Windows Version 14* (State College, PA: Minitab, 2003).

7. Montgomery, D. C., *Design and Analysis of Experiments,* 5th ed. (New York: John Wiley, 2001).

8. Neter, J., M. H. Kutner, C. Nachtsheim, and W. Wasserman, *Applied Linear Statistical Models,* 4th ed. (Homewood, IL: Richard D. Irwin, 1996).

CHAPTER 8

CONTROL PHASE OF THE DMAIC MODEL

CHAPTER OUTLINE

LEARNING OBJECTIVES

After reading this chapter, you will be able to:

- Reduce the effects of collateral damage
- Standardize process improvements in the Xs
- Maintain control of the Xs
- Develop a control plan for the process owner
- Identify and document the benefits and costs of the project
- Input the project into a Six Sigma database
- Diffuse the improvements throughout the organization
- Present the control phase in a tollgate review (if team member)
- Conduct a control phase tollgate review (if champion or process owner)

INTRODUCTION

The control phase is about ensuring that the optimized settings of the Xs are locked into place and are insensitive to human and environmental noise. Additionally, team members reduce the risks of collateral damage to related processes caused by the newly optimized settings of the Xs in the process under study. Team members spread the process improvements throughout the organization and hand the process over to the process owner for continual turning of the Plan-Do-Study-Act (PDSA) cycle. Finally, team members disband and celebrate their success.

8.1 REDUCE THE EFFECTS OF COLLATERAL DAMAGE TO RELATED PROCESSES

The control phase can be used to explore the risks created by the optimized settings of the Xs to other (related) processes that were not the focus of the original project. For example, the distribution of cycle times for step 1 in a process is stable, normally distributed with a mean of 100 minutes and a standard deviation of 10 minutes, and the distribution of cycle times for step 2 in the process is stable, normally distributed with a mean of 75 minutes and a standard deviation of 10 minutes. The above process is experiencing a bottleneck in step 1 because the cycle times in step 1 are usually greater than the cycle times in step 2. If step 1 is improved through the application of the DMAIC model and the distribution of cycle times becomes stable and normally distributed with a mean of 40 minutes and a standard deviation of 10 minutes, then the bottleneck in the process shifts from step 1 to step 2. This is an example of the collateral damage to related processes that can be caused by Six Sigma projects. This type of collateral damage is not necessarily a bad thing. However, the process improvement in step 1 uncovered a weakness in step 2. The control phase seeks to mitigate the collateral damage (risks) to processes that were not part of the focus of the current Six Sigma project.

Team members identify the risk elements (collateral damage) to related processes using the techniques discussed in Section 7.6.

A format for a risk abatement plan is shown in Table 8.1.

8.2 STANDARDIZE PROCESS IMPROVEMENTS IN THE Xs

The International Standards Organization (ISO) is a system of documenting what you do and doing what you document. It is a critical first step to improvement of a process or an entire organization; it is standardization of a process. Team members standardize process improvements by answering the following questions.

TABLE 8.1 Format for a Risk Abatement Plan

Potential risk elements for process i	Potential harm for the risk elements from process i	Risk Element score		Counter-measure	Risk owner	Completion date for counter-measure
		Before	After			

1. Who is involved at the revised step of the process?
2. What should they be doing after standardization of the revised standard operating procedures?
3. Why should they follow the revised standard operating procedures?
4. Where should they be doing the revised process procedure?
5. When should they be doing the revised process procedure?
6. How should they be doing the revised process procedure?
7. How much will it cost to do the revised process procedure?
8. Is additional training needed to perform the revised process procedure?
9. How often should the revised process procedure be monitored?
10. Who will monitor the revised process procedure?
11. Who will make decisions on the future outputs of the revised process procedure?

The answers to the above questions are formalized in training manuals, training programs for existing and new employees, and, if appropriate, International Standards Organization (ISO) documentation.

ISO 9000 and ISO 14000

The ISO 9000 and ISO 14000 families of standards are among ISO's most widely known and successful standards. ISO 9000 has become an international reference for quality requirements in business to business dealings, and ISO 14000 looks set to achieve at least as much, if not more, in helping organizations to meet their environmental challenges.

Generic Table of Contents of an ISO Standard

A generic table of contents for an ISO product specification is shown in Table 8.2.

TABLE 8.2 Generic Table of Contents from an ISO Type Standard

- Applicable documents
  - Internal documents
    - Drawing of product
    - Drawing of package
    - Specifications for component parts
  - External documents
    - Regulations
    - Accepted standards
- Product description
  - Features of product
  - Variations of product features
- Product provisions
  - Functioning of product (general, operating characteristics, acceptable noise level, acceptable pollution, etc.)
  - Materials specifications
  - Workmanship specifications
  - Safety requirements
  - Dimensions (specifications)
  - Finish appearance
  - Marking
- Manufacture
  - Fabrication
  - Painting
  - Assembly
- Shipping
  - Packaging
    - Requirements
    - Tests
  - Marking and labeling
- Inspection

8.3 MAINTAIN CONTROL OF THE XS

Team members monitor each X for future stability and capability using control charts (see Chapter 14). Four future scenarios are possible for an X.

1. The X remains stable and capable at the desired level. This is the desired scenario.
2. The X remains stable but not capable. In this case, the process owner must work to gain the desired capability for the X.
3. The X is not stable, but it happens to be capable at the current time. This is a dangerous situation because the Xs seem okay but can go out of control at any time, and the process owner is not in control of the process. In this case, the X can cause havoc on one or more CTQs.
4. The X is not stable and not capable. In this case, the process owner must improve the X or suffer potentially dire consequences to one or more CTQs.

TABLE 8.3 Generic QC Process Chart

Revised process	Experiment	Monitor	Standardize and PDSA
Original best practice flowchart is replaced with the revised best practice flowchart in ISO documentation.	Employees use the revised process.	Employees collect data on the CTQs and Xs, and analyze the data to understand the stability and capability of the CTQs and Xs.	If a CTQ or X is stable and capable, repeat the PDSA cycle for further improvements in the process. If a CTQ or X is not stable or capable, go back to the plan phase and revise the best practice flowchart.
Appropriate personnel are trained in the working of the revised process using training materials such as training manuals or instructional videotapes.			
Employees learn operational definitions for the CTQs and Xs, including nominal values and specification limits.			
Employees learn how to monitor the CTQs and Xs using the approved sampling plans.			
Employees learn what to do with defective output.			

8.4 Develop a Control Plan for the Process Owner

Team members develop a control plan for monitoring the *X*s and CTQs for the process owner. A **control plan** takes the form of a **QC (quality control) process chart**. The QC process chart is shown in Table 8.3.

Returning to the MSD case study discussed in Chapters 4–7, team members develop a control plan for the Paper-Shuffling Department (PSD) that requires a monthly sampling of the boxes of MSDs in inventory. The purpose of the sampling plan is to check whether the boxes of MSDs being purchased are either small Office Optimum MSDs with ridges or large Ibix MSDs with ridges. The percentage of nonconforming boxes of MSDs will be plotted on a *p*-chart (see Section 14.5). PSD management will use the *p*-chart to highlight violations of the new and improved purchasing process. The *p*-chart will be the basis for continuously turning the PDSA cycle for the purchasing process.

Table 8.4 shows a technical example of a control plan for a white film production process. The dosage (column 3) applied in the coating step (column 2) of the white film process (column 1) is examined in row 2 of Table 8.4. Dosage requires a nominal value of 22.5 with a lower specification limit of 22 and an upper specification limit of 23 (column 5). The current process sigma is 3.92 (column 6) with respect to the nominal and specification limits. The UIL-1700 is the measurement technique (column 7) used to collect dosage data. A sample of 35 points per panel (column 8) is drawn every hour (column 9) from the coating step of the white film process. The coating step of the white film process is controlled through an automatic timer (column 10). Finally, the reaction to a data point outside of the specification limits (column 11) is "cross-check" the measurement for accuracy. If a data point is out of a specification limit, initiate a study of the dosage step of the white film process to reduce variation.

8.5 Identify and Document the Benefits and Costs of the Project

Team members document the actual benefits (realized benefits to date) and potential benefits (future benefits), as well as the hard costs and soft costs of the Six Sigma project. Benefits include, but are not limited to:

1. Improved financial performance
2. Improved safety (fewer accidents and fewer unsafe behaviors)
3. Decreased cycle time
4. Identification of additional improvement opportunities (potential Six Sigma projects)
5. Improved work environment (increased joy in work) for employees

Returning to the MSD case study, team members checked the business indicator from the PSD dashboard (see Table 4.1 on page 63) and determined that production costs in the PSD decreased, probably due to the MSD Six Sigma project (see Figure 8.1). The MSD project took effect in month 73 of Figure 8.1.

TABLE 8.4 Technical Control Plan for the White Film Process

Control Plan

1	2	3	4	5	6	7	8	9	10	11
Process	**Process Step**	**Input**	**Output**	**Process Specification (Target, LSL, USL)**	**Process Sigma**	**Measurement Technique**	**Sample Size**	**Sample Frequency**	**Control Method**	**Reaction Plan**
White film	Coating	Dosage		22.5, 22, 23	3.92	UII-1700		1/hr	Auto-timer	Cross check
			Coating Height	24, 23, 25	3.45	Micrometer	35 pts per panel	1/hr	Coating & pump speed	Adjust previous
			Coating width	14, 12, 16	3.78	Laser Measuring Device		1/hr		None in place
			Coating length	36, 34, 38	4.02	Laser Measuring Device		1/hr		None in place
		Vacuum		35" Hg		Vacuum gauge		1/hr	Monitor	Compare guages, look for blockage
		Coating	Coating thickness	18, 17.5, 18.5	4.01	ATI beta guage	480 pts per patch	Every patch	Calibration	Correlate to micrometer
			Dancing	0, 0, 1	2.34	Leica 0–3 scale		1/hr	clean mask, monitor dosage	Check mask checkdosage
			Delamination	0, 0, 1	3.07	Visual 0–3 scale		1/hr	Dev. time, vacuum	Clean vacuum grooves & system
	Developer	Wash time	Delamination	see above						
		% flow rate	Stripes	No stripes	N/A	N/A	100% inspection	Every patch		Adjust wash time & flowrate

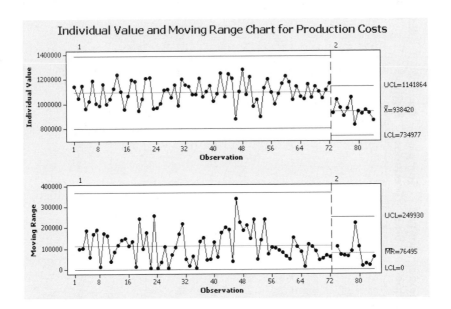

FIGURE 8.1 Minitab Individual and Moving Range Chart of Production Costs in the PSD Before and After the MSD Six Sigma Project

8.6 INPUT PROJECT INTO THE SIX SIGMA DATABASE

The black belt (or green belt) facilitating the Six Sigma project enters the project into the organization's database (Quality Tracking System). The database is used to spread the newly discovered improvements and/or innovations from Six Sigma projects throughout the entire organization.

8.7 DIFFUSE THE IMPROVEMENTS THROUGHOUT THE ORGANIZATION

The **diffusion** portion of the control phase explains how to spread improvements among the different areas within an organization and from one organization to another organization (for example, suppliers, subcontractors, and regulators, to name a few). How to diffuse improvements is not obvious. For example, creating a newsletter or having a meeting for all interested persons is not the way to reliably spread improvements. Other methods are needed. This section discusses such methods for both inter (between)- and intra (within)-firm diffusion [see References 1 and 2].

All potential adopters of process improvements fall into one of five adopter categories: innovator, early adopter, early majority, late majority, and laggard [see Reference 2]. **Innovators** are frequently the gatekeepers of new ideas into their organization. They are venturesome, cosmopolites, friendly with a clique of innovators, possess substantial financial resources, and understand complex technical knowledge. However, they may not be respected by the members of their organization. They are considered to be unreliable by their near peers, due to their attraction to new things. **Early adopters** are the embodiment of successful, discrete use of ideas. They are the key to spreading process improvements. Early adopters are well respected by their peers, localites, opinion leaders, and role models for other members of their organization. **Early majority** deliberate for some time before adopting new ideas and interact frequently with their peers. They are not opinion leaders. **Late majority** require peer pressure to adopt an improvement. They have limited economic resources that require the removal of uncertainty surrounding an innovation. **Laggards** are suspicious of change, and their reference point is in the past. They are very localite and are near isolates in their organization.

Successful diffusion of an improvement to a process must consider several factors.

- It must involve opinion leaders. Team members identify opinion leaders by asking themselves: "Who would we go to for advice about the process under study within our organization?" They prepare a motivational plan to induce opinion leaders to try the process improvement. The motivational plan must have the commitment of the champion and process owner, and should consider a balance of extrinsic and intrinsic motivators.

- It must provide a process improvement that is adequately developed and not too costly for potential adopters within the organization.

- It must not exceed the learning capacity of potential adopters.

- It must not exceed the process owner's ability to communicate the improvement to his/her direct reports.

- It must utilize any informal relationships between potential adopters and the Six Sigma team members.

If the above five factors do not exist or do not exist effectively, the window of opportunity for the spread of the improvement begins to close. Additionally, team members must develop user-friendly training programs (e.g., courseware, locations, time of day, to name a few issues) for both the process owner and his or her employees concerning the process improvement(s).

8.8 CONTROL PHASE TOLLGATE REVIEW

A checklist of items that can form the basis of a control phase tollgate review is shown in Table 8.5.

TABLE 8.5 Improve Phase Tollgate Review Checklist

1) Risk abatement plan and mistake-proofing	(Satisfactory . . . Needs Improvement)
• Risk management	(Satisfactory . . . Needs Improvement)
• Mistake proofing	(Satisfactory . . . Needs Improvement)
• FMEA	(Satisfactory . . . Needs Improvement)
2) Standardize revised process	(Satisfactory . . . Needs Improvement)
3) Input from the Finance department	(Satisfactory . . . Needs Improvement)
4) Input from IT department	(Satisfactory . . . Needs Improvement)
5) Sign-off from Champion	(Yes . . . No)
6) Sign-off from Process Owner	(Yes . . . No)
7) Complete lessons learned	(Satisfactory . . . Needs Improvement)
8) Project entered into data base	(Yes . . . No)
9) Train relevant personnel in revised process	(Satisfactory . . . Needs Improvement)
10) Process owner turns PDSA cycle	(Satisfactory . . . Needs Improvement)
11) Team disbands and celebrate success	(Yes . . . No)
12) Spread lessons learned throughout org.	(Satisfactory . . . Needs Improvement)

SUMMARY

The control phase locks in the optimized settings of the *X*s while reducing the likelihood of collateral damage to related processes due to the improved process. Team members diffuse the process improvements throughout the organization and hand the process over to the process owner. The process owner keeps turning the PDSA cycle for the revised process, forever! Finally, team members disband and celebrate their success.

REFERENCES

1. Cool, Karen, D. Igemar, and G. Szulanski, "Diffusion of Innovations Within Organizations: Electronic Switching in the Bell System, 1971–1982," *Organization Science*, 8, 5, September/October 1997, pp. 543–559.

2. Rogers, Everett, *Diffusion of Innovations*, 4th edition, (New York: The Free Press, 1995).

3. N. K. Shimbun (Editor), Poka-Yoke, "Improving Product Quality by Preventing Defects," *Factory Magazine*, 1989.

SIX SIGMA TOOLS AND METHODS

BASICS OF STATISTICAL STUDIES

CHAPTER OUTLINE

LEARNING OBJECTIVES

After reading this chapter, you will be able to:

- Use basic statistics in Six Sigma management
- Distinguish between enumerative and analytic studies
- Distinguish between different sampling methods
- Develop graphs for attribute data
- Develop graphs for measurement data
- Describe the properties of central tendency, variation, and shape in measurement data
- Use Minitab to select samples, obtain graphs, and compute descriptive statistics

9.1 Introduction to Statistics

In this chapter, we begin the third part of this text, "Six Sigma Tools and Methods." These tools and methods usually involve a sometimes dreaded word—*statistics*. What exactly do we mean by statistics and why is statistics such an integral part of Six Sigma management? To understand the importance of statistics for improving quality, you need only go back to a famous 1925 quote of Walter Shewhart, widely considered to be the father of quality control:

> The long-range contribution of statistics depends not so much upon getting a lot of highly trained statisticians into industry as it does in creating a statistically minded generation of physicists, chemists, engineers and others who will in any way have a hand in developing and directing the production processes of tomorrow.

This quote is consistent with the goal of the next six chapters. We have no intention of making you a statistician after reading through Chapter 14. However, we do intend to provide the proper foundation so that you will be able to use statistical methods as an integral part of Six Sigma management. We hope to achieve this goal by using Minitab 14 statistical software to minimize your need for formulas and computations.

The definition of *statistics*, according to Deming [see Reference 5], is to study and understand variation in processes and populations, interactions among the variables in processes and populations, operational definitions (definitions of process and population variables that promote effective communication between people), and ultimately, to take action to reduce variation in a process or population. Hence, statistics can be broadly defined as the study of data to provide a basis for action on a population or process. Statistics is often divided into two branches, descriptive statistics and inferential statistics.

Descriptive statistics focus on the collection, analysis, presentation, and description of a set of data. For example, the United States Census Bureau has been collecting data every 10 years since 1790 and has been developing improved descriptive statistical methods to analyze the data. Another example of the application of descriptive statistics is the description of the employee benefits used by the employees of an organization in fiscal year 2003.

Inferential statistics focus on making decisions about a large set of data, called the **population,** from a subset of the data, called the **sample.** The invention of the computer eased the computational burden of statistical methods and opened up access to these methods to a wide audience. Today, the preferred approach is to use statistical software such as Minitab (as we will do in this book) to do the computations involved in using various statistical methods.

9.2 Enumerative and Analytic Studies

There are two types of statistical studies, enumerative and analytic. The purposes of the two types of studies are different, so, it is important to understand the distinction between them.

Enumerative studies are used to draw conclusions about a population. A common example of an enumerative study is a political poll in which a sample of registered voters is selected from a list of all registered voters in a particular geographical area as of December 2003. Based on the results of the sample, statistical inferences are made about the entire voter registration list in the geographical area as of December 2003. Another example of an enumerative study is a study of the average weight of roofing shingles manufactured by a factory in 2003. Based on a sample of shingles selected, inferences can be made about the average weight of the shingles manufactured in 2003.

Other examples of enumerative studies are the estimation of the number of residents in California who are harmed by an earthquake and the number of hospital beds required to care for them. These are enumerative studies because they investigate the number of people in need at a specific point in time. Dynamic questions such as why the people are where they are or why they need the supplies that they need are not considered in an enumerative study. A final example of an enumerative study is to assay a sample of peanuts from a truckload of peanuts to determine an appropriate price. All of these examples are time-specific and static; there is no reference to the past or the future.

Analytic studies are used to study the cause-and-effect systems of a process to improve the future functioning of a process. An example of an analytic study related to the roofing shingles previously mentioned is to study why there was variation in the average weight of the roofing shingles manufactured over time and what factors could be causing this variation to improve the future production of shingles. Another example of an analytic study is determining why spinach production in an area is low and how it can be increased in the future. Other examples of analytic studies are comparing the output of two paper machines over time to determine whether one is more productive and comparing ways of marketing a financial service to increase market share. All of these examples focus on the future, not on the past or present. The information gathered is used to make dynamic decisions to improve the future functioning of a process.

Distinguishing Enumerative and Analytic Studies

A simple rule for distinguishing between an enumerative study and an analytic study is as follows: If a 100% sample answers the question under investigation, the study is enumerative; if not, the study is analytic.

9.3 TYPES OF SAMPLING

Before we go any further, it is important to define some terms. A **population** is the entire group of units, items, services, people, etc., under investigation. A **frame** is a physical list of the units in the population. The **gap** is the difference between the units in the population and the units in the frame.

If the units in the gap are distributed like the units in the frame, no problems should occur due to the gap. However, if the units in the gap are not distributed like the units in the frame, a systematic bias could result from the analysis of the frame. For example, if the frame of Miami residents over 18 years of age is the voter registration list, then a statistical analysis of the people on the list may contain bias if the distribution of people 18 and older is different for people on the list (frame) and people not on the list (gap). An example of where this difference might have an impact is if a survey was conducted to determine attitudes toward handgun control and the voter registration list underrepresented members of the National Rifle Association.

A **sample** is the portion of a population that is selected to gather information to provide a basis for action on the population. Rather than taking a complete census of the whole population, statistical sampling procedures focus on collecting a small portion of the larger population. For example, 50 accounts receivable drawn from a list, or frame, of 10,000 accounts receivable constitute a sample. The resulting sample provides information that can be used to estimate characteristics of the entire frame.

There are four main reasons for drawing a sample. These are depicted in Exhibit 9.1.

Exhibit 9.1 | **Reasons for Drawing a Sample**

1. A sample is less time-consuming than a census.
2. A sample is less costly to administer than a census.
3. A sample is less cumbersome and more practical to administer than a census.
4. A sample provides higher quality data than a census.

There are two kinds of samples: nonprobability samples and probability samples.

A **nonprobability sample** is one in which the items or individuals included are chosen without the benefit of a frame, and hence, the individual units in the population have an unknown probability of occurrence.

Nonprobability samples choose units without the benefit of a frame, and hence, without a known probability of selection (and in some cases, participants have self-selected). In this case, the theory of statistical inference should not be applied to the sample data. For example, many companies conduct surveys by giving visitors to their Web site the opportunity to complete survey forms and submit them electronically. The response to these surveys can provide large amounts of data in a timely fashion, but the sample is composed of self-selected Web users; there is no frame. Nonprobability samples are selected for convenience (**convenience sample**), based on the opinion of an expert (**judgment sample**) or on a desired proportional representation of certain classes of items, units, or people in the sample (**quota sample**). Nonprobability samples are all subject to an unknown degree of bias. Bias is caused by the absence of a frame and the ensuing classes of items or people that may be systematically denied representation in the sample (the gap).

Nonprobability samples have the potential advantages of convenience, speed, and lower cost. On the other hand, they have two major disadvantages: potential selection bias and the ensuing lack of generalizability of the results. These disadvantages more than offset the advantages. Therefore, you should restrict the use of nonprobability sampling methods to situations in which you want to obtain rough approximations at low cost or to small-scale initial or pilot studies that will later be followed up by more rigorous investigations. Probability sampling should be used whenever possible because it is the only method by which valid statistical inferences can be made from a sample.

> A **probability sample** is one in which the items or individuals are chosen from a frame, and hence, the individual units in the population have a known probability of selection from the frame.

The four types of probability samples most commonly used are simple random, stratified, systematic, and cluster. These sampling methods vary from one another in their cost, accuracy, and complexity.

Simple Random Sample

A **simple random sample** is a sample in which every sample of a fixed size has the same chance of selection as every other sample of that size. Simple random sampling is the most elementary random sampling technique. It forms the basis for the other random sampling techniques. With simple random sampling, n is used to represent the sample size, and N is used to represent the frame size. Every item or person in the frame is numbered from 1 to N. The chance that any particular member of the frame is selected on the first draw is $1/N$.

A random sample is selected using random numbers to draw the items in the sample from the frame to eliminate bias and hold uncertainty within known limits. For example, in Appendix 9.3 on page 277, Minitab is used to draw a simple random sample of items from a frame of items.

Two important points to remember are that different samples of size n will yield different sample statistics, and different methods of measurement will yield different sample statistics. Random samples, however, do not have bias, and the sampling error can be held to known limits by increasing the sample size. These are the advantages of probability sampling over nonprobability sampling.

Stratified Sample

A **stratified sample** is a sample in which the N items in the frame are divided into subpopulations, or strata, according to some common characteristic. A simple random sample is drawn within each of the strata, and the results from the separate simple random samples are combined. Stratified sampling is useful to decrease the sample size, and, consequently to lower the cost of a sample. A stratified sample will have a smaller sample size than a simple random sample if the items are similar within a stratum (called *homogeneity*) and the strata are different from each other (called *heterogeneity*). As an example of stratified sampling, suppose that a company has workers located at several facilities in a geographical area. The workers within each location are similar to each other with respect to the characteristic being studied, but the workers at the different locations are different from each other with respect to the characteristic being studied. Rather than take a simple random sample of all workers, it is cost-efficient to sample the workers by location, then combine the results into a single estimate of a characteristic being studied.

Systematic Sample

A **systematic sample** is a sample in which the N individuals or items in the frame are placed into k groups by dividing the size of the frame N by the desired sample size n. To obtain a systematic sample, the first individual or item to be selected is chosen at random from the k individuals or items in the first group in the frame, and the rest of the sample is obtained by selecting every kth individual or item thereafter from the entire frame.

If the frame consists of a listing of prenumbered checks, sales receipts, or invoices, or if the frame pertains to student registration listings or a preset number of consecutive items coming off an assembly line, a systematic sample is faster and easier to obtain than a simple random sample. In such situations, the systematic sample is a convenient mechanism for obtaining the desired data.

A shortcoming of a systematic sample occurs if the frame has a pattern. For example, if homes are being assessed, every fifth home is a corner house, and the random number selected is 5, then the entire sample will consist of corner houses. Corner houses are known to have higher assessed values than other houses. Consequently, the average assessed value of the homes in the sample will be inflated, due to the corner house phenomenon.

Cluster Sample

A **cluster sample** is a sample in which the N individuals or items in the frame are divided into many *clusters*. Clusters are naturally occurring subdivisions of a frame, such as counties, election districts, city blocks, apartment buildings, factories, or families. A random sampling of clusters is then taken, and all individuals or items in each selected cluster are studied and used to compute the results.

Cluster sampling methods are more cost-effective than simple random sampling methods if the population is spread over a wide geographic region. Cluster samples are very useful to cut down on travel time. However, cluster sampling methods tend to be less efficient than either simple random sampling methods or stratified sampling methods. It often requires a larger overall sample size to obtain results as precise as those that would be obtained from more efficient procedures.

A detailed discussion of systematic sampling, stratified sampling, and cluster sampling procedures can be found in Reference 4.

9.4 TYPES OF VARIABLES

Numerical information collected about a product, service, process, individual, item, or thing is called **data.** Because no two things are exactly alike, data inherently varies. Each characteristic of interest is referred to as a **variable.** Data are classified into two types, attribute data and measurement data.

      Attribute data (also referred to as classification or count data) occurs when a variable is either classified into categories or used to count occurrences of a phenomenon. Attribute data places an item or person into one of two or more categories. For example, gender has only two categories. In other cases, there are many possible categories into which the variable of interest can be classified. For example, there could be many reasons for a defective product. Regardless of the number of categories, the data consists of the number or frequency of items in a particular category, whether it is the number of voters in a sample who prefer a particular candidate in an election or the number of occurrences of each reason for a defective product. Count data consists of the number of occurrences of a phenomenon in an item or person. For example, the number of blemishes in a yard of fabric or the number of cars entering a highway at a certain location during a specific time period.

      Measurement data (also referred to as *continuous* or *variables data*) results from a measurement taken on an item or person of interest. Any value can theoretically occur, limited only by the precision of the measuring process. For example, height, weight, temperature, and cycle time are examples of measurement data.

9.5 OPERATIONAL DEFINITIONS

Operational definitions were discussed in Chapter 5. Recall, major problems occur when the measurement definitions for CTQs are inconsistent over time or vary from individual to individual. Ambiguous definitions, such as defective, safe, round, and hot, have no meaning that can be communicated unless they are operationally defined.

      An **operational definition** is a definition that provides communicable meaning to the users of the definition.

      A recent example [see Reference 3] that illustrates the importance of operation definitions refers to the 2000 U. S. Presidential election and the disputed ballots in the state of Florida. A review of 175,010 Florida ballots that were rejected for either no presidential vote or votes for two or more candidates was conducted with the help of the National Opinion Research Center of the University of Chicago. Nine operational definitions were used to evaluate the ballots to determine whether they should be counted. The nine operational definitions led to different results. Three of the operational definitions (including one pursued by Al Gore) led to margins of victory for George Bush that ranged from 225 to 493 votes. Six of the operational definitions (including one pursued by George Bush) led to margins of victory for Al Gore that ranged from 42 to 171 votes.

9.6 INTRODUCTION TO GRAPHICS

Graphics is a term that refers to the visual representation of data. Graphics have been used by civilizations throughout recorded history. The usefulness of graphics can be summarized in an 1801 quote by Playfair [Reference 1] that stated:

> I have succeeded in proposing and putting into practice a new and useful mode of stating accounts . . . as much information may be obtained in five minutes as would require whole days to imprint on the memory, in a lasting manner, by a table of figures.

More recently, the widespread availability of statistical and spreadsheet software for personal computers has enabled users to quickly develop many different graphs, even for large data sets. In this text, the Minitab statistical software package will be used to obtain a wide variety of graphs.

9.7 GRAPHING ATTRIBUTE DATA

When dealing with attribute data, responses are tallied into categories, and the frequency or percentage in each category is obtained. Three widely used graphs, the bar chart, the Pareto diagram, and the line chart, will be discussed.

The Bar Chart

A **bar chart** presents each category of an attribute type variable as a bar whose length is the frequency or percentage of observations falling into a category. To illustrate a bar chart, we examine data from a large injection molding company that manufactures plastic molded components used in computer keyboards, washing machines, automobiles, and television sets. The data presented in Table 9.1 is based on all computer keyboards produced during a 3-month period.

Figure 9.1 is a Minitab bar chart of the causes of defects in the computer keyboards.

The bar for the defects due to warpage in Figure 9.1 stands out because there are almost 2,000 defective keyboards due to warpage. In addition, you can see that there are a large number of damaged keyboards (more than 1,000) and keyboards with pin marks (more than 800).

The Pareto Diagram

A **Pareto diagram** is a special type of bar chart in which the categories of an attribute type variable are listed on the *X*-axis, the frequencies in each category (listed from largest to smallest frequency) are shown on the left side *Y*-axis, and the cumulative percentage of frequencies are shown on the right side *Y*-axis. Regardless of frequency, the "Other" category is always placed at

TABLE 9.1 Summary Table of Causes of Defects in Computer Keyboards in a 3-Month Period

Cause	Frequency	Percentage
Black Spot	413	6.53
Damage	1,039	16.43
Jetting	258	4.08
Pin mark	834	13.19
Scratches	442	6.99
Shot mold	275	4.35
Silver streak	413	6.53
Sink mark	371	5.87
Spray mark	292	4.62
Warpage	1,987	31.42
Total	6,324	100.01*

Keyboard *Error due to rounding.
Source: U. H. Acharya and C. Mahesh, "Winning Back the Customer's Confidence: A Case Study on the Application of Design of Experiments to an Injection Molding Process," *Quality Engineering,* 11, 1999, 357–363.

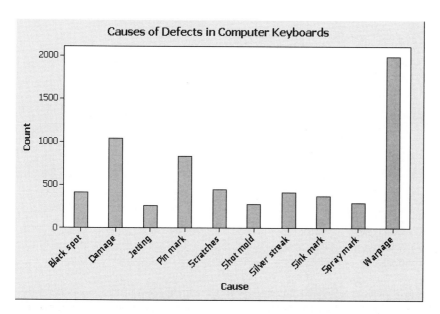

FIGURE 9.1 Minitab Bar Chart of the Causes of Defects in the Computer Keyboards

the right side of the *X*-axis. The main principle behind the Pareto diagram is to separate the "vital few response categories" from the "trivial many response categories," enabling you to focus on the critical categories. The Pareto diagram promotes prioritization of effort which discourages micromanagement. Figure 9.2 is a Minitab Pareto diagram of the causes of defects in the computer keyboards. From Figure 9.2, you see that warpage is the first category listed (with 31.4% percent of the defects) followed by damage (with 16.4% percent), followed by pin mark (with 13.2%). The two most frequently occurring categories, warpage and damage, account for 47.8% of the defects; the three most frequently occurring categories, warpage, damage, and pin mark, account for 61.0% of the corrections, and so on. 31.4% of the defects are accounted for by only 10% of the categories (One out of 10 categories). Thus, the priority problem is warpage.

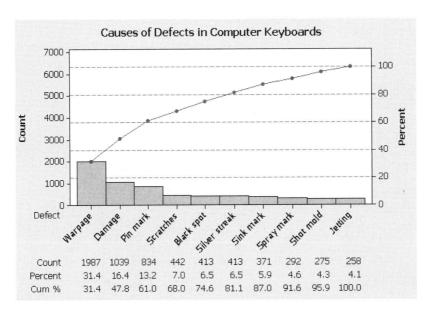

FIGURE 9.2 Minitab Pareto Diagram of the Causes of Defects in the Computer Keyboards

Line Chart

A **line chart** is a graph of an attribute type variable with the CTQ or *X* plotted on the vertical-axis and time plotted on the horizontal axis. It is useful for obtaining a dynamic picture of the output of a process.

The line chart is illustrated by using data concerning a medical transcription service that enters medical data on patient files for hospitals. The service studied ways to improve the turnaround time (defined as the time between receiving data and time the client receives completed files). After studying the process, the service determined that transmission errors increased turnaround time. A transmission error was defined as data transmitted that did not go through as planned and needed to be retransmitted. Each day, a sample of 125 record transmissions were randomly selected and evaluated for errors. Table 9.2 presents the number and proportion of transmissions with errors in samples of 125 records transmitted.

Figure 9.3 presents the line chart obtained from Minitab for these data. A horizontal line is plotted so that half the observations are at or above the horizontal line and half the observations are at or below the horizontal line.

Figure 9.3 clearly shows a great deal of fluctuation in the proportion of transmission errors from day to day. The highest number of errors occurred on day 23 (September 3), but a large

TABLE 9.2 Daily Number of Transmission Errors in 125 Records Transmitted

Date	Number of Errors	Proportion of Errors	Date	Number of Errors	Proportion of Errors
August:			23	4	0.032
1	6	0.048	26	6	0.048
2	3	0.024	27	3	0.024
5	4	0.032	28	5	0.040
6	4	0.032	29	1	0.008
7	9	0.072	30	3	0.024
8	0	0.000	September:		
9	0	0.000	3	14	0.112
12	8	0.064	4	6	0.048
13	4	0.032	5	7	0.056
14	3	0.024	6	3	0.024
15	4	0.032	9	10	0.080
16	1	0.008	10	7	0.056
19	10	0.080	11	5	0.040
20	9	0.072	12	0	0.000
21	3	0.024	13	3	0.024
22	1	0.008			

 TRANSMIT

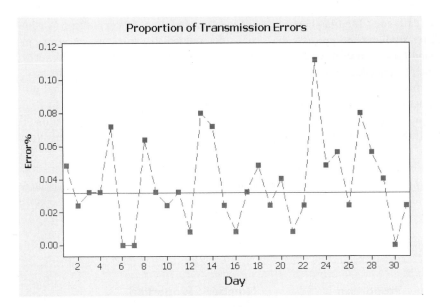

FIGURE 9.3 Minitab Line Chart of Transmission Errors

number of errors also occurred on days 5, 8, 13, 14, and 27. The medical transcription service needs to study the process to determine the reasons for the variation. Are the variations due to special causes? Or are the variations due to common causes? Methods for studying these issues using control charts are discussed in Chapter 14.

9.8 GRAPHING MEASUREMENT DATA

Histogram

A **histogram** is a special bar chart for measurement data. In the histogram, the data is grouped into adjacent numerical categories, for example, 100 to less than 200, 200 to less than 300, 300 to less than 400, and so on. Minitab can be used to both organize the data into groups and plot the histogram. The difference between a bar chart and a histogram is that the X axis on a bar chart is a listing of categories, whereas the X axis on a histogram is a measurement scale. In addition, there are no gaps between adjacent bars.

Data concerning the viscosity (resistance to flow) of a chemical product produced in 120 batches is used to illustrate the histogram. Assume that the viscosity of the chemical needs to be between 13 and 18 to meet company specifications. Figure 9.4 illustrates a histogram of the viscosity for these 120 batches.

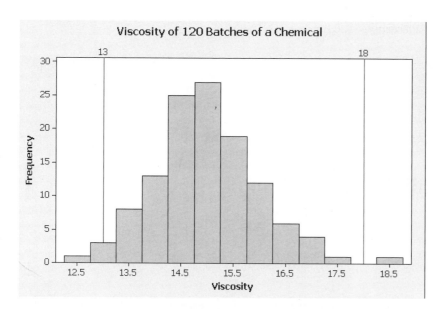

FIGURE 9.4 Minitab Histogram of the Viscosity of a Chemical

(Source: Holmes and Mergen, "Parabolic Control Limits for the Exponentially Weighted Moving Average Control Charts," (1992) *Quality Engineering*, 4(4), pp. 487–495)

◉WEB CHEMICAL

Minitab groups the data into numerical classes. For these data, notice tick marks at 12.5, 13.5, 14.5, 15.5, 16.5, 17.5, and 18.5. These tick marks are located at the midpoint of the class interval, so the first class whose midpoint is at 12.5 contains values between 12.25 to less than 12.75, the second class contains values between 12.75 to less than 13.25, and so on. Minitab also displays reference lines at the specification limits of 13 and 18, respectively. Most of the viscosity values shown in Figure 9.4 are in the center of the distribution, with very few values either below 13 or above 18. The distribution appears to be approximately bell-shaped with a heavy concentration of viscosities between 14 and 16.

The Dot Plot

A **dot plot** is a graph of measurement data in which dots are stacked vertically on the horizontal axis for each value of the variable of interest. Figure 9.5 is a dot plot of the viscosity of 120 batches of a chemical, for which a histogram was presented in Figure 9.4.

Notice that the dot plot for these data looks different from the histogram. This occurs because the histogram groups the data into class intervals, whereas the dot plot presents each data

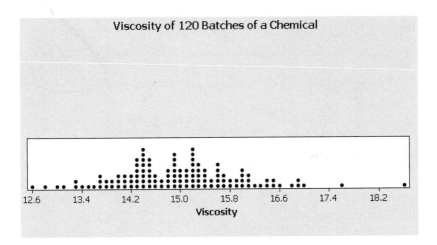

FIGURE 9.5 Minitab Dot Plot of the Viscosity of a Chemical

value, with the height representing the frequency at each horizontal (viscosity) value. Nevertheless, the dot plot shows a concentration of values in the center of the distribution between 14 and 16 and clearly shows which batches have viscosities below 13 or above 18.

The Run Chart

When data are collected over time, the variable of interest should be plotted in time order before any other graphs are plotted, descriptive statistics are calculated, or statistical analyses performed. The reason for this is the possible existence of a **lurking variable,** one that has an important effect on the CTQ or X being studied but has not been considered in the statistical study. A **run chart** is a type of line chart in which all of the measurements at a particular time for a CTQ or X are plotted on the Y axis at that time period, and time is plotted on the X axis. Referring to the data concerning the viscosity of a chemical, Figure 9.6 illustrates the run chart obtained from Minitab in batch order.

From Figure 9.6, observe that although there is a great deal of variation in the viscosities, there does not appear to be a pattern in the viscosities in the order of the production of the batch. In Chapter 14, you will learn how to determine if only common causes are present in the viscosity measures. If so, then the histogram and the dot plot previously shown can be used to evaluate the distribution of the viscosity.

9.9 MEASURES OF CENTRAL TENDENCY

Although the graphs we have studied in Sections 9.7 and 9.8 are extremely useful for getting a visual picture of what the distribution of a CTQ or X looks like, it is important to compute measures of central tendency or location. Three measures of central tendency will be developed, the

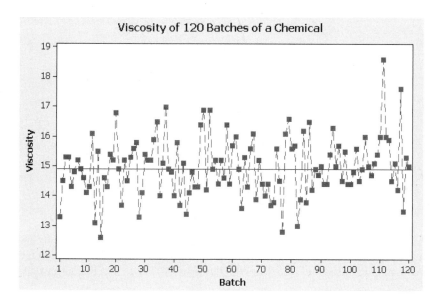

FIGURE 9.6 Run Chart Obtained from Minitab of the Viscosity of a Chemical

arithmetic mean (often called the *mean* or average), the **median,** and the **mode.** If these measures are computed from a sample, they are **statistics.** If they are computed from a frame, they are **parameters.** (To distinguish sample statistics and population parameters, Roman letters are used for sample statistics, and Greek letters are used for population parameters.)

The Arithmetic Mean

The **arithmetic mean** (also called the *mean* or average) is the most commonly used measure of central tendency. It is calculated by summing the observed numerical values of a variable, then dividing the total by the number of observations involved.

For a sample containing a set of n observations $X_1, X_2, \ldots, X_n$, the arithmetic mean of a sample (given by the symbol $\overline{X}$, called *X bar*) is written as

$$\overline{X} = \frac{\text{sum of the observations}}{\text{number of observations}}$$

To illustrate the computation of the sample mean, consider the following example related to your personal life, the time it takes to get ready to go to work in the morning. Many people wonder why it seems to take longer than they anticipate to get ready to leave for work, but virtually no one has actually measured the time it actually takes to get ready in the morning. Suppose the time to get ready is operationally defined as the time in minutes (rounded to the nearest minute) from when you get out of bed to when you leave your home. Suppose you collect these data for a period of 2 weeks, 10 working days, with the following results:

Day	1	2	3	4	5	6	7	8	9	10
Time (minutes)	39	29	43	52	39	44	40	31	44	35

The arithmetic mean time is computed from

$$\overline{X} = \frac{\text{sum of the observations}}{\text{number of observations}}$$

$$\overline{X} = \frac{396}{10} = 39.6$$

The mean time to get ready is 39.6 minutes, even though not one individual day in the sample actually had that value. Note that the calculation of the mean is based on all the observations in the set of data. No other commonly used measure of central tendency possesses this characteristic.

CAUTION   **When to Use the Arithmetic Mean**

Because its computation is based on every observation, the arithmetic mean is greatly affected by any extreme value or values. In such instances, the arithmetic mean presents a distorted representation of what the data are conveying. Thus, the mean is not the best measure of central tendency to use for describing or summarizing a set of data that has extreme values.

To demonstrate the effect that extreme values have when summarizing and describing the property of central tendency, suppose that the highest value of 52 minutes was actually 98 minutes. In this case, the mean is equal to

$$\overline{X} = \frac{\text{sum of the observations}}{\text{number of observations}}$$

$$\overline{X} = \frac{442}{10} = 44.2$$

The revised mean, because it is greatly affected by the extreme value of 98 minutes, is actually greater than 9 of the 10 values. Thus, it is not very representative of the central tendency of the time to get ready for the 10 days.

Using Summation Notation in Equations (optional)

Although the formula for the arithmetic mean can be represented by a few words, for virtually every other equation used in statistics, that is not feasible. In statistics, formulas are represented using a notation called summation notation.* Instead of using the formula with words

$$\overline{X} = \frac{\text{sum of the observations}}{\text{number of observations}}$$

in statistics, the formula with symbols is

$$\overline{X} = \frac{X_1 + X_2 + \cdots + X_n}{n}$$

where

X_1 is the value for observation 1
X_2 is the value for observation 2

.

.

X_n is the value for observation n, the last value in the sample
n = the number of observations in the sample
Using summation notation, the term

$$\sum_{i=1}^{n} X_i$$

(meaning the summation of all the X_i values from the first X value X_1 to the last X value X_n) replaces the written X values in the formula above. Thus,

$$\sum_{i=1}^{n} X_i = X_1 + X_2 + \cdots + X_n$$

Using this summation notation, the arithmetic mean of the sample is expressed as:

$$\overline{X} = \frac{\sum_{i=1}^{n} X_i}{n} \tag{9.1}$$

where

$\overline{X}$ = sample arithmetic mean
n = number of observations or sample size
X_i = ith observation of the variable X

$\displaystyle\sum_{i=1}^{n} X_i$ = summation of all X_i values in the sample.

---

*See Appendix A for a review of arithmetic and algebra and Appendix B for a discussion of summation notation.

The Median

The **median** is the middle value in a set of data that has been ordered from the lowest to the highest value. If there are no ties, half the observations will be smaller than the median, and half will be larger. The median is not affected by any extreme values in a set of data. Whenever an extreme value is present, the median is preferred instead of the mean in describing the central tendency of a set of data.

To calculate the median from a set of data, you must first organize the data into an **ordered array** that lists the values from smallest to largest. Then the median is obtained as:

Median

The median is the value such that 50% of the observations are smaller and 50% of the observations are larger.

$$\text{Median} = \frac{n + 1}{2} \text{ ranked observation} \tag{9.2}$$

where n = the number of observations

Equation (9.2) is used to find the place in the ordered set of values that corresponds to the median value by following one of two rules:

Rule 1   If there is an *odd* number of observations in the data set, the median is the numerical value corresponding to the $(n + 1)/2$ ordered observation.

Rule 2   If there is an *even* number of observations in the data set, then by convention, the median is taken to be the average of the two observations in the middle of the data set.

To compute the median for the sample of 10 times to get ready in the morning, the raw data are placed in order as follows:

29   31   35   39   39   40   43   44   44   52

Ordered observation:

1   2   3   4   5   6   7   8   9   10
                          ↑

Median = 39.5

Using rule 2 for the even-sized sample of 10 days, the median corresponds to the $(10 + 1)/2 = 5.5$ ranked value, halfway between the fifth-ranked value and the sixth-ranked value. Because the fifth-ranked value is 39 and the sixth-ranked value is 40, the median is the average of 39 and 40, or 39.5. The median of 39.5 means that for half of the days, the time to get ready is less than or equal to 39.5 minutes, and for half of the days, the time to get ready is greater than or equal to 39.5 minutes

To illustrate the computation of the median when there is odd number of values, the median for the second week (5 days) of the study (days 6 through 10) can be computed. The times for these days were

    44   40   31   44   35

Placing these values in order results in the following

    31   35   40   44   44

Ordered observation:

    1   2   3   4   5
                ↑
          Median = 40

Using rule 1 for the odd number of 5 days, the median corresponds to the $(5 + 1)/2 =$ third-ranked value. The third-ranked value is 40 minutes.

The Mode

The **mode** is the value in a set of data that appears most frequently. Unlike the arithmetic mean, the mode is not affected by the occurrence of any extreme values. The mode is used only for descriptive purposes, because it is more variable from sample to sample than other measures of central tendency. For measurement variables, a mode often does not exist or there are several modes. Referring to the times for the 10 days, there are two modes, 39 minutes and 44 minutes, because each of these values occurs twice.

Quartiles

While the median is the value that splits the ordered values in half (50% of the values are smaller, and 50% of the values are larger), the quartiles are descriptive measures that split the ordered data into four quarters.

The quartiles are defined in equations (9.3) and (9.4)

First Quartile Q_1

The **first quartile, Q_1,** is the value such that 25% of the values are smaller and 75% are larger.

$$Q_1 = \frac{n + 1}{4} \text{ ordered observation} \tag{9.3}$$

where n = sample size

Third Quartile Q_3

The **third quartile Q_3,** is the value such that 75% of the values are smaller and 25% are larger.

$$Q_3 = \frac{3(n + 1)}{4} \text{ ordered observation} \tag{9.4}$$

where n = sample size

Using the sample of 10 times to get ready in the morning, the raw data are placed in order as follows:

29   31   35   39   39   40   43   44   44   52

Ordered observation:

1   2   3   4   5   6   7   8   9   10

The first quartile is the $(n + 1)/4$ or $(10 + 1)/4 = 2.75$-ranked value, 75% past the second-ranked value. Because the second-ranked value is 31 and the third ranked value is 35 (and their difference is $35 - 31 = 4$), the first quartile is 34 [because $31 + 3/4(4) = 31 + 3 = 34$]. This means that on 25% of the days, the time to get ready is less than or equal to 34 minutes, and on 75% of the days, the time to get ready is greater than or equal to 34 minutes.

The third quartile is the $3(n + 1)/4$ or $3(10 + 1)/4 = 8.25$-ranked value, 25% past the eighth-ranked value. Because the eighth-ranked value is 44 and the ninth-ranked value is also 44, the third quartile is 44 [$44 + 1/4(0)$]. This is interpreted to mean that on 75% of the days, the time to get ready is less than or equal to 44 minutes, and on 25% of the days, the time to get ready is greater than or equal to 44 minutes.

Descriptive Statistics: Time

Variable	Total Count	Mean	Standard Deviation	Variance	Sum	Minimum	Q1	Median	Q3
Time	10	39.60	6.77	45.82	396.00	29.00	34.00	39.50	44.00

Variable	Maximum	Range	Skewness
Time	52.00	23.00	0.09

FIGURE 9.7 Minitab Descriptive Statistics for the Time to Get Ready in the Morning Data

In circumstances where there is a large number of data values, it is impractical to manually compute descriptive statistics, such as the mean, median, and quartiles. Statistical software such as Minitab should be used. Figure 9.7 illustrates descriptive statistics obtained from Minitab for the time to get ready in the morning data. Additional descriptive statistics included in Figure 9.7 will be discussed in Sections 9.10 and 9.11.

As a second application of descriptive statistics, recall that in Section 9.8, a histogram, dot plot, and run chart were obtained for the viscosity (resistance to flow) of a chemical product produced in 120 batches. Figure 9.8 illustrates descriptive statistics obtained from Minitab for the viscosity of a chemical product.

Descriptive Statistics: Viscosity

Variable	Total Count	Mean	Standard Deviation	Variance	Minimum	Q1	Median	Q3
Viscosity	120	14.978	1.007	1.014	12.600	14.300	14.900	15.600

Variable	Maximum	Range	Skewness
Viscosity	18.60	6.00	0.42

FIGURE 9.8 Minitab Descriptive Statistics for the Viscosity of a Chemical Product

From Figure 9.8, you see that the mean of 14.978 is very close to the median of 14.9. The median of 14.9 tells you that half of the batches have a viscosity of 14.9 or less, and half the batches have a viscosity of 14.9 or more. The first quartile of 14.3 tells you that 25% of the batches have a viscosity at or less than 14.3, and the third quartile tells you that 75% of the batches have a viscosity of 15.6 or less (and 25% have a viscosity of 15.6 and more). The minimum value of 12.6 and the maximum value of 18.6 provide evidence that at least some values are outside the specification limits of 13–18.

9.10 MEASURES OF VARIATION

A second important property that describes a set of numerical data is variation. **Variation** is the amount of **dispersion,** or spread, in the data. Three measures of variation include the range, the variance, and the standard deviation.

The Range

The **range** is the difference between the *largest* and *smallest* values in a set of data.

Range

The range is equal to the largest value minus the smallest value.

Range = largest value − smallest value (9.5)

Using the data on the time to get ready in the morning,

$$\text{Range} = \text{largest value} - \text{smallest value}$$
$$\text{Range} = 52 - 29 = 23 \text{ minutes.}$$

This means that the largest difference between any 2 days in the time to get ready in the morning is 23 minutes.

Referring to the data concerning the viscosity of a chemical, in Figure 9.8 on page 249, observe that the range is 6.0. This means that the largest difference in the viscosity of any two batches of the chemical is 6.0.

The Variance and the Standard Deviation

Although the range is a measure of the total spread, it does not consider *how* the values are distributed around the mean. Two commonly used measures of variation that do take into account how all the values in the data are distributed around the mean are the **variance** and the **standard deviation.** These measures evaluate how the values fluctuate about the mean.

In developing a measure of variation around the mean, the simplest measure might just take the difference between each value and the mean, and sum these differences. However, if you did that, you would find that because the mean is the balance point in a set of data, for every set of data, these differences would sum to zero. A measure of variation used in statistics that differs from data set to data set *squares* the difference between each value and the mean, then sums these squared differences. This quantity is called the **sum of squares** (or SS) and will be encountered again in Chapters 11–13. If the sum of squares for all observations is divided by the number of observations minus 1 (in the case of sample data), the resulting statistic is the sample **variance.**[*] The square root of the sample **variance** (S^2) is called the sample **standard deviation** (S). This statistic is the most widely used measure of variation. The steps for computing the variance and the standard deviation of a sample of data are presented in Exhibit 9.2.

The computation of the variance and standard deviation using the steps of Exhibit 9.2 is illustrated in Table 9.3 for the time to get ready in the morning data. Note that the sum of the differences between the individual values and the mean is equal to zero.

---

[*]We will not discuss why we divide by the sample size minus 1 and not just the sample size. It is discussed in [Reference 2].

Exhibit 9.2	**Computing S^2 and S**

To compute S^2, the sample variance, do the following:
1. Obtain the difference between each value and the mean.
2. Square each difference.
3. Add the squared differences.
4. Divide this total by $n - 1$.

To compute S, the sample standard deviation, take the square root of the variance.

TABLE 9.3 Computing the Sample Variance and Sample Standard Deviation for the Time to Get Ready in the Morning Data

Time (*X*)	Difference between *X* and the mean	Squared differences around the mean
39	−0.6	0.36
29	−10.6	112.36
43	3.4	11.56
52	12.4	153.76
39	−0.6	0.36
44	4.4	19.36
40	0.4	0.16
31	−8.6	73.96
44	4.4	19.36
35	−4.6	21.16
Mean = 39.6	Sum of differences = 0	Sum of squared differences = 412.4

The sample variance S^2 is obtained by dividing the sum of the squared differences computed in step 3 (412.4) by the sample size (10) minus 1.

$$\text{Sample variance } (S^2) = \frac{412.4}{9} = 45.82$$

Because the variance is in squared units (in squared minutes for these data), to obtain the standard deviation, you take the squared root of the variance. Thus

$$\text{Sample standard deviation } (S) = \sqrt{45.82} = 6.77$$

   In Figure 9.8 on page 249, the standard deviation is labeled "StDev" by Minitab and is computed as 1.007. How can this value be interpreted? The standard deviation helps you to know how a set of data clusters or distributes around its mean. For almost all sets of data that have a single mode, most of the observed values lie within an interval of plus or minus 3 standard deviations above and below the arithmetic mean. Therefore, knowledge of the arithmetic mean and the standard deviation usually helps define the range in which most of the data values are clustering. Thus, for the viscosity of the chemical shown in Figure 9.8 on page 249, it is reasonable to state that most of the batches will have a viscosity between the mean of $14.978 \pm (3)(1.007)$ or 11.957 and 17.999.

   As summarized in Exhibit 9.3, the following statements about the range, variance, and standard deviation can be made.

Exhibit 9.3 1. The more spread out, or dispersed, the data are, the larger will be the range, the variance, and the standard deviation.

2. The more concentrated or homogeneous the data is, the smaller will be the range, the variance, and the standard deviation.

3. If the values are all the same (so that there is no variation in the data), the range, variance, and standard deviation will all be zero.

4. The range, variance, or standard deviation will always be greater than or equal to zero.

These three measures of variation will be used extensively in Chapters 10–14.

Equations for the Variance and Standard Deviation (optional)

$$S^2 = \frac{\sum_{i=1}^{n}(X_i - \overline{X})^2}{n - 1} \tag{9.6}$$

$$S = \sqrt{\frac{\sum_{i=1}^{n}(X_i - \overline{X})^2}{n - 1}} \tag{9.7}$$

where

$\overline{X}$ = sample arithmetic mean

n = sample size

X_i = ith value of the variable X

$\sum_{i=1}^{n}(X - \overline{X})^2$ = summation of all the squared differences between the X values and $\overline{X}$

Using the results of Table 9.3 and Equations (9.6) and (9.7),

$$S^2 = \frac{\sum_{i=1}^{n}(X_i - \overline{X})^2}{n - 1}$$

$$S^2 = \frac{412.4}{10 - 1} = 45.82$$

$$S = \sqrt{45.82} = 6.77$$

9.11 THE SHAPE OF DISTRIBUTIONS

Shape

Shape is a third important property of a set of data The shape is the manner in which the data are distributed. Either a histogram or a dot plot can be used to study the shape of a distribution of data.

Either the distribution of the data is **symmetrical** or it is not symmetrical. To determine the shape of a data set, you compare the mean with the median. If these two measures are equal, the CTQ or X is considered to be symmetrical (or zero-skewed). If the mean is greater than the median, the variable is described as *positive,* or **right-skewed.** If the mean is less than the median, the variable is called *negative,* or **left-skewed.** Thus,

mean $>$ median: positive, or right-skewness
mean $=$ median: symmetry, or zero-skewness
mean $<$ median: negative, or left-skewness

Positive skewness arises when the mean is increased by some unusually high values. Negative skewness occurs when the mean is reduced by some extremely low values. The distribution of a CTQ or X is symmetrical when there are no really extreme values in a particular direction so that low and high values balance each other out. Figure 9.9 depicts the shapes of three data sets.

The data in panel A are negative, or left-skewed. In this panel, there is a long tail and distortion to the left that is caused by extremely small values. These extremely small values pull the mean downward so that the mean is less than the median. The data in panel B are symmetrical; each half of the curve is a mirror image of the other half of the curve. The low and high values on the scale balance, and the mean equals the median. The data in panel C are positive, or right-skewed. In this panel, there is a long tail on the right of the distribution and a distortion to the right that is caused by extremely large values. These extremely large values pull the mean upward so that the mean is greater than the median.

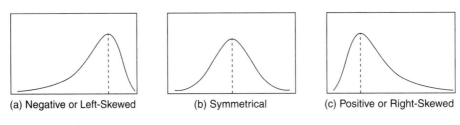

(a) Negative or Left-Skewed   (b) Symmetrical   (c) Positive or Right-Skewed

FIGURE 9.9 A comparison of Three Data Sets Differing in Shape

Referring to the viscosity of the batch of chemical illustrated in the histogram of Figure 9.4 on page 241 and the dot plot of Figure 9.5 on page 242, the distribution appears to be approximately symmetric. In Figure 9.8 on page 249, Minitab displays a skewness measure (that is based on the cubed differences around the mean) equal to 0.42. This gives reinforcement to the notion that the batches of the chemical are approximately symmetric or perhaps slightly right-skewed.

In addition to determining whether a set of data is symmetric or skewed, of particular concern is whether there is more than one concentration of data in the distribution of values. A distribution with two concentrations of data is called **bimodal.** The existence of a bimodal distribution is often a signal that data from two groups (such as two production shifts) have been inappropriately combined into a single group.

As an illustration of a bimodal distribution, a bank collected data on a sample of 200 customers who arrived during peak times in order to determine the waiting time to conduct a transaction 🔧 **BIMODAL.MTW.** Figure 9.10 presents a histogram obtained from Minitab of the waiting times.

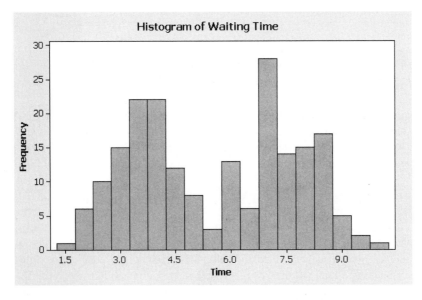

FIGURE 9.10 Minitab Histogram of the Waiting Times at a Bank

There appear to be two peaks in the distribution of waiting times. One is between 3.5 and 4.0, and the other is between 7 and 8. In fact, the data collected is based on a sample 100 customers from two different branches of the bank. The peak time for the first branch from which the data was collected was Friday from 12 noon until 2 p.m. (the branch was located in the central business district of a city). The peak time for the second branch from which the data was collected was Friday from 5 p.m. until 7 p.m. (the branch was located in a residential neighborhood).

Figure 9.11 is a dot plot obtained from Minitab of the waiting times for each of the banks. From Figure 9.11 it is clear that the distribution of the waiting times is different for the two banks. The distribution for bank 1 (located in the business district) is concentrated between 3 and 4 minutes, whereas the distribution for bank 2 (located in a residential neighborhood) is concentrated between 7 and 8 minutes.

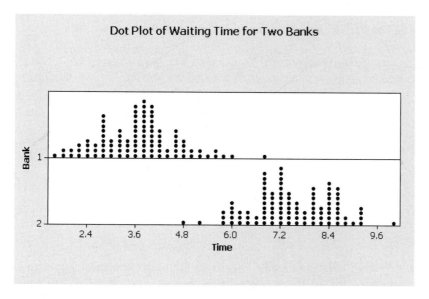

FIGURE 9.11 Minitab Dot Plot of the Waiting Times for Two Banks

The Five-Number Summary

The **five-number summary** provides another way to determine the shape of the distribution.

A **five-number summary** consists of:

Smallest value Q_1 Median Q_3 *largest value*

If the data are perfectly symmetrical, the relationship among the various measures in the five-number summary is expressed as in Exhibit 9.4.

Exhibit 9.4	**Using the Five-Number Summary to Recognize Symmetry in Data**

1. The distance from the smallest value to the median equals the distance from the median to the largest value.
2. The distance from the smallest value to Q_1 equals the distance from Q_3 to the largest value.

If the data are skewed, the relationship among the various measures of location is expressed as in Exhibit 9.5.

Exhibit 9.5	**Using the Five-Number Summary to Recognize Skewness in Data**

1. In right-skewed distributions, the distance from the median to the largest value is greater than the distance from the smallest value to the median.
2. In right-skewed distributions, the distance from Q_3 to the largest value is greater than the distance from the smallest value to Q_1.
3. In left-skewed distributions, the distance from the smallest value to the median is greater than the distance from the median to the largest value.
4. In left-skewed distributions, the distance from the smallest value to Q_1 is greater than the distance from Q_3 to the largest value.

Referring to the descriptive statistics for the viscosity of the batch of chemical illustrated in Figure 9.8 on page 249, notice that the distance between the third quartile and the median, equal to 0.7(15.6–14.9), is about the same as the distance between the first quartile and the median, equal to 0.6 (14.9–14.3). However, the distance between the maximum value and the median, equal to 3.7 (18.6–14.9), is greater than the distance between the median and the minimum value, equal to 2.3 (14.9–12.6). This may indicate an extreme, or outlier, value in the upper tail of the distribution of the viscosity.

The Box-and-Whisker Plot

The **box-and-whisker plot** is a graphical representation of the five-number summary that consists of the smallest value, the first quartile (or 25th percentile), the median, the third quartile (or 75th percentile), and the largest value. The line drawn within the box represents the location of the median value in the data. The line at the lower end of the box represents the location of Q_1, and the line at the upper end of the box represents the location of Q_3. Thus, the box contains the middle 50% of the observations in the distribution. The lower 25% of the data are represented by a line (i.e., a *whisker*) connecting the lower end of the box to the location of the smallest value. Similarly, the upper 25% of the data are represented by a line connecting the upper end of the box to the largest value. Figure 9.12 demonstrates the relationship between the box-and-whisker plot and the polygon. Four different types of distributions are depicted with their box-and-whisker plot and corresponding polygon.

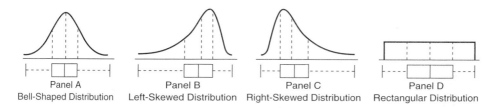

| Panel A | Panel B | Panel C | Panel D |
| Bell-Shaped Distribution | Left-Skewed Distribution | Right-Skewed Distribution | Rectangular Distribution |

FIGURE 9.12 Four Hypothetical Distributions Examined Through Their Box-and-Whisker Plots and Corresponding Distributions

Note: Area under each distribution is split into quartiles corresponding to the five-number summary for the respective box-and-whisker plot

When a data set is perfectly symmetrical, as is the case in Figure 9.12(A) and (D), the mean and median are the same. In addition, the length of the left (or lower) whisker will equal the length of the right (or upper) whisker, and the median line will divide the box in half.

When the data set is left-skewed as in Figure 9.12(B), the few small observations distort the mean toward the left tail. For this hypothetical left-skewed distribution, 75% of all data values are found between the left (or lower) edge of the box (Q_1) and the end of the right (or upper) whisker ($X_{largest}$). Therefore, the long left (or lower) whisker contains the distribution of only the smallest 25% of the observations, demonstrating the distortion from symmetry in this data set.

For the right-skewed data set in Figure 9.12(c) the concentration of data points will be on the low end of the scale (i.e., the left side of the box-and-whisker plot). Here, 75% of all data values are found between the beginning of the left (or lower) whisker (smallest value) and the right (or upper) edge of the box (Q_3) and the remaining 25% of the observations are dispersed along the long right (or upper) whisker at the upper end of the scale.

Figure 9.13 represents the box-and-whisker plot obtained from Minitab of the time to get ready in the morning.

Minitab displays the box-and-whisker plot vertically from bottom (low) to top (high). The box-and-whisker plot seems to indicate an approximately symmetric distribution of the time to get ready. The median line in the middle of the box is approximately equidistant between the ends of the box, and the length of the whiskers does not appear to be very different.

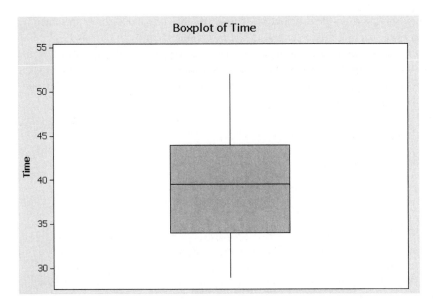

FIGURE 9.13 Minitab Box-and-Whisker Plot of the Time to Get Ready in the Morning

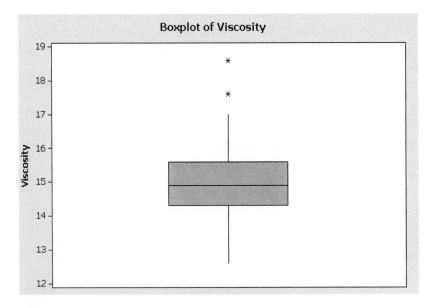

FIGURE 9.14 Minitab Box-and-Whisker Plot of the Viscosity of a Chemical

Figure 9.14 presents the box-and-whisker plot obtained from Minitab of the viscosity of a chemical.

Notice that asterisks appear at the top part of the box-and-whisker plot. These represent extreme values, or outliers, in the data. Other than these extreme values, the remainder of the distribution appears approximately symmetric.

The box-and-whisker plot is particularly useful when there are two or more groups to be compared. In such a situation, separate box-and-whisker plots are shown side by side using the same vertical axis scale, so you can directly compare the different groups in terms of central tendency, variation, and shape.

SUMMARY

This chapter has provided an introduction to the field of statistics and why statistics is such a vital tool in Six Sigma management. Some basic principles were defined, and different types of sampling methods were discussed. Various graphical presentations were illustrated for different types of variables. The properties of central tendency, variation, and shape were explained for measurement data.

REFERENCES

1. Beninger, J. M., and D. L. Robyn, "Quantitative Graphics in Statistics, "*The American Statistician,* 32, 1978, 1–11.

2. Berenson, M. L., D. M. Levine, and T. C. Krehbiel, *Basic Business Statistics: Concepts and Applications,* Ninth Ed. (Upper Saddle River, NJ: Prentice Hall, 2004).

3. Calmes, J. and E. P., Foldessy, "In Election Review, Bush Wins with No Supreme Court Help," *Wall Street Journal,* November 12, 2001, A1, A14.

4. Cochran, W. G. *Sampling Techniques,* Third Ed. (New York: John Wiley, 1977).

5. Deming, W. E. *Some Theory of Sampling,* (New York: John Wiley, 1950).

6. Hahn, G. J. and W. Q. Meeker, "Assumptions for Statistical Inference," *The American Statistician,* 1993, 47, 1–11.

7. Minitab Version 14 (State College, PA: Minitab, 2004).

Appendix 9.1

Using Windows

The step-by-step instructions for using Minitab require that you are familiar with basic Microsoft Windows procedures and objects. You can use this section to either learn or review these concepts.

You point and select objects onscreen by using a mouse or other pointing device in Microsoft Windows. The graphical user interface of Windows expects pointing devices to contain two buttons, one designated as the primary button and the other as the secondary button. Moving the pointing device and pressing and releasing these buttons in different ways determines which one of the standard mouse operations is executed (see Exhibit A9.1).

By default, Microsoft Windows defines the left mouse button as the primary button and the right button as the secondary button (this gives rise to the term *right-click*), but the definitions can be swapped by changing the appropriate Windows user settings.

Opening Programs

Microsoft Windows includes three methods of using a mouse to open a program (see Exhibit A9.2). Which way you choose is partly personal preference and partly determined by how the program has been set up.

When you open a program, Microsoft Windows opens an **application window.** The application window of Minitab contains a title bar, resize and close application window buttons, a menu bar containing a list of pull-down menus, a toolbar that contains icons represent-

---

Exhibit A9.1

Standard Mouse Operations

Click: Move the mouse pointer over an object and press the primary button. For some objects, the verb **select** is used to describe this action, as in the phrase "select the entry for the program."

Drag: Move the mouse pointer over an object. Then, while pressing and holding down the primary button, move the mouse pointer somewhere else on the screen and release the primary button. Dragging either moves objects to another screen location or allows you to select multiple items.

Double-click: Move the mouse pointer over an object and click the primary button twice in rapid succession.

Right-click: Move the mouse pointer over an object and click the secondary button.

---

ing menu shortcuts, and a worksheet area of rows and columns for making entries (see Figure A9.1).

You operate the program directly in the application window by making entries and selecting choices from the pull-down menus.

| Exhibit A9.2 | **Methods of Opening Programs in Microsoft Windows** |

Program icon click: Double-click the Windows desktop icon representing the program (in some Windows versions, this requires only a single click.)

Start menu entry selection: Press the Windows key (or click the onscreen Start button) and select the Programs or All Programs choice. From the menu list that appears, select the entry for the program. Sometimes, you will find the program entry on a submenu, so several selections may be required.

File icon click: Double-click the Windows desktop icon representing a file of a type that Windows associates with a specific program. For example, if you click an icon for an .mtw workbook file, both Minitab and the Minitab worksheet open.

Throughout this text, the procedures for using the statistical programs are written presuming that you will be using either the first or second method because these two methods *always* allow you to verify program settings before you use your data. Should you choose to use the third method, you will still be able to use those procedures.

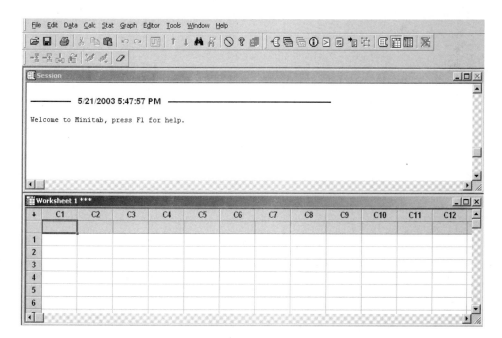

FIGURE A9.1 Minitab Application Window

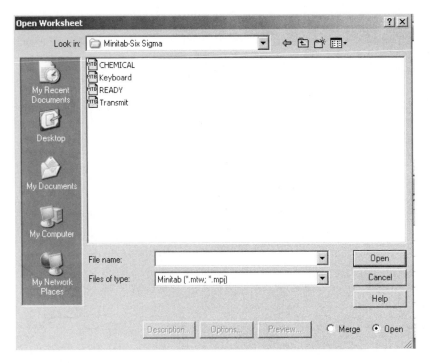

FIGURE A9.2 Panel A Minitab Open Worksheet Dialog Box

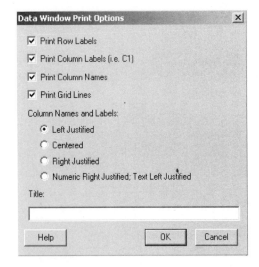

FIGURE A9.2 Panel B Minitab Print Worksheet Dialog Box

Data entries are made directly into worksheet cells to which you navigate by using either the mouse or the cursor keys. Some menu selections directly perform a function or task, but many more lead to dialog boxes in which you enter information and settings for a procedure. The Open Worksheet and Print Worksheet dialog boxes from Minitab (see Figure A9.2) contain the types of objects commonly found in the dialog boxes. Exhibit A9.3 further explains these objects.

Note that in the Open Worksheet dialog box, the Files of Type: drop-down list box by default lists Minitab (*.mtw). To change the selection to another type of file, click the down arrow and select the desired file type (such as Excel [*.xls]).

Exhibit A9.3

Common Dialog Box Objects

Drop-down list box: Displays a list of choices when the drop-down button, located on the right edge of the box, is clicked.

List box: Displays a list of choices for selection. Should the list exceed the dimensions of the list box, the list box will include **scroll buttons** and a **slider** that you can click to display the other choices of the list.

Edit box: Provides an area into which a value can be edited or typed. Edit boxes are often combined with either a drop-down list or **spinner buttons** to provide alternatives to the direct typing of a value.

Option buttons: Represent a set of mutually exclusive choices. Selecting an option button always deselects, or clears, the other option buttons in the set, thereby allowing only one choice to be made for that set.

Check box: Allows the selection of optional actions. Unlike option buttons, more than one check box can be selected at a time.

OK command button: Causes the program to execute some action using the current values and settings of the dialog box. As in the Open Worksheet dialog box shown in Figure A9.2 Panel A, this button sometimes contains a different label, such as Open (in Panel A), Save, or Finish.

Cancel command button: Closes a dialog box and cancels the operation represented by the dialog box. In most contexts, clicking the Cancel button is equivalent to clicking the **Close button** on the title bar.

Help command button: Displays a help message or help window for the dialog box. Many dialog boxes also include the **Question mark button** on the title bar that performs a similar function.

Making Mistakes and Correcting Entries

If you make an error while entering data, you can usually do one of the following three things to correct the error.

1. Press the Escape key to cancel the current entry.
2. Press the Backspace key to erase typed characters to the left of the cursor one character at a time.
3. Press the Delete key to erase characters to the right of the cursor one character at a time.

For errors in the middle of an entry, you can also drag the mouse over the in-error text, then type the replacement text. Selecting Delete from the Edit menu will undo any typing, as well.

Appendix 9.2 presents the basic operating procedures for the Minitab statistical program that is featured in this book.

How This Book Represents Multiple Menu Selections

From this point forward, when this book describes a procedure that involves two or more consecutive menu selections, the selections appear in boldfaced type and are chained together with the right arrow character ($\rightarrow$). For example, the phrase "select the Open Worksheet choice from the File pull-down menu" is written as "select **File** $\rightarrow$ **Open Worksheet**" in subsequent pages.

A P P E N D I X   9 . 2

INTRODUCTION TO MINITAB

Minitab Overview

Minitab is an example of a statistical package, a set of programs designed to perform statistical analysis to a high degree of numerical accuracy. Minitab initially evolved from efforts at the Pennsylvania State University to improve the teaching of statistics and quickly spread to many other colleges and universities. Today, while maintaining its academic base, Minitab has become a commercial product that is used in many large corporations and is widely used by companies involved in Six Sigma management.

In Minitab, you create and open **projects** to store all of your data and results. A **session,** or log of activities, a **Project Manager** that summarizes the project contents, and any worksheets or graphs used are the components that form a project. Project components are displayed in separate windows inside the Minitab application window. By default, you will see only the session and one worksheet window when you begin a new project in Minitab. (You can bring any window to the front by selecting the desired window in the Minitab Windows menu.) You can open and save an entire project or, as is done in this text, open and save worksheets.

Minitab's statistical rigor, availability for many different types of computer systems, and commercial acceptance make this program a great tool for using statistics in Six Sigma management.

Using Minitab Worksheets

You use a Minitab worksheet to enter data for variables by column. Minitab worksheets are organized as numbered rows and columns numbered in the form *Cn,* in which C1 is the first column. You enter variable labels in a special unnumbered row that precedes row 1. Unlike worksheets in program such as Microsoft Excel, currently Minitab worksheets do not accept formulas and do not automatically recalculate themselves when you change the values of the supporting data.

By default, Minitab names opened worksheets serially in the form of Worksheet1, Worksheet2, and so on. Better names are ones that reflect the content of the worksheets, such as CHEMICAL for a worksheet that contains data for the viscosity of a chemical. To give a sheet a descriptive name, open the Project Manager window, right-click the icon for the worksheet, select **Rename** from the shortcut menu, and type in the new name.

Opening and Saving Worksheets and other Components

You open worksheets to use data that have been created by you or others at an earlier time. To open a Minitab worksheet, first select **File → Open Worksheet.** In the Open Worksheet dialog box that appears (see Figure A9.3):

1. Select the appropriate folder (also known as a directory) from the Look in: drop-down list box.

2. Check, and select, if necessary, the proper Files of type: value from the drop-down list at the bottom of the dialog box. Typically, you will not need to make this selection because the default choice Minitab will list all Minitab worksheets and projects. However, to list all Microsoft Excel files, select Excel (*.xls); to list every file in the folder, select All.

3. If necessary, change the display of files in the central files list box by clicking the rightmost (View menu) button on the top row of buttons and selecting the appropriate view from the drop-down list.

4. Select the file to be opened from the files list box. If the file does not appear, verify that steps 1, 2, and 3 were done correctly.

5. Click the **OK** button.

To open a Minitab Project that can include the session, worksheets, and graphs, select Minitab Project in step 2 above or select the similar **File → Open Project.** Individual graphs can be opened as well by selecting **File → Open Graph.**

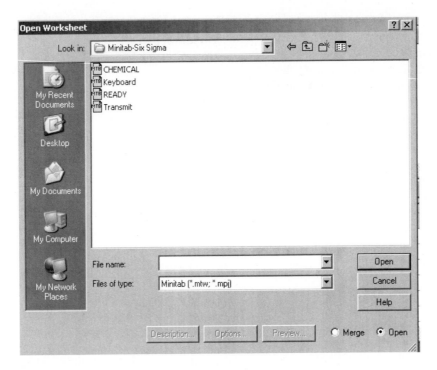

FIGURE A9.3 Minitab Open Worksheet Dialog Box

You can save a worksheet individually to assure its future availability, to protect yourself against a system failure, or to later import it into another project. To save a worksheet, select the worksheet's window, then select **File → Save Current Worksheet As.** In the Save Worksheet As dialog box that appears (see Figure A9.4):

1. Select the appropriate folder from the Save in: drop-down list box.

2. Check and select, if necessary, the proper Save as: type value from the drop-down list at the bottom of the dialog box. Typically, you will want to accept the default choice, Minitab, but select Minitab Portable to use the data on a different type of computer system or

select an earlier version, such as Minitab 13, to use the data in that earlier version.

3. Enter (or edit) the name of the file in the File name: edit box.

4. Optionally, click the Description button and in the Worksheet Description dialog box (not shown), enter documentary information and click the OK button.

5. Click the **OK** button (in the Save Worksheet As dialog box).

To save a Minitab Project, select the similar **File → Save Project As.** The Save Project As dialog box (not shown), contains an Options button that displays the Save Project—Options dialog box in which you can indicate which project components other than worksheets

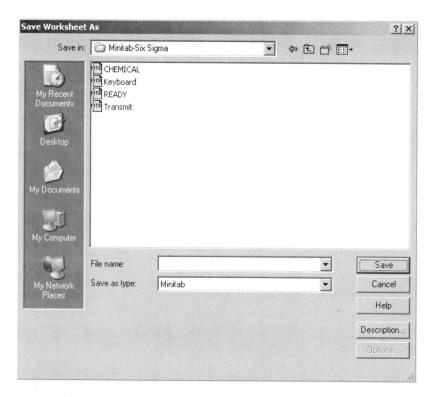

FIGURE A9.4 Minitab Save Worksheet as Dialog Box

(session, dialog settings, graphs, and Project Manager content) will be saved.

Individual graphs and the session can also be saved separately by first selecting their windows, then selecting the similar **File → Save Graph As** or **File → Save Session As,** as appropriate. Minitab graphs can be saved in either a Minitab graph format or any one of several common graphics formats, and Session files can be saved as simple or formatted text files.

You can repeat a save procedure and save a worksheet, project, or other component using a second name as an easy way to create a backup copy that can be used should some problem make your original file unusable.

Printing Worksheets, Graphs, and Sessions

Printing components gives you the means to study and review data and results away from the computer screen. To print a specific worksheet, graph, or session:

1. Select the window of the worksheet, graph, or session to be printed.

2. Select **File → Print** *object,* where *object* is either Worksheet, Graph, or Session Window, depending on the component window you selected.

3. If you are printing a worksheet, select formatting options and add a title in the

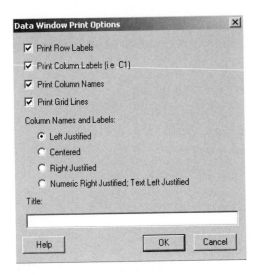

FIGURE A9.5 Minitab Data Window Print Options Dialog Box

Data Window Print Options dialog box that appears, then click the **OK** button in that dialog box (see Figure A9.5).

4. In the Print dialog box that appears, select the printer to be used, set the Number of copies to the proper value, and click the **OK** button.

After printing, you should verify the contents of your printout. Most printing problems or failures will trigger the display of an informational dialog box. Click the OK button of any such dialog box and correct the problem noted before attempting a second print operation.

A P P E N D I X 9 . 3

USING MINITAB FOR CHARTS AND DESCRIPTIVE STATISTICS

In this chapter, several charts along with descriptive statistics have been developed. Some of these as well as others not discussed in this book can be obtained using Minitab. If you have not already read Appendix A9.2, Introduction to Minitab, you should do so now.

Obtaining a Bar Chart

To obtain the bar chart in Figure 9.1 on page 237, open the 🌐 **KEYBOARD** worksheet. Select **Graph → Bar Chart.**

1. In the Bar Charts dialog box (see Figure A9.6), in the Bars represent: drop-down list box, select **Values from a table.** Select the **Simple** choice. Click the **OK** button.

2. In the Bar Chart—Values from a table, one column of values, Simple dialog box (see Figure A9.7), enter **C2** or **Frequency** in the Categorical Variables: edit box. Enter **Cause** in the Categorical variable: edit box. Click the **OK** button.

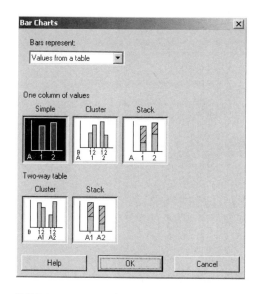

FIGURE A9.6 Minitab Bar Charts Dialog Box

To select colors for the bars and borders in the bar chart:

1. Right-click on any of the bars of the bar chart.

2. Select Edit Bars.

3. In the Attributes tab of the Edit bars dialog box (see Figure A9.8), enter selections for Fill pattern and Border and Fill Lines.

Obtaining a Pareto Diagram

To obtain the Pareto diagram of Figure 9.2 on page 238, open the **KEYBOARD.MTW** worksheet. Note that this data set contains the causes of the defects in column C1 and the frequency of defects in column C2. Select **Stat → Quality Tools → Pareto Chart.** In the Pareto Chart dialog box (see Figure A9.9):

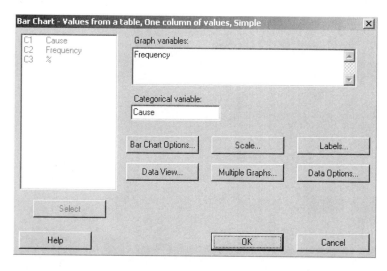

FIGURE A9.7 Minitab Bar Chart—Values from a Table, One Column of Values, Simple Dialog Box

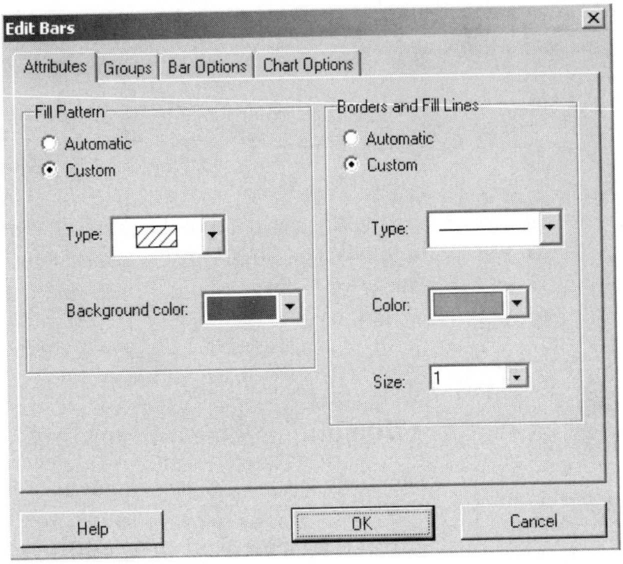

FIGURE A9.8 Minitab Edit Bars Dialog Box

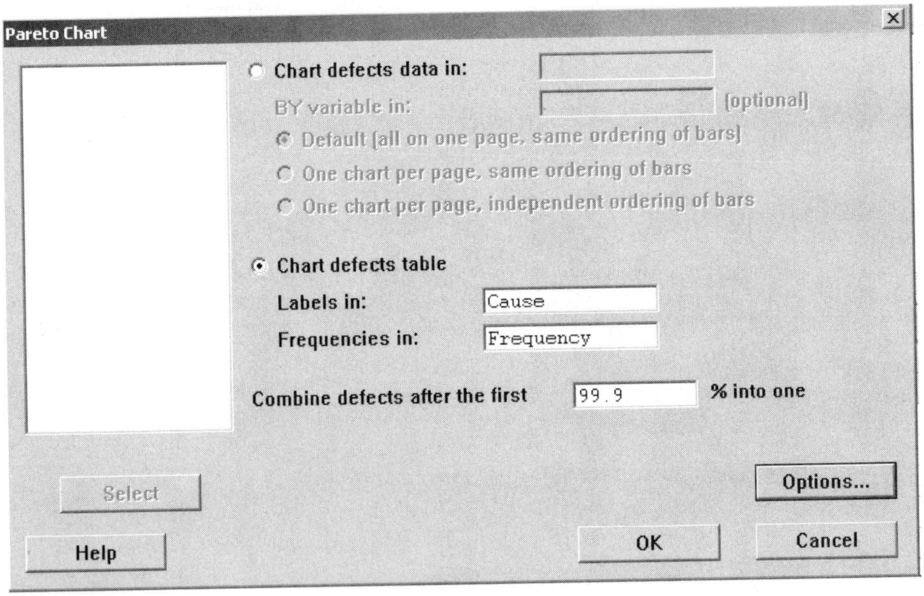

FIGURE A9.9 Minitab Pareto Chart Dialog Box

1. Select the **Chart defects table** option button.

2. In the Labels in: edit box, enter **C1** or **Cause.**

3. In the Frequencies in: edit box, enter **C2** or **Frequency.**

4. In the Combine defects after the first edit box, enter **99.9.**

5. Click the **OK** button.

If the variable of interest is located in a single column and is in raw form with each row indicating a type of error, you select the Charts defects data in: option button and enter the appropriate column number or variable name in the Chart defects data in: edit box.

To select colors for the bars and borders in the Pareto diagram:

1. Right-click on any of the bars of the Pareto diagram.

2. Select Edit Bars.

3. In the Attributes tab of the Edit bars dialog box, enter selections for Fill pattern and Border and Fill Lines (see Figure A9.8).

Obtaining a Run Chart

To obtain the run chart in Figure 9.3 on page 240, open the 🌐 **TRANSMIT** worksheet. To obtain a run chart of the percentage of errors,

1. Enter the label Error% in column C3.

2. Select **Calc → Calculator.**

3. In the Calculator dialog box (see Figure A9.10), enter **C3** or **Error%** in the Store

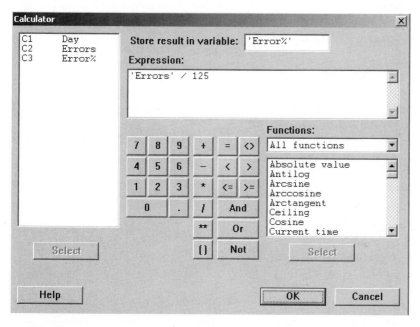

FIGURE A9.10 Minitab Calculator Dialog Box

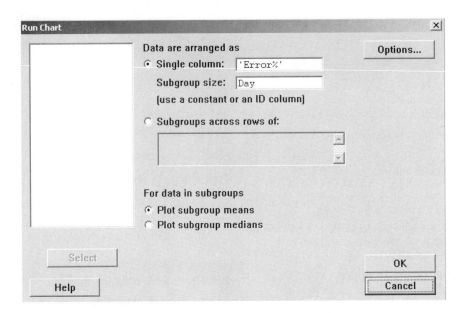

FIGURE A9.11 Minitab Run Chart Dialog Box

result in variable: edit box. To obtain the percentage of errors, enter **Errors / 125** in the Expression edit box. Click the **OK** button.

4. Select **Stat → Quality Tools → Run Chart.**

5. In the Run Chart dialog box (see Figure A9.11), select the Single column: option button. Enter **C3** or **Error%** in the edit box. Enter **C1** or **Day** in the Subgroup size: edit box. Click the **OK** button.

Obtaining a Histogram

To obtain the histogram in Figure 9.4 on page 241, open the 🖴 **CHEMICAL.MTW** worksheet. Select **Graph → Histogram.**

1. In the Histograms dialog box (see Figure A9.12), select **Simple.** Click the **OK** button.

2. In the Histogram—Simple dialog box (see Figure A9.13), enter **C2** or **Viscosity** in the Graph variables: edit box. To obtain reference lines, select the **Scale** button.

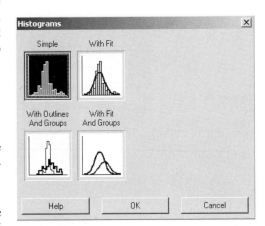

FIGURE A9.12 Minitab Histograms Dialog Box

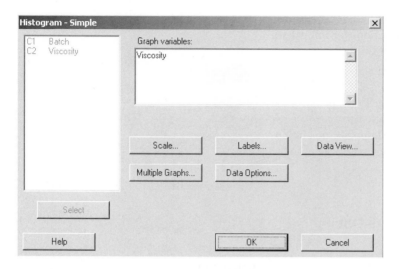

FIGURE A9.13 Minitab Histogram—Simple Dialog Box

3. In the Histogram-Scale dialog box (see Figure A9.14), select the **Reference Lines** tab. Enter **13** and **18** in the Show reference lines at X (data scale) positions. Click the **OK** button to return to the Histogram—Simple dialog box. Click the **OK** button to obtain the histogram.

To select colors for the bars and borders in the histogram:

1. Right-click on any of the bars of the histogram.

2. Select Edit Bars.

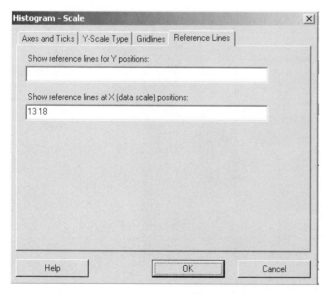

FIGURE A9.14 Minitab Histogram—Scale Dialog Box

3. In the Attributes tab of the Edit bars dialog box, enter selections for Fill pattern and Border and Fill Lines.

4. To define your own class groupings, select the Binning tab. Select the Midpoints option button to specify midpoints or the Cutpoint option button to specify class limits. Select the Midpoint/Cutpoint option button. Enter the set of values in the edit box.

Using Minitab to Obtain a Dot Plot

To obtain a Dot plot using Minitab, open the **CHEMICAL.MTW** worksheet. Select **Graph → Dotplot,** then do the following:

1. In the Dotplots dialog box (see Figure A9.15), select the **One Y Simple** choice. If dot plots of more than one group are desired, select the **One Y With Groups** Choice.

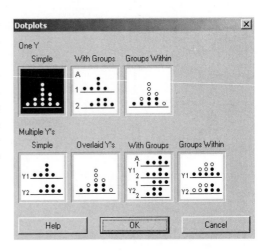

FIGURE A9.15 Minitab Dotplots Dialog Box

2. In the Dotplot—One Y, Simple dialog box (see Figure A9.16), in the Graph variables: edit box, enter **C2** or **Viscosity.** Click the **OK** button.

The output obtained will be similar to Figure 9.5 on page 242.

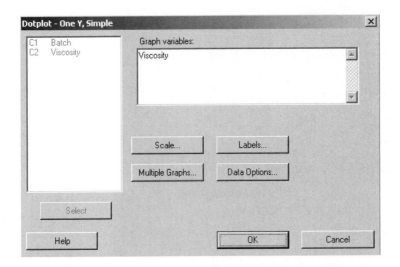

FIGURE A9.16 Minitab Dotplot—One Y, Simple Dialog Box

Obtaining Descriptive Statistics

To obtain the descriptive statistics for the viscosity of the chemical shown in Figure 9.8 on page 249, open the 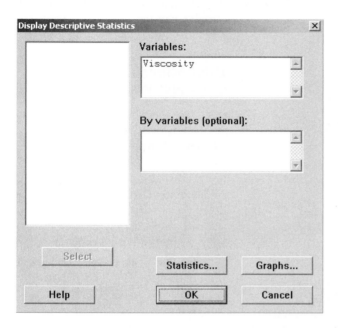 CHEMICAL.MTW worksheet. Select **Stat → Basic Statistics → Display Descriptive Statistics.**

FIGURE A9.17 Minitab Display Descriptive Statistics Dialog Box

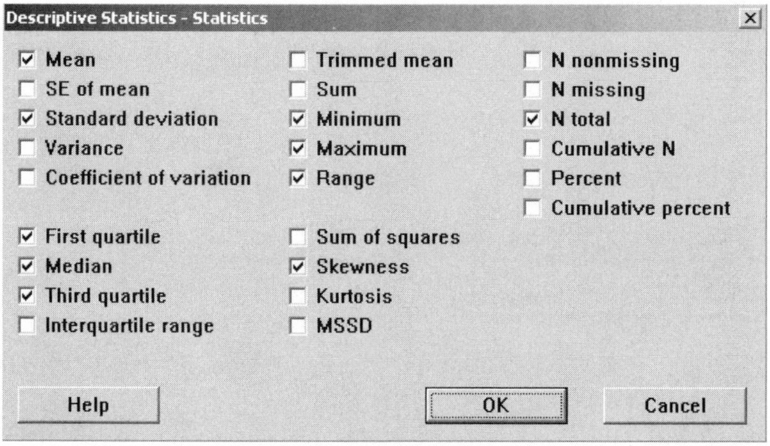

FIGURE A9.18 Minitab Display Descriptive Statistics—Statistics Dialog Box

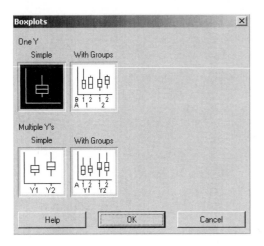

FIGURE A9.19 Minitab Boxplots Dialog Box

1. In the Display Descriptive Statistics dialog box (see Figure A9.17), enter **C2** or **Viscosity** in the Variables: edit box.

2. Select the **Statistics** button. In the Display Descriptive Statistics—Statistics dialog box (see Figure A9.18), select the **Mean, Standard deviation, First quartile, Median, Third quartile, Minimum, Maximum, Range, Skew-**

ness, and **N total** (the sample size) check boxes (see Figure A9.18), Click the **OK** button to return to the Display Descriptive Statistics dialog box. Click the **OK** button again to obtain the descriptive statistics.

Using Minitab to Obtain a Box-and-Whisker Plot

To obtain a box-and-whisker plot using Minitab, open the **CHEMICAL.MTW** worksheet. Select **Graph → Boxplot.**

1. In the Boxplots dialog box (see Figure A9.19), select the **One Y Simple** choice. If you want to obtain a side-by-side box-and-whisker plot for two or more groups, select the **One Y With Groups** choice.

2. In the Boxplot—One Y, Simple dialog box (see Figure A9.20), enter **C2** or **Viscosity** in the Graph variables: edit box. Click the **OK** button.

The output obtained will be similar to Figure 9.14 on page 258.

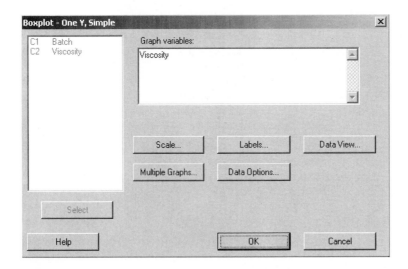

FIGURE A9.20 Minitab Boxplots—One Y, Simple Dialog Box

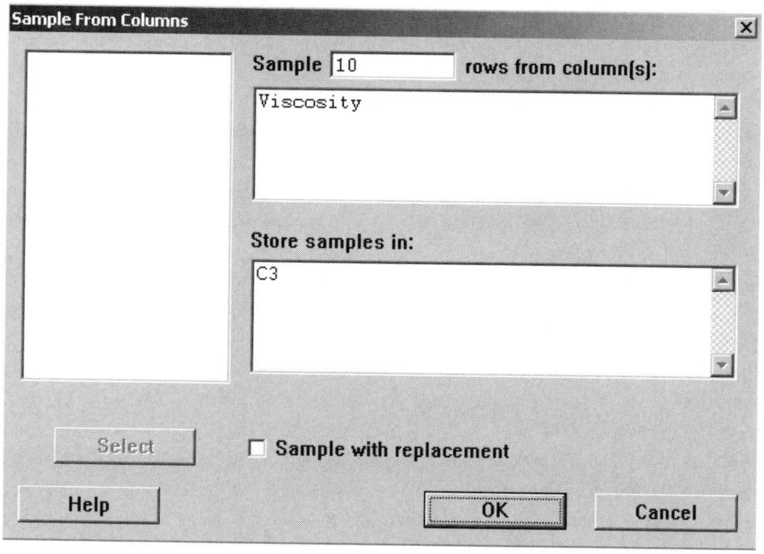

FIGURE A9.21 Minitab Sample From Columns Dialog Box

Using Minitab to Select a Random Sample

To obtain a random sample from a population using Minitab, open the **CHEMICAL.MTW** worksheet. Select **Calc → Random Data → Sample from Columns,** then do the following:

1. In the Sample From Columns dialog box (see Figure A9.21), enter **10** in the Sample rows from column(s): edit box.

2. Enter **Viscosity** or **C2** in the edit box. Enter **C3** in the Store samples in: edit box. Click the **OK** button.

Figure A9.22 illustrates the sample results. Note that if these instructions are repeated, a different sample of 10 data points would be selected.

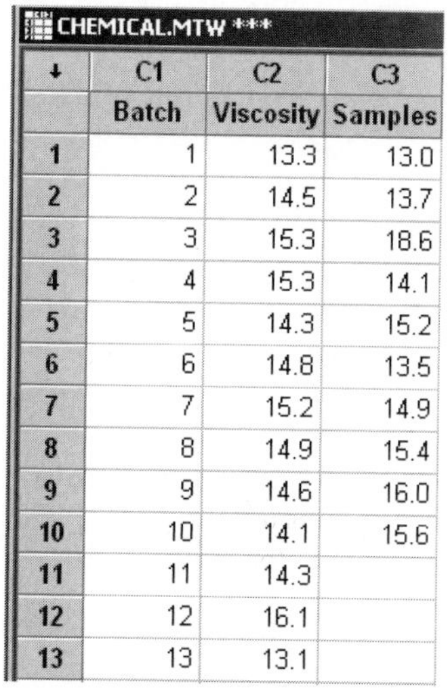

	C1	C2	C3
↓	Batch	Viscosity	Samples
1	1	13.3	13.0
2	2	14.5	13.7
3	3	15.3	18.6
4	4	15.3	14.1
5	5	14.3	15.2
6	6	14.8	13.5
7	7	15.2	14.9
8	8	14.9	15.4
9	9	14.6	16.0
10	10	14.1	15.6
11	11	14.3	
12	12	16.1	
13	13	13.1	

CHEMICAL.MTW *

FIGURE A9.22 Minitab Sample of 10 Viscosities selected from a Population of 120 Viscosities

PROBABILITY AND PROBABILITY DISTRIBUTIONS

CHAPTER OUTLINE

LEARNING OBJECTIVES

After reading this chapter, you will be able to:

- Understand basic probability concepts
- Understand the basic properties of a probability distribution
- Be able to compute the mean and standard deviation of a probability distribution
- Understand when to use the binomial, Poisson, and normal distributions and how to compute probabilities using these distributions
- Use a normal probability plot to evaluate whether a set of data is normally distributed

10.1 Introduction to Probability

The word *probability* is often used as a synonym for *chance, likelihood,* or *possibility*—words that you hear all the time with respect to the behavior of cycle times, safety (accidents), or quality of products or services. A **probability** is just the numeric value representing the chance, likelihood, or possibility that a particular event will occur, such as a defective customer transaction, a cycle time greater than 20 minutes, or an OSHA (Occupational Safety and Health Administration) reportable accident. In all these instances, the probability attached is a proportion or fraction whose values range *between 0 and 1, inclusively.*

The basic elements of probability theory are the individual outcomes of a particular process, such as an experimental trial or a natural phenomenon. Each possible type of occurrence is referred to as an **event**. Each individual or distinct outcome is referred to as an **elementary event**. For example, when making a sales call, the two possible outcomes are close and fail to close. Each of these represents an elementary event. When rolling a standard six-sided die (see Figure 10.1), in which the six faces of the die contain either one, two, three, four, five, or six dots, there are six possible elementary events. An event can be any one of these elementary events, or a set of several of them. For example, the event of an *even number of dots* is represented by three elementary events (i.e., two, four, or six dots).

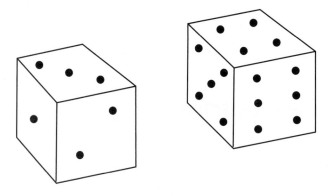

FIGURE 10.1 The Six Sides of a Pair of Dice

There are three distinct approaches for assigning probability to an event occurring: the classical approach; the empirical (relative frequency) approach; and the subjective approach.

The **classical approach** for assigning probability is based on prior knowledge of the population involved. Classical probability often assumes that all elementary events are equally likely to occur. When this is true, *P(A)*, the probability that a particular event *A* will occur is defined by:

$$\text{Probability of event } A = \frac{\text{number of ways } A \text{ can occur}}{\text{total number of elementary events}}$$

Probability of Event A (optional)

$$P(A) = \frac{X_A}{T} \tag{10.1}$$

where

X_A = number of ways A can occur and

T = total number of elementary events.

Classical probability is illustrated by referring to the standard six-sided die shown in Figure 10.1. If the die is rolled a single time, the probability of obtaining the face with three dots is 1/6, because there is only one face that contains exactly three dots out of a total of six possible faces (i.e., elementary events). The assumption made by the classical approach is that the die rolling process is totally random and has no memory, so that each of the six faces is equally likely to occur on each and every roll of the die. Thus, on any roll, the probability of obtaining the face with three dots remains 1/6. In the long run, assuming that the process is working properly, you would theoretically expect 1,000 out of 6,000 rolls to result in a face with three dots.

The **empirical (relative frequency) approach to probability** states that if an experiment were conducted a large number of times (say, M times), the probability of event A occurring is:

$$P(A) = \frac{k}{M} \tag{10.2}$$

where

k = the number of times A occurred during these experiments and

M = the maximum number of times that event A could have occurred during these experiments.

For example, suppose that in processing bank loans, a study of the most recent 500 loan applications indicated that the type of loan requested was omitted 12 times. Consequently, the relative frequency probability of omitting the type of loan requested is:

$$P(\text{omit type of loan requested}) = \frac{12}{500} = 0.024$$

Analytic studies are conducted to determine process characteristics. However, process characteristics have a past and present and will have a future. Thus, there is no frame from which classical probabilities can be calculated. Probabilities concerning process characteristics must be obtained empirically, through experimentation, and must therefore be relative frequency probabilities. For example, a newly hired worker is expected to perform an administrative operation, entering data from sales slips into a computer terminal. Is it possible to predict the percentage of entries per hour that will be in error? Unfortunately not; the best you can do is to train workers properly, then observe them performing their jobs over a long period of time. If a worker's efforts represent a stable system (more on this in Chapter 14), you can compute the relative frequency of sales slips entered per hour, with errors as an estimate of the probability of a sales slip's being entered with errors. This relative frequency probability can be used to predict the percentage of sales slips per hour entered with errors.

It is not always possible to use the classical approach or the empirical approach when assigning probabilities. In many circumstances, where either the number of elementary events or actual data is not available for the calculation of relative frequencies, the **subjective approach** is often used. Subjective probabilities can be based on expert opinion or even gut feelings or hunches. Whereas the process knowledge-based classical approach and the observed databased empirical approach to probability assignment are considered *objective*, a subjective approach to probability assessment is used when individuals employ various modes of intuition to judge the likely outcome of an event. Different individuals might provide differing assessments as to what future traffic patterns will be, what the weather will be like tomorrow, or what future economic conditions will be.

10.2 SOME RULES OF PROBABILITY

There are several basic rules that govern the theory of probability.

Rule 1: A probability is a number between 0 and 1 that is assigned to an event or outcome of some process or experiment.

The smallest possible probability value is zero. An event or outcome that has a probability of zero is called a *null event* and has no chance of occurring. In the case of the die, the event of obtaining a face of seven has a probability of zero because such an event cannot occur. No event can possibly have a probability below zero.

The largest possible probability value is 1.0. An event or outcome that has a probability of 1.0 is called a *certain event* and must occur. When rolling a single die, the event of obtaining a face with fewer than seven dots has a probability of 1.0 because it is certain that one of the elementary events of one, two, three, four, five, or six dots must occur. This set of elementary events is also considered to be **collectively exhaustive,** because one of them must occur. No event can have a probability above 1.0.

> Rule 2: The event that *A* does not occur is called "*A* complement" or simply "not *A*" and is given the symbol *A'*. If *P(A)* represents the probability of event *A* occurring, 1 – *P(A)* represents the probability of event *A* not occurring or *P(A')*.

For example, in the case of the bank loan application, the complement of observing that the type of loan requested was omitted is observing that the type of loan requested is checked. Because the probability of omitting the type of loan request is 12/500, the probability of not omitting the type of loan request is 1–[12/500] = 488/500 or

P (Not omitting loan request) = 1 – P(omitting loan request)

= 1 – 12/500

= 488/500
= 0.976

> Rule 3: If two events *A* and *B* are *mutually exclusive,* the probability of both events *A* and *B* occurring simultaneously is zero.

If two events are **mutually exclusive,** they *cannot* occur at the same time. When rolling a standard six-sided die in which the six faces of the die contain either one, two, three, four, five, or six dots, there are six possible elementary events. On one roll of a single die, the face of the die cannot have three dots *and* also have four dots. It can have one or the other, but not both.

> Rule 4: If two events *A* and *B* are *mutually exclusive,* the probability of either event *A or* event *B* occurring is the sum of their separate probabilities

In the example concerning the single die, if you wanted to determine the probability of obtaining a face that has two dots *or* three dots, then:

P(face 2 *or* 3) = P (face 2) + P (face 3)

$$= \frac{1}{6} + \frac{1}{6}$$

$$P(\text{face 2 } or \text{ 3}) = \frac{2}{6} = \frac{1}{3} = 0.333$$

This addition rule for mutually exclusive events can be extended to consider cases in which there are more than two events. In the case of the die, suppose you wanted to know the probability of obtaining an even-numbered outcome (i.e., two, four, or six dots). Then:

$$P(\text{even}) = P(\text{face 2 } or \text{ 4 } or \text{ 6}) = P(\text{face 2}) + P(\text{face 4}) + P(\text{face 6})$$

$$= \frac{1}{6} + \frac{1}{6} + \frac{1}{6}$$

$$= \frac{3}{6} = \frac{1}{2}$$

$$P(\text{even}) = P(\text{face 2 } or \text{ 4 } or \text{ 6}) = 0.50$$

Rule 5: If events in a set are mutually exclusive and collectively exhaustive, the sum of their probabilities must add to 1.0.

In the example of the single die, the events of a face with an even number of dots and a face with an odd number of dots are mutually exclusive and collectively exhaustive. They are mutually exclusive because even and odd cannot occur simultaneously on the roll of a single die. They are also collectively exhaustive because either even or odd must occur on a particular roll. Therefore, the probability of a face with an even *or* odd number of dots is:

$$P(\text{even } or \text{ odd}) = P(\text{face 2 } or \text{ 4 } or \text{ 6}) + P(\text{face 1 } or \text{ 3 } or \text{ 5})$$

$$= \frac{3}{6} + \frac{3}{6}$$

$$P(\text{even } or \text{ odd}) = \frac{6}{6} = 1.0$$

Rule 6: If two events *A* and *B* are *not* mutually exclusive, the probability of either event *A or* event *B* occurring is the sum of their separate probabilities minus the probability of their simultaneous occurrence (called *joint probability*).

To illustrate this rule, consider the example concerning the die. The events of a face with an even number of dots and a face with fewer than 5 dots are not mutually exclusive because the result two dots and the result four dots each satisfy the criteria of having an even number of dots and also having fewer than five dots. Thus, to determine the probability of having a face with an even number of dots or having a face with fewer than five dots, you add the probability of having a face with an even number of dots to the probability of having a face with fewer than five dots, then subtract the joint probability of simultaneously having a face with an even number of dots and having a face with fewer than five dots. The reason that this joint probability must be subtracted is that it has already been included twice in computing the probability of having a face with an even number of dots and having a face with fewer than five dots. Therefore, because it has been "double counted," it must be subtracted to provide the correct result. Thus:

P (having a face with an even number of dots *or* having a face with fewer than five dots)
= *P (having a face with an even number of dots)* + *P (having a face with fewer than five dots)*
− *P* (having a face with an even number of dots *and* having a face with fewer than five dots)

$$= \frac{3}{6} + \frac{4}{6} - \frac{2}{6}$$

$$= \frac{5}{6}$$

$$= 0.833$$

Rule 7: If two events *A and B* are *independent,* the probability of both events *A and B* occurring is equal to the product of their respective probabilities. Two events are **independent** if the occurrence of one event in no way affects the probability of the second event.

In the case of rolling a single die twice, it is reasonable to assume that the result of the first roll is independent of the result of the second roll. Thus, to determine the probability that you would obtain the face that contains five dots on *each* of two rolls, you have:

$$P(5 \text{ dots on roll } 1 \textit{ and } 5 \text{ dots on roll } 2) = P(5 \text{ dots on roll } 1) \times P(5 \text{ dots on roll } 2)$$

$$= \frac{1}{6} \times \frac{1}{6}$$

$$= \frac{1}{36}$$

Rule 8: If two events *A and B* are *not* independent, the probability of both events *A and B* occurring is the product of the probability of event *A* times the conditional probability of event *B* occurring, given that event *A* has occurred.

To show an example of events that are not independent, consider a standard deck of 52 cards that contains four suits (hearts, diamonds, clubs, and spades), each having 13 cards (Ace, 2, 3, 4, 5, 6, 7, 8, 9, 10, Jack, Queen, and King). If the deck was thoroughly shuffled and you selected two cards from the deck, what is the probability that both cards are hearts?

The probability that the first card selected is a heart is 13/52 or 1/4, because 13 of the 52 cards are hearts. However, because the second card is selected without returning the first card to the deck, the number of cards remaining after the first selection is 51. If the first card is a heart, the probability that the second is a heart is 12/51, because 12 hearts remain in the deck. Therefore:

$$P(\text{heart on first and heart on second}) = \left(\left(\frac{13}{52} \right) \left(\frac{12}{51} \right) \right)$$

$$= \frac{156}{2,652}$$
$$= 0.0588$$

Thus, there is a 5.88% chance that both cards selected will be hearts.

10.3 PROBABILITY DISTRIBUTIONS

Now that probability has been defined and some rules of probability have been illustrated, we can examine a variable that has many different outcomes. Consider the number of possible closes that can occur in three independent sales calls in which the probability of a close is 0.5 on each sales call. This example assumes that based on past history, you know that each time a sales person makes a sales call, the result (close or fail) is independent of any other sales call and the probability of closing a sale on any randomly selected call is 0.50.

The possible outcomes that can occur in terms of the number of closes are as shown in Table 10.1.

TABLE 10.1 Outcomes of Three Sales Calls

No. possible outcomes	First sales call	Second sales call	Third sales call
1	Close	Close	Close
2	Close	Close	Fail to close
3	Close	Fail to close	Close
4	Close	Fail to close	Fail to close
5	Fail to close	Close	Close
6	Fail to close	Close	Fail to close
7	Fail to close	Fail to close	Close
8	Fail to close	Fail to close	Fail to close

The probability of occurrence of a particular outcome (for example, first sales call is close [C_1], second sales call is close [C_2], and third sales call is close [C_3]) is obtained by extending Rule 7 of probability (see page 285) to the case of three events. Thus,

$$P(C_1 \text{ and } C_2 \text{ and } C_3) = P(C_1) \times P(C_2) \times P(C_3)$$

Because each sales call has a probability of Close of 0.5,

$$P(C_1 \text{ and } C_2 \text{ and } C_3) = (0.5)\,(0.5)\,(0.5) = 0.125.$$

Another way of looking at this example is to consider each of the rows in Table 10.1 as a distinct elementary event. Because the event C_1 and C_2 and C_3 can occur only one way, and there are eight elementary events,

$$\text{Probability of event } C_1 \text{ and } C_2 \text{ and } C_3 = \frac{\text{number of ways event can occur}}{\text{total number of elementary events}}$$

$$P(C_1 \text{ and } C_2 \text{ and } C_3) = \frac{1}{8} = 0.125$$

Similar calculations can be made for each of the other seven possible outcomes, because in this instance, the probability that the outcome of a sales call is a close is 0.5; therefore, the probability of being a close is the same as the probability of being a fail to close. The results are organized in terms of the probability of obtaining a particular number of closes in three independent sales calls. The results for all the possible outcomes* are summarized in Table 10.2.

TABLE 10.2 Distribution of the Number of Closes in Three Independent Sales Calls in Which the Probability of a Close is 0.50

Number of closes	Frequency	Probability
0	1	0.125
1	3	0.375
2	3	0.375
3	1	0.125
	8	1.000

Table 10.2 is an example of a probability distribution for a discrete variable. A **discrete variable** is one that is based on a count of the number of occurrences of an attribute, such as number of closes, number of defective items, or number of blemishes in a yard of wallpaper.

---

*This is actually an example of a process that follows the binomial distribution which will be covered in Section 10.4.

> A **probability distribution** for a discrete random variable is a listing of all possible distinct outcomes and their probabilities of occurring. Because all possible outcomes are listed, the sum of the probabilities must add to 1.0.

Table 10.2 satisfies this definition of the probability distribution because all outcomes (0, 1, 2, and 3 closes) are listed, and the sum of the probabilities adds to 1.0.

The Average or Expected Value of a Random Variable

The mean (μ) of a probability distribution is also called the **expected value** of the distribution. The mean (μ) of a probability distribution is obtained by multiplying each possible outcome X by its corresponding probability, then summing the resulting products.

Mean = sum of [each value $\times$ the probability of each value]

If there are three sales calls per day (Table 10.2), you can calculate the mean or expected value of the number of closes as done in Table 10.3:

Mean = sum of [each value $\times$ the probability of each value]

Mean = $(0)(0.125) + (1)(0.375) + (2)(0.375) + (3)(0.125)$

$= 0 + 0.375 + 0.750 + 0.375$
$= 1.50$

Notice that in this example, the average or expected value of the number of Closes is 1.5, a value for the number of closes that is impossible. The average of 1.5 closes tells you that, in the long run, if you make three sales calls per day for many days, the average number of closes you can expect is 1.5.

Mean of a Probability Distribution (optional)

$$\mu = \sum_{i=1}^{N} X_i P(X_i) \tag{10.3}$$

where

X = random variable of interest

X_i = ith outcome of X

$P(X_i)$ = probability of occurrence of the ith outcome of X

$i = 1, 2, \ldots, N$

N = the number of outcomes for X

TABLE 10.3 Computing the Expected Value of a Probability Distribution

Number of Closes	Probability	(number of closes) × (probability)
0	0.125	$(0) \times (0.125) = 0$
1	0.375	$(1) \times (0.375) = 0.375$
2	0.375	$(2) \times (0.375) = 0.75$
3	0.125	$(3) \times (0.125) = 0.375$
		$= 1.50$

Standard Deviation of a Random Variable (σ)

As was the case with sample data, the standard deviation of a probability distribution is a measure of variation around the mean or expected value. This summary measure is obtained by multiplying the squared difference between each possible value and the mean by its corresponding probability, summing the resulting products, then taking the square root of this result.

σ = standard deviation = square root of [sum of (squared differences between a value and the mean) × (probability of the value)]

If there are three sales calls per day (Table 10.2 on page 287), you can calculate the standard deviation of the number of closes as is done in Table 10.4

σ = standard deviation = square root of [sum of (squared differences between a value and the mean) × (probability of the value)]

$\sigma^2 = (0 - 1.5)^2(0.125) + (1 - 1.5)^2(0.375) + (2 - 1.5)^2(0.375) + (3 - 1.5)^2(0.125)$

$= 2.25(0.125) + .25(.375) + .25(.375) + 2.25(.125)$

$= 0.75$

and

$\sigma = \sqrt{0.75} = 0.866$

Standard Deviation of a Probability Distribution (optional)

$$\sigma = \sqrt{\sum_{i=1}^{N} (X_i - \mu)^2 P(X_i)} \tag{10.4}$$

where

X = random variable of interest

X_i = ith outcome of X

$P(X_i)$ = probability of occurrence of ith outcome of X

$i = 1, 2, \ldots, N$

N = number of outcomes for X

TABLE 10.4 Computing the Standard Deviation of a Probability Distribution

Number of Closes	Probability	(number of closes – average number of closes)^2 × (probability)
0	0.125	$(0 - 1.5)^2 \times (0.125) = 2.25 \times (0.125) = 0.28125$
1	0.375	$(1 - 1.5)^2 \times (0.375) = 0.25 \times (0.375) = 0.09375$
2	0.375	$(2 - 1.5)^2 \times (0.375) = 0.25 \times (0.375) = 0.09375$
3	0.125	$(3 - 1.5)^2 \times (0.125) = 2.25 \times (0.125) = 0.28125$
		$\sigma = \sqrt{0.75} = 0.866$

One common application for the mean and standard deviation of a probability distribution is in finance. Suppose that you are deciding between two alternative investments. Investment A is a mutual fund whose portfolio consists of a combination of stocks that make up the Dow Jones Industrial Average. Investment B consists of shares of a growth stock. You estimate the returns (per $1,000 investment) for each investment alternative under three economic conditions (recession, stable economy, and expanding economy); you also provide your subjective probability of the occurrence of each economic condition. The results are summarized in Table 10.5.

The mean return for the two investments is computed as follows.

Mean for the Dow Jones fund = $(-100)(0.2) + (100)(0.5) + (250)(0.3) = \$105$
Mean for the Growth stock = $(-200)(0.2) + (50)(0.5) + (350)(0.3) = \$90$

TABLE 10.5 Estimated Return for Two Investments under Three Economic Conditions

Probability	Economic condition	Investment	
		Dow Jones fund (A)	Growth stock (B)
0.2	Recession	−$100	−$200
0.5	Stable economy	+ 100	+ 50
0.3	Expanding economy	+ 250	+ 350

You can calculate the standard deviation for the two investments as is done in Tables 10.6 and 10.7

σ = standard deviation = square root of [sum of (squared differences between a value and the mean) × (probability of the value)]

$$\sigma_A = \sqrt{(0.2)(-100 - 105)^2 + (0.5)(100 - 105)^2 + (0.3)(250 - 105)^2}$$
$$= \sqrt{14,725}$$
$$= \$121.35$$

TABLE 10.6 Computing the Variance for Dow Jones Fund (A)

Probability	Economic Event	Dow Jones Fund (A)	(return − average return)² × probability
0.2	Recession	−$100	$(-100 - 105)^2 \times (0.2) = (42,025) \times (0.2)$ $= 8,405$
0.5	Stable economy	+ 100	$(100 - 105)^2 \times (0.5) = (25) \times (0.5) = 12.5$
0.3	Expanding economy	+ 250	$(250 - 105)^2 \times (0.3) = (21,025) \times (0.3)$ $= 6,307.5$ $\sigma = \sqrt{14,725} = \$121.35$

TABLE 10.7 Computing the Standard Deviation for Growth Stock (B)

Probability	Economic Event	Growth Stock (B)	(return − average return)² × probability
0.2	Recession	−$200	$(-200 - 90)^2 \times (0.2) = (84,100) \times (0.2)$ $= 16,820$
0.5	Stable economy	+ 50	$(50 - 90)^2 \times (0.5) = (1,600) \times (0.5) = 800$
0.3	Expanding economy	+ 350	$(350 - 90)^2 \times (0.3) = (67,600) \times (0.3)$ $= 20,280$ $\sigma = \sqrt{37,900} = \$194.68$

$$\sigma_B = \sqrt{(0.2)(-200 - 90)^2 + (0.5)(50 - 90)^2 + (0.3)(350 - 90)^2}$$
$$= \sqrt{37,900}$$
$$= \$194.68$$

Thus, the Dow Jones fund has a higher mean return than the growth fund and has a lower standard deviation, indicating less variation in the return under the different economic conditions. Having a higher return with less variation makes the Dow Jones fund a more desirable investment than the growth fund.

In this section, the concept of a probability distribution and the mean or expected value and standard deviation of a discrete probability distribution were defined. In the remainder of the chapter, two specific discrete probability distributions that are important in statistics and Six Sigma management will be developed, along with a very important distribution, the normal distribution, which is used for measurement or continuous data.

10.4 BINOMIAL DISTRIBUTION

Many studies involving probability distributions are based on attribute data that results from classifying the outcomes of a variable (key indicator) into only two categories, arbitrarily called *success* or *failure, defect* or *conforming, on time* or *late*, etc. When classifying each outcome as either a success or a failure, it is not important which outcome is classified as a success and which is classified as a failure. For example, in the context of statistical process control (see Chapter 14), an item that has failed inspection could be classified as a success, because the goal in process control is usually to study nonconformances. In such circumstances, the binomial probability distribution can be used to analyze the number of nonconforming items in a sample of *n* units.

Binomial distribution has four essential properties, as shown in Exhibit 10.1.

Exhibit 10.1   **Properties of the Binomial Distribution**

1. The sample consists of a fixed number of observations, called *n*.
2. Each elementary event is classified into one of two mutually exclusive and collectively exhaustive categories, usually called *success* or *failure*.
3. The probability of an outcome being classified as success, *p*, is constant from observation to observation, and the probability of an outcome being classified as failure, 1 − *p*, is constant over all observations.
4. The outcome (success or failure) of any observation is independent of the outcome of any other observation.

To demonstrate an application of the binomial distribution, suppose that three sales calls are made per day, and the probability of a close is 0.50 on any randomly selected sales call. The sales call data fits the binomial distribution if:

1. There is a fixed number of observations (three sales calls per day),
2. Each observation is classified into one of two categories (close or fail to close),
3. The probability of a close is the same on all sales calls ($p = 0.5$), and
4. The outcome on one sales call is independent of the outcome on any other sales call.

To determine the probability of obtaining one close in three sales calls, from Table 10.1 on page 286, observe that of the eight possible outcomes, there are three ways of obtaining one close in three sales calls.

Close	Fail to close	Fail to close
Fail to close	Close	Fail to close
Fail to close	Fail to close	Close

Because there are eight equally likely possible outcomes, the probability of one close in three sales calls is 3/8 = 0.375, as shown in Table 10.2 on page 287.

In most cases, the probability of success (closing on a sales call) is not 0.5. In addition, the number of observations is usually much greater than three. The equation for determining the probability of a particular number of successes (X) for a given number of observations n can be developed by realizing that the result for one close in three sales calls was obtained as the product of:

number of ways to obtain one close in three sales calls × probability of one close in three sales calls in a specific order.

From Table 10.1, there are three ways to obtain one close in three sales calls. The probability of one close in three sales calls in a specific order (such as close-fail to close-fail to close) is equal to:

$$P(C_1 \text{ and } F_2 \text{ and } F_3) = P(C_1) \times P(F_2) \times P(F_3)$$

If p = the probability of a close, then $(1 - p)$ equals the probability of a fail to close. Then:

$$P(C_1) \times P(F_2) \times P(F_3) = p \times (1 - p) \times (1 - p)$$
$$= p \times (1 - p)^2$$
$$= (0.5) \times (1 - 0.5)^2$$
$$= 0.125$$

Multiplying $3 \times 0.125 = 0.375$

This is the probability of obtaining one close in three sales calls in any order of occurrence.

A similar intuitive derivation can be done for any combination of *n*, the number of observations; *p*, the probability of success; and *X*, the number of successes. Instead, however, Minitab can be used as illustrated in Figure 10.2.

```
Binomial with n = 3 and p = 0.5

x   P( X = x )
0      0.125
1      0.375
2      0.375
3      0.125
```

FIGURE 10.2 Minitab Binomial Distribution Calculations for *n* = 3 and *p* = 0.5

Minitab computes the probability of success for *X* = 0, 1, . . ., *n*.

Binomial Distribution (optional)

$$p(X = x|n, p) = \frac{n!}{x!(n - x)!}p^x(1 - p)^{n-x} \tag{10.5}$$

where

$P(X = x \,|n, p)$ = the probability that $X = x$, given a knowledge of *n* and *p*

n = sample size

p = probability of success

$1 - p$ = probability of failure

x = number of successes in the sample ($X = 0,1,2,\ldots, n$)

$n! = (n)(n-1)(n-2)\ldots (1)$.

0! is defined as equal to 1.

To determine the probability of one close in three sales calls,

$n = 3$, $p = 0.5$, and $x = 1$. Using Equation (10.5),

$$P(X = 1|n = 3, p = 0.5) = \frac{3!}{1!(3-1)!}(0.5)^1(1-(0.5))^{3-1}$$

$$= \frac{3!}{1!(2)!}(0.5)^1(1-(0.5))^2 = 3(0.5)^1(0.5)^2 = 3(0.5)^3$$

$$= 3(0.125) = 0.375$$

As a second example of the binomial distribution, suppose that five sales calls are made per day, but the probability of a close on any randomly selected sales call is a stable 0.16 from historical records. What is the probability of obtaining at least four (either four or five) closes in these five sales calls? Figure 10.3 illustrates Minitab output for this example.

```
Binomial with n = 5 and p = 0.16

x   P( X = x )
0     0.418212
1     0.398297
2     0.151732
3     0.028901
4     0.002753
5     0.000105
```

FIGURE 10.3 Minitab Binomial Distribution Calculations for $n = 5$ and $p = 0.16$

From Figure 10.3:

$P(X = 4|n = 5, p = 0.16) = 0.002753$
$P(X = 5|n = 5, p = 0.16) = 0.000105$

Thus, the probability of four or more closes = 0.002753 + 0.000105 = 0.002858, or 2.858 in a thousand.

Characteristics of the Binomial Distribution

Each time a set of parameters n and p is specified, a particular binomial probability distribution can be generated.

Shape. Binomial distributions can be symmetrical or skewed. Whenever $p = 0.5$, the binomial distribution will be symmetrical, regardless of how large or small the value of n. However, when $p \neq 0.5$, the distribution will be skewed. If $p < 0.5$, the distribution will be positive, or right-skewed; if $p > 0.5$, the distribution will be negative, or left-skewed. The closer p is to 0.5 and the larger the number of observations in the sample, n, the more symmetrical the distribution will be.

Mean. The mean of a binomial distribution is the product of the sample size, n, and the probability of success, p.

Mean = sample size × probability of success

Mean of the Binomial Distribution (optional)

$$\mu = np \tag{10.6}$$

For example, when dealing with three independent sales calls and $p = 0.5$, the mean was 1.5, the product of the sample size $n = 3$, and the probability of a close is a stable $p = 0.5$.

Mean = $3 \times 0.5 = 1.5$

Standard Deviation. The standard deviation of a binomial distribution is equal to the square root of the product of the sample size n, the probability of success p, and the probability of failure $(1 - p)$.

Standard deviation = square root [sample size × probability of success × (1 – probability of success]

Standard Deviation of the Binomial Distribution (optional)

$$\sigma_x = \sqrt{np(1 - p)} \tag{10.7}$$

For example, when dealing with three independent sales calls and the probability of a close is a stable $p = 0.5$, the standard deviation is 0.866, the square root of the product of the sample size 3, the probability of success 0.5, and the probability of failure $(1 - 0.5)$.

Standard deviation = square root $[3 \times (0.5) \times (1 - 0.5)] = 0.866$

10.5 POISSON DISTRIBUTION

Many studies are based on counts of the number of nonconformities or defects per *area of opportunity*. An **area of opportunity** is a continuous unit of time, space, or area in which more than one occurrence of an event can occur. Examples are the number of surface defects on a new refrigerator, the number of network failures in a day, or the number of accidents in a factory in a month. In such circumstances, the **Poisson probability distribution** can be used to calculate probabilities. This includes applications to the theory of area of opportunity control charts that will be discussed in Section 14.4. Exhibit 10.2 describes the properties that must exist in a specific situation to use Poisson distribution.

Exhibit 10.2	**The Poisson Distribution**

The Poisson distribution is used in situations that have the following properties:
1. You are counting the number of times a particular event occurs in a given area of opportunity. The area of opportunity is defined by time, space, geography, etc.
2. The probability that an event will occur in a given area of opportunity is the same for all of the areas of opportunity.
3. The number of events that occur in one area of opportunity is independent of the number of events that occur in other areas of opportunity.
4. The probability that two or more events will occur in an area of opportunity approaches zero as the area of opportunity becomes smaller.

Consider the number of customers arriving during the lunch hour at a bank located in the central business district in a large city. Of interest to you is the number of customers that arrive each minute. Does this situation match the four properties of Poisson distribution given in Exhibit 10.2? First, the *event* of interest is a customer arriving, and the given *area of opportunity* is defined as a 1-minute interval at the bank during lunch hour. Will zero customers arrive, one customer arrive, two customers arrive, etc.? Second, it is reasonable to assume that the probability that a customer arrives during a randomly selected 1-minute interval is the same for all 1-minute intervals. Third, the arrival of one customer in any 1-minute interval has no effect on (i.e., is statistically independent of) the arrival of any other customer in any other 1-minute interval. Finally, the probability that two or more customers will arrive in a given time period approaches zero as the time interval becomes small. For example, there is virtually no probability that two customers will arrive in a time interval with a width of $1/100^{th}$ of a second. Thus, the Poisson distribution (see Equation (10.8)) can be used to compute probabilities concerning the number of customers arriving at the bank in a 1-minute time interval during the lunch hour.

To demonstrate the application of the Poisson probability distribution, suppose that past data indicates that the average arrival of customers during the lunch hour is three per minute. To find the probability of the arrival of a particular number of customers in the next minute, Minitab can be used.

```
Poisson with mu = 3

x    P( X = x )
0      0.049787
1      0.149361
2      0.224042
3      0.224042
4      0.168031
5      0.100819
6      0.050409
7      0.021604
8      0.008102
9      0.002701
10     0.000810
11     0.000221
12     0.000055
```

FIGURE 10.4 Minitab Poisson Distribution Calculations for an Average of Three Arrivals Per Minute

Figure 10.4 illustrates the probability of the number of arrivals, from zero arrivals up to 12 arrivals. For example, observe that with an average of three arrivals per minute, the probability of zero arrivals is 0.049787, the probability of one arrival is 0.149361, the probability of two arrivals is 0.224042, whereas the probability of 12 arrivals is only 0.000055. Thus, to obtain the probability of two or fewer arrivals, you would add the probability of zero arrivals (0.049787), one arrival (0.149361), and two arrivals (0.224042) to obtain a final result of 0.42319.

Probability of two or fewer arrivals = 0.049787 + 0.149361 + 0.224042 = 0.42319

Thus, there is a 42.319% chance that two or fewer customers will arrive in the next minute if the average number of arrivals is three per minute.

Poisson Distribution (optional)

$$P(X = x|\lambda) = \frac{e^{-\lambda}\lambda^x}{x!} \tag{10.8}$$

where

$P(X = x|\lambda)$ = the probability that $X = x$, given a knowledge of λ

λ = average number of nonconformities per area of opportunity*

---

*It should be noted that λ is equal to DPU (defects per unit), when the number of DPU is distributed according to a Poisson distribution. Therefore, $P\{X = 0 \text{ Defects}\} = \dfrac{e^{-\lambda}\lambda^x}{x!} = \dfrac{e^{-\lambda}\lambda^0}{0!} = \exp(-\lambda) = \exp(-\text{DPU})$
= Yield as used in Chapter 2.

e = mathematical constant approximated by 2.71828

x = number of successes per area of opportunity in the sample ($X = 0,1,2,...,\infty$)

To determine the probability of exactly 2 arrivals in the next minute, given an average of three arrivals per minute in the bank during lunch hour, using equation (10.8)

$$P(X = 2|\lambda = 3) = \frac{e^{-3}(3)^2}{2!}$$

$$= \frac{(2.71828)^{-3}(3)^2}{2!}$$

$$= \frac{9}{(2.71828)^3(2)}$$

$$= 0.224042$$

Characteristics of the Poisson Distribution

Each time the mean is specified, a particular Poisson probability distribution is generated. A Poisson distribution will be right-skewed but will approach symmetry with a peak in the center as the mean gets large. An important property of Poisson distribution is that the mean and the variance are equal. In the example concerning the number of arrivals at a bank, the mean or expected number of arrivals is three per minute, and the standard deviation is the square root of 3, which is 1.732 arrivals per minute.

10.6 NORMAL DISTRIBUTION

This section focuses on the normal distribution. The normal distribution is a continuous, bell-shaped distribution used for measurement data. Continuous distributions differ from discrete distributions, such as the binomial and Poisson distributions, in the following ways:

1. Any value within the range of the variable can occur, rather than just specific (i.e., integer) values. For example, cycle time can be measured to as many decimal places as are appropriate.

2. The probability of occurrence of a specific value of X is zero. For example, the probability of a cycle time being measured at exactly 3.0000000000 seconds approaches zero as the number of digits to the right of the decimal points gets larger.

3. Probabilities can be obtained by cumulating an area under a curve. For example, the probability of obtaining a cycle time between 2.00 and 3.00 minutes can be obtained if the form of the curve is known and stable.

The normal distribution is used to represent a wide variety of continuous measurement data (variables, or CTQs and Xs). Many natural phenomena have been found to follow a normal distribution, for example, the cycle time to complete an activity, measurement errors, the dimension of industrial parts, and voltage output. An example of a normal distribution is depicted in Figure 10.5. Additionally, statistical inference utilizes the normal distribution (see Chapters 11–13).

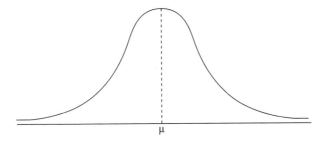

FIGURE 10.5 The Normal Distribution

The normal distribution has several important theoretical properties, as illustrated in Exhibit 10.3.

Exhibit 10.3 **Properties of the Normal Distribution**

1. It is bell-shaped and symmetrical in appearance.
2. Its measures of central tendency (mean, median, and mode) are all identical.
3. Its probabilities are determined by two characteristics, its mean, μ, and its standard deviation, σ.
4. It has a theoretically infinite range.

Probability under the normal curve can be found either by using a table of the normal distribution (see Table C.1 in Appendix C) or by having Minitab compute the probability. Table C.1 provides the area or probability *less than* a specific number of standard deviation units (called Z, or standardized normal units) from the mean.

$$\text{standardized normal units} = Z = \frac{\text{individual value} - \text{mean}}{\text{standard deviation}}$$

Table C.1 provides this probability for standard deviation (Z) units ranging from –3.99 to +6.0. To illustrate how to find a probability or area under the standard normal curve (which has a mean of 0 and a standard deviation of 1), examine Figure 10.6 below.

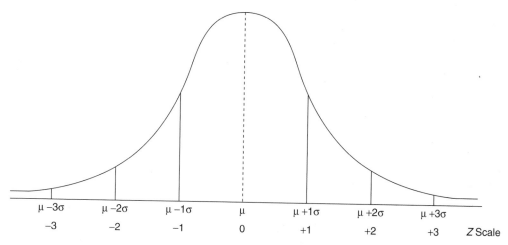

FIGURE 10.6 The Standard Normal Distribution

First, the probability of obtaining a value that is *less* than 3 standard deviations below the mean (–3σ) is computed using Table 10.8. Table 10.8 is extracted from the complete table of the normal distribution shown in Appendix C, Table C.1.

From Table 10.8, the probability of obtaining a value less than –3.00 standard deviation (or Z) units is 0.00135, or 0.135%.

Next, the probability of obtaining a value that is less than 3 standard deviations *above* the mean (+3σ) is computed using Table 10.9. Table 10.9, extracted from the complete normal table shown in Appendix C, Table C.1, shows the area below +3.00 standard deviation (or Z) units.

From Table 10.9, the probability of obtaining a value less than +3 standard deviation (or Z) units is 0.99865, or 99.865%.

The complement of the probability of obtaining a value less than +3 standard deviation (or Z) units is the probability of obtaining a value above 3 standard deviation (or Z) units. This is illustrated in Figure 10.7 on page 304.

Thus, the probability of obtaining a value above 3 standard deviation (or Z) units is equal to $1.0 - 0.99865 = 0.00135$. As shown in Figure 10.7, observe that the area above +3σ is the same as the area below –3σ. This occurs because the normal distribution is symmetric so that each half of the curve is a mirror image of the other half of the curve. The area that is more than 3 standard deviations from the mean is equal to the sum of the area below –3σ (0.00135) and the area above +3σ (0.00135). This is equal to $0.00135 + 0.00135 = 0.0027$, or 0.27%. Stated another way, there is a 27 out of 10,000 (or 2,700 out of a million) chance of obtaining a value that is more than 3 standard deviations from the mean. The complement of this statement is that there is a $1 - 0.0027 = 0.9973$, or 99.73% chance of obtaining a value that is *within* 3 standard deviations of the mean. Table 10.10 on page 304 summarizes this information for several different standard deviation units.

TABLE 10.8 Obtaining a Cumulative Area Below −3 Standard Deviations

Z	.00	.01	.02	.03	.04	.05	.06	.07	.08	.09
	.	.	.	.	.	.	.	.	.	.
	.	.	.	.	.	.	.	.	.	.
−3.0 →	0.00135	0.00131	0.00126	0.00122	0.00118	0.00114	0.00111	0.00107	0.00103	0.00100

Source: Extracted from Appendix C, Table C.1.

TABLE 10.9 Obtaining a Cumulative Area Below ⁺3 Standard Deviations

z	.00	.01	.02	.03	.04	.05	.06	.07	.08	.09
	.	.	.	.	.	.	.	.	.	.
	.	.	.	.	.	.	.	.	.	.
	.	.	.	.	.	.	.	.	.	.
+3.0 →	0.99865	0.99869	0.99874	0.99878	0.99882	0.99886	0.99889	0.99893	0.99897	0.99900

Source: Extracted from Appendix C, Table C.1.

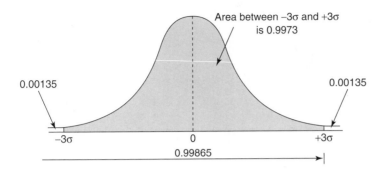

FIGURE 10.7 Computing the Probability or Area Under the Normal Curve

TABLE 10.10 Normal Probabilities for Selected Numbers of Standard Deviation Units

Number of standard deviation units	Probability or area outside these units	Probability or area within these units
-1σ to $+1\sigma$	0.3174	0.6826
-2σ to $+2\sigma$	0.0456	0.9544
-3σ to $+3\sigma$	0.0027	0.9973
-6σ to $+6\sigma$	0.000000002	0.999999998

The previous example involved using the normal tables to find an area under the normal curve that corresponded to a specific Z value. There are many circumstances when you want to do the opposite of this—you want to find the Z value that corresponds to a specific area. For example, you might want to find the Z value that corresponds to a cumulative area of 1%, 5%, 95%, or 99%. You might also want to find lower and upper Z values between which 95% of the area under the curve is contained.

In order to accomplish this, instead of starting with the Z value and looking up the cumulative area less than Z in the table, you locate the cumulative area in the body of the standard normal table and then determine the Z value that corresponds to this cumulative area. Suppose that you want to find the Z values such that 95% of the normal curve is contained between a lower Z value and an upper Z value with 2.5% below the lower Z value, and 2.5% above the upper Z value. Using Figure 10.8, you determine that you need to find the Z value that corresponds to a cumulative area of 0.025 and the Z value that corresponds to a cumulative area of 0.975.

Table 10.11 on page 306 contains a portion of Table C.1 that is needed to find the Z value that corresponds to a cumulative area of 0.025. Table 10.12 on page 307 contains a portion of Table C.1 that is needed to find the Z value that corresponds to a cumulative area of 0.975.

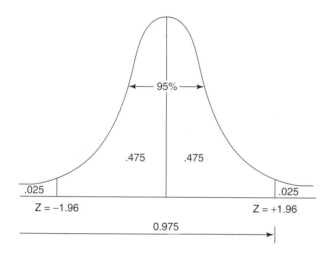

FIGURE 10.8 Finding the *Z* Value Corresponding to a Given Area

To find the *Z* value that corresponds to a cumulative area of 0.025, you look in the body of Table 10.11 until you see the value of 0.025 (or the closest value to 0.025) Then you determine the row and column that this value corresponds to. Locating the value of 0.025, you see that it is located in the –1.9 row and the .06 column. Thus the *Z* value that corresponds to a cumulative area of 0.025 is –1.96.

To find the *Z* value that corresponds to a cumulative area of 0.975, you look in the body of Table 10.12 until you see the value of 0.975 (or the closest value to 0.975). Then you determine the row and column that this value corresponds to. Locating the value of 0.975, you see that it is located in the 1.9 row and the .06 column. Thus, the *Z* value that corresponds to a cumulative area of 0.975 is 1.96. Taking this result along with the *Z* value of –1.96 for a cumulative area of 0.025 means that 95% of all the values will be between $Z = -1.96$ and $Z = 1.96$.

The computation of any probability or area under the normal curve can be done using Minitab. Figure 10.9 on page 308 displays the probability of obtaining a value less than -3σ.

In Figure 10.9, the mean of the distribution is zero, and the standard deviation is 1.0 (this is called a *standardized normal distribution*). To learn how to obtain a normal probability for a distribution that has a mean that is not equal to zero and/or a standard deviation that is not equal to 1, you can examine the following example.

Suppose that an industrial sewing machine uses ball bearings that are targeted to have a diameter of 0.50 inch. The specification limits under which the ball bearing can operate are 0.49 inch (LSL) and 0.51 inch (USL). Past experience has indicated that the actual diameter is stable (see Chapter 14) and approximately normally distributed, with a mean $\mu = 0.503$ inch and a standard deviation $\sigma = 0.004$ inch. Suppose that you want to determine the proportion of all ball bearings that have a diameter between 0.49 and 0.51 inch; that is, within specification limits (For our purposes this is the same as determining the probability that a single ball bearing will have a

TABLE 10.11 Partial Table C.1 for Finding Z value that Corresponds to a Cumulative Area of 0.025

z	.00	.01	.02	.03	.04	.05	.06	.07	.08	.09
.	.	.	.	.	.	.	.	.	.	.
-2.0	0.0228	0.0222	0.0217	0.0212	0.0207	0.0202	0.0197	0.0192	0.0188	0.0183
-1.9	0.0287	0.0281	0.0274	0.0268	0.0262	0.0256	0.0250	0.0244	0.0239	0.0233

TABLE 10.12 Partial Table C.1 for Finding Z Value that Corresponds to a Cumulative Area of 0.975

z	.00	.01	.02	.03	.04	.05	.06	.07	.08	.09
⋮	⋮	⋮	⋮	⋮	⋮	⋮		⋮	⋮	⋮
1.9	0.9713	0.9719	0.9726	0.9732	0.9738	0.9744	0.9750	0.9756	0.9761	0.9767
2.0	0.9772	0.9778	0.9783	0.9788	0.9793	0.9798	0.9803	0.9808	0.9812	0.9817

Cumulative Distribution Function

```
Normal with mean = 0 and standard deviation = 1

x   P( X <= x )
-3    0.0013499
```

FIGURE 10.9 Minitab Normal Probabilities.

diameter between 0.49 and 0.51 inch.) The answer is found by using Table C.1, the table in Appendix C of the probabilities of the cumulative standardized normal distribution.

To find this probability, the diameters must first be converted to a standardized normal units by subtracting the mean and dividing by the standard deviation. Thus:

$$\text{Standardized normal units} = Z = \frac{\text{individual value} - \text{mean}}{\text{standard deviation}}$$

$$\text{Standardized normal units} = Z = \frac{0.49 - 0.503}{0.004} = -3.25$$

$$\text{Standardized normal units} = Z = \frac{0.51 - 0.503}{0.004} = 1.75$$

The diameter of 0.490 inch is 3.25 standard deviation (or Z) units below the mean of 0.503 and the diameter of 0.51 is 1.75 standard deviations above the mean of 0.503. The appropriate areas can be found using either Table C.1, Appendix C or by using Minitab. Figure 10.10 illustrates the use of Table C.1, whereas Figure 10.11 displays Minitab output.

The area below 0.49 is 0.00058, whereas the area below 0.51 is 0.9599. Thus the area or probability of obtaining a value between 0.49 and 0.51 inch is 0.9599 – 0.00058 = 0.95932. The

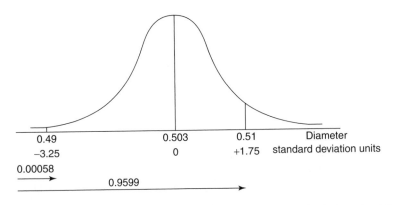

FIGURE 10.10 Computing the Probability Between 0 and +1 Standard Deviation Units.

```
Normal with mean = 0.503 and standard deviation = 0.004

   x    P( X <= x )
0.49      0.000577
0.51      0.959941
```

FIGURE 10.11 Obtaining Normal Probabilities Using Minitab for the Area Below 0 and +1 Standard Deviation Units.

proportion of the ball bearings meeting customer specification is 0.95932. Thus, the proportion of ball bearings failing to meet customer specifications is 0.04068 or a DPMO = 40,680.

10.7 NORMAL PROBABILITY PLOT

The normal probability plot is a graphical device for helping to evaluate whether a set of data follows a normal distribution. Minitab uses an approach to the normal probability plot that transforms the vertical Y axis in a special way so that if the data are normally distributed, a plot of the data from lowest to highest will follow a straight line. If the data are left-skewed, the curve will rise more rapidly at first, then level off. If the data are right-skewed, the data will rise more slowly at first, then rise at a faster rate for higher values of the variable being plotted. Figure 10.12 illustrates the typical shape of normal probability plots for a left-skewed distribution (panel A), a normal distribution (panel B), and a right-skewed distribution (panel C).

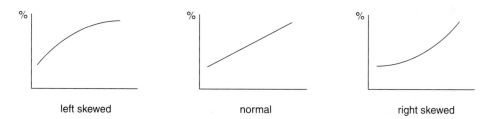

FIGURE 10.12 Normal Probability Plots for a Left-Skewed Distribution, a Normal Distribution, and a Right-Skewed Distribution

To illustrate the normal probability plot, the chemical viscosity data discussed in Section 9.8 can be used. Figure 10.13 is a Minitab normal probability plot of the viscosity of a 120 batches of a chemical. Consistent with the results of the histogram on page 241, the straight line that the data follow in this normal probability plot (with the exception of two outlier points) appears to indicate that the viscosity is approximately normally distributed.

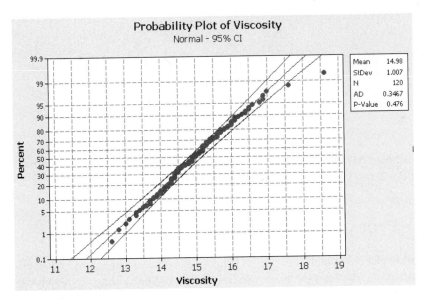

FIGURE 10.13 Minitab Normal Probability Plot of the Viscosity of 120 Batches of a Chemical

SUMMARY

This chapter covered the basic concepts of probability and discussed the binomial, Poisson, and normal distributions. First, some rules of probability were discussed, followed by the development and definition of the probability distribution. Then, the circumstances in which binomial, Poisson, and normal distributions could be used were emphasized, along with how to compute probabilities for each of these distributions. Finally, the normal probability plot was introduced as a tool for evaluating whether a set of data approximately follows a normal distribution.

REFERENCES

1. Berenson, M. L., D. M. Levine, and T. C. Krehbiel, *Basic Business Statistics: Concepts and Applications*, 9th ed. (Upper Saddle River, NJ: Prentice Hall, 2004).

2. Levine, D. M. , P. C. Ramsey, R. K. Smidt, *Applied Statistics for Engineers and Scientists using Microsoft Excel and Minitab* (Upper Saddle River, NJ: Prentice Hall, 2001).

3. *Minitab Version 14* (State College, PA: Minitab, 2004).

APPENDIX 10.1

USING MINITAB FOR PROBABILITY DISTRIBUTIONS

Using Minitab to Obtain Binomial Probabilities

Minitab can be used to compute binomial probabilities. Referring to the example in Section 10.4 in which $n = 3$ and $p = 0.5$, to find the binomial probabilities shown in Figure 10.2 on page 294:

1. Enter **0 1 2 3** in the first four rows of column C1. Label column C1 **Closes**.

2. Select **Calc** → **Probability Distributions** → **Binomial**.

3. In the Binomial Distribution dialog box (see Figure A10.1), select the **Probability** option button. Enter **3** in the Number of trials: edit box and **.5** in the Probability of success: edit box. Enter **C1** or **Closes** in the Input column: edit box. Click the **OK** button.

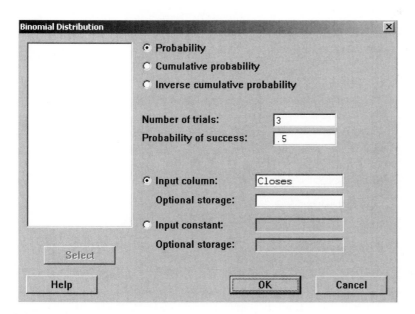

FIGURE A10.1 Binomial Distribution Dialog Box

Using Minitab to Obtain Poisson Probabilities

Minitab can be used to compute Poisson probabilities. Referring to the example in Section 10.5 in which the mean = 3, to find the Poisson probabilities shown in Figure 10.4 on page 298:

1. Enter **0 1 2 3 4 5 6 7 8 9 10 11 12** in the first 13 rows of column C1. Label column C1 **Arrivals.**

2. Select **Calc → Probability Distributions → Poisson.**

3. In the Poisson Distribution dialog box (see Figure A10.2), select the **Probability option button.** Enter **3** in the Mean: edit box. Enter **C1** or **Arrivals** in the Input column: edit box. Click the **OK** button.

Using Minitab to Obtain Normal Probabilities

Minitab can be used to compute normal probabilities. Referring to the example in Section 10.6 in which $\mu = 0$ and $\sigma = 1$, to find the probability below –3 standard deviations:

1. Enter **–3** in the first row of column C1.

2. Select **Calc → Probability Distributions → Normal.**

3. In the Normal Distribution dialog box (see Figure A10.3), select the **Cumulative probability options button.** Enter **0** in the Mean: edit box and **1** in the Standard deviation: edit box. Enter **C1** in the Input column: edit box. Click the **OK** button.

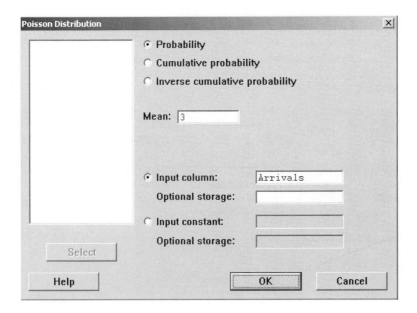

FIGURE A10.2 Poisson Distribution Dialog Box

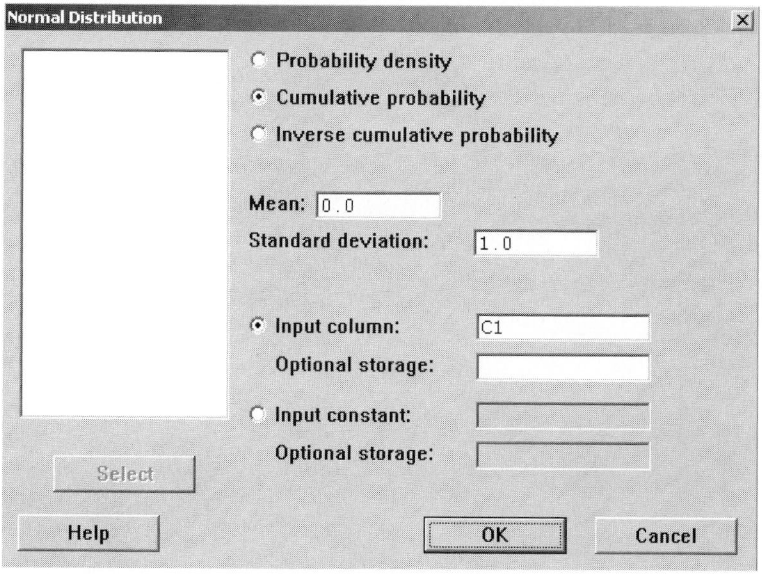

FIGURE A10.3 Normal Distribution Dialog Box

Using Minitab to Obtain a Normal Probability Plot

To obtain a normal probability plot using Minitab, open the **CHEMICAL.MTW** worksheet. Select **Graph → Probability Plot,** then do the following:

1. In the Probability Plots dialog box, select the **Single** choice.

2. In the Probability Plot—Single dialog box (see Figure A10.4), in the Graph variables: edit box, enter **C2** or **Viscosity**.

3. Select the **Distribution** option button. In the Probability Plot—Distribution dialog box (see Figure A10.5), select the Distribution tab. In the Distribution: drop-down list box, select **Normal.** Click the **OK** button to return to the Probability Plot—Single dialog box.

4. Click the **OK** button to obtain the normal probability plot.

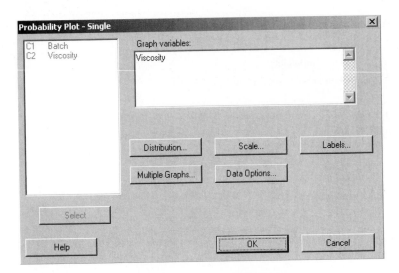

FIGURE A10.4 Probability Plot—Single Dialog Box

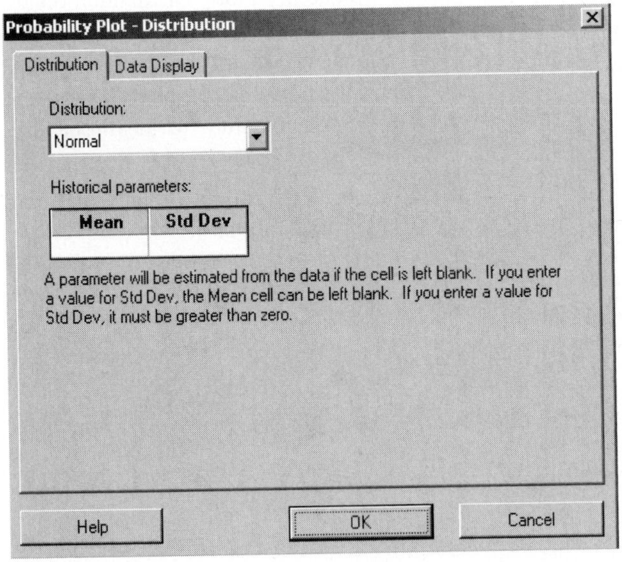

FIGURE A10.5 Probability Plot—Distribution Dialog Box

SAMPLING DISTRIBUTIONS AND INTERVAL ESTIMATION

CHAPTER OUTLINE

LEARNING OBJECTIVES

After reading this chapter, you will be able to:

- Understand the concept of a sampling distribution
- Understand the concept of a confidence interval
- Obtain confidence interval estimates for the mean and the proportion
- Obtain a prediction interval for a forecasted value
- Understand the difference between a confidence interval and a prediction interval

INTRODUCTION

In Chapter 9, the basic concepts of statistics were introduced, and a variety of useful graphs and descriptive statistical measures were developed. In Chapter 10, the rules of probability were discussed, the probability distribution was defined, and some specific probability distributions used in Six Sigma management, such as the binomial, Poisson, and normal distributions, were studied.

11.1 SAMPLING DISTRIBUTIONS

Basic Concepts

In this chapter, we build on these topics to provide the foundation for using statistical inference in this and the next two chapters. In Section 9.1, *inferential statistics* were defined as those in which conclusions about a large set of data, called the frame, are made from a subset of the data, called the **sample.** Enumerative studies frequently utilize a random sample that is selected from a frame [see Reference 3], something that is at least theoretically possible to attain. In the case of analytical studies, although a population does not exist because it is not possible to obtain a frame of future output, nevertheless the methods of statistical inference are considered to be useful (along with graphical methods) by Six Sigma experts.

In enumerative or analytical studies, the key focus is on using the results of a sample statistic to draw conclusions about a population characteristic. In practice, only one sample is usually selected. However, statisticians have developed the theory necessary that allows you to draw conclusions about an entire population based on only a single sample. This is accomplished through the concept of the sampling distribution.

The **sampling distribution** consists of the distribution of a sample statistic (such as the mean) for all possible samples of a given size *n*.

For example, if a population consists of 1,000 items, the sampling distribution of the mean for samples of 15 items would be obtained by taking *every single* different sample of 15 items from the population of 1,000 items, computing the mean, then arranging all the sample means in a distribution. Actually doing the selection is an involved, time-consuming task that is not necessary in practice. You primarily need to understand the following principles:

1. Every sample statistic has a sampling distribution.
2. A specific sample statistic is used to estimate its corresponding population characteristic.

Statisticians have extensively studied sampling distributions for many different statistics. Some of these well-known sampling distributions are used extensively, in this chapter and continuing through Chapter 13.

Sampling Distribution of the Mean

The mean is the most widely used measure in statistics. Recall from Section 9.9 that the mean is calculated by summing the observed numerical values, then dividing the sum by the number of observations.

$$\text{arithmetic mean} = \frac{\text{sum of all the values}}{\text{number of values}}$$

Because the mean is based on the computation of all the values in the sample, it is subject to a great deal of variation from sample to sample, especially when extreme values, or **outliers,** are present. Statisticians have developed the **Central Limit Theorem** that states that regardless of the shape of the distribution of the individual values in a population:

As the sample size gets *large enough,* the sampling distribution of the mean can be approximated by a normal distribution.

Figure 11.1 represents the sampling distribution of the mean for three different populations. For each population, the sampling distribution of the sample mean is shown for all samples of $n = 2$, $n = 5$, and $n = 30$.

Panel A of Figure 11.1 illustrates the sampling distribution of the mean selected from a population that is normally distributed. When the population is normally distributed, the sampling distribution of the mean is normally distributed, regardless of the sample size. As the sample size increases, the variability of the sample mean from sample to sample decreases. This is due to the fact that the influence of extreme values on an individual mean becomes smaller as the sample size gets larger.

Panel B of Figure 11.1 displays the sampling distribution from a population with a uniform (or rectangular) distribution. When samples of size $n = 2$ are selected, there is a peaking, or *central limiting,* effect already working in which there are more sample means in the center than there are individual values in the population. For $n = 5$, the sampling distribution is bell-shaped and approximately normal. When $n = 30$, the sampling distribution appears to be very similar to a normal distribution. In general, the larger the sample size, the more closely the sampling distribution will follow a normal distribution. As with all cases, the mean of each sampling distribution is equal to the mean of the population, and the variability decreases as the sample size increases.

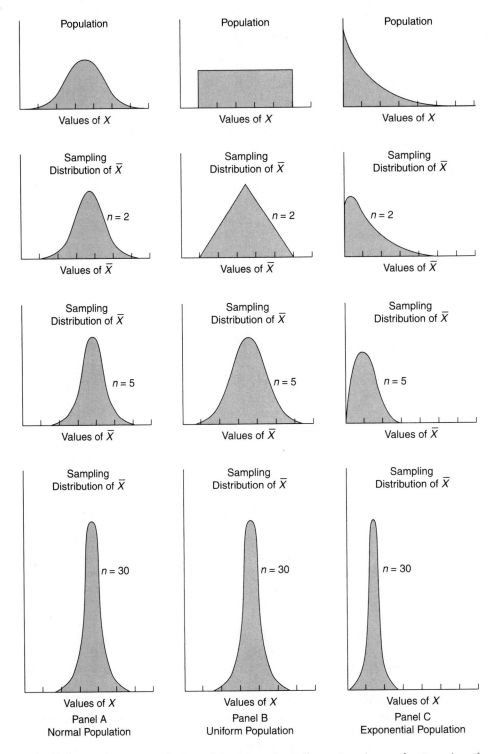

FIGURE 11.1 Sampling Distribution of the Mean for Different Populations for Samples of $n = 2$, 5, and 30.

Panel C of Figure 11.1 presents an exponential distribution. This population is heavily skewed to the right. When $n = 2$, the sampling distribution is still highly skewed to the right but less so than the distribution of the population. For $n = 5$, the sampling distribution is approximately symmetric, with only a slight skew to the right. When $n = 30$, the sampling distribution appears to be approximately normally distributed. Again, the mean of each sampling distribution is equal to the mean of the population, and the variability decreases as the sample size increases.

The results displayed in these statistical distributions (normal, uniform, exponential) allow statisticians to draw the following conclusions as presented in Exhibit 11.1.

Exhibit 11.1 **Normality and the Sampling Distribution of the Mean**

1. For most population distributions, regardless of shape, the sampling distribution of the mean is approximately normally distributed if samples of at least 30 observations are selected.

2. If the population distribution is fairly symmetrical, the sampling distribution of the mean is approximately normal if samples of at least 15 observations are selected.

3. If the population is normally distributed, the sampling distribution of the mean is normally distributed, regardless of the sample size.

Sampling Distribution of the Proportion

In Chapter 9, the simplest form of attribute data was defined in which a variable was classified into one of only two categories. The proportion of successes in each category follows a binomial distribution, as discussed in Section 10.4. However, the normal distribution can be used to approximate the binomial distribution when the average number of successes and the number of failures are *each* at least five. In most cases in which you are making inferences about the proportion, the sample size is more than sufficient to meet the conditions for using the normal approximation [see Reference 5].

11.2 BASIC CONCEPTS OF CONFIDENCE INTERVALS

The development of the sampling distribution of the statistic of interest is crucial for being able to use the sample statistic to draw a conclusion about a population parameter. However, the results of a sample statistic, such as the mean, obtained from a single sample provides only a **point estimate** of the population parameter. This point estimate is a single value and will almost certainly not be the same if a different sample is selected. Thus, statisticians have developed the concept of an interval estimate in which the value of the characteristic for the entire population is estimated with a specific degree of certainty with a lower and upper limit.

To develop the concept of the interval estimate, return to the example concerning the viscosity of 120 batches of a chemical, 🌐 **CHEMICAL** first discussed in Chapter 9. For now, consider these 120 batches to be the population. Although in an actual situation the population characteristics are rarely known, for this population, the mean, μ, = 14.978, and the standard deviation, σ, is 1.003.

To examine the variation of the sample mean from sample to sample, 20 different samples of $n = 10$ were selected from this population of 120 batches. The results for these samples are summarized in Figure 11.2.

Descriptive Statistics: Sample 1, Sample 2, Sample 3, Sample 4, Sample 5, ...

Variable	Mean	StDev	Minimum	Median	Maximum	Range
Sample 1	14.690	0.858	13.400	14.600	16.100	2.700
Sample 2	15.310	0.590	14.500	15.300	16.300	1.800
Sample 3	14.650	0.824	13.300	14.650	16.000	2.700
Sample 4	14.910	1.049	13.700	14.850	16.900	3.200
Sample 5	14.780	0.847	13.700	14.650	16.500	2.800
Sample 6	14.630	1.145	12.600	14.350	16.600	4.000
Sample 7	14.610	1.034	12.800	14.900	16.400	3.600
Sample 8	15.040	1.422	13.600	14.700	18.600	5.000
Sample 9	15.340	1.055	13.700	15.650	16.800	3.100
Sample 10	15.370	0.572	14.300	15.300	16.200	1.900
Sample 11	15.230	0.864	14.200	15.100	16.900	2.700
Sample 12	15.160	0.749	14.400	14.950	16.900	2.500
Sample 13	15.120	0.840	14.000	15.150	16.600	2.600
Sample 14	14.860	0.696	14.200	14.750	16.500	2.300
Sample 15	15.680	0.750	14.400	15.450	17.000	2.600
Sample 16	15.130	0.699	14.000	15.150	16.300	2.300
Sample 17	14.470	0.715	13.300	14.600	15.300	2.000
Sample 18	15.250	0.985	13.800	15.150	16.800	3.000
Sample 19	14.720	0.888	13.300	14.500	16.000	2.700
Sample 20	15.400	0.968	14.300	15.150	17.600	3.300

FIGURE 11.2 Minitab Sample Statistics for 20 Samples of $n = 10$ Selected from the Population of 120 Batches

From Figure 11.2, you can see the following:

1. The sample statistics differ from sample to sample. The sample means vary from 14.47 to 15.68, the sample standard deviations vary from 0.572 to 1.422, the sample medians vary from 14.35 to 15.65, and the sample ranges vary from 1.8 to 3.6.

2. Some of the sample means are higher than the population mean of 14.978, and some of the sample means are lower than the population mean.

3. Some of the sample standard deviations are higher than the population standard deviation of 1.003, and some of the sample standard deviations are lower than the population standard deviation.

4. The variation in the sample range from sample to sample is much more than the variation in the sample standard deviation.

The fact that sample statistics vary from sample to sample is called **sampling error.** Sampling error is the variation that occurs due to selecting a single sample from the population. The size of the sampling error is primarily based on the variation in the population and on the size of the sample selected. Larger samples will have less sampling error, but will be more costly to obtain.

Because *only one sample is actually selected in practice,* statisticians have developed methods for estimating the population parameter that consists of an interval with a lower and upper limit, rather than a single value. This interval is called a **confidence interval estimate.** Using the data concerning the viscosity of the chemical illustrated in Figure 11.2, 95% confidence interval estimates of the population mean viscosity for each of the 20 samples of $n = 10$ previously selected are illustrated in Figure 11.3.

```
Variable    N     Mean    StDev   SE Mean       95% CI
Sample 1    10  14.6900   0.8582   0.3172   (14.0683, 15.3117)
Sample 2    10  15.3100   0.5896   0.3172   (14.6883, 15.9317)
Sample 3    10  14.6500   0.8236   0.3172   (14.0283, 15.2717)
Sample 4    10  14.9100   1.0493   0.3172   (14.2883, 15.5317)
Sample 5    10  14.7800   0.8470   0.3172   (14.1583, 15.4017)
Sample 6    10  14.6300   1.1451   0.3172   (14.0083, 15.2517)
Sample 7    10  14.6100   1.0344   0.3172   (13.9883, 15.2317)
Sample 8    10  15.0400   1.4222   0.3172   (14.4183, 15.6617)
Sample 9    10  15.3400   1.0554   0.3172   (14.7183, 15.9617)
Sample 10   10  15.3700   0.5716   0.3172   (14.7483, 15.9917)
Sample 11   10  15.2300   0.8642   0.3172   (14.6083, 15.8517)
Sample 12   10  15.1600   0.7486   0.3172   (14.5383, 15.7817)
Sample 13   10  15.1200   0.8404   0.3172   (14.4983, 15.7417)
Sample 14   10  14.8600   0.6963   0.3172   (14.2383, 15.4817)
Sample 15   10  15.6800   0.7495   0.3172   (15.0583, 16.3017)
Sample 16   10  15.1300   0.6993   0.3172   (14.5083, 15.7517)
Sample 17   10  14.4700   0.7150   0.3172   (13.8483, 15.0917)
Sample 18   10  15.2500   0.9846   0.3172   (14.6283, 15.8717)
Sample 19   10  14.7200   0.8879   0.3172   (14.0983, 15.3417)
Sample 20   10  15.4000   0.9684   0.3172   (14.7783, 16.0217)
```

FIGURE 11.3 Minitab Confidence Interval Estimates of the Mean for 20 Samples of $n = 10$ Selected from the Population of 120 Batches

Begin by examining the first sample selected. The sample mean is 14.69, the sample standard deviation is 0.8582, and the interval estimate for the population mean is 14.0683–15.3117. You do not know for sure whether this interval estimate is actually correct because in an actual study you rarely know the actual value of the population mean. However, *in the example concerning the batches of the chemical,* the population mean is known to be 14.978. If you examine the interval 14.0683–15.3117, you see that the population mean of 14.978 is included *between* these lower and upper limits. Thus, the first sample provides a correct estimate of the population mean in the form of an interval estimate. Looking over the other 19 samples, you see that similar results occur for all the other samples *except* for sample 15. For each of the intervals generated (other than sample 15), the population mean of 14.978 is located *somewhere* within the interval.

However, in the case of sample 15 the sample mean is 15.68, and the interval is 15.0583 to 16.3017. The population mean of 14.978 is *not* located within the interval, and any estimate of the population mean made using this interval is incorrect.

In practice, the dilemma concerning the interval estimate has two aspects. Only one sample is actually selected, and you have no way to be 100% certain whether your interval correctly estimates the population characteristic of interest. However, by setting the level of certainty at a value below 100% and using an interval estimate of the population parameter of interest, you can obtain an inference about the population with a given degree of certainty.

In general, a **95% confidence interval estimate** can be interpreted to mean that if all possible samples of the same size *n* were selected, 95% of them would include the population parameter somewhere within the interval, and 5% would not.

Although 95% is the most common confidence level used, if more confidence is needed, 99% is typically used, whereas if less confidence is needed, 90% is typically used. However, there is a trade-off between the level of confidence and the width of the interval. For a given sample size, if you want more confidence that your interval will be correct, you will have a wider interval and, thus, more sampling error.

The fundamental concepts of confidence interval estimation remain the same, regardless of the population characteristics being estimated. To develop a confidence interval estimate, you need to know the sample statistic used to estimate the population characteristic and the sampling distribution for the sample statistic.

11.3 CONFIDENCE INTERVAL ESTIMATE FOR THE MEAN (σ UNKNOWN)

The most common confidence interval estimate involves estimating the mean of a population. In virtually all cases, the population mean is estimated from sample data in which only the sample mean and sample standard deviation are available, not the standard deviation of the population. For this situation, statisticians [see Reference 1] have developed a sampling distribution called the *t* **distribution** to obtain a confidence interval estimate of the mean. The confidence interval estimate for the mean is illustrated in the following example.

Allowable stress for a material is the maximum stress at which you can be reasonably certain that failure will not occur. In aircraft design, because weight is an important consideration, composite materials are being used with increasing frequency. These materials can provide the strength and stiffness of metallic components with less weight. A sample of 25 specimens of composite material was selected, and the results are presented in Table 11.1.

TABLE 11.1 Tensile Strength of 25 Specimens of Composite Material (in 1,000 psi)

203.41	209.58	213.35	218.56	242.76
185.97	190.67	207.88	210.80	231.46
184.41	200.73	206.51	209.84	212.15
160.44	180.95	201.95	204.60	219.51
174.63	185.34	205.59	212.00	225.25

🌐 **TENSILE**

Source: M. G. Vangel, " New Methods for One-Sided Tolerance Limits for a One-Way Balanced Random-Effects ANOVA Model," *Technometrics*, 34, 1992, pp. 176–185. Reprinted with permission from *Technometrics*. Copyright 1992 by the American Statistical Association. All rights reserved.

Figure 11.4 represents the Minitab confidence interval estimate of the population mean for the tensile strength of the 25 specimens.

One-Sample T: Strength

```
Variable   N     Mean   StDev  SE Mean       95% CI
Strength   25  203.934  18.320   3.664  (196.371, 211.496)
```

FIGURE 11.4 Minitab Confidence Interval Estimate of the Population Mean for the Tensile Strength of the 25 Specimens.

Thus, you conclude with 95% confidence that the average tensile strength of the composite material is between 196.37 and 211.50 (in 1,000 pounds per square inch [psi]).

Figure 11.5 displays the normal probability plot of the tensile strength.

CAUTION **Assumptions of the Confidence Interval Estimate for the Mean**

The *t* distribution assumes that the variable being studied is normally distributed. In practice, however, as long as the sample size is large enough and the population is not very skewed, the *t* distribution can be used to estimate the population mean when the population standard deviation σ is unknown. You should be concerned about the validity of the confidence interval primarily when dealing with a small sample size and a skewed population distribution. The assumption of normality in the population can be assessed by evaluating the shape of the sample data using a histogram, box-and-whisker plot, or normal probability plot.

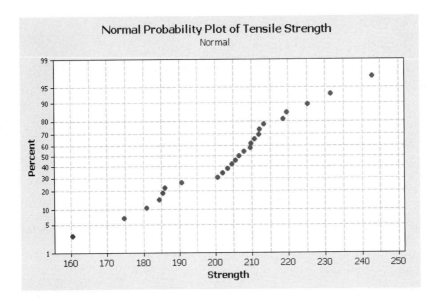

FIGURE 11.5 Minitab Normal Probability Plot of Tensile Strength

You see that the points on the normal probability plot appear to be distributed across an approximately straight line from lowest to highest value. Thus, there appears to be little reason to suspect a serious departure from the normality assumption that would affect the validity of the confidence interval estimate.

Equation for Confidence Interval for a Mean [σ Unknown] (optional)

$$\overline{X} \pm t_{n-1}\frac{S}{\sqrt{n}}$$

or   (11.1)

$$\overline{X} - t_{n-1}\frac{S}{\sqrt{n}} \leq \mu \leq \overline{X} + t_{n-1}\frac{S}{\sqrt{n}}$$

where t_{n-1} is the critical value of the t distribution with $n-1$ degrees of freedom for an area of $\alpha/2$ in the upper tail.

Using the Minitab output shown in Figure 11.4, $\overline{X} = 203.93$, and $S = 18.32$. Because $n = 25$, there are $25 - 1 = 24$ degrees of freedom. For 95% confidence, the area in the upper tail of the t distribution is $0.05/2 = 0.025$. Using Table C.2 in Appendix C, the critical value for the row with 24 degrees of freedom and the column with an area of 0.025 is 2.0639. Using equation (11.1):

$$\overline{X} \pm t_{n-1}\frac{S}{\sqrt{n}}$$

$$= 203.93 \pm (2.0639)\frac{18.3204}{\sqrt{25}}$$

$$= 203.93 \pm 7.56$$

$$196.37 \leq \mu \leq 211.50$$

11.4 PREDICTION INTERVAL ESTIMATE FOR A FUTURE INDIVIDUAL VALUE

In addition to the need to obtain a confidence interval estimate for the population mean, often you need to predict the outcome of a future individual value [see Reference 4]. Although the form of the prediction interval is similar to the confidence interval estimate of the mean shown in Equation (11.1), the interpretation of the prediction interval is different. The prediction interval is estimating an observable future individual value X_f, *not* an unknown population parameter μ. Because Minitab currently does not compute a prediction interval, the prediction interval is shown in Equation (11.2).

$$\overline{X} \pm t_{n-1}S\sqrt{1 + \frac{1}{n}}$$

$$\overline{X} - t_{n-1}S\sqrt{1 + \frac{1}{n}} \leq X_f \leq \overline{X} + t_{n-1}S\sqrt{1 + \frac{1}{n}}$$

$$(11.2)$$

Returning to the example concerning the tensile strength of composite material for aircraft design, suppose that you wanted to obtain a 95% prediction interval estimate of the future tensile strength of an individual specimen of composite material. Using Equation (11.2),

$$\overline{X} \pm t_{n-1}S\sqrt{1 + \frac{1}{n}}$$

$$= 203.93 \pm (2.0639)(18.3204)\sqrt{1 + \frac{1}{25}}$$

$$= 203.93 \pm 38.56$$

$$165.37 \le X_f \le 242.49$$

Thus, you predict with 95% assurance that the value of a future individual tensile strength will be between 165.37 and 242.49 thousands of psi. This result differs markedly from the confidence interval estimate of the population mean. The prediction interval is substantially wider because you are estimating a *future individual value,* not the population mean.

11.5 CONFIDENCE INTERVAL ESTIMATION FOR THE PROPORTION

A confidence interval estimate for an attribute can be developed to estimate the proportion of successes in a given category. Instead of using the sample mean to estimate the population mean, you use the sample proportion of successes (p):

$$\text{Proportion of successes} = \frac{\text{number of successes}}{\text{sample size}}$$

to estimate the population proportion (π). The sample statistic p follows a binomial distribution that can be approximated by the normal distribution for most studies.

To demonstrate the confidence interval estimate of the proportion, you can examine the situation faced by the quality engineer for a large city newspaper. In the production of a newspaper, an important quality characteristic relates to the proportion of newspapers that are printed even though a nonconforming attribute, such as excessive ruboff, improper page setup, missing pages, or duplicate pages, is present. Because it is impractical (and would be extremely time-consuming and expensive) to examine every newspaper printed, a random sample of 200 newspapers is selected for study. Suppose that, in a sample of 200, a total of 35 contain some type of nonconformance. Figure 11.6 consists of a Minitab 95% confidence interval estimate for the percentage of nonconforming newspapers.

Therefore, 95% of all confidence intervals computed from a random sample of 200 newspapers will contain the population proportion. Since the population proportion is unknown, the interval 12.2% to 22.8% may be one of the 95% of the intervals containing the population proportion. There is a 5% chance of obtaining an interval that does not include the population proportion.

```
Sample   X    N   Sample p        95% CI
1       35  200   0.175000   (0.122340, 0.227660).
```

FIGURE 11.6 Minitab 95% Confidence Interval Estimate for the Proportion of Nonconforming Newspapers

Equation for the Confidence Interval Estimate for the Proportion (optional)

$$p \pm Z\sqrt{\frac{p(1-p)}{n}}$$

or (11.3)

$$p - Z\sqrt{\frac{p(1-p)}{n}} \leq \pi \leq p + Z\sqrt{\frac{p(1-p)}{n}}$$

where

$p = X/n$ = sample proportion

π = population proportion

Z = critical value from the normal distribution

n = sample size

For these data, $p = 35/200 = 0.175$. For a 95% level of confidence, the lower tail area of 0.025 provides a Z value from the normal distribution of -1.96, and the upper tail area of 0.025 provides a Z value from the normal distribution of $+1.96$. Using Equation (11.3),

$$p \pm Z\sqrt{\frac{p(1-p)}{n}}$$

$$= .175 \pm (1.96)\sqrt{\frac{(.175)(.825)}{200}}$$

$$= .175 \pm (1.96)(.0269)$$

$$= .175 \pm .053$$

$$.122 \leq \pi \leq .228$$

For a given sample size, confidence intervals for proportions often seem to be wider than those for measurement variables. With continuous variables, the measurement on each respondent contributes more information than for a categorical variable. In other words, a categorical variable with only two possible values is a very crude measure, compared with a continuous variable, so each observation contributes only a little information about the parameter being estimated.

Assumptions of the Confidence Interval Estimate for the Proportion

In most studies, the number of successes and failures is sufficiently large that the normal distribution provides an excellent approximation to the binomial distribution. If there are fewer than an average five successes or failures in the data, the confidence intervals computed using Minitab can be adjusted to provide more exact intervals [see Reference 5].

SUMMARY

In this chapter, the concept of the sampling distribution of a statistic served as the foundation for developing confidence interval estimates of the mean and the proportion. The assumption of each confidence interval was stated, and methods for evaluating the validity of the assumption were shown. In addition, the distinction was made between the confidence interval and the prediction interval.

REFERENCES

1. Berenson, M. L., D. M. Levine, and T. C. Krehbiel, *Basic Business Statistics: Concepts and Applications,* 9th ed. (Upper Saddle River, NJ: Prentice Hall, 2004).

2. Cochran, W. G. *Sampling Techniques,* 3rd ed. (New York: John Wiley, 1977).

3. Hahn, G. J. and W. Q. Meeker, "Assumptions for Statistical Inference," *The American Statistician,* 1993, 47, pp. 1–11.

4. Hahn, G. J. and W. Nelson, "A Survey of Prediction Intervals and their Applications," *Journal of Quality Technology,* 1973, 5, pp. 178–188.

5. Minitab Version 14 (State College, PA: Minitab, 2004).

A P P E N D I X 1 1 . 1

USING MINITAB TO OBTAIN CONFIDENCE INTERVALS

Obtaining the Confidence Interval Estimate for the Mean

To obtain the confidence interval estimate of the mean tensile strength illustrated in Figure 11.4 on page 323, open the **TENSILE.MTW** worksheet. Select **Stat → Basic Statistics → 1-Sample t.**

1. In the 1-Sample t (Test and Confidence Interval) dialog box (see Figure A11.1),

enter **C1** or **Strength** in the Samples in columns: edit box. (If you have summarized data instead of the actual data, select the Summarized data option button and enter values for the sample size, mean, and standard deviation.)

2. Click the **Options** button. In the 1-Sample t—Options dialog box (see Figure A11.2), enter **95** in the Confidence level: edit box. Click the **OK** button to

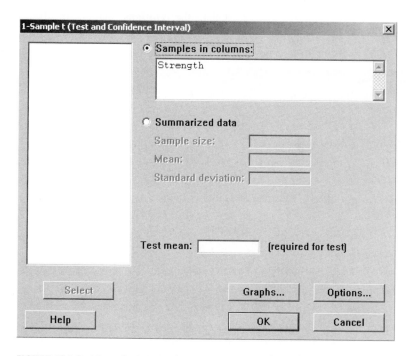

FIGURE A11.1 Minitab 1-Sample t (Test and Confidence Interval) Dialog Box

return to the 1-Sample t (Test and Confidence Interval) dialog box. (Click the Graphs button to obtain a histogram

or box-and-whisker plot.) Click the **OK** button.

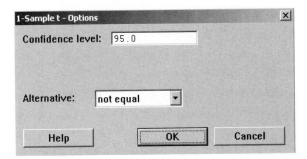

FIGURE A11.2 Minitab 1-Sample t— Options Dialog Box

Obtaining the Confidence Interval Estimate for the Proportion

To obtain the confidence interval estimate of the proportion of nonconforming newspapers illustrated in Figure 11.6 on page 326, select **Stat → Basic Statistics → 1 Proportion.**

1. In the 1 Proportion (Test and Confidence Interval) dialog box (see Figure A11.3), select the **Summarized data** option button. Enter **200** in the Number of trials: edit box. Enter **35** in the Number of events: edit box.

2. Click the **Options** button. In the 1 Proportion—Options dialog box (see

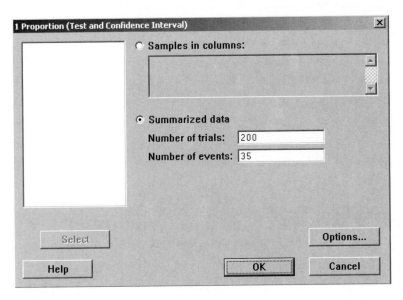

FIGURE A11.3 Minitab 1 Proportion (Test and Confidence Interval) Dialog Box

Figure A11.4), enter **95** in the Confidence level: edit box. Select the **Use test and interval based on the normal distribution** check box (uncheck this if this selection is not desired). Click the **OK** button to return to the 1 Proportion (Test and Confidence Interval) dialog box. Click the **OK** button.

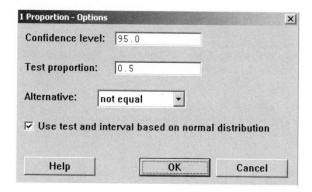

FIGURE A11.4 Minitab 1 Proportion— Options Dialog Box

HYPOTHESIS TESTING

CHAPTER OUTLINE

LEARNING OBJECTIVES

After reading this chapter, you will be able to:

- Understand the basic principles of hypothesis testing
- Understand the assumptions of hypothesis testing and know what to do if the assumptions are violated
- Test for differences between means, proportions, and variances using hypothesis tests

INTRODUCTION

In Chapter 11, the concept of a sampling distribution was developed, and confidence intervals were used to estimate population parameters. In this chapter, the focus is on hypothesis testing to make inferences about the hypothesized values of two or more population parameters using sample statistics. The variable of interest is the CTQ, and the populations of interest are the different levels of an *X*. For example, the CTQ could be the hardness of a steel plate, and the populations of interest might be the different methods used to manufacture the steel plate. These methods are referred to as **hypothesis testing** or **tests of statistical significance.** These procedures are used for enumerative studies and for guidance in designed experiments.

12.1 FUNDAMENTAL CONCEPTS OF HYPOTHESIS TESTING

Hypothesis testing typically begins with some theory, claim, or assertion about a particular characteristic (CTQ) of one or more populations (levels of an *X*). For example, a study may be designed to determine whether the accounts receivable (CTQ) were higher in market segment 1 ($X = 1$) or market segment 2 ($X = 2$) in 2003. To state this quantitatively, CTQ = $f(X)$, where CTQ = accounts receivable, and $X = 1$ if market segment 1 and $X = 2$ if market segment 2. *X* either is or is not a statistically significant predictor of CTQ. A sample of accounts is drawn from each market segment. If the accounts receivable in 2003 are similar in both market segments, the means and the standard deviations should be similar in both market segments.

The hypothesis that the mean 2003 account receivables are equal in the market segments (no statistically significant difference in the mean accounts receivable between market segments) is referred to as the **null hypothesis.** A null hypothesis is always a statement containing no difference between a parameter and a specific value, or no difference between the parameters for two or more populations. The symbol H_0 is commonly used to identify the null hypothesis. Because the experimenter wants to compare the mean yield of a CTQ for the low and high levels of an *X*, the null hypothesis is stated as either:

$$H_{0A}: \mu_1 = \mu_2 \text{ or } \mu_1 - \mu_2 = 0$$

$$H_{0B}: \mu_1 \leq \mu_2 \text{ or } \mu_1 - \mu_2 \leq 0$$

$$H_{0C}: \mu_1 \geq \mu_2 \text{ or } \mu_1 - \mu_2 \geq 0$$

H_{0A} is used to test the null hypothesis of no difference between two population means when there is no information about which population has the higher mean. H_{0B} is used to test the null hypothesis when there is information that the mean of population 1 is less than or equal to the mean of population 2. H_{0C} is used to test the null hypothesis when there is information that the mean of population 1 is greater than or equal to the mean of population 2.

Even though information is obtained only from a sample, the null hypothesis is written in terms of the population parameters. This is because you are interested in the population of responses that might ever be studied. The sample statistics are used to make inferences about the population parameters. The logic and theory of hypothesis testing requires that the null hypothesis is considered true until evidence in the form of sample data indicates that is false. If the null hypothesis is considered false, something else must be true.

Whenever a null hypothesis is specified, an **alternative hypothesis** or one that must be true if the null hypothesis is found to be false must also be specified. The **alternative hypothesis** (H_1) is the opposite of the null hypothesis (H_0). For the difference between the mean of the two groups, this is stated as either:

$$H_{1A} : \mu_1 \neq \mu_2 \text{ or } \mu_1 - \mu_2 \neq 0$$

$$H_{1B} : \mu_1 > \mu_2 \text{ or } \mu_1 - \mu_2 > 0$$
$$H_{1C}: \mu_1 < \mu_2 \text{ or } \mu_1 - \mu_2 < 0.$$

H_{1A} is used to state the alternative hypothesis that there is a statistically significant difference between two population means when there is no information about which population has the higher mean. H_{1B} is used to state the alternative hypothesis that the mean of population 1 is statistically significantly greater than the mean of population 2. H_{1C} is used to state the alternative hypothesis that the mean of population 1 is statistically significantly less than the mean of population 2.

The alternative hypothesis represents the conclusion reached by rejecting the null hypothesis if there were sufficient evidence from sample information to decide that the null hypothesis is unlikely to be true. In the example concerning the difference between the 2003 mean accounts receivable in two market segments, if the difference between the means is sufficiently large, the null hypothesis is rejected in favor of the alternative hypothesis that the two 2003 market segment means are different.

Hypothesis-testing procedures or statistical tests of significance are designed so that rejection of the null hypothesis is based on evidence from the sample that the alternative hypothesis is far more likely to be true. However, *failure to reject the null hypothesis is not proof that the null hypothesis is true.* If you fail to reject the null hypothesis, you can only conclude that there is insufficient evidence to warrant its rejection.

A summary of the null and alternative hypotheses is presented in Exhibit 12.1.

| Exhibit 12.1 | **The Null and Alternative Hypotheses** |

The following key points summarize the null and alternative hypotheses:

1. The null hypothesis (H_0) represents the status quo or current belief in a situation, that is, that the X has no influence on the CTQ.

2. The alternative hypothesis (H_1) is the opposite of the null hypothesis and represents a research claim or specific inference you would like to study, that is, that the X has a statistically significant influence on the CTQ.

3. If you reject the null hypothesis, you have statistical proof that the alternative hypothesis is true.

4. If you do not reject the null hypothesis, you have failed to prove the alternative hypothesis. The failure to prove the alternative hypothesis does not mean that you have proven the null hypothesis.

5. The null hypothesis (H_0) always refers to a specified value of the *population parameter* (such as μ), not a *sample statistic* (such as $\overline{X}$).

6. The statement of the null hypothesis *always* contains an equal sign regarding the specified value of the parameter (for example, H_0: $\mu_1 = \mu_2$).

7. The statement of the alternative hypothesis *never* contains an equal sign regarding the specified value of the parameter (for example, H_1: $\mu_1 \neq \mu_2$).

The Critical Value of the Test Statistic

The logic behind the hypothesis-testing methodology is based on using sample information to determine the plausibility of the null hypothesis.

The null hypothesis for the accounts receivable problem is that the mean 2003 accounts receivable for the market segment 1 is equal to the mean 2003 accounts receivable for market segment 2, H_0: $\mu_1 = \mu_2$. Sample data is collected, and the 2003 sample mean accounts receivable for each of the two market segments is computed. Sample statistics are estimates of population parameters and will likely differ from the population parameters because of chance or sampling error. If in fact there is no difference between the two market segments, you expect the sample means to be very close to each other. When this occurs, there is insufficient evidence to reject the null hypothesis.

If there is a large difference between the sample statistics for the two groups, your instinct is to conclude that the null hypothesis is unlikely to be true. Here you reject the null hypothesis. In either case, the decision is reached because of the belief that randomly selected samples reflect the underlying frames from which they are drawn.

Unfortunately, the decision-making process is not always so clear-cut and cannot be left to an individual's subjective judgment as to the meaning of "very close" or "very different." Determining what is very close and what is very different is arbitrary without using operational definitions. Hypothesis-testing procedures provide operational definitions for evaluating such differences and enable you to quantify the decision-making process so that the probability of obtaining a given sample result can be found if the null hypothesis were true. This is achieved by first determining the sampling distribution for the sample statistic of interest, then computing the particular *test statistic* based on the given sample result. The sampling distribution for the test statistic often follows a well-known statistical distribution, such as the normal distribution or the *t*-distribution. In such circumstances, you will be able to determine the likelihood of a null hypothesis being true.

Regions of Rejection and Nonrejection

The sampling distribution of the test statistic is divided into two regions, a **region of rejection** (sometimes called the **critical region**) and a **region of nonrejection** (see Figure 12.1). If the test statistic falls into the region of nonrejection, the null hypothesis is not rejected. In the test for the accounts receivable for the two market segments in 2003, you would conclude that the mean accounts receivable is the same for the two market segments in 2003. If the test statistic falls into the rejection region, the null hypothesis is rejected. In this case, you would conclude that the average accounts receivable is different between the two market segments in 2003.

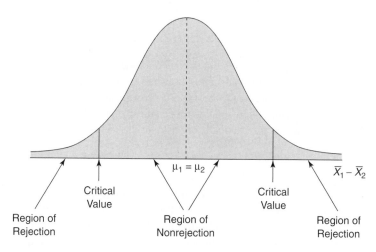

FIGURE 12.1 Regions of Rejection and Nonrejection in Hypothesis Testing

The region of rejection consists of the values of the test statistic that are unlikely to occur if the null hypothesis is true. These values are not so unlikely to occur if the null hypothesis is false. Therefore, if you observe a value of the test statistic that falls into the *rejection region,* the null hypothesis is rejected because that value is unlikely if the null hypothesis is true.

To make a decision concerning the null hypothesis, you first determine the **critical value** of the test statistic. The critical value divides the nonrejection region from the rejection region. However, the determination of the critical value is directly related to the risks involved in using only sample evidence to make decisions about a population parameter.

Risks in Decision Making Using Hypothesis-Testing Methodology

There are risks that an incorrect conclusion will be reached when using a sample statistic to make decisions about a population parameter. In fact, two different types of errors can occur when applying hypothesis-testing methodology, Type I and Type II.

A **Type I error** occurs if the null hypothesis H_0 is rejected when in fact it is true and should not be rejected. The probability of a Type I error occurring is α. A good way to remember the definition of the Type I error is ART, Alpha-Reject H_0-True.

A **Type II error** occurs if the null hypothesis H_0 is not rejected when in fact it is false and should be rejected. The probability of a Type II error occurring is β. A good way to remember the definition of the Type II error is BAF, Beta-Accept H_0-False.

In the accounts receivable problem, the Type I error occurs if you conclude (based on sample information) that the mean 2003 accounts receivable is different between the two market segments when in fact there is no difference. On the other hand, the Type II error occurs if you conclude (based on sample information) that the mean 2003 accounts receivable is not different between the two market segments when in fact there is a statistically significant difference.

Level of Significance

The probability of committing a Type I error, denoted by α, is referred to as the **level of significance** of the statistical test. Traditionally, you control the Type I error by deciding the risk level of α you are willing to tolerate in terms of rejecting the null hypothesis when it is true. Because the level of significance is specified before the hypothesis test is performed, the risk of committing a Type I error, α, is directly under the control of the individual performing the test. Researchers traditionally select α levels of 0.05 or 0.01. The choice of selecting a particular risk level for making a Type I error is dependent on the cost of making a Type I error. Once the value for α is specified, the rejection region is known, because α is the probability of rejection under the null hypothesis. From this fact, the critical value or values that divide the rejection and non-rejection regions are determined.

The Confidence Coefficient

The complement $(1 - \alpha)$ of the probability of a Type I error is called the **confidence coefficient,** which when multiplied by 100% yields the confidence level studied in Section 11.2–11.5.

The **confidence coefficient,** denoted by $1 - \alpha$, is the probability that the null hypothesis H_0 is not rejected when it is true and should not be rejected.

In terms of hypothesis-testing methodology, this coefficient represents the probability of concluding that the specified value of the parameter being tested under the null hypothesis may be true when, in fact, it is true. In the accounts receivable example, the confidence coefficient measures the probability of concluding that there is no statistically significant difference between the two market segments when in fact there is actually no difference.

The β Risk

The probability of committing a Type II error, called β, is often referred to as the *consumer's risk* level. Unlike the Type I error which you control by the selection of α, the probability of making a Type II error is dependent on the difference between the hypothesized and actual value of the population parameter. Because large differences are easier to find, if the difference between the hypothesized value and the corresponding population parameter is large, β the probability of committing a Type II error will likely be small. If the difference between the hypothesized value and the corresponding parameter value is small, the probability of committing a Type II error β is large.

The Power of a Test

The complement $(1 - \beta)$ of the probability of a Type II error is called the **power of a statistical test.**

> The **power of a statistical test**, denoted by $1 - \beta$, is the conditional probability of rejecting the null hypothesis when it is false and should be rejected.

In the accounts receivable example, the power of the test is the probability of concluding that there is a statistically significant difference in the means of the two market segments when in fact there actually is a difference. Table 12.1 illustrates the results of the two possible decisions (do not reject H_0 or reject H_0) that can occur in any hypothesis test. Depending on the specific decision, one of two types of errors may occur or one of two types of correct conclusions will be reached.

TABLE 12.1 Hypothesis Testing and Decision Making

	Actual situation	
Statistical decision	**H_0 True**	**H_0 False**
Do not reject H_0	Correct decision confidence = $1 - \alpha$	Type II error $P(\text{Type II error}) = \beta$
Reject H_0	Type I error $P(\text{Type I error}) = \alpha$	Correct decision power = $1 - \beta$

One way you can control the probability of making a Type II error in a study is to increase the size of the sample. Larger sample sizes generally permit you to detect even very small differences between the hypothesized and actual values of the population parameter. For a given level of α, increasing the sample size will decrease β and, therefore increase the power of the test to detect that the null hypothesis H_0 is false. Of course, there is always a limit to resources. Thus, for a given sample size, you must consider the trade-off between the two possible types of errors. Because you can directly control the risk of the Type I error, you can reduce your risk by selecting a lower level for α. For example, if the negative consequences associated with making a Type I error are substantial, you can select α to be 0.01 instead of 0.05. However, when α is decreased, β will be increased, so a reduction in risk of Type I error will result in an increased risk of Type II error. If, you wish to reduce β, the risk of Type II error, you could select a larger value for α. Therefore, if it is important to try to avoid a Type II error, you can select α to be 0.05 instead of 0.01.

Now that the level of significance has been defined, you need to make a distinction between a statistically significant difference and a practically significant difference between population parameters. Given a large enough sample size, you will always be able to detect a statistically significant difference between population parameters. This is because no two things in nature are exactly equal. So with a large enough sample size, you can always detect the natural difference between two populations. Consequently, in some cases, a better type of null hypothesis might be: H_0: $\mu_1 - \mu_2 \geq \Delta$, where Δ is a practically significant difference between the population means.

The steps of hypothesis testing are summarized in Exhibit 12.2.

| **Exhibit 12.2** | **Seven-Step Method of Hypothesis Testing** |

1. State the null hypothesis, H_0 and the alternative hypothesis H_1. The null hypothesis must be stated in statistical terms, using population parameters. In testing whether there is a difference in the means of the two populations, the null hypothesis states that $\mu_1 = \mu_2$ and the alternative hypothesis states that $\mu_1 \neq \mu_2$

2. Choose the level of significance, α. The level of significance is specified according to the relative importance of the risks of committing Type I and Type II errors in the problem. In other words, the Type I error is set by the decision maker as the probability she or he is willing to accept in rejecting the null hypothesis when it is in fact true. This error is associated with the most serious error that can occur with respect to the decision being made by the hypothesis test. For example, if a person has limited funds, this error would involve taking an action that could cause the person to lose his or her bankroll, as opposed to incurring the cost of a lost opportunity.

3. Choose the sample size, *n*. The sample size is determined after taking into account the specified risks of committing Type I and Type II errors (i.e., selected levels of α and β) and considering budget constraints in carrying out the study.

4. Determine the appropriate statistical technique and corresponding test statistic.

5. Set up the critical values that divide the rejection and nonrejection regions. Once the null and alternative hypotheses are specified and the level of significance and sample size are determined, the critical values for the appropriate statistical distribution can be found so that the rejection and nonrejection regions can be specified.

6. Collect the data and compute the sample value of the appropriate test statistic. Determine whether the test statistic has fallen into the rejection or the nonrejection region. Compare the computed value of the test statistic with the critical values for the appropriate sampling distribution to determine whether it falls into the rejection or nonrejection region.

7. Make the statistical decision. If the test statistic falls into the nonrejection region, the null hypothesis H_0 cannot be rejected. If the test statistic falls into the rejection region, the null hypothesis is rejected in favor of the alternative hypothesis. Express the statistical decision in terms of the problem.

The *p*-Value Approach to Hypothesis Testing

Modern statistical software can compute a probability value known as the *p*-value. This approach to hypothesis testing has increasingly gained acceptance and is commonly substituted for the critical value approach.

The **p-value** is the probability of obtaining a test statistic equal to or more extreme than the result obtained from the sample data, given that the null hypothesis H_0 is true.

The *p*-value is often referred to as the *observed level of significance.* This is the smallest level at which H_0 can be rejected for a given set of data. The decision rule in the *p*-value approach for rejecting H_0 is:

- If the *p*-value is greater than or equal to α, the null hypothesis is not rejected.
- If the *p*-value is less than α, the null hypothesis is rejected.

Many people confuse this rule, mistakenly believing that a high *p*-value is grounds for rejection. You can avoid this confusion by informally remembering "If the *p*-value is *low*, then H_0 must go."

A summary of the *p*-value approach for hypothesis testing is displayed in Exhibit 12.3.

Exhibit 12.3 | **Six Steps of Hypothesis Testing Using the *p*-Value Approach**

1. State the null hypothesis, H_0 and the alternative hypothesis, H_1.
2. Choose the level of significance, α and the sample size, n.
3. Determine the appropriate statistical technique and corresponding test statistic.
4. Collect the data and compute the sample value of the appropriate test statistic.
5. Calculate the *p*-value based on the test statistic and compare the *p*-value to α.
6. Make the statistical decision. If the *p*-value is greater than or equal to α, the null hypothesis is not rejected. If the *p*-value is less than α, the null hypothesis is rejected. Express the statistical decision in the context of the problem.

12.2 TESTING FOR THE DIFFERENCE BETWEEN TWO PROPORTIONS

Often you want to analyze differences between two populations in the number of nonconforming or defective occurrences. The sample statistics needed to analyze these differences are the proportion of occurrences in population 1 and the proportion of occurrences in population 2. With sufficient sample size in each group, the sampling distribution of the difference between the two proportions approximately follows a normal distribution.

Table 12.2 summarizes some findings from a study that was conducted as part of a legal case at a semiconductor manufacturing facility for 2003. The study provided defect data for a

TABLE 12.2 Cross-Classification of Whether a Particle is Present and the Condition of the Wafer

Particles present	Condition of wafer based on frequencies		
	Good	Bad	Total
Yes	14	36	50
No	320	80	400
Total	334	116	450

sample of 450 wafers. Of 334 wafers that were classified as good, 320 had no particle found on the die that produced the wafer. Of 116 wafers that were classified as bad, 80 had no particle found on the die that produced the wafer.

The objective of the test of hypothesis is to determine whether the proportion of wafers with no particle is the same for good and bad wafers using a level of significance of $\alpha = 0.05$.

For these 2003 data, the proportion of good wafers without particles is $320/334 = 0.9581$, and the proportion of bad wafers without particles is $80/116 = 0.6897$.

Because the number of "successes" (having no particles) in the groups (320 and 80) is large, as is the number of "failures" (having a particle) in the groups (14 and 36), the sampling distribution for the difference between the two proportions is approximately normally distributed. The null and alternative hypotheses are:

$H_0: \pi_1 = \pi_2$ or $\pi_1 - \pi_2 = 0$ (No difference between the two proportions)

$H_1: \pi_1 \neq \pi_2$ or $\pi_1 - \pi_2 \neq 0$ (There is a difference between the two proportions)

Figure 12.2 illustrates Minitab output for the yield improvement experiment.

Test and CI for Two Proportions

```
Sample    X    N   Sample p
1        320  334  0.958084
2         80  116  0.689655


Difference = p (1) - p (2)
Estimate for difference:  0.268429
95% CI for difference:  (0.181539, 0.355318)
Test for difference = 0 (vs not = 0):  Z = 7.93  P-Value = 0.000
```

FIGURE 12.2 Minitab Output for the Difference Between Two Proportions for the Yield Improvement Experiment

There are two approaches to making a decision using a hypothesis test, the critical value approach and the *p*-value approach. In this first example of hypothesis testing, both approaches will be illustrated. For other tests of hypothesis used in this book, because Minitab software will be used, the *p*-value approach will be emphasized.

Using the critical value approach, regions of rejection and nonrejection must be defined. As stated previously, the sampling distribution of the difference between two proportions approximately follows the normal distribution. Selecting a level of significance of 0.05 provides a lower tail area of 0.025 and an upper tail area of 0.025. Using the cumulative normal distribution table (Table C.1 in Appendix C), the lower critical value of 0.025 corresponds to a Z value of -1.96, and an upper critical value of 0.025 (cumulative area of 0.975) corresponds to an upper critical value of $+1.96$ (see Figure 12.3). The decision rule is:

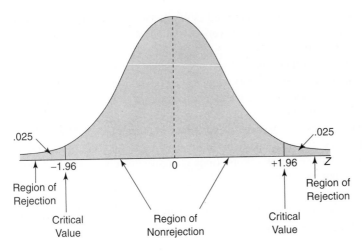

FIGURE 12.3 Testing a Hypothesis for the Difference Between Two Proportions at the 0.05 Level of Significance

Reject H_0 if $Z < -1.96$

or if $Z > +1.96$;

otherwise, do not reject H_0.

From Figure 12.2, the test statistic $Z = +7.93$. Because $Z = +7.93$ is greater than the upper critical value of $+1.96$, the null hypothesis is rejected. Alternatively, using the *p*-value approach, the *p*-value $= 0.0000$. Because the *p*-value $= 0.0000$ is *less than* the level of significance $\alpha = 0.05$, the null hypothesis is rejected. This means that the chance of obtaining a Z value greater than 7.93 is virtually zero (0.0000). You conclude that there is a difference in the proportion of wafers that have no particles between the good and bad wafers for 2003, the timeframe of the lawsuit. Clearly, the good wafers are much more likely to have no particles than the bad wafers. This information can be used in court concerning the state of the manufacturing facility in 2003.

The steps of the critical value approach for this example are summarized as follows:

Step 1:

H_0: $\pi_1 = \pi_2$ (no difference between the two proportions)
H_1: $\pi_1 \neq \pi_2$ (statistically significant difference between the two proportions)

Step 2:

$\alpha = 0.05$

Step 3:

A sample of 450 wafers is selected.

Step 4:

The test for the difference between two proportions follows a normal distribution.

Step 5:

The decision rule is Reject H_0 if $Z < -1.96$ or if $Z > +1.96$; otherwise, do not reject H_0.

Step 6:

$Z = +7.93$ $Z = +7.93$ is greater than the upper critical value of $+1.96$.

Step 7:

The null hypothesis is rejected. You conclude that there is a difference in the proportion of wafers that have no particles between the good and bad wafers for 2003.
The steps of the *p*-value approach for this example are summarized as follows:

Steps 1–3 Same as steps 1–4 of the critical value approach.

Step 4:

$Z = +7.93$

Step 5:

The *p*-value (obtained from Minitab) is 0.0000 which is less than $\alpha = 0.05$.

Step 6:

Reject the null hypothesis. You conclude that there is a difference in the proportion of wafers that have no particles between the good and bad wafers in 2003.

These steps for hypothesis testing are used for all hypothesis tests subsequently discussed in this book.

Equation for the Z Test for the Difference Between Two Proportions (optional)

$$Z = \frac{(p_1 - p_2) - (\pi_1 - \pi_2)}{\sqrt{\overline{p}(1 - \overline{p})\left(\dfrac{1}{n_1} + \dfrac{1}{n_2}\right)}}$$

(12.1)

with

$$\overline{p} = \frac{X_1 + X_2}{n_1 + n_2} \qquad p_1 = \frac{X_1}{n_1} \qquad p_2 = \frac{X_2}{n_2}$$

where

p_1 = proportion of successes in sample 1

X_1 = number of successes in sample 1

n_1 = sample size from population 1

π_1 = proportion of successes in population 1

p_2 = proportion of successes in sample 2

X_2 = number of successes in sample 2

n_2 = sample size from population 2

π_2 = proportion of successes in population 2

For the example concerning the presence of particles on the wafers, using Equation (12.1) where

$$p_1 = \frac{X_1}{n_1} = \frac{320}{334} = 0.9581 \qquad p_2 = \frac{X_2}{n_2} = \frac{80}{116} = 0.6897$$

and

$$\bar{p} = \frac{X_1 + X_2}{n_1 + n_2} = \frac{320 + 80}{334 + 116} = \frac{400}{450} = 0.8889$$

so that

$$Z = \frac{(0.9581 - 0.6897) - (0)}{\sqrt{0.8889(1 - 0.8889)\left(\dfrac{1}{334} + \dfrac{1}{116}\right)}}$$

$$= \frac{0.2684}{\sqrt{(0.09876)(0.0116)}}$$

$$= \frac{0.2684}{\sqrt{0.0011456}}$$

$$= \frac{0.2684}{0.03385} = +7.93$$

12.3 TESTING FOR THE DIFFERENCE BETWEEN THE MEANS OF TWO INDEPENDENT GROUPS

Many studies are designed to compare two independent populations where the response of interest is a measurement on a continuous variable. Two different tests of hypotheses for the difference between the means are usually used, a pooled-variance t test in which the variances in the two populations are assumed to be equal and a separate-variance t test in which the variances in the two populations are not assumed to be equal.

Pooled-Variance t Test for the Difference in Two Means

The pooled-variance t test requires that the two sample variances be combined or pooled into one estimate of the variance common in the two groups, assuming that the population variances in the two populations are equal. The test statistic is based on the difference in the sample means of the two groups. The sampling distribution for the difference in the two sample means approximately follows the t distribution (see assumptions on page 349).

The null hypothesis of no difference in the means of two independent populations is

H_0: $\mu_1 = \mu_2$ (the two population means are equal)

and the alternative hypothesis is

H_1: $\mu_1 \neq \mu_2$ (the two population means are not equal)

To illustrate this test of hypothesis for the difference between two means, an experiment is designed to compare differences in average surface hardness of steel plates used in intaglio printing (measured in indentation numbers), based on two different surface conditions—untreated versus treated by light polishing with emery paper. This experiment is important to a legal case concerning the surface steel hardness of steel plates in a facility in the 2003 time period. In the experiment, 40 steel plates are randomly assigned, 20 that are untreated and 20 that are lightly polished. The results are displayed in Table 12.3.

The objective of the test of hypothesis is to determine whether the mean surface hardness is the same for untreated and treated steel plates for 2003. A level of significance of $\alpha = 0.05$ has been selected for making the decision.

Figure 12.4 illustrates Minitab output for the difference in the mean surface hardness between treated and untreated steel plates.

From Figure 12.4, the t statistic is $+4.12$, and the p-value is 0.000. Because the p-value is 0.000, which is less than $\alpha = 0.05$, the null hypothesis is rejected. This means that the chance of obtaining a t value greater than $+4.12$ is 0.000. You can conclude that the mean surface hardness is higher for the untreated steel plates (sample average of 165.09) than for the treated steel plates (sample average of 155.70) in 2003.

TABLE 12.3 Surface Hardness of 20 Untreated Steel Plates and 20 Treated Steel Plates

Untreated	Treated
164.368	158.239
159.018	138.216
153.871	168.006
165.096	149.654
157.184	145.456
154.496	168.178
160.920	154.321
164.917	162.763
169.091	161.020
175.276	167.706
177.135	150.226
163.903	155.620
167.802	151.233
160.818	158.653
167.433	151.204
163.538	150.869
164.525	161.657
171.230	157.016
174.964	156.127
166.311	147.920

 INTAGLIO

```
Two-sample T for Untreated vs Treated

            N    Mean   StDev  SE Mean
Untreated  20   165.09   6.46    1.4
Treated    20   155.70   7.90    1.8


Difference = mu (Untreated) - mu (Treated)
Estimate for difference:  9.39061
95% CI for difference:  (4.77274, 14.00848)
T-Test of difference = 0 (vs not =): T-Value = 4.12  P-Value = 0.000  DF = 38
Both use Pooled StDev = 7.2135
```

FIGURE 12.4 Minitab Output of the Pooled-Variance *t* Test for the Difference in Hardness Between Steel Plates

---

CAUTION   Checking the Assumptions of the Pooled-Variance *t* Test

In testing for the difference between the means, the assumption is made that the populations are normally distributed with equal variances. For situations in which the two populations have equal variances, the pooled-variance *t* test is **robust** (not sensitive) to moderate departures from the assumption of normality, provided that the sample sizes are large. In these situations, the pooled-variance *t* test can be used without serious effect on its power.

On the other hand, if the data in each group cannot be assumed to be from normally distributed populations, two choices exist. A *nonparametric* procedure, such as the *Wilcoxon rank sum test* [see References 1 and 2], can be used that does not depend on the assumption of normality for the two populations. Alternatively a transformation [see Reference 2] on each of the outcomes can be made and the pooled-variance *t* test can then be used.

To check the assumption of normality in each of the two groups, a side-by-side box-and-whisker plot is obtained (see Figure 12.5).

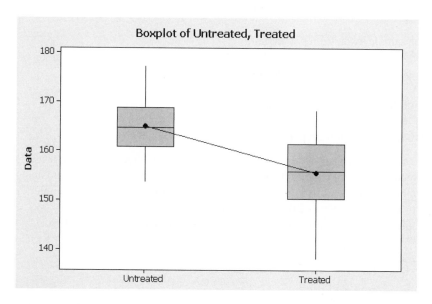

FIGURE 12.5 Side-by-Side Box-and-Whisker Plot of Untreated and Treated Steel Plates Obtained from Minitab

From Figure 12.5 you can see that there is only moderate departure from normality, so the assumption of normality needed for the *t*-test does not appear to be seriously violated.

Equation for the Pooled-Variance *t* Test for the Difference Between Two Means (optional)

$$t = \frac{(\overline{X}_1 - \overline{X}_2) - (\mu_1 - \mu_2)}{\sqrt{S_p^2\left(\dfrac{1}{n_1} + \dfrac{1}{n_2}\right)}} \tag{12.2}$$

where

$$S_p^2 = \frac{(n_1 - 1)S_1^2 + (n_2 - 1)S_2^2}{(n_1 - 1) + (n_2 - 1)}$$

and

S_p^2 = pooled variance

$\overline{X}_1$ = mean of the sample taken from population 1

S_1^2 = variance of the sample taken from population 1

n_1 = size of the sample taken from population 1

$\overline{X}_2$ = mean of the sample taken from population 2

S_2^2 = variance of the sample taken from population 2

n_2 = size of the sample taken from population 2

The test statistic *t* follows a *t* distribution with $n_1 + n_2 - 2$ degrees of freedom. The $n_1 + n_2 - 2$ degrees of freedom are derived from the fact that there are $n_1 - 1$ degrees of freedom in group 1 (the sample size minus 1) and $n_2 - 1$ degrees of freedom in group 2 (the sample size minus 1), for a total of $n_1 + n_2 - 2$ degrees of freedom.

For the example concerning the surface hardness of steel plates, using Equation (12.2),

$$t = \frac{(\overline{X}_1 - \overline{X}_2) - (\mu_1 - \mu_2)}{\sqrt{S_p^2\left(\dfrac{1}{n_1} + \dfrac{1}{n_2}\right)}}$$

where

$$S_p^2 = \frac{(n_1 - 1)S_1^2 + (n_2 - 1)S_2^2}{(n_1 - 1) + (n_2 - 1)}$$

$$= \frac{19(6.46)^2 + 19(7.90)^2}{19 + 19} = 52.0708$$

Therefore:

$$t = \frac{165.09 - 155.70}{\sqrt{52.0708\left(\dfrac{1}{20} + \dfrac{1}{20}\right)}} = \frac{9.39}{\sqrt{5.20708}} = +4.12$$

Using the $\alpha = 0.05$ level of significance, with $20 + 20 - 2 = 38$ degrees of freedom, the critical value of t (see table C.2 in Appendix C) is 2.0244 (0.025 in the upper tail of the t distribution).
Because

$$t = +4.12 > 2.0244,$$

you reject H_0.

Separate-Variance t Test for Differences in Two Means

In the pooled variance test for the difference between the means of two independent populations, the sample variances were pooled together into a common estimate because the assumption was made that the population variances were equal. However, if this assumption cannot be made, the pooled-variance t test is inappropriate. As a result, the **separate-variance t test** [see References 1 and 2] is used. Although the computations for the separate-variance t test are complicated, Minitab can be used to perform them. Figure 12.6 presents Minitab output of this separate-variance t test for these steel plates.

```
Two-sample T for Untreated vs Treated

            N    Mean   StDev   SE Mean
Untreated  20  165.09   6.46     1.4
Treated    20  155.70   7.90     1.8


Difference = mu (Untreated) - mu (Treated)
Estimate for difference:  9.39061
95% CI for difference:  (4.76430, 14.01692)
T-Test of difference = 0 (vs not =): T-Value = 4.12  P-Value = 0.000  DF = 36
```

FIGURE 12.6 Minitab Output of the Separate-Variance t Test for the Steel Plate Data

From Figure 12.6, the test statistic for $t = +4.12$ (there are 36 degrees of freedom), and the p-value is $0.000 < 0.05$. For these data, the results from the two different t tests led to the same decision and conclusions. The assumption of equality of population variances had no real effect on the results. Sometimes, however, the results from the pooled- and separate-variance t tests conflict because the assumption of equal variances is violated. This is why it is so important to evaluate the assumptions and use those results as a guide in the appropriate selection of a test procedure. In the next section, the F test and the Levene test are used to determine whether there is evidence of a difference in the two population variances. The results of these tests can help you determine which of the t tests (pooled-variance or separate-variance) is more appropriate.

12.4 TESTING FOR THE DIFFERENCES BETWEEN TWO VARIANCES

Often it is necessary to test whether two independent populations have the same variance. One important reason to test for the difference in the variances of two populations is the need to determine whether the pooled-variance t test is appropriate.

The F Test for the Ratio of Two Variances

The test statistic for the difference between the variances of two independent populations is based on the ratio of the two sample variances. The sampling distribution follows the F distribution (see assumptions on page 353).

The null hypothesis of equality of variances

$$H_0: \quad \sigma_1^2 = \sigma_2^2$$

is tested against the alternative hypothesis that the two population variances are not equal

$$H_1: \quad \sigma_1^2 \neq \sigma_2^2$$

To illustrate this test for the difference between two variances, return to the legal case previously discussed concerning the differences in surface hardness of steel plates used in intaglio printing (measured in indentation numbers), based on two different surface conditions—untreated versus treated by light polishing with emery paper.

The objective of the test of hypothesis is to determine whether the variance in surface hardness is the same for untreated and treated steel plates at the $\alpha = 0.05$ level of significance.

Figure 12.7 illustrates Minitab output for the difference in the variance of surface hardness between treated and untreated steel plates.

From Figure 12.7, the F statistic is 0.67, and the p-value is 0.388. Because the p-value is 0.388, which is greater than $\alpha = 0.05$, the null hypothesis is not rejected. This means that the

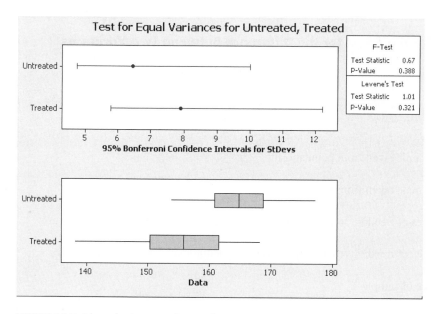

FIGURE 12.7 Minitab Output of Tests for Variances of the Difference in Hardness Between Treated and Untreated Steel Plates

chance of obtaining an *F* value greater than 0.67 is 0.388. You can conclude that there is insufficient evidence of a difference in the variance of surface hardness between the untreated steel plates and the treated steel plates.

> **CAUTION**   **Checking the Assumptions of the *F* Test for the Differences Between Two Variances**
>
> In testing for a difference in two variances using the *F* test, the assumption is made that each of the two populations is normally distributed. This test is *very* sensitive to the normality assumption. If box-and-whisker plots or normal probability plots suggest even a mild departure from normality for either of the two populations, you should not use the *F* test. In such a case, another test, such as the Levene test, should be used.

Equation for the *F* Test for the Difference Between Two Variances (optional)

$$F = \frac{S_1^2}{S_2^2} \tag{12.3}$$

where

n_1 = size of sample taken from population 1

n_2 = size of sample taken from population 2

$n_1 - 1$ = degrees of freedom from sample 1 (i.e., the numerator degrees of freedom)

$n_2 - 1$ = degrees of freedom from sample 2 (i.e., the denominator degrees of freedom)

S_1^2 = variance of sample 1

S_2^2 = variance of sample 2

The test statistic *F* follows an *F* distribution with $n_1 - 1$ and $n_2 - 1$ degrees of freedom For the example concerning the surface hardness of steel plates, using Equation (12.3),

$$F = \frac{S_1^2}{S_2^2}$$

$$= \frac{(6.46)^2}{(7.90)^2} = 0.67$$

The Levene Test for the Difference Between Variances

Although the *F* test for the ratio of two variances is a simple test, it is very sensitive to the assumption that each of the two populations follows the normal distribution. The Levene test for differences between variances is robust (not very sensitive) to lack of normality. The Levene test is based on the idea that if the variation in the two groups does not differ, a *t* test of the absolute differences from each group median can be used to test the null hypothesis of equal variances. Thus, the absolute value of the difference between each observation and the median of the group is obtained, and a one-way **analysis of variance** (ANOVA; see Section 12.5) is carried out on these *absolute differences*. Figure 12.7 provides the test statistic for the Levene test. The test statistic is 1.01, and the *p*-value is 0.321. Because the *p*-value is 0.321, which is greater than $\alpha = 0.05$, the null hypothesis is not rejected. You can conclude that there is insufficient evidence of a difference in the variance of the surfaces between the untreated steel plates and the treated steel plates. For these data, the results of the F test for differences between variances and the Levene test are similar. However, remember that if there is any departure from normality in the data, the F test is inappropriate, and the more robust Levene test should be used.

12.5 ONE-WAY ANOVA: TESTING FOR DIFFERENCES AMONG THE MEANS OF THREE OR MORE GROUPS

Sometimes a hypothesis test involves testing for differences in the mean level of a CTQ or Y for an X with three or more levels. A factor (X) such as baking temperature may have several *numerical levels* (e.g., 300 degrees, 350 degrees, 400 degrees, 450 degrees) or a factor such as preferred level may have several *categorical levels* (low, medium, high). This type of hypothesis test is called a **completely randomized design.**

F Test for Differences in Three or More Means

When the numerical measurements (values of the CTQ) across the groups (levels of the X) are continuous and certain assumptions are met (see pages 360–361), the methodology known as **analysis of variance (ANOVA)** is used to compare the populations means of the CTQ for each level of X. The ANOVA procedure used for completely randomized designs is referred to as a **one-way ANOVA.** In a sense, the term *analysis of variance* is misleading because the objective is to analyze differences among the population means, not the variances. However, unlike the t test, which compares differences in two means, the one-way ANOVA compares the differences among three or more population means simultaneously. This is accomplished through an analysis of the variation among the populations and also within the populations. In ANOVA, the total variation of the measurements in all the populations is subdivided into variation that is due to differences *among* the populations and variation that is due to variation *within* the populations (see Figure 12.8). **Within-group (population) variation** is considered **experimental error. Among-group (population) variation** is attributable to **treatment effects,** which represent the effect of the factor (levels of X) used in the experiment on the CTQ or Y.

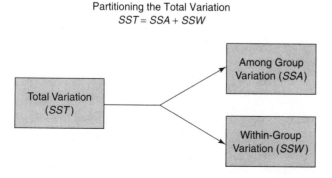

Partitioning the Total Variation
$SST = SSA + SSW$

FIGURE 12.8 Partitioning the Total Variation in a One-Way ANOVA

The total variation of all the measurements is also called the **sum of squares total** (*SST*) because it represents the sum of the squared differences between each individual observation and the **overall or grand mean.** The among-group variation, also called the **sum of squares among groups** (*SSA*), represents the sum of the squared differences between the sample mean of each group and the overall or grand mean, weighted by the sample size in each group. The within-group variation, called the **sum of squares within groups** (*SSW*), measures the difference between each observation and the mean of its own group and cumulates the squares of these differences over all groups.

The ANOVA procedure derives its name from the fact that the comparison of the means of the groups is achieved by analyzing variances. In Section 9.10 on page 252, the variance was computed as a sum of squared differences around the mean, divided by the sample size minus 1. This sample size minus 1 represents the actual number of values that are free to vary once the mean is known and is called **degrees of freedom.** In the Analysis of Variance, there are three different variances: the variance among groups, the variance within groups, and the total variance. These variances are referred to in the ANOVA terminology as **mean squares.** The mean square among groups (*MSA*) is equal to the *SSA* divided by the number of groups minus 1. The mean square within groups (*MSW*) is equal to the *SSW* divided by the sample size minus the number of groups. The mean square total (*MST*) is equal to the *SST* divided by the sample size minus one.

To test the null hypothesis

H_0: All the population means are equal

against the alternative

H_1: Not all the population means are equal

the test statistic *F* is computed as the ratio of two of the variances, *MSA* to *MSW*.

The results of an analysis of variance are usually displayed in an **ANOVA summary table,** the format for which is presented in Table 12.4. The entries in this table include the sources of variation (i.e., among-group, within-group, and total), the degrees of freedom, the sums of squares, the mean squares (i.e., the variances), and the calculated *F* statistic. In addition, the *p*-value is included in the ANOVA table obtained from Minitab.

TABLE 12.4 ANOVA Summary Table

Source	Degrees of freedom	Sum of squares	Mean square (variance)	F
Among groups	$c - 1$	SSA	$MSA = \dfrac{SSA}{c - 1}$	$F = \dfrac{MSA}{MSW}$
Within groups	$n - c$	SSW	$MSW = \dfrac{SSW}{n - c}$	
Total	$n - 1$	SST		

To illustrate the one-way ANOVA F test, consider the manufacture of integrated circuits in a particular facility that is being sued by a customer concerning its output for the 2003 time-frame. Integrated circuits are produced on silicon wafers, which are ground to target thickness during an early stage of the production process. The wafers are positioned in various locations on a grinder and kept in place throughout a vacuum decompression process. The goal of this particular study is to determine whether the thickness of a wafer is the same at different positions on the wafer for a legal case. To accomplish this, a sample of 30 wafers is selected, and the thickness of each wafer at five different positions (positions 1, 2, 18, 19, and 28) is measured. The results are presented in Table 12.5.

Figure 12.9 displays the ANOVA results obtained from Minitab for the wafer positions.

TABLE 12.5 Thickness of Wafers in an Integrated Circuit Manufacturing Process

Position 1	Position 2	Position 18	Position 19	Position 28
240	243	250	253	248
238	242	245	251	247
239	242	246	250	248
235	237	246	249	246
240	241	246	247	249
240	243	244	248	245
240	243	244	249	246
245	250	250	247	248
238	240	245	248	246
240	242	246	249	248
240	243	246	250	248
241	245	243	247	245
247	245	255	250	249
237	239	243	247	246
242	244	245	248	245
237	239	242	247	245
242	244	246	251	248
243	245	247	252	249
243	245	248	251	250
244	246	246	250	246
241	239	244	250	246
242	245	248	251	249
242	245	248	243	246
241	244	245	249	247
236	239	241	246	242
243	246	247	252	247

(continued)

TABLE 12.5 Thickness of Wafers in an Integrated Circuit Manufacturing Process (*continued*)

Position 1	Position 2	Position 18	Position 19	Position 28
241	243	245	248	246
239	240	242	243	244
239	240	250	252	250
241	243	249	255	253

CIRCUITS

Source: K. C. B. Roes and R. J. M. M. Does, " Shewhart-Type Charts in Nonstandard Situations," *Technometrics*, 37, 1995, pp. 15–24. Reprinted with permission from *Technometrics*. Copyright 1995 by the American Statistical Association.

```
One-way ANOVA: Position 1, Position 2, Position 18, Position 19, Position 28

Source    DF      SS      MS      F       P
Factor     4  1417.73  354.43  51.00  0.000
Error    145  1007.77    6.95
Total    149  2425.50

S = 2.636   R-Sq = 58.45%   R-Sq(adj) = 57.31%
```

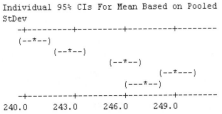

```
                                  Individual 95% CIs For Mean Based on Pooled
                                  StDev
Level        N    Mean  StDev    -+---------+---------+---------+--------
Position 1  30  240.53   2.62    (--*--)
Position 2  30  242.73   2.79         (--*--)
Position 18 30  246.07   2.90                     (--*--)
Position 19 30  249.10   2.66                            (--*---)
Position 28 30  247.07   2.15                       (---*--)
                                  -+---------+---------+---------+--------
                                 240.0     243.0     246.0     249.0
```

```
Pooled StDev = 2.64
```

FIGURE 12.9 Minitab ANOVA for the Wafer Positions

From Figure 12.9, the *F* statistic is 51.00, and the *p*-value is 0.000. Because the *p*-value is 0.000, which is less than $\alpha = 0.05$, the null hypothesis is rejected. This means that the chance of obtaining an *F* statistic greater than 51.00 is virtually zero (0.000). You can conclude that the mean thickness of the wafers is not the same for all the positions for the lawsuit. From Figure 12.9, you see that the mean for position 1 is 240.53; for position 2, it is 242.73; for position 18, it is 246.07; for position 19, it is 249.10; and for position 28, it is 247.07.

After performing the one-way ANOVA and finding a significant difference between the means of the positions, what is not yet known is which positions differ from each other. All that

---

Using the Critical Value Approach for ANOVA (optional)

To use the critical value approach in ANOVA, you refer to the table of the F statistic (Table C.3 in Appendix C). Two sets of degrees of freedom are required to obtain the critical value of the F statistic: the numerator degrees of freedom, which are equal to the number of groups minus 1; and the denominator degrees of freedom, which are equal to the sample size minus the number of groups. For the integrated circuit example, because there are five groups of 30 wafers each and a total sample size of $(30)(5) = 150$ wafers, the numerator degrees of freedom are equal to $5 - 1 = 4$, and the denominator degrees of freedom are equal to $150 - 5 = 145$. Selecting the $\alpha = 0.05$ level of significance, you see that in Table C.3, there is no entry for exactly 145 degrees of freedom, so you scan down to the intersection of the column with 4 degrees of freedom and the row with 120 degrees of freedom (the closest value to 145), and you find a critical value of F of 2.45.

Because the decision rule is to reject H_0 if $F >$ critical value of F, and

$F = 51.00 > 2.45$, you reject H_0.

---

is known is that there is sufficient evidence to state that the population means are not all the same. In other words, at least one or some combination of means is statistically significantly different from some other means. To determine exactly which positions differ, all possible pairwise comparisons between the positions can be made using a procedure developed by John Tukey [see References 1, 3, and 4].

Multiple Comparisons: The Tukey Procedure

In the integrated circuit example, the one-way ANOVA F test was used to determine whether there was a difference between the positions. Once differences in the means of the groups are found, it is important that the groups that are different are determined.

Although many procedures are available [see References 3 and 4], the **Tukey multiple comparison procedure** will be used to determine which of the means are statistically significantly different. This method is an example of a **post hoc** comparison procedure, because the hypotheses of interest are formulated *after* the data have been inspected. The Tukey procedure enables you to simultaneously examine comparisons between all pairs of groups. Figure 12.10 represents Minitab output for the wafer thickness for all pairs of positions.

In Figure 12.10, position 1 is compared with all other positions, then position 2 is compared with the remaining positions (18, 19, and 28), then position 18 is compared with the remaining positions (19 and 28), and position 19 is compared with the remaining position (28). For each pairwise comparison, Minitab shows the lower and upper limits of the interval, the pairwise difference, and a plot of the interval. Any intervals that do *not* include zero are considered significant. The 95% simultaneous confidence means that there is 95% confidence that the *entire set of intervals* is correctly estimating the pairwise differences in the population. Thus, only the

```
Tukey 95% Simultaneous Confidence Intervals
All Pairwise Comparisons

Individual confidence level = 99.36%


Position 1 subtracted from:

             Lower  Center  Upper   ------+---------+---------+---------+---
Position 2   0.318   2.200   4.082               (--*---)
Position 18  3.651   5.533   7.415                    (---*---)
Position 19  6.685   8.567  10.449                         (---*---)
Position 28  4.651   6.533   8.415                      (---*---)
                                    ------+---------+---------+---------+---
                                        -5.0       0.0       5.0      10.0


Position 2 subtracted from:

             Lower  Center  Upper   ------+---------+---------+---------+---
Position 18  1.451   3.333   5.215             (---*--)
Position 19  4.485   6.367   8.249                  (---*--)
Position 28  2.451   4.333   6.215               (---*--)
                                    ------+---------+---------+---------+---


Position 18 subtracted from:

             Lower  Center  Upper   ------+---------+---------+---------+---
Position 19  1.151   3.033   4.915              (---*---)
Position 28 -0.882   1.000   2.882          (---*---)
                                    ------+---------+---------+---------+---
                                        -5.0       0.0       5.0      10.0


Position 19 subtracted from:

             Lower  Center  Upper   ------+---------+---------+---------+---
Position 28 -3.915  -2.033  -0.151         (---*---)
                                    ------+---------+---------+---------+---
                                        -5.0       0.0       5.0      10.0
```

FIGURE 12.10 Minitab Tukey Multiple Comparisons for all Pairs of Positions

difference in mean thickness between position 18 and 28 (whose interval is from −0.882 to 2.882) is not considered different. All the other positions differ in average thickness.

ANOVA Assumptions

To use the one-way ANOVA *F* test, you must make three assumptions about the underlying populations:

1. Randomness and independence
2. Normality
3. Homogeneity of variance

The first assumption, **randomness and independence,** always must be met because the validity of any experiment depends on random sampling and/or the randomization process. To avoid biases in the outcomes, it is essential that either the obtained samples of data be considered as randomly and independently drawn from the populations or that the items or subjects in a study be randomly assigned to the levels of the factor of interest (i.e., the *treatment groups or levels of X*). Departures from this assumption can seriously affect inferences from the ANOVA. These problems are discussed more thoroughly in Reference 3.

The second assumption, **normality,** states that the values in each sampled group are drawn from normally distributed populations. Just as in the case of the *t* test, the one-way ANOVA *F* test is fairly robust against departures from the normal distribution. As long as the distributions are not extremely different from a normal distribution, the level of significance of the ANOVA *F* test is usually not greatly affected by lack of normality, particularly for large samples. When only the normality assumption is seriously violated, *nonparametric* alternatives to the one-way ANOVA *F* test are available [see References 1 and 2].

The third assumption, **homogeneity of variance,** states that the variance within each population should be equal for all populations (that is, $\sigma_1^2 = \sigma_2^2 = \cdots = \sigma_c^2$). This assumption is needed to combine or pool the variances within the groups into a single within-group source of variation *SSW.* If there are equal sample sizes in each group, inferences based on the *F* distribution may not be seriously affected by unequal variances. If, however, there are unequal sample sizes in different groups, unequal variances from group to group can have serious effects on any inferences developed from the ANOVA procedures. Thus, when possible, there should be equal sample sizes in all groups.

One way to evaluate the assumptions is to plot a side-by-side box-and-whisker plot of the groups to study their central tendency, variation, and shape. Figure 12.11 represents the Minitab box-and-whisker plot of the thickness for the five wafer positions.

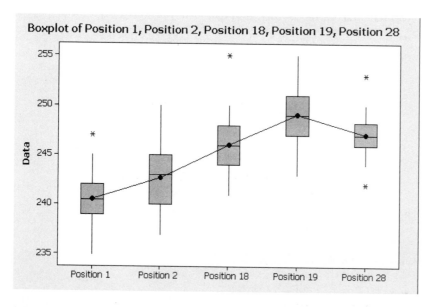

FIGURE 12.11 Minitab Box-and-Whisker Plot of the Thickness for the Five Wafer Positions

From Figure 12.11, there appears to be very little difference in the variation and very little skewness in wafer thickness for the five positions.

Levene's Test for Homogeneity of Variance

Although the one-way ANOVA *F* test is relatively robust with respect to the assumption of equal group variances, large departures from this assumption may seriously affect the level of significance and the power of the test. Therefore, various procedures have been developed to more formally test the assumption of homogeneity of variance. Perhaps the most powerful is the Levene procedure [see References 1 and 2]. You test for the equality of the population variances

H_o: All the population variances are equal

against the alternative

H_1: Not all the population variances are equal

The Levene test is based on the idea that if the variation within the groups does not differ, an ANOVA of the absolute differences from each group median can be used to test the null hypothesis of equal variances. Thus, you compute the absolute value of the difference between each observation and the median of the group, and a one-way ANOVA is carried out on these *absolute differences*. Figure 12.12 represents Minitab output of the Levene test for the wafer thickness of the five positions.

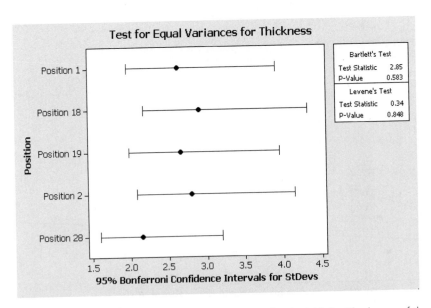

FIGURE 12.12 Minitab Output of the Levene Test for the Wafer Thickness of the Five Positions

From Figure 12.12, the value of the F test statistic for the Levene test is 0.34, and the p-value is 0.848. Because the p-value of 0.848 is greater than $\alpha = 0.05$, the null hypothesis is not rejected. The p-value means that the probability of obtaining an F statistic greater than 0.34 is 0.848. Thus, there is insufficient evidence to conclude that any of the variances in wafer thickness are different.

Figure 12.12 also contains the test statistic for Bartlett's test for the differences between variances. This test should be used only when the data comes from a normal distribution. In addition, Figure 12.12 provides a set of confidence intervals for the standard deviation in each group [see Reference 2].

SUMMARY

This chapter provided an introduction to the fundamental concepts of hypothesis testing. You learned how to test for the difference in the proportions, means, and variances in two groups. In addition, the ANOVA testing method was developed to determine whether differences exist in the means of more than two groups. This ANOVA method will be extended in Chapter 13 to the more general situation in which several factors are being studied.

REFERENCES

1. Berenson, M. L., D. M. Levine, and T. C. Krehbiel, *Basic Business Statistics: Concepts and Applications,* 9th ed. (Upper Saddle River, NJ: Prentice Hall, 2004)

2. *Minitab for Windows Version 14* (State College, PA: Minitab, 2003).

3. Montgomery, D. C., *Design and Analysis of Experiments,* 5th ed. (New York: John Wiley, 2001).

4. Neter, J., M. H. Kutner, C. Nachtsheim, and W. Wasserman, *Applied Linear Statistical Models,* 4th ed. (Homewood, IL: Richard D. Irwin, 1996).

APPENDIX 12.1

USING MINITAB FOR HYPOTHESIS TESTING

Testing for the Difference Between Two Proportions

To test the hypothesis for the difference in the proportion of good and bad wafers with no particles illustrated in Figure 12.2 on page 343, select **Stat → Basic Statistics → 2 Proportions.**

1. In the 2 Proportions (Test and Confidence Interval) dialog box (see Figure A12.1), select the **Summarized data** option button. In the First: row, enter **334** in the Trials: edit box and **320** in the Events: edit box. In the Second: row, en-

ter **116** in the Trials: edit box and **80** in the Events: edit box.

2. Click the **Options** button. In the 2 Proportions—Options dialog box (see Figure A12.2) enter **95** in the Confidence level: edit box. Enter **0.0** in the Test difference: edit box. Select **not equal** in the Alternative: drop-down list box. Select the **Use pooled estimate of p for test** check box (uncheck this if this selection is not desired). Click the **OK** button to return to the 2-Proportions (Test and Confidence Interval) dialog box. Click the **OK** button.

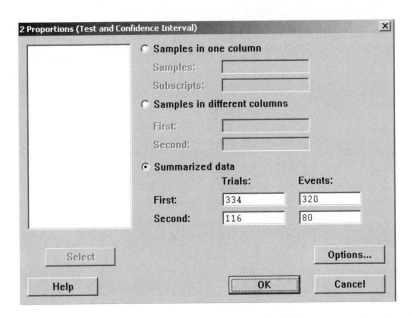

FIGURE A12.1 Minitab 2 Proportions (Test and Confidence Interval) Dialog Box

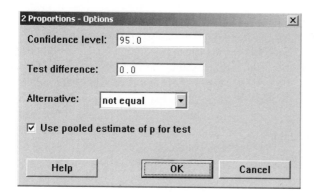

Testing for the Difference Between the Means of Two Independent Samples

To test for the difference in the mean surface hardness of steel plates illustrated in Figure 12.4 on page 348, open the **INTAGLIO.MTW** worksheet. Select **Stat → Basic Statistics → 2-Sample t.**

1. In the 2-Sample t (Test and Confidence Interval) dialog box (see Figure A12.3), select the **Samples in different columns** option button. In the First: edit box, enter **C1** or **Untreated.** In the Second: edit box, enter **C2** or **Treated.** (If you have summarized data instead of the actual data, select the Summarized data option button and enter values for the sample

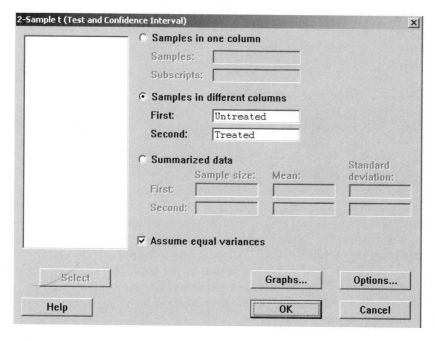

FIGURE A12.3 Minitab 2-Sample t (Test and Confidence Interval) Dialog Box

size, mean, and standard deviation.) For the pooled-variance *t* test, select the Assume equal variances check box. For the separate variance *t* test, leave this box unchecked.

2. Click the **Graphs** button. In the 2-Sample t–Graphs dialog box (see Figure A12.4), select the **Boxplots of data** check box. Click the **OK** button to return to the 2-Sample t (Test and Confidence Interval) dialog box.

3. Click the **Options** button. In the 2-Sample t–Options dialog box (see Figure A12.5), enter **95** in the Confidence level: edit box. Enter **0.0** in the Test difference: edit box. Select **not equal** in the Alternative: drop-down list box. Click the **OK** button to return to the 2-Sample t (Test and Confidence Interval) dialog box. Click the **OK** button.

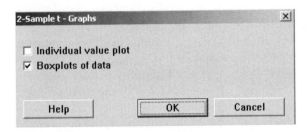

FIGURE A12.4 Minitab 2-Sample t—Graphs Dialog Box

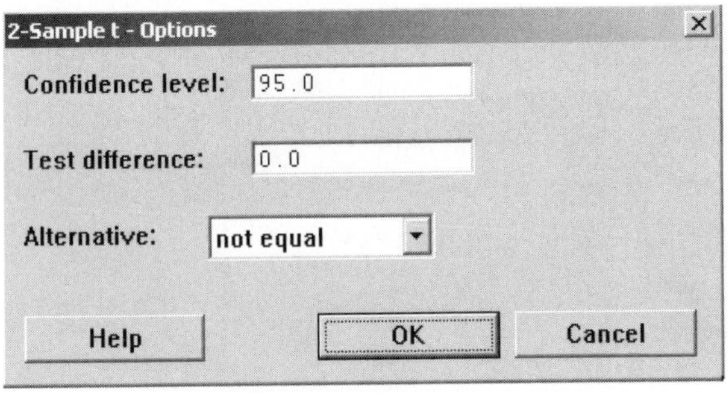

FIGURE A12.5 Minitab 2-Sample t—Options Dialog Box

Testing for the Difference Between Two Variances

To test for the difference in the variances of the surface hardness of steel plates illustrated in Figure 12.7 on page 353, open the **INTAGLIO.MTW** worksheet. Select **Stat → Basic Statistics → 2 Variances.**

1. In the 2 Variances dialog box (see Figure A12.6), select the **Samples in different** columns option button. In the First: edit box, enter **C1** or **Untreated.** In the Second: edit box, enter **C2** or **Treated.** (If you have summarized data instead of the actual data, select the Summarized data option button and enter values for the sample size and variance.)

2. Click the **OK** button.

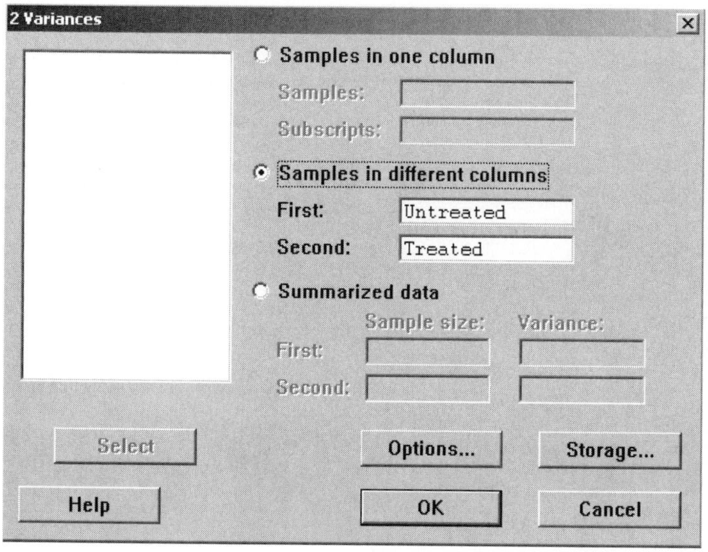

FIGURE A12.6 Minitab 2 Variances Dialog Box

Obtaining a One-Way ANOVA with Multiple Comparisons

To obtain the ANOVA for the thickness of the wafer positions illustrated in Figures 12.9–12.11 on pages 358, 360–361, open the **CIRCUITS.MTW** worksheet. Note that the data have been stored in an unstacked format with each position in a separate column. Select **Stat → ANOVA → One-Way (Unstacked).**

1. In the One-Way Analysis of Variance dialog box (see Figure A12.7), enter **C2** or **'Position 1', C3** or **'Position 2', C4** or **'Position 18', C5** or **'Position 19',** and **C6** or **'Position 28'** in the Responses (in separate columns): edit box. Enter **95** in the Confidence level: edit box.

2. Click the **Comparisons** button. In the One-Way Multiple Comparisons dialog box (see Figure A12.8), select the **Tukey's, family error rate:** check box. Enter **5** in the edit box for 95% simulta-

neous confidence intervals. Click the **OK** button to return to the One-Way Analysis of Variance dialog box.

3. Click the **Graphs** button. In the One-Way Analysis of Variance–Graphs dialog box (see Figure A12.9), select the **Boxplots of data** check box. Click the **OK** button to return to the One-Way Analysis of Variance dialog box.

4. Click the **OK** button.

Testing for Equal Variances in the Analysis of Variance

To obtain the Levene test for the difference in the variance of the thickness of the wafer positions illustrated in Figure 12.12 on page 362, open the **CIRCUITS.MTW** worksheet. To perform the Levene test in the ANOVA, you need to stack the data. Select **Data → Stack → Columns.** Then, in the Stack Columns dialog box:

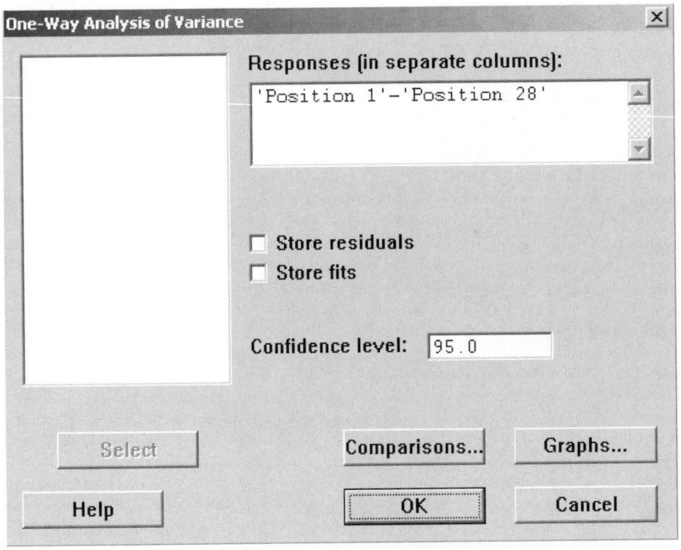

FIGURE A12.7 Minitab One-Way Analysis of Variance Dialog Box

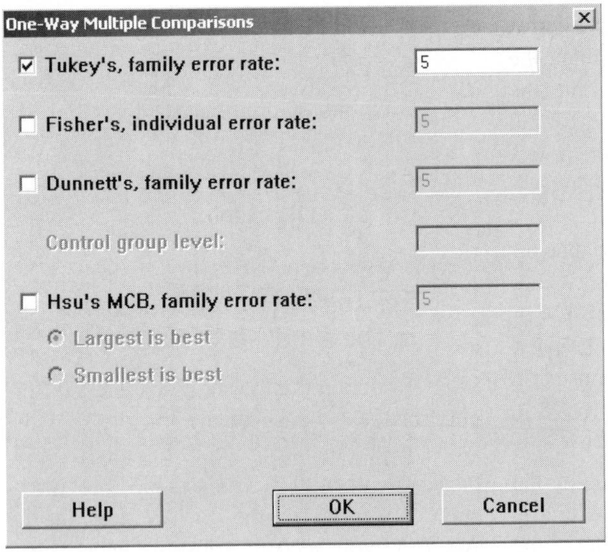

FIGURE 12.8 Minitab One-Way Multiple Comparisons Dialog Box

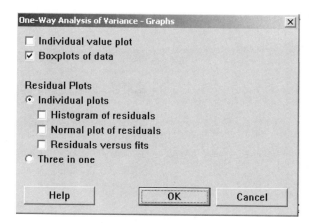

FIGURE 12.9 Minitab One-Way Analysis of Variance—Graphs Dialog Box

1. Enter **C2** or **'Position 1'**, **C3** or **'Position 2'**, **C4** or **'Position 18'**, **C5** or **'Position 19'**, and **C6** or **'Position 28'** in the Stack the following columns: edit box.

2. Select the **Column of current worksheet:** option button. Enter **C7** in the edit box. Enter **C8** in the Store the Subscript in: edit box. Click the **OK** button.

3. Label **C7 Thickness** and **C8 Position.**

4. Select **Stat → ANOVA → Test for Equal Variances.** In the Test for Equal Variances dialog box (see Figure A12.10), enter **C7** or **Thickness** in the Response: edit box and **C8** or **Position** in the Factors: edit box. Enter **95.0** in the Confidence level: edit box. Click the **OK** button.

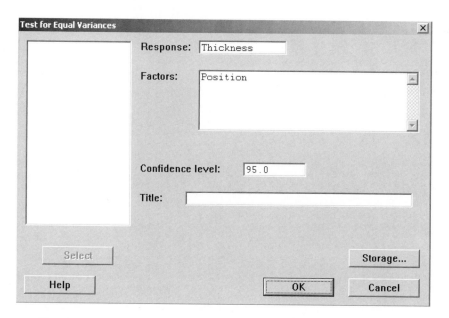

FIGURE A12.10 Minitab Test for Equal Variances dialog box

DESIGN OF EXPERIMENTS

CHAPTER OUTLINE

LEARNING OBJECTIVES

After reading this chapter, you will be able to:

- Understand the basic concepts of experimental design
- Conduct 2^k factorial designs and interpret the effect of interactions
- Conduct fractional factorial designs.

13.1 DESIGN OF EXPERIMENTS: BACKGROUND AND RATIONALE

Design of Experiments (DoE) is a collection of statistical methods for studying the relationships between **independent variables,** the Xs, and their interactions (also called *factors, input variables,* or *process variables*) on a **dependent variable,** the Y (or CTQ). Additionally, design of experiments can be used to minimize the effects of background variables on understanding the relationships between the X(s) and Y. A **background variable** (also called **noise variable** or

lurking variable) is a variable that can potentially affect the dependent variable (Y or CTQ) in an experiment, but is not of interest as an independent variable (X).

The concepts of experimental design discussed in this chapter represent an *active* intervention into a process by Six Sigma team members; that is, process changes are planned and tested by team members, and the data caused by those changes is studied to determine the effect of the process change. This kind of experiment does more than passively collect data from a functioning process; rather, it actively intervenes in the function of the process to conduct experiments concerning the effects of the Xs and their interactions on a Y.

The ideas involved in the design of experiments are not new. They were originally developed by R. A. Fisher in England early in the twentieth century [References 1 and 4]. His original work focused on improving agricultural experimentation. Fisher's contributions to experimental design were based on several fundamental principles. First, Fisher developed an experimental strategy that purposely designed experiments to simultaneously study several factors of interest. This approach was considered novel, because it contrasted with the scientific method as practiced in the nineteenth century of varying only one factor at a time. Second, he developed the concept of randomization that allows for the control and measurement of variation resulting from factors not considered in the experiment. Fisher realized that, in conducting an agricultural experiment in the field, not all factors could even be foreseen (background variables). Thus, he determined the particular treatment levels received by each plot of land (the individual observations) by a method of random assignment. Any differences between different plots that received the same treatment could be considered to be due to random variation or experimental error.

The methods of experimental design have been used not only in agricultural experimentation, but also in industrial applications [see Reference 1]. They form a critical component of the statistical methods used in Six Sigma management, particularly in the analyze and improve phases of the DMAIC model.

13.2 TWO-FACTOR FACTORIAL DESIGNS

In this section, we begin the study of experimental designs in which more than one factor (X) is examined simultaneously. These experimental designs are called **factorial designs** because they simultaneously evaluate the effects of two or more factors (Xs). This section discusses the simplest factorial design, the two-factor design. In addition, although any number of levels of a factor can be included in a design, for pedagogical simplicity, only the special circumstance in which there are two levels (or treatments) for each factor of interest will be considered in this book. Designs that contain more than two levels of a factor are logical extensions of the two-level case. In addition, this text only considers situations in which there are equal numbers of **replicates** (that is, the sample size) for each combination of the levels of the factors (Xs).

Owing to the complexity of the calculations involved, particularly as the number of levels of each factor increases and the number of *replications* in each cell increases, statistical software such as Minitab is usually used both to design experiments and to analyze data obtained from them.

Recall from Figure 12.8 (page 355), that in the one-way completely randomized design model, the **sum of squares total** (*SST*) is subdivided into **sum of squares among groups** (*SSA*) and **sum of squares within groups** (*SSW*). For the two-factor factorial design model with equal replication in each cell, the **sum of squares total** (*SST*) is subdivided into **sum of squares due to factor A or X_A** (*SSA*), **sum of squares due to factor B or X_B** (or *SSB*), **sum of squares due to the interacting effect of A and B** (*SSAB*), and **sum of squares due to inherent random error** (*SSE*). This partitioning of the *SST* is displayed in Figure 13.1.

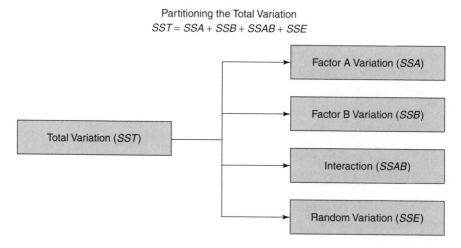

Partitioning the Total Variation
$$SST = SSA + SSB + SSAB + SSE$$

FIGURE 13.1 Partitioning the Total Variation in a Two-Factor Factorial Design Model

The *SST* represents the total variation among all the observations around the grand mean of the CTQ. The *SSA* represents the differences among the various mean levels of factor *A* and the grand mean of the CTQ. The *SSB* represents the differences among the various mean levels of factor *B* and the grand mean of the CTQ. The *SSAB* represents the effect of the combinations of factor *A* and factor *B* on the CTQ. The *SSE* represents the differences among the individual observations of the CTQ within each cell (combinations of one level of X_A and one level of X_B) and the corresponding cell mean. If each sum of squares is divided by its associated degrees of freedom, you obtain the four variances or mean square terms (*MSA, MSB, MSAB,* and *MSE*) needed for analysis of variance (ANOVA)

If the levels of factor *A* and factor *B* have been *specifically selected* for analysis (rather than being *randomly selected* from a population of possible levels[*]), there are three tests of hypotheses in the two-way ANOVA.

1. Test of no difference due to factor *A* (mean level of the CTQ is not affected by factor *A*):

H_0: All levels of factor *A* have the same mean value of the CTQ
against the alternative.

H_1: Not all levels of factor *A* have the same mean value of the CTQ.

---

[*]A discussion of random effects models is beyond the scope of this book [see References 6, 9, and 10].

This test of hypothesis consists of an F test of MSA divided by MSE.

2. Test of no difference due to factor B (mean level of the CTQ is not affected by factor B):

H_0: All levels of factor B have the same mean value of the CTQ
against the alternative.

H_1: Not all levels of factor B have the same mean value of the CTQ.

This test of hypothesis consists of an F test of MSB divided by MSE.

3. Test of no interaction of factors A and B:

H_0: The interaction between factors A and B on the CTQ does not effect the mean level of the CTQ

against the alternative.

H_1: There is an interacting effect between factors A and B on the CTQ.

This test of hypothesis consists of an F test of $MSAB$ divided by MSE.

The entire set of steps is summarized in the ANOVA table of Table 13.1.

TABLE 13.1 ANOVA Table for the Two-Factor Model with Replication

Source	Degrees of freedom	Sum of squares	Mean square (variance)	F
A	$r-1$	SSA	$MSA = \dfrac{SSA}{r-1}$	$F = \dfrac{MSA}{MSE}$
B	$c-1$	SSB	$MSB = \dfrac{SSB}{c-1}$	$F = \dfrac{MSB}{MSE}$
AB	$(r-1)(c-1)$	SSAB	$MSAB = \dfrac{SSAB}{(r-1)(c-1)}$	$F = \dfrac{MSAB}{MSE}$
Error	$rc(n'-1)$	SSE	$MSE = \dfrac{SSE}{rc(n'-1)}$	
Total	$n-1$	SST		

r = the number of levels of factor A
c = the number of levels of factor B
n' = the number of values (replications) for each cell, assuming each cell has an equal number of replications
n = the total number of observations in the experiment.

A study concerning the distortion of drive gears (CTQ) in automobiles will be used to illustrate the two-factor design. The factors included were the tooth size of the gear (X_1) and the part positioning (X_2). A study of eight gears for each tooth size and part positioning combination is displayed in Table 13.2.

TABLE 13.2 Distortion of Gears (CTQ) Based on Tooth Size (X_1) and Part Positioning (X_2)

Tooth size	Part positioning	
	X_2 = Low	X_2 = High
X_1 = Low	18.0	13.5
	16.5	8.5
	26.0	11.5
	22.5	16.0
	21.5	−4.5
	21.0	4.0
	30.0	1.0
	24.5	9.0
X_1 = High	27.5	17.5
	19.5	11.5
	31.0	10.0
	27.0	1.0
	17.0	14.5
	14.0	3.5
	18.0	7.5
	17.5	6.5

GEAR

Source: D. R. Bingham and R. R. Sitter, "Design Issues in Fractional Factorial Split-Plot Experiments," *Journal of Quality Technology*, 33, 2001, pp. 2–15. Copyright © 2001 American Society for Quality. Reprinted with permission.

The particular design in this example is called a 2 × 2 design with eight replications. The first number refers to the number of levels for the first factor, and the second number refers to the number of levels for the second factor. This design is also referred to as a 2^2 design, where the exponent indicates that there are two factors each with two treatment levels. Figure 13.2 represents Minitab output for these data.

From Figure 13.2, the tests of hypotheses are as follows (at the $\alpha = 0.05$ level of significance):

```
Source               DF      SS       MS      F      P
Tooth Size            1     0.63     0.63    0.02   0.892
Part Positioning      1  1519.38  1519.38   45.47   0.000
Interaction           1    14.45    14.45    0.43   0.516
Error                28   935.59    33.41
Total                31  2470.05

S = 5.780   R-Sq = 62.12%   R-Sq(adj) = 58.06%

Individual 95% CIs For Mean Based on
Tooth           Pooled StDev
Size     Mean   -----+---------+---------+---------+----
High   15.2188       (------------------*------------------)
Low    14.9375  (------------------*------------------)
                -----+---------+---------+---------+----
                   12.8      14.4      16.0      17.6

                       Individual 95% CIs For Mean Based on Pooled
                       StDev
Part Positioning   Mean   +---------+---------+---------+---------
High              8.1875  (-----*-----)
Low              21.9688                          (-----*-----)
                          +---------+---------+---------+---------
                         5.0      10.0      15.0      20.0
```

FIGURE 13.2 Minitab Two-way ANOVA Results for the Drive Gear Data

1. Test for interaction: Because the F statistic for the interaction effect = 0.43 and the p-value is 0.516 > 0.05, the decision is not to reject the null hypothesis. There is insufficient evidence of any interaction between tooth size and part position.

2. Test for tooth size: Because the F statistic for the tooth size = 0.02 and the p-value is 0.892 > 0.05, the decision is not to reject the null hypothesis. There is insufficient evidence of any effect of tooth size on distortion of the gears.

3. Test for part positioning: Because the F statistic for the part positioning = 45.47 and the p-value is 0.000 < 0.05, the decision is to reject the null hypothesis. There is evidence of an effect of part positioning on distortion of the gears. The distortion is much higher for low part positioning than for high part positioning.

From Table 13.2, the averages for each combination of tooth size and part positioning can be obtained. These are presented in Table 13.3.

TABLE 13.3 Average Distortion of Gears Based on Tooth Size and Part Positioning

Tooth size	Part positioning		
	Low	**High**	**Row average**
Low	22.5000	7.3750	14.93750
High	21.4375	9.0000	15.21875
Column average	21.9688	8.1875	15.08000

From Table 13.3, several conclusions can be reached. In terms of the individual factors (called the **main effects**), there is very little difference in the average distortion (CTQ) between the low and high levels of tooth size, or X_1 (14.9375 vs. 15.2188). The size of the effect for tooth size is 15.2188 − 14.9375 = 0.2813. However, there is a substantial difference in the average distortion (CTQ) between the low and high levels of part positioning, or X_2. The low level of part positioning has a average distortion of 21.9688, and the high level of part positioning has a average distortion of 8.1875. Thus, the effect due to part positioning is 21.9688 − 8.1875 = 13.7813. These two main effects are illustrated in the Minitab main effects plot in Figure 13.3.

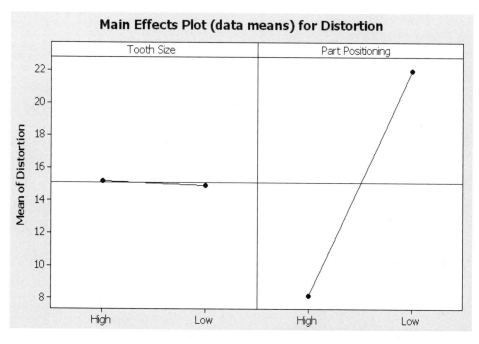

FIGURE 13.3 Minitab Main Effects Plot of Tooth Size and Part Positioning

Now that the main effects of tooth size and parts positioning have been studied, the question remains as to what is meant by interaction? **Interaction** can first be examined by considering what would be meant by the absence of interaction.

If there is no interaction between two factors (*A* and *B*), then any difference in the dependent or response variable (CTQ) between the two levels of factor *A* (X_A) would be the same at each level of factor *B* (X_B).

In terms of the factors in this example, if there was no interaction between tooth size and part positioning, any difference in distortion between low tooth size and high tooth size would be the same under conditions of low part positioning as under conditions of high part positioning. From Table 13.3, you see that for a low level of tooth size, the difference in distortion between low and high levels of part positioning is 15.125, and for a high level of tooth size, the difference in distortion between low and high levels of part positioning is 12.4375.

The interaction between two factors can be presented in an interaction plot. If there is no interaction between the factors, the lines for the two levels will be approximately parallel. Figure 13.4 contains a Minitab interaction plot for the gear example.

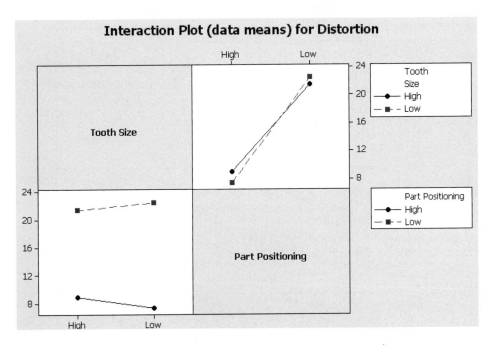

FIGURE 13.4 Minitab Interaction Plot for Distortion for the Gear Example

Either the bottom left or the top right panels of this plot can be used, depending on whether you want to focus on tooth size or part positioning. Referring to the upper right panel, the levels on the horizontal axis represent the part positioning levels for each tooth size. Referring to the lower left panel, the levels on the horizontal axis represent the tooth size levels for each part positioning. An examination of either panel shows that the lines are roughly parallel, indicating very little interaction between the tooth size and part positioning factors.

To study an example that has a clear interaction present, consider the manufacture of rolling bearings (see Reference 2). The factors studied were outer ring osculation, or X_A (factor A)

and cage design, or X_B (factor *B*). The results in terms of the life of the bearings (CTQ) are presented in Table 13.4.

TABLE 13.4 Life of Roller Bearings (CTQ) Based on Ring Osculation (X_A) and Cage Design (X_B)

	Cage design	
Ring osculation	X_B **= Low**	X_B **= High**
X_A = Low	17	19
	26	16
X_A = High	· 25	21
	85	128

⊕ **BEARINGS**

Source: Box, G.E.P., "Do Interactions Matter?" *Quality Engineering,* 2, 1990, pp. 365–369.

From Table 13.4, the averages for each combination of ring osculation and cage design are computed and presented in Table 13.5.

TABLE 13.5 Average Life of Roller Bearings (CTQ) Based on Ring Osculation (X_A) and Cage Design (X_B)

	Cage design		
Ring osculation	X_B **= Low**	X_B **= High**	**Row average**
X_A = Low	21.50	17.5	19.500
X_A = High	55.00	74.5	64.750
Column average	38.25	46.0	42.125

The main effects plot for these data is displayed in Figure 13.5 and the interaction plot is presented in Figure 13.6.

From Table 13.5 and Figure 13.5, the life of the roller bearings is much higher at the high level of ring osculation than at the low level of ring osculation (64.75 vs. 19.5). In addition, the life of the roller bearings is slightly higher at the high level of cage design than at the low level of cage design (46 vs. 38.25). However, a further study of Table 13.5 and an examination of Figure 13.6 reveal that there is an interaction effect between ring osculation and cage design. This is

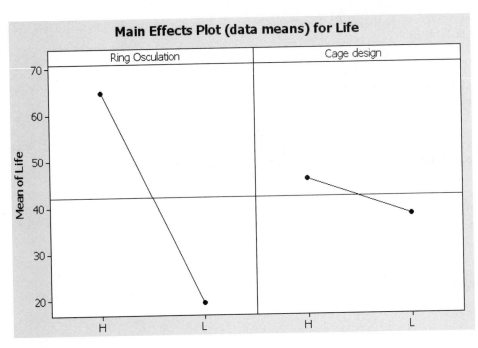

FIGURE 13.5 Minitab Main Effects Plot for the Life of Roller Bearings

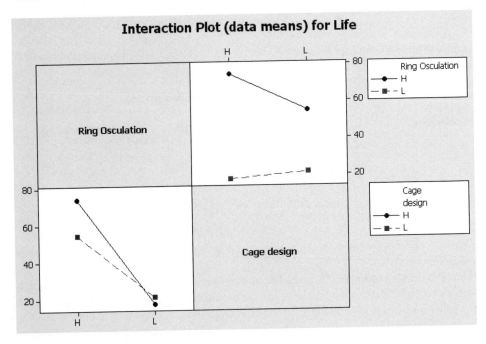

FIGURE 13.6 Interaction Plot for the Life of Roller Bearings

clearly apparent in the lower left panel of Figure 13.6. At the low level of ring osculation, there is very little difference in the life of the roller bearing for the two cage designs. However, at the high level of ring osculation, the life of the roller bearings is much higher at the high level of cage design than at the low level of cage design (74.5 vs. 55). The existence of this interaction effect complicates the interpretation of the main effects. You cannot conclude that there is a difference in the average life of low and high ring osculation because the difference is not the same for the two cage designs. Likewise, you cannot conclude that there is a difference in the average life of the two cage designs because the difference is not the same for both types of ring oscillations. In sum, the interaction effect takes precedence over any interpretation of main effects.

Notation for Interaction Effects. Determining the magnitude of the effect of each factor and interaction becomes complex when many factors are involved. A special notation is used to represent the treatment combinations, that is, the simultaneous combinations of the different levels of each of the Xs or factors. The steps involved in this notation are as follows.

1. A shorthand notation is used to define the factors by assigning a letter, such as *A, B,* or *C,* to each factor.

2. One level of each factor is designated as the low level, and the other level is designated as the high level. The high and low levels are defined by the nature of the factor (e.g., high speed vs. low speed). In cases where levels are not defined by the factor being studied, it is common practice to set the current operating level as the low level.

3. A table is developed in which the columns represent the factors and their interactions, and the rows represent the different combinations, called **treatment combinations,** created by setting the factors at their different levels. Treatment combinations are defined only by the high levels of the factors. For example, in a two-factor design, if only the high level of factor *A* is present, the treatment combination is specified as *a.* If only the high level of factor *B* is present, the treatment combination is specified as *b.* If the high levels of factors *A* and *B* are present, the treatment combination is specified as *ab.* The treatment combination that contains the low level of all the factors is specified as (1).

4. Each factor is listed in a column. For each factor, a minus (−) sign is included in the row if the low level is present and a plus (+) sign is included if the high level of the factor is present. The sign for an interaction effect is the product of the signs that define the interaction. Thus, the sign for the *AB* interaction is the product of the signs in the particular row for factors *A* and *B* (for example, if the row has a plus sign for A and a plus sign for B or a minus sign for *A* and a minus sign for *B,* the interaction *AB* sign is a plus. If the row has a plus sign for *A* and a minus sign for *B* or a minus sign for *A* and a plus sign for *B,* the interaction *AB* sign is a minus).

The treatment combinations for the data of Table 13.3 on page 376, using the special notation, are displayed in Table 13.6.

TABLE 13.6 Obtaining Average Effects for Factors A, B, and AB in the 2^2 Design for the Drive Gears Data

Treatment combination	Notation	Average Response	Tooth size A	Part positioning B	AB
Low tooth size, low part positioning	(1)	22.5000	−	−	+
High tooth size, low part positioning	a	21.4375	+	−	−
Low tooth size, high part positioning	b	7.3750	−	+	−
High tooth size, high part positioning	ab	9.0000	+	+	+

Computing the Estimated Effects (optional)

The average effect for each factor or interaction is obtained by multiplying the average response for the row by the sign in the column and summing these products over all the rows. This sum is then divided by the number of plus signs used in obtaining the effect.

For a two-factor design, the average effects for factor A, factor B, and the interaction of A and B are as follows.

$$A = \frac{1}{2}(a + ab - b - (1)) \tag{13.1a}$$

$$B = \frac{1}{2}(b + ab - a - (1)) \tag{13.1b}$$

$$AB = \frac{1}{2}(ab - a - b + (1)) \tag{13.1c}$$

From equations (13.1a–13.1c) and Table 13.6:

$$A = \frac{1}{2}(21.4375 + 9.0000 - 22.5000 - 7.3750)$$

$$= \frac{0.5625}{2}$$

$$= 0.28125$$

Thus, the average for the high tooth size is 0.28125 greater than the average for the low tooth size, a conclusion previously stated on page 377.

$$B = \frac{1}{2}(7.3750 + 9.0000 - 22.50000 - 21.4375)$$

$$= -\frac{27.5625}{2}$$

$$= -13.78125$$

Thus, the average for the high part positioning is 13.78125 lower for high part positioning than for low part positioning.

$$AB = \frac{1}{2}(22.5000 + 9.0000 - 21.4375 - 7.3750)$$

$$= -\frac{2.6875}{2}$$

$$= 1.34375$$

The interaction means that the average effect of combining the high level of tooth size and part positioning is 1.34375 greater than the average difference between the gears at the two tooth sizes. This is obtained from the fact that the average distortion for high tooth size and high part positioning is 1.625 greater than the average distortion for low tooth size and high part positioning (9.0 as compared with 7.375), whereas the difference in the average distortion for high tooth size as compared with low tooth size is 0.28125 (14.9375 – 15.21875). The difference between 1.625 and 0.28125 is the interaction effect of 1.34375. The above information is provided in tabular form below.

		Part Position		
		High	Low	Average
Tooth Size	High	9.0000	21.43750	15.218750
	Low	7.3750	22.50000	14.937500
	Average	8.1875	21.96875	15.078125

13.3 2^K FACTORIAL DESIGNS

The two-factor factorial design is the most elementary of all factorial designs. In this section, the concepts developed for the two-factor 2^2 design in Section 13.2 are extended to the more general factorial design that has three or more factors. With this design, there are 2^k treatment combinations, where k = the number of factors, for example, $2^3 = 2 \times 2 \times 2 = 8$ treatment combinations. Table 13.7 extends the format of Table 13.6 to the 2^3 design in standard order. **Standard order** is an arrangement for listing trials in which the first factor alternates between – and +, the second factor alternates between –,– and +,+, the third factor alternates between –,–,–,– and +,+,+,+, and so on.

TABLE 13.7 Obtaining Effects for Factors *A*, *B*, *C*, and Interactions *AB*, *AC*, *BC*, and *ABC* in the 2^3 Design in Standard Order

	Contrast						
Notation	**A**	**B**	**C**	**AB**	**AC**	**BC**	**ABC**
(1)	−	−	−	+	+	+	−
a	+	−	−	−	−	+	+
b	−	+	−	−	+	−	+
ab	+	+	−	+	−	−	−
c	−	−	+	+	−	−	+
ac	+	−	+	−	+	−	−
bc	−	+	+	−	−	+	−
abc	+	+	+	+	+	+	+

To illustrate the 2^3 design, suppose that in the roller bearing example discussed in Table 13.4 on page 379, in addition to ring osculation and cage design, there was a third factor, the heat treatment used. Each treatment combination consisted of a single replication. The results from this experiment are presented in Table 13.8.

TABLE 13.8 Results for a 2^3 Design Involving the Life of Roller Bearings (CTQ) Based on Ring Osculation (X_A), Cage Design (X_B), and Heat Treatment (X_C) Treatment Combinations

Ring osculation	Cage design	Heat treatment	Notation	Life
Low	Low	Low	(1)	17
High	Low	Low	*a*	25
Low	High	Low	*b*	19
High	High	Low	*ab*	21
Low	Low	High	*c*	26
High	Low	High	*ac*	85
Low	High	High	*bc*	16
High	High	High	*abc*	128

Source: Box, G.E.P., "Do Interactions Matter?" *Quality Engineering*, 2, 1990, pp. 365–369.

The eight treatment combinations (and their responses) are presented in the form of a cube in Figure 13.7.

Figure 13.8 represents Minitab output of the estimated effects of ring osculation, cage design, and heat treatment on the relative life of the roller bearings.

The main effects plot for these data is displayed in Figure 13.9 and the interaction plot is presented in Figure 13.10.

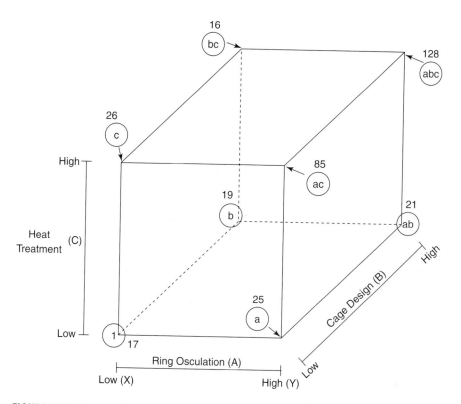

FIGURE 13.7 Geometric Representation of the 2^3 Design (Source: Table 13.7)

```
Term                              Effect    Coef
Constant                                  42.125
Ring Osculation                   45.250  22.625
Cage design                        7.750   3.875
Heat treatment                    43.250  21.625
Ring Osculation*Cage design       11.750   5.875
Ring Osculation*Heat treatment    40.250  20.125
Cage design*Heat treatment         8.750   4.375
Ring Osculation*Cage design*      14.750   7.375
  Heat treatment

S = *

Analysis of Variance for Relative life (coded units)

Source              DF   Seq SS   Adj SS   Adj MS   F   p
Main Effects         3   7956.4   7956.4   2652.1   *   *
2-Way Interactions   3   3669.4   3669.4   1223.1   *   *
3-Way Interactions   1    435.1    435.1    435.1   *   *
Residual Error       0      *        *        *
Total                7  12060.9
```

FIGURE 13.8 Minitab Output of the Estimated Effects of Ring Osculation, Cage Design, and Heat Treatment on the Relative Life of the Roller Bearings

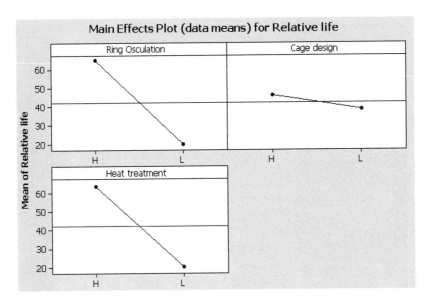

FIGURE 13.9 Minitab Main Effects Plot for the Life of Roller Bearings in the 2^3 Experiment

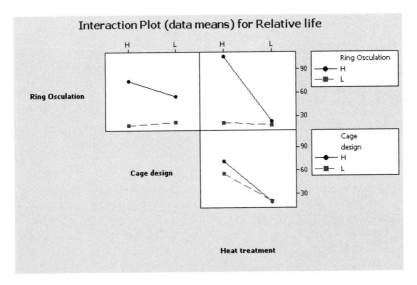

FIGURE 13.10 Minitab Interaction Plot for the Life of Roller Bearings in the 2^3 Experiment

From the effects shown in Figure 13.8, the main effects plot illustrated in Figure 13.9, and the interaction plot in Figure 13.10, you can conclude that:

1. The average life is 45.25 greater for high ring osculation than for low ring osculation.
2. The average life is 7.75 greater for high cage design than for low cage design.
3. The average life is 43.25 greater for high heat treatment than for low heat treatment.
4. The interactions range from 8.75 for *BC* (Cage Design-Heat Treatment) to 40.25 for *AC* (Ring Osculation-Heat Treatment). The effects of *A* (Ring Osculation) and *C* (Heat Treatment) are interacting due to the large effect caused by the presence of the high level of ring osculation and the high level of heat treatment. This interacting effect means that the average difference in the life for high ring osculation as compared with low ring osculation is 40.25 higher for high heat treatment than for the average of low and high heat treatments.

In many instances (such as in this example), it may not be possible or may be prohibitively expensive to obtain more than one replication for each treatment combination. When this is the case, you are unable to obtain a separate measure of the error variance and, therefore, not able to conduct an ANOVA of the effects and interactions. However, a preliminary screening step using a **half-normal plot** [see Reference 5] can be used to screen out interactions that do not appear to have any effect and combine them into an error variance. This is a type of normal probability plot in which the estimated effects in rank order are plotted on normal probability paper.

The estimated effects and their associated cumulative probabilities for the roller bearing example are provided in the normal probability plot of Figure 13.11.

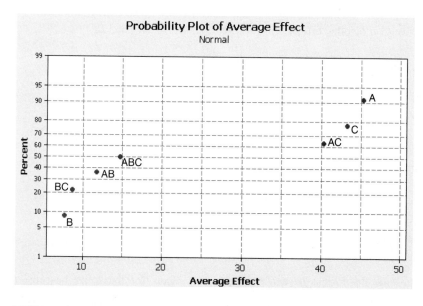

FIGURE 13.11 Minitab Normal Probability Plot for the 2^3 Design for the Roller Bearing Example

The normal probability plot is used to determine which factors and interaction effects are not important (and thus, not different from zero). Any factors or interactions whose observed effects are due to chance are expected to be randomly distributed around zero, with some being slightly below zero and others being slightly above zero. These effects will tend to fall along a straight line. The effects that may be important have average values different from zero and are located a substantial distance away from the hypothetical vertical line that represents no effect.

From Figure 13.11, observe that although all effects seem different from zero, the most important effects are *A, C,* and *AC*. These results are consistent with those seen in the main effects plot and the interaction plot of Figures 13.9 and 13.10.

Computing the Estimated Effects and Interaction Effects (optional)

For each of the main effects, the estimated effect consists of the average at the high level of the factor minus the average at the low level of the factor. Thus, for factors *A, B,* and *C:*

$$A = \frac{1}{4}[a + ab + ac + abc - (1) - b - c - bc] \tag{13.4a}$$

$$B = \frac{1}{4}[b + ab + bc + abc - (1) - a - c - ac] \tag{13.4b}$$

$$C = \frac{1}{4}[c + ac + bc + abc - (1) - a - b - ab] \tag{13.4c}$$

The two-way interactions are measured as one-half the difference in the average of one effect at the two levels of the other effect. Thus, for interactions *AB, AC,* and *BC:*

$$AB = \frac{1}{4}[abc - bc + ab - b - ac + c - a + (1)] \tag{13.5a}$$

$$AC = \frac{1}{4}[(1) - a + b - ab - c + ac - bc + abc] \tag{13.5b}$$

$$BC = \frac{1}{4}[(1) + a - b - ab - c - ac + bc + abc] \tag{13.5c}$$

The *ABC* interaction is defined as the average difference in the *AB* interaction for the two levels of factor *C*. Thus:

$$ABC = \frac{1}{4}[abc - bc - ac + c - ab + b + a - (1)] \tag{13.6}$$

Table 13.9 represents the format needed to obtain the effects for the roller bearing example.

TABLE 13.9 Obtaining Effects for Factors A, B, and C and Interactions AB, AC, BC, and ABC in the 2^3 Design

					Contrast			
Notation	**Life**	A	B	C	AB	AC	BC	ABC
(1)	17	−	−	−	+	+	+	−
a	25	+	−	−	−	−	+	+
b	19	−	+	−	−	+	−	+
ab	21	+	+	−	+	−	−	−
c	26	−	−	+	+	−	−	+
ac	85	+	−	+	−	+	−	−
bc	16	−	+	+	−	−	+	−
abc	128	+	+	+	+	+	+	+

From Table 13.9 and Equations (13.4), (13.5), and (13.6):

$$A = \frac{-17 + 25 - 19 + 21 - 26 + 85 - 16 + 128}{4}$$

$$= \frac{181}{4}$$

$$= 45.25$$

$$B = \frac{-17 - 25 + 19 + 21 - 26 - 85 + 16 + 128}{4}$$

$$= \frac{31}{4}$$

$$= 7.75$$

$$C = \frac{-17 - 25 - 19 - 21 + 26 + 85 + 16 + 128}{4}$$

$$= \frac{173}{4}$$

$$= 43.25$$

$$AB = \frac{+17 - 25 - 19 + 21 + 26 - 85 - 16 + 128}{4}$$

$$= \frac{47}{4}$$

$$= 11.75$$

$$AC = \frac{+17 - 25 + 19 - 21 - 26 + 85 - 16 + 128}{4}$$

$$= \frac{161}{4}$$

$$= 40.25$$

$$BC = \frac{+17 + 25 - 19 - 21 - 26 - 85 + 16 + 128}{4}$$

$$= \frac{35}{4}$$

$$= 8.75$$

$$ABC = \frac{-17 + 25 + 19 - 21 + 26 - 85 - 16 + 128}{4}$$

$$= \frac{59}{4}$$

$$= 14.75$$

The AC interaction effect can be studied further by reorganizing the results of Table 13.8 into Table 13.10 which focuses on these two factors.

From Table 13.10, the average life for high ring osculation is 5 more than for low ring osculation when low heat treatment is used, but is 85.5 more for high ring osculation than for low ring osculation when high heat treatment is used. The difference of $85.5 - 5 = 80.5$, divided by 2 (to account for the two levels of factor C), represents the interaction effect of 40.25 for factors A (ring osculation) and C (heat treatment).

TABLE 13.10 The Roller Bearing 2^3 Design Organized by Ring Osculation and Heat treatment

	Heat treatment	
Ring osculation	**Low**	**High**
Low	17 19 Cell mean = 18	26 16 Cell mean = 21
High	25 21 Cell mean = 23	85 128 Cell mean = 106.5

To study a factorial design that has more than three factors (Xs), consider an experiment involving a cake mix. Each year, millions of cake mixes are sold by food processing companies. A cake mix consists of a packet containing flour, shortening, and egg powder that will (it is hoped) provide a good-tasting cake. One issue in determining the amount of these ingredients to include in the packet to maximize the tastiness of the cake relates to the fact that consumers might not precisely follow the recommended oven temperature and baking time. An experiment is conducted in which each factor is tested at a higher level than called for in the instructions and at a lower level than called for in the instructions. The goal of the experiment is to determine which factors have an effect on the taste rating of the cake and the levels of the factors that will provide the cake with the highest taste rating. Five factors were to be considered, flour, shortening, egg powder, oven temperature, and baking time. Only one observation for each of the $2^5 = 32$ treatment combinations was obtained. The taste rating for each treatment combination is presented in Table 13.11.

TABLE 13.11 Taste Rating for Cake Mix Combinations

Treatment combination	Oven temp (A)	Baking time (B)	Flour (C)	Shortening (D)	Egg powder (E)	Rating score (Y)
(1)	−	−	−	−	−	1.1
a	+	−	−	−	−	3.8
b	−	+	−	−	−	3.7
ab	+	+	−	−	−	4.5
c	−	−	+	−	−	4.2
ac	+	−	+	−	−	5.2
bc	−	+	+	−	−	3.1
abc	+	+	+	−	−	3.9

(continued)

TABLE 13.11 Taste Rating for Cake Mix Combinations (continued)

Treatment combination	Oven temp (A)	Baking time (B)	Flour (C)	Shortening (D)	Egg powder (E)	Rating score (Y)
d	−	−	−	+	−	5.7
ad	+	−	−	+	−	4.9
bd	−	+	−	+	−	5.1
abd	+	+	−	+	−	6.4
cd	−	−	+	+	−	6.8
acd	+	−	+	+	−	6.0
bcd	−	+	+	+	−	6.3
abcd	+	+	+	+	−	5.5
e	−	−	−	−	+	6.4
ae	+	−	−	−	+	4.3
be	−	+	−	−	+	6.7
abe	+	+	−	−	+	5.8
ce	−	−	+	−	+	6.5
ace	+	−	+	−	+	5.9
bce	−	+	+	−	+	6.4
abce	+	+	+	−	+	5.0
de	−	−	−	+	+	1.3
ade	+	−	−	+	+	2.1
bde	−	+	−	+	+	2.9
abde	+	+	−	+	+	5.2
cde	−	−	+	+	+	3.5
acde	+	−	+	+	+	5.7
bcde	−	+	+	+	+	3.0
abcde	+	+	+	+	+	5.4

🔵 **CAKE**

Figure 13.12 presents the estimated effects obtained from Minitab for the cake mix design.

Figure 13.13 on page 394 is a Minitab normal probability plot of the estimated effects for the cake mix design.

From Figure 13.13, you see that only effects *C, BC, DE,* and *ADE* plot far away from a straight line that is approximately zero on the *X* axis. Minitab indicates that these terms are statistically significant, according to criteria developed by Lenth [see Reference 7]. From Figure 13.13, factor *C* (Egg Powder), the *BC* (Shortening–Egg Powder) interaction, the *DE* (Oven Temperature–Bake Time) interaction, and the *ADE* (Flour–Oven Temperature–Bake Time) interaction are far from a hypothetical vertical line at zero. Thus, a reasonable approach is to consider

```
Estimated Effects and Coefficients for Rating (coded units)

Term                                        Effect    Coef
Constant                                              4.759
Flour                                        0.431    0.216
Shortening                                   0.344    0.172
Egg Powder                                   0.781    0.391
ovenTemp                                    -0.044   -0.022
BakeTime                                    -0.006   -0.003
Flour*Shortening                             0.131    0.066
Flour*Egg Powder                            -0.081   -0.041
Flour*ovenTemp                               0.394    0.197
Flour*BakeTime                              -0.094   -0.047
Shortening*Egg Powder                       -0.994   -0.497
Shortening*ovenTemp                          0.131    0.066
Shortening*BakeTime                          0.244    0.122
Egg Powder*ovenTemp                          0.294    0.147
Egg Powder*BakeTime                          0.056    0.028
ovenTemp*BakeTime                           -2.194   -1.097
Flour*Shortening*Egg Powder                 -0.231   -0.116
Flour*Shortening*ovenTemp                    0.344    0.172
Flour*Egg Powder*ovenTemp                    0.006    0.003
Flour*Shortening*BakeTime                    0.131    0.066
Flour*Egg Powder*BakeTime                    0.394    0.197
Flour*ovenTemp*BakeTime                      1.194    0.597
Shortening*Egg Powder*ovenTemp               0.069    0.034
Shortening*Egg Powder*BakeTime              -0.044   -0.022
Shortening*ovenTemp*BakeTime                 0.256    0.128
Egg Powder*ovenTemp*BakeTime                 0.394    0.197
Flour*Shortening*Egg Powder*ovenTemp        -0.194   -0.097
Flour*Shortening*Egg Powder*BakeTime        -0.181   -0.091
Flour*Shortening*ovenTemp*BakeTime          -0.181   -0.091
Flour*Egg Powder*ovenTemp*BakeTime           0.056    0.028
Shortening*Egg Powder*ovenTemp*             -0.406   -0.203
  BakeTime
Flour*Shortening*Egg Powder*                 0.281    0.141
  ovenTemp*BakeTime
```

FIGURE 13.12 Minitab Estimated Effects for the Cake Mix Example

all third-order interactions (except *ADE*), all fourth-order interactions, and the single fifth-order interaction (*ABCDE*) as consisting only of random error. These effects can be eliminated from the ANOVA model and combined to obtain an estimate of the error variance. The ANOVA model computed by Minitab with these effects combined into an error variance is displayed in Figure 13.14.

From Figure 13.14, using the 0.05 level of significance, you see that factor *C* (Egg Powder) with a *p*-value of 0.007, the *BC* (Shortening–Egg Powder) interaction (*p*-value = 0.001), the *DE* (Oven Temperature–Bake Time) interaction (*p*-value = 0.000), and the *ADE* (Flour–Oven Temperature–Bake Time) interaction (*p*-value = 0.000) are all highly significant. The significance of these interactions complicates any interpretation of the main effects. Although egg powder significantly affects taste rating (with high amount providing a better rating than low amount), the significance of the shortening–egg powder interaction means that the difference in egg powder is not the same for the two levels of shortening. Because neither effect *D* nor *E* was

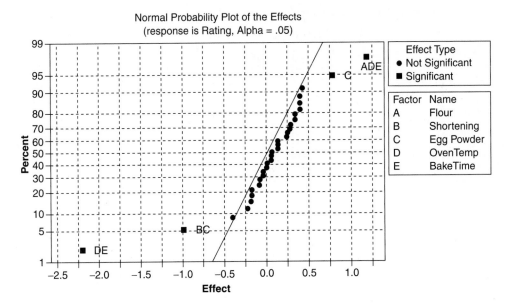

FIGURE 13.13 Minitab Normal Probability Plot of the Estimated Effects for the Cake Mix Design

Term	Effect	Coef	SE Coef	T	P
Constant		4.759	0.1240	38.40	0.000
Flour	0.431	0.216	0.1240	1.74	0.102
Shortening	0.344	0.172	0.1240	1.39	0.186
Egg Powder	0.781	0.391	0.1240	3.15	0.007
ovenTemp	-0.044	-0.022	0.1240	-0.18	0.862
BakeTime	-0.006	-0.003	0.1240	-0.03	0.980
Flour*Shortening	0.131	0.066	0.1240	0.53	0.604
Flour*Egg Powder	-0.081	-0.041	0.1240	-0.33	0.748
Flour*ovenTemp	0.394	0.197	0.1240	1.59	0.133
Flour*BakeTime	-0.094	-0.047	0.1240	-0.38	0.711
Shortening*Egg Powder	-0.994	-0.497	0.1240	-4.01	0.001
Shortening*ovenTemp	0.131	0.066	0.1240	0.53	0.604
Shortening*BakeTime	0.244	0.122	0.1240	0.98	0.341
Egg Powder*ovenTemp	0.294	0.147	0.1240	1.18	0.254
Egg Powder*BakeTime	0.056	0.028	0.1240	0.23	0.824
ovenTemp*BakeTime	-2.194	-1.097	0.1240	-8.85	0.000
Flour*ovenTemp*BakeTime	1.194	0.597	0.1240	4.82	0.000

Analysis of Variance for Rating (coded units)

Source	DF	Seq SS	Adj SS	Adj MS	F	P
Main Effects	5	7.332	7.332	1.4663	2.98	0.046
2-Way Interactions	10	49.231	49.231	4.9231	10.01	0.000
3-Way Interactions	1	11.400	11.400	11.4003	23.19	0.000
Residual Error	15	7.375	7.375	0.4916		

FIGURE 13.14 Minitab ANOVA Model for the Cake Mix Example

significant, the significance of the *DE* (Oven Temperature–Bake Time) interaction indicates a crossing effect (see Figure 13.16). This occurs because the rating is high for low oven temperature and high baking time and for high oven temperature and low baking time. The significance of the *ADE* (Flour–Oven Temperature–Bake Time) interaction means that the interaction of oven temperature and baking time is not the same for low and high amounts of flour.

Figure 13.15 presents a main effects plot, and Figure 13.16 consists of an interaction plot for the cake mix design.

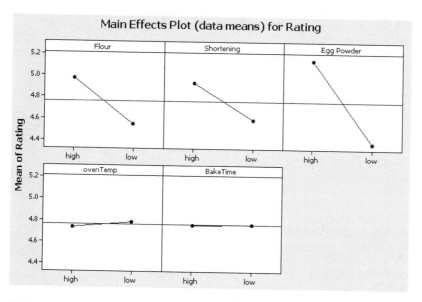

FIGURE 13.15 Minitab Main Effects Plot for the Cake Mix Design

To further your understanding of these results, the interaction plots in Figure 13.16 can be examined along with Tables 13.12–13.15, which provide the average values for combinations of shortening and egg powder, oven temperature and baking temperature, and oven temperature and baking time for each level of flour.

From Figure 13.16 and Table 13.12, you see that for low levels of shortening, the rating is much better for the high level of egg powder (5.475) than for the low level of egg powder (3.70). For a high level of shortening, the results are quite different. The rating is slightly better for low egg powder (5.0375) than for high egg powder (4.825).

Turning to the interaction of oven temperature and baking time, from Figure 13.16 and Table 13.13, you see that the average rating is best for low oven temperature and high baking time (5.875) or high oven temperature and low baking time (5.8375). The rating is worse when there is both low oven temperature and low baking time (3.6875) or high oven temperature and high baking time (3.6375). However, the interaction of oven temperature and baking time is different for each of the two levels of flour. From Tables 13.14 and 13.15, the interaction seen in Table 13.13 is much more pronounced for the low level of flour than for the high level of flour.

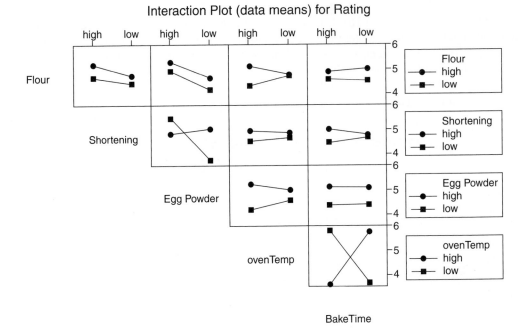

FIGURE 13.16 Minitab Interaction Plot for the Cake Mix Design

TABLE 13.12 Average Rating for Each Level
of Shortening and Egg Powder

	Egg powder	
Shortening	**Low**	**High**
Low	3.7000	5.475
High	5.0375	4.825

Thus, how can you choose the level of flour, shortening, and egg powder that will result in the highest rating? Based on these results, you probably should choose high flour, low shortening, and high egg powder. The rationale for this is as follows.

1. Based on Tables 13.14 and 13.15, using a high level of flour will improve the rating and reduce the effect of oven temperature and baking time.

2. Based on Table 13.12, using a low level of shortening and a high level of egg powder provides the best rating.

3. In addition, the consumer should be warned not to use oven temperature and baking time that are both too low or both too high.

TABLE 13.13 Average Rating for Each Level of Oven Temperature and Baking Time

	Baking time	
Oven temperature	**Low**	**High**
Low	3.6875	5.8750
High	5.8375	3.6375

TABLE 13.14 Average Rating for Each Level of Oven Temperature and Baking Time for the Low Level of Flour

	Baking time	
Oven temperature	**Low**	**High**
Low	3.025	6.500
High	5.975	2.675

TABLE 13.15 Average Rating for Each Level of Oven Temperature and Baking Time for the High Level of Flour

	Baking time	
Oven temperature	**Low**	**High**
Low	4.35	5.25
High	5.70	4.60

13.4 FRACTIONAL FACTORIAL DESIGNS

When four or more factors (Xs) are to be considered, simultaneously running all possible treatment combinations often becomes costly or impossible. For example, 4 factors each with 2 levels involve 16 treatment combinations; 5 factors each with 2 levels involve 32 treatment combinations; and 7 factors each with 2 levels involve 128 treatment combinations. Thus, as the number of factors in an experiment increases, there needs to be a rational way of choosing a subset of the treatment combinations so that a cost-effective experiment with meaningful results can be undertaken. One way to do this is through the use of a fractional factorial design.

In a **fractional factorial design,** only a subset of all possible treatment combinations is used. As a consequence of reducing experimental size, not all the effects can be independently estimated. In other words, there is a loss of information. If the experiment is designed appropriately, higher order interactions often can be confounded with lower order terms. The higher order interaction effects are assumed to be negligible, so what remains are relatively good estimates of the lower order interactions. If the experimental size is reduced too much, lower order interactions, such as two-factor interactions, may become confounded with main effects or other two-factor interactions. It is advantageous to use fractional designs that allow good estimates of main effects and two-factor interactions. One approach is to choose the treatment combinations so that each main effect can be independently estimated without being confused or **confounded** with any estimate of the two-factor interactions. When a main effect or an interaction is confounded, its effect cannot be isolated from the main effect of some other factor or interaction.

Designs in which main effects are confounded with two-way interactions (such as *A* being confounded with *BC*) are called **resolution III designs.** In other words, confounding main effects (one factor) with two-way interactions (two factors) yields Resolution III designs (one factor + two-way interaction = Resolution III design).

In **Resolution IV designs,** a two-way interaction such as *AB* is confounded with another two-way interaction such as *CD* (two-way interaction + two-way interaction = Resolution IV design), or a main effect such as A is confounded with a three-way interaction such as *BCD* (one factor + three-way interaction = Resolution IV design).

In **Resolution V designs,** main effects and two-way interactions are confounded with three-way or higher order interactions (such as *ABC* or *ABCD*). In other words, confounding main effects (one factor) with four-way interactions (four factors) yields Resolution V designs (one factor + four-way interaction = Resolution V design. Also, confounding two-way interactions (two factors) with three-way interactions (three factors) yields Resolution V designs (two-way interaction + three-way interaction = Resolution V design).

Choosing the Treatment Combinations

The discussion of how to choose a subset of the treatment combinations begins by referring to the 2^4 design. Table 13.16 presents the 16 possible treatment combinations for this full factorial design, along with the pattern of pluses and minuses for the main effects (the columns headed by *A, B, C,* and *D*) and the *ABCD* interaction.

In a fractional factorial design with four factors in which half the treatment combinations are chosen, only eight treatment combinations are available from the possible 16 combinations. With only eight treatment combinations, you cannot obtain as much information as compared with the full factorial 2^4 design, in which there are 16 combinations. If you are willing to assume that the four-way interaction, *ABCD,* is not significant, the fraction or subset of eight treatment combinations (called a *half-replicate*) out of the possible 16 could be selected, so that either:

1. The eight treatment combinations all have a plus sign in the column headed by *ABCD* or

2. The eight treatment combinations all have a minus sign in the column headed by *ABCD.*

If you use such a design, the *ABCD* interaction would be considered as the **defining contrast,** from which the factors and interactions that are confounded with each other could be determined. With *ABCD* as the defining contrast, factor *A* is confounded with interaction *BCD* because *A* and

TABLE 13.16 Treatment Combinations for the 2^4 Design in Standard Order

Notation	A	B	C	D	ABCD
(1)	−	−	−	−	+
a	+	−	−	−	−
b	−	+	−	−	−
ab	+	+	−	−	+
c	−	−	+	−	−
ac	+	−	+	−	+
bc	−	+	+	−	+
abc	+	+	+	−	−
d	−	−	−	+	−
ad	+	−	−	+	+
bd	−	+	−	+	+
abd	+	+	−	+	−
cd	−	−	+	+	+
acd	+	−	+	+	−
bcd	−	+	+	+	−
abcd	+	+	+	+	+

ABCD differ only by *BCD*. *BCD* is also called an **alias** of *A*, because the effects of *BCD* and *A* cannot be separated in this fractional factorial design. Thus, the *A* main effect is equivalent to the *BCD* interaction. If you are willing to assume that the *BCD* interaction is negligible, when you evaluate the average main effect of *A*, you state that this is the effect of factor *A* (even though it could have been the effect of the *BCD* interaction). If the half-replicate chosen has a plus sign in column *ABCD*, then *A* is confounded with *BCD*. If the half-replicate chosen has a minus sign in column *ABCD*, then *A* is confounded with −*BCD*. In a similar manner, *B* is confounded with *ACD*; *C* is confounded with *ABD*; *D* is confounded with *ABC*; *AB* is confounded with *CD*; *AC* is confounded with *BD*, and *AD* is confounded with *BC*. Thus, this design is a Resolution IV design.

From this pattern of confounded effects, observe that in this design (which is called a 2^{4-1} fractional factorial design) the two-factor or two-way interaction terms are confounded with each other. Thus, you cannot separate *AB* and *CD*, *AC* and *BD*, and *AD* and *BC*. If any of these interaction terms are found to be important, you will not be able to know whether the effect is due to one term or the other.

As a first example of a fractional factorial design, a 2^{4-1} design in which eight treatments have been chosen from the total of 16 possible combinations and the defining contrast is *ABCD* is considered. In addition to the experimental design used in Section 13.3, Box (see Reference 3) reported on another experiment in which four factors were used to study the average life of bearings produced. The four factors were the manufacturing process for the balls (standard or modified), the cage design (standard or modified), the type of grease (standard or modified), and the amount of grease (normal or large). A half-replicate of a full factorial design was used. The full factorial design is shown in Table 13.17.

TABLE 13.17 Sixteen Treatment Combinations in a 2^4 Experiment in Standard Order

Notation	Average life (Y)	A	B	C	D	Defining contrast
						ABCD
(1)		−	−	−	−	+
a		+	−	−	−	−
b		−	+	−	−	−
ab		+	+	−	−	+
c		−	−	+	−	−
ac		+	−	+	−	+
bc		−	+	+	−	+
abc		+	+	+	−	−
d		−	−	−	+	−
ad		+	−	−	+	+
bd		−	+	−	+	+
abd		+	+	−	+	−
cd		−	−	+	+	+
acd		+	−	+	+	−
bcd		−	+	+	+	−
abcd		+	+	+	+	+

The half-replicate (using only the plus signs from the *ABCD* column) from the defining contrast (*ABCD*) is shown in Table 13.18.

In this design, the two-way interactions are confounded with each other, specifically, *AB* with *CD*, *AC* with *BD*, and *AD* with *BC*. This is a Resolution IV design.

Using the results presented in Table 13.18, for this 2^{4-1} design, you can evaluate $2^{4-1} - 1 = 7$ effects (*A, B, C, D, AB, AC,* and *AD*), as long as you realize that *A* is confounded with *BCD*, *B* is confounded with *ACD*, *C* is confounded with *ABD*, *D* is confounded with *ABC*, *AB* is confounded with *CD*, *AC* is confounded with *BD*, and *AD* is confounded with *BC*. The average effects for these factors obtained from Minitab are presented in Figure 13.17.

These average effects are depicted in Figure 13.18 on page 402 in a normal probability plot of the effects. Figure 13.19 on page 402 is a main effects plot, and Figure 13.20 on page 403 is an interaction plot.

From Figure 13.18, you see that factor *A* and possibly factor *B* appear to plot away from this line. From Figure 13.19, it appears that average life is higher for modified ball bearings than for standard ball bearings and that average life may be higher for a modified cage design than for a standard cage design. From Figure 13.20, none of the interactions appear to be important.

TABLE 13.18 Average Life for Eight Treatment Combinations in the 2^{4-1} Experiment in Standard Order

Notation	Average life	A	B	C	D	AB+ CD	AC+ BD	AD+ BC
(1)	0.31	−	−	−	−	+	+	+
ab	2.17	+	+	−	−	+	−	−
ac	1.37	+	−	+	−	−	+	−
bc	0.92	−	+	+	−	−	−	+
ad	1.38	+	−	−	+	−	−	+
bd	0.73	−	+	−	+	−	+	−
cd	0.95	−	−	+	+	+	−	−
abcd	2.57	+	+	+	+	+	+	+

BEARINGS2

Source: Reprinted from Box, G.E.P., "What Can You Find out from Eight Experimental Runs," *Quality Engineering*, 4, 1992, pp. 619–627.

```
Factorial Fit: Average life versus balls, Cage design, ...

Estimated Effects and Coefficients for Average life (coded units)

Term                      Effect     Coef
Constant                            1.30000
balls                    1.14500    0.57250
Cage design              0.59500    0.29750
Grease                   0.30500    0.15250
Amount of grease         0.21500    0.10750
balls*Cage design        0.40000    0.20000
balls*Grease            -0.11000   -0.05500
balls*Amount of grease  -0.01000   -0.00500
```

FIGURE 13.17 Minitab Estimated Effects for the Roller Bearing Fractional Factorial Design

Now that the topic of fractional factorial designs has been introduced with the 2^{4-1} design, a second example involving a 2^{5-1} design will be considered. This experiment was conducted to study the process of using carbon dioxide to extract oil from peanuts in a production process. The response variable (CTQ) was the amount of oil that could dissolve in the carbon dioxide (the solubility). Five factors (Xs) were to be studied. They are labeled as follows: A = carbon dioxide pressure, B = carbon dioxide temperature, C = peanut moisture, D = carbon dioxide flow rate, E = peanut particle size. Two levels of each factor (low and high) were chosen. A half-replicate of a 2^5 design was selected, due to budgetary constraints. The standard order matrix for a full factorial 2^5 design is shown in Table 13.19.

The results of the half-replicate experiment (using the minus signs in the $ABCDE$ column) are presented in Table 13.20 on page 404.

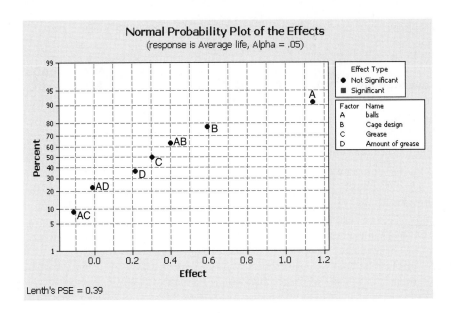

FIGURE 13.18 Minitab Normal Probability Plot for the 2^{4-1} Design for the Roller Bearing Experiment

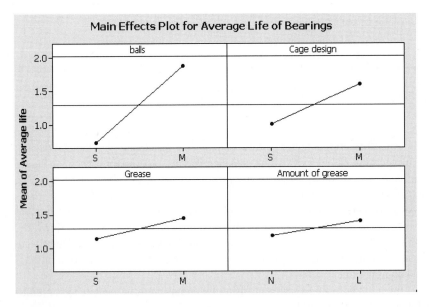

FIGURE 13.19 Minitab Main Effects Plot for the 2^{4-1} Design for the Roller Bearing Experiment

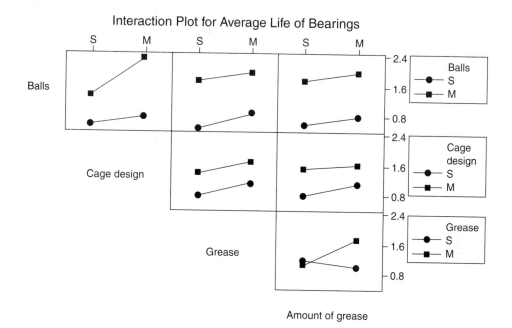

FIGURE 13.20 Minitab Interaction Plot for the 2^{4-1} Design for the Roller Bearing Experiment

TABLE 13.19 Standard Order Design Matrix for a Full Factorial 2^5 Experiment

Notation	Response variable (Y)	A	B	C	D	E	ABCDE
(1)		−	−	−	−	−	−
a		+	−	−	−	−	+
b		−	+	−	−	−	+
ab		+	+	−	−	−	−
c		−	−	+	−	−	+
ac		+	−	+	−	−	−
bc		−	+	+	−	−	−
abc		+	+	+	−	−	+
d		−	−	−	+	−	+
ad		+	−	−	+	−	−
bd		−	+	−	+	−	−
abd		+	+	−	+	−	+
cd		−	−	+	+	−	−
acd		+	−	+	+	−	+
bde		−	+	+	+	−	+

(continued)

TABLE 13.19 Standard Order Design Matrix for a Full Factorial 2^5 Experiment (continued)

Notation	Response variable (Y)	A	B	C	D	E	ABCDE
abcd		+	+	+	+	−	−
e		−	−	−	−	+	+
ae		+	−	−	−	+	−
be		−	+	−	−	+	−
abe		+	+	−	−	+	+
ce		−	−	+	−	+	−
ace		+	−	+	−	+	+
bce		−	+	+	−	+	+
abce		+	+	+	−	+	−
de		−	−	−	+	+	−
ade		+	−	−	+	+	+
bde		−	+	−	+	+	+
abde		+	+	−	+	+	−
cde		−	−	+	+	+	+
acde		+	−	+	+	+	−
bcde		−	+	+	+	+	−
abcde		+	+	+	+	+	+

TABLE 13.20 Data for the Peanut Oil Experiment

Treatment Combination	Response	Treatment Combination	Response
(1)	29.2	de	22.4
ae	23.0	ad	37.2
be	37.0	bd	31.3
ab	139.7	abde	148.6
ce	23.3	cd	22.9
ac	38.3	acde	36.2
bc	42.6	bcde	33.6
abce	141.4	abcd	172.6

PEANUT

Source: Kilgo, M., "An Application of Fractional Factorial Experimental Designs," *Quality Engineering*, 1, 1989, pp. 45–54.

The subset or fraction of 16 treatment combinations used in Table 13.20 is based on the five-factor interaction *ABCDE* as the defining contrast. This produces a Resolution V design in which all main effects and two-factor interactions can be estimated independently of each other. Each main effect is confounded with a four-factor interaction, and each two-factor interaction is confounded with a three-factor interaction. For this design, the set of confounded effects is summarized in Table 13.21.

TABLE 13.21 Confounded Effects for the 2^{5-1} Design with *ABCDE* as the Defining Contrast

Effect	Confounded with	Effect	Confounded with
A	BCDE	AE	BCD
B	ACDE	BC	ADE
C	ABDE	BD	ACE
D	ABCE	BE	ACD
E	ABCD	CD	ABE
AB	CDE	CE	ABD
AC	BDE	DE	ABC
AD	BCE		

The average effects for these factors (obtained from Minitab) are presented in Figure 13.21.

```
Estimated Effects and Coefficients for Amount dissolved (coded units)

Term                                  Effect    Coef
Constant                                       61.206
CO2 pressure                          61.837   30.919
CO2 temperature                       64.287   32.144
peanut moisture                        5.312    2.656
CO2 flow rate                          3.788    1.894
Peanut particle size                  -6.038   -3.019
CO2 pressure*CO2 temperature          52.613   26.306
CO2 pressure*peanut moisture           4.688    2.344
CO2 pressure*CO2 flow rate             9.263    4.631
CO2 pressure*Peanut particle size     -3.613   -1.806
CO2 temperature*peanut moisture        3.088    1.544
CO2 temperature*CO2 flow rate          2.563    1.281
CO2 temperature*Peanut particle size  -0.363   -0.181
peanut moisture*CO2 flow rate          1.137    0.569
peanut moisture*Peanut particle size  -4.437   -2.219
CO2 flow rate*Peanut particle size     0.237    0.119
```

FIGURE 13.21 Minitab Estimated Effects for the Peanut Oil Fractional Factorial Design

Figure 13.22 is a normal probability plot of the estimated effects for the peanut oil experiment.

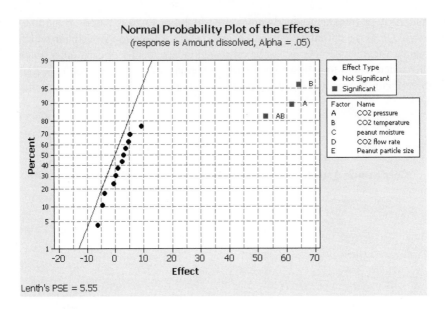

FIGURE 13.22 Minitab Normal Probability Plot for the Peanut Oil Experiment

From Figure 13.22, you see that factors *A* and *B* and the *AB* interaction plot far away from the straight line that is approximately zero on the *X* axis. Minitab indicates that these terms are statistically significant according to criteria developed by Lenth [see Reference 7]. Thus, a reasonable approach is to consider all interactions except *AB* as consisting only of random error. These effects can be eliminated from the ANOVA model and combined to estimate an error variance. The ANOVA model obtained from Minitab with these effects combined into an error variance is displayed in Figure 13.23.

From Figure 13.23, you see that the main effects of carbon dioxide pressure and carbon dioxide temperature are highly significantly with *p*-values of 0.000. The interaction of carbon dioxide pressure and carbon dioxide temperature is also highly significant with a *p*-value of 0.000.

Figure 13.24 is a main effects plot, and Figure 13.25 is an interaction plot.

From Figure 13.24, you see that the average amount dissolved is higher for high carbon dioxide pressure than for low carbon dioxide pressure and is higher for high carbon dioxide temperature than for low carbon dioxide temperature. However, the interaction plot displayed in Figure 13.25 indicates a clear interaction of carbon dioxide pressure and temperature. High carbon dioxide pressure combined with high carbon dioxide temperature greatly increases the average amount of oil dissolved.

In this section, we have discussed two examples of fractional factorial designs that are used when it is not feasible to evaluate all possible treatment combinations. These two designs are only a small subset of the variety of fractional factorial designs that are available for selection. The 2^{4-1} and 2^{5-1} designs are examples of designs that involve the selection of a half-replicate

```
Estimated Effects and Coefficients for Amount dissolved (coded units)

Term                         Effect    Coef  SE Coef       T      P
Constant                              61.206    2.096   29.21  0.000
CO2 pressure                 61.837   30.919    2.096   14.75  0.000
CO2 temperature              64.287   32.144    2.096   15.34  0.000
peanut moisture               5.312    2.656    2.096    1.27  0.237
CO2 flow rate                 3.788    1.894    2.096    0.90  0.390
Peanut particle size         -6.038   -3.019    2.096   -1.44  0.184
CO2 pressure*CO2 temperature 52.613   26.306    2.096   12.55  0.000


S = 8.38223   R-Sq = 98.56%   R-Sq(adj) = 97.60%


Analysis of Variance for Amount dissolved (coded units)

Source              DF   Seq SS   Adj SS   Adj MS       F      P
Main Effects         5  32143.1  32143.1   6428.6   91.50  0.000
2-Way Interactions   1  11072.3  11072.3  11072.3  157.59  0.000
Residual Error       9    632.4    632.4     70.3
Total               15  43847.8
```

FIGURE 13.23 ANOVA Model Obtained from Minitab for the Peanut Oil Example

(8 out of 16 or 16 out of 32 treatment combinations) of a full factorial design. Other designs might involve a quarter-replicate (such as 2^{5-2} and 2^{6-2} designs) or even smaller portions of a factorial design in which only main effects can be estimated (for instance, a 2^{15-11} design). Discussion of such designs are beyond the scope of this text. For further information, see References 6, 9, and 10).

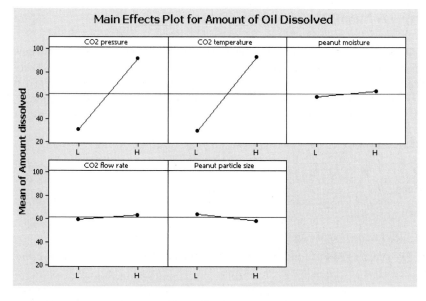

FIGURE 13.24 Minitab Main Effects Plot for the Peanut Oil Experiment

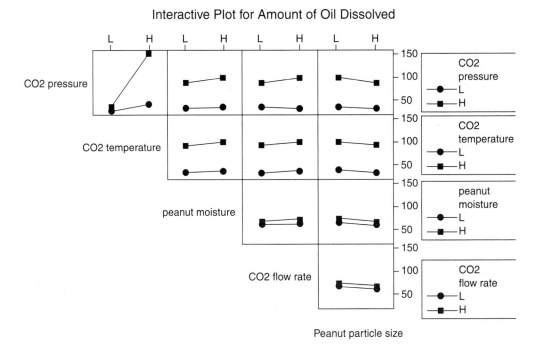

FIGURE 13.25 Minitab Interaction Plot for the Peanut Oil Experiment

SUMMARY AND OVERVIEW

In this chapter, the basic aspects of design of experiments have been developed. You have seen how the factorial design, by allowing for the measurement of the size of interaction effects, offers a substantial benefit as compared with the one-factor design approach. Although several designs were discussed, you should be aware that the topics covered in this book have barely "scratched the surface" of the subject of the design of experiments. For further information, see References 6, 9, and 10.

REFERENCES

1. Bisgaard, S., "Industrial Use of Statistically Designed Experiments: Case Study References and Some Historical Anecdotes," *Quality Engineering,* 4, 1992, pp. 547–562.

2. Box, G.E.P., "Do Interactions Matter?" *Quality Engineering,* 2, 1990, pp. 365–369.

3. Box, G.E.P., "What Can you Find out from Eight Experimental Runs," *Quality Engineering,* 4, 1992, pp. 619–627.

4. Box, J. F., "R. A. Fisher and the Design of Experiments," *American Statistician,* 34, 1980, pp. 1–10.

5. Daniel, C., "Use of Half-Normal Plots in Interpreting Factorial Two-Level Experiments," *Technometrics,* 1, 1959, pp. 311–341.

6. Hicks, C. R. and K. V. Turner, *Fundamental Concepts in the Design of Experiments,* 5th ed. (New York: Oxford University Press, 1999).

7. Lenth, R. V., "Quick and Easy Analysis of Unreplicated Factorials," *Technometrics,* 31, 1989, pp. 469–473.

8. *Minitab for Windows Version 14* (State College, PA: Minitab, 2004).

9. Montgomery, D. C., *Design and Analysis of Experiments,* 5th ed. (New York: John Wiley, 2001).

10. Neter, J., M. H. Kutner, C. Nachtsheim, and W. Wasserman, *Applied Linear Statistical Models,* 4th ed. (Homewood, IL: Richard D. Irwin, 1996).

A P P E N D I X 1 3 . 1

USING MINITAB FOR THE DESIGN OF EXPERIMENTS

Using Minitab for the Two-Way ANOVA

To obtain a two-way ANOVA using Minitab, open the **GEAR.MTW** worksheet. Select **Stat → ANOVA → Two-Way,** then do the following:

1. In the Two-Way Analysis of Variance dialog box (see Figure A13.1), enter **C3** or **Distortion** in the Responses: edit box.

2. In the Row Factor: edit box, enter **C1** or **'Tooth Size'.** Select the **Display means** check box.

3. In the Column Factor: edit box, enter **C2** or **'Part Positioning'.** Select the **Display means** check box.

4. Click the **OK** button.

Using Minitab for a Main Effects Plot

To obtain a main effects plot using Minitab, open the **GEAR.MTW** worksheet. Select **Stat → ANOVA → Main Effects Plot,** then do the following:

1. In the Main Effects Plot dialog box (see Figure A13.2), enter **C3** or **Distortion** in the Responses: edit box.

2. In the Factors: edit box, enter **C1** or **'Tooth Size'** and **C2** or **'Part Positioning'.**

3. Click the **OK** button.

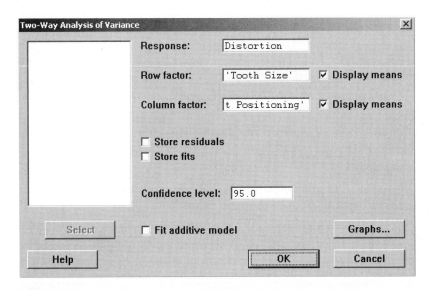

FIGURE A13.1 Minitab Two-Way Analysis of Variance Dialog Box

Using Minitab for an Interaction Plot

To obtain an interaction plot using Minitab, open the **GEAR.MTW** worksheet. Select **Stat → ANOVA → Interactions Plot,** then do the following:

1. In the Interactions Plot dialog box (see Figure A13.3), enter **C3** or **Distortion** in the Responses: edit box.

2. In the Factors: edit box, enter **C1** or **'Tooth Size'** and **C2** or **'Part Positioning'.**

3. Click the **OK** button.

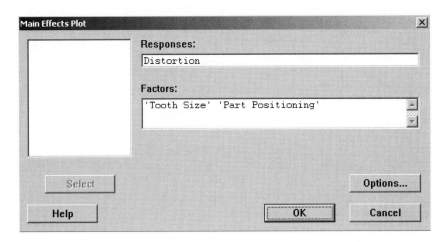

FIGURE A 13.2 Minitab Main Effects Plot Dialog Box

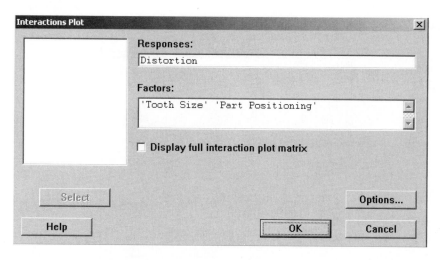

FIGURE A 13.3 Minitab Interactions Plot Dialog Box

Using Minitab for a Factorial Design

To obtain the estimated effects and ANOVA in a factorial design along with a normal probability plot of the effects, open the **CAKE.MTW** worksheet. Select **Stat → DOE → Factorial → Analyze Factorial Design**, then do the following:

1. Click **Yes** in the Minitab dialog box (see Figure A13.4) that appears because Minitab has not yet created a design.

2. In the Define Custom Factorial Design dialog box (see Figure A13.5), enter **C1** or **Flour, C2** or **Shortening, C3** or **'Egg Powder', C4** or **ovenTemp, C5** or **BakeTime** in the Factors: edit box. Select the **2-level factorial** option button. Click the **Low/High** button.

3. Enter the low and high values for each factor in the Design Custom Factorial Design—Low/High dialog box (see Figure A13.6). Click the **OK** button to return to the Design Custom Factorial Design dialog box. Click the **OK** button.

4. In the Analyze Factorial Design dialog box (see Figure A13.7), enter **C6** or **Rating** in the Responses: edit box.

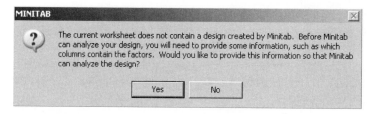

FIGURE A13.4 Minitab Dialog Box to Create a Design

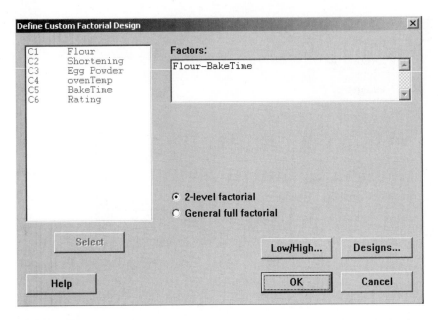

FIGURE A13.5 Minitab Define Custom Factorial Design Dialog Box

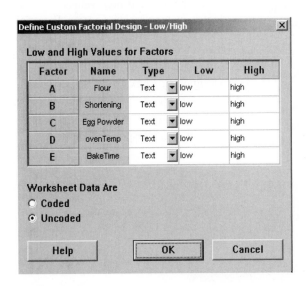

FIGURE A13.6 Minitab Define Custom Factorial Design—Low/High Dialog Box

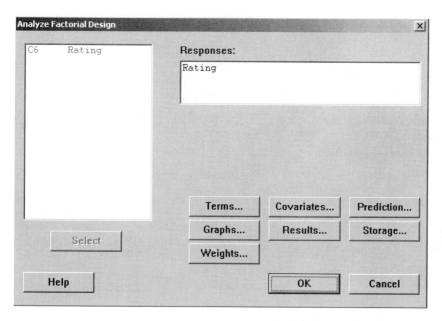

FIGURE A13.7 Minitab Analyze Factorial Design Dialog Box

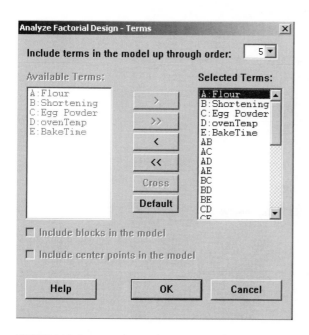

FIGURE A13.8 Minitab Analyze Factorial Design—Terms Dialog Box

5. Click the **Terms** button. In the Analyze Factorial Design—Terms dialog box (see Figure A13.8), because this is a full factorial design, the Include terms in the model up through order: drop-down list box is **5.** (Use arrow keys to add terms and delete terms if desired.) Click the **OK** button.

6. In the Analyze Factorial Design dialog box (Figure A13.7), click the **Graphs** button. In the Analyze Factorial Design—Graphs dialog box (see Figure A13.9), under Effects Plots, select the **Normal** check box to obtain a normal probability plot for the effects. (Select Pareto to obtain a Pareto diagram of the effects.) Click the **OK** button.

7. In the Analyze Factorial Design dialog box (Figure A13.7), click the **OK** button.

Using Minitab for a Fractional Factorial Design

Follow the steps shown for the factorial design, except for step 5. In the Analyze Factorial Design—Terms dialog box, enter the value in the edit box that indicates the highest interactions included in the model. For example, in the 2^{4-1} fractional factorial design used for the roller bearing example, open the **BEARINGS2.MTW** worksheet. In the Analyze Factorial Design—Terms dialog box (Figure A13.10), enter **2** in the Include terms in the model up through order: edit box because only the *AB, AC, AD, BC, BD,* and *CD* interactions are to be included.

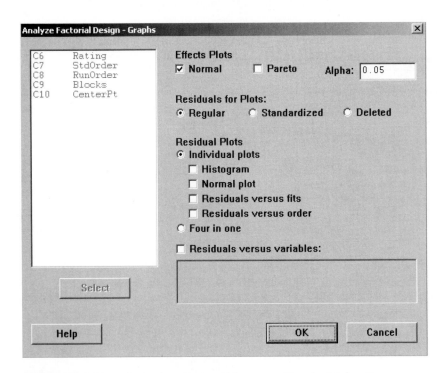

FIGURE A13.9 Minitab Analyze Factorial Design—Graphs Dialog Box

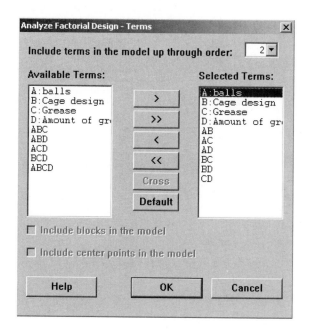

FIGURE A13.10 Minitab Analyze Factorial Design—Terms dialog box

CONTROL CHARTS FOR SIX SIGMA MANAGEMENT

CHAPTER OUTLINE

LEARNING OBJECTIVES

After reading this chapter, you will be able to:

- Understand the purpose of control charts
- Know which control chart to use for a particular type of data
- Construct and interpret various control charts

14.1 Basic Concepts of Control Charts

The **control chart** is a tool for distinguishing between the common causes of variation (variation due to the system itself) and special causes of variation (variation due to factors external to the system) for a CTQ or an X. It is used to assess and monitor the stability of a CTQ or an X (presence of only common causes of variation). The data for a control chart is obtained from a subgroup or sample of items selected at each observation session.

Control charts can be divided into two categories that are determined by the type of data used to monitor a process. These two broad categories are called **attribute control charts** and **measurement (variable) control charts.** In Chapter 9, attribute data was defined as classification data (e.g., conforming or nonconforming) or count data (e.g., number of defects per area of opportunity). Attribute control charts are used to evaluate CTQs or Xs that are defined by attribute data. The attribute control charts covered in this chapter are:

1. Proportion nonconforming charts (*p*-charts) for classification data
   a. Proportion of nonconformities for constant subgroup size
   b. Proportion of nonconformities for variable subgroup size
2. Area of opportunity charts for attribute data
   a. Number of defects charts (*c*-charts) for constant areas of opportunity
   b. Number of defects per unit charts (*u*-charts) for variable areas of opportunity

If the CTQ or X is measured on a continuous scale, such as height, weight, or temperature, a variables control chart is used. **Variables (measurement) control charts** contain two sections: One studies process variability, and the other studies central tendency. The variables control charts covered in this chapter are:

1. Charts based on subgroups of size $n \geq 2$
   a. Mean and range charts ($\overline{X}$ and *R*-charts) for subgroups of size $2 \leq n \leq 10$
   b. Mean and standard deviation charts ($\overline{X}$ and *S*-charts) for subgroups of size $n \geq 10$
2. Charts based on individual measurements (X and moving range charts) for subgroups of size $n = 1$

Figure 14.15 on page 454 is a flow diagram that can help in deciding which type of chart is most appropriate for a given situation. Control charts are an important statistical tool in Six Sigma management. They are used at every stage of the DMAIC model (see Chapters 4–8 for examples).

The distinction between the two causes of variation is crucial because special causes of variation are considered to be those that are not due to the process, whereas common causes of variation are due to the process. Only management can change the process.

> **Special or assignable causes of variation** create fluctuations or patterns in data that are not inherent to a process. Special causes of variation are the responsibility of workers and engineers. Workers and engineers identify and, if possible, resolve special causes of variation. If they cannot resolve a special cause of variation, they enlist the aid of management. **Chance or common causes of variation** create fluctuations or patterns in data that are due to the system itself, for example, the fluctuations caused by hiring, training, and supervisory policies and practices. Common causes of variation are the responsibility of management. Only management can change the policies and procedures that define the common causes of variation in a system.

One experiment that is useful to help you appreciate the distinction between common and special causes of variation was developed by Walter Shewhart more than 80 years ago. The experiment requires that you repeatedly write the letter "A" over and over again in a horizontal line across a piece of paper.

AAAAᴀᴀᴀAAᴀᴀᴀAᴀᴀᴀᴀ

When you do this, you will immediately notice that the "A"s are all similar, but not exactly the same. Additionally, you may notice as much as a 10%, 20%, or even 30% difference in the size of the "A"s from letter to letter. This difference is due to common cause variation. Nothing special happened that caused the differences in the size of the "A"s. If you had gotten more sleep last night, or drank less coffee today, your hand might be steadier, and your "A"s would be more similar. You probably realize that it would be foolish to try to explain why the largest "A" was so big and the smallest "A" was so small. However, you may be aware that, in accounting, it is common practice to try to explain this type of variation when it appears as discrepancies between the actual and budgeted expense items. These types of discrepancies may represent a common cause system of variation. If this is the case, it is dangerous to treat common causes of variation as special causes of variation. The danger of this confusion is explained below.

There are two types of errors that control charts help prevent. The first type of error involves the belief that an observed value represents special cause variation when in fact it is due to the common cause variation of the system. Treating common causes of variation as special cause variation can result in tampering with or overadjustment of a process with an accompanying increase in variation. The second type of error involves treating special cause variation as though it were common cause variation and not taking corrective action when it is necessary. Although these errors can still occur when a control chart is used, they are far less likely.

14.2 THE FUNNEL EXPERIMENT

The **funnel experiment** [see Reference 1] is a teaching aid that is frequently employed to explain the destructive effects of the first type of error; that is, treating a common cause of variation as a special cause of variation (remember the A's). This is called *overcontrol of the process,* or **tampering.** If management tampers with a process, they will increase the process's variation and reduce their ability to manage that process. The equipment needed for the funnel experiment* shown in Figure 14.1 includes:

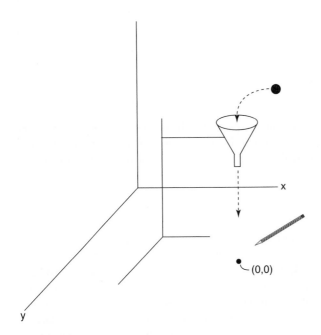

FIGURE 14.1 Funnel Experiment Equipment

1. A kitchen funnel
2. A marble that will fall through the funnel
3. A flat surface (e.g., a table top)
4. A pencil
5. A holder for the funnel (chemistry stand for holding test tubes)

---

*The funnel experiment can also be conducted using a device called a quincunx.

The funnel experiment involves the following five steps:

1. Designate a point on the flat surface as a target and consider this target to be the point of origin in a two-dimensional space, where X and Y represent the axes of the surface. Hence, the target (X, Y) is $(0,0)$.
2. Drop a marble through the funnel to hit the target.
3. Mark the spot where the marble comes to rest on the surface with a pencil.
4. Adjust the positioning of the funnel to better hit the target. Drop the marble through the funnel again and mark the spot where the marble comes to rest on the surface.
5. Repeat step (4) through 50 drops.

A rule for adjusting the funnel's position in relation to the target is needed to perform the fourth step. There are four rules, and the second rule can be handled in two ways.

Rule 1. Set the funnel over the target at $(0,0)$ and leave the funnel fixed through all 50 drops. This rule will produce a stable pattern (only common causes of variation) of points on the surface; this pattern will approximate a circle, as shown in Figure 14.2. The variance of the diameters of all circles produced by repeated experimentation using Rule 1 will be smaller than the variance resulting from any other rule used in the fourth step of the experiment.

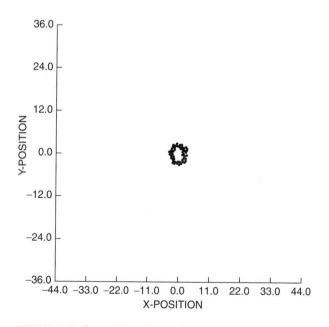

FIGURE 14.2 Illustrating Rule 1 of the Funnel Experiment

Management's use of the first rule demonstrates an understanding of the distinction between special and common variation, and the different types of managerial action required for each type of variation. Management using rule 1 understands that only common variation is present and that reduction of variation (creating a smaller circle) requires the system to be fundamentally changed. This could be accomplished by lowering the funnel closer to the table, making a longer barrel on the funnel, or creating a rounded barrel for the funnel.

Rule 2. The funnel is set over the target at (0,0) prior to the initial drop. Let (X_k, Y_k) represent the point where the kth marble dropped through the funnel comes to rest on the surface. Rule 2 states that the funnel should be moved the distance $(-X_k, -Y_k)$ from its last resting point. In essence, this is an adjustment rule with a memory of the last resting point. This rule will produce a stable pattern of resting points on the surface, which will approximate a circle. However, the variance of the diameters of all circles produced by repeated experimentation using rule 2 will have double the variance of the circular pattern produced using rule 1, as Figure 14.3 shows.

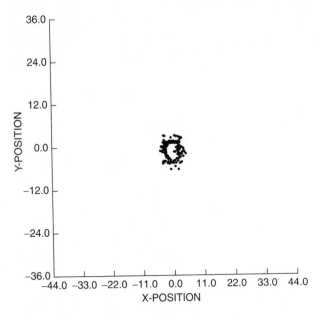

FIGURE 14.3 Illustrating Rule 2 of the Funnel Experiment

In terms of its application to management actions, rule 2 implies that the process is being tampered with by people with inadequate knowledge of how to manage the process to reduce its variation. It implies acting on common variation as though it were special variation. Rule 2 is commonly used as a method of attempting to make things better in a process. Here are three examples of rule 2 management.

1. Automatic process control. The automatic adjustment of a process to hold output within specified tolerance limits is an example of rule 2, assuming adjustments to the process are made from the last process measurement. This type of process adjustment procedure is frequently called **rule-based process control** (RPC). RPC is widely used in industry.

2. Operator adjustment. Operator adjustment to compensate for a unit of output not being on target, or nominal, is an example of rule 2, assuming that adjustments to the process are made from the last process measurement [see Reference 3, pp. 359–360].

3. Stock market. The stock market's reaction to good or bad news is often an overreaction to phenomena.

Rule 2a. A variant on rule 2 is often employed in industry. Rule 2a states if (X_k, Y_k) is within a circle centered at (0,0) with diameter d_{spec}, don't adjust the funnel. But if (X_k, Y_k) is outside the circle centered at (0,0) with diameter d_{spec}, use the adjustment rule specified in rule 2. Rule 2a creates a "dead-band" in which no process adjustment takes place.

An example of rule 2a can be seen in variance analysis in cost accounting. As stated in Section 14.1, one method of monitoring performance in an organization is the use of efficiency and spending variances for the areas of direct labor, direct materials, and overhead. This is called *variance analysis.* Traditionally, manufacturers in the United States have relied on variance analysis to evaluate performance. If the actual performance of a line item is more than 10% under budget, it is believed to indicate that excellent work is being done. If the actual performance of a line item is more than 10% over budget, the converse is assumed to be true.

Variance analysis may cause employees to react inappropriately to accounting variances, that is, variance analysis forces employees to react to variances as though they were due only to special causes, as opposed to common causes. In the long run, variance analysis doubles the variation of stable processes being managed in accordance with cost accounting principles.

Rule 3. The funnel is set over the target at (0,0) prior to the initial drop. Let (X_k, Y_k) represent the point where the kth marble dropped through the funnel comes to rest on the surface. Rule 3 states that the funnel should be moved a distance $(-X_k, -Y_k)$ from the target (0,0). In essence, this is an adjustment rule with no memory of the last resting point. This rule will produce an unstable, explosive pattern of resting points on the surface; as k increases without bound, the pattern will move farther and farther away from the target in some symmetrical pattern, such as the bow-tie-shaped pattern in Figure 14.4.

Rule 3, like rule 2, is commonly used as a method of attempting to improve the process. Rule 3 implies that the process is being tampered with by people with inadequate knowledge of how to manage the process to reduce its variation. It implies acting on common variation as though it were special variation. The following are five examples of rule 3.

1. Automatic process control. The automatic adjustment of a process to hold output within specified tolerance limits is an example of rule 3, assuming that adjustments to the process are made from the target and not the last process measurement.

2. Operator adjustment. Operator adjustment to compensate for a unit of output not being on target is an example of rule 3, assuming that adjustments to the process are made from the target and not the last process measurement.

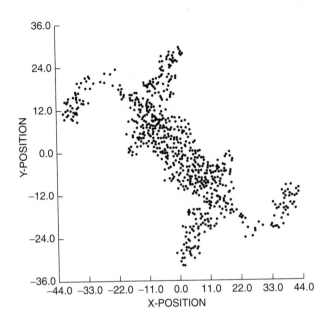

FIGURE 14.4 Illustrating Rule 3 of the Funnel Experiment

3. Setting the current period's goal based on last period's overage or underage. A sales quota policy that states that if you are short of this month's goal by $25,000, you must increase next month's goal by $25,000 is an example of rule 3.

4. Setting the inspection policy for the kth batch based on the $(k - 1^{st})$ batch's record. An inspection policy that recommends tightened or loosened inspection for a batch of material based on the history of the prior batch is an example of rule 3.

5. Making up the previous period's shortage during the current period. A production policy that requires production personnel to make up any shortages from last month's production run in this month's production run is an example of rule 3.

Rule 4. The funnel is set over the target at (0,0) prior to the initial drop. Let (X_k, Y_k) represent the point where the kth marble dropped through the funnel comes to rest on the surface. Rule 4 states that the funnel should be moved to the resting point, (X_k, Y_k). In essence, this is an adjustment rule with no memory of either the last resting point or the position of the target at (0,0). This rule will produce an unstable, explosive pattern of resting points on the surface as k increases without bound, and it will eventually move farther and farther away from the target at (0,0) in one direction, as shown in Figure 14.5.

Rule 4 is commonly used as a method of attempting to make things better in a process. Rule 4 implies that the process is being tampered with by people with inadequate knowledge of how to manage the process to reduce its variation. It implies acting on common variation as though it were special variation. Many of the following eight examples were discussed by Deming [see References 2 and 3].

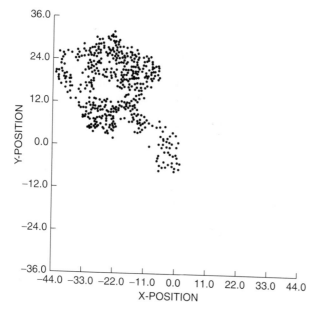

FIGURE 14.5 Illustrating Rule 4 of the Funnel Experiment

1. Make it like the last one. Using the last unit of output as the standard for the next unit of output will eventually produce material bearing no resemblance to the original piece—an example of rule 4. A possible solution to this problem is to use a master piece as a point of comparison. A common complaint is that "we sold the master (model) piece" so a standard is no longer available for comparison purposes.

2. On-the-job training. Deming cites [Reference 3, p. 329] "A frightening example of rule 4. . . where people on a job train a new worker. This worker is then ready in a few days to help to train a new worker. The methods taught deteriorate without limit. Who would know?" Possible solutions to this problem are to formalize training with a video presentation or to utilize a master in the subject matter to do the training, to get a consistent and desired message to the trainees.

3. Budgeting. Setting the next period's budget as a percentage of the last period's budget is an example of rule 4.

4. Policy setting. If they lack a mission statement to guide them and a theory of management, executives meeting to establish policy for an organization will set policies that become increasingly less consistent and more confusing, so that eventually their policies will damage the organization.

5. Engineering changes. Engineering changes to a product or process based on the latest version of a design without regard to the original design are made in accordance with rule 4. Eventually, the current design will bear no resemblance to the original design.

6. Policy surveys. An executive who changes policy based on results of the latest employee survey in a stream of employee surveys is operating under rule 4. Eventually, the policy will have no bearing on its original intended purpose.

7. Adjusting work standards to reflect current performance. An organization that adjusts work standards to reflect current conditions is using rule 4. Work standards should be replaced with control charts that allow management to understand the capability of a process and take action to improve the process by reducing the variation in the process.

8. Collective bargaining. Union-management negotiations in which successive contracts are a reaction to current conditions is an example of rule 4.

The funnel experiment illustrates how a system is improved by process improvement, not by overcontrol of variation. In the funnel experiment, the diameter of the circle created under rule 1 is reduced by moving the funnel closer to the surface or by straightening and lengthening the tube portion of the funnel. Both of these methods for improvement are system changes. In terms of an organization, the corresponding reduction of variation also involves system changes. Because management is responsible for the system, only management can make the necessary changes to reduce this variation in the system.

14.3 CONTROL LIMITS AND PATTERNS

The most typical form of a control chart sets control limits at plus or minus three standard deviations of the statistic of interest (the average, the range, the proportion, etc.). In general, this is stated as:

Obtaining Control Limits

Process average of the statistic $\pm\,3$ [standard deviations of the statistic]   (14.1)

so that

Upper control limit (UCL) = average of the statistic + 3 [standard deviations of the statistic]

Lower control limit (LCL) = average of the statistic – 3 [standard deviations of the statistic]

Once these control limits are computed from the data, the control chart is evaluated by discerning any nonrandom pattern that might exist in the data. Figure 14.6 illustrates three different patterns.

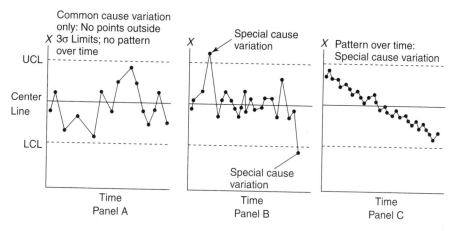

FIGURE 14.6 Three Control Chart Patterns

In panel A of Figure 14.6, there does not appear to be any pattern in the ordering of values over time, and there are no points that fall outside the 3 standard deviation control limits. It appears that the process is stable and contains only common cause variation. Panel B, on the contrary, contains two points that fall outside the 3 standard deviation control limits. Each of these points should be investigated to determine the special causes that led to their occurrence. Although Panel C does not have any points outside the control limits, it has a series of consecutive points above the average value (the center line), as well as a series of consecutive points below the average value. In addition, a long-term overall downward trend in the value of the variable is clearly visible.

Control limits are often called **Three-Sigma limits.** In practice, virtually all of a process's output will be located within a Three-Sigma interval of the process mean, provided that the process is stable. Further, virtually all the sample means for a given subgroup size will be located within a 3 standard error interval around the process mean, provided that the process is stable. This provides a basis for distinguishing between common and special variation for the process statistics.

14.4 RULES FOR DETERMINING OUT-OF-CONTROL POINTS

The simplest rule for detecting the presence of a special cause is one or more points falling beyond the ±3 standard deviation (sigma) limits of the chart. The control chart can be made more sensitive and effective in detecting out-of-control points by considering other signals and patterns that are unlikely to occur by chance alone. For example, if only common causes are operating, you would expect the points plotted to approximately follow a bell-shaped normal distribution. Figure 14.7 presents a control chart in which the area between the UCL and LCL is subdivided into bands, each of which is 1 standard deviation wide. These additional limits, or **zone boundaries,** are useful in detecting other unlikely patterns of data points.

Exhibit 14.1 provides some rules for deciding when a process is out of control.

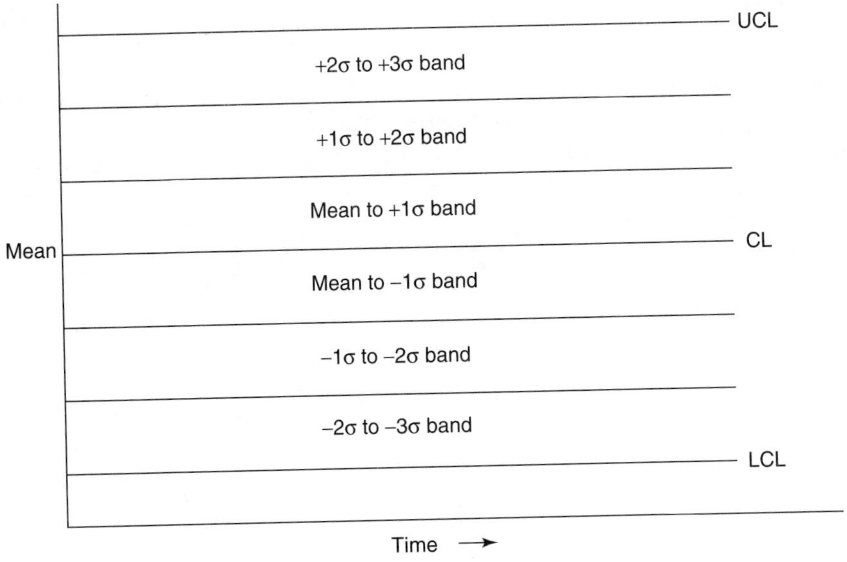

FIGURE 14.7 A Control Chart Showing Bands, Each of Which is 1 Standard Deviation Wide

---

| Exhibit 14.1 | **Some Rules for Deciding When a Process is out of Control** |

Conclude that the process is out of control if any of the following events occur:

1. A point falls above the UCL or below the LCL.
2. Two of three *consecutive points* fall above the +2 standard deviation limits or two of three *consecutive points* fall below the −2 standard deviation limits.
3. Four of five *consecutive points* fall above the +1 standard deviation limit or four of five *consecutive points* fall below the −1 standard deviation limit.
4. Eight or more *consecutive points* lie above the center line or eight or more *consecutive points* lie below the center line.
5. Eight or more *consecutive points* move upward in value or eight or more *consecutive points* move downward in value.
6. **An unusually small number of consecutive points above and below the centerline are present (a sawtooth pattern).
7. Thirteen consecutive points fall within zone C on either side of the centerline.

**Rules 6 and 7 are used to determine whether a process is unusually noisy (high variability) or unusually quiet (low variability).

If only common causes are operating, each of these events is statistically unlikely to occur. For example, the probability of obtaining eight consecutive points on a given side of the center line by chance alone is $(0.5)^8 = 0.0039$. (This is based on the binomial distribution [see Section 10.4.]) Consequently, either a low-probability event occurred (eight points in a row on one side of the center line) or a special cause of variation is present in the process. Many statisticians agree that if the probability of an event is less than 1/100 (in this case, 0.0039), it is reasonable to assume the event is due to a special cause of variation, not due to the occurrence of a low-probability common cause of variation (event).

The presence of one or more of these low-probability events indicates that one or more special causes *may* be operating, thereby resulting in a process that is out of a state of statistical control. Rules 2–7 should be used with statistical knowledge because, in some situations, they can increase the false alarm rate. Other rules for special causes have been developed and are incorporated within the control chart features of Minitab. Different rules may be considered appropriate for specific charts (see Appendix 14.1).

14.5 THE *p*-CHART

The *p*-chart is used to study classification type attribute data, for example, the proportion of nonconforming items by month. Subgroup sizes in a *p*-chart may remain constant or may vary. The *p*-chart assumes that:

1. There are only two possible outcomes for an event. An item must be found to be either conforming or nonconforming.

2. The probability, *p,* of a nonconforming item is constant over time.

3. Successive items are independent over time.

4. Subgroups are of sufficient size to detect an out-of-control event. A general rule for subgroup size for a *p*-chart is that the subgroup size should be large enough to detect a special cause of variation if it exists. Frequently, subgroup sizes are between 50 and 500 per subgroup, depending on the variable being studied.

5. Subgroup frequency, how often you draw a subgroup from the process under study, should be often enough to detect changes in the process under study. This requires expertise in the process under study. If the process can change very quickly, more frequent sampling is needed to detect special causes of variation. If the process changes slowly, less frequent sampling is needed to detect a special cause of variation.

As an illustration of the *p*-chart, consider the case of an importer of decorative lawn gnomes. Some gnomes are cracked or broken before or during transit, rendering them useless scrap. The fraction of cracked or broken gnomes is naturally of concern to the firm. Each day, a sample of 100 lawn gnomes is drawn from the total of all gnomes received from each lawn gnome vendor. Table 14.1 presents the sample results for 30 days of incoming shipments for a particular vendor.

TABLE 14.1 Number of Cracked or Broken Lawn Gnomes for a Sample of 30 Days

Day	Sample size	Number cracked	Day	Sample size	Number cracked
1	100	14	16	100	3
2	100	2	17	100	8
3	100	11	18	100	4
4	100	4	19	100	2
5	100	9	20	100	5
6	100	7	21	100	5
7	100	4	22	100	7
8	100	6	23	100	9
9	100	3	24	100	1
10	100	2	25	100	3
11	100	3	26	100	12
12	100	8	27	100	9
13	100	4	28	100	3
14	100	15	29	100	6
15	100	5	30	100	9

GNOMES

These data are appropriate for a *p*-chart because each gnome is classified as cracked or not cracked. The probability of a cracked gnome is assumed to be constant from gnome to gnome and each gnome is considered independent of the other gnomes.

Figure 14.8 illustrates the *p*-chart obtained from Minitab for the cracked lawn gnomes data.

From Figure 14.8, you see that the process lacks control. On day 1, the proportion of cracked gnomes (14/100 = 0.14) is above the UCL, and on day 14, the proportion of cracked gnomes (15/100 = 0.15) is above the UCL. None of the other rules presented in Exhibit 14.1 seems to be violated. There are no instances when two of three consecutive points lie in zone A on one side of the center line; there are no instances when four of five consecutive points lie in zone B or beyond on one side of the center line; there are no instances when eight consecutive points move upward or downward; nor are there eight consecutive points on one side of the center line, etc.

Nevertheless, the incoming flow of ceramic lawn gnomes needs further examination. The special causes of these erratic shifts in the fraction of cracked or broken gnomes should be studied and eliminated so that expectations for usable portions can be stabilized. Only after this is done can improvements be made in the process.

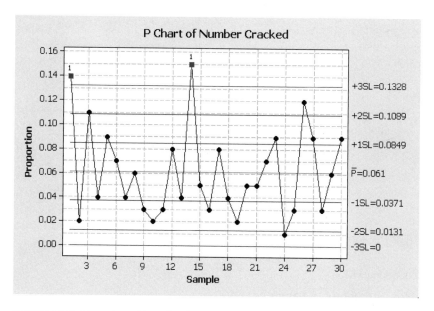

FIGURE 14.8 Minitab *p*-Chart for the Cracked Lawn Gnome Data

Obtaining the LCL and UCL for the *p*-Chart (optional)

$$LCL = \overline{p} - 3\sqrt{\frac{\overline{p}(1 - \overline{p})}{\overline{n}}} \qquad \text{(14.2a)}$$

$$UCL = \overline{p} + 3\sqrt{\frac{\overline{p}(1 - \overline{p})}{\overline{n}}} \qquad \text{(14.2b)}$$

where X_i = number of nonconforming items in subgroup i

n_i = sample or subgroup size for subgroup i

$p_i = X_i / n_i$ = proportion of nonconforming items in subgroup i

k = number of subgroups taken

$\overline{n}$ = average subgroup size

$\overline{p}$ = average proportion of nonconforming items

$$\bar{n} = \frac{\sum_{i=1}^{k} n_i}{k} = \frac{\text{total sample size}}{\text{number of groups}}$$

$$\text{and } \bar{p} = \frac{\sum_{i=1}^{k} X_i}{\sum_{i=1}^{k} n_i} = \frac{\text{total number of nonconformances}}{\text{total sample size}}$$

For the data of Table 14.1, the number of cracked lawn gnomes is 183, and the total sample size is 3,000. Thus:

$$\bar{p} = \frac{183}{3,000} = 0.061 \text{ and } \bar{n} = 100$$

so that, using equation (14.2):

$$LCL = 0.061 - 3\sqrt{\frac{(0.061)(1 - 0.061)}{100}}$$

$$= 0.061 - 0.072$$

$$= -0.011$$

$$= 0$$

Therefore, LCL is set at zero.

$$UCL = 0.061 + 3\sqrt{\frac{(0.061)(1 - 0.061)}{100}}$$

$$= 0.061 + 0.072$$

$$= 0.133$$

In many instances, unlike the example concerning the lawn gnomes, the subgroup size will vary. Consider the case of a small manufacturer of low-tension electric insulators. The insulators are sold to wholesalers who subsequently sell them to electrical contractors. Each day during a 1-month period, the manufacturer inspects the production of a given shift; the number inspected varies somewhat. Based on carefully laid out operational definitions, some of the production is deemed nonconforming and is downgraded. Table 14.2 illustrates the results for 25 days.

TABLE 14.2 Number of Nonconforming Insulators for 25 Days

Day	Number inspected	Nonconforming	Day	Number inspected	Nonconforming
1	350	22	14	355	21
2	420	27	15	410	26
3	405	20	16	414	21
4	390	12	17	366	24
5	410	23	18	377	22
6	384	23	19	404	24
7	392	25	20	387	26
8	415	26	21	402	27
9	364	24	22	358	30
10	377	29	23	411	28
11	409	12	24	404	17
12	376	36	25	390	26
13	399	23			

INSULATORS

Figure 14.9 illustrates the *p* chart obtained from Minitab for the nonconforming insulators. Due to the different subgroup sizes, the values obtained from Minitab for the UCL, LCL, and the zones are different for each subgroup. None of the points are outside the control limits, and none of the rules concerning consecutive points have been violated. Thus, any improvement in the proportion of nonconforming insulators must come from management changing the system.

14.6 THE *c*-CHART

A defective item is a nonconforming unit. It must be discarded, reworked, returned, sold, scrapped, or downgraded. It is unusable for its intended purpose in its present form. A defect, however, is an imperfection of some type that does not necessarily render the entire item defective or unusable, but is undesirable. One or more defects may not make an entire item defective. An assembled piece of machinery such as a car, dishwasher, or air conditioner may have one or more defects that may not render the entire item defective, but may cause it to be downgraded or may necessitate its being reworked.

When there are multiple opportunities for defects or imperfections in a given continuous unit (such as a large sheet of fabric or a week in a call center), each unit is called an **area of**

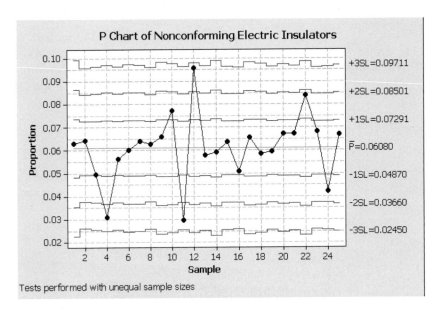

FIGURE 14.9 Minitab *p*-Chart for the Nonconforming Insulators

opportunity; each area of opportunity is a subgroup. The *c*-chart is used when the areas of opportunity are of constant size, whereas the *u*-chart is used when the areas of opportunity are not of constant size.

Subgroups should be of sufficient size to detect an out-of-control event. A general rule for subgroup size for a *c*-chart is that the subgroup size should be large enough to detect a special cause of variation if it exists. This is operationally defined as the average number of defects per area of opportunity being at least 2.0. Additionally, subgroup frequency should be often enough to detect changes in the process under study. This requires expertise in the process under study. If the process can change very quickly, more frequent sampling is needed to detect special causes of variation. If the process changes slowly, less frequent sampling is needed to detect a special cause of variation.

To illustrate the *c*-chart, consider the number of customer complaints received by a company per week. Each week is an area of opportunity. Results of the complaints per week produce the data in Table 14.3.

The assumptions necessary for using the *c*-chart are well met here because the weeks are long enough to be considered continuous areas of opportunity; complaints are discrete events and seem to be independent of one another, and they are relatively rare. Even if these conditions are not precisely met, the *c*-chart is fairly robust, or insensitive to small departures from the assumptions.

Figure 14.10 illustrates the *c*-chart obtained from Minitab for the number of complaints per week.

From Figure 14.10, the number of complaints appears to be stable around a center line or mean of 6.0. None of the weeks is outside the control limits, and none of the rules concerning zones has been violated.

TABLE 14.3 Complaints per week for 25 weeks

Week	Number of complaints	Week	Number of complaints
1	4	14	9
2	5	15	0
3	5	16	2
4	10	17	6
5	6	18	10
6	4	19	3
7	5	20	7
8	6	21	4
9	3	22	8
10	6	23	7
11	6	24	9
12	7	25	7
13	11		

COMPLAINTS

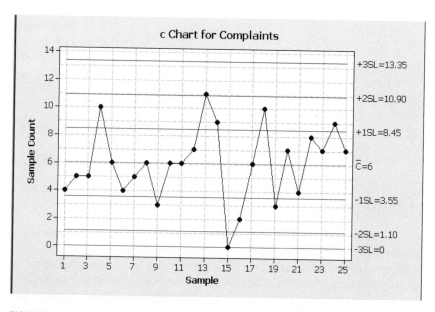

FIGURE 14.10 Minitab c-Chart for the Number of Complaints Per Week

---

Obtaining Upper and Lower Control Limits for the *c*-Chart (optional)

$$LCL = \bar{c} - 3\sqrt{\bar{c}} \qquad\qquad\qquad (14.3a)$$

$$UCL = \bar{c} + 3\sqrt{\bar{c}} \qquad\qquad\qquad (14.3b)$$

where

$$\bar{c} = \frac{\sum_{i=1}^{k} c_i}{k} = \frac{\text{total number of occurrences}}{\text{number of units}}$$

$\bar{c}$ = average number of occurrences

k = number of units sampled

c_i = number of occurrences in unit i

For the data of Table 14.3, the total number of complaints is 150 for the 25 weeks. Thus:

$$\bar{c} = \frac{\text{total number of occurrences}}{\text{number of units}}$$

$$= \frac{150}{25} = 6.0$$

$$LCL = 6.0 - 3\sqrt{6.0}$$
$$= 6.0 - 7.35 = -1.35, \text{ so LCL} = 0.0$$
$$UCL = 6.0 + 3\sqrt{6.0}$$
$$= 6.0 + 7.35 = 13.35$$

14.7 THE *u*-CHART

In some applications, the areas of opportunity vary in size. Generally, the construction and interpretation of control charts are easier when the area of opportunity remains constant, but from time to time changes in the area may be unavoidable. For example, samples taken from a roll of paper may need to be manually torn from rolls, so that the areas of opportunity will vary; and the number of typing errors in a document will have areas of opportunity that will vary with the lengths of the documents. When the areas vary, the control chart used is a *u*-chart.

The *u*-chart is similar to the *c*-chart in that it is a control chart for the count of the number of events, such as the number of defects (nonconformities over a given area of opportunity). The fundamental difference lies in the fact that during construction of a *c*-chart, the area of opportunity remains constant from observation to observation, whereas this is not a requirement for the *u*-chart. Instead, the *u*-chart considers the number of events (such as complaints or other defects) as a fraction of the total size of the area of opportunity in which these events were possible, thus circumventing the problem of having different areas of opportunity for different observations. The characteristic used for the chart, *u*, is the ratio of the number of events to the area of opportunity in which the events occur.

As with the *c*-chart, subgroups should be of sufficient size to detect an out-of-control event. A general rule for subgroup size for a *u*-chart is that the subgroup size should be large enough to detect a special cause of variation if it exists. Additionally, subgroup frequency should be often enough to detect changes in the process under study. This requires expertise in the process under study. If the process can change very quickly, more frequent sampling is needed to detect special causes of variation. If the process changes slowly, less frequent sampling is needed to detect a special cause of variation.

To illustrate a *u*-chart, consider the case of the manufacture of a certain grade of paper. The paper is produced in rolls, with samples taken five times daily. Because of the nature of the process, the square footage of each sample varies from inspection lot to inspection lot. Hence, the *u*-chart should be used. Table 14.4 shows the data on the number of defects for the past 30 inspection lots.

TABLE 14.4 Number of Defects in Rolls of Paper

Lots	Square feet (00)	Defects	Lots	Square feet (00)	Defects
1	2.0	5	16	1.8	4
2	2.5	7	17	0.8	1
3	1.0	3	18	1.0	2
4	0.9	2	19	1.4	3
5	1.2	4	20	1.2	4
6	0.8	1	21	2.5	2
7	2.0	10	22	1.3	3
8	2.2	5	23	2.2	1
9	1.4	4	24	2.0	5
10	0.8	2	25	1.0	2
11	1.7	1	26	1.6	4
12	0.9	2	27	2.5	12
13	2.0	5	28	0.8	1
14	2.5	12	29	1.5	5
15	2.3	4	30	2.1	4

PAPER

Figure 14.11 illustrates the *u*-chart obtained from Minitab for the paper rolls data.

From Figure 14.11, the number of defects per unit appears to be stable around a center line, or mean, of 2.505. No points indicate a lack of control, so there is no reason to believe that any special variation is present. If sources of special variation were detected, we would identify the source or sources of the special variation, eliminate them from the system if detrimental, or incorporate them into the system if beneficial; drop the data points from the data set; and reconstruct and reanalyze the control chart.

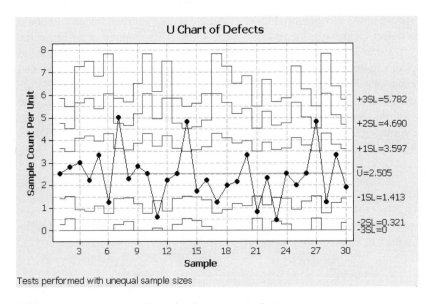

FIGURE 14.11 Minitab *u*-Chart for the Paper Rolls Data

Obtaining Control Limits for the *u*-Chart (optional)

$$u_i = \frac{c_i}{a_i} \tag{14.4}$$

where

c_i = number of events observed in inspection unit i

a_i = the size of the area of opportunity, inspection unit, or subgroup of items i

The average number of events per area of opportunity equals:

$$\bar{u} = \frac{\sum\limits_{i=1}^{k} c_i}{\sum\limits_{i=1}^{k} a_i} \qquad (14.5)$$

where

c_i = number of events observed in inspection unit i

a_i = the size of the ith area of opportunity, inspection unit, or subgroup

k = number of areas of opportunity

$$UCL = \bar{u} + 3\sqrt{\frac{\bar{u}}{a_i}} \qquad (14.6a)$$

$$LCL = \bar{u} - 3\sqrt{\frac{\bar{u}}{a_i}} \qquad (14.6b)$$

For the data of Table 14.4:

Total number of defects = 120, total area of opportunity = 47.9

$$\bar{u} = \frac{\sum\limits_{i=1}^{k} c_i}{\sum\limits_{i=1}^{k} a_i}$$

$$\bar{u} = \frac{120}{47.9}$$

$$= 2.505$$

$$UCL = 2.505 + 3\sqrt{\frac{2.505}{a_i}}$$

$$LCL = 2.505 - 3\sqrt{\frac{2.505}{a_i}}$$

The control limits will vary according to the area of opportunity for each subgroup.

14.8 CONTROL CHARTS FOR THE MEAN AND RANGE

Variables control charts are used to study a process when a characteristic is a measurement, for example, cycle time, processing time, waiting time, height, area, temperature, cost, or revenue. Measurement data provides more information than attribute data; consequently, variables charts are more sensitive in detecting special cause variation than are attribute charts. Variables charts are typically used in pairs. One chart studies the variation in a process, and the other studies the process average. The chart that studies variability must be examined before the chart that studies the process average. This is so because the chart that studies the process average assumes that the process variability is stable over time. One of the most commonly employed pair of charts is the $\overline{X}$ chart and the R-chart. When these charts are used, the subgroup range, R, is plotted on the

TABLE 14.5 Vial Weights for Six Vials Selected During 22 Time Periods

Observation	Time	1	2	3	4	5	6
1	9:30	52.22	52.85	52.41	52.55	53.10	52.47
2	9:35	52.25	52.14	51.79	52.18	52.26	51.94
3	9:40	52.37	52.69	52.26	52.53	52.34	52.81
4	9:45	52.46	52.32	52.34	52.08	52.07	52.07
5	9:50	52.06	52.35	51.85	52.02	52.30	52.20
6	9:55	52.59	51.79	52.20	51.90	51.88	52.83
7	10:00	51.82	52.12	52.47	51.82	52.49	52.60
8	10:05	52.51	52.80	52.00	52.47	51.91	51.74
9	10:10	52.13	52.26	52.00	51.89	52.11	52.27
10	10:15	51.18	52.31	51.24	51.59	51.46	51.47
11	10:20	51.74	52.23	52.23	51.70	52.12	52.12
12	10:25	52.38	52.20	52.06	52.08	52.10	52.01
13	10:30	51.68	52.06	51.90	51.78	51.85	51.40
14	10:35	51.84	52.15	52.18	52.07	52.22	51.78
15	10:40	51.98	52.31	51.71	51.97	52.11	52.10
16	10:45	52.32	52.43	53.00	52.26	52.15	52.36
17	10:50	51.92	52.67	52.80	52.89	52.56	52.23
18	10:55	51.94	51.96	52.73	52.72	51.94	52.99
19	11:00	51.39	51.59	52.44	51.94	51.39	51.67
20	11:05	51.55	51.77	52.41	52.32	51.22	52.04
21	11:10	51.97	51.52	51.48	52.35	51.45	52.19
22	11:15	52.15	51.67	51.67	52.16	52.07	51.81

 VIALS

R-chart, which monitors process variability of the process, and the subgroup average, $\overline{X}$, is plotted on the $\overline{X}$ chart, which monitors the central tendency of the process.

Subgroups should be of sufficient size to detect an out-of-control event, as with attribute control charts. The common subgroup sizes for $\overline{X}$–*R*-charts are between 2 and 10 items. If a larger subgroup size is required, an $\overline{X}$–*S*-chart is needed to detect special causes of variation in the process. Additionally, subgroup frequency should be often enough to detect changes in the process under study. This requires expertise in the process under study. If the process can change very quickly, more frequent sampling is needed to detect special causes of variation. If the process changes slowly, less frequent sampling is needed to detect a special cause of variation.

To illustrate the *R*- and $\overline{X}$ charts, consider a large pharmaceutical firm that provides vials filled to a specification of 52.0 grams. The firm's management has embarked on a program of statistical process control and has decided to use variables control charts for this filling process to detect special causes of variation. Samples of six vials are selected every 5-minutes during a 105-minute period. Each set of six measurements makes up a subgroup. Table 14.5 lists the vial weights for 22 subgroups.

Figure 14.12 illustrates the *R*- and $\overline{X}$ charts obtained from Minitab for the vials filled data.

In Figure 14.12, the bottom portion is the *R*-chart, and the top portion is the $\overline{X}$ chart. First, the *R*-chart is examined for signs of special variation. None of the points on the *R*-chart is outside of the control limits and there are no other signals indicating a lack of control. Thus, there are no indications of special sources of variation on the *R*-chart.

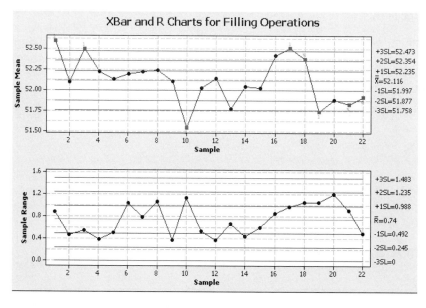

FIGURE 14.12 Minitab *R*- and $\overline{X}$ Charts for the Vials Filled Data.

Obtaining the Lower and Upper Control Limits for the Range (optional)

$$LCL = \overline{R} - 3\overline{R}\frac{d_3}{d_2} \qquad (14.7a)$$

$$UCL = \overline{R} + 3\overline{R}\frac{d_3}{d_2} \qquad (14.7b)$$

where

$$\overline{R} = \frac{\sum\limits_{i=1}^{k} R_i}{k} = \frac{\text{sum of the ranges}}{\text{number of subgroups}}$$

Referring to Equations (14.7a) and (14.7b), instead of using the d_2 and d_3 factors, the calculations can be simplified by utilizing the **D_3 factor,** equal to $1 - 3(d_3/d_2)$, and the **D_4 factor,** equal to $1 + 3(d_3/d_2)$, to obtain the control limits as shown in Equations (14.8a) and (14.8b). Values for these factors for different subgroup sizes are listed in Appendix C, Table C.4.

$$LCL = D_3\overline{R} \qquad (14.8a)$$

$$UCL = D_4\overline{R} \qquad (14.8b)$$

For the data of Table 14.5:

Sum of the ranges = 16.28 and number of subgroups = 22.

Thus:

$$\overline{R} = \frac{\text{sum of the ranges}}{\text{number of subgroups}}$$

$$= \frac{16.28}{22} = 0.74$$

For a subgroup size = 6, $D_3 = 0$, and $D_4 = 2.004$

$$LCL = (0)(0.74) = 0$$

$$UCL = (2.004)(0.74) = 1.483$$

Obtaining Lower and Upper Control Limits for the Mean (optional)

$$LCL = \bar{\bar{X}} - 3\frac{\bar{R}}{d_2\sqrt{n}} \qquad\qquad (14.9a)$$

$$UCL = \bar{\bar{X}} + 3\frac{\bar{R}}{d_2\sqrt{n}} \qquad\qquad (14.9b)$$

where

$$\bar{\bar{X}} = \frac{\displaystyle\sum_{i=1}^{k}\bar{X}_i}{k} = \frac{\text{sum of the sample means}}{\text{number of subgroups}}$$

$$\bar{R} = \frac{\displaystyle\sum_{i=1}^{k}R_i}{k} = \frac{\text{sum of the ranges}}{\text{number of subgroups}}$$

$\bar{X}_i$ = the sample mean of n observations at time i

R_i = the range of n observations at time i

k = number of subgroups

Referring to Equations (14.9a) and (14.9b), the calculations are simplified by utilizing the **A₂ factor,** equal to $3/(d_2\sqrt{n})$, to obtain the control limits as displayed in Equations (14.10a) and (14.10b). Values for these factors for different subgroup sizes are listed in Appendix C, Table C.4.

$$LCL = \bar{\bar{X}} - A_2\bar{R} \qquad\qquad (14.10a)$$

$$UCL = \bar{\bar{X}} + A_2\bar{R} \qquad\qquad (14.10b)$$

For the data of Table 14.5:

Sum of the ranges = 16.28, sum of the sample means = 1,146.55, and number of subgroups = 22.

Thus:

$$\bar{R} = \frac{\text{sum of the ranges}}{\text{number of subgroups}}$$

$$= \frac{16.28}{22} = 0.74$$

$$\overline{\overline{X}} = \frac{\text{sum of the sample means}}{\text{number of subgroups}}$$

$$= \frac{1{,}146.55}{22} = 52.12$$

For a subgroup size = 6, $A_2 = 0.483$

$LCL = 52.12 - (0.483)(0.74) = 51.76$
$UCL = 52.12 + (0.483)(0.74) = 52.47$

Now you can examine the $\overline{X}$ chart. Notice that a total of five points on the $\overline{X}$ chart are outside of the control limits and points 16, 17, and 18 are above +2 standard deviations (2 out of 3 points 2 sigma or beyond rule). This indicates a lack of control. Further investigation is warranted to determine the source(s) of these special variations. Once the special sources of variation have been identified, a revised process (flow chart) can be developed and put in place to make the process robust against the special causes.

14.9 CONTROL CHARTS FOR THE MEAN AND THE STANDARD DEVIATION

As the sample size n increases, the range becomes increasingly less efficient as a measure of variability. Because the range ignores all information between the two most extreme values, as the sample size increases, the range will use a smaller proportion of the information available in a sample. In addition, the probability of observing an extreme value in a sample increases as n gets larger. A single extreme value will result in an unduly large value for the sample range and will inflate the estimate of process variability. Thus, as the subgroup size increases, the individual subgroup standard deviations provide a better estimate of the process standard deviation than does the range.

Subgroups should be of sufficient size to detect an out-of-control event, as with $\overline{X}-R$-charts. The common subgroup sizes for $\overline{X}-S$-charts are 11 or more items. Additionally, subgroup frequency should be often enough to detect changes in the process under study. This requires expertise in the process under study. If the process can change very quickly, more frequent sampling is needed to detect special causes of variation. If the process changes slowly, less frequent sampling is needed to detect a special cause of variation.

To illustrate the S- and $\overline{X}$ charts, consider the cycle time for a banking operation. Cycle time data is collected for the first 10 transactions every half-hour for twenty time periods as summarized in Table 14.6

Figure 14.13 illustrates the S- and $\overline{X}$ charts obtained from Minitab for the cycle times data.

TABLE 14.6 Cycle Times for the First 10 Transactions for 20 Time Periods

8:30	9:00	9:30	10:00	10:30	11:00	11:30
2.08	2.14	2.30	2.01	2.06	2.14	2.07
2.26	2.02	2.10	2.10	2.12	2.22	2.05
2.13	2.14	2.20	2.15	1.98	2.18	1.97
1.94	1.94	2.25	1.97	2.12	2.27	2.05
2.30	2.30	2.05	2.25	2.20	2.17	2.16
2.15	2.08	1.95	2.12	2.02	2.26	2.02
2.07	1.94	2.10	2.10	2.19	2.15	2.02
2.02	2.12	2.16	1.90	2.03	2.07	2.14
2.22	2.15	2.37	2.04	2.02	2.02	2.07
2.18	2.36	1.98	2.08	2.09	2.36	2.00

12:00	12:30	13:00	13:30	14:00	14:30	15:00
2.08	2.13	2.13	2.24	2.25	2.03	2.08
2.31	1.90	2.16	2.34	1.91	2.10	1.92
2.12	2.12	2.12	2.40	1.96	2.24	2.14
2.18	2.04	2.22	2.26	2.04	2.20	2.20
2.15	2.40	2.12	2.13	1.93	2.25	2.02
2.17	2.12	2.07	2.15	2.08	2.03	2.04
1.98	2.15	2.04	2.08	2.29	2.06	1.94
2.05	2.01	2.28	2.02	2.42	2.19	2.05
2.00	2.30	2.12	2.05	2.10	2.13	2.12
2.26	2.14	2.10	2.18	2.00	2.20	2.06

15:30	16:00	16:30	17:00	17:30	18:00	
2.04	1.92	2.12	1.98	2.08	2.22	
2.14	2.10	2.30	2.30	2.12	2.05	
2.18	2.13	2.01	2.31	2.11	1.93	
2.12	2.02	2.20	2.12	2.22	2.08	
2.00	1.93	2.11	2.08	2.00	2.15	
2.02	2.17	1.93	2.10	1.95	2.27	
2.05	2.24	2.02	2.15	2.15	1.95	
2.34	1.98	2.25	2.35	2.14	2.11	
2.12	2.34	2.05	2.12	2.28	2.12	
2.05	2.12	2.10	2.26	2.31	2.10	

 CYCLETIME2

In Figure 14.13, the bottom portion is the *S*-chart, and the top portion is the $\overline{X}$ chart. First, the *S*-chart is examined for signs of special variation. None of the points on the *S*-chart is outside of the control limits, and there are no other signals indicating a lack of control. Thus, there are no indications of special sources of variation on the *S*-chart. Now the $\overline{X}$ chart can be examined. There are no indications of a lack of control, so the process can be considered to be stable and the output to be predictable with respect to time, as long as conditions remain the same.

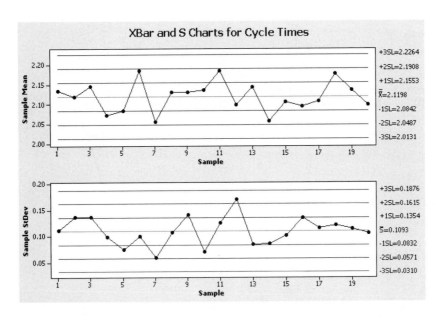

FIGURE 14.13 Minitab *S*- and $\overline{X}$ Charts for the Cycle Time Data

Obtaining the Lower and Upper Control Limits for the Standard Deviation (optional)

$$\overline{S} = \frac{\sum_{i=1}^{k} S_i}{k} = \frac{\text{sum of the sample standard deviations}}{\text{number of subgroups}}$$

where

S_i = the sample standard deviation for sample or subgroup i

k = number of subgroups

$$UCL(s) = \overline{S} + 3\overline{S}\frac{\sqrt{1 - c_4^2}}{c_4} \tag{14.11a}$$

$$LCL(s) = \overline{S} - 3\overline{S}\frac{\sqrt{1 - c_4^2}}{c_4} \tag{14.11b}$$

where c_4 is a control chart factor (see Appendix C, Table C.4) that represents the relationship between the sample standard deviations and the process standard deviation for varying subgroup sizes.

Because c_4 is constant for a given sample size, the term $\left(1 + \dfrac{3\sqrt{1 - c_4^2}}{c_4}\right)$ can be replaced by tabled values of control chart factor B_4 and the term $\left(1 - \dfrac{3\sqrt{1 - c_4^2}}{c_4}\right)$ can be replaced by control chart factor B_3 (see Appendix C, Table C.4). The factors B_4 and B_3 can be used to simplify equations (14.11a) and (14.11b).

$$UCL(s) = B_4\overline{S} \tag{14.12a}$$

and

$$LCL(s) = B_3\overline{S} \tag{14.12b}$$

For the data of Table 14.6, the sum of the sample standard deviations = 2.19 and the number of subgroups = 20.

$$\overline{S} = \frac{\text{sum of the sample standard deviations}}{\text{number of subgroups}}$$

$$= \frac{2.19}{20} = 0.11$$

With a subgroup size of 10, $B_4 = 1.716$ and $B_3 = 0.284$

$UCL = (1.716)(0.11) = 0.188$

$LCL = (0.284)(0.11) = 0.031$

Obtaining Lower and Upper Control Limits for the Mean (optional)

$$UCL(\overline{X}) == \overline{\overline{X}} + 3 - \frac{\overline{S}}{c_4\sqrt{n}} \tag{14.13a}$$

and

$$LCL(\overline{X}) == \overline{\overline{X}} - 3\frac{\overline{S}}{c_4\sqrt{n}} \tag{14.13b}$$

where

c_4 = a control chart factor that represents the relationship between subgroup standard deviations and the process standard deviation for varying subgroup sizes.

n = the subgroup size.

Because $\dfrac{3}{c_4\sqrt{n}}$ is a constant term for a given subgroup size, the equations for the upper and lower control limits can be simplified by using tabled values (see Appendix C, Table C.4) of $\dfrac{3}{c_4\sqrt{n}}$ called A_3.

$$UCL(\overline{X}) = \overline{\overline{X}} + A_3\overline{S} \tag{14.14a}$$

$$LCL(\overline{X}) = \overline{\overline{X}} - A_3\overline{S} \tag{14.14b}$$

For the data of Table 14.6, the sum of the sample standard deviations = 2.19, the sum of the sample means = 42.43, and the number of subgroups = 20.

$$\overline{S} = \frac{\text{sum of the sample standard deviations}}{\text{number of subgroups}}$$

$$= \frac{2.19}{20} = 0.11$$

$$\overline{\overline{X}} = \frac{\text{sum of the sample means}}{\text{number of subgroups}}$$

$$= \frac{42.43}{20} = 2.12$$

With a subgroup size of 10, $A_3 = 0.975$

$$UCL = 2.12 + (0.975)(0.11) = 2.226$$

$$LCL = 2.12 + (0.975)(0.11) = 2.013$$

14.10 INDIVIDUAL VALUE AND MOVING RANGE CHARTS

Often, a situation occurs where only a single value is observed per subgroup. Perhaps measurements must be taken at relatively long intervals, or the measurements are destructive and/or expensive; or perhaps they represent a single batch where only one measurement is appropriate, such as the total yield of a homogeneous chemical batch process; or the measurements may be monthly or quarterly revenue or cost data. Whatever the case, there are circumstances when data must be taken as individual units that cannot be conveniently divided into subgroups.

Individual value charts have two parts, one that charts the process variability and the other that charts the process average. The two parts are used in tandem, as with the $\bar{X}$ and R-charts. Stability must first be established in the portion charting the variability because the estimate of the process variability provides the basis for the control limits of the portion charting the process average.

Single measurements of variables are considered a subgroup of size one. Hence, there is no variability within the subgroups themselves. An estimate of the process variability must be made in some other way. The estimate of variability used for individual value charts is based on the point-to-point variation in the sequence of single values, measured by the moving range (the absolute value of the difference between each data point and the one that immediately preceded it).

TABLE 14.7 Revenues in Millions for 30 Months for A-744

Month	Revenue (000, 000)	Month	Revenue (000, 000)
January 2002	1.242	April 2003	1.253
February 2002	1.289	May 2003	1.257
March 2002	1.186	June 2003	1.275
April 2002	1.197	July 2003	1.232
May 2002	1.252	August 2003	1.201
June 2002	1.221	September 2003	1.281
July 2002	1.299	October 2003	1.274
August 2002	1.323	November 2003	1.234
September 2002	1.323	December 2003	1.187
October 2002	1.314	January 2004	1.196
November 2002	1.299	February 2004	1.282
December 2002	1.225	March 2004	1.322
January 2003	1.185	April 2004	1.258
February 2003	1.194	May 2004	1.261
March 2003	1.235	June 2004	1.201

 REVENUE

As before, subgroup frequency should be often enough to detect changes in the process under study. This requires expertise in the process under study. If the process can change very quickly, more frequent sampling is needed to detect special causes of variation. If the process changes slowly, less frequent sampling is needed to detect a special cause of variation.

To illustrate the individual value chart, consider the monthly revenues for a chemical company of a liquid chemical product, A-744. Shipments of A-744 to customers are made each month. Table 14.7 shows the monthly revenues for A-744.

Figure 14.14 illustrates the moving range and individual value charts obtained from Minitab for the monthly revenue data.

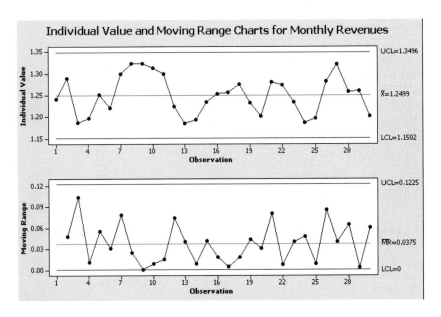

FIGURE 14.14 Minitab Moving Range and Individual Value Charts for the Monthly Revenue

In Figure 14.14, the bottom portion is the moving range chart, and the top portion is the individual value chart. First, the moving range chart is examined for signs of special variation. None of the points on the moving range chart is outside of the control limits, and there are no other signals indicating a lack of control. Thus, there are no indications of special sources of variation on the moving range chart. Now the individual value chart can be examined. There are no indications of a lack of control, so the process can be considered to be stable and the revenue to be predictable with respect to time, as long as conditions remain the same.

Obtaining Control Limits for the Moving Range (optional)

$$MR_i = |X_{i+1} - X_i| \tag{14.15}$$

where

k = the number of samples or subgroups

$||$ = the absolute value

X_{i+1} = the value for observation $i + 1$

X_i = the value for observation i

Because each value of MR_i requires two successive observations for its calculation, for any set of k observations there will be only $k - 1$ values of the moving range. For example, the first moving range value $MR_1 = |X_2 - X_1|$, the second moving range value $MR_2 = |X_3 - X_2|$, and the last moving range value $MR_{k-1} = |X_k - X_{k-1}|$.

$$\overline{MR} = \frac{\sum_{i=1}^{k-1} MR_i}{k - 1} = \frac{\text{sum of the moving ranges}}{\text{number of subgroups} - 1} \tag{14.16}$$

$$UCL(MR) = D_4 \overline{MR} \tag{14.17a}$$

$$LCL(MR) = D_3 \overline{MR} \tag{14.17b}$$

where D_4 and D_3 are control chart factors from Appendix C, Table C.4.

Because each moving range value is based on two consecutive observations, the subgroup size for each moving range is 2. From Table C.4, with $n = 2$, D_4 is 3.267, and D_3 is 0.00. Therefore:

$$UCL(MR) = 3.267 \overline{MR} \tag{14.18a}$$

$$LCL(MR) = 0.00 \overline{MR} \tag{14.18b}$$

For the data of Table 14.7:
The sum of the moving ranges = 1.087.
Thus:

$$\overline{MR} = \frac{\text{sum of the moving ranges}}{\text{number of subgroups} - 1}$$

$$= \frac{1.087}{29} = 0.037$$

$$UCL = (3.267)(0.037) = 0.122$$

$$LCL = (0)(0.037) = 0$$

Obtaining Control Limits for the Individual Value Chart (optional)

$$UCL(X) = \overline{X} + 3\frac{\overline{MR}}{d_2} \qquad\qquad (14.19a)$$

$$LCL(X) = \overline{X} - 3\frac{\overline{MR}}{d_2} \qquad\qquad (14.19b)$$

Because $3/d_2$ is a constant for a given subgroup size, the control chart factor E_2 presented in Appendix C, Table C.4 can be used, so that:

$$UCL(X) = \overline{X} + E_2\overline{MR} \qquad\qquad (14.20a)$$

$$LCL(X) = \overline{X} - E_2\overline{MR} \qquad\qquad (14.20b)$$

Because each of the moving ranges used to calculate $\overline{MR}$ is calculated from two consecutive observations, the subgroup size is equal to 2. Whenever $n = 2$, the value of $E_2 = 2.66$. Therefore:

$$UCL(X) = \overline{X} + 2.66\overline{MR} \qquad\qquad (14.21a)$$

$$LCL(X) = \overline{X} - 2.66\overline{MR} \qquad\qquad (14.21b)$$

For the data of Table 14.7,
The sum of the revenues = 37.498, and the sum of the moving ranges = 1.087.
Thus:

$$\overline{MR} = \frac{\text{sum of the moving ranges}}{\text{number of subgroups} - 1}$$

$$= \frac{1.087}{29} = 0.037$$

$$\overline{X} = \frac{37.498}{30}$$

$$= 1.25$$

$$UCL = 1.25 + 2.66(0.037) = 1.349$$

$$LCL = 1.25 - 2.66(0.037) = 1.15$$

SUMMARY

In this chapter, both attribute and variables control charts have been discussed. As a road map for this chapter, Figure 14.15 presents a flow diagram useful in selecting the control chart appropriate for monitoring your process.

REFERENCES

1. Boardman, T. J. and H. Iyer, *The Funnel Experiment* (Fort Collins, CO: Colorado State University, 1986.)

2. Deming, W. Edwards, *Out of the Crisis* (Cambridge, MA: Massachusetts Institute for Technology Center for Advanced Engineering Study, 1986).

3. Deming, W. Edwards, *The New Economics for Industry, Government, Education* (Cambridge, MA: Massachusetts Institute for Technology Center for Advanced Engineering Study, 1993).

4. Gitlow, H. G., A. Oppenheim, R. Oppenheim, and D. M. Levine, *Quality Management: Tools and Methods for Improvement,* 3rd ed. (New York: McGraw-Hill-Irwin, 2005)

5. Levine, D. M., P. C. Ramsey, and R. K. Smidt, *Applied Statistics for Engineers and Scientists using Microsoft Excel and Minitab* (Upper Saddle River, NJ: Prentice Hall, 2001).

6. *Minitab for Windows Version 14* (State College, PA: Minitab, 2004).

7. Montgomery, D. C., *Introduction to Statistical Quality Control,* 4th ed. (New York: John Wiley, 2000).

8. Shewhart, W. A., *Economic Control of Quality of Manufactured Product* (New York: Van Nostrand-Reinhard, 1931, reprinted by the American Society for Quality Control, Milwaukee, 1980).

6. Shewhart, W. A., and W. E. Deming, *Statistical Methods from the Viewpoint of Quality Control.* (Washington, D.C.: Graduate School, Department of Agriculture, 1939; Dover Press, 1986).

7. Western Electric, *Statistical Quality Control Handbook.* (Indianapolis, IN: Western Electric Corporation, 1956).

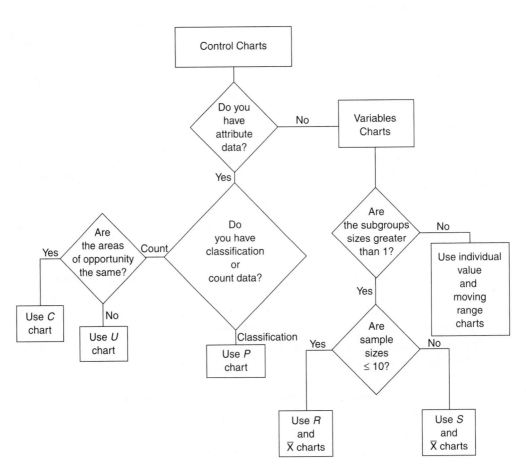

FIGURE 14.15 Flow Diagram for Selecting the Control Chart Appropriate for Monitoring a Process.

A P P E N D I X   1 4 . 1

USING MINITAB FOR CONTROL CHARTS

Using Minitab to Obtain Zone Limits

To plot zone limits on any of the control charts discussed in this appendix, open to the initial dialog box for the control chart being developed and do the following:

1. Click the **Scale** button. Click the **Gridlines** tab. Select the **Y major ticks, Y minor ticks,** and **X major ticks** check boxes. Click the **OK** button to return to the previous dialog box.

2. Click the **Options** button. Select the **S limits** tab. In the Display Control limits at: edit box, enter **1 2 3** in the edit box. Click the **OK** button to return to the initial dialog box.

Using Minitab for the *p*-Chart

To illustrate how to obtain a *p*-chart, refer to the data of Figure 14.8 on page 431 concerning the number of broken tiles. Open the **GNOMES.MTW** worksheet.

1. Select **Stat → Control Charts → Attribute Charts → P.** In the P Chart dialog box (see Figure A14.1), enter **C3** or **'Number Cracked'** in the Variable(s): edit box. Because the subgroup sizes are equal, enter **100** in the **Subgroup sizes:** edit box. Click the **P Chart Options** button.

2. In the P Chart—Options dialog box, click the **Tests** tab (see Figure A14.2). In the drop-down list box select **Perform all tests for special causes.** Click the **OK**

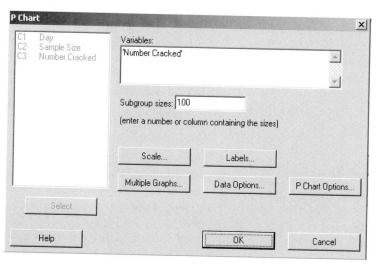

FIGURE A14.1 Minitab P Chart Dialog Box

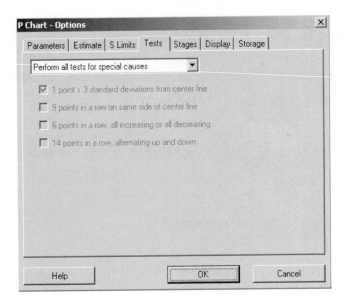

FIGURE A14.2 Minitab P Chart—Options Dialog Box, Tests Tab

button to return to the P Chart dialog box. (These values will stay intact until Minitab is restarted.)

3. If there are points that should be omitted when estimating the center line and control limits, click the **Estimate** tab in the P Chart—Options dialog box (see Figure A14.3). Enter the points to be omitted in the edit box shown. Click the **OK** button to return to the P Chart dialog box. In the P Chart dialog box, click the **OK** button to obtain the *p*-chart.

Using Minitab for the *c*-Chart

To illustrate how to obtain a *c*-chart, refer to the data of Figure 14.10 on page 435 concerning the number of customer complaints. Open the **COMPLAINTS.MTW** worksheet.

1. Select **Stat** → **Control Charts** → **Attribute Charts** → **C.** In the C Chart dialog box (see Figure A14.4), enter **C2** or **COMPLAINTS** in the Variable(s): edit box.

2. Click the **C Chart Options** button. In the C Chart—Options dialog box, click the **Tests** tab. In the drop-down list box select **Perform all tests for special causes.** Click the **OK** button to return to the C Chart dialog box. (These values will stay intact until Minitab is restarted.) Click the **OK** button to obtain the *c*-chart.

3. If there are points that should be omitted when estimating the center line and control limits, click the **Estimate** tab in the C Chart—Options dialog box. Enter the points to be omitted in the edit box shown. Click the **OK** button to return to the C Chart dialog box.

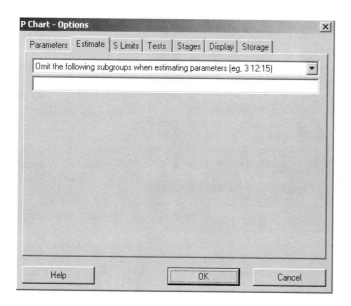

FIGURE A14.3 Minitab P Chart—Options Dialog Box, Estimate Tab

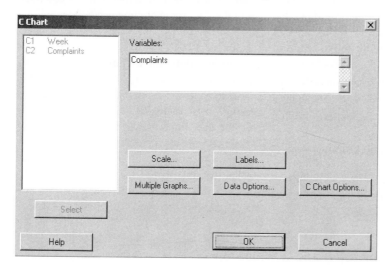

FIGURE A14.4 Minitab C chart Dialog Box

Using Minitab for the *u*-Chart

To illustrate how to obtain a *u*-chart, refer to the data of Figure 14.11 on page 438 concerning the number of defects in a lot of paper. Open the **PAPER.MTW** worksheet.

1. Select **Stat → Control Charts → Attribute Charts → U.** In the U Chart dialog box (see Figure A14.5), enter **C3** or **Defects** in the Variable(s): edit box. In the Subgroups sizes: edit box, enter **C2** or **'Square Feet (00)'.**

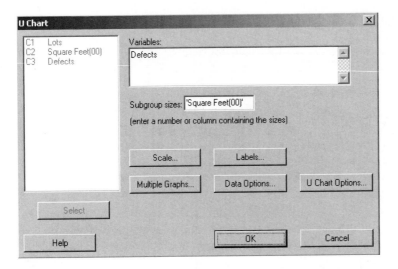

FIGURE A14.5 Minitab U Chart Dialog Box

2. In the U Chart—Options dialog box, click the **Tests** tab. In the drop-down list box, select **Perform all tests for special causes.** Click the **OK** button to return to the U Chart dialog box. (These values will stay intact until Minitab is restarted.) Click the **OK** button to obtain the *u*-chart.

3. If there are points that should be omitted when estimating the center line and control limits, click the **Estimate** tab in the U Chart—Options dialog box. Enter the points to be omitted in the edit box shown. Click the **OK** button to return to the U Chart dialog box.

Using Minitab for the R and $\overline{X}$ Charts

R and $\overline{X}$ charts can be obtained from Minitab by selecting **Stat → Control Charts → Variable Charts for Subgroups → Xbar-R** from the menu bar. The format for entering the variable name is different, depending on whether the data are stacked down a single

column or unstacked across a set of columns, with the data for each time period located in a single row. If the data for the variable of interest are stacked down a single column, choose **All observations for a chart are in one column** in the drop-down list box and enter the variable name in the edit box below. If the subgroups are unstacked with each row representing the data for a single time period, choose **Observations for a subgroup are in one row of columns** in the drop-down list box and enter the variable names for the data in the edit box below.

To illustrate how to obtain R and $\overline{X}$ charts, refer to the data of Figure 14.12 on page 441 concerning the weight of vials. Open the **VIALS.MTW** worksheet.

1. Select **Stat → Control Charts → Variable Charts for Subgroups → Xbar-R.** Since the data are unstacked, select **Observations for a subgroup are in one row of columns** in the drop-down list box. In the Xbar-R Chart dialog box (see Figure A14.6) enter **C3** or

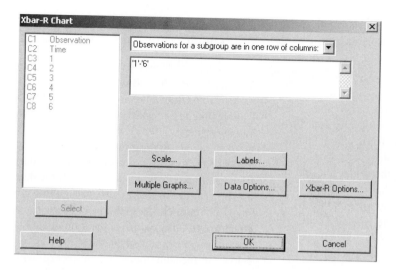

FIGURE A14.6 Minitab Xbar-R Chart—Dialog Box

1, C4 or **2, C5** or **3, C6** or **4, C7** or **5,** and **C8** or **6,** in the edit box. Click the **Xbar-R Options** button.

2. In the Xbar-R Chart—Options dialog box (see Figure A14.7), click the **Tests** tab. In the drop-down list box, select

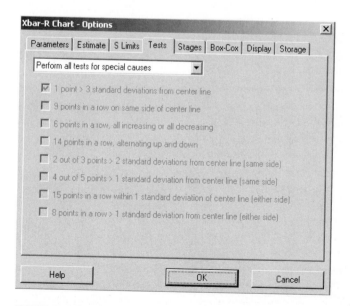

FIGURE A14.7 Minitab Xbar-R Chart—Options Dialog Box, Tests Tab

Perform all tests for special causes. Click the **OK** button to return to the Xbar-R Chart—dialog box. (These values will stay intact until Minitab is restarted.)

3. Click the **Estimate** tab in the Xbar-R Chart—Options dialog box (see Figure A14.8). Click the **Rbar** option button, If there are points that should be omitted when estimating the center line and control limits, enter the points to be omitted in the edit box shown. Click the **OK** button to return to the Xbar-R Chart—dialog box. (Note: When obtaining more than one set of R and $\overline{X}$ charts in the same session, be sure to reset the values of the points to be omitted before obtaining new charts.)

4. In the Xbar-R Chart dialog box, click the **OK** button to obtain the R and $\overline{X}$ charts.

Using Minitab for the S and $\overline{X}$ Charts

S and $\overline{X}$ charts can be obtained from Minitab by selecting **Stat → Control Charts → Variable Charts for Subgroups → Xbar-S** from the menu bar. The format for entering the variable name is different, depending on whether the data are stacked down a single column or unstacked across a set of columns with the data for each time period in a single row. If the data for the variable of interest are stacked down a single column, choose **All observations for a chart are in one column** in the drop-down list box and enter the variable name in the edit box below. If the subgroups are unstacked with each row representing the data for a single time period, choose **Observations for a subgroup are in one row of columns** in the drop-down list box and enter the variable names for the data in the edit box below.

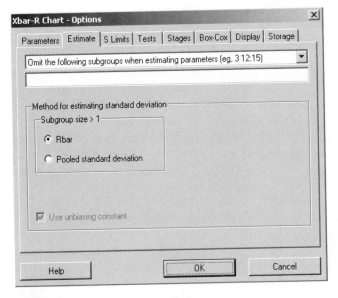

FIGURE A14.8 Minitab Xbar-R Chart—Options Dialog Box, Estimate Tab

To illustrate how to obtain S and $\overline{X}$ charts, refer to the data of Figure 14.13 on page 446 concerning the cycle time of transactions. Open the **CYCLETIME2.MTW** worksheet.

1. Select **Stat → Control Charts → Variable Charts for Subgroups → Xbar-S.** Since the data are stacked, select **All observations for a chart are in one column** in the drop-down list box. In the Xbar-S Chart dialog box (see Figure A14.9) enter 'Cycle Time' in the edit box. In the Subgroup sizes, edit box, enter **10.** Click the **Xbar-S Options** button.

2. In the Xbar-S Chart—Options dialog box, click the **Tests** tab. In the drop-down list box select **Perform all tests for special causes.** Click the **OK** button to return to the Xbar-S Chart dialog box. (These values will stay intact until Minitab is restarted.)

3. Click the **Estimate** tab in the Xbar-S Chart—Options dialog box. Click the **Sbar** option button. If there are points that should be omitted when estimating the center line and control limits, enter the points to be omitted in the edit box shown. Click the **OK** button to return to the Xbar-S Chart dialog box. (Note: When obtaining more than one set of S and $\overline{X}$ charts in the same session, be sure to reset the values of the points to be omitted before obtaining new charts.)

4. In the Xbar-S Chart—dialog box, click the **OK** button to obtain the S and $\overline{X}$ charts.

Using Minitab for the Individual Value and Moving Range Charts

Individual value and moving range charts can be obtained from Minitab by selecting **Stat → Control Charts → Variable Charts for**

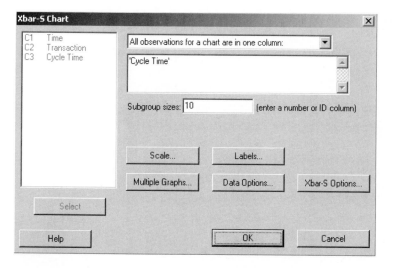

FIGURE A14.9 Minitab Xbar-S Chart—Dialog Box

Individuals → **I-MR** from the menu bar. To illustrate how to obtain individual value and moving range charts, refer to the data of Figure 14.14 on page 450 concerning monthly revenues. Open the **REVENUE .MTW** worksheet.

1. Select **Stat** → **Control Charts** → **Variable Charts for Individuals** → **I-MR.** In the Individuals-Moving Range Chart—dialog box (see Figure A14.10) enter **REVENUE** in the Variable(s): edit box. Click the **I-MR Options** button.

2. In the Individuals-Moving Range Chart— Options dialog box, click the **Tests** tab. Select the **Perform the following tests for special causes** in the drop-down list box. Select the **1 point > 3 standard deviations from center line** check box. Click the **OK** button to return to the I-

MR Chart dialog box. (These values will stay intact until Minitab is restarted.)

3. Click the **Estimate** tab in the Individual-Moving Range Chart—Options dialog box. Click the **Average moving range** option button. If there are points that should be omitted when estimating the center line and control limits, enter the points to be omitted in the edit box shown. Click the **OK** button to return to the Individuals-Moving Range Chart dialog box. (Note: When obtaining more than one set of individual value and moving range charts in the same session, be sure to reset the values of the points to be omitted before obtaining new charts.)

4. In the Individuals-Moving Range Chart dialog box, click the **OK** button to obtain the individual value and moving range charts.

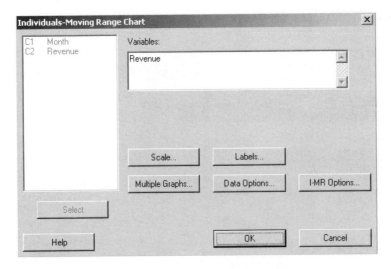

FIGURE A14.10 Minitab Individuals-Moving Range Chart Dialog Box

ADDITIONAL TOOLS AND METHODS

CHAPTER OUTLINE

LEARNING OBJECTIVES

After reading this chapter, you will be able to:

- Brainstorm for ideas about improving a process, product, or service
- Use an affinity diagram to identify the structure for a set of ideas generated in a brainstorming session
- Use a cause-and-effect diagram or matrix to understand the relationships between the CTQ(s) and Xs
- Use check sheets to collect data
- Use stratification to identify the root cause(s) of variation in a CTQ or an X
- Schedule a project using a Gantt chart

INTRODUCTION

In addition to the quantitative tools discussed in Chapters 9–14, this chapter presents several additional diagnostic techniques and tools. The techniques and tools are brainstorming, affinity diagrams, cause-and-effect diagrams, check sheets, stratification, and Gantt charts.

15.1 BRAINSTORMING

Brainstorming is a technique used to elicit a large number of ideas from a Six Sigma team using its collective thinking power. It normally takes place in a structured session involving between 3 and 12 people, with 5 or 6 people being the optimal group size. The group should include a variety of people, not all of whom should be technical experts in the particular area under study.

The team leader (Green Belt or Black Belt) keeps the team members focused, prevents distractions, keeps ideas flowing, and records the outputs (or makes sure that team members record their own outputs). The brainstorming session should be a closed-door meeting to prevent distractions. Seating should be arranged in a U-shape or circle to promote the flow of ideas among group members.

Procedure

The following steps are recommended *prior to* a brainstorming session:

1. Clearly define the subject of the brainstorming session. This is important. You do not want to have any arguments over the purpose of the brainstorming session at the beginning of the first meeting.
2. Conduct library and Internet research on the topic. You do not want the participants in the brainstorming session to reinvent the wheel.
3. Prepare a list of the ideas identified in step 2 and provide a copy to each of the participants before the session.
4. Identify all members of the brainstorming group and select the facilitator (Green Belt or Black Belt).
5. Invite all participants to the brainstorming session and remind them to study the list of ideas provided to them on the topic.

The following steps are recommended *at* a brainstorming session.

1. The facilitator posts the topic so that it can be clearly seen by all team members.
2. Each team member prepares a list of ideas about the topic on a piece of paper or on 3×5 cards with one idea per card. This should take no longer than 10 minutes. Remind the group members to add to the list of ideas provided to them prior to the brainstorming session.
3. In a circular fashion, each team member reads one idea at a time from his/her list of ideas. As ideas are read, the facilitator records and displays each idea on a flip chart; alternatively, each team member places his or her 3×5 card in one pile in the middle of the team members. Team members continue reading in this circular fashion until all the ideas on everyone's list are read. Finally, team members ignore any structure that might exist among the 3×5 cards.
4. If a member's next idea is a duplicate of a previously stated idea, that member goes on to the next idea on his or her list.
5. After each idea is read by a group member, the leader requests all other team members to think of new ideas. Hearing others' ideas may result in new ideas. This is called *piggy-backing*. Piggybacking is a very important part of brainstorming. Without piggybacking, team members could mail in their brainstormed ideas. Piggybacking is where the synergistic and creative magic of brainstorming occurs. The leader continues asking each group member in turn for new ideas until no one can think of any more.
6. Members are free to pass on each go-around but should be encouraged to add something.
7. If the group reaches an impasse, the leader can ask for everyone's "wildest idea." A wild idea can stimulate a valid one from someone else.
8. Brainstorming continues until all team members pass.

Rules

The following rules should be observed by the participants to ensure that participation is not inhibited:

1. Do not criticize anyone's ideas, by word or gesture.
2. Do not discuss any ideas during the session, except for clarification.
3. Do not hesitate to suggest an idea because it sounds "silly." Many times, such an idea can lead to the problem solution.
4. Do not allow any group member to present more than one idea at a time.
5. Do not allow the group to be dominated by one or two people.
6. Do not let brainstorming become a gripe session.

Example

A brainstorming session was conducted at a private university during 2003 to identify crises. Internet and library searches were performed prior to the brainstorming session. The purpose of the searches was to identify crises at other universities. The results of these searches were input into the brainstorming session.

The members of the brainstorming session were top-level administrators from selected divisions within the university. All members were viewed by senior management as being capable of identifying current crises and potential threats to the university. A list of 174 crises was the outcome of that brainstorming session. A partial listing (74 of the 174) of the crises is shown in Table 15.1.

TABLE 15.1 Partial Brainstormed List of Crises Facing a Private University

1. Local funding drying up.
2. Federal funding drying up.
3. State funding drying up.
4. Grant dollars as a percentage of applications declining.
5. Competition for research awards increasing.
6. No mandatory retirement age.
7. Some faculty unable to get grants.
8. Insufficient teaching load to cover all courses offered.
9. Focus on teaching, as opposed to learning.
10. Business universities adding competition.
11. Students focusing on getting a job, not on education for self-improvement.
12. K–12 not doing its job.
13. U.S. population becoming more diversified.
14. Drop in number of high school graduates.
15. Majority of high school students less able to afford university education.
16. Low faculty productivity.
17. Some universities have lowered entrance qualifications.
18. We are *not* focusing on the nontraditional students.
19. Our schedule is set for the convenience of faculty and traditional students.
20. Faculty are not student-focused.
21. We need to focus on K–80 education.
22. We must use our resources more effectively.
23. Security costs are much higher.
24. Security is vital to our image.
25. The Internet communicates image issues quickly and worldwide.
26. More money earmarked for federal regulations.

(continued)

TABLE 15.1 Partial Brainstormed List of Crises Facing a Private University (continued)

27. Insurance rates have increased substantially.
28. Need to beef up the use of technology.
29. Need to use more interactive instruction.
30. Need to educate staff and faculty that "education is a business."
31. Use carrots to drive change—not the stick.
32. Need to solicit ideas for change from the staff.
33. We need to change our culture here.
34. We do not work well together.
35. We do not communicate among ourselves.
36. We do not have the freedom to change gradually.
37. We need to create or plan a crisis to get people moving.
38. We can no longer afford to be all things to all people.
39. We are good at finding crises but not good at solving them.
40. Academia has difficulty defining its stakeholders.
41. It is easier to do something and apologize than to ask permission.
42. University is a culture of asking permission.
43. Some colleges within the university have "passé" curriculum.
44. Change is talked about not financially supported.
45. We allocate resources in ways that do not reward innovation.
46. Funding is not based on strategic planning.
47. Getting information technology is a crisis.
48. Getting information technology used is a crisis.
49. Difficult to change the culture and attitudes of people so they will use technology.
50. We need better classrooms for our students.
51. We need better dorm rooms for our students.
52. Our dorm rooms need to be built with the future in mind.
53. Professors view themselves as independent contractors, not as employees.
54. Need to build trust with faculty.
55. Security for access to scholarly communications is an issue.
56. The Internet is changing the definition of publishing.
57. Issues of "ownership" of information and charging for access need to be addressed.
58. How scholars communicate is changing.
59. Technology is changing the need for libraries in current format.
60. We have a crisis in our social contract with society.
61. People do not trust institutions any more.
62. Concerns about research ethics.
63. People are "bitter" about their "contract" with the university.
64. Some organizations and people are more "loyal" than others.

(continued)

TABLE 15.1 Partial Brainstormed List of Crises Facing a Private University (continued)

65. We do not communicate the "depth" we have.
66. We do not share or use the capability of one part of the university with other parts of the university.
67. We need more entrepreneurial managers.
68. Need to shift from "industrial age" to "information age" model.
69. People need different skills at different times—JIT (just in time) training.
70. Old attitude: "If we sit here—people will come to us."
71. We need more endowment.
72. We need more dollars to use to change things.
73. University needs to be more aggressive and open to dollar-generating innovations.
74. Poor relationship between our image and what we offer.

Sometimes ideas that are generated in a brainstorming session are inappropriate, not polite, or "politically incorrect." Consequently, people may not verbalize them due to fear of criticism or fear of offending someone. This is a weakness of brainstorming because a very offensive idea could possibly stimulate someone to think of a fantastic idea.

15.2 AFFINITY DIAGRAM

An **affinity diagram** is used to organize verbal and pictorial data consisting of facts, opinions, intuition, and experience into natural clusters that bring out the latent structure of the problem under study. Frequently, the input into an affinity diagram is the output of a brainstorming session.

Construction

Constructing an affinity diagram begins with identifying a problem. Team composition usually consists of the same people and facilitator who participated in the brainstorming session about the problem under study.

A team should take the following steps to construct an affinity diagram:

1. The team leader transfers all the ideas generated from a brainstorming session to 3 × 5 cards, recording one idea per card, or collects each team member's 3 × 5 cards.

2. The team leader spreads all the 3 × 5 cards on a large surface (table) in no particular order, but all cards face the same direction.

3. *In silence,* all team members simultaneously move the cards into clusters so that the cards in a cluster seem to be related; that is, they have an unspoken affinity (underlying theme) for each other. One team member may move a card to one cluster, and another team member may move the card back to its former cluster. This may go on for a time, but the card will eventually find a home cluster. Clustering is finished once team members stop moving cards. If clustering continues for too long, too few piles may remain, thereby hiding the

latent structure of the problem. Cards that do not fit into any cluster should be placed in a miscellaneous cluster.

4. After team members agree that the clusters are complete (usually, 3–15 clusters emerge), they study the cards in each cluster and prepare a header card that states the underlying theme for each cluster. The header card should contain simply the theme represented by the cards in the cluster. For example, the header card should not say "Infrastructure." Rather, it should say "Improve the buildings and grounds of the company." The team leader prepares the header cards.

5. The team leader transfers the information from the header cards and 3×5 cards onto a flip chart, or "butcher paper" (usually rolled paper 36 inches in width) and draws a circle around each cluster. The transfer of information involves either rewriting the header cards and ideas from the clusters onto the flip chart or taping the header cards and 3×5 cards from each cluster onto the flip chart. Related clusters are joined with connecting lines. Team members then discuss each cluster's relationship to the problem under study and make any necessary changes to the affinity diagram.

6. The underlying structure of the problem, usually typified by the names of the header cards, is used to understand the product, service, or process problem under study.

An Example

A subset of the affinity diagram developed from the 174 brainstormed crises facing a private university (see Table 15.1) is shown in Table 15.2.

TABLE 15.2 Affinity Diagram of Crises Facing a Private University

Inadequate Educational System

Poor productivity
Insufficient teaching load to cover all courses offered
Low faculty productivity
Our schedule is set for the convenience of faculty and traditional students
No mandatory retirement age
Some faculty unable to get grants
Ineffective educational philosophy
Focus on teaching as opposed to learning
Faculty are not student-focused
Need to educate staff and faculty that "education is a business"
Use carrots to drive change—not the stick
Need to solicit ideas for change from the staff
Some colleges within the university have "passé" curriculum

(continued)

TABLE 15.2 Affinity Diagram of Crises Facing a Private University (continued)

Dysfunctional Culture

We need to change our culture here
We do not work well together
We do not communicate among ourselves
We do not have the freedom to change gradually
We are good at finding crises but not good at solving them
It is easier to do something and apologize than to ask permission
University is a culture of asking permission
Change is talked about, not financially supported
We allocate resources in ways that do not reward innovation
Funding is not based on strategic planning
Difficult to change the culture and attitudes of people so they will use technology
Professors view themselves as independent contractors, not as employees
Need to build trust with faculty
We have a crisis in our social contract with society
We do not communicate the "depth" we have
We do not share the capability between parts of the university
We need more entrepreneurial managers
People need different skills at different times

Ineffective Internal Systems to Support the Future

Insufficient technology
Keep up with technology
The Internet communicates image issues quickly and worldwide
Need to beef up the use of technology
Security for access to scholarly communications is an issue
The Internet is changing the definition of publishing
Issues of "ownership" of information and charging for access need to be addressed
How scholars communicate is changing
Technology is changing the need for libraries in current format
Need to shift from "industrial age" to "information age" model
Insufficient infrastructure
Keep up with infrastructure
We must use our resources more effectively
We need better classrooms for our students
We need better dorm rooms for our students
Our dorm rooms need to be built with the future in mind
Getting information technology is a crisis
Getting information technology used is a crisis

(continued)

TABLE 15.2 Affinity Diagram of Crises Facing a Private University (continued)

Unclear Understanding of Identity

We need to focus on K–80 education
We are *not* focusing on the nontraditional students
Need to use more interactive instruction
We need to get people moving
We can no longer afford to be all things to all people
Academia has difficulty defining its stakeholders
Poor relationship between our image and what we offer

Increasingly Hostile External Environment

Safety on campus
Security is an increasing problem
Security costs are much higher
Security is vital to our image
Competitive environment
Business universities adding competition
Some universities have lowered entrance qualifications
Old attitude: "If we sit here—people will come to us"
K–12 not doing its job
Changing stakeholders
Students focusing on getting a job, not on education for self-improvement
U.S. population is becoming more diversified
Drop in number of high school graduates
Majority of high school students less able to afford university education
People do not trust institutions any more
People are "bitter" about their "contract" with the university
Some organizations and people are more "loyal" than others
Concerns about research ethics

Decreasing Resource Base

Need dollars to change things
Need to be more aggressive and open to dollar-generating innovations
Local funding drying up
Federal funding drying up
State funding drying up
Grant dollars as a percentage of applications declining
Competition for research awards increasing
More money earmarked for federal regulations
Insurance rates have increased substantially
We need more endowment

The six major themes (crises) in the diagram and their subthemes (crises) have been organized and reworded to enhance clarity and communicability to stakeholders of the university. As you can see from Table 15.2, the underlying themes are:

1. inadequate educational system
2. dysfunctional culture
3. ineffective internal systems to support the future
4. unclear understanding of identity
5. increasingly hostile external environment
6. decreasing resource base

15.3 Cause-and-Effect Diagram and Matrix

A **Cause and Effect (C&E) diagram** is a tool used to organize the possible factors (Xs) that could negatively impact the stability, center, spread, and shape of a CTQ. Cause-and-effect diagrams were discussed briefly in Chapter 6. The data analyzed by a cause-and-effect diagram usually comes from a brainstorming session. Cause-and-effect diagrams are also known as *Ishikawa diagrams* or *fishbone diagrams*. Figure 15.1 shows an example of a cause-and-effect diagram for errors in producing printed airline tickets (CTQ) with major causes and subcauses (Xs).

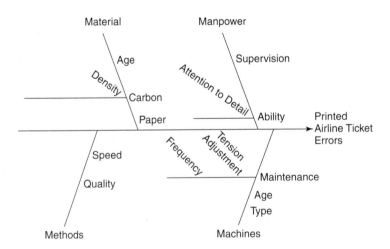

FIGURE 15.1 Minitab Cause-and-Effect Diagram for Printed Airline Ticket Errors

Construction

The following steps are recommended for constructing a cause-and-effect diagram.

1. The team leader (Green Belt or Black Belt) posts the problem (called an *effect*) for a cause-and-effect diagram in a visible location.

2. Team members are frequently the same individuals who participated in the brainstorming session about the problem (or effect) under study.

3. Team members identify the major causes of the effect under study using a list of universal major causes: machines, methods, material, manpower, and environment (see Figure 15.1).

4. Team members brainstorm for subcauses of each universal cause and prepare one 3 × 5 card for each subcause, or the team uses the 3 × 5 cards from a brainstorming session. Next, they classify each card into one or more of the universal major causes. Team members keep subdividing causes into subcauses and sub-subcauses. This procedure creates subclusters and sub-subclusters of potential causes for each major universal cause.

5. Next, team members brainstorm to fill in the "holes" in the cause and effect diagram.

6. Finally, team members circle the most likely subcause(s) of the effect (problem).

Constructing a Cause-and-Effect Diagram Using an Affinity Diagram

A particularly effective technique for constructing a cause-and-effect diagram is to combine an affinity diagram and a cause-and-effect diagram. This simply involves substituting the header cards from an affinity diagram for the major universal causes on a cause-and-effect diagram. The advantage of this method is that a structure for the causes is created that is tailor made to the problem under study. An example of a cause-and-effect diagram constructed using an affinity diagram to understand the crises facing a university can be seen in Figure 15.2.

A **Cause and Effect (C&E) matrix** is a tool used to organize the possible causes of problems (*X*s) for several CTQs simultaneously and to assist team members in the identification of the most probable causes (*X*s) for each CTQ. A cause-and-effect matrix is a multivariate cause-and-effect diagram. Cause-and-Effect matrices were discussed in detail in Chapter 6.

15.4 CHECK SHEETS

Check sheets are used in Six Sigma projects to collect data on *X*s and CTQs in a format that permits efficient and easy analysis by team members. Three types of check sheets will be discussed: attribute check sheets, measurement check sheets, and defect location check sheets.

Attribute Check Sheet

An **attribute check sheet** is used to gather data about defects in a process. The logical way to collect data about a defect is to determine the number and percentage of defects generated by

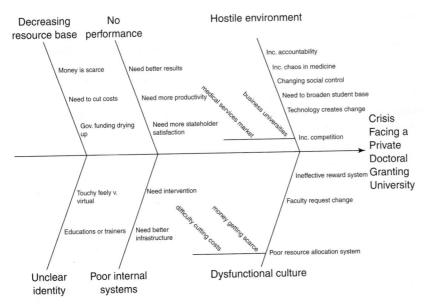

FIGURE 15.2 Minitab Cause-and-Effect Diagram of Crisis Facing a Private University

each cause. Table 15.3 shows an attribute check sheet for the causes of defective responses to telephone calls in a call center.

TABLE 15.3 Attribute Check Sheet of Defects in a Call Center

Type of defect	Frequency	Percentage
Improper use of English language	2	2.9
Grammatical errors in speech	6	8.6
Inappropriate use of words	3	4.3
Rude response	3	4.3
Didn't know answer to question	25	35.7
Call took too much time	30	42.9
Not available	1	1.4
Total	70	100.1*

*rounding error

This check sheet was created by tallying each type of call defect during four 2-hour time periods for 1 week. It shows the types of defects and how many of each type occurred during the week. Keeping track of these data provides management with information on which to base improvement actions. Assuming that the call center process is stable with respect to defective calls (see Chapter 14), the process owner's next step is to construct a bar chart called a *Pareto diagram* (see Section 9.7) of the reasons why "call took too much time" and why the operator "did not know the answer to a question." A good place to start studying the "call took too much time" problem is to create a log sheet for a randomly selected sample of calls per day. This may bring to light the biggest contributing factors of long calls. A good place to start studying the "did not know the answer to the question" problem is to create a log sheet of the questions being asked for a randomly selected sample of calls per day. This may shed light on the questions for which operators most frequently did not know the answer. It makes sense that the same sample of calls per day is used to study the above two problems. It would not be surprising if one of the major reasons for "calls took to long" is that the operator "did not know the answer to a question."

Measurement Check Sheet

Gathering data about a product, service, or process also involves collecting information about measurements, such as cycle time, temperature, size, length, weight, and diameter. This data is best represented on a frequency distribution on a measurement check sheet. Table 15.4 is a measurement check sheet showing the frequency distribution of cycle times to answer 508 customers' questions that came into a call center between 8:00 a.m. and 5:00 p.m. on January 16, 2004.

This type of check sheet is a simple way to examine the distribution of a CTQ or X and its relationship to specification limits (the boundaries of what is considered an acceptable cycle time). The number and percentage of items outside the specification limit are easy to identify so that appropriate action can be taken to reduce the number of defective calls. For example, if a survey of customers revealed that a call that takes 20 minutes or more to answer is unacceptable (upper specification limit ≥ 20), we see that 12% (61/508) of the cycle times for calls are out of specification.

TABLE 15.4 Measurement Check Sheet of Cycle Times into a Call Center on January 16, 2004

Cycle time (minutes)	Frequency
05 < 10 minutes	36
10 < 15 minutes	178
15 < 20 minutes	233
20 < 25 minutes	53
25 < 30 minutes	8
Total	508

Defect Location Check Sheet

Another way to gather information about defects in a product is to use a defect location check sheet. A defect location check sheet is a picture of a product (or a portion of it) on which an inspector indicates the location and nature of a defect. The inspector is sometimes the person actually doing the work. Figure 15.3 shows a defect location check sheet for collecting data regarding defects on a cube. It shows the location of a defect on the front panel of a cube. The location is marked with an X. Suppose that an analysis of multiple check sheets reveals that many Xs are in the upper left corner of the cube. If this is so, further analysis might shed light on the type of defect in the upper left corner. In turn, this might lead employees to identify the root cause of the defects. This, of course, leads to improvements in the cube production process.

FIGURE 15.3 Defect Location Check Sheet for a Cube

15.5 STRATIFICATION

Stratification is a procedure used to describe the systematic subdivision of a data set. It can be used to break down a problem to discover its root causes and set into motion appropriate corrective actions. Stratification is important to the proper functioning of the DMAIC model. Stratification is illustrated in this section using several of the basic tools described earlier in this book.

Stratification and Pareto Diagrams

Figure 15.4 shows 110 observations classified into categories such as *A, B, C,* etc. By breaking each category into subcategories (for example, stratifying the 50 items in *A* into A_1–A_6 and the 40 items in *B* into B_1–B_4), you can focus on the root causes of a problem to establish a corrective action.

In general, when all categories in a Pareto diagram for a CTQ are approximately the same size, as in Figure 15.5(a) on page 478, stratifying on another *X* should be done until a Pareto diagram like the one in Figure 15.5(b) is found. Figure 15.5(a) is called an *old mountain stratification* (the mountain is worn flat) because no category or categories emerge as the significant few on which to take improvement action. Figure 15.5(b) is called a *new mountain stratification* (the

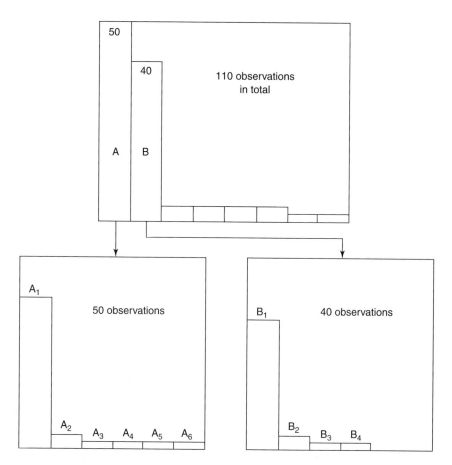

FIGURE 15.4 Pareto Diagrams with Stratification

mountain is young and has high peaks) because one or two categories emerge as the obvious start-ing points for improvement action. It is critical that anyone using a Pareto diagram continue to stratify a CTQ by different Xs until a new mountain Pareto diagram emerges from the analysis. This may require the development of a hypothesis on which Xs should be used for stratification in the Pareto diagram (see the analyze phase of the DMAIC model). Without a new mountain Pareto diagram, there is an absence of a significant few categories and, hence, no prioritization.

For example, a factory kept records on a quarterly basis concerning OSHA (Occupational Safety and Health Administration)-reportable accidents over a 5-year period. There were 5,000 accidents in total. The safety director constructed a c-chart of the data that indicated that the number of accidents per month were a stable and predictable process. Further, he created Pareto diagrams that revealed old mountain structure for accidents broken out by location of accident in the mill, age of person injured, and time of day of the accident, as well as several other

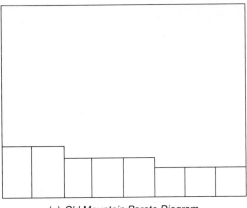

(a) Old Mountain Pareto Diagram

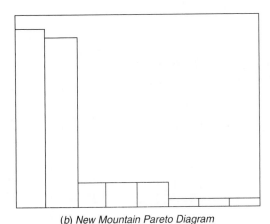

(b) New Mountain Pareto Diagram

FIGURE 15.5 Types of Pareto Diagrams

characteristics. The safety director conducted some research through the trade association and literature and discovered that the body part injured and type of injury are the two most likely characteristics with which to stratify the accident data. Subsequently, he prepared a Pareto diagram that used body part *and* type of injury as the stratifying characteristics. The analysis revealed that 60% of all accidents ($n = 3,000$) were due to "strains and sprains to the back." "Strains and sprains to the back" was the most significant type of accident in this example. Further stratification of the 1,800 "strains and sprains to the back" accidents by "the method used to lift during the accident" (an X discovered in a review of the safety literature) caused the safety director to require a training program on proper lifting techniques, as opposed to giving everyone a back brace, changing the rules on what can be lifted, etc.

Stratification and Cause-and-Effect (C&E) Diagrams

Figure 15.6 shows how stratification is used to identify root causes (Xs) that impact CTQs using cause-and-effect diagrams. We see that a second-tier cause-and-effect diagram can be constructed to study in depth any cause (X) shown on a first-tier cause-and-effect diagram, and so on. Stratification continues until the root causes of problems in a CTQ are identified, making possible improvement action(s).

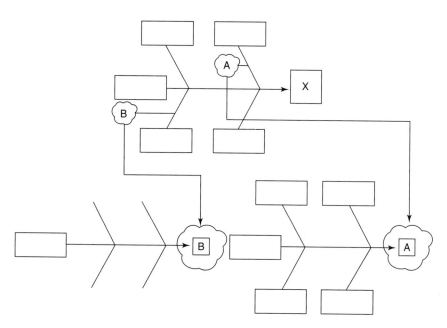

FIGURE 15.6 Stratification and Cause-and-Effect Diagrams

Stratification with Pareto Diagrams and Cause-and-Effect Diagrams

A Pareto diagram is shown in Figure 15.7(a). A cause-and-effect diagram focusing exclusively on one of the bars in the Pareto diagram in Figure 15.7(a) is shown in Figure 15.7(b). This is the correct way to stratify a Pareto diagram to study the root causes of a problem in depth. A cause-and-effect diagram focusing on all the bars in the Pareto diagram in Figure 15.7(a) is shown in Figure 15.7(c). This is the incorrect way to stratify a Pareto diagram to study a problem's root cause(s) in depth. A cause-and-effect diagram should be used to stratify one bar at a time from a Pareto diagram to get an in-depth understanding of the corresponding cause (bar) before any other cause (bar) is studied. It is like peeling an onion to get at its heart.

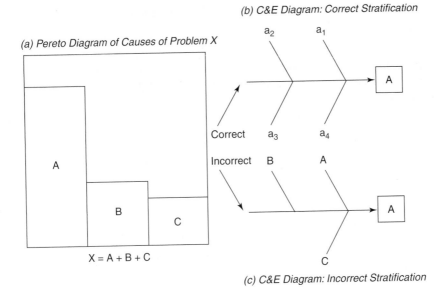

(a) Pereto Diagram of Causes of Problem X

(b) C&E Diagram: Correct Stratification

(c) C&E Diagram: Incorrect Stratification

FIGURE 15.7 Stratification with Pareto Diagrams and Cause-and-Effect Diagrams

Stratification with Control Charts, Pareto Diagrams, and Cause-and-Effect Diagrams

A Pareto diagram can be used to identify common causes of variation from a stable process (see Figure 15.8). These common causes of variation can be stratified through Pareto diagrams or cause-and-effect diagrams to determine root causes of problems and identify appropriate improvement actions.

Other Combinations of Tools for Stratification

The tools and techniques in this book can be used in combination to identify a problem's (CTQ's) root causes (Xs). Once you have determined the root cause(s), you can develop appropriate improvement actions, make a revised flow chart, and work the DMAIC model.

15.6 GANTT CHARTS

A **Gantt chart** is a simple scheduling tool that plots tasks and subtasks against time for a Six Sigma project. Once a list of tasks and subtasks has been created for a Six Sigma project, responsibilities can be assigned for each task. Next, team members identify start and stop dates for each task and subtask. Any comments relevant to a task or subtask are indicated on the Gantt chart. A generic Gantt chart is shown in Table 15.5. A Gantt chart is useful to identify tasks that

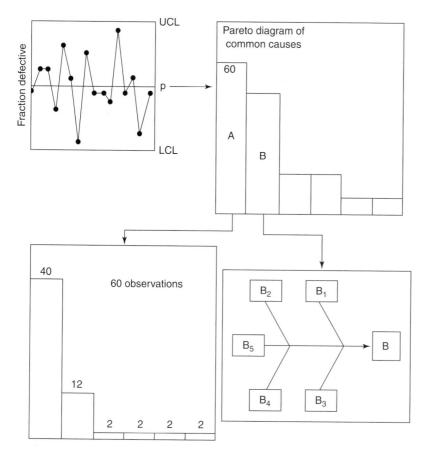

FIGURE 15.8 Stratification with Control Charts, Pareto Diagrams, and Cause-and-Effect Diagrams

can be accomplished in parallel, tasks that cannot start or stop until another task has started or stopped, and time periods that have too many or too few tasks.

Construction

Each task or subtask is listed on the vertical axis, as are the person(s) or area(s) responsible for its completion. The horizontal axis is time. It shows the anticipated and actual duration of each task by a bar of the appropriate length. The left end of the bar indicates the earliest start time, and the right end of the bar indicates the latest stop time for the task. For example, Table 15.6 shows that activity C cannot start before the end of time period 5 because activity B must be completed before activity C can begin. As each activity is completed, the appropriate bar is shaded.

TABLE 15.5 Generic Gantt Chart

Tasks	Responsibility	Timeline (month)																		Comments
		J	F	M	A	M	J	J	A	S	O	N	D	J	F	M	A	M	J	
Task 1																				
Subtask 1a																				
Subtask 1b																				
Task 2																				
Task 3																				
Subtask 3a																				
Subtask 3b																				
Subtask 3c																				

TABLE 15.6 Example of a Gantt Chart

Timeline

Tasks	Responsibility	1	2	3	4	5	6	7	8	9	10	11	12	13	14	15	16	17	18	19
A	HG	▓	▓	▓																
B	HG	█	█	█	█	█														
C	RO					█	█	█												
D	RO							█	█	█	█	█								
E	AO									█	█	█	█	█	█	█	█			
F	AO										█	█								
G	AO												█	█	█					
H	AO													█	█					
I	HG						█	█	█	█	█	█	█	█	█	█	█	█	█	█

SUMMARY

This chapter presented diagnostic techniques and tools that can be used to help resolve special causes of variation and remove common causes of variation from a process. The techniques discussed in this chapter are brainstorming, affinity diagrams, cause and effect diagrams, check sheets, stratification, and Gantt charts.

Brainstorming is a way to elicit a large number of ideas from a group of people in a short period of time. Members of the group use their collective thinking power to generate ideas and unrestrained thoughts.

An affinity diagram is used to organize and consolidate an extensive and unorganized amount of verbal, pictorial, and/or audio data concerning a problem. The data usually consists of facts, opinions, intuition, and experience. Frequently, the input into an affinity diagram is the output of a brainstorming session.

A Cause-and-Effect (C&E) diagram is a tool used to organize the possible causes of a problem, select the most probable cause, and verify the cause and effect relationship between the most probable cause and the problem (effect) under study, to direct appropriate action to resolving the problem (effect). The data analyzed by a cause-and-effect diagram usually comes from a brainstorming session.

Check sheets are used for collecting or gathering data in a logical format. The data collected can be used in constructing a control chart, a Pareto diagram, or a histogram.

Stratification is a procedure used to describe the systematic subdivision of process data to obtain a detailed understanding of the process's structure. Stratification can be used to break down a problem, to discover its root causes, and set into motion appropriate corrective actions, called *countermeasures*.

A Gantt chart is a scheduling tool for relatively small projects. It is a bar chart that plots tasks and subtasks against time. Once a list of tasks and subtasks has been created for a project, responsibilities can be assigned for each task or subtask, and beginning and finishing dates can be scheduled for each task and subtask.

Individually, the above tools and techniques are powerful aids for improvement of a process. However, they take on their true strength when they are used as an integrated system of tools and techniques for diagnosing a process.

REFERENCES

1. Gitlow, H., Oppenheim, A. Oppenheim, R., and Levine, D., *Quality Management* 3rd ed. (New York: McGraw-Hill-Irwin, 2004).

Appendix 15.1

Using Minitab for the Cause-and-Effect Diagram

To illustrate how to obtain a cause-and-effect diagram, refer to the data of Figure 15.1 on page 472 concerning printed airline ticket errors. Open the **FIGURE15-1.MTW** worksheet. Note that the entries on each branch and subbranch of the cause-and-effect diagram have been entered in columns C1–C7, respectively (see Figure A15.1). Select **Stat** → **Quality Tools** → **Cause-and-Effect.**

1. In the Cause-and-Effect diagram dialog box (see Figure A15.2), in the Causes column, enter **C4** in the Manpower row, **C6** in the Machines row, **C1** in the Material row, and **C3** in the Methods row.

2. Click the **Sub** button in the Manpower row. In the Cause-and-Effect diagram—Sub-Branches dialog box (see Figure A15.3), enter **C5** in the Ability row of the Causes column. Click the **OK** button to return to the Cause-and-Effect Diagram dialog box.

3. Click the **Sub** button in the Machines row. In the Cause-and-Effect Diagram—Sub-Branches dialog box, enter **C7** in the Maintenance row of the Causes column. Click the **OK** button to return to the Cause-and-Effect Diagram dialog box.

4. Click the **Sub** button in the Material row. In the Cause-and-Effect Diagram—Sub-Branches dialog box, enter **C2** in the Carbon row of the Causes column. Click the **OK** button to return to the Cause-and-Effect Diagram dialog box.

5. Click the **OK** button.

↓	C1-T	C2-T	C3-T	C4-T	C5-T	C6-T	C7-T
	C1-T	C2-T	C3-T	C4-T	C5-T	C6-T	C7-T
1	Age	Density	Quality	Supervision	Atention to Detail	Type	Frequency
2	Carbon		Speed	Ability		Age	Tension Adjustment
3	Paper					Maintenance	
4							

FIGURE A15.1 Minitab Worksheet Showing Cause and Subcause Entries

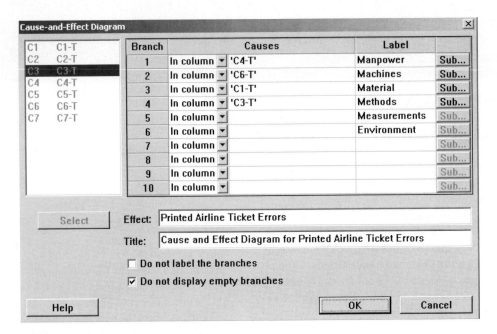

FIGURE A15.2 Minitab Cause-and-Effect Diagram Dialog Box

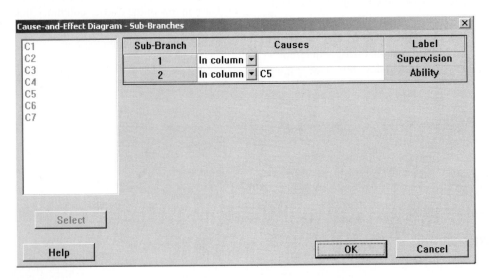

FIGURE A15.3 Minitab Cause-and-Effect Diagram—Sub-Branches Dialog Box for the Manpower Row

Six Sigma Case Studies

Paper Organizers International: A Fictitious Six Sigma Green Belt Case Study

CHAPTER OUTLINE

LEARNING OBJECTIVES

After reading this chapter, you will be able to:

* Conduct a Six Sigma DMAIC project
* Use the tools and methods of the Define, Measure, Analyze, Improve, and Control Phases

16.1 BACKGROUND OF THE CASE STUDY

The Company

Paper Organizers International (POI) offers a full range of filing, organizing, and paper shuffling services. To accomplish these tasks, POI purchases metallic securing devices* (MSDs), staplers, hole punchers, folders, three-ring binders, and a full range of related products to serve its customers' paper-handling needs. The employees, or internal customers, of Paper Organizers International use Metallic Securing Devices (MSDs) to organize piles of paper pending placement into folders or binders.

The Purchasing Department of POI has noticed an increase in complaints from employees in the Paper-Shuffling Department (PSD) about MSDs breaking and failing to keep papers together. This creates opportunities for client papers to be mixed together. The Purchasing Department would like to improve the process for purchasing MSDs to eliminate complaints from employees in the Paper Shuffling Department.

Origin of the MSD Six Sigma Project

POI's mission statement is "Put the **R**ight **I**nformation in the Right **P**lace," **RIP** it! To accomplish this mission, POI has established a cascading set of business objectives and business indicators, which ultimately result in potential Six Sigma projects, see Table 16.1 on page 491.

The monthly production costs in the PSD are shown on the Individual and Moving Range chart in Figure 16.1 (see the next to last row in the fourth column in Table 16.1).

Figure 16.1 on page 492 indicates that production costs are stable (no special causes such as points beyond a control limit or too many sequences up and down, etc.) in the PSD with an average monthly cost of $1,096,880.00 and a standard deviation of $99,000 ($\overline{R}/d_2 = $111,672/1.128$). Additionally, production costs are approximately normally distributed (see Figure 16.2 on page 492). Team members discovered that PSD management considers monthly production costs to be very high, given the volume of work being processed by the department.

The four potential Six Sigma projects shown in the rightmost column of Table 16.1 are prioritized for attention in Table 16.2. Table 16.2 on page 493 is a Cause-and-Effect-type matrix (see Section 4.1) that weights the importance of each potential Six Sigma project to each of POI's business objectives.

The cell values are assigned by top management and are defined as follows: 0 = no relationship, 1 = weak relationship, 3 = moderate relationship, and 9 = strong relationship. The Finance Department developed the importance weights for each business objective to maximize the impact of Six Sigma projects on the bottom line of the organization. Consequently, the most critical project with respect to the business objectives is the MSD quality project; see 4.95 in the last row of Table 16.2. The champion and process owner of the MSD process prepared an initial project charter and presented it to the members of the MSD quality project team.

---

*The idea for a Six Sigma case study focusing on Metallic Securing Device (paper clips) was adapted from an exercise developed by Oriel Inc. (Madison, WI) for Johnson & Johnson.

TABLE 16.1 POI's Business Objectives and Indicators with Potential Six Sigma Projects

President		Director of Paper Shuffling Department (PSD)		
Business objectives	Business indicators	Area objectives	Area indicators	Potential Six Sigma projects
Increase the number of orders	Number of orders/month (c-chart)	Increase the number of orders in PSD	Number of orders in PSD/month (c-chart)	New customer promotions project
Increase the number of POI services (filing, organizing, etc.) utilized by each customer	Average/and standard deviation of number of services utilized per customer/quarter ($\overline{X}$ and S-charts)	Increase the number of services utilized by each customer in PSD	Average and standard deviation of number of services utilized per PSD customer/quarter ($\overline{X}$ and S-charts)	Existing customer promotions project
Minimize production costs	Production costs/month (I and MR charts)	Minimize production costs in PSD	Production costs in PSD/month (Figure 16.1; I and MR charts)	MSD quality project
Eliminate employee complaints	Number of employee complaints/month (c-chart)	Eliminate employee complaints from PSD	Number of employee complaints from PSD/month (c-chart)	Employee morale project

16.2 DEFINE PHASE

The Define phase has three components: business case with a project objective, SIPOC analysis, and Voice of the Customer (VoC) analysis.

Prepare a Business Case with a Project Objective

Preparing a business case requires team members to answer the following eight partially redundant questions. Some of the answers can be obtained from the draft project objective completed by the champion and process owner. The redundancy in the questions helps team members distill the critical elements of the business case.

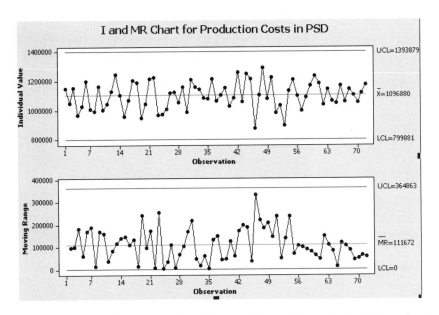

FIGURE 16.1 Minitab Individual and Moving Range Chart of Monthly Production Costs in the PSD

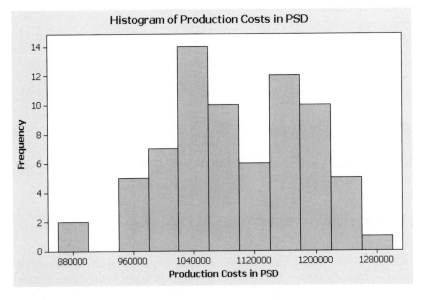

FIGURE 16.2 Minitab Histogram of Monthly Production Costs in the PSD

TABLE 16.2 Prioritization of Potential Six Sigma Projects

Business objectives			Potential Six Sigma projects			
			New customer promotions project	**Existing customer promotions project**	**MSD quality project**	**Employee morale project**
Increase the number of orders	W e i g h t s	.35	3	3	0	0
Increase the number of POI services utilized by each customer		.10	1	3	0	0
Minimize production costs		.40	0	0	9	3
Eliminate employee complaints		.15	0	0	9	9
Weighted average of potential Six Sigma projects			1.15	1.35	4.95*	2.55

*4.95 = (0.35 × 0) + (0.10 × 0) + (0.40 × 9) + (0.15 × 9)

Question: What is the name of the process?

Answer: MSD Purchasing Process. The first step in the supply chain for the MSD process is the process for purchasing MSDs. Hence, the first operation to be investigated by MSD quality project team members is the process for purchasing MSDs. Team members may study other factors that affect the quality of MSDs, such as the method of use or shelf-life at a later time.

Question: What is the aim of the process?

Answer: The aim of the purchasing process as it relates to this project is to purchase MSDs that improve the productivity and morale of the employees in the PSD and decrease production costs.

Question: What is the business case (economic rationale) for the project? This is answered by addressing the following subquestions:

Question: Why do the MSD project at all?

Answer: According to a judgment sample of three employees and two managers from the PSD, team members determined that MSDs that cannot withstand four or more bends are unacceptable because they are unlikely to remain intact throughout the paper shuffling processes and will not hold papers tightly. This is called *durability.* Defective MSDs create costs for POI; for example: (a) papers from different clients may get mixed together if not properly bound, requiring additional processing time, (b) employees may have to use multiple MSDs for one project, creating additional material costs, and (c) employees get frustrated and do not perform their jobs efficiently and productively, consequently increasing labor costs. Additionally, team members discovered that a large proportion of the boxes containing MSDs arrive to the PSD with five or more broken MSDs. This is called *functionality*. This creates additional processing costs for POI; for example, (a) increased unit costs and (b) frustrated and nonproductive employees and managers. Team members used the same judgment sample as above and determined that approximately 60% of individual MSDs do not meet durability criteria, and 60% of MSD boxes do not meet functionality criteria (see the survey questionnaire in Table 16.3 and the data matrix in Table 16.4).

TABLE 16.3 Survey Questionnaire

Survey

Name: _____
1. Please estimate the percentage of MSDs that cannot withstand four or more bends. _____
2. Please estimate the percentage of MSD boxes that contain greater than five broken MSDs. _____

TABLE 16.4 Survey Data

Survey Number	**Response Q1**	**Response Q2**
1	55%	70%
2	50%	55%
3	60%	65%
4	65%	60%
5	70%	50%
Average	60%	60%

Question: Why do the MSD project now?

Answer: Because the PSD is experiencing very high monthly production costs (see Figures 16.1 and 16.2) and because internal customers, including managers and hourly employees, are submitting an increased number of complaints: 14 in the first quarter, 18 in the second quarter, and 32 in the third quarter, as recorded in the Purchasing Department's complaint log for the fiscal year 2003. There are 100 hourly workers in the PSD.

Question: What business objectives are supported by the MSD quality project?

Answer: The MSD project is most strongly related to the "minimize production costs" and "eliminate employee complaints" business objectives (see Table 16.2).

Question: What are the consequences of not doing the project?

Answer: The consequences of not doing the project are decreased profit margins due to higher production costs and increased employee complaints due to frustration with materials.

Question: What projects have higher or equal priority?

Answer: At this time, the MSD quality project has the highest priority (4.95) (see the bottom row of Table 16.2).

Question: What is the problem statement? What is the pain?

Answer: Low-quality MSDs create additional production costs and employee frustration.

Question: What is the goal (desired state) for this project?

Answer: The Champion and Process Owner of the MSD process initially determined that a 100-fold improvement in MSD quality (durability and functionality) should be the goal for the Six Sigma project. They derived the concept of a 100-fold improvement from Motorola's 1986 stated improvement rate of tenfold every 2 years, or a 100-fold every 4 years during the kickoff of the Six Sigma effort. Because 100-fold improvement means the defects per million opportunities (DPMO) would decrease from 600,000 to 6,000, and a DPMO of 6,210 represents a Four Sigma process, team members decided to use Four Sigma as the goal for the MSD project.

Question: What is the project scope? This is answered by answering the following subquestions:

Question: What are the process boundaries?

Answer: The starting point for the project is when the Purchasing Department receives purchase orders from the PSD. The stopping point for the project is when the PSD places MSDs into inventory.

Question: What, if anything, is out of bounds?

Answer: The project team cannot change the way employees handle or use MSDs.

Question: What resources are available for the project?

Answer: The budget for the MSD project is $30,000.00. This includes estimated hourly salaries of project participants. Team members Brian Mercurio and Jeremy Pressman are the only project participants who will incur additional job responsibilities as a result of the project. Budget estimates show "opportunity cost" and "hard costs" (see Table 16.5). The estimated hard costs ($10,500) and expected opportunity costs ($15,540) are less than the budget of $30,000.

Question: Who can approve expenditures?

Answer: Only the Process Owner, Dana Rasis, can approve expenditures.

TABLE 16.5 Estimated Labor Costs for the Project

Name	Position	Estimated salary/ hour	Expected number of hours per week	Expected opportunity costs for 21 weeks	Expected hard costs for 21 weeks (direct labor costs)
Adam Johnson	Champion	$100	2	$4,200	
Dana Rasis	Process Owner	$50	2	$2,100	
Bettina Arguelles	Green Belt	$50	5	$5,250	
Brian Mercurio	Team member	$25	10	$0	$5,250
Jeremy Pressman	Team member	$25	10	$0	$5,250
Lindsey Barton	Finance rep.	$45	2	$1,890	
Mary Montano	IT rep.	$50	2	$2,100	
Total				$15,540	$10,500

Question: How much can the team spend beyond $30,000.00 without seeking additional authority?

Answer: Nothing.

Question: What are the obstacles and constraints of the project?

Answer: The team must work within a $30,000 budget and a 21-week time constraint.

Question: What time commitment is expected of team members?

Answer: Team members are expected to be present at weekly Friday morning meetings from 8:00 a.m. until 9:00 a.m. Team members are also expected to provide progress of project tasks at each meeting. Completion of project tasks will require additional hours of work per week.

Question: What will happen to each team member's regular job while working on the project?

Answer: If any, overtime hours will be compensated for team members and support staff. The estimated rate for overtime labor is 1.5 times normal labor. Overtime labor is not included in the budget in Table 16.5.

Question: Is there a Gantt chart for the project?

Answer: A Gantt chart is shown in Table 16.6.

Question: What are the benefits of the project?

Answer: The soft benefits of the project include eliminating complaints from the PSD and increasing employee morale. The hard (financial) benefits of the project are minimizing labor costs and material costs. The hard cost benefits are estimated on page 498.

The labor costs of the current and proposed systems are presented in Table 16.7.

TABLE 16.6 Gantt Chart for the MSD Project

Steps	Resp.	1	2	3	4	5	6	7	8	9	10	11	12	13	14	15	16	17	18	19	20	21
																	Week					
Define	BA	X	X	X	X																	
Measure	BA					X	X															
Analyze	BA								X	X	X											
Improve	BA											X	X	X	X	X	X					
Control	BA																	X	X	X	X	X

TABLE 16.7 Labor Costs

---

100 employees in the Paper Shuffling Department (PSD)

× 40 hours/week/paper shuffling employee

× 10% of time devoted to clipping

@ 400 hours/week devoted to clipping in PSD

× $25/hour/paper-shuffling employee

$10,000/week devoted to clipping

× 50 weeks/year

$500,000/year devoted to clipping

× 0.60 defective clips (judgment sample estimate of durability of the current system) Broken clips are not selected for use on jobs. This makes 0.6 a conservative estimate of the percentage of defective clips in the current system.*

$300,000/year on defective clipping for current system

× 0.0062 defective clips (durability of the proposed system)**

$3,100/year on defective clipping for proposed system

---

*This conservative estimate does not include problems arising from defective clips not detected until after they have been used and have caused failure on the job.

**Again, broken clips are not selected for use on jobs.

Hence, a lower bound on the estimated annual savings on labor costs from improving the MSD purchasing process is $296,900 ($300,000 – $3,100). The PSD incurs a 10% annual employee turnover. To capitalize on savings in labor costs, the department will now hire 4 new employees instead of 10 new employees, for a savings of 6 full-time employees ($296,900/$25 = 11,876 hours; 11,876/40 hours per week/50 weeks per year = 5.938 = ~ 6 employees saved). Alternatively, the PSD may now serve more customers with its current employee base.

The material costs of the current system are shown in Table 16.8.

Hence, the annual savings on material costs from improving MSD purchasing process is $44,820 ($75,000 – $30,180). This yields a lower bound on the estimated annual total hard benefit savings of $341,720.00.

Question: What are the roles and responsibilities of team members?

Answer: The roles and responsibilities of team members are shown in Table 16.9.

Do A SIPOC Analysis

The second part of the define phase requires that team members perform a SIPOC analysis. A SIPOC analysis is a simple tool for identifying the suppliers and their inputs into a process, the high-level steps of a process, the outputs of the process, and the customer segments interested in the outputs. A SIPOC analysis of POI's Purchasing Department is shown in Figure 16.3 on page 500.

TABLE 16.8 Material Costs

100 employees in the Paper Shuffling Department

× 60 projects/week/paper-shuffling employee
× 50 weeks/year
@ 300,000 projects/year requiring 3,000,000 MSDs (10 clips per project on average)
× 0.60 defective clips (judgment sample estimate of current system).
7,500,000* clips must be used to complete 300,000 projects
× 0.01/clip
@ $75,000/year on clips in current system
× 0.0062 defective clips **(proposed system)**
3,018,000** clips must be used to complete 300,000 projects
× .01/clip
@ $30,180/year on clips in proposed system

*1/(1 − 0.6) = 2.5 clips needed to get a good clip. So 3,000,000 × 2.5 = 7,500,000.
**1/(1 − 0.0062) = 1.006 clips needed to get a good clip. So 3,000,000 × 1.006 = 3,018,000.

TABLE 16.9 Roles and Responsibilities

Project Name: MSD Purchasing Process

Role	Responsibility	Stakeholder		Supervisor's signature
		Signature	Date	
Champion	Adam Johnson	AJ	9/1/2003	
Process Owner	Dana Rasis	DR	9/1/2003	
Green Belt	Bettina Arguelles	BA	9/2/2003	
Team member 1	Bryan Mercurio	BM	9/3/2003	
Team member 2	Jeremy Pressmen	JP	9/3/2003	
Finance rep	Lindsey Barton	LB	9/4/2003	
IT rep	Michelle Montano	MM	9/4/2003	

Conduct a "Voice of the Customer" Analysis

The third part of the define phase involves team members collecting and analyzing VoC data. VoC data is verbal or written information collected from a sample of users in a selected market segment. The questionnaire used to collect data from users of MSDs in the PSD is shown in Table 16.10 on page 501.

Team members analyze the "Voice of the Customer" (VoC) data by market segment (see column 1 of Table 16.11 on page 502). Next, they use all the raw VoC data points (see column 2 of

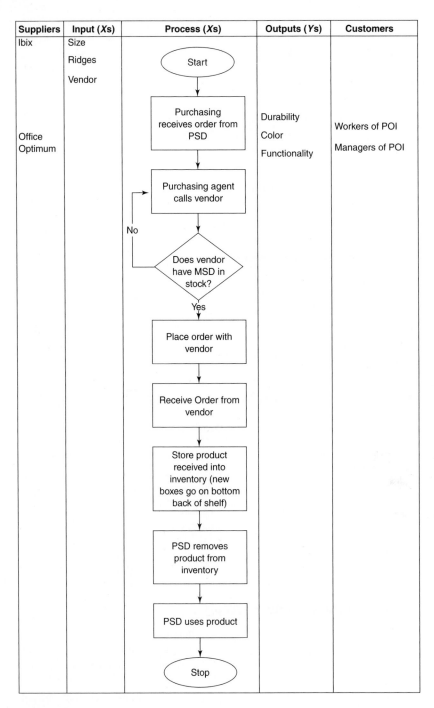

Suppliers	Input (*Xs*)	Process (*Xs*)	Outputs (*Ys*)	Customers
Ibix	Size			
	Ridges			
	Vendor			
Office Optimum			Durability Color Functionality	Workers of POI Managers of POI

FIGURE 16.3 SIPOC Analysis

TABLE 16.10 Voice of the Customer Questionnaire

Questions*
What emotions come to mind when you think about MSDs?
What needs and wants come to mind when you think about MSDs?
What complaints or problems would you like to mention about MSDs?

*These questions do not consider the opinions, feelings, and attitudes of the upstream, downstream, and external customers of the PSD.

Table 16.11) to create affinity diagram themes [see References 3 and 5 and Chapter 15], called *focus points* (see boldface numbers linking columns 2 and 3 in column 3 in Table 16.11). Next, team members identify the engineering issue underlying each focus point, called *cognitive issues* (see column 4 in Table 16.11). Then team members convert each cognitive issue into one or more quantitative engineering variable, called *critical-to-quality* (CTQ) variables (see column 5 in Table 16.11). Finally, team members develop technical specifications for each CTQ (see column 6 of Table 16.11).

A Kano questionnaire (see Table 16.12 on page 504) is a tool used by team members to classify a set of CTQs (see column 1 in Table 16.12) into an appropriate Kano quality category (see columns 2 and 3 in Table 16.12) from a large sample of regular users of a product, service, or process (see Chapter 4). There are six common Kano categories:

1. One-way (O)—User satisfaction is proportional to the performance of the feature; the lower the performance, the lower the user satisfaction; the higher the performance, the higher the user satisfaction.

2. Must-be (M)—User satisfaction is not proportional to the performance of the feature; the lower the performance, the lower the user satisfaction, but high performance creates feelings of indifference to the feature.

3. Attractive (A)—Again, user satisfaction is not proportional to the performance of the feature; low levels of performance create feelings of indifference to the feature, but high levels of performance create feelings of delight to the feature.

4. Indifferent (I)—User does not care about the feature.

5. Questionable (Q)—User response does not make sense (e.g., delighted if feature is present and delighted if feature is absent).

6. Reverse (R)—User offers responses opposite the responses expected by individuals conducting the Kano survey (e.g., "do not like it" if feature is present and "delighted" if feature is absent).

Additionally, team members use a Kano questionnaire to classify CTQs into their appropriate Kano cost category (see column 4 in Table 16.12). There are three common Kano cost categories:

1. Approximately, 80% of users are willing to pay at least a 10% cost increase for a new feature or a new product or service, above current offerings of products or services.

TABLE 16.11 Analysis Table for Voice of the Customer Data

1	2	3	4	5	6
Selected market segment	**Raw VoC data**	**Affinity diagram theme** (focus point)	**Driving issue** (cognitive issue)	**CTQ**	**Tech specs**
Paper organizing managers					
	"My employees are frustrated about the MSDs. They complain that they break too fast." 1 & 2	Variation in durability 1	Durability	Ability to withstand bending	≥ 4 bends without breaking
	"My employees are complaining that the MSDs are not holding up during the organizing process." 1	Variation in color 2	Color	Number of different MSD colors	= 1 color of MSDs
	"The employees are also complaining that the color of the MSDs change from one day to the next. It seems to be confusing them." 2	Variation in functionality 3	Functionality	Number of broken MSDs in a box	≤ 5 broken MSDs in a box
	"My employees are very unhappy with the purple and blue MSDs. They would prefer only one color of MSDs be used consistently." 2				
	"My employees say that more than five MSDs per box arrive broken." 3				
	"I've heard from numerous employees that the MSDs coming straight from inventory are already broken." 3				

Hourly employees

"The MSDs are falling apart before we are ready to file the papers into binders. An MSD should be able to take at least four bends." 1

"The MSDs aren't helping us to do our work efficiently." 1 & 2

"I would prefer if we used only one color of MSDs." 2

"I don't understand why we use different colors of MSDs." 2

"The MSDs just break when trying to bend them over the paper stacks. They should take at least four bends." 1

"It is very frustrating when you open a brand new box of MSDs and find that more than five of the clips are already broken." 3

"It is very time-consuming to sift out the broken MSDs from a brand new box coming straight from inventory." 3

2. Approximately, 60% of users are willing pay at least a 10% cost increase for a new feature or a new product or service, above current offerings of products or services.

3. Approximately, 10% of users are willing to pay a 10% cost increase for a new feature or a new product or service, above current offerings of products or services.

TABLE 16.12 Kano Questionnaire for MSDs

CTQs	How would you feel if the following CTQ were **present** in the product?	How would you feel if the CTQ were **not** present in the product?	What percentage of cost increase, over current costs, would you be willing to pay for this CTQ?
Ability to withstand ≥ 4 bends	Delighted [ ] Expect it and like it [ ] No feeling [ ] Live with it [ ] Do not like it [ ] Other [ ]	Delighted [ ] Expect it and like it [ ] No feeling [ ] Live with it [ ] Do not like it [ ] Other [ ]	0% [ ] 10% [ ] 20% [ ] 30% [ ] 40% or more [ ]
= One color of MSDs	Delighted [ ] Expect it and like it [ ] No feeling [ ] Live with it [ ] Do not like it [ ] Other [ ]	Delighted [ ] Expect it and like it [ ] No feeling [ ] Live with it [ ] Do not like it [ ] Other [ ]	0% [ ] 10% [ ] 20% [ ] 30% [ ] 40% or more [ ]
≤ 5 Broken MSDs in a box	Delighted [ ] Expect it and like it [ ] No feeling [ ] Live with it [ ] Do not like it [ ] Other [ ]	Delighted [ ] Expect it and like it [ ] No feeling [ ] Live with it [ ] Do not like it [ ] Other [ ]	0% [ ] 10% [ ] 20% [ ] 30% [ ] 40% or more [ ]

The questionnaire in Table 16.12 was given to the 100 paper shufflers in the PSD. Table 16.13 is used to classify the survey responses from each of the 100 paper shufflers for each of the CTQs into their Kano categories.

TABLE 16.13 Classification Table for Responses to a Kano Questionnaire

		Not present question response (see column 3 in Table 16.12)				
Present Question Response (see column 2 in Table 16.12)		Delighted	Expect it and like it	No feeling	Live with it	Do not like it
	Delighted	Q	A	A	A	O
	Expect it and like it	R	I	I	I	M
	No feeling	R	I	I	I	M
	Live with it	R	I	I	I	M
	Do not like it	R	R	R	R	Q

For example, if one of the paper shufflers answered the Kano survey about durability as is shown in Table 16.14, the CTQ would be classified as "attractive" for that paper shuffler (see Table 16.13 for classification table).

TABLE 16.14 One Paper Shuffler's Kano Questionnaire for MSDs

CTQs	How would you feel if the following CTQ were **present** in the product?	How would you feel if the CTQ were **not present** in the product?
Durability: Ability to withstand ≥ 4 bends	Delighted [X] Expect it and like it [ ] No feeling [ ] Live with it [ ] Do not like it [ ] Other [ ]	Delighted [ ] Expect it and like it [ ] No feeling [X] Live with it [ ] Do not like it [ ] Other [ ]

The responses for the 100 paper shufflers are tabulated in Table 16.15.

Durability is a must-be quality characteristic, and its presence is required to achieve employee indifference. Its absence creates employee dissatisfaction. The PSD is not willing to pay more for durable MSDs. Functionality is a one-way quality characteristic. Its absence is related to employee dissatisfaction, and its presence is related to employee satisfaction. The PSD is not willing to pay more for functional MSDs. Color is an indifferent quality characteristic. PSD employees do not care about it and are not willing to pay more for MSDs that are uniform in color.

The final step of a VoC analysis is to define each CTQ (see Table 16.16).

Returning to the first part of the Define phase, team members can now define the project's objectives.

TABLE 16.15 Tabulated Responses to Kano Questionnaire

CTQs	Kano quality category	Kano cost category
Durability: Ability to withstand four or more bends	M = 80 O = 20 M = 35	0% = 100
Color: Only 1 color per box	O = 15 I = 50	0% = 100
Functionality: Less than or equal to five broken MSDs in a box	M = 10 O = 90	0% = 100

TABLE 16.16 Definition of CTQs

CTQ	Definition of unit	Definition of opportunity for defect	Definition of defect	Kano Category
Durability: Ability to withstand bending	MSD	MSD	Break < 4 bends	Must-be: Fundamental to the delivery of the most basic level of customer satisfaction.
Color: Number of different MSD colors	1 box of MSDs	MSD	MSD colors in one box > 1	Indifferent: Far less critical than durability to paper shufflers.
Functionality: Number of broken MSDs in a box	1 box of MSDs	MSD	Broken MSDs in one box > 5	One-way: Improving the number of functional MSDs in a box will improve employee satisfaction in a linear fashion.

Project Objective 1: Decrease (direction) the percentage of MSDs that cannot withstand four or more bends without breaking (measure) bought by the Purchasing Department (process) to 0.62% (goal) by January 1, 2004 (deadline). Go for Four Sigma!

Project Objective 2: Decrease (direction) the percentage of boxes of MSDs with more than five broken clips (measure) bought by the Purchasing Department (process) to 0.62% (goal) by January 1, 2004 (deadline). Go for Four Sigma!

A correlation exists between the project objectives. A broken MSD cannot withstand four or more bends because it is already broken. Improving the percentage of functional MSDs per box will increase the percentage of MSDs that can withstand four or more bends.

16.3 MEASURE PHASE

The Measure phase has three steps. They are: operationally define each CTQ, perform a gage R&R study on each CTQ, and develop a baseline for each CTQ.

Operationally Define Each CTQ

Team members operationally define durability and functionality by establishing criteria for durability and functionality, developing a test for each set of criteria, and formulating a decision rule for each criteria. The operational definitions for durability and functionality are shown below.

Operational Definition for CTQ1: Durability. *Criteria* for a selected MSD can be seen in Figure 16.4.

1. Bend Zero: Closed clip

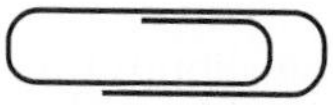

2. Bend One: Open clip

3. Bend Two: Closed clip

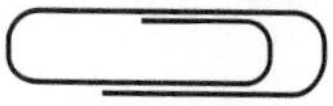

4. Bend Three: repeat bend One
5. Bend Four: repeat bend Two
6. Bend ?: repeat until break
7. Count number of successful bends. Do not count the bend the break occurs on.

FIGURE 16.4 Criteria for Number of Bends of an MSD

Test for a selected MSD:

1. Select the top front box of MSDs on the shelf in the inventory room.
2. Close your eyes, then open the box of MSDs, then haphazardly select one intact MSD. No switching is allowed.
3. Utilize the criteria for the selected MSD.
4. Count the number of bends until breaking.

Decision for a selected MSD:

1. If the number of bends is ≥ 4, then MSD is conforming.
2. If the number of bends is < 4, then MSD is defective.

Operational Definition for CTQ2: Functionality. *Criteria* for a box of MSDs: Count the number of "broken" clips. A clip is "broken" if it is in two pieces, regardless of the relative sizes of the pieces. It is a fact that clips can be broken only into two pieces.
Test for a box of MSDs:

1. Select the top front box of MSDs on the shelf in the inventory room.
2. Count the number of "broken" clips.

Decision for a box of MSDs:

1. If the number of MSDs that are broken ≤ 5, then the box of MSDs is conforming.
2. If the number of MSDs that are broken > 5, then the box of MSDs is defective.

The same box of MSDs is used for both operational definitions.

Perform a Gage R&R Study on Each CTQ

Team members conduct an attribute Gage R&R (repeatability and reproducibility) study on the measurement system of each CTQ to determine whether it is adequate for the needs of the project. Gage R&R is only part of a measurement system analysis. Linearity, stability, and calibration are also components of a measurement system analysis that can be conducted. These components were not studied as part of this Six Sigma project. The measurement of durability requires a destructive test.

Therefore, a simple Gage R&R study was not done for durability at this time. In the near future, an operational definition of the testing process for durability will be established, and testing will be audited to assure consistency. The measurement system for functionality is studied using the following sampling plan.

1. A shelf in the storage area contains boxes of MSDs purchased throughout the week. There are different types of MSD boxes in the storage area (different vendors, sizes, etc.).
2. The Gage R&R study required two inspectors to sample the same 10 boxes of MSDs twice.
3. The top 10 boxes on the front of the shelf were selected for the Gage R&R study.
4. The study is repeated as is deemed necessary by PSD management.

Two PSD managers have the responsibility of inspecting the MSDs for functionality; they are called *Inspector 1* (Tom) and *Inspector 2* (Jerry). Both Tom and Jerry counted the number of defective MSDs, twice, in random order. The functionality data is shown in Table 16.17 but not in random order.

TABLE 16.17 Gage R&R Data for Functionality

Box	Inspector	Count	Fuctionality	Box	Inspector	Count	Fuctionality
1	1	1	10	6	1	1	9
1	1	2	10	6	1	2	9
1	2	1	10	6	2	1	9
1	2	2	10	6	2	2	9
2	1	1	9	7	1	1	6
2	1	2	9	7	1	2	6
2	2	1	9	7	2	1	6
2	2	2	9	7	2	2	6
3	1	1	5	8	1	1	6
3	1	2	5	8	1	2	6
3	2	1	5	8	2	1	6
3	2	2	5	8	2	2	6
4	1	1	4	9	1	1	9
4	1	2	4	9	1	2	9
4	2	1	4	9	2	1	9
4	2	2	4	9	2	2	9
5	1	1	5	10	1	1	11
5	1	2	5	10	1	2	11
5	2	1	5	10	2	1	11
5	2	2	5	10	2	2	11

WEB GAGER&R-FUNCTIONALITY 2

A Gage run chart shows that there is no variation within inspectors or between inspectors, as seen in Figure 16.5. All the variation is between the 10 boxes of MSDs. Therefore, the measurement system is acceptable to measure functionality. The same is true for durability.

Develop a Baseline for Each CTQ

Team members conduct a study (as part of routine business) to determine the baseline capability for each CTQ. At the beginning of each hour, one box of MSDs is selected from the storage area. The procedure for selecting a box of MSDs is simply to select the top-frontmost box on the shelf. The selection process was not altered during a sampling period of two 8-hour shifts. Baseline capability data is shown in Table 16.18.

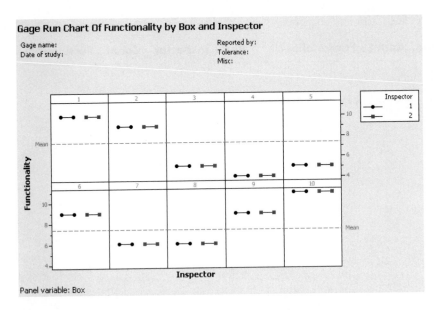

FIGURE 16.5 Minitab Gage Run Chart for Functionality

TABLE 16.18 Baseline Capability Data

Hour	Durability	Functionality	Hour	Durability	Functionality
Shift 1—Hour 1	5	12	Shift 2—Hour 1	12	6
Shift 1—Hour 2	7	4	Shift 2—Hour 2	9	6
Shift 1—Hour 3	3	8	Shift 2—Hour 3	3	9
Shift 1—Hour 4	2	6	Shift 2—Hour 4	1	5
Shift 1—Hour 5	9	1	Shift 2—Hour 5	1	4
Shift 1—Hour 6	2	5	Shift 2—Hour 6	1	5
Shift 1—Hour 7	1	11	Shift 2—Hour 7	1	9
Shift 1—Hour 8	1	9	Shift 2—Hour 8	4	10
Yield	6/16 = 0.375	6/16 = 0.375			

 BASELINE

The yields for durability and functionality are both 0.375, as determined by the number of tests out of 16 trials shown in Table 16.18 that met their respective CTQ's (i.e., at least four bends for durability, no more than five broken MSDs per box for functionality). This indicates very poor levels of durability and functionality for the MSDs received into the PSD and supports the initial yield estimates of 40.0%, or 60% defective MSDs (see Table 16.4).

An individuals and moving range (I-MR) chart for the durability baseline data indicates that the variability of durability is not stable over time (see the bottom panel of Figure 16.6). An investigation of the range between the eight and ninth MSDs did not reveal any obvious special cause of variation that could be used to improve the durability of MSDs.

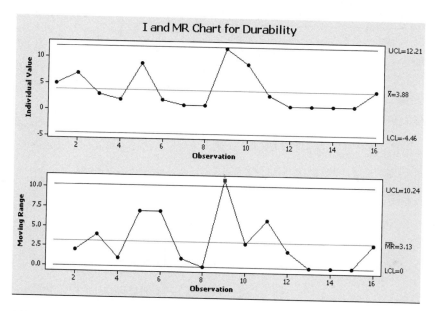

FIGURE 16.6 Minitab Individual and Moving Range Chart for Baseline Durability Data

The I-MR chart assumes approximate normality of the CTQ (durability). The durability data is not normally distributed, as shown in Figure 16.7.

Hence, use of the durability I-MR chart is not advised at this time. However, the distribution of durability may approximate a Poisson distribution. Consequently, team members constructed a c-chart** for the "count of bends" before each MSD breaks, which is displayed in Figure 16.8.

Figure 16.8 indicated a possible special cause Shift 2—Hour 1 when 12 bends were observed for the durability test. Further investigation and notes related to the test did not reveal any obvious differences between the MSD tested and the others, although during the first hour, the tester indicated that he may have bent the MSD slower than usual during the test, which may have caused less stress and consequently more bends.

**If the durability were measured using a continuous measurement system allowing for a fractional number of bends before breaking, then a log or similar transformation of the distribution may be appropriate before using an I-MR charting procedure.

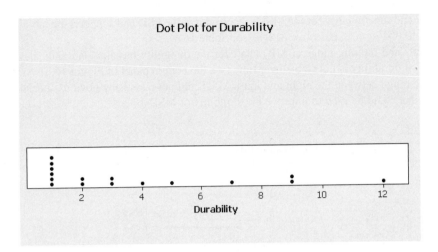

FIGURE 16.7 Minitab Dot Plot of Baseline Durability Data

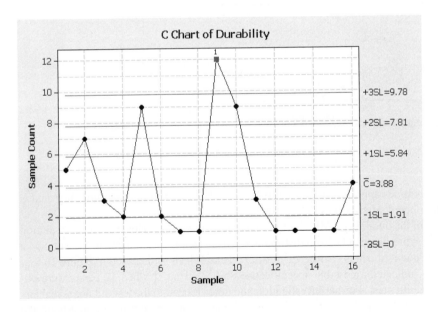

FIGURE 16.8 Minitab c-Chart for Durability

A *c*-chart for functionality shown in Figure 16.9 indicates that it is stable over time.

    The functionality data (see Figure 16.10) appears to be approximately Poisson distributed.

    Hence, use of the functionality *c*-chart is acceptable at this time. Finally, team members estimate the current process performance for each CTQ in Table 16.19.

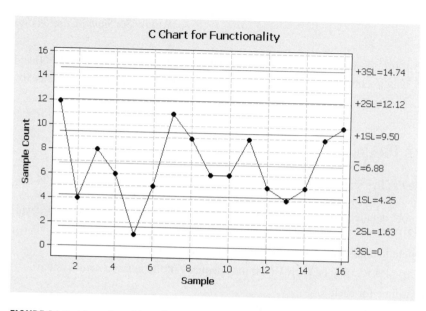

FIGURE 16.9 Minitab c-Chart for Functionality Baseline Data

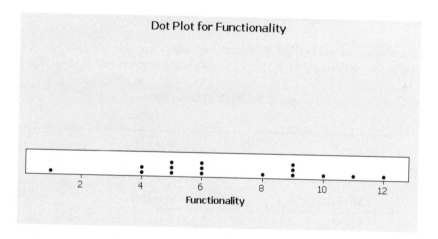

FIGURE 16.10 Minitab Dot Plot for Functionality Baseline Data

TABLE 16.19 Current Process Performance for CTQs

CTQs	Yield		DPMO	
	Current	**Desired**	**Current**	**Desired**
Durability	37.50%	99.38%	625,000	6,210
Functionality	37.50%	99.38%	625,000	6,210

513

Notice the desired 100-fold improvement shown in the DPMO columns (Current = 625,000 and Desired = 6,210). This is consistent with the goals stated in the Define phase of the DMAIC model.

16.4 ANALYZE PHASE

The Analyze phase has five steps:

1. Develop a more detailed process map (that is, more detailed than the process map developed in the SIPOC analysis of the Define phase).
2. Construct operational definitions for each input or process variable (called Xs).
3. Perform a Gage R&R study on each X (test the adequacy of the measurement system).
4. Develop a baseline for each X.
5. Develop hypotheses between the Xs and Ys.

The Ys are the output measures used to determine whether the CTQs are met.

Team members prepare a detailed process map identifying and linking the Xs and Ys, as shown in Figure 16.11.

Team members develop an operational definition for each X variable identified on the process map. The operational definitions for X_1, X_2, X_3, and X_8 relate to individual MSDs and are shown below.

Criteria: Each X conforms to either one or the other of the options.

X_1	Vendor	Ibix	Office Optimum
X_2	Size	Small (stock size)	Large (stock size)
X_3	Ridges	With ridges	Without ridges
X_8	Type of usage	Large stack of paper (number of papers is 10 or more)	Small stack of paper (number of papers is 9 or less)

Test: Select MSD.

Decision: Determine X_1, X_2, X_3, and X_8 options for the selected MSD.

The operational definitions for the procedures used to measure X_4, X_5, X_6, and X_7 are shown below.

Criteria: Compute the cycle time in days by subtracting the order date from the date on the bill of lading.

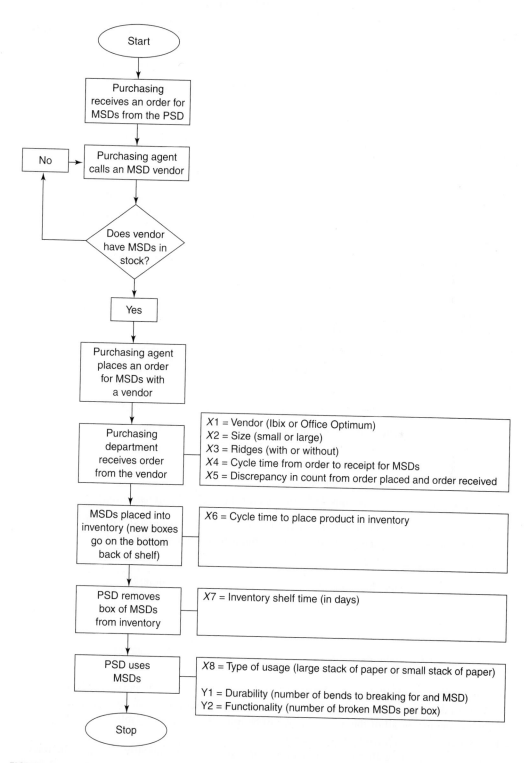

FIGURE 16.11 Process Map Linking CTQs and Xs for the MSD Purchasing Process

X_4	Cycle time from order to receipt for MSDs	In days

Test: Select a box of MSDs upon receipt of shipment from vendor. Compute the cycle time.

Decision: Determine X_4 for the selected box of MSDs.

Criteria: Count the number of boxes of MSD received for a given order. Subtract the number of boxes ordered from the number of boxes received for the order under study.

X_5	Discrepancy in count from order placed and order received	In boxes of MSDs by order

Test: Select a particular purchase order for MSDs.

Decision: Compute the value of X_5 in number of boxes for the selected purchase order.

Criteria: Compute the cycle time in days to place a shipment of MSDs in inventory by subtracting the date the shipment was received from the date the order was placed in inventory.

X_6	Cycle time to place product in inventory	In days

Test: Select a particular purchase order.

Decision: Compute the value of X_6 in days for the selected purchase order.

Criteria: Compute the inventory shelf-time in days for a box of MSDs by subtracting the date the box was placed in inventory from the date the box was removed from inventory.

X_7	Inventory shelf time	In days

Test: Select a box of MSDs.

Decision: Compute the value of X_7 in days for the selected box of MSDs.

Team members conduct Gage R&R studies for the Xs. Recall that the purpose of a Gage R&R study is to determine the adequacy of the measurement system for an X. In this case, the measurement systems for all of the Xs are known to be reliable and reproducible. Hence, Gage R&R studies were not conducted by team members.

Team members gather baseline data on durability (Y_1) functionality (Y_2), and the relevant Xs using the following sampling plan. For a 2-week period, the first box of MSDs brought to the

PSD each hour was selected as a sample. This yielded a sample of 80 boxes of MSDs, which can be seen Table 16.20.

TABLE 16.20 Baseline Data

Sample	Day	Hour	X_1	X_2	X_3	X_7	Dur	Fun
1	Mon	1	1	0	0	7	2	5
2	Mon	2	0	1	0	7	2	9
3	Mon	3	0	0	1	7	10	7
4	Mon	4	0	1	0	7	1	4
5	Mon	5	0	0	0	7	7	3
6	Mon	6	0	1	1	7	2	5
7	Mon	7	0	1	1	7	1	9
8	Mon	8	0	0	0	7	7	5
9	Tue	1	0	1	0	8	2	8
10	Tue	2	0	1	0	8	1	7
11	Tue	3	0	1	0	8	1	13
12	Tue	4	1	1	1	8	9	5
13	Tue	5	1	1	0	8	9	9
14	Tue	6	1	1	1	8	10	11
15	Tue	7	1	1	1	8	10	11
16	Tue	8	0	0	1	8	8	9
17	Wed	1	1	1	1	9	8	11
18	Wed	2	1	0	0	9	1	11
19	Wed	3	1	1	1	9	10	11
20	Wed	4	0	0	0	9	7	11
21	Wed	5	1	1	1	9	9	9
22	Wed	6	0	0	1	9	9	5
23	Wed	7	1	0	1	9	2	11
24	Wed	8	1	0	0	9	1	10
25	Thu	1	1	0	1	10	1	14
26	Thu	2	0	1	1	10	1	10
27	Thu	3	1	1	1	10	8	13
28	Thu	4	0	0	1	10	10	12
29	Thu	5	0	0	0	10	7	14
30	Thu	6	0	1	1	10	3	13
31	Thu	7	0	0	0	10	9	13

(continued)

For each sampled box, team members determined the durability (Y_1) and functionality (Y_2) measurements. Furthermore, information concerning the vendor (X_1), size of the MSD (X_2), whether the MSD has ridges (X_3), and inventory shelf-life is recorded (X_7).

TABLE 16.20 Baseline Data (continued)

Sample	Day	Hour	X_1	X_2	X_3	X_7	Dur	Fun
32	Thu	8	1	1	1	10	8	11
33	Fri	1	0	1	0	1	2	0
34	Fri	2	0	1	0	1	2	1
35	Fri	3	0	1	0	1	1	6
36	Fri	4	0	1	0	1	3	3
37	Fri	5	0	1	0	1	2	2
38	Fri	6	1	1	0	1	10	6
39	Fri	7	0	0	1	1	10	0
40	Fri	8	0	1	0	1	2	0
41	Mon	1	0	1	1	4	3	4
42	Mon	2	0	1	0	4	3	7
43	Mon	3	0	1	1	4	3	3
44	Mon	4	0	0	0	4	10	2
45	Mon	5	1	1	0	4	8	5
46	Mon	6	0	1	1	4	3	4
47	Mon	7	1	0	0	4	1	4
48	Mon	8	0	0	1	4	10	5
49	Tue	1	1	1	1	5	11	6
50	Tue	2	1	0	1	5	3	4
51	Tue	3	1	1	0	5	10	6
52	Tue	4	1	0	1	5	3	5
53	Tue	5	1	0	0	5	2	4
54	Tue	6	0	0	0	5	9	5
55	Tue	7	0	0	1	5	9	5
56	Tue	8	0	1	0	5	3	7
57	Wed	1	0	0	1	6	9	5
58	Wed	2	1	1	0	6	9	7
59	Wed	3	0	0	0	6	9	5
60	Wed	4	1	0	0	6	2	6
61	Wed	5	1	0	1	6	2	5
62	Wed	6	1	1	1	6	10	5
63	Wed	7	0	1	0	6	1	7
64	Wed	8	0	1	0	6	2	5
65	Thu	1	0	0	1	7	10	7
66	Thu	2	1	1	0	7	9	5
67	Thu	3	1	0	0	7	1	7

(continued)

TABLE 16.20 Baseline Data (continued) (continued)

Sample	Day	Hour	X_1	X_2	X_3	X_7	Dur	Fun
68	Thu	4	0	1	0	7	2	5
69	Thu	5	1	0	1	7	1	6
70	Thu	6	0	1	0	7	1	5
71	Thu	7	1	0	0	7	1	8
72	Thu	8	1	1	1	7	10	5
73	Fri	1	0	1	1	8	3	7
74	Fri	2	1	1	1	8	9	7
75	Fri	3	1	0	0	8	1	13
76	Fri	4	0	1	1	8	2	8
77	Fri	5	0	1	1	8	3	9
78	Fri	6	1	1	1	8	8	10
79	Fri	7	1	0	1	8	3	11
80	Fri	8	0	0	1	8	10	11

DATAMINING

X_1 = vendor (0 = Office Optimum and 1 = Ibix)
X_2 = size (0 = small and 1 = large)
X_3 = ridges (0 = without and 1 = with)
X_7 = inventory shelf-time, in days

The Purchasing Department will separately study cycle time from order to receipt of order (X_4), discrepancy between ordered and received box counts (X_5), and cycle time from receipt of order to placement in inventory (X_6). These last factors may influence such concerns as choice of vendor, ordering procedures, and inventory control, but they do not impact durability and functionality. Furthermore, the MSDs are not tested after they are used, so the type of usage (X_8) is not studied here. As was indicated in the Define phase, certain variables (e.g., X_4, X_5, X_6, and X_7) can be addressed in subsequent Six Sigma projects.

The baseline data revealed that the yield for durability is 0.4625 (37/80) and the yield for functionality is 0.425 (34/80), as shown in Table 16.21. As before, this indicates very poor levels for the CTQs in the PSD. For comparison purposes, the judgment sample carried out by the team during the Define phase showed that the yield was approximately 40% (i.e., the team assumed the failure rate was approximately 60%) for both durability and functionality. The slightly increased yields in this study can be due to natural variation in the process. The baseline data also showed that 56.25% of all MSDs are from Office Optimum (X_1), 42.50% of MSDs are small (X_2), 50.00% of all MSDs are without ridges (X_3), and the average shelf-time for boxes of MSDs (X_7) is 6.5 days, with a standard deviation of 2.5 days (see Table 16.21).

Team members develop hypotheses [$Y = f(X)$] about the relationships between the Xs and the Ys to identify the Xs that are critical to improving the center, spread, and shape of the Ys with respect to customer specifications. This is accomplished through data mining. **Data mining** is a method used to analyze passive data; that is, data that is collected as a consequence of operating a process. In this case, the baseline data in Table 16.20 is the passive data set that will be subject

TABLE 16.21 Basic Statistics on Baseline Data

Variable		Proportion	Mean	Standard deviation
Y_1: Durability	Four or more bends/clip	0.4625	5.213	3.703
Y_2: Functionality	Five or fewer broken/box	0.4250	7.025	3.438
X_1: Vendor	0 = Office Optimum 1 = Ibix	0.5625 0.4375		
X_2: Size	0 = Small 1 = Large	0.4250 0.5750		
X_3: Ridges	0 = Without ridges 1 = With ridges	0.5000 0.5000		
X_7: Inventory shelf-time	Shelf-time in days		6.5000	2.5160

to data mining procedures. Dot plots or box plots of durability (Y_1) and functionality (Y_2) stratified by X_1, X_2, X_3, and X_7 can be used to generate some hypotheses about main effects (i.e., the individual effects of each X on Y_1 and Y_2). Interaction plots can be used to generate hypotheses about interaction effects (i.e., those effects on Y_1 or Y_2 for which the influence of one X variable depends on the level or value of another X variable) if all combinations of levels of X variables

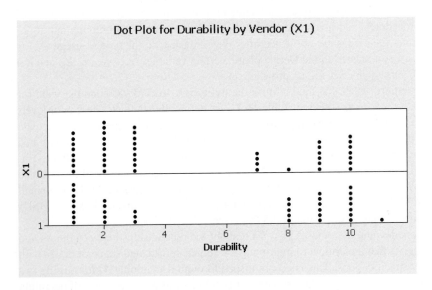

FIGURE 16.12 Minitab Dot Plot for Durability by X_1 (i.e., Vendor)

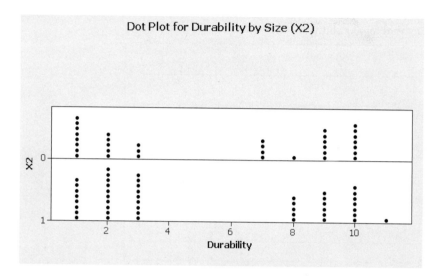

FIGURE 16.13 Minitab Dot Plot for Durability by X_2 (i.e., Size)

are studied. If not all combinations of levels of X variables are studied, then interaction effects are often not discovered.

Team members constructed dot plots from the baseline data in Table 16.20 to check whether any of the Xs (i.e., main effects) impact durability (Y_1) and functionality (Y_2). The dot plots for durability are shown in Figures 16.12–16.15. The dot plots for functionality are shown in Figures 16.16–16.19.

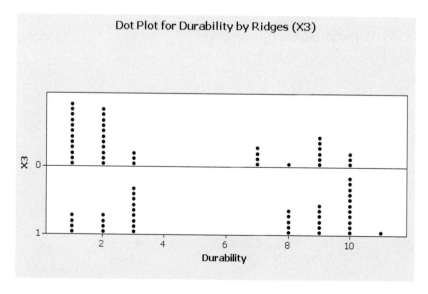

FIGURE 16.14 Minitab Dot Plot for Durability by X_3 (i.e., Ridges)

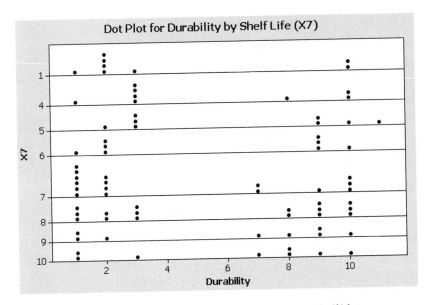

FIGURE 16.15 Minitab Dot Plot for Durability by X_7 (i.e., Shelf-life)

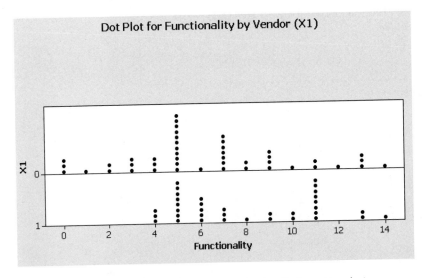

FIGURE 16.16 Minitab Dot Plot for Functionality by X_1 (i.e., Vendor)

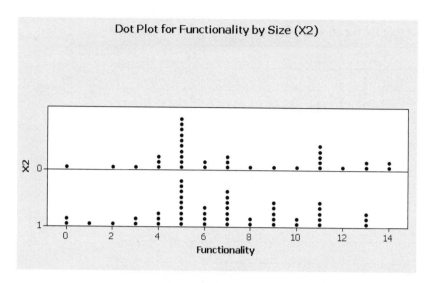

FIGURE 16.17 Minitab Dot Plot for Functionality by X_2 (i.e., Size)

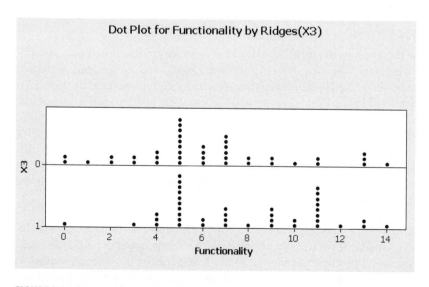

FIGURE 16.18 Minitab Dot Plot for Functionality by X_3 (i.e., Ridges)

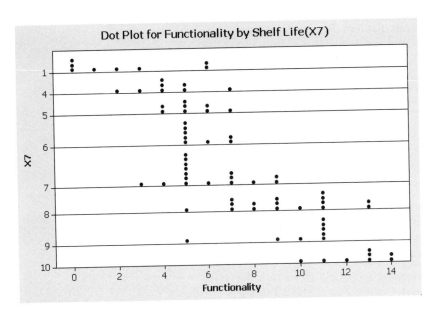

FIGURE 16.19 Minitab Dot Plot for Functionality by X_7 (i.e., Shelf-life)

The dot plots for durability (Y_1) indicate: (1) the values of durability tend to be low or high, with a significant gap between 4 and 6 for X_1, X_2, X_3, and X_7, and (2) the variation in durability is about the same for all levels of X_1, X_2, X_3, and X_7. The dot plots for functionality (Y_2) indicate: (1) the values of functionality tend to be lower when $X_1 = 0$ than when $X_1 = 1$, (2) the variation in functionality is about the same for all levels of X_2 and X_3, and (3) the values of functionality tend to be lower for low values of X_7.

Discussion of the Analysis of Durability. Because there are no clear differences in variation (i.e., spread) of durability for each of the levels of X_1, X_2, X_3, and X_7, the team wondered whether there might be differences in the average (i.e., center) for each level of the individual Xs. Team members constructed a main effects plot for durability to study differences in averages (see Figure 16.20).

Figure 16.20 indicates that for the ranges of shelf-life observed, there is no clear pattern for the relationship of shelf-life (X_7) to the average durability. On the other hand, it appears that ridges (i.e., $X_3 = 1$) have a positive relationship to the average durability. At first glance, it would seem that better results for average durability are seen when the vendor Ibix is chosen using small MSDs (i.e., $X_1 = 1$ and $X_2 = 0$), whereas using large MSDs from Office Optimum (i.e., $X_1 = 0$ and $X_2 = 1$) yields worse results.

While discussing the dot plots and main effects plot, it is dangerous to make any conclusions without knowing whether there are interaction effects. An interaction effect is present when the amount of change introduced by changing one of the Xs depends on the value of another X. In that case, it is misleading to choose the best value of the Xs individually without first considering the interactions between the Xs. Consequently, team members did an interaction plot for X_1, X_2, and X_3. X_7 was not included in the interaction plot because the main effects plot indicated

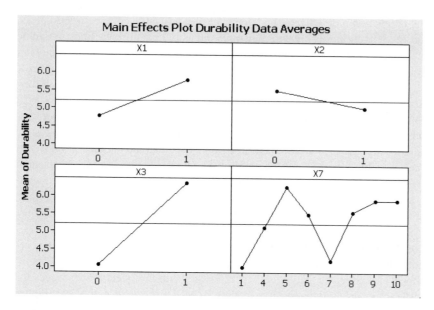

FIGURE 16.20 Minitab Main Effects Plot for Durability by X_1, X_2, X_3, and X_7.

no clear pattern or relationship with durability (Y_1). All combinations of levels of the X variables must be present to draw an interaction plot. This is often not the case with passive data (i.e., no plan was put in place to insure all combinations were observed in the data-gathering phase). Fortunately, although not all combinations were observed equally often, they were all present. Figure 16.21 is the interaction plot for durability.

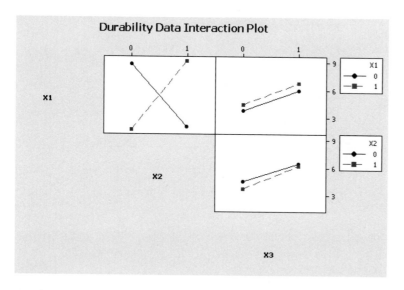

FIGURE 16.21 Minitab Interaction Effects Plot for Durability by X_1, X_2, and X_3

Surprise! The interaction plot indicates that there is a possible interaction between X_1 (i.e., vendor) and X_2 (i.e., size). How is this known? When there is no interaction, the lines should be parallel to each other, indicating that the amount of change in average durability when moving from one level of each X variable to another level should be the same for all values of another X variable. This plot shows the lines on the graph of X_1 and X_2 not only are not parallel, but they cross. The average durability is the highest when either large Ibix MSDs (i.e., $X_1 = 1$ and $X_2 = 1$) or small Office Optimum MSDs (i.e., $X_1 = 0$ and $X_2 = 0$) are used. This means the choice of vendor may depend on the size of MSD required. The main effects plot suggests that the best results for average durability occurs when small MSDs from Ibix are used, but the interactions plot suggests this combination yields a bad average durability. To study all of this further, the team decides that during the Improve phase, they will run a full factorial design to examine the relationship of X_1, X_2, and X_3 on durability (Y_1) because the main effects plot indicates potential patterns. Again, there does not appear to be a relationship between durability (Y_1) and X_7.

Discussion of the Analysis of Functionality. Figures 16.22 and 16.23 show the main effects and interaction effects plots for functionality (Y_2).

The main effects plot indicates that higher values of shelf-life (X_7) yield higher values for functionality (Y_2). The team surmised that the longer a box of MSDs sets in inventory (i.e., higher

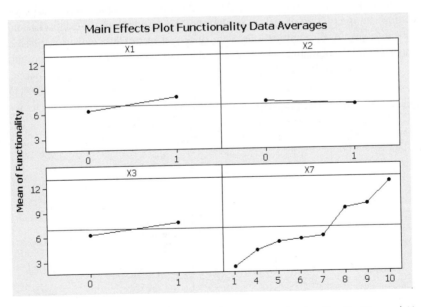

FIGURE 16.22 Minitab Main Effects Plot for Functionality by X_1, X_2, X_3, and X_7.

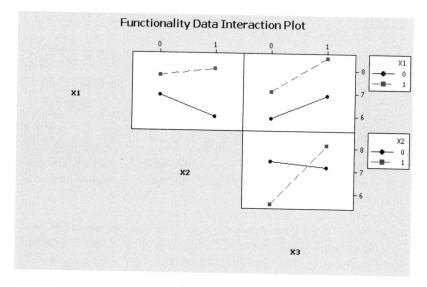

FIGURE 16.23 Minitab Interaction Effects Plot for Functionality by X_1, X_2, and X_3

values of shelf-life), the higher will be the count of broken MSDs (i.e., functionality will be high). From a practical standpoint, the team felt comfortable with this conclusion. They decided the Purchasing Department should put a Six Sigma project in place to investigate whether the potential benefit of either a "just-in-time" MSD ordering process or the establishment of better inventory handling procedures will solve the problem.

The interaction effect plot indicates a potential interaction between the X_2 (i.e., size) and X_3 (i.e., ridges). Better results for functionality (i.e., low values) were observed for large MSDs without ridges (i.e., $X_2 = 1$ and $X_3 = 0$). Why this may be the case needs to be studied further. Also, there may be an interaction between X_1 (i.e., vendor) and X_2 (i.e., size), but it appears that better results are observed whenever Office Optimum is used (i.e., $X_1 = 0$). In other words, the average count of broken MSDs is lower (i.e., functionality average is lower) whenever Office Optimum is the vendor.

Analyze Phase Summary. The Analyze phase resulted in the following hypotheses:

Hypothesis 1: Durability $= f(X_1 = $ Vendor, $X_2 = $ Size, $X_3 = $ Ridges) with a strong interaction effect between X_1 and X_2.

Hypothesis 2: Functionality $= f(X_1 = $ vendor, $X_2 = $ size, $X_3 = $ ridges, $X_7 = $ shelf-life), the primary driver being X_7 with some main effect due to X_1 and an interaction effect between X_2 and X_3.

X_7 is the main driver of the distribution of functionality (Y_2) and is under the control of the employees of POI. Hence, team members restructured Hypothesis 2 as follows: Functionality $= f(X_1 = $ vendor, $X_2 = $ size, $X_3 = $ ridges) for each fixed level of X_7 (shelf-life).

16.5 IMPROVE PHASE

The Improve phase involves designing experiments to understand the relationship between the Ys and the vital few Xs and major noise variables (see Chapter 13); generating the actions needed to implement the levels of the vital few Xs that optimize the shape, spread, and center of the distributions of the Ys; developing action plans; and conducting pilot tests of the action plans.

Team members conducted an experimental design to determine the effect of X_1 (vendor), X_2 (size), and X_3 (ridges), and their interactions, on the Ys, with $X_7 = 0$ (no shelf-life—MSDs are tested immediately upon arrival to POI before they are placed in inventory). A 2^3 full factorial design with two replications (16 trials) was performed for durability and functionality. The factor conditions for vendor (X_1) are Office Optimum (-1) or Ibix (1); the factor conditions for size (X_2) are small (-1) or large (1), and the factors conditions for ridges (X_3) are without ridges (-1) or with ridges (1). The experiment was set up in two blocks to increase experimental reliability, with the first eight runs conducted in the morning and the second eight runs conducted in the afternoon. The runs were randomized within each block. The purpose of the blocks and randomization is to help prevent lurking (background) variables that are related to time (e.g., time of day and order in which data is collected) from confusing the results. Additional information can be gathered because 16 trials were run, rather than the minimum of 8 trials, especially regarding potential interactions. The data from the 2^3 full factorial design (with two replications in run order, the first eight runs constituting the first replicate) is shown in Table 16.22.

TABLE 16.22 Durability and Functionality Data

Std order	Run order	Vendor	Size	Ridges	Durability	Functionality
2	1	Ibix	Small	Without	1	8
4	2	Ibix	Large	Without	9	9
3	3	Office Optimum	Large	Without	1	8
8	4	Ibix	Large	With	11	8
5	5	Office Optimum	Small	With	10	0
6	6	Ibix	Small	With	4	2
7	7	Office Optimum	Large	With	4	3
1	8	Office Optimum	Small	Without	10	2
16	9	Ibix	Large	With	9	3
10	10	Ibix	Small	Without	3	0
12	11	Ibix	Large	Without	9	0
14	12	Ibix	Small	With	3	7
13	13	Office Optimum	Small	With	9	6
11	14	Office Optimum	Large	Without	2	4
9	15	Office Optimum	Small	Without	8	1
15	16	Office Optimum	Large	With	2	4

FACTORIAL MTW

Pareto charts showing which of the vital few *X*s and the interactions between them have a statistically significant effect on durability (Y_1) and functionality (Y_2) at the 10% level of significance can be seen in Figures 6.24 and 6.25, respectively.

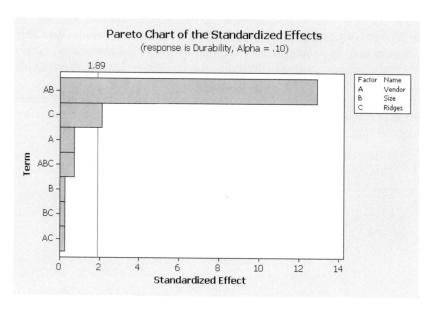

FIGURE 16.24 Minitab Pareto Chart of Effects for Durability

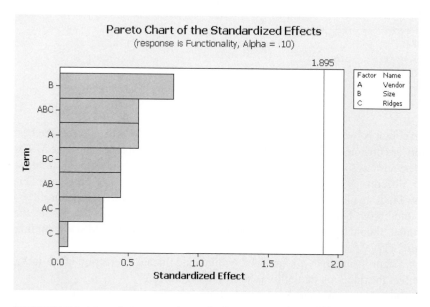

FIGURE 16.25 Minitab Pareto Chart of Effects for Functionality

The major effects (i.e., those that have significance level less than 0.10—in other words, over 90% confidence level) for durability are the interaction of vendor and size and the main effect due to ridges. There are no significant effects due to vendor, size, or ridges present for functionality. This indicates that because the effect of shelf-life was held constant in this designed experiment, although it was shown to affect functionality in the data mining analysis, the team can restrict its attention to improving functionality by addressing shelf-life first. Because durability is the only outcome influenced by vendor, size, or ridges in this designed experiment, further consideration in this study will be restricted to durability. Another project can address shelf-life and its effect on functionality.

Because interaction effects should be interpreted prior to studying main effects, the team decided to construct an interaction effect plot for vendor and size. Figure 16.26 is the interaction effect plot for vendor and size, relative to durability.

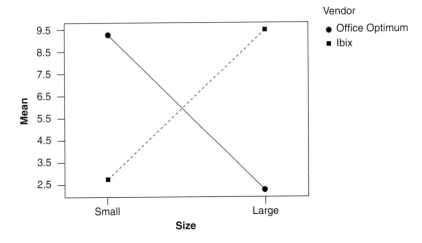

FIGURE 16.26 Minitab Interaction Effect Plot for Vendor and Size, Relative to Durability

The interaction effect plot between size and vendor shown in Figure 16.26 indicates that the best results for durability are obtained using small MSDs supplied by Office Optimum or large MSDs supplied by Ibix. The reasons for this interaction may be due to factors such as materials used for each size of MSD, differences in supplier processes for each size of MSD, or other supplier-dependent reasons. Team members can ask each vendor why its sizes show significant differences in average durability, if there is a preference to use only one vendor. Otherwise, the Purchasing Department should buy small MSDs from Office Optimum or large MSDs from Ibix to optimize durability (Y_1).

The only significant main effect not involved within a significant interaction effect is X_3, ridges. The main effect for ridges on durability is shown in Figure 16.27.

This plot indicates that the average durability is about $6.5 - 5.4 = 1.1$ more when an MSD with ridges is used rather than an MSD without ridges. Therefore, because ridges is a main effect

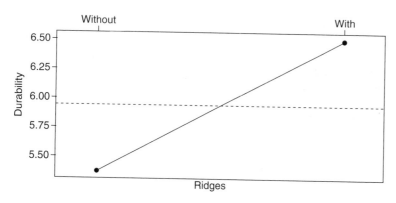

FIGURE 16.27 Minitab Main Effect Plot for Ridges, Relative to Durability

independent of any interaction effects, the right selection of MSDs is to use Office Optimum for small MSDs with ridges and Ibix for large MSDs with ridges. If the experimental results from Table 16.22 are used, the average durability for Office Optimum's small MSDs with ridges is (10 + 9) / 2 = 9.5, and the average durability for Ibix's large MSDs with ridges is (11 + 9) / 2 = 10.0. Both averages are well above the required corresponding CTQ of at least 4. As long as the variation (spread) of results is small enough so that no individual durability result is far from these averages, the team is successful with respect to durability. The variation in these results can be monitored using control charts after changing the purchasing process for selecting MSDs.

The team members decided to purchase all MSDs with ridges. In addition, the choice of vendor and size will be as follows: (vendor = Office Optimum) and (size = small) or (vendor = Ibix) and (size = large) to maximize average durability. In addition, the team decided to take on another project to reduce shelf-life to less than 5 days to address functionality. The revised flowchart for the Purchasing Department incorporating the findings of the Six Sigma project is shown in Figure 16.28.

The team members conducted a pilot test of the revised best practice (see the flowchart in Figure 16.28). Data for durability from the pilot test is shown in Table 16.23.

Table 16.23 on page 533 indicates that the rolled throughput yield (RTY) for durability is 100%. Functionality was also tested (not shown here), using shelf-life = 0 days; that is, the MSDs were tested immediately upon arrival to POI before they were placed in inventory. This resulted in an RTY of 75%, which is better than the baseline RTY. The effect on functionality of shelf-life and inventory control procedures will be investigated in subsequent projects if management decides these projects should be chartered.

Figure 16.29 on page 534 shows that durability is in control, with a higher mean number of bends for all MSDs in the pilot test. The test pilot data shown in Table 16.23 includes results for both small MSDs from Office Optimum and large MSDs from Ibix. Subsequently, team members realized that, with all things being equal, large MSDs from Ibix should have a higher average durability than small MSDs from Office Optimum. Consequently, team members constructed two control charts, one for small MSDs from Office Optimum and another for large MSDs from Ibix (Figures 16.30 on page 534 and 16.31 on page 535, respectively).

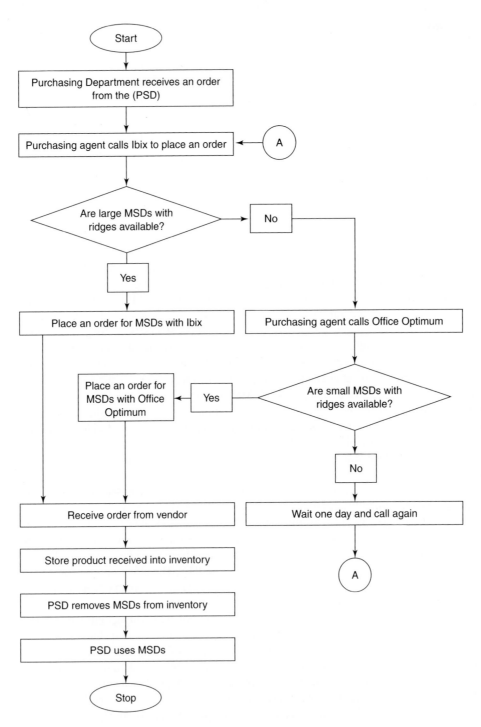

FIGURE 16.28 Revised Flowchart of the Purchasing Department

TABLE 16.23 Data from the Pilot Test

Hour	Vendor	Size	Ridges	Durability
Shift 1 — Hour 1	Office Optimum	Small	With	10
	Ibix	Large	With	11
Shift 1 — Hour 2	Office Optimum	Small	With	7
	Ibix	Large	With	11
Shift 1 — Hour 3	Office Optimum	Small	With	10
	Ibix	Large	With	11
Shift 1—Hour 4	Office Optimum	Small	With	8
	Ibix	Large	With	11
Shift 1—Hour 5	Office Optimum	Small	With	9
	Ibix	Large	With	10
Shift 1—Hour 6	Office Optimum	Small	With	9
	Ibix	Large	With	9
Shift 1—Hour 7	Office Optimum	Small	With	8
	Ibix	Large	With	11
Shift 1—Hour 8	Office Optimum	Small	With	9
	Ibix	Large	With	10
Shift 2—Hour 1	Office Optimum	Small	With	9
	Ibix	Large	With	11
Shift 2—Hour 2	Office Optimum	Small	With	8
	Ibix	Large	With	10
Shift 2—Hour 3	Office Optimum	Small	With	10
	Ibix	Large	With	9
Shift 2—Hour 4	Office Optimum	Small	With	7
	Ibix	Large	With	9
Shift 2—Hour 5	Office Optimum	Small	With	7
	Ibix	Large	With	10
Shift 2—Hour 6	Office Optimum	Small	With	9
	Ibix	Large	With	11
Shift 2—Hour 7	Office Optimum	Small	With	10
	Ibix	Large	With	9
Shift 2—Hour 8	Office Optimum	Small	With	8
	Ibix	Large	With	11
RTY				32/32 = 1

PILOT

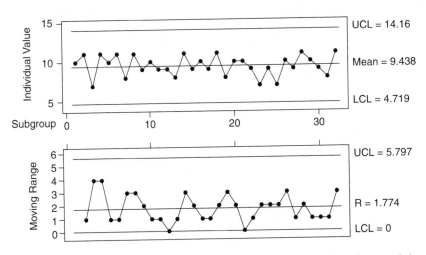

FIGURE 16.29 Minitab Individual Value and Moving Range Chart for Durability

Figures 16.29, 16.30, and 16.31 show that durability (Y_1) is in control, but it is dangerous to compute any process capability statistics due to the small sample sizes. However, estimates for the mean and standard deviation of small MSDs from Office Optimum are 8.625 and 1.05 (calculated from the data but not shown here), respectively. The mean and standard deviation for large MSDs from Ibix are 10.25 and 0.83, respectively. Because the CTQ for durability requires the number of bends to be four or more, this requirement is 4.4 standard deviations below the mean for small MSDs from Office Optimum and 7.5 standard deviations below the mean for large MSDs from Ibix. Team members all agreed that as long as the process for both small MSDs from Office Optimum with ridges and large MSDs from Ibix with ridges remain in control, it is extremely unlikely that the MSDs will fail the CTQ for durability (Y_1).

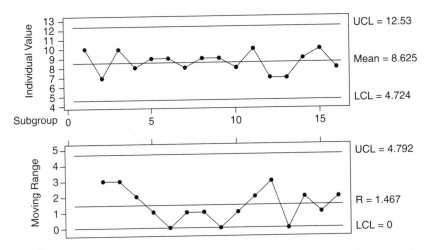

FIGURE 16.30 Minitab Individual Value and Moving Range Chart for Durability of Small MSDs from Office Optimum

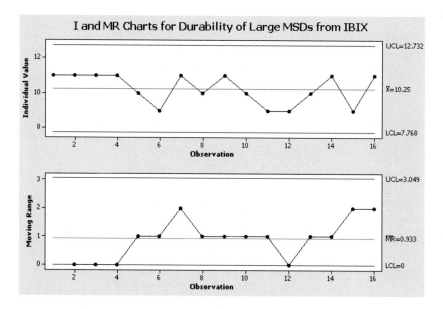

FIGURE 16.31 Minitab Individual Value and Moving Range Chart for Durability of Large MSDs from Ibix

16.6 CONTROL PHASE

The Control phase involves mistake proofing the improvements and/or innovations discovered in the Six Sigma project; establishing a risk management plan to minimize the risk of failure of product, service, or process; documenting the improvement and/or innovation in ISO 9000 documentation; and preparing a control plan for the process owners who will inherit the improved or innovated product, service, or process; turning the process over to the process owner; and disbanding the team and celebrating their success.

Team members identified and prioritized two problems while mistake proofing the process improvements discovered in the improve phase. They are: (1) Purchasing agents do not specify "with ridges" on a purchase order and (2) purchasing agents do not consider that the choice of vendor depends on the size of the MSDs being requested on the purchase order. Team members created solutions that make both errors impossible. They are: (1) The purchase-order entry system does not process an order unless "with ridges" is specified on the purchase order and (2) the purchase-order entry system does not process an order unless Office Optimum is the selected vendor for small MSDs and Ibix is the selected vendor for large MSDs.

Team members use risk management to identify two risk elements. They are: (1) failing to train new purchasing agents in the revised purchasing process shown in Figure 16.28 on page 532 and (2) Office Optimum and Ibix are out of MSDs with ridges. Team members assigned risk ratings to both risk elements, as shown in Table 16.24.

Both risk elements must be dealt with in risk abatement plans. The risk abatement plan for "failing to train new purchasing agents" is to document the revised purchasing process in training manuals. The risk abatement plan for "vendor out of MSDs with ridges" is for POI to

TABLE 16.24 Risk Elements for Purchasing Process

Risk elements	Risk category	Likelihood of occurrence	Impact of occurrence	Risk element score	
Failing to train new purchasing agents	Performance	5	5	25	High
Vendor out of MSDs with ridges	Materials	2	5	10	Medium

Scale: 1–5, with 5 being the highest.

request that both Office Optimum and Ibix manufacture only MSDs with ridges, due to their superior durability. This is a reasonable and acceptable suggestion to POI, Office Optimum, and Ibix because the cost structures for manufacturing MSDs with and without ridges are equal, and neither Office Optimum nor Ibix has other customers requesting MSDs without ridges. Office Optimum and Ibix agree to produce only MSDs with ridges after a 6-month trial period in which they check incoming purchase orders for requests for MSDs without ridges. If the trial period reveals no requests for MSDs without ridges, the POI Purchasing Department will revise Figure 16.28 and the appropriate ISO 9000 documentation to reflect the possibility of purchasing only MSDs with ridges. Additionally, Office Optimum and Ibix thanked POI for pointing out to them that average durability is higher for MSDs with ridges than for MSDs without ridges. Both vendors claim that they are going to experiment with possible different ridge patterns to increase durability and decrease costs. Both vendors stated that they anticipate decreased costs from producing only MSDs with ridges because of the lower amortized costs of having only one production line.

Team members prepare ISO 9000 documentation for the revisions to the training manual for the purchasing process from Figure 16.28.

Team members develop a control plan for the PSD that requires a monthly sampling of the boxes of MSDs in inventory. The purpose of the sampling plan is to check whether the boxes of MSDs being purchased are either small Office Optimum MSDs with ridges or large Ibix MSDs with ridges. The percentage of nonconforming boxes of MSDs will be plotted on a p-chart. PSD management will use the p-chart to highlight violations of the new and improved purchasing process shown in Figure 16.28. The p-chart will be the basis for continuously turning the Plan-Do-Study-Act (PDSA) cycle for the revised purchasing process.

Team members check the business indicator from the PSD and determine that production costs in the PSD decreased, probably due to the MSD Six Sigma project (see Figure 16.32). The MSD project took effect in month 73 of Figure 16.32.

Conclusion

This chapter presented a Six Sigma case study. It is time for the champion and black belt to disband the project team, turn the improved process over to the Purchasing Department for continuing turns of the PDSA cycle, and celebrate the project's success with team members.

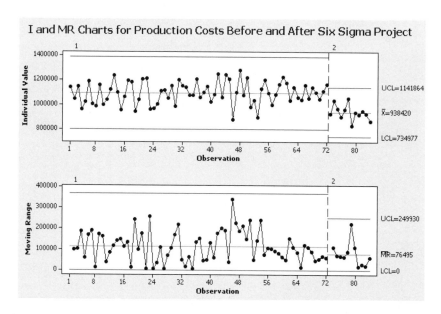

FIGURE 16.32 Individuals and Moving Range Chart Obtained from Minitab of Production Costs in the PSD Before and After the MSD Six Sigma Project

REFERENCES

1. Gitlow, H., "Innovation on Demand," *Quality Engineering,* 11, 1998–1999, pp. 79–89.

2. Gitlow, H., A. Oppenheim, R. Oppenheim, and D. Levine *Quality Management,* 3rd ed. (New York: McGraw-Hill-Irwin, 2005).

3. Deming, W. E., *The New Economics: For Industry, Government, Education,* (Cambridge, MA: M.I.T., Center for Advanced Engineering Study, 1994).

4. Deming W. E., *Out of the Crisis* (Cambridge, MA: M.I.T., Center for Advanced Engineering Study, 1986).

5. Gitlow H. and Gitlow S., *The Deming Guide to Quality and Competitive Position* (Englewood Cliffs, NJ: Prentice Hall, 1987).

6. Gitlow, H. and PMI, *Planning for Quality, Productivity and Competitive Position* (Homewood, IL: Richard D. Irwin, pp. 83–89, 1990).

7. Rasis, D., Gitlow, H. and Popovich, E., "Paper Organizers International: A Fictitious Six Sigma Green Belt Case Study—Part 1," *Quality Engineering,* 15, 2003, pp. 127–145.

8. Rasis, D., Gitlow, H., and Popovich, E., "Paper Organizers International: A Fictitious Green Belt Case Study—Part 2," *Quality Engineering,* 15, 2003, pp. 259–274.

A PAPER HELICOPTER EXPERIMENT CASE STUDY

CHAPTER OUTLINE

LEARNING OBJECTIVES

After reading this chapter you will be able to:

- Conduct a Six Sigma DMAIC project
- Use the tools and methods of the Define, Measure, Analyze, Improve, and Control phases

INTRODUCTION

This chapter presents an application of the Six Sigma DMAIC model to a version of G.E.P. Box's famous "paper helicopter" experiment [References 1, 3, and 4]. The intent of this chapter is to present the reader with a case study for structuring a Six Sigma project.

17.1 BACKGROUND

Lilliputia is one of the countries portrayed in *Gulliver's Travels* by Jonathan Swift and is a member of the Small Countries Treaty Organization (SCTO). In the last couple of decades it has been plagued by a violent splinter faction known as the Lilliputian Freedom Fighters (LFF). The LFF is known for its takeovers of cities, as well as its radical social and political doctrine. As a result, Lilliputia is in a state of unrest.

In an effort to halt the advancing LFF, Emperor Nova approved a large military budget. The money was primarily spent to refine siege engines and tactics to reclaim lost cities. This strategy was highly successful but very costly in casualties, time, and money. The cost of the siege strategy led to a new tactic involving attacks by air. As a result, the Lilliputian National Army (LNA) commissioned an Army Air Corps (AAC).

Early experience with the AAC and its fleet of helicopters showed that this new tactic was much better than the previous siege tactic. Sieges were ending far sooner as a result of the air power.

The Lilliputian National Dashboard lists Emperor Nova's key objectives and indicators, as well as his high-priority projects, in Table 17.1. Note that the key objectives and indicators that led to the high-priority projects have been denoted with bold and italicized fonts. These projects are summarized by importance in Table 17.2.

TABLE 17.1 Lilliputian Government Dashboard

Emperor's key objectives	Emperor's key indicators	Direct report key objectives	Direct report key indicators	Projects
1) Rule justly and fairly	*c*-charts of broken laws	A) Advise for better legal policy	*c*-charts of broken laws	Study of stoning murderers
			I-MR charts of losses from crimes	Determining actuarial rate
		B) Enforcement of laws	*c*-charts of broken laws	
	c-chart of court appeals	C) Minimization of appeals	*c*-charts of number of appeals	
			Pareto diagram of appeal reasons	Elimination of judge bias
2) Keep citizens safe	*p*-chart of lands held by LFF	A) Elimination of LFF	*c*-charts of LFF casualties by week	
		B) Equipment efficiency	*c*-charts of LNA casualties by week	
			$\bar{X}$ and *S*-charts of catapult accuracy	

(continued)

TABLE 17.1 Lilliputian Government Dashboard (continued)

Emperor's key objectives	Emperor's key indicators	Direct report key objectives	Direct report key indicators	Projects
			I-MR charts of helicopter flight times between repair actions	*Increased flight time; electronic reconnaissance implementation*
			I-MR charts of helicopter maintenance times	
			Pareto charts of repair reasons	Helicopter landing process
			p-chart of scrapped equipment	
		C) Maximization of morale	Enlisted Likert scale X̄ and R-charts	*Equipment repainting; barracks food quality*
3) Strong national appearance	Budget updates and logbooks	A) Budget tracking	Pareto diagram of expenditures	Continuous tracking
			I-MR charts of expenditures	Continuous tracking
			X̄ and R-chart of economic output	Continuous tracking
	Dignitary home location tracking	B) Marketing Lilliputia	Map with push pins on each visitor's home	Gage R&R of maps
			X̄ and R-chart of exports and imports	
	c-chart of celebrations	C) Keeping morale of citizenry	Citizenry Likert scale X̄ and S-charts	
			c-chart of patriotic parades and events	Improving celebration locations

The AAC is designed for rapid deployment of LNA ground forces and as an attack unit. The only aircraft in service is a line of helicopters which have not been performing at the levels expected by the senior officers in the LNA (see Figure 17.1 on page 543).

As a result, the commanding general for the AAC decided to champion an effort to improve the helicopters to increase the morale of his personnel and to create a more effective fighting machine for the AAC.

TABLE 17.2 Importance of Potential Projects by Military Business Objectives

| | | Weights | Potential projects for the Six Sigma team | | | | |
			Increased flight time	Equipment repainting	Helicopter landing process	Barracks food quality	Electronic reconnaissance implementation
Military business objectives	Attack capability	0.40	9	0	3	0	3
	Scouting	0.30	9	1	0	0	9
	Military cargo transportation	0.20	9	0	3	0	0
	Morale	0.10	3	3	3	9	1
Weighted average of CTQs			8.4*	0.6	2.1	0.9	4.0

*8.4 = 0.4(9) + 0.3(9) + 0.2(9) + 0.1(3)

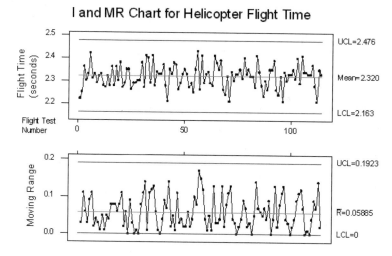

FIGURE 17.1 Minitab Individual Value and Moving Range Charts for Key Indicator Data from the Lilliputian Dashboard

17.2 DEFINE PHASE

The Define phase consists of three steps: the business case, the SIPOC analysis, and the Voice of the Customer (VoC) analysis. Each step is presented as follows.

Business Case

The business case for the project is built by answering a series of eight questions.

Question: What is the name of the product or process?

Answer: Helicopter production process.

Question: What is the aim of the product or process?

Answer: To build the best helicopters possible for the AAC.

Question: What is the economic rationale for doing the project? This question is addressed by a series of subquestions.

Question: Why do the helicopter project at all?

Answer: Strategists and scientists have determined that the best military action is to have a helicopter with extended flying time to be able to launch a complete payload of rockets.

Question: Why do the project now?

Answer: According to intelligence operatives, there is a credible threat of an invasion attempt in the next six to twelve months. Production of new units will require an estimated two months. The project must be started now to have a new design in the required time.

Question: What business objectives are supported by the helicopter production project?

Answer: The helicopter construction project is directly related to the "keep citizens" safe objective.

Question: What are the consequences of not doing the project?

Answer: Detailed analysis of previous battles shows that without air power the LFF will continue to be successful in their efforts.

Question: What projects have higher or equal priority?

Answer: Table 17.2 shows that the helicopter construction process is the highest priority project.

Question: What is the pain?

Answer: Multiple types of pain exist: for example, the deaths of soldiers, fear of decreased national security, a loss of national pride, and possibly national independence.

Question: What is the goal for this project?

Answer: The project hopes to deliver payloads of 24 rockets in the course of normal missions.

Question: What is the project scope? This is answered by the following subquestions.

Question: What are the process boundaries?

Answer: A better helicopter must be constructed utilizing existing materials.

Question: What, if anything, is out of bounds?

Answer: The project cannot research new materials. Also, once built, the prototypes cannot be altered due to a constraint imposed by the fabrication processes of the highly technical materials being used.

Question: What resources are available for the project?

Answer: The total budget for the project is 18.3 million gold florins. The Lilliputian government funding, through the LNA, constitutes the majority of this budget with 15 million gold florins for materials. Each prototype costs 100,000 gold florins, and testing costs an additional 10,000 gold florins per prototype. The remaining 3.3 million gold florins are devoted to building prototypes from the new design specifications and pilot testing them. This funding is not a lump sum but is instead a conglomerate of funds from both the military research budget, as well as a chunk of 15 million gold florins coming directly from the budget of the AAC. The premise behind the contribution of the ACC is that by spending additional money for better helicopters and purchasing fewer of the improved aircraft, a more effective force will be deployed for battle. An additional 300,000 gold florins will be provided from The National Technical University in testing facilities and scientists, as well as 3 million gold florins from various private investors. This private money will be rewarded with information for potential long-term relationships, as well as for future innovations and business opportunities.

Prototypes come in lots of two, so 200,000 gold florins must be allocated for each prototype. Labor will be provided by Design Engineer Adam Johnson and Captain Scott Widener. Their effort will not be charged to any department, because their salaries have already been paid.

Question: Who can approve expenditures?

Answer: The team must approve expenditures.

Question: How much can be spent beyond the budget without additional authorization?

Answer: Nothing can be spent beyond the budgeted 18.3 million gold florins.

Question: What are the obstacles and constraints of the project?

Answer: The team must work within the budget and finish within 20 weeks.

Question: What time commitment is expected of the team members?

Answer: Each team member is expected to devote 35 hours per week to the project.

Question: What will happen to each team member's regular job while working on the project?

Answer: Regular work is not to be neglected, but relegated to a secondary importance status.

Question: Is there a Gantt chart for the project?

Answer:

Month	Jan. 2003	Feb. 2003	March 2003	April 2003	May 2003
Define	██				
Measure		██			
Analyze			██		
Improve				██	
Control					██

Question: What are the benefits of the project?

Answer:

- Soft benefits:
  - National unity and pride
  - Feelings of safety from superior machines defending the country
  - Safety of aircrews
- Hard (measurable) benefits as summarized by LNA's Office of Accounting:

	Previous Cost	Improved Cost	Savings
VARIABLE COSTS			
Mission Cost[1]	GF25,000	GF25,000	
Expected Number of Combat Missions per Year	100	100	
Combat Mission Cost per Year	GF2,500,000	GF2,500,000	GF0
Expected Additional Missions to Complete Objectives[2]	20	0	
Additional Mission Cost per Year	GF500,000	GF0	GF500,000
Total Expected Yearly Transportation Costs	GF3,000,000	GF2,500,000	GF500,000
Rocket Cost	GF1,000	GF1,000	
Expected Total Combat Missions per Year[3]	120	100	
Rockets per Mission	24	24	
Total Expected Yearly Ammunition Costs	GF2,880,000	GF2,400,000	GF480,000
Expected Pilot Losses Due to Equipment Failure	10.00%	0.01%	
Expected Total Combat Missions per Year	120	100	
Pilot Training Costs	GF10,000	GF10,000	
Total Actuarial Cost Prediction to Replace Pilots	GF120,000	GF100	GF119,900
TOTAL VARIABLE COSTS TRACKED BY AAC	GF6,000,000	GF4,900,100	GF1,099,900
FIXED COSTS			
Sun Super Catapult Development Programs[4]	GF1,000,000	GF0	
AAC Airport Maintenance and Expansion[5]	GF2,000,000	GF2,000,000	
Total Yearly Fixed Costs	GF3,000,000	GF2,000,000	GF1,000,000
TOTAL COSTS			
Combined Total Variable and Fixed Costs	GF9,000,000	GF6,900,100	GF2,099,900
Benefit of Project	**GF2,099,900**		

GF=gold florin.

[1] The mission cost is known by the accountants, and this takes into account all costs associated with the mission that are not related to weaponry.

[2] Additional missions are based on the current mission failure rate of 20%. The belief is that by getting helicopters that can empty all 24 of their rockets, additional missions will be unnecessary.

[3] Total number of combat missions per year plus additional missions to complete objectives.

[4] The LNA is trying to phase out the Sun Super catapults, and a more successful AAC will allow this phasing out to begin sooner.

[5] The AAC is expanding its capabilities throughout Lilliputia on a 10-year plan.

Each siege that ends sooner due to overwhelming airpower saves approximately 10 million additional gold florins due to less expended equipment, casualties, and all supporting materials. These savings become highly dependent on the number of sieges that actually occur and are considered to be an additional bonus on top of improving the process itself, because they are not guaranteed and are dependent on the speed of winning the battle. Current predictions show that there is a 70% chance that there will be no sieges this year, because the LFF may attack. However, if a force is mobilized, there is a 25% chance that one siege could be completed by year end and a 5% chance of two sieges completed by year end. Consequently, the expected savings due to fewer seiges is GF3,500,000 [(0.7 × 0) + (0.25 × 10,000,000) + (0.05 × 20,000,000)]. With nearly a third of the country currently threatened by LFF forces, additional sieges are almost a certainty. In the end, the project will save GF2,099,900, plus an additional GF 3,500,000 in the first year the helicopter is used by the ACC.

Question: What are the roles and responsibilities of the team members?

Answer:

Role	**Responsibility**
Champion	Howard Gitlow, Brigadier General
Technical Advisor	Edward Popovich, Scientist
Team Leader (Black Belt)	Scott Widener, Captain
Design and Manufacturing Engineer	Adam Johnson, Design Engineer

SIPOC Analysis

SIPOC analysis is a tool used to identify and display how the components of a process fit together. SIPOC is an acronym that stands for Suppliers-Inputs-Processes-Outputs-Customers. The suppliers provide the inputs that the process then uses to create outputs, which are sent to customers.

SIPOC analysis of the ACC helicopter production process is shown in Figure 17.2.

Suppliers	Inputs	Processes	Outputs	Customers
Georgia Pacific	Paper	Helicopter Requisition	Battle Ready Helicopters	Lilliputian National Army
Officemate	Paper Clips	Helicopter Production	Flight Times ≥ 2.6 Seconds	Lilliputian Civilians
3M	Tape	(see Figure 17.3)	Payloads ≥ 24 Rockets	Lilliputian Freedom Fighters
Xerox	Wing Length			
	Body Design	Helicopter Flight		
	Air Crews			
Lilliputian Citizens	Lilliputian Labor			
Lilliputian National Army	Maintenace Crews	Helicopter Repair	Repaired Helicopters	

FIGURE 17.2 SIPOC Analysis of the Helicopter Production Process

A flowchart of the ACC helicopter production process is shown in Figure 17.3.

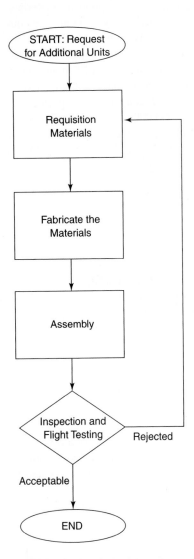

FIGURE 17.3 Executive Flowchart of the Current Production Process

The outputs from the SIPOC analysis are potential critical-to-quality (CTQ) characteristics for the Six Sigma project.

The helicopter production process requires the equipment shown in Figure 17.4 and consists of a high-density polyethylene cutting board, a utility knife, and a generic straight-edge ruler.

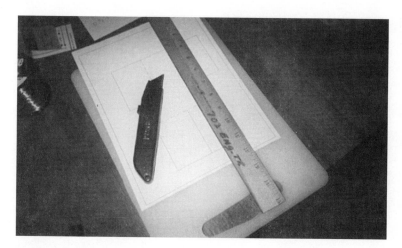

FIGURE 17.4 Manufacturing Equipment

This equipment is then used to cut down the paper into the shape of the template shown in Figure 17.5. The arrows on the figure indicate the directions that the paper is to be folded. A sample of the folding can be seen in Figure 17.6.

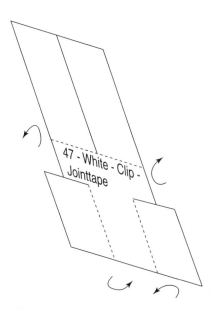

47 - White - Clip - Jointtape

FIGURE 17.5 Helicopter Template and How it is To Be Folded

The completely folded helicopter should look like Figure 17.7.

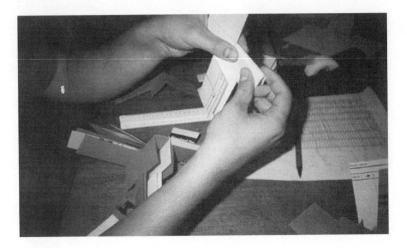

FIGURE 17.6 Folding a Helicopter

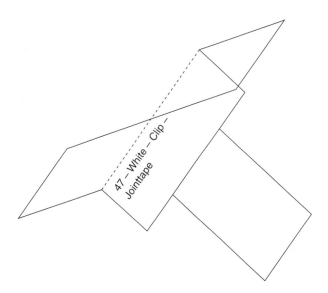

FIGURE 17.7 Isometric View of a Completed Helicopter

VoC Analysis

The information shown in Table 17.3 was attained by interviewing stakeholders of the system concerning their feelings about the current helicopter production process and its outputs. The interviews have been shortened, and key points from each interview are noted. The original words of the stakeholder were left in the original context, so as not to lose their meaning by trying to clean it up and determine the individual stakeholder's intent.

TABLE 17.3 Affinitized Voice of the Customer Information

Selected customer segments	Raw information from customers	Affinitized to key objectives from the National Dashboard
General Quinn	1) Lack of air support is scaring my troops on the ground, leading to low morale. They need to launch at least 24 rockets to clear the LFF positions.	2C
	2) How am I supposed to plan a battle when the helicopter cannot get me any information?	2A
Air Marshal Domi	1) I need to know exactly what these new machines will be able to do.	2B
	2) My current fleet is not up to an acceptable standard because they don't launch all of their rockets.	2B
	3) If the attack comes, I will fight it, with or without your new-fangled machines.	2A
Loadmaster Roberts	1) Any cargo will break unless the descent is slowed, so we have to rely on trucks and wagons.	2B
	2) Moving cargo by air would make deployment much easier!	2A
Pilot Sundin	1) Go to war in these copters? No way! Not until they fly at least 2.6 seconds	2C
Pilot Nolan	1) These things fly like box cars!	2B
	2) How can I retrieve good scouting pictures when I come back to the ground so quickly?	2B
	3) Are they serious about using these for attacks? I need at least 2.6 seconds to fire my ordnance.	2C
Maintenance Crew Chief Healey	1) Will any new designs make these things easier to repair?	2B
Citizen Lumme	1) Whatever … I just want to be safe from attacks.	3C
Citizen Belak	1) I am worried about the safety of my brothers in those choppers.	3C
Citizen Kaberle	1) Attacks are supposedly coming soon.	3C
	2) I believe in our military.	3C

These statements were then affinitized, meaning that groups of statements with similar intents were placed into categories. This was done to assess similarities across different stakeholder groups, as well as to help identify common problems in the process from the stakeholder viewpoint.

In this case, these groups of statements were then related back to the Dashboard shown in Table 17.1 on page 540 to further clarify what actions should be taken and who should be responsible for these.

Project Objective

To develop a better helicopter production process (process) for the LNA's AAC that will increase (direction) the flight time (measure) in mission service to at least 2.6 seconds (goal). This project is to be completed by May 9, 2003 (deadline).

17.3 MEASURE PHASE

Introduction

The measurement phase contains three steps: operationally defining each CTQ, conducting Gage Reproducibility and Repeatability (R&R) studies on each CTQ, and developing a baseline for each CTQ. Each step is presented as follows.

Operationally Defining Each CTQ

From the define phase, the team members decided that there are two CTQs, flight time and payload delivery. However, an interesting cause-and-effect (C & E) relationship appears between the flight time and the payload delivery. A long enough flight time allows for a complete firing of all of the rockets. Consequently, this project will only focus on the flight time CTQ. Flight time needs to be operationally defined so that all stakeholders agree on what constitutes flight time. To accomplish this, three parameters need to be established:

1. Criteria for the flight time
2. Test for the flight time
3. Decision resulting from this test

Criteria for Flight Time: Flight time is defined as the time that the helicopter is supported only by its aerodynamic properties. Therefore, flight time is the time elapsed from a helicopter leaving the test rig until the helicopter hits the ground. Figure 17.8 shows the testing facilities, and Figure 17.9 shows a sample helicopter.

Before discussing the actual test for flight, the facilities and the flight-testing rig were designed to allow all of the helicopters to be tested under the same conditions. The atmosphere is controlled to eliminate significant variations in prevailing winds, temperature, or humidity, which could impact the results. Inside of this testing facility is an altitude standardizer, which is shown in Figure 17.10.

FIGURE 17.8 Testing Facility

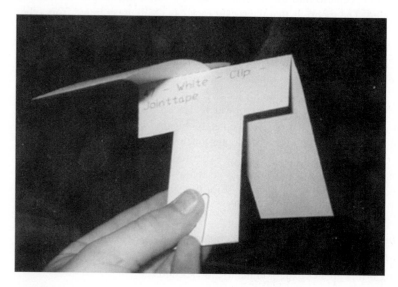

FIGURE 17.9 Sample Helicopter

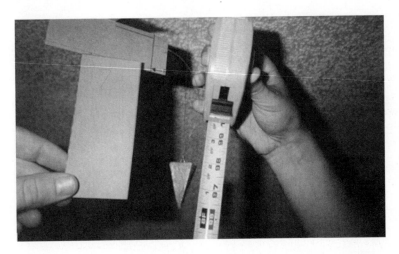

FIGURE 17.10 Altitude Standardizer

This standardizer is used to ensure that all helicopters fly the same distance so that the times can be compared. The helicopter bodies and wings are of different sizes, so the "nose" of the helicopter is lined up with the bottom of the altitude standardizer's plumb bob for dropping. This is especially important, because this should be the first part of the helicopter to hit the ground.

The height of the altitude standardizer is set at 8 feet, which is determined by scaling the actual worst-case battlefield scenario into the laboratory setting. From this height, the rack of rockets needs to be emptied. The theory is that the rocket rack can easily be emptied from other higher altitudes.

In addition, this is also an optimal altitude from which to scout troop movements on the ground. Therefore, maximizing the time in the air with the camera increases the quality of the information that can be returned to the LNA command centers across Lilliputia for further analysis and battle planning.

Timings are taken with a newly calibrated stopwatch. The stopwatch is zeroed out at the beginning of each run and is started when the helicopter is released from the testing rig. The watch is allowed to run until the any part of the helicopter touches the ground.

The time shown on the watch is recorded on the experiment design spreadsheet with the precision of hundredths of a second. A flight time is considered defective if it is less than 2.60 seconds, the lower specification limit as discovered from the stakeholders in Figure 17.2 and Table 17.3 on page 551.

Test for Flight Time: The flight time of each helicopter drop.

Decision for Flight Time: A flight time is defective if it is less than 2.60 seconds. A flight time is conforming if it is greater than or equal to 2.60 seconds.

Conducting a Gage R&R Study of the Flight Time

Lilliputian scientists and statisticians were brought in from around the nation to test the validity of the measurement system for flight time. Each specialist was given a sample film from the drop of the current Prototype 1 aircraft, as well as a randomly chosen new prototypes, 21, 38, and 59. The scientists determined that the measurement system was adequate. However, it needed to be tested for confirmation. Two flight test engineers, Adam and Jill, were chosen to determine the validity of the test method. Adam is the most senior flight testing engineer, and Jill is the least senior flight testing engineer. They were chosen to cover the widest spread of possible experience levels.

Films of the drops were taken to ensure that flight test engineers had the same visual perspectives. In addition, this reduced the number of drops needed by 50% and allowed delegation of that money elsewhere within the budget, instead of further swelling the overhead costs. Based on films of test drops, the engineers were asked to determine the flight time of the helicopter in each trial, using the same stopwatch used in the laboratory. Each scientist observed the same drops, and the results are shown in Table 17.4, blocked by operator, to show the precision of the measurements. The results were then analyzed with a Gage R&R run chart (Figure 17.11).

TABLE 17.4 Raw Data from the Gage R&R Study

	Helicopter #1	Helicopter #21	Helicopter #38	Helicopter #59
	Descent time (sec)	Descent time (sec)	Descent time (sec)	Descent time (sec)
Adam	2.56	2.14	2.29	1.91
Adam	2.63	2.19	2.36	1.93
Adam	2.63	2.19	2.32	**1.82**
Jill	**2.82**	2.18	2.35	1.88
Jill	2.76	2.23	2.28	1.88
Jill	2.63	2.12	2.38	1.94

 HELICOPTER

The Gage R&R run chart in Figure 17.11 gives a visual interpretation as to how the individual measurements compared with each other, by the prototype used in the test, as well as a depiction of how similar the measurements of each inspector were on a given aircraft. The overall range was 1.00 seconds (1.82–2.82 seconds). The ranges between drops by operator were 0.26 seconds (2.56–2.82 seconds) for helicopter 1, which was the baseline prototype. The remaining three prototypes saw similar variation within the test drops. Prototype 59 had a range of 0.12 seconds (1.82–1.94 seconds) between the operators, helicopter 38 had a range of 0.10 seconds (2.28–2.38 seconds), and helicopter 21 had a range of 0.11 seconds (2.12–2.23 seconds). Although this appears to be a very strong measurement system, the statement is qualitative. To validate this

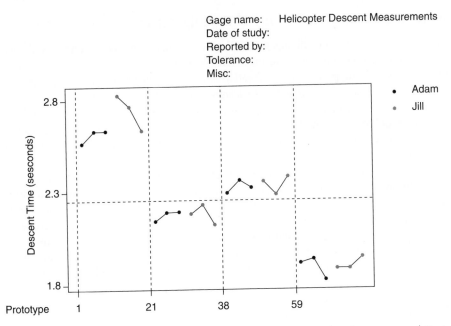

Gage name: Helicopter Descent Measurements
Date of study:
Reported by:
Tolerance:
Misc:

FIGURE 17.11 Minitab Gage R&R Run Chart of Descent Times by Operator and Prototype

observation, a crossed analysis of variance (ANOVA) was run to show the numerical relationships between the variables (see Figure 17.12).

Interpretation of the Minitab Analysis of the Gage R&R

Looking at the upper left panel in Figure 17.12, Components of Variation, the largest source of variation between the measurements is from the prototype, or part, used in the test. The Components of Variation graph indicates that the prototype comprises 96.21% of the entire variation (see the upper left corner of Table 17.5).

This leaves only 3.79% of the remaining variation to account for differences between the operators and their ability to repeat their own measurements. It is of note that the $\overline{X}$ Chart by Operator, shown in lower left panel of Figure 17.12, shows special causes due to the prototype, 1 or 59, as the major sources of all variation. The left middle panel of Figure 17.12 shows the R-chart by Operator to be in control, indicating that the variation is common variation. This reveals that the range within drops for helicopters are in control whereas the drop times are out of control. They are out of control because the two prototypes have different flight characteristics that generate different flight times. The ranges are in control because the drops are reproducible and repeatable. The R-chart shows that the time differences for the same test can be almost 0.3 seconds, indicating that if the test results are near 2.6 seconds, there may not be assurance that the minimum requirement of 2.6 seconds is actually met. The discrimination between test results is no greater than 0.3 seconds, meaning two test results that differ less than that are not necessar-

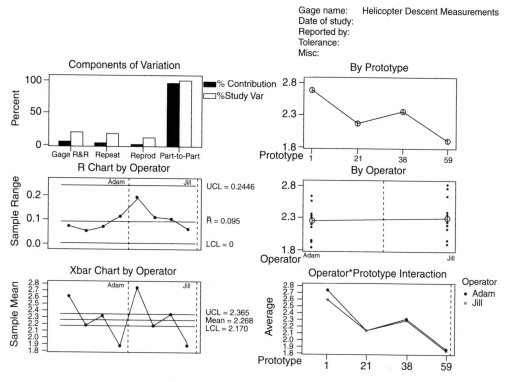

FIGURE 17.12 Minitab Gage R&R ANOVA Output

TABLE 17.5 Percentage of Contribution Table

%Contribution

Source	VarComp	(of VarComp)
Total Gage R&R	0.00411	3.79
Repeatability	0.00293	2.70
Reproducibility	0.00118	1.09
Operator	0.00035	0.32
Operator*Prototype	0.00083	0.77
Part-to-Part	0.10437	96.21
Total Variation	0.10848	100.00

ily implying a true difference. In that case, films of each test will be used to verify actual results that are near 2.6 seconds, similar to using a film at a horse race to determine the winner in a "photo finish."

The By Prototype chart, the upper right panel of Figure 17.12, and the By Operator chart, middle right panel of Figure 17.12, also verify that the variation results from the prototypes and not operators. The fact that there is a slope in the line in the By Prototype panel indicates that the expected mean flight time is affected by the prototype, and the fact that the line in the By Operator panel is nearly horizontal indicates that the expected mean flight time is not affected by the operator.

Finally, in the remaining 3.71% of variation not accounted for by the difference in prototype, there is no evidence of any interactions between prototypes and the operators, as evidenced by the nearly parallel lines in the Operator*Prototype Interaction plot shown in the lower right panel of Figure 17.12. This indicates that only main effect differences exist in the measurements, and further improvements to the measurement scheme are possible and not restrained by an interaction. Some may note that Adam, the more experienced of the two testers, has an average flight time for Prototype 1 that is slightly lower than the mean observed by Jill. This will be monitored during the test to see whether Jill consistently records longer flight times than Adam for those helicopters that tend to fly longer.

However, given that there is only 3.71% variation due to the measurement system, the current measurement system is deemed acceptable, using the 1–10 rule. The 1–10 rule states that a measurement system is acceptable if the variation in the system is less than 1% in the R&R of the measurements. Likewise, if the value is between 1% and 10%, the measurements are questionable but could be used if necessary. Anything over 10% is deemed to be unacceptable. In this case, there is 3.71% variation from the R&R, so this measurement system is marginal for the project. If the VoC (USL–LSL) clearly contains the Voice of the Process (VoP; distribution of the CTQ), which includes measurement error, then the measurement system is adequate, and as a result, a baseline can be established for the CTQ.

Gage R&R standards that arose from the automobile industry use a 10–30 rule, which applies to the standard deviations of the Gage R&R, not the variance component of the Gage R&R. Recall that the standard deviation is the square root of the variance; hence, if the variation percentages goals are 1% and 10%, the goals for the standard deviations are 10% and approximately 30%. Minitab estimates the standard deviation percentages with what is labeled *% Study Var,* and the variance components are labeled *%Contribution.* Variance components add up to the total; hence, the total percentage is 100%. Standard deviation percentages for the components of Gage R&R and parts will sum to more than 100% because they are not actually percentages; they are the square root of the %Contribution.

Develop a Baseline for Each CTQ

All Prototype 1 units undergo the same testing as described in the operational definition before being sent to the battlefields. Given the fact that the measurement system already used in the flight testing of the helicopters by the AAC was deemed to be adequate, the current control charts of the Prototype 1 times can be used as a baseline, which come from Figure 17.1 on page 543.

According to Figure 17.1, the mean baseline is 2.320 seconds, and the process is in control with a standard deviation of 0.052 seconds ($\overline{R}/d_2 = 0.05885/1.1317$). From this information and by having a reliable measurement system to produce these results, a histogram can be plotted to determine the shape of the distribution of the current process outputs (see Figure 17.13). Figure 17.13 shows an approximately normal distribution. This is further verified because the *p*-value for the Anderson-Darling normality test is 0.107, as shown in Figure 17.14.

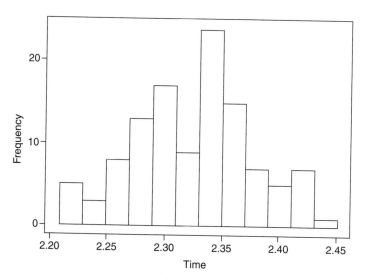

FIGURE 17.13 Minitab Histogram of the Current Process Flight Times

Therefore, flight time can now be explained in terms of process sigmas. Although most time-related tests will yield skewed data, the data shown in Figure 17.13 appears to be normally distributed because the average is far enough above zero with a small standard deviation.

The Define phase stated that the ultimate aim of the process was a flight time of at least 2.6 seconds (LSL) to minimize the unlaunched rockets and their associated expenses. This has repeatedly been a problem plaguing the AAC. This causes additional aircraft and pilots to be placed in harm's way, with the potential for additional losses. Looking at the individual control chart for the current Prototype 1 in Figure 17.1 and noting that the upper control limit is only 2.476 seconds shows that currently, no helicopters are meeting this specification of 2.600 seconds. Note that it is acceptable to use specification limits to compare with control limits for data presented on individual control charts. Therefore, the yield is zero. The resulting defects per million opportunities (DPMO) are calculated, and the DPMO can then be converted into a process sigma value. The results of these calculations are summarized in Table 17.6 on page 561.

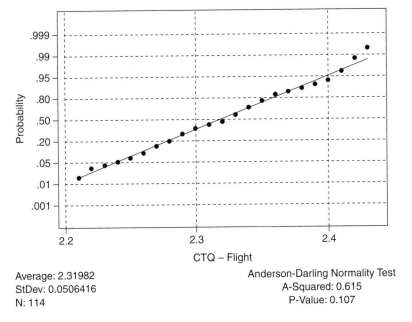

FIGURE 17.14 Minitab Normality Test of the Current Process Outputs

If the current yield is less than 6.68% (in fact, it is 0.00000002%) in a stable and normally distributed process, the process sigma value is negative. For convenience, the current process sigma is set at 0.00 in Table 17.6.

17.4 ANALYZE PHASE

The analyze phase contains five components:

1. Developing a detailed process map or flowchart
2. Constructing operational definitions for each process variable (X)
3. Running a Gage R&R study on each X
4. Developing a baseline for each X
5. Developing hypotheses about the relationships between each CTQ and the Xs

Process Map

The process map is quite detailed and lengthy when compared with Figure 17.3 and is shown in Figure 17.15. On the process map, note that each X has been identified and placed in the step where it is "manufactured" into the process.

TABLE 17.6 Process Sigma Calculation Outputs

CTQ	Yield			DPMO			Process sigma		
	Current	Desired	Gap	Current	Desired	Gap	Current	Desired	Gap
Flight Time	0.00000002%	99.9000000%	99.89999998%	999999.98	1000.00	998999.98	0.00	4.59	4.59

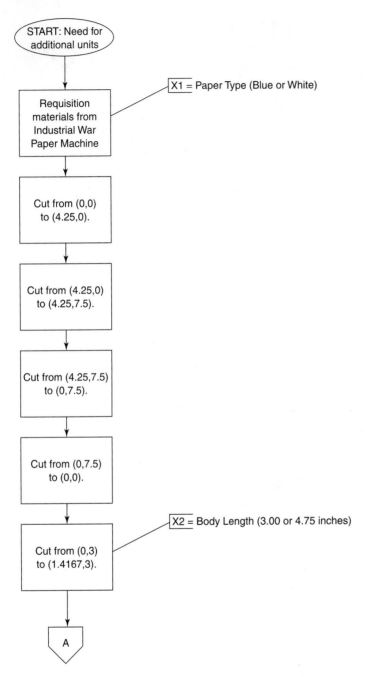

FIGURE 17.15 Flowchart of the LNA ACC Helicopter Construction Process with Xs

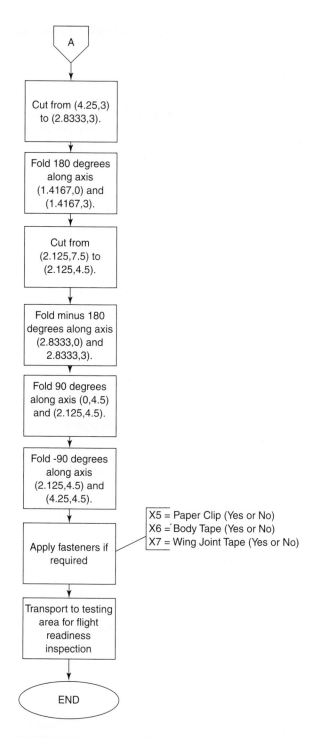

FIGURE 17.15 (Continued)

Operationally Defining Each *X*

Criteria: All of the *X*s are defined in terms of a binary decision as laid out by the engineers from the LNA Aeronautical Laboratories. As a result, Table 17.7, has been used to summarize what the dimensions are for the allowable levels for each *X*. Three of these *X*s are length measurements and are denoted in inches. However, these length measurements remain binary, because they are fixed to two levels.

TABLE 17.7 Levels for the Individual *X*s

Label	Component	Level "low"	Level "high"	Measuring scale	Notes
X1	Paper type	White	Blue	NA	White is a 20-pound bond, and blue is a 24-pound bond paper
X2	Body length	3.00	4.75	Inches	
X3	Body width	1.42	2.00	Inches	
X4	Wing length	3.00	4.75	Inches	
X5	Paper clip	No	Yes	NA	Paper clips are standard office supply clips
X6	Body tape	No	Yes	NA	Wrapped around the body to hold it closed in flight
X7	Wing joint tape	No	Yes	NA	Small square placed on the joint to hold the wings down in flight

Test: Select a given helicopter prototype.

Decision: Identify the properties of all seven components.

Gage R&R Studies of Each *X*

Gage R&R studies were not conducted on the *X*s because they are binary variables and their values are inherently obvious. Therefore, the assumption is that all of the measurements used for the *X*s are acceptable.

Developing Baselines for Each *X*

The *X*s are all binary variables, making it unnecessary to collect baseline data to check for stability.

Relationships Among the *X*s and the CTQ

Given that the relationship between the *X*s and the CTQ is unknown, it is a reasonable assumption that all seven *X*s are contributing factors to the flight time. Therefore, the following relationship is developed to express the flight time as a function of the *X*s.

CTQ = $f(X_1, X_2, X_3, X_4, X_5, X_6, X_7,$ Potential Interactions, Error)

or,

Flight Time = f(Paper Type Effects, Body Length Effects, Body Width Effects, Wing Length Effects, Paper Clip Effects, Body Tape Effects, Wing Joint Tape Effects, Potential Interaction Effects, Error Effects)

A designed experiment will be run in the Improve phase to identify the critical *X*s, establish any interactions among the *X*s, and ultimately, improve the design of the helicopters.

17.5 IMPROVE PHASE

The Improve phase of the DMAIC model has three steps. The first step is to design and run experiments to isolate the significant *X*s and their interactions (see Chapter 13 for details). The second step is to interpret the results of these experiments and to develop settings for the *X*s which optimize the spread, shape, and center of the CTQ(s). Finally, the third step is to test the settings of the *X*s by conducting a pilot study.

Design of Experiments

Designing the Experiment. The designed experiment contained seven *X*s, which were identified in the Analyze phase of the project. The experiment was initially viewed as a full factorial design with a replication, resulting in 2^7 trials run twice, which would have required 256 independent trials.

Realizing that the total material budget for the experiment is 15 million gold florins and that the costs of production are essentially fixed for retooling machines and changing the setups, the LNA's financial analysts have concluded that each prototype, including overhead expenses, cost about 100,000 gold florins, and the testing, including overhead expenses, was an additional 10,000 gold florins. Considering that these numbers included the overhead, which covered salaries of the workers and staff, essentially the entire budget could be dumped into this experiment. This was the AAC's motivation for allocating funds away from helicopter purchases and into development. As a result of this, quick arithmetic showed that 128 total runs were possible, with a small pool of leftover money in the budget to help offset any potential bumps along the way. It is worth noting that these numbers do not include the 3.3 million gold florins that were allocated to the pilot test.

A total of 128 runs for the experiment was compatible with the time constraint, and as a result, it was the number of trials chosen for the experiment. The problem became that of experimental clarity.

Running 128 individual trials in the full factorial design, which would then be replicated, requires a total of 256 individual trials. This will fully show all interactions and relationships between the variables, but it requires too much time and resources. Therefore, reducing the design to a half-fractional factorial, requiring 64 randomized individual trials plus a randomized replication for 128 total individual trials, is a better solution. However, the cost of saving the time and money of the trials is the inability to distinguish between the effects of certain interactions. This is known as *confounding*.

Potential Confounding Problems. The half-fractional factorial design reduces the number of runs by half, but these savings reduce the experiment's clarity in terms of confounding. This 2^{7-1} design has a resolution of VII (see Chapter 13 for a discussion of the resolution of a design). In this case, this means that the main effects and two-way interactions will not be confounded with each other. The main effects are confounded with the six-way interactions, the two-way interactions are confounded with the five-way interactions, and the three-way interactors are confounded with the four-way interactions. This confounding is acceptable because field expertise dictates that high order interactions are safely ignored.

Given that the six-factor interactions are extremely rare, as are five-factor interactions, as previously indicated, the chances of significantly confounding the main effects or the two-factor interactions are very small. The problem lies in the three-factor interactions being confounded by the four-factor interactions. Because three-factor interactions do happen, although not very often, and four-factor interactions are more uncommon than three-factor interactions, the chances of these effectively clouding each other is small, especially when weighed against the costs of running a full factorial to ensure that all of the effects are isolated. Therefore, the Lilliputians have not backed themselves into a corner through confounding as it might seem; instead, they have taken a calculated risk to minimize the cost and duration of the experiment.

Gearing up for Running the Experiment. Two aircraft of each of the 64 prototypes were manufactured. This ensured that two separate aircraft were available for testing, which served two purposes. First, this helped to determine within-prototype variation and second, in the event of a catastrophe, a second unit was available.

The aircraft were manufactured using the same processes as in full scale production. A miniature Industrial War Paper Machine is in the job shop and workers used the same tools as were found on the production lines. The workers tirelessly worked to churn out these aircraft, because time remained a factor.

The work continued furiously using the usual flowchart up to flight testing. Flight testing was done in the laboratory instead of the usual facilities. However, the inspection was still performed to ensure that each aircraft, were it standard, would be fully functional, operable, and ready for use in the field.

The team is also proud to report that although these were special aircraft, the production process in the job shop produced no defective units despite the pressure that the workers were under. They did a great job.

Running the Experiment. The experiment was run in a laboratory similar to the ones used on the production lines. As each aircraft was manufactured, it was marked with a number corresponding to which aircraft it was on the design layout. As an example, the aircraft marked 39 was the thirty-ninth aircraft on the design layout, which also meant it would be the thirty-ninth aircraft tested. The design layout was randomized to curb the effects of lurking variables, so the thirty-ninth aircraft was the thirty-ninth random aircraft, not the thirty-ninth aircraft from the standard order of a 2^{7-1} fractional factorial experiment. Each aircraft was individually dropped, and the times were recorded and saved in a Minitab worksheet.

Interpretation of the Experiments

Preliminary Interpretation. Figure 17.16 shows a Pareto chart (standardized effects) indicating which variables impacted the flight time most significantly.

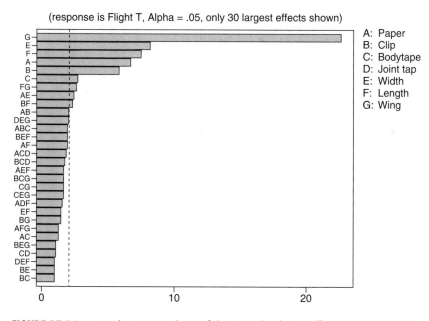

FIGURE 17.16 Minitab Pareto Chart of the Standardized Effects

The larger bars, or the ones that extend past the dotted line, which represents the 5% level of significance, are potential *X*s of interest. The main effects, with the exception of D, are the most important in the explanation of the *X*s' impact on the flight time. Furthermore, Figure 17.16 shows that there are potentially four two-way interactions: *FG, AE, BF,* and *AB,* that could be working in this design.

In-Depth Analysis. At this stage, the group had an idea of where to look to improve the flowchart for the process, but confirmation was needed. This involved actually studying the ANOVA output for the experiment and digging out the statistically significant factors.

The second part of Table 17.8, "Analysis of Variance for Flight," numerically reiterates the impact of the two-way interactions and the main effects that was illustrated in the Figure 17.16. This gives some further insight as to what will actually be found in the first part of Table 17.8, "Estimated Effects and Coefficients for Flight Time."

TABLE 17.8 Original Minitab ANOVA Output

Estimated Effects and Coefficients for Flight Time (coded units)

Term	Effect	Coef	SE Coef	T	P
Constant		2.10523	0.01089	193.39	0.000
Paper	0.14734	0.07367	0.01089	6.77	0.000
Clip	−0.12797	−0.06398	0.01089	−5.88	0.000
Bodytape	−0.05828	−0.02914	0.01089	−2.68	0.009
Jointtape	−0.00516	−0.00258	0.01089	−0.24	0.814
Width	−0.17797	−0.08898	0.01089	−8.17	0.000
Length	−0.16391	−0.08195	0.01089	−7.53	0.000
Wing	0.49297	0.24648	0.01089	22.64	0.000
Paper*Clip	−0.04484	−0.02242	0.01089	−2.06	0.043
Paper*Bodytape	−0.02641	−0.01320	0.01089	−1.21	0.230
Paper*Jointtape	−0.01828	−0.00914	0.01089	−0.84	0.404
Paper*Width	−0.05172	−0.02586	0.01089	−2.38	0.021
Paper*Length	−0.04078	−0.02039	0.01089	−1.87	0.066
Paper*Wing	−0.01328	−0.00664	0.01089	−0.61	0.544
Clip*Bodytape	0.01953	0.00977	0.01089	0.90	0.373
Clip*Jointtape	−0.01859	−0.00930	0.01089	−0.85	0.396
Clip*Width	0.01984	0.00992	0.01089	0.91	0.365
Clip*Length	−0.04984	−0.02492	0.01089	−2.29	0.025
Clip*Wing	0.03016	0.01508	0.01089	1.39	0.171
Bodytape*Jointtape	−0.02141	−0.01070	0.01089	−0.98	0.329
Bodytape*Width	−0.01797	−0.00898	0.01089	−0.83	0.412
Bodytape*Length	0.01672	0.00836	0.01089	0.77	0.445
Bodytape*Wing	0.03359	0.01680	0.01089	1.54	0.128
Jointtap*Width	−0.01797	−0.00898	0.01089	−0.83	0.412
Jointtap*Length	0.01672	0.00836	0.01089	0.77	0.445
Jointtap*Wing	−0.00703	−0.00352	0.01089	−0.32	0.748
Width*Length	−0.03047	−0.01523	0.01089	−1.40	0.166

(continued)

TABLE 17.8 Original Minitab ANOVA Output (continued)

Estimated Effects and Coefficients for Flight Time (coded units)

Term	Effect	Coef	SE Coef	T	P
Width*Wing	0.00078	0.00039	0.01089	0.04	0.971
Length*Wing	−0.05516	−0.02758	0.01089	−2.53	0.014
Paper*Clip*Bodytape	0.04141	0.02070	0.01089	1.90	0.062
Paper*Clip*Jointtape	0.00078	0.00039	0.01089	0.04	0.971
Paper*Clip*Width	−0.00391	−0.00195	0.01089	−0.18	0.858
Paper*Clip*Length	−0.00297	−0.00148	0.01089	−0.14	0.892
Paper*Clip*Wing	0.01641	0.00820	0.01089	0.75	0.454
Paper*Bodytape*Jointtape	−0.03953	−0.01977	0.01089	−1.82	0.074
Paper*Bodytape*Width	0.01703	0.00852	0.01089	0.78	0.437
Paper*Bodytape*Length	0.00734	0.00367	0.01089	0.34	0.737
Paper*Bodytape*Wing	−0.00766	−0.00383	0.01089	−0.35	0.726
Paper*Jointtap*Width	−0.01672	−0.00836	0.01089	−0.77	0.445
Paper*Jointtap*Length	0.03234	0.01617	0.01089	1.49	0.142
Paper*Jointtap*Wing	0.00297	0.00148	0.01089	0.14	0.892
Paper*Width*Length	0.03453	0.01727	0.01089	1.59	0.118
Paper*Width*Wing	−0.01609	−0.00805	0.01089	−0.74	0.462
Paper*Length*Wing	−0.02766	−0.01383	0.01089	−1.27	0.209
Clip*Bodytape*Jointtape	0.03641	0.01820	0.01089	1.67	0.099
Clip*Bodytape*Width	−0.01141	−0.00570	0.01089	−0.52	0.602
Clip*Bodytape*Length	−0.01297	−0.00648	0.01089	−0.60	0.553
Clip*Bodytape*Wing	−0.03422	−0.01711	0.01089	−1.57	0.121
Clip*Jointtap*Width	−0.01516	−0.00758	0.01089	−0.70	0.489
Clip*Jointtap*Length	0.00078	0.00039	0.01089	0.04	0.971
Clip*Jointtap*Wing	0.00391	0.00195	0.01089	0.18	0.858
Clip*Width*Length	0.04109	0.02055	0.01089	1.89	0.064
Clip*Width*Wing	0.02172	0.01086	0.01089	1.00	0.322
Clip*Length*Wing	0.00328	0.00164	0.01089	0.15	0.881
Bodytape*Jointtap*Width	−0.00422	−0.00211	0.01089	−0.19	0.847
Bodytape*Jointtap*Length	−0.00641	−0.00320	0.01089	−0.29	0.770
Bodytape*Jointtap*Wing	−0.01391	−0.00695	0.01089	−0.64	0.525
Bodytape*Width*Length	0.00766	0.00383	0.01089	0.35	0.726
Bodytape*Width*Wing	−0.03359	−0.01680	0.01089	−1.54	0.128
Bodytape*Length*Wing	0.01734	0.00867	0.01089	0.80	0.429
Jointtap*Width*Length	0.02078	0.01039	0.01089	0.95	0.343
Jointtap*Width*Wing	−0.04234	−0.02117	0.01089	−1.94	0.056
Jointtap*Length*Wing	−0.00516	−0.00258	0.01089	−0.24	0.814
Width*Length*Wing	0.00703	0.00352	0.01089	0.32	0.748

(continued)

TABLE 17.8 Original Minitab ANOVA Output (continued)

Estimated Effects and Coefficients for Flight Time (coded units)

Analysis of Variance for Flight Time (coded units)

Source	DF	Seq SS	Adj SS	Adj MS	F	P
Main Effects	7	10.9781	10.9781	1.56830	103.40	0.000
2–Way Interactions	21	0.6043	0.6043	0.02878	1.90	0.026
3–Way Interactions	35	0.5369	0.5369	0.01534	1.01	0.473
Residual Error	64	0.9707	0.9707	0.01517		
Pure Error	64	0.9708	0.9708	0.01517		
	Total		127	13.0900		

The first part of Table 17.8 shows the *p*-values for each main effect and interaction component. All effects that are statistically significant are indicated by a *p*-value less than 0.05. The statistically significant main effects and interactions have been condensed in Table 17.9.

TABLE 17.9 Significant Effects from Table 17.8

Term	Effect	Coef	SE Coef	T	P
Constant		2.10523	0.01089	193.39	0.000
Paper	0.14734	0.07367	0.01089	6.77	0.000
Clip	−0.12797	−0.06398	0.01089	−5.88	0.000
Bodytape	−0.05828	−0.02914	0.01089	−2.68	0.009
Width	−0.17797	−0.08898	0.01089	−8.17	0.000
Length	−0.16391	−0.08195	0.01089	−7.53	0.000
Wing	0.49297	0.24648	0.01089	22.64	0.000
Paper*Clip	−0.04484	−0.02242	0.01089	−2.06	0.043
Paper*Width	−0.05172	−0.02586	0.01089	−2.38	0.021
Clip*Length	−0.04984	−0.02492	0.01089	−2.29	0.025
Length*Wing	−0.05516	−0.02758	0.01089	−2.53	0.014

Figure 17.17 shows that wing length is the most significant *X*. Paper, clip, width, and length are of secondary importance. Body taping and joint taping are the least significant of all the factors.

Formulation of a Design. All interactions supercede all main effects in determining the value at which each individual design factor should be set. With this in mind, you should start at the bottom of Table 17.9 and work up, analyzing each significant interaction. The first interaction is Length*Wing and looking at the interaction plot in Figure 17.18, you can see that the longer wing, 4.75 inches, and the shorter length, 3.00 inches, optimize the flight time, because that is the highest point within the box where the Length and Wing columns or rows intersect. Both

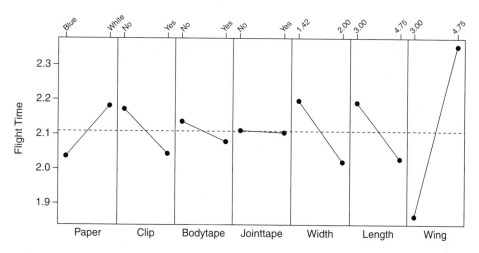

FIGURE 17.17 Minitab Main Effects Plot (Data Means) of Flight Times for the Helicopters

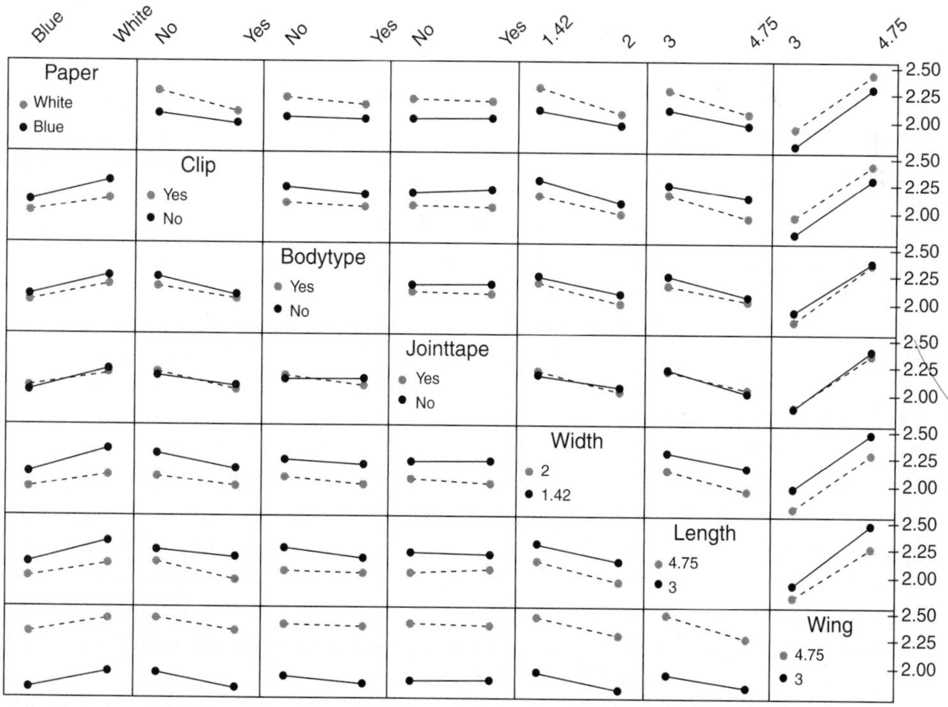

FIGURE 17.18 Minitab Interaction Plot on Flight Times for the Helicopters

combinations in the table will yield the same result, because the two plots are inverses of each other. The next interaction is Clip*Length. Using the same methods to find the highest point within the relevant boxes on Figure 17.18, the length should be 3.00 inches, and no paper clip should be used. Continuing up Table 17.9, the next interaction is Paper*Width. Using the relevant boxes in Figure 17.18 indicates that the width of the helicopter's body should be 1.42 inches and that the helicopter should be made with white paper. The final interaction is Paper*Clip. Using Figure 17.18 indicates that white paper should be used with no paper clip. These results are then compiled and summarized in Table 17.10.

TABLE 17.10 Factors Determined Through Analysis of Interactions

Variable name	Variable	Optimizing value
Paper	Paper type	White paper
Clip	Paper clip	No clip
Bodytape	Body tape	Unknown
Jointtape	Joint tape	Unknown
Width	Body width	1.42 Inches
Length	Body length	3.00 Inches
Wing	Wing length	4.75 Inches

In Table 17.10 there is no indication for the factors labeled *Bodytape* or *Jointtape*. This is because there were no interactions for these factors. As a result, no known information can be displayed.

When all of the interactions from Table 17.9 have been analyzed, the *main effects* or *single-factor effects* can be analyzed. The analysis for these is found in Figure 17.17. The first of these effects from Table 17.9 is *Wing*. Consulting Figure 17.17, the optimal wing length is 4.75 inches. This is consistent with the wing length that was determined by analyzing the relevant interaction. If there is a conflict between the analyses of the interactions and the main effects, in general, the interaction effect is given consideration first.

The next two items found in Table 17.9, *Length* and *Width,* show that the analysis of the main effects for best results is consistent with the interaction analysis. However, the next item in Table 17.9, *Bodytape,* must be considered.

Bodytape is listed as one of the unknowns in Table 17.10. Therefore, the main effect is relevant to determining the level for the factor in the final design of the aircraft. Consulting Figure 17.17, observe that in the Bodytape box, the line is tipped slightly up on the left side. Reading the top shows that the high side is associated with no taping; therefore, the main effect indicates that there should be no tape on the body. This value can then be added to the table for the final design.

Continuing along with the analysis of Table 17.9, two more factors are found, *Clip* and *Paper,* yet both of these were determined by interaction. A summary of the analysis of Table 17.9 to achieve a final design is shown in Table 17.11.

The problem that remains is that there is still no solution to the joint tape problem, which is listed as an unknown in Table 17.11. Because this was not listed as a significant factor in either the interactions or the main effects, the level of this factor is essentially irrelevant to the design. Ideally,

TABLE 17.11 Final Design Parameters Based on Main Effect and Interaction Analysis

Variable name	Variable	Optimizing value
Paper	Paper type	White paper
Clip	Paper clip	No clip
Bodytape	Body tape	No tape
Jointtape	Joint tape	Unknown
Width	Body width	1.42 Inches
Length	Body length	3.00 Inches
Wing	Wing length	4.75 Inches

the AAC would like to eliminate costs, and as a result, not taping the joint would save some labor and extra material. Furthermore, this decision is justified by the main effect shown in Figure 17.17 related to joint tape. The line in that box is almost horizontal, indicating no effect, hence its lack of significance. (If there is some other CTQ that is impacted by joint tape, such as the time to provide helicopter maintenance, it is reasonable to consider taping the joint. In our case, we do not see any reason to use joint tape.). Therefore, the finalized design parameters, taking into account interactions, main effects, and cost-cutting moves, are summarized in Table 17.12.

TABLE 17.12 Design Parameters for New Aircraft

Variable name	Variable	Optimizing value
Paper	Paper type	White paper
Clip	Paper clip	No clip
Bodytape	Body tape	No tape
Jointtape	Joint tape	No tape
Width	Body width	1.42 Inches
Length	Body length	3.00 Inches
Wing	Wing length	4.75 Inches

Pilot Study

The final section of the Improve phase is taking the optimized design and conducting a pilot study to determine its effectiveness in improving the distribution of the CTQ. A revised flowchart can be seen in Figure 17.19.

A scaled production line was assembled and the new improved prototypes were built.

It was determined that the new helicopters required 62 man-days to build versus the previous 60 man-days, due to complications with the longer wing structures. The chief concern of the LNA and the AAC was the flight times of these new aircraft.

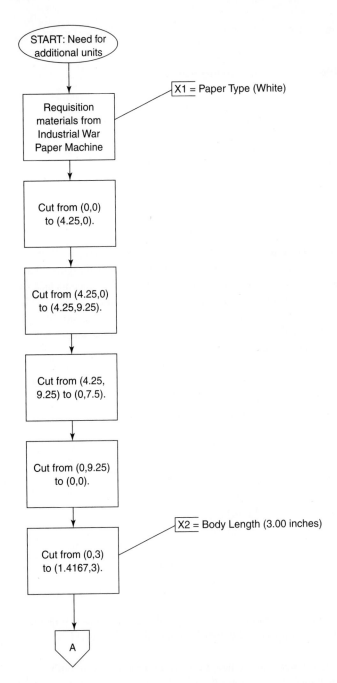

FIGURE 17.19 Improved LNA ACC Helicopter Construction Flowchart

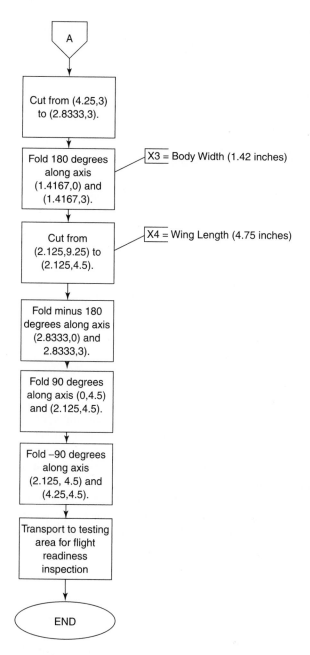

FIGURE 17.19 (Continued)

As each helicopter rolled off the line, it received the same tests as in a full-scale production version. The results of those flight times are shown in Figure 17.20.

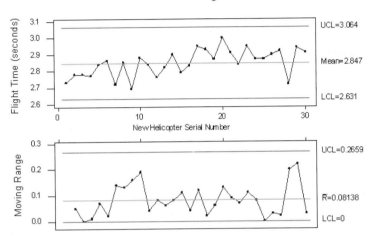

FIGURE 17.20 Minitab I and MR Chart of Flight Times for Helicopters Built Based on the Improved Flowchart

The new flowchart has resulted in a stable process, with a lower control limit above the lower specification limit of 2.60 seconds and with a much higher mean flight time than the mean flight time of 2.320 seconds from the original process shown in Figure 17.15. However, the variation has increased as a result of this upward shift in flight time; $\bar{R}$ has increased from 0.05885 seconds in Figure 17.15 to 0.08138 seconds in Figure 17.19. When the variation increases as the mean time increases, this is often indicative of a skewed time distribution. However, the skewness in time distributions is usually to the right (greater values) side. In other words, higher values may appear as part of the new process, but that is acceptable because the goal was to exceed 2.6 seconds.

The flight times have improved significantly. Figure 17.21, shows the distributions of the former Prototype 1 units and the newly developed units.

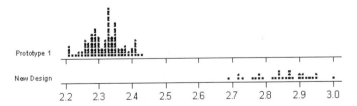

FIGURE 17.21 Minitab Dot Plot Comparing the Distributions of the New Helicopters Against Prototype 1

TABLE 17.13 Process Capability with the New Design

CTQ	Yield			DPMO			Sigma		
	Current	Desired	Gap	Current	Desired	Gap	Current	Desired	Gap
Flight Time	99.9088600%	99.9000000%	−0.0088600%	911.14	1000.00	−88.86	4.62	4.59	−0.03

The key item from Figure 17.21 is that the mean of the distribution has shifted upward, which was the primary goal of the project; unfortunately, the amount of dispersion in the measurements has also increased.

Based on this information from the pilot study, the new flowchart is confirmed as being improved, as shown in Table 17.13, and now must be implemented for use by the AAC so that the new helicopters can be delivered as quickly as possible.

17.6 CONTROL PHASE

The Control phase is comprised of four steps:

1. Standardization
2. Mistake-proofing
3. Documentation
4. Giving control of the process back to the process owner

Standardization

Standardization was not viewed to be a significant problem, given that the process already operates from a single flowchart. Reasonable care will be taken to ensure that the new process flowchart is posted and incorporated on the production floor. Further problems will be addressed in the rest of the Control phase.

Mistake-Proofing

Team members identified potential risk elements that could be carried through the process by using failure mode effects analysis (FMEA). These risk elements are:

1. Employees not being educated about the new wing length
2. Employees folding the body in the wrong directions, i.e., folding at positive 180 degrees for both folds or vice versa
3. Employees folding the wings in the same direction, i.e., folding both wings at positive 90 degrees or vice versa
4. Employees folding the wings at angles other than ± 90 degrees
5. Management or the process owner tampering with the process

Table 17.14 shows the FMEA for the helicopter production process. Each of the risk elements is subjected to a rating on a 1–10 scale on likelihood of occurrence, severity, and likelihood of detection, with high numbers being more problematic. The risk priority number (RPN) is then calculated as the product of those three inputs.

TABLE 17.14 Failure Mode Effects Analysis (FMEA)

Risk elements	Failure mode	Likelihood of occurrence	Severity	Likelihood of detection	RPN	Action	Likelihood of occurrence	Severity	Likelihood of detection	RPN
1) Employee awareness of wing length	Incorrect wing length	8	9	5	360	Helicopter education seminar	5	5	4	100
2) Incorrect body folds	Single-edge folds	6	2	2	24	Redesign of template and warning sign with picture of correct fold	2	2	2	8
3) Incorrect wing folds by direction	Wings facing the same direction	2	10	1	20	Redesign of template and integration of wing tolerance tool	1	10	1	10
4) Incorrect wing folds by angle	Unbalanced wings	9	3	5	135	Integration of wing tolerance tool	2	3	1	6
5) Process tampering	Process spiraling into chaos	7	8	6	336	New process flow-chart and control plan	5	5	6	150

Risk Element 1—Employee Awareness of the New Wing Length—RPN = 360.
Employee education will alleviate many of the employee awareness problems concerning the
new wing length by teaching the employees exactly how their jobs relate to the operation and
structure of the entire helicopter. This awareness can be instilled through a short one-day training
course. This can help to reduce, but not eliminate, the ignorance as decisions come down to the
individual employees on the production floor.

Another measure that could be implemented to avoid confusion and potential mistakes
about the wing length would be to lock in the calibrations of the War Paper Machine (see Risk element
4) such that only one wing length could be cut. This would remove the wing length decision
from the employees and could reduce the RPN to 100. Furthermore, a completed mockup of
the helicopter can be kept on display nearby for quick visual comparison and as a guide.

Risk Element 5—Tampering with the Process—RPN = 336. The process can deteriorate
if the Process Owner unjustifiably tampers with it. Therefore, the Process Owner will be
thoroughly educated with regard to the impact of process tampering by performing the famous
funnel experiment [Reference 2]. The RPN should drop to 150, based on the educational program.
This remains a very real potential risk and should be monitored.

Risk Element 4—Incorrect Wing Folds by Angle—RPN = 135. Folding the wings at
the wrong angle is a definite problem because the Lilliputian workers cannot reliably fold at a
90-degree angle. However, if this happens, the helicopter can still fly, and this problem can easily
be circumvented using the "wing tolerance tool." This is a tool that was designed by the
Lilliputian Engineering Corps following the Six Sigma group's specifications. The angle of the
wings must be within one degree of specification, 90 degrees, for the tool to fit onto the helicopter.
A sketch of the specifications for the wing tolerance tool is shown in Figure 17.22.

Figure 17.23 illustrates the use of the wing tolerance tool.

The wing tolerance tool dictates that a wing be within one degree of 90 degrees, the current
engineering tolerance. This tool is designed so that employees can slide it onto the helicopter
from both sides. If the tool fits, the wings are within one degree of nominal. It also ensures that
they are folded in the correct directions, which relates back to risk element 3. The wing tolerance
tool creates a non–value-added mass inspection step in the manufacturing process. Mass inspection
should be used only if the cost of inspection divided by the cost of a dysfunctional helicopter
is less than the percentage of helicopters that are defective. This is determined by using the *kp*
rule for a stable process [see Reference 2].

$$\frac{\text{Cost of Inspection}}{\text{Cost of Defect}} > \text{Percent Defective} \Rightarrow 0\% \text{ inspection and}$$

$$\frac{\text{Cost of Inspection}}{\text{Cost of Defect}} < \text{Percent Defective} \Rightarrow 100\% \text{ inspection}$$

Figure 17.24 on page 582 shows a stable *p*-chart indicating that approximately 10% of old helicopters
exhibited defective wing angles ($\bar{p} = 0.10$). The cost of inspection is very low, (GF50 per
inspection).

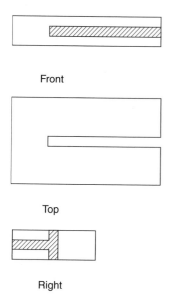

Front

Top

Right

FIGURE 17.22 Wing Tolerance Tool Specifications

The cost of building a defective helicopter may include the cost of unlaunched rockets because a defective wing can have an adverse impact on flight time. The worst case is that is may cost lives due to the opportunity cost of not launching rockets. This cost far exceeds GF500. Therefore, mass inspection is justified and the wing tolerance tool is to be used.

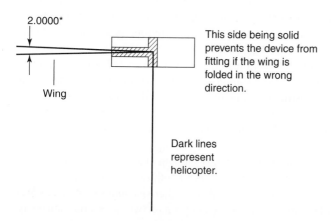

FIGURE 17.23 Wing Tolerance Tool in Use

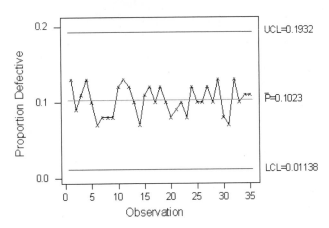

FIGURE 17.24 Minitab *p*-Chart of Defective Wing Angles

$$\left[\frac{\text{Cost of inspection}}{\text{Cost of defect}}\right] < p$$

$$\left[\frac{\text{GF50}}{\text{Cost of defect}} < 0.10\right]$$

Cost of defect > GF500

Given these measures, risk element 4 can almost be eliminated, and as a result, the RPN drops to a value of 6.

Risk Element 2—Incorrect Body Folds—RPN = 24. The problem of folding the body in the wrong directions can be circumvented by requiring employees to check that the body has two edges when inspecting from either side. If the folds are made improperly, one side will only have one edge, and the other side has two edges, as shown in Figure 17.25.

Figure 17.25 will be posted on the production floor and will be included in the training manual. In addition to this common-sense circumvention measure for risk element 2, there is an additional precaution that incorporates instructions into the design, as illustrated in Figure 17.26.

Employees should be able to read the word *Outside* and should not be able to read the word *Inside* on a completed helicopter. However, this is not a substitute for the first control measure because this precaution is not capable of preventing the body folding problem by itself.

Although it may seem a simpler solution to have text on both sides of the paper, the War Paper Machine does not replicate designs that require objects on both sides of the paper. Forcing it to do so would create an endless cycle of recalibration that is otherwise unnecessary. The War Paper Machine prints on only one side of the paper and cannot print on two sides simultaneously. After printing the first side, an employee would need to determine placement of the original design so that it lines up with the placement of the already printed design for manufacturing. Then

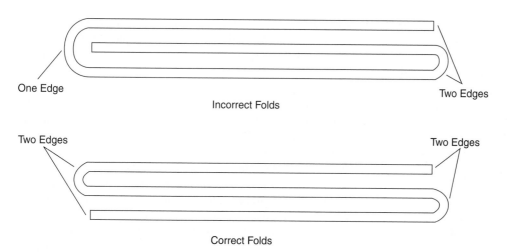

One Edge

Two Edges

Incorrect Folds

Two Edges

Two Edges

Correct Folds

FIGURE 17.25 Correct and Incorrect Body Folds

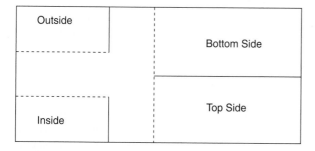

FIGURE 17.26 New War Paper Design

the paper that has one side printed would have to be evenly fed back into the War Paper Machine. The design on both sides of the paper would need to be in perfect alignment for this to work. Figure 17.27 shows a picture of the War Paper Machine.

FIGURE 17.27 The War Paper Machine

With regard to aesthetic and operational consistency, the helicopters are to be painted within LNA convention. Therefore, the words will not be visible at the time of deployment.

Given these precautionary measures, risk element 2 can almost be eliminated as well, and as a result, the RPN drops to 8.

Risk Element 3—Incorrect Wing Folds by Direction—RPN = 20. This risk is catastrophic to the helicopter and its pilot, but it is blatantly obvious with even the most routine inspection because it will appear as though the helicopter is missing a wing. Because of easy detection, this has not been a problem in the past. However, reducing the risk is quite simple. The design of the helicopter template has been modified to make it easier to determine folds, as shown in Figure 17.26. The words *Bottom Side* should be visible only from below the helicopter and vice versa for *Top Side*. The new design should be communicated to all relevant employees.

A wing tolerance tool was developed for risk element 4, incorrect wing folds by angle, that will provide an additional control for risk element 3. Use of the wing tolerance tool will make it nearly impossible for incorrect wing folds to go undetected. Therefore, the RPN drops to 10.

It is worth noting that all of these items do not directly impact the new flowchart for the helicopter construction process that was generated in the Improve phase, but are instead supplemental, in that they impact the flowcharts of other processes. For example, the redesigned templates would change the helicopter tool and die flowchart, and the helicopter construction employee training flowchart would need to be updated to account for teaching the new body-folding mechanisms, as well as a thorough understanding of how the helicopter works.

Documentation

The primary piece of documentation required is the new flowchart that was generated in the Improve phase. This flowchart needs to be inserted into all relevant training manuals, as well as into any standard operating procedures kept on the production floor. Also included among the documentation items that should be on the production floor are copies of all of the control charts so that the actual process outputs can be monitored. Operational definitions should be in all relevant training manuals and distributed. ISO documentation needs to include the new standard operating procedure (see Figure 17.15 on page 562).

Returning Process Control to the Process Owner

The final step of the Control phase is returning control of the process back to the Process Owner which requires a control plan so that the process improvements are not lost. A big piece of this control plan is the documentation described in the previous section. A copy of the revised flowchart must go to the Process Owner for future planning for the iterations of the Plan-Do-Study-Act cycle, also known as the PDSA or Deming Cycle.

Control charts are also part of the control plan. Employees must be trained in how to use these charts. By having the charts in progress, there will be less resistance to the change because employees simply have to keep the new system going instead of developing a whole new system. This can also be used as a way to show commitment from management and the LNA that this is a serious change and not a new manufacturing fad.

The final part of the control plan is to make sure that the Process Owner has adequate help taking over the process. The Process Owner and his or her employees need to be able to get in contact with the Six Sigma Black Belt in the event that he or she runs into trouble or becomes confused as to what to do. Keeping lines of communication open is key to making sure that the process does not revert back to a state of chaos.

This concludes the project. This process will now be turned over to the Process Owner with control plans for future PDSA cycles, and the team will now disband, celebrate its success, and take on other projects.

SUMMARY

The purpose of this chapter was to demonstrate an application of the DMAIC model. This was done by breaking each phase into a manageable set of components to improve a fictional helicopter production process. This chapter can be used as a model for other Six Sigma projects, as well as a guide to the use of selected Six Sigma tools and methods.

REFERENCES

1. Box, G.E.P., "Teaching Engineers Experimental Design with a Paper Helicopter," *Quality Engineering,* 4, 3, 1992, pp. 453–459.

2. Gitlow, H. G., A. Oppenheim, R. Oppenheim, and D. M. Levine, *Quality Management* 3rd ed. (New York: McGraw-Hill-Irwin, 2005).

3. Johnson, A., Widener, S., Popovich, E., Niggley, J., and Gitlow, H., A "Six Sigma" Black Belt Case Study: G.E.P. Box's Paper Helicopter Experiment—Part A, *Quality Engineering,* 2004.

4. Johnson, A., Widener, S., Popovich, E., and Gitlow, H., A "Six Sigma" Black Belt Case Study: G.E.P. Box's Paper Helicopter Experiment—Part B, *Quality Engineering,* 2004.

SIX SIGMA CERTIFICATION

SIX SIGMA CHAMPION CERTIFICATION AT THE UNIVERSITY OF MIAMI

CHAPTER OUTLINE

LEARNING OBJECTIVES

After reading this chapter, you will be able to:

* Understand the procedure for Six Sigma champion training and certification at the University of Miami
* Study sample questions and answers for the Six Sigma Champion examination at the University of Miami

INTRODUCTION

At this point, you are probably interested in obtaining certification as a Six Sigma Champion or Green Belt. This chapter provides information on certification as a Six Sigma Champion at the University of Miami. Six Sigma Green Belt certification at the University of Miami is discussed in Chapter 19.

The Department of Management Science, the Institute for the Study of Quality, and the McLamore Executive Education Center, all of the University of Miami, jointly offer Six Sigma education, training, and certification. The objective of the Six Sigma program at the University of Miami is to provide a comprehensive, fair, and independent source for Six Sigma education and training, certification examination, project review, and ultimately, Six Sigma certification. You can obtain information about Six Sigma at the University of Miami by going to the following URL:

http://sba07.bus.miami.edu/dev_new/sections/exec/six_sigma/

18.1 CERTIFICATION AT THE UNIVERSITY OF MIAMI

There are six types of Six Sigma certifications offered through the University of Miami:

1. Champion
2. Yellow Belt
3. Green Belt
4. Brown Belt
5. Black Belt
6. Master Black Belt

A Champion is an individual who wishes to become aware of the theory and practice of Six Sigma management and can review projects, remove impediments to projects, and secure adequate resources and support for projects. A Yellow Belt is an individual who is aware of the theory and practice of Six Sigma and can provide support to team members (for example, data collection) but is not sufficiently trained in statistical methods to perform the duties of a Six Sigma process improvement team member. A Yellow Belt has passed the Champion and Green Belt certification examinations but has not completed a Six Sigma project. A Green Belt is an individual who understands statistical methods and is a member of one or more Six Sigma process improvement teams. She or he is not sufficiently trained to lead a complex Six Sigma team but is trained to lead a simple Six Sigma project. A Green Belt has passed the Six Sigma Champion and Green Belt certification examinations and has completed a Six Sigma project. A Brown Belt is an individual who has a deep understanding of statistical methods and can lead a team. She or he is a Green Belt and has passed the Black Belt certification examinations, but has not completed two Six Sigma projects. A Black Belt is an individual who possesses a deep understanding of statistical methods and has successfully led two or more Six Sigma projects that have resulted in dramatic quality improvements and cost reductions. A Master Black Belt is an individual who has successfully supervised two or more Black Belts while they worked with projects that led to dramatic quality improvements and/or cost reductions in their organizations. Levels of Yellow, Green, Brown, and Black Belt do not specify hierarchy on the organizational charts. A senior executive might do well to be Yellow or Green Belt certified; in fact, this would be a good goal for all executives who have Black Belts, Master Black Belts, and/or Champions reporting to them. This chapter is concerned only with Six Sigma Champion certification.

18.2 CHAMPION CERTIFICATION EXAMINATION

Six Sigma Champion Certification examinations are offered to interested individuals and organizations at secure remote locations. You will have to work with University of Miami personnel to find an approved secure location for your examination, for example, a local university or high school. These examinations are open to anyone wishing certification. You should study Chapters 1–8 in this book before sitting for the Champion certification examination. The Champion certification examination does not require the statistical rigor of Green Belt certification discussed in Chapters 9–15. However, you are still required to understand the definition of Six Sigma and be able to compute a process sigma. A Champion certificate is awarded upon successful completion of the Champion certification examination. All participants are expected to score 100% on a certification examination. A passing grade of 80% is required on the first pass of the examination to take a follow-up examination covering only the parts of the first examination that were answered incorrectly. If a participant fails to achieve a grade of 80% or better on the first pass or fails to attain a grade of 100% on the second pass, he or she is required to begin the certification process from the start and incur all costs.

18.3 COST FOR CHAMPION CERTIFICATION EXAMINATION

The cost in 2004 (subject to change) for sitting for the Champion examination is $3,000 per examination.

18.4 APPLICATION PROCESS

The University of Miami actively seeks participants who demonstrate seriousness of educational purpose. Admission is selective and is offered to those applicants whose credentials are academically sound and work experience reflects interest in Six Sigma management.

To receive a complete application packet, contact Executive Director, McLamore Executive Education Center, School of Business Administration, University of Miami, Coral Gables, FL, 33124 or send email to **sixsigma@miami.edu.**

18.5 SAMPLE CHAMPION CERTIFICATION EXAMINATION QUESTIONS WITH ANSWERS

Question: A service has 10 steps and each step has only one defect opportunity. If the DPMO is 2,700 for each step, what is Rolled Throughput Yield (RTY) of the final service? What is the process sigma for the final service?

Answer: Yield at each step = 0.9973, RTY = $(0.9973)^{10}$ = 0.973326, DPO = 1 − RTY = 0.026674, DPMO = 26,674, Process sigma = between 3.4 and 3.5.

Question: Define special causes of variation.

Answer: Special causes of variation are due to factors that are external to the system.

Question: Define common causes of variation. Give a few examples.

Answer: Common causes of variation are due to the system itself. Examples include: hiring, training, and supervisory practices; management style; and stress level.

Question: Explain the Taguchi Loss Function view of quality. Draw a picture.

Answer: Dr. Genichi Taguchi developed the continuous improvement view of quality when he invented the Taguchi Loss Function. The Taguchi Loss Function explains that losses begin to accrue as soon as a product or service deviates from nominal. Under his loss function, the never-ending reduction of process variation around nominal without capital investment makes sense.

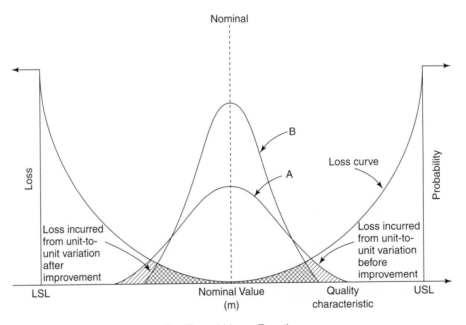

The Taguchi Loss Function

Losses incurred from unit-to-unit variation before process improvement (see distribution A) is greater than the losses incurred from unit-to-unit variation after process improvement (see distribution B). The Taguchi Loss Function promotes the continual reduction of variation of the output of a process around the nominal value, absent capital investment.

Question: Explain the origin of the 1.5 sigma shift of the process mean to the definition of Six Sigma management.

Answer: Through experience, managers have discovered that it is typical for process variation to increase over time. This variation increase has been shown to be similar to a process mean shifting between 1 and 2 sigma over time. Hence, 1.5 sigma has been established as an industrial standard for describing typical process shift.

Question: Explain how the DMAIC model promotes Six Sigma management.

Answer: The DMAIC model is a roadmap for improving chronic problems or performance gaps that exist in a process. It is used to determine the key upstream variables (Xs) in a process that impact the outcome performance of CTQs, optimize the relationships between these upstream variables (Xs) and the outcomes (CTQs), and improve the process based on the discovered relationships.

Question: Explain the origin of the 3.4 DPMO in Six Sigma management.

Answer: If a process generates output that is stable, normally distributed, and centered on the nominal value, which occupies only one-half the distance allowed by specifications (see center normal distribution), then the process will produce only 1 defective part per billion opportunities at the closest specification limit. If the process mean is allowed to vary 1.5 standard deviations in either direction for the above process (see right and left normal distributions), then the process will produce 3.4 DPMO at the closest specification limit.

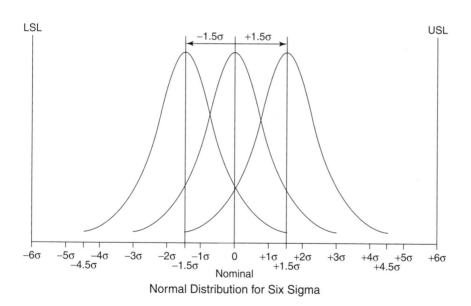

Normal Distribution for Six Sigma

Question: Construct a dashboard explaining the relationship between the mission statement and Six Sigma projects. Make sure you include objectives and indicators in your answer.

Answer:

Mission: To be A, B, and C						
President		**Vice Presidents (V.P.)**		**Direct Reports (D.R.)**		
Business objectives	**Business indicators**	**V.P. Business objectives**	**V.P. Business indicators**	**D.R. Business objectives**	**D.R. Business indicators**	**Six Sigma projects**
A	A1	A11	A111			
	A2	A21	A211			
			A212			
		A22	A221			
B	B1					
C	C1					

Question: What are steps of the define phase of the DMAIC model?

Answer: The Define phase of the DMAIC model has three components:

1. *Prepare the background material for a project charter. This material includes a business case, problem statement, goal statement, scope, milestones and schedule, benefits, roles, and project objective.*
2. *Conduct an SIPOC analysis.*
3. *Perform a Voice of the Customer analysis.*

Question: What are steps of the Measure Phase of the DMAIC model?

Answer: The activities required in the Measure phase of the DMAIC model include:

1. *Operationally defining the CTQ(s).*
2. *Establishing the validity of the measurement system for each CTQ.*
3. *Collecting baseline data for each CTQ.*
4. *Establishing baseline capabilities for each CTQ (RTY, DPMO, and process sigma).*

The Measure phase often includes analysis of well-understood Xs as DMAIC addresses chronic problems in existing processes, which implies there is likelihood of some knowledge of some of the Xs.

Question: What are steps of the Analyze phase of the DMAIC model?

Answer: The steps required by the analyze phase of the DMAIC model include:
1. *Identify the Xs for each CTQ using process maps, QFD and/or Cause and Effect matrices.*
2. *Reduce the number of Xs using FMEA analysis.*
3. *Develop operational definitions for the high-risk Xs.*
4. *Establish the validity of the measurement system for each critical X.*
5. *Collect baseline data for the high-risk Xs.*
6. *Estimate process capability for the high-risk Xs.*

(Many practitioners would include steps 1–6 above in the Measure phase.)

7. *Control high-risk Xs with control charts.*
8. *Identify major noise variables with data mining.*
9. *Use screening designs to reduce the number of Xs.*
10. *Develop hypotheses relating the Xs to the CTQs.*

Question: What are steps of the improve phase of the DMAIC model?

Answer: The steps required in the Improve phase include:

1. *Conduct a designed experiment to understand the relationship between the Xs and the CTQ.*
2. *Optimize the relationship between the Xs and the CTQ.*
3. *Avoid potential problems in the optimized Xs.*
4. *Conduct a pilot test.*
5. *Identify the actions required to realize the optimized relationship between the Xs and the CTQ.*

Question: What are steps of the Control phase of the DMAIC model?

Answer: The Control phase of the DMAIC model includes:

1. *Reduce the effects of collateral damage to related processes.*
2. *Standardize improvements (International Standards Organization [ISO]).*
3. *Develop a control plan for the process owner.*
4. *Identify and document benefits and costs of the project.*
5. *Turn the improved process over to the process owner for continual turning of the PDSA cycle.*
6. *Input the project into Six Sigma database.*
7. *Diffuse the improvements throughout the organization.*
8. *Disband the team and celebrate its success.*

Summary

The purpose of this chapter is to explain the procedure for attaining Six Sigma Champion training and certification at the University of Miami, School of Business Administration, McLamore Executive Education Center. Additionally, sample questions and answers are provided for the Six Sigma Champion certification examination.

Six Sigma Green Belt Certification at the University of Miami

CHAPTER OUTLINE

19.1 Green Belt Basics
19.2 Green Belt Certification Examination Review Questions with Answers
19.3 Green Belt Case Study Project

LEARNING OBJECTIVES:

After reading this chapter, you will be able to:

- Pursue Six Sigma Green Belt certification at the University of Miami
- Study sample questions and answers for the University of Miami Six Sigma Green Belt certification examination.
- Begin one possible Six Sigma project required for Green Belt certification at the University of Miami

INTRODUCTION

At this point, you may be interested in obtaining certification as a Six Sigma Green Belt. This chapter explains the procedure for Six Sigma Green Belt certification at the University of Miami, provides sample questions and answers for the Green Belt certification examination, and provides the information needed to begin one possible Six Sigma project required for Green Belt certification. Remember, if you pass the Green Belt certification examination, but have not yet completed the Green Belt project, the University of Miami awards you a Six Sigma Yellow Belt to signify your level of achievement. You can obtain information about Six Sigma Green Belt training and certification at the University of Miami by going to the following URL:

http://sba07.bus.miami.edu/dev_new/sections/exec/six_sigma/

19.1 Green Belt Basics

Green Belt Certification Examinations and Project Reviews

Green Belt certification examinations and project reviews are offered for interested individuals and organizations. An advisory board of academics and Six Sigma professionals supervises the development of all certification examinations.

Certification examinations for Six Sigma Green Belt are offered to interested individuals and organizations at secure locations. You will have to work with University of Miami personnel to find an approved secure location for your certification examination, such as a local university or high school. These examinations are open to anyone wishing certification. It is strongly suggested that you study this book before sitting for a certification examination. All persons interested in sitting for the Green Belt examination must first pass the Champion examination at the University of Miami. A Green Belt is awarded after passing the Green Belt certification examination and successfully completing a Six Sigma project or case study. All participants are expected to score 100% on a certification examination. A passing grade of 80% on the first pass of the examination is required to take a follow-up examination covering only the parts of the first examination that were answered incorrectly. If a participant fails to achieve a grade of 80% or better on the first pass or fails to attain a grade of 100% on the second pass, he or she is required to begin the certification process from the start and incur all costs.

A laptop computer with the most current version of the Minitab statistical software and Microsoft Word is required to sit for the Green Belt certification examination. Minitab is one of the most popular statistical software packages for Six Sigma. You can rent or purchase Minitab from **www.minitab.com**

Costs for Certification Examinations and Dossier Reviews

The cost for sitting for the Green Belt examination is $3,000 per examination. Time spent by University faculty critiquing Six Sigma Green Belt case studies is charged at $500 per hour. Critiquing rarely exceeds 4 hours, but it is possible that your project will take more than 4 hours. The costs stated above are for 2004 and are subject to change.

Application Process

The University of Miami actively seeks participants who demonstrate seriousness of educational purpose. Admission is selective and is offered to those applicants whose credentials are academically sound and work experience reflects interest in Six Sigma management. To receive a complete application packet, contact Executive Director, McLamore Executive Education Center, School of Business Administration, University of Miami, Coral Gables, FL, 33124 (e-mail: sixsigma@miami.edu).

19.2 SAMPLE GREEN BELT CERTIFICATION EXAMINATION QUESTIONS WITH ANSWERS

Green Belt certification examinations assume that that the participant has successfully completed the Champion certification examination at the University of Miami. This section presents only questions beyond the Champion certification level. However, Green Belt certification examinations are cumulative in that they cover the material required for both Champion and Green Belt certification.

Question: Provide a nontechnical definition for Six Sigma management.

Answer: Six Sigma management is an organizational initiative designed to create breakthrough improvements in manufacturing, service, and administrative processes. For example, Motorola established a goal to reduce defects tenfold, with a 50% reduction in cycle time every 2 years.

Question: Define a process. Draw a picture.

Answer: A process is the vehicle for transforming inputs into outputs, see Figure 19.1. Feedback loops are used to move data to appropriate points in the process for decision-making purposes.

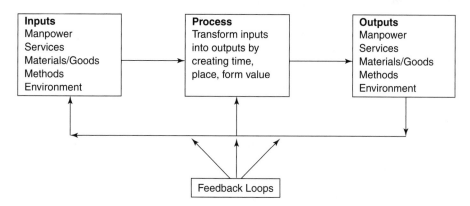

FIGURE 19.1 A Process

Question: Describe the three types of feedback loops (none, special only, common, and special cause).

Answer:

- *No feedback loop: A process without a feedback loop will deteriorate and decay due to entropy.*
- *Special cause only feedback loop: A process in which all feedback is treated as special will exhibit a doubling or explosion in the variation of its output.*
- *Special and common cause feedback loop: A process in which feedback is statistically recognized as common cause or special cause will experience improvement of its output.*

Question: Explain the origin of the 6 and 3.4 in Six Sigma management. Use a diagram that includes the Voice of the Customer and the Voice of the Process, see Figures 19.2 and 19.3.

Answer:

Voice of Customer equals Voice of Process	Voice of Customer equals Voice of Process
• Process is stable and centered on nominal. • 0.0 sigma shift in the mean results in 1,350 DPMO at each specification limit. • See Figure 19.2.	• Process is stable. • 1.5 sigma shift in the mean results in 66,807 DPMO at the nearest specification limit. • See Figure 19.3.

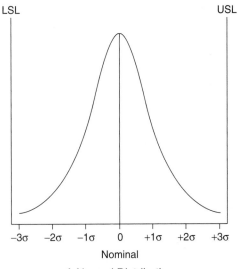

A Normal Distribution

FIGURE 19.2 Centered 3 Sigma Process

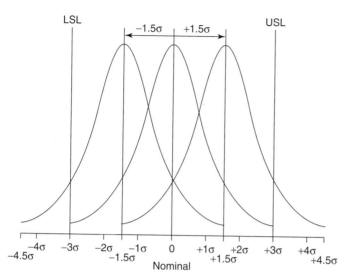

A Normal Distribution for Six Sigma

FIGURE 19.3 3 Sigma Process with Drift in the Mean

Through continuous process improvement, the variation of the process is reduced. Thus, the relationship between Voice of Customer and Voice of Process moves to a better level; Voice of Process is half the Voice of Customer, that is, the process improves from a Three-Sigma process to a Six-Sigma process.

Voice of Process is half Voice of Customer	Voice of Process is half Voice of Customer
• Process is stable and centered on nominal. • 0.0 sigma shift in the mean results in 1 defect per billion opportunities at each specification limit. • See Figure 19.4	• Process is stable. • 1.5 sigma shift in the mean results in 3.4 DPMO at the nearest specification limit. • See Figure 19.5.

Question: Describe the roles and responsibilities of a Process Owner.

Answer:

1. *A Process Owner has the authority to change a process.*
2. *A Process Owner should be identified and designated early in a Six Sigma project.*
3. *A Process Owner is responsible for managing and holding the gains for the improved process and for improving and innovating the process in the future.*
4. *A Process Owner empowers people in the process.*

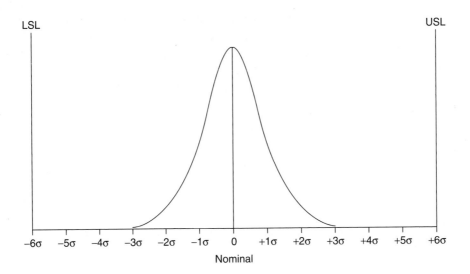

FIGURE 19.4 Centered Six Sigma Process

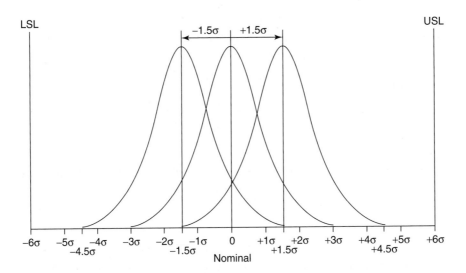

FIGURE 19.5 Six Sigma Process with Drift in the Mean

5. *A Process Owner works with the project team. (This can also be a Champion role.)*

6. *A Process Owner coordinates team logistics. (This can also be a Master Black Belt or Black Belt role.)*

7. *A Process Owner negotiates resources for the team. (This can also be a Champion role.)*

8. *A Process Owner links process and organizational objectives.*

9. *A Process Owner understands their process' capability and its relationship to the organization.*

10. *A Process Owner ensures that customers' needs take priority. (This is also mainly the responsibility of the top executives of an organization.)*

11. *Process Owner optimizes the entire organization, not just a component of the organization.*

Question: Describe the roles and responsibilities of a Champion.

Answer:

1. *A Champion should be a member of the Executive Committee or at least a trusted direct report of a member of the Executive Committee. Champions take a very active sponsorship and leadership role in implementing Six Sigma projects.*

2. *A Champion translates strategic measures into a project (coordinates with Executive Committee).*

3. *A Champion selects the Team Leader.*

4. *A Champion develops and negotiates the project charter.*

5. *A Champion removes obstacles to the project.*

6. *A Champion obtains resources and helps the team control the budget.*

7. *A Champion reviews team progress.*

8. *A Champion helps keep the team focused.*

9. *A Champion assures use of Six Sigma methods and tools.*

10. *A Champion is the liaison between executive management and the project leader.*

Question: Describe the roles and responsibilities of a Black Belt.

Answer:

1. *A Black Belt is a full-time change agent who may not be an expert in the process under study.*

2. *A Black Belt serves as team leader.*

3. *A Black Belt is a master of Six Sigma theory and methods (e.g., the DMAIC model).*

4. *A Black Belt provides guidance and training to team members.*

5. *A Black Belt helps the team refine a project charter (assuming that Champion/Process Owner drafted the initial charter).*

6. *A Black Belt interfaces with the Champion and Master Black Belt.*

7. *A Black Belt helps the team analyze data and design experiments.*

8. *A Black Belt provides training in tools and team functions.*

9. *A Black Belt helps the team prepare for reviews.*

10. *A Black Belt recommends strategic Six Sigma projects.*

11. *A Black Belt leads and coaches Green Belts leading lower level teams.*

Question: Describe the roles and responsibilities of a Green Belt.

Answer:

1. *A Green Belt is a part-time (25%) project leader or member and provides most of the functions of a Black Belt (Team Leader) for lower level project teams.*
2. *Green Belts are the "work horses" of Six Sigma management. Most managers should be or become Green Belts.*
3. *For lower level teams, a Green Belt:*

   - *Refines a draft project charter (Process Owners and Champions should coauthor the first draft)*
   - *Reviews the draft charter with Champion*
   - *Selects team members*
   - *Facilitates the team*
   - *Communicates with the Champion, the Process Owner, and other stakeholders of the process*
   - *Analyzes data*
   - *Provides training in basic tools*
   - *Coordinates team efforts with higher level teams*
   - *Completes documentation*
   - *Completes the control plan*
   - *Spreads the lessons learned*

Question: Describe the roles and responsibilities of a Master Black Belt.

Answer: A Master Black Belt is a proven leader and change agent for Six Sigma management. A Master Black Belt provides technical expertise in Six Sigma management.

1. *Teaches Black Belts and Green Belts.*
2. *Mentors Black Belts and Green Belts.*
3. *Coordinates several Black Belt projects simultaneously.*
4. *Improves and innovates the Six Sigma process.*
5. *Counsels top management on Six Sigma management.*

Question: Create a service example to explain rolled throughput yield, DPO, DPMO, process sigma.

Answer: A service has four steps and each step has only one opportunity for a defect. The yield of step 1 is 0.99, the yield of step 2 is 0.95, the yield of step 3 is 0.99, and the yield of step 4 is 0.97. The four steps are independent of each other. What is the rolled throughput yield (RTY), the DPO, the DPMO, and the process sigma?

$RTY = 0.99 \times 0 .95 \times 0.99 \times 0.97 = 0.903$

$DPO = 1.0 - RTY = 0.097$

$DPMO = 97,000$

Process Sigma = approximately 2.8

Question: Construct a table that shows how to prioritize potential Strategic Six Sigma projects based on their relationships with business objectives. Explain how the table functions to accomplish its aim.

Answer:

				Six Sigma Project		
				Project 1	**Project 2**	**Project 11**
BO	BO1	W e i g h t s	W1			
	BO2		W2			
	BOm		Wm			
Weighted average of Projects						

- W_is are developed by the Finance Department. The sum of $W_i = 1.0$.
- Cell values are determined by team members with the strong guidance of the Finance Department 0 = no relationship, 1 = weak, 3 = moderate, 9 = strong.

The weighted averages that are shown in the last row of the columns are ranked from smallest to largest. The largest average is considered the highest priority project. Alternatively, a control chart could be used to find a project with a weighted average that is out of control on the high side from the other project's averages.

Question: Give an example of a project objective. Label each of the five parts of the project charter.

Answer: Decrease (direction) of the number of customer complaints (CTQ measure) caused by at-home repairs (process) from 20 per day to 0 per day (CTQ target) by March 1, 2004 (deadline).

Question: Explain *SIPOC analysis*. Construct a chart to illustrate your explanation.

*Answer: SIPOC analysis is a simple tool for identifying the **S**uppliers and their **I**nputs into a **P**rocess, the high-level steps of a process, the **O**utputs of the process, and the **C**ustomer (market) segments interested in the outputs, see Figure 19.6.*

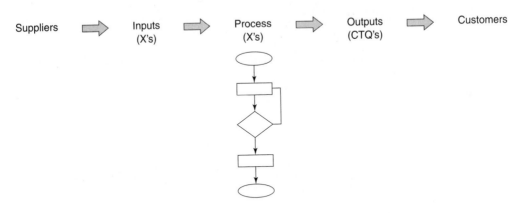

FIGURE 19.6 SIPOC Analysis

Question: Define CTQ.

Answer: CTQ stands for Critical-to-Quality characteristic. It is a characteristic of a process, product, or service that is critical to the satisfaction of a stakeholder.

Question: Define *X.*

Answer: Xs are the inputs and process steps that cause variation in the outputs of a process (CTQs).

Question: What is the tactic of Six Sigma management with respect to *X*s?

Answer:

- *Define vital few* Xs
- *Identify level of critical* Xs *that optimize the CTQ(s); that is, stability, spread, shape, and center of CTQ(s)*
- *Select best actions needed to implement levels of critical* Xs
- *Do it again*

Question: Define must-be, one-way, and attractive qualities that can result from a Kano survey. Make sure your answer is based on the dimensions of performance and satisfaction. Draw a picture to illustrate your explanation.

Answer:

Must-be: User satisfaction is not proportional to the performance of the feature. The lower the performance, the lower the user satisfaction, but high performance creates feelings of indifference to the feature, see Figure 19.7.

One-way: User satisfaction is proportional to the performance of the feature; the lower the performance, the lower the user satisfaction, and the higher the performance, the higher the user satisfaction, see Figure 19.7.

Attractive: User satisfaction is not proportional to the performance of the feature; low levels of performance create feelings of indifference to the feature, but high levels of performance create feelings of delight to the feature, see Figure 19.7.

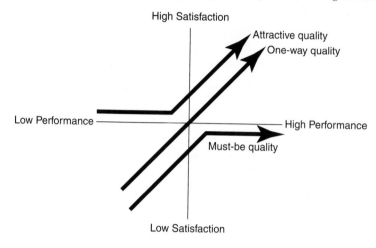

FIGURE 19.7

Question: Provide an example of a question on a Kano survey.

Answer: See Table 19.1

TABLE 19.1 Kano Questionnaire

Column 1	Column 2	Column 3	Column 4
CTQs	How would you feel if the following CTQ were **present?**	How would you feel if the CTQ were **not present?**	What percentage cost increase over current costs would you be willing to pay for this CTQ?
Study center in the dormitory	Delighted [ ] Expect it sand like it [ ] No feeling [ ] Live with it [ ] Do not like it [ ] Other [ ]	Delighted [ ] Expect it and like it [ ] No feeling [ ] Live with it [ ] Do not like it [ ] Other [ ]	0% [ ] 10% [ ] 20% [ ] 30% [ ] 40% or more [ ]

Question: Give examples of classification attribute data. Explain why each example is classification attribute data.

Answer: Examples of classification attribute data: classifying employees by department, classifying cars by manufacturers, and so on. Each example is classification attribute data because the item is classified into one of two or more categories.

Question: Give examples of count (area of opportunity) attribute data. Explain why each example is area of opportunity attribute data.

Answer: Examples of count attribute data: number of union grievances per week, number of typing errors on a page, number of chocolate chips in a cookie. Each example is count attribute data because it shows the number of occurrences (count) per unit.

Question: Give examples of measurement data. Explain why each example is measurement data.

Answer: Examples of measurement data: cycle time, weight, and temperature. Measurement data is continuous data.

Question: What is the purpose of an operational definition?

Answer: An operational definition promotes effective communication between people by putting communicable meaning into a word or term.

Question: Create an operational definition for "12-pound bar" that results in attribute data.

Answer:

Criteria: Select a bar from inventory. Place it on a digital scale. If the digital readout is between 11.999 and 12.001, inclusive, the bar is classified as 12 pounds. If the digital readout is not between 11.999 and 12.001, inclusive, the bar is classified as not 12 pounds.

Test: Select a particular bar and put it on the scale. Record the digital readout.

Decision:

If $11.999 \leq$ digital readout ≤ 12.001, bar = 12 pounds.

If digital readout < 11.999 or digital readout > 12.001, bar $\neq 12$ pounds.

Question: Create an operational definition for "12-pound bar" that results in measurement data.

Answer:

Criteria: Select a bar from inventory. Use a digital scale to weigh the bar.

Test: Select a particular bar and put it on the digital scale. Record the digital readout.

Decision: Use digital readout for weight of bar.

A customer wants to buy chocolate bars with a nominal weight of 6.0 ounces and will accept a tolerance of 0.05 ounces either side of nominal. As a supplier of chocolate bars, you believe that your process produces chocolate rectangles that are cut from larger blocks of chocolate and then packaged as 6-ounce bars. Every 15 minutes, three chocolate bars are weighed prior to packaging. Table 19.2 shows the weights for each bar examined in a 7-hour day.

Question: Use Minitab to construct a run chart and a histogram from this data set.

TABLE 19.2 Weights of Chocolate Bars

Time	Observation #	Weight (oz)	Time	Observation #	Weight (oz)
	1	6.01		1	6.03
9:15	2	5.99	12:45	2	6.02
	3	6.01		3	6.03
	1	5.98		1	6.03
9:30	2	5.99	1:00	2	6.00
	3	6.01		3	6.01
	1	6.03		1	6.04
9:45	2	6.02	1:15	2	6.02
	3	6.02		3	6.03
	1	6.02		1	6.05
10:00	2	6.03	1:30	2	6.02
	3	6.02		3	6.04
	1	6.00		1	6.03
10:15	2	5.99	1:45	2	6.04
	3	6.01		3	6.01
	1	5.99		1	6.02
10:30	2	6.00	2:00	2	6.02
	3	6.00		3	6.02
	1	6.02		1	6.04
10:45	2	6.01	2:15	2	6.05
	3	6.00		3	6.03
	1	6.01		1	6.06
11:00	2	6.03	2:30	2	6.03
	3	6.01		3	6.04
	1	6.01		1	6.05
11:15	2	6.02	2:45	2	6.04
	3	6.00		3	6.02
	1	6.00		1	6.05
11:30	2	6.02	3:00	2	6.04
	3	6.01		3	6.03
	1	6.04		1	6.04
11:45	2	6.02	3:15	2	6.06
	3	6.03		3	6.05
	1	6.02		1	6.05
12:00	2	6.01	3:30	2	6.03
	3	6.00		3	6.04
	1	6.03		1	6.03
12:15	2	6.02	3:45	2	6.04
	3	6.04		3	6.03

(continued)

(cont.)

Time	Observation #	Weight (oz)	Time	Observation #	Weight (oz)
12:30	1	6.02	4:00	1	6.06
	2	6.02		2	6.06
	3	6.03		3	6.05

CHOCOLATE

Answer: See Figures 19.8–19.10

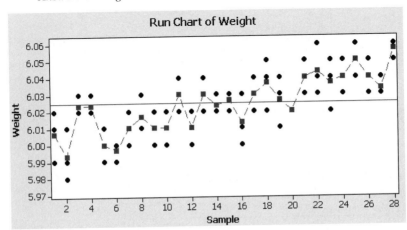

FIGURE 19.8 Minitab Run Chart of Chocolate Bar Weights

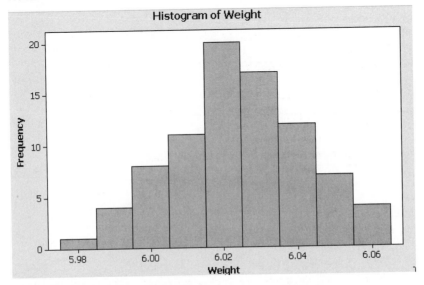

FIGURE 19.9 Minitab Histogram of Chocolate Bar Weights

Question: Interpret the charts. What conclusions about the distribution of the weights can you reach based on these charts?

Answer: The histogram (see Figure 19.9) shows that the chocolate bars are approximately normally distributed, but the average weight is more than 6.00 ounces. The run chart (see Figure 19.8) shows that the observed weights plotted over time have upward drift in the weights of chocolate bars throughout the day. The run chart also indicates the need for action on the process.

Question: Use Minitab to construct an $\overline{X}$ and R-chart from this data set. Is the process stable? If no, at what times is it unstable?

Answer:

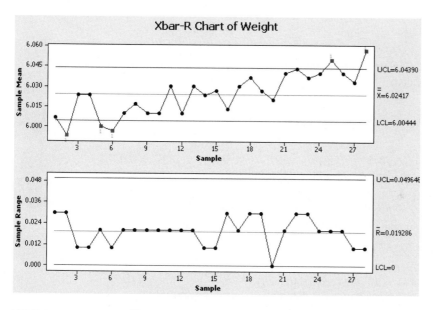

FIGURE 19.10 Minitab $\overline{X}$–R Chart of Chocolate Bar Weights

No, at 9:30 a.m., 10:15 a.m., 10:30 a.m., 3:15 p.m., and 4:00 p.m, see Figure 19.10.

Question: What is the overall process mean?

Answer: 6.024

Question: What is the estimate of the process standard deviation?

Answer:

$$(\overline{R}/d_2) = (0.019286/1.693) = 0.01139.$$

Question: Why did you use this formula versus another formula?

Answer: $(\overline{R} \div d_2)$ was used instead of the formula for the sample standard deviation because $(\overline{R} \div d_2)$ considers only short-term variation, whereas the formula for the sample standard considers long-term variation. $(\overline{R} \div d_2)$ assumes that the process is stable. If *the process is not stable, the out-of-control points will jump out of the control limits based on* $(\overline{R} \div d_2)$. *The* $(\overline{R} \div d_2)$ *limits are tighter than limits based on the sample standard deviation.*

Question: State the LSL and USL for the above process.

Answer:

LSL = 5.95 and USL = 6.05

Question: Calculate the actual process yield using the empirical data.

Answer:

80 ÷ 84 = 0.952

Question: Calculate the theoretical process yield using the normal distribution. Is this a reasonable calculation? If yes, why? If no, why not?

Answer:

$Z_{LSL} = (5.95 - 6.024)/ 0.01139 = -6.4969$, *hence,* $P(X < -6.4969) = 0.0000$

$Z_{USL} = (6.05 - 6.024)/ 0.01139 = 2.2827$, *hence,* $P(X > 2.2827) = 0.0112$
$P (5.95 \leq X \leq 6.05) = 1 - 0.0000 - 0.0112 = 0.9888$

The above calculation is not reasonable because the process is not in statistical control.

Question: Compute the actual DPMO from the empirical data.

Answer:

DPO = 1 - RTY = 1 - 0.952 = 0.048
DPMO = 1,000,000 × DPO = 1,000,000 × 0.048 = 48,000 DPMO

Question: Compute the theoretical DPMO using the normal distribution. Is this a reasonable calculation? If yes, why? If no, why not?

Answer:

DPO = 0.0112
DPMO = 1,000,000 × 0.0112 = 11,200

The DPMO calculation is not reasonable because the process is not stable at this time.

Question: Compute the process sigma. Which DPMO should you use? Why?

Answer: Process sigma assuming a 1.5 sigma shift in the mean for the empirical DPMO of 11,200 is 3.1 to 3.2.

Process sigma assuming a 1.5 sigma shift in the mean for the theoretical DPMO of 48,000 is 3.7 to 3.8.

Neither DPMO should be used because the process is not stable. A process sigma calculation is not appropriate for this process at this time.

Consider the data in Table 19.3.

TABLE 19.3 Defective Entries

Day	Number of entries inspected	Number of defective entries	Fraction of defective entries
1	200	6	0.03
2	200	6	0.03
3	200	6	0.03
4	200	5	0.025
5	200	0	0
6	200	0	0
7	200	6	0.03
8	200	14	0.07
9	200	4	0.02
10	200	0	0
11	200	1	0.005
12	200	8	0.04
13	200	2	0.01
14	200	4	0.02
15	200	7	0.035
16	200	1	0.005
17	200	3	0.015
18	200	1	0.005
19	200	4	0.02
20	200	0	0
21	200	4	0.02
22	200	15	0.075
23	200	4	0.02
24	200	1	0.005
Totals	4,800	102	

DEFECTIVES

Question: What type of data is in the above matrix?

Answer: Classification type attribute data.

Question: *What type of control chart should be used to study the above data?*

Answer: p-chart with constant subgroup size.

Question: Use Minitab to construct a control chart for the above data.

Answer: See Figure 19.11.

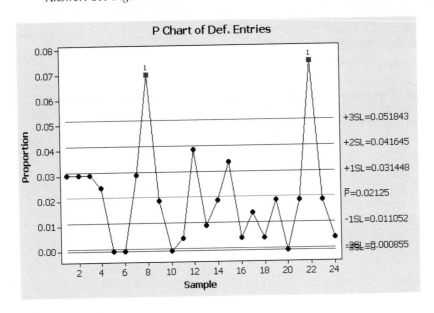

FIGURE 19.11 Minitab *p*-Chart of Defective Entries

Question: Is the process stable? If not, on what days is it not stable?

Answer: Days 8 and 22 are beyond the upper control limit, see Figure 19.11.

Analyze the following data set.

TABLE 19.4 Accident Data

Monthly accident data is listed across the rows for 36 months

25	22	22	14	21	14	19	17	13	22	18	22	23	26	21
26	15	26	16	31	19	16	27	24	13	22	24	24	25	22
17	27	24	22	24	21									

Question: What type of data is in the above matrix?

Answer: Count type attribute data

Question: What type of control chart should be used to study the above data?

Answer: c-chart

Question: Use Minitab to construct a control chart for the above data.

Answer: See Figure 19.12.

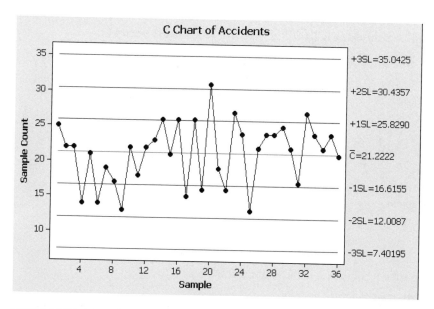

FIGURE 19.12 Minitab c-Chart of Accidents

Question: Is the process stable? If not, in what months is it not stable?

Answer: Yes, see Figure 19.12.

The following represents 3 years of weekly sales data for the Latin American Division of a hospital supply company, see Table 19.5.

TABLE 19.5 Hospital Supply Data

Weekly Hospital Supply data is listed across the rows for 3 years

20,594.0	39,447.7	34,884.9	30,895.5	24,420.5	25,774.4	21,847.8
32,095.5	37,328.1	26,053.5	34,475.1	23,539.9	29,721.0	36,508.4
31,972.7	20,496.3	31,970.9	21,406.3	20,123.7	25,977.4	22,057.3
29,258.7	27,054.7	19,044.3	19,096.2	12,629.3	21,780.3	8,161.7
29,876.2	30,136.4	26,456.7	30,099.8	20,265.1	30,219.2	18,621.7
30,116.9	22,898.7	23,167.3	12,889.2	22,943.3	26,445.9	17,671.1
22,689.7	32,186.2	27,144.3	40,109.7	23,210.1	24,863.2	16,859.6
23,640.8	32,579.6	16,155.0	29,424.0	19,994.2	37,201.9	36,673.1
24,034.6	20,082.6	31,597.9	12,122.8	15,737.4	35,017.2	16,550.8
19,720.4	21,028.6	22,531.0	29,792.0	17,870.4	25,190.8	26,550.6
13,394.4	29,292.0	29,478.6	11,839.4	26,331.7	29,647.5	24,929.8
24,959.7	6,594.5	17,086.2	4,945.2	23,232.7	17,871.3	22,874.1
28,181.8	26,110.9	18,595.0	28,770.3	18,607.7	38,645.3	21,746.6
23,092.9	32,058.7	31,578.4	29,364.7	6,872.8	13,886.7	38,049.8

(continued)

Weekly Hospital Supply data is listed across the rows for 3 years

32,245.3	26,072.7	27,118.6	24,881.4	27,277.2	30,522.2	33,493.6
35,899.3	27,833.8	20,321.1	36,236.4	29,992.1	25,029.5	23,004.0
33,282.1	28,741.1	17,702.2	25,963.0	13,915.7	25,416.9	21,448.6
27,494.1	21,020.7	33,265.4	35,491.0	27,897.6	19,611.2	14,903.2
30,608.8	14,694.7	29,046.7	36,153.4	34,614.4	24,937.3	28,996.3
5,991.3	9,056.1	31,705.0	32,959.2	11,831.6	24,567.5	21,397.9
21,335.7	19,655.3	27,238.7	19,239.4	31,899.1	22,663.4	18,906.8
14,227.5	29,180.8	25,484.7	23,547.2	25,919.4	14,761.7	18,666.0
26,977.7	17,805.9					

HOSPITAL

Question: What type of data is in the above matrix?

Answer: Measurement data

Question: What type of control chart should be used to study the above data?

Answer: An I-MR chart should be used due to measurement data and a subgroup size of one, see Figure 19.13.

Question: Use Minitab to construct a control chart for the data in Table 19.5.

Answer:

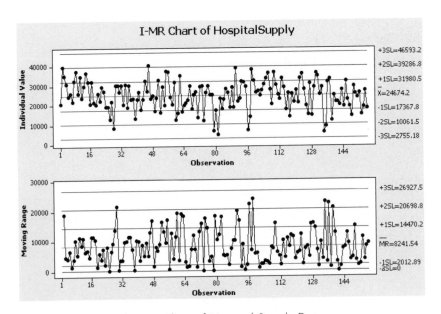

FIGURE 19.13 Minitab I-MR Chart of Hospital Supply Data

Question: Is the process stable? If not, in what weeks is it not stable?

Answer: The process is stable, see Figure 19.13.

Question: Explain the purpose of a Gage R&R study.

Answer: The purpose of a Gage R&R study is to define the validity of a measurement system, specifically, to estimate the proportion of observed variation due to unit-to-unit variation and measurement variation.

Question: Construct a Gage R&R run chart from the data in Table 19.6.

TABLE 19.6 Gage R&R Data

Inspector	Reading	CTQ	Inspector	Reading	CTQ
1	1	10	1	1	7
1	2	10	1	2	7
2	1	9	2	1	7
2	2	10	2	2	7
1	1	8	1	1	7
1	2	7	1	2	7
2	1	8	2	1	8
2	2	8	2	2	7
1	1	9	1	1	7
1	2	9	1	2	8
2	1	9	2	1	8
2	2	10	2	2	8
1	1	5	1	1	6
1	2	5	1	2	6
2	1	5	2	1	6
2	2	6	2	2	6

 GAGE

Answer: See Figure 19.14.

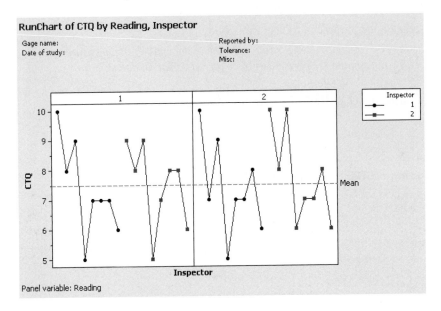

FIGURE 19.14 Minitab Gage R&R Run Chart

Question: Explain how flowcharts can be constructed to identify and highlight the non–value-added steps in a process.

Answer: See Figure 19.15.

Value Added Steps or Xs	Non Value Added Steps or Xs

NOTE: Show cycle times for each step or X.

FIGURE 19.15 Generic VA/NVA Chart

Question: Explain the relationship between $Y = f(X)$ and a flowchart with respect to Six Sigma management.

Answer: As you can see from Figure 19.16, $CTQ_1 = f(X_1, X_2, X_3, X_4, X_5)$

CTQ,

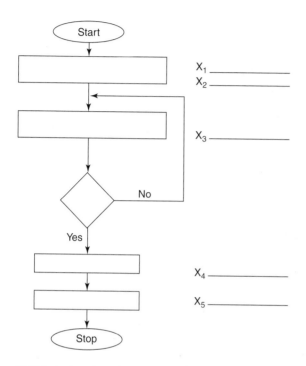

FIGURE 19.16 Flowchart with CTQs and *X*s

Question: Explain how failure modes and effects analysis (FMEA) is used to identify the *X*s that cause CTQs to be out of specification. Construct a table to illustrate your explanation.

Answer: Failure mode and effects analysis (FMEA) is used to identify, estimate, prioritize, and reduce the risk of failure in CTQs through the development of countermeasures based on Xs. There are 10 steps to conducting a FMEA, see Table 19.7. First, team members identify the critical parameters and their potential failure modes through brainstorming or other tools, that is, ways in which the design might fail (columns 1 and 2 of Table 19.7). Second, team members identify the potential effect of each failure (consequences of that failure) and rate its severity (columns 3 and 4 of Table 19.7). The definition of the severity scale is shown in Table 19.8 on page 621. Third, team members identify causes of the effects and rate their likelihood of occurrence (columns 5 and 6 of Table 19.7). The definition of the likelihood of occurrence scale is shown in Table 19.9 on page 621. Fifth, team members identify the current controls for detecting each failure mode and rate the organization's ability to detect each failure mode (columns 7 and 8 of Table 19.7). The definition of the detection scale is shown in Table 19.10 on page 622. Sixth, team members calculate the RPN (Risk Priority Number) for each failure mode by multiplying the

TABLE 19.7 Format for an FMEA

1	2	3	4	5	6	7	8	9	10	11	12	13	14	15	16
Critical parameter	Potential failure mode	Potential failure effect	Severity	Potential causes	Occur-rence	Current controls	Detec-tion	RPN	Recom-mended action	Respon-sibility and target date	Action taken	Severity	Occur-rence	Detec-tion	RPN

Before RPN =   After RPN =

values in columns 4, 6, and 8 (column 9 of Table 19.7). Seventh, team members identify recommended actions and contingency plans, persons responsible, and target completion dates for reducing or eliminating each failure mode (columns 10 and 11 of Table 19.7). Eight, team members identify the date the action was taken to reduce or eliminate each failure mode (column 12 of Table 19.7). Ninth, team members rank the severity (column 12 of Table 19.7), occurrence (column 13 of Table 19.7), and detection (column 14 of Table 19.7) of each failure mode after the recommended action (column 10 of Table 19.7) has been put into motion. Tenth, team members multiply the values in columns 13, 14, and 15 of Table 19.7 to calculate the RPN for each failure mode after the recommended action (column 16 of Table 19.7) has been put into motion.

TABLE 19.8 Definition of "Severity" scale = likely impact of failure

Impact	Rating	Criteria: A failure could...
Bad	10	Injure a customer or employee
\/	9	Be illegal
\/	8	Render the unit unfit for use
\/	7	Cause extreme customer dissatisfaction
\/	6	Result in partial malfunction
\/	5	Cause a loss of performance likely to result in a complaint
\/	4	Cause minor performance loss
\/	3	Cause a minor nuisance; can be overcome with no loss
\/	2	Be unnoticed; minor effect on performance
Good	1	Be unnoticed and not affect the performance

TABLE 19.9 Definition of "Occurrence" scale = frequency of failure

Impact	Rating	Time period	Probability of occurrence
Bad	10	More than once per day	> 30%
\/	9	Once every 3–4 days	≤ 30%
\/	8	Once per week	≤ 5%
\/	7	Once per month	≤ 1%
\/	6	Once every 3 months	≤ 0.3 per 1,000
\/	5	Once every 6 months	≤ 1 per 10,000
\/	4	Once per year	≤ 6 per 100,000
\/	3	Once every 1–3 years	≤ 6 per million (approx. Six Sigma)
\/	2	Once every 3–6 years	≤ 3 per 10 million
Good	1	Once every 6–100 years	≤ 2 per billion

TABLE 19.10 Definition of "Detection" scale = ability to detect failure

Impact	Rating	Definition
Bad	10	Defect caused by failure is not detectable
\/	9	Occasional units are checked for defects
\/	8	Units are systematically sampled and inspected
\/	7	All units are manually inspected
\/	6	Manual inspection with mistake-proofing modifications
\/	5	Process is monitored with control charts and manually inspected
\/	4	Control charts used with an immediate reaction to out-of-control condition
\/	3	Control charts used as above with 100% inspection surrounding out-of-control condition
\/	2	Control charts used to improve the process
Good	1	Defect is obvious and can be kept from the customer or control charts are used for process improvement to yield a no-inspection system with routine monitoring

Question: Define capability of the process in statistical terms.

Answer: Capability is a measure of the relative relationship between the Voice of the Process and the Voice of the Customer. This relationship considers the differential between the mean and nominal of the process. The capability of a stable and normally distributed process is defined as 99.73% of its output will be in the interval between LNL (mean $- 3[\overline{R}/d_2]$) and UNL (mean $+ 3[\overline{R}/d_2]$), given measurement data and a subgroup size between 2 and 10, inclusive.

Question: Construct a dot plot for the CTQ. Construct dot plots to study the CTQ for the different levels of X_1 and X_2. Construct main effects plots and interaction plots for the following data set. Use the data in Table 19.4.

TABLE 19.11 Dot Plot Data

X_1	X_2	CTQ
−1	−1	8
+1	−1	9
−1	+1	14
+1	+1	13
−1	−1	7
+1	−1	8
−1	+1	15
+1	+1	14

CTQ

Answer: See Figures 19.17–19.22.

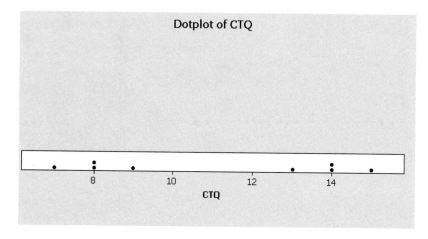

FIGURE 19.17 Minitab Dot Plot of CTQ

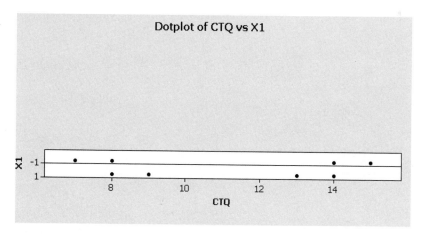

FIGURE 19.18 Minitab Dot Plot of CTQ vs. X_1

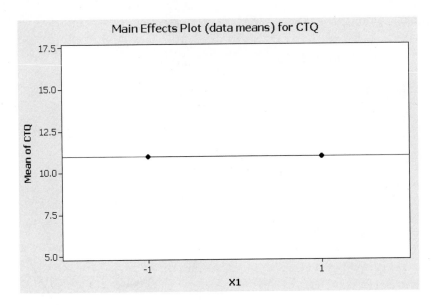

FIGURE 19.19 Minitab Main Effects Plot for CTQ vs. X_1

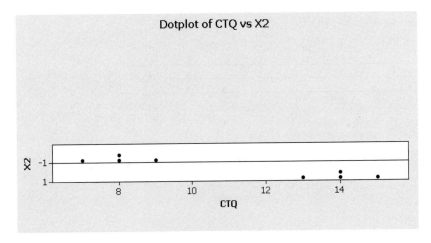

FIGURE 19.20 Minitab Dot Plot of CTQ vs. X_2

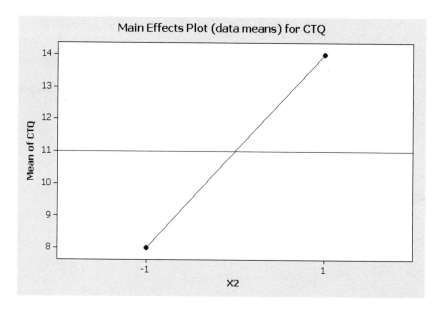

FIGURE 19.21 Minitab Main Effects Plot for CTQ vs. X_1

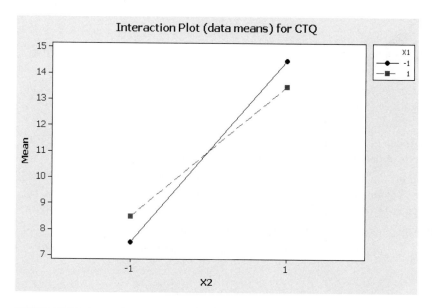

FIGURE 19.22 Minitab Interaction Plot for CTQ

There is an interaction between X_1 and X_2 that will affect the CTQ. The interaction is seen in the crossed lines, see Figure 19.22.

Question: Explain the purpose of a 2^k full factorial design.

Answer: The purpose of a 2^k full factorial design is to understand the relationships between a set of Xs, each with only two levels, and the interactions of the Xs, on a CTQ.

Question: Create the standard order matrix for a 2^3 full factorial design.

Answer: See Table 19.12.

TABLE 19.12 Standard Order Matrix

Test	X_1	X_2	X_3
1	−	−	−
2	+	−	−
3	−	+	−
4	+	+	−
5	−	−	+
6	+	−	+
7	−	+	+
8	+	+	+

Question: Explain how the standard order matrix for a 2^3 full factorial design is used to estimate the effects of one main factor on the CTQ.

Answer: Add up the values of the CTQ for which the X is +, then add up the values of the CTQ for which X is −; finally, divide the difference of the sums by the number of plus signs.

Question: Explain how the coefficient pattern for a 2^3 full factorial design is used to estimate the effects of one interaction factor (X_iX_j) on the CTQ.

Answer: *Multiply the signs of X_i and X_j to create a new variable, X_iX_j. Next, add up the values of the CTQ for which the interaction X_iX_j is +, then add up the values of the CTQ for which X_iX_j is −; finally, divide the difference of the sums by the number of plus signs.*

Question: Why randomize runs in an experimental design?

Answer: Randomization is done in experimental designs to remove the effects of lurking variables.

Multiple Choice Questions (correct answer is in boldface type):

1. A 2^3 full factorial design with two replications provides information about:
   a) main factor effects
   b) two-way interactions
   c) three-way interaction
   d) all of the above

2. A 2^3 full factorial design attempts to prevent the effect of lurking variables by
   a) replication
   b) randomization
   c) interaction
   d) none of the above
   e) all of the above

3. A 2^3 full factorial design with two replications per cell requires _____ runs.
   a) 2
   b) 3
   c) 4
   d) 8
   e) 16

4. A 2^3 full factorial design can be physically represented by which shape?
   a) square
   b) cube
   c) rectangle
   d) circle
   e) none of the above

5. The purpose of a full factorial design is to:
   a) provide information on the effects of main factors
   b) provide information on the effects of interactions
   c) if possible, remove the effects of lurking variables
   d) all of the above
   e) none of the above

6. Use the design matrix in Table 19.13 to answer the following questions.

TABLE 19.13 Design Matrix

Test	X_1	X_2	X_3	CTQ
1	−	−	−	6
2	+	−	−	7
3	−	+	−	8
4	+	+	−	7
5	−	−	+	3
6	+	−	+	4
7	−	+	+	4
8	+	+	+	5

7. The above design matrix layout is called:

   a) random order

   b) run order

   c) standard order

   d) none of the above

   e) all of the above

8. Compute the average effect of X_3:

   a) +12

   b) −3

   c) −4

   d) +15

   e) none of the above

   [3+4+4+5]/4−{6+7+8+7]/4 = 4−7 = −3

9. Compute the average effect of the interaction between X_1 and X_3.

   a) −2

   b) +1/2

   c) +3

   d) 1/3

   e) none of the above

   [6+8+4+5]/4−[7+7+3+4]/4=23/4−21/4=1/2

Question: Explain the purpose of a pilot test.

Answer: A pilot test serves four purposes. First, it validates a revised best practice method. Second, it highlights the risks (e.g., FMEA) involved in using the revised best practice method. Third, it promotes a smooth implementation of the revised best practice method. Finally, it facilitates buy-in by the stakeholders of revised best practice method.

Question: Analyze the following 2^3 full factorial design with two replications in Table 19.14 using Minitab.

TABLE 19.14 2^3 Full Factorial Design with Two Replications

StdOrder	RunOrder	CenterPt	Blocks	A	B	C	CTQ
15	1	1	1	−1	1	1	30
1	2	1	1	−1	−1	−1	21
8	3	1	1	1	1	1	100
12	4	1	1	1	1	−1	29
3	5	1	1	−1	1	−1	26
2	6	1	1	1	−1	−1	23
13	7	1	1	−1	−1	1	19
16	8	1	1	1	1	1	99
7	9	1	1	−1	1	1	31
11	10	1	1	−1	1	−1	32
14	11	1	1	1	−1	1	24
10	12	1	1	1	−1	−1	20
4	13	1	1	1	1	−1	34
6	14	1	1	1	−1	1	34
9	15	1	1	−1	−1	−1	28
5	16	1	1	−1	−1	1	30

🌐 **CTQ2.MTW**

Answer: Analysis of Variance for CTQ (coded units). See Figures 19.23–19.25.

Source	DF	Seq SS	Adj SS	Adj MS	F	P
Main Effects	3	4884.7	4884.7	1628.25	76.18	0.000
2-Way Interactions	3	3555.0	3555.0	1185.00	55.44	0.000
3-Way Interactions	1	870.2	870.2	870.25	40.71	0.000
Residual Error	8	171.0	171.0	21.37		
Pure Error	8	171.0	171.0	21.38		
Total	15	9481.0				

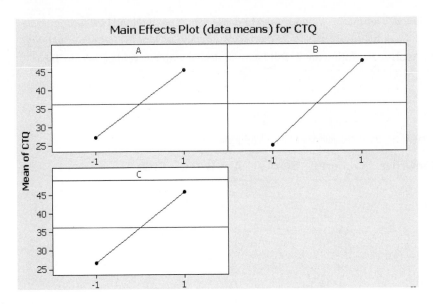

FIGURE 19.23 Minitab Main Effects Plot for CTQ

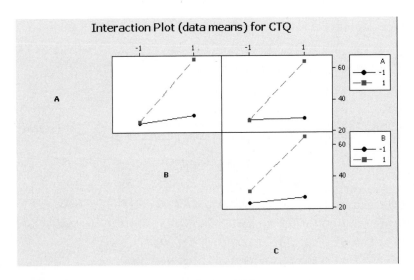

FIGURE 19.24 Minitab Interaction Plot for CTQ

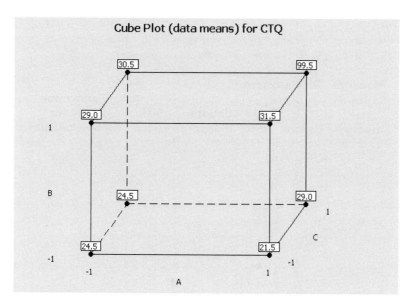

FIGURE 19.25 Cube Plot for CTQ

The high-high-high 3-way interaction rules the experiment. To maximize CTQ, set all factors at the high level.

Question: Explain the purpose of risk management.

Answer: The purpose of risk management is to maintain control and minimize the risk of failure of product, service, or process by using risk abatement plans.

Question: List the steps involved in developing a risk abatement plan.

Answer: Team members construct risk abatement plans for risk elements with high- and medium-risk elements (column 1); that is, a risk element score of 16–25 (column 4). Next, team members identify the potential harm for each risk element (column 2) and measure each risk element (column 3). Team members identify process, product, or service changes called countermeasures to reduce the risk for each high- and medium-risk element (Xs) [column 6]. Next, team members estimate the risk element score after the risk abatement plan is set into motion (column 5). Team members identify the risk element owner (column 7) and set a completion date for the risk abatement plan to become operational (column 8). Finally, team members document the risk abatement plans.

A format for a risk abatement plan is shown in Table 19.15.

TABLE 19.15 Format for a Risk Abatement Plan

1	2	3	4	5	6	7	8
Potential risk element	Potential harm	Measure for risk element	Risk element score		Counter-measure	Risk owner	Completion date for countermeasure
			Before	After			

Team members carry out all risk abatement plans. They document the lessons learned for each risk element and transfer the knowledge to other relevant risk elements. Next, team members incorporate the risk abatement plans into a control plan for the Process Owner. Team members turn the process control plan over to the Process Owner. Finally, the Process Owner continuously turns the PDSA cycle to continue improving the process, product, or service.

Question: Explain the purpose of mistake proofing. Explain the functioning of mistake proofing.

Answer: Mistake proofing is used to create "robust steps" in a process, service, or components of a product, denoted as Xs, that are not susceptible to human error. It is used on the critical parameters shown in column 1 in Table 19.16 and on the potential failure modes shown in column 2 of Table 19.16. Column 12 in Table 19.16 is used to list a mistake-proofing solution to potential failure modes (column 2). There are many types of mistake-proofing solutions to prevent failure modes, for example, alarms that indicate danger to an operator, color coding medical records by type (green for pediatric and orange for geriatric), or a hand harness for a press to prevent an operator from getting his/her hands crushed in the press. Team members can brainstorm for mistake-proofing solutions to potential failure modes or they can review the literature on mistake-proofing techniques.

TABLE 19.16 Format for an FMEA

1	2	3	4	5	6	7	8	9	10	11	12	13	14	15	16
Critical Parameter	Potential Failure mode	Potential Failure effect	Severity	Potential Causes	Occur-rence	Current controls	Detec-tion	RPN	Recom-mended	Respon-sibility and target date	Action taken	Severity	Occur-rence	Detec-tion	RPN

Before RPN =   After RPN =

Question: Explain why standardization is such an important part of Six Sigma.

Answer: Standardization of a process creates a known best practice flowchart that can be improved by one or more employees, perhaps a Six Sigma project team. There are multiple variations of a process without standardization. The lack of standardization makes process improvement very difficult because there is not one process to be improved; rather, there are many versions of the same process.

Question: Explain the function of control charts in the control phase of the DMAIC model.

Answer: Control charts are important in the Control phase of the DMAIC model because they can be used to monitor stability of the Xs and the CTQs. Also, control charts promote process monitoring and work toward the elimination of mass inspection.

Question: Explain the purpose of a QC process chart. Draw a QC chart to illustrate your explanation.

Answer: The purpose of a QC process chart is to monitor implementation of revised best practice methods, see Table 19.17.

TABLE 19.17 QC Process Chart

PLAN/DO		STUDY			ACT		
Flowchart		**CTQs and Xs**			**Corrective action**		
Revised best practice flowchart for doing the process.	Show how revised step should be done or provide a reference that describes the revised step.	Identify CTQs and Xs.	Specify CTQs and Xs.	Describe CTQs and/or Xs should be monitored (e.g., run chart.) Who should monitor?	State corrective actions to prevent future problem.	Formalize procedures for operators enabling them to deal with problems.	Who needs what data to improve the best practice method?
					What should be done with defective output? Who should do it?	Update the training process to include revised best practice.	
						Update training manual.	
						Use statistical methods to determine if and when an employee reaches a state of statistical control from a particular training program.	

Question: Explain the purpose of documentation in Six Sigma management.

Answer: Documentation has at least four purposes in Six Sigma. First, it provides a permanent record of the project and details for the future owner of the process. Second, it ensures that the improvement and rationale are documented so that the problem does not come back. Third, it ensures that the knowledge gained by the team is saved and shared. Finally, it documents vital information about the project from which others can benefit.

19.3 CASE STUDY FOR GREEN BELT CERTIFICATION

Introduction

The purpose of the following case study is to provide you with a Six Sigma project to achieve your Green Belt certification without having to rely on an organization other than the University of Miami. We understand that some readers may not currently be employed, or if employed, may not have the opportunity to do a case study on the job.

The case study requires you to enter into the fictitious world of Lilliputia (of *Gulliver's Travels* fame) and to accept a position as a Six Sigma Green Belt with Catapult International (CI). Your job is to work with Catapult International employees, customers, and suppliers to resolve problems they are experiencing with the newly released Sun Super catapult, see Figure 19.26.

FIGURE 19.26 Sun Super Catapult

Sun Super Catapult Supplies

The following items are required for the case study.

1. 1 Sun Super catapult (one catapult costs $350 as of 2004 and is an important aid to illustrate many statistical concepts). For more information, contact Lightning Calculator (248) 641–7030 (www.qualitytng.com).

2. 1 roll of tin foil to mark where catapult stones (balls) land with respect to a target. It is important to use the tin foil to avoid difficulties in collecting catapult throw data.

Background Information

Catapult International (CI) is a munitions manufacturer that specializes in single-arm catapults. The Lilliputian National Army (LNA) is the firm's largest customer, accounting for more than 65% of its revenues over the last 5 years. CI has been the sole source of supply for catapults for the LNA, based on the quality of its product and its competitive pricing practices.

Emperor Nova, the twenty-second Emperor of Lilliputia, has been fighting with the Lilliputian Freedom Fighters (LFF) for more than 20 years to put down a secession attempt. The LFF had gained control of approximately 45% of the country. It has built numerous fortified castles across the land to provide strongholds for its army and to maintain control of its territory. To conquer the LFF and reunite his country, Emperor Nova's army needs to defeat the LFF in battle and reduce its castles to rubble. The favored siege engine for this is CI's Mars I catapult.

By the time of Emperor Nova's rule, siege warfare had developed into a science, with a large number of munitions manufacturers, such as CI, competing to provide the various munitions necessary to wage war. Munitions manufacturers were in the habit of introducing new models every 5 years and discontinuing production and support of their old models shortly following the launch of a new model. In keeping with this corporate strategy, CI recently launched its Sun Super catapult and discontinued production of its Mars I catapult.

The Mars I catapult had been capable of consistently throwing 8-ounce stones (a ball) to hit targets at a distance of 80 inches. The tolerance on the catapult was that stones could be up to 2 inches short or long of the intended target. The Sun Super catapult was marketed as having the same target reliability as the Mars I with the added value of requiring less maintenance and repair time. Immediately following their purchase of 100 new Sun Super catapults, the LNA started experiencing problems with the new equipment. The following problems were reported to CI:

- Several Sun Super catapults were out of order during key military operations.
- Several soldiers were injured while operating the Sun Super catapult.
- The Sun Super catapult did not appear to be as accurate as the Mars I.
- The Sun Super catapult was more difficult to operate than the Mars I.

CI set up a Six Sigma team to resolve the above problems to salvage its contract with the LNA and maintain its good relationship with the personnel of the LNA.

Practical Aspects of the Case Study

Purpose. The case study provides you with the opportunity to do a Six Sigma Green Belt project using a toy catapult. All data is obtained by experimenting with your catapult or by collecting data from stakeholders. Stakeholder data is presented in the "Background Information for the Define Phase" section on page 637. Please follow the MSD case study in Chapter 16 or the helicopter case study in Chapter 17 for format, tools, and methods.

Background Information for the Define Phase. Table 19.18 presents five potential Six Sigma projects that resulted from CI's dashboard. They are listed in the columns of the following matrix. CI's business objectives are shown in the rows of the following matrix. Further, the Finance Department determined the "weights" for the four business objectives.

TABLE 19.18 Six Sigma Projects Priority Matrix

Business objectives			Hit rate	Maintenance and Reliability Time	Instructions	Preventive maintenance	Injury rate
Increase sales	W E	.40	9	3	3	3	3
Retain customers	I G	.30	9	3	3	3	3
Avoid lawsuits	H T	.15	3	1	1	1	9
Decrease costs	S	.15	1	1	3	1	9
Weighted Average of CTQs			6.9	2.4	2.7	2.4	4.8

Scale: 0 = No relationship, 1 = Weak, 3 = Moderate, 9 = Strong.

The process improvement team will have the following resources for the project:

- Exclusive use of a Sun Super catapult for test purposes (your personal catapult)
- Unlimited access to the catapult test site for the duration of the project
- Two design engineers and two manufacturing engineers available full time to assist with the project

The process improvement team will have the following limitations during the project:

- The project must be completed within 21 weeks.
- The team must not exceed its 1,000 gold piece (GP) budget, see Table 19.19.
- Release of patent information to nonemployees of CI is not authorized.

TABLE 19.19 Budget for Hit Rate Project

Budget item	Planned
Overtime	200 GP
Ammunition	150 GP
Salary for Design Engineers	150 GP
Materials	350 GP
Salary for Manufacturing Engineers	150 GP
Total budget	1,000 GP

Overtime was determined based on the following allocation rates received from human resources:

Team members—2 GP/hour

Team Leader & Process Owner—3 GP/hour

Green Belt—4 GP/hour

Finance & IT reps—5 GP/hour

Black Belt and Champion—exempt, no charge for overtime. Project commensurate with normal duties.

Voice of the Customer (VoC) data was collected from each significant market segment. The raw VoC data by market segment is shown in Table 19.20.

TABLE 19.20 Voice of the Customer

Selected market segment(s)	Raw VoC data
Army personnel	
General	1.1) I can't afford to lose people to injuries when the equipment breaks.
	1.2) The catapult is useless if it doesn't hit the target.
	1.3) More than a couple of hours is too much down time. I need my catapult to be reliable for at least 2,000 throws.
Captain	2.1) I need a quick response when the catapults break.
	2.2) Preventive maintenance needs to take up less time.
Sergeant	3.1) My job is to hit the target every time I shoot.

Selected market segment(s)	Raw VoC data
Sergeant	3.2) The instructions need to be easy to understand — my people aren't scientists.
Sergeant	3.3) I need better instructions on how to conduct preventive maintenance.
Private	4.1) I can't read.
	4.2) I heard people get hurt using this machine; I don't want that to happen to me!
Internal customers	
Sales force	5.1) The catapults need to be reliable for me to be able to sell them.
	5.2) Every time there is an injury, the story spreads to everyone; each time, it increases in severity.
	5.3) The customers are concerned with preventive maintenance schedules and catapult down time.
Rapid response repair force	6.1) The customers aren't happy when it takes us a long time to get there.
	6.2) The catapults need to be designed with the capability of completing any repairs within 12 hours.

An affinity diagram of the raw VoC data is shown in Table 19.21.

TABLE 19.21 Affinity Diagram

Raw VoC data	Affinity diagram theme(s)	Clarified affinity theme	Quantitative view of clarified theme	CTQ(s) for each quantitative view	Tech specs for each CTQ
1.2, 3.1, 5.1	Hit rate	The product does hit the target with sufficient reliability.	Improve the hit rate.	CTQ1: Improve hit rate beyond 99%, the level of the Mars I.	Hit rate of 3.4 DPMO
1.3, 2.1, 5.3, 6.1, 6.2	Down time for maintenance & repair (M&R)	M&R takes too much time	Decrease the time required for M&R	CTQ2: Decrease M&R time to less than 24 hours, the level of the Mars I	Down time must not exceed 24 consecutive hours
3.2, 3.3, 4.1	Easy instructions	Instructions for use must be easy to understand	Design instructions that are easy to understand	CTQ3: Design instructions that are mistake-proof	Instructions must be understood by all personnel who have completed basic training
2.2, 5.3, 6.2	Down time for preventive maintenance	Preventive maintenance is required too frequently	Decrease the frequency of required preventive maintenance	CTQ4: Decrease frequency of preventive maintenance to once per 2,000 throws	Preventive maintenance must not be required more than once per 2,000 throws

Raw VoC data	Affinity diagram theme(s)	Clarified affinity theme	Quantitative view of clarified theme	CTQ(s) for each quantitative view	Tech specs for each CTQ
1.1, 4.2, 5.2	Injuries	Injuries are unacceptable to customers, end users, and internal sales force	Eliminate injuries resulting from use of the catapult	CTQ5: Determine what causes injuries and mistake proof the catapult	Injury rate must be equal to zero

NOTE　It is not necessary to conduct a Kano analysis for this case study.

All CTQs are defined in Table 19.22.

TABLE 19.22 Definition of CTQs

CTQ	Definition of a unit	Definition of an opportunity for a defect	Definition of a defect
1. Hit rate	Battle or training session	Throw	Throw that misses the target by more than 2 inches in distance, given a target 80 inches away from the catapult.
2. M & R time	Catapult	Preventive maintenance or catapult breaks	If the preventive maintenance or repairs result in the catapult being unavailable for more than 24 hours
3. Mistake-proof instructions	Trainee	Trainee	Trained person who is incapable of operating the catapult
			(continued)

CTQ	Definition of a unit	Definition of an opportunity for a defect	Definition of a defect
4. Less than 1 M&R period per 2,000 throws	2,000 consecutive throws	One Throw	Catapult requires maintenance or repair more than once in any 2,000 consecutive throws
5. No injuries from	Catapult	Injury	Injury to one or more person operation during operation

A SIPOC analysis (see Table 19.23) revealed the following information.

TABLE 19.23 SIPOC Analysis

Suppliers	Inputs (*Xs*)	Process 1 Catapult construction process	Outputs (CTQs)	Customers
Materials vendors	Precut lumber	Procurement request Receipt incoming materials	Hit rate	LNA of Command
Design architect >	Nuts & bolts >	Production of catapults Inspection	M&R time >	LNA operators >
Production equipment	Rubber bands Saws, drills, and files Pins Screws	Shipping Assembly at destination	Ease of use Preventive maintenance Injuries	CI sales force CI rapid response force

Supplier		Inputs (Xs)		Process 2 LNA Catapult purchase process		Outputs (CTQs)		Customer
CI		Unassembled catapult		Order catapult Receive catapult		Completed catapult		LNA
	>	Instructions	>	Assemble catapult Test catapult Feedback to CI	>	Hit rate of 99.99966%	>	

Supplier		Inputs (Xs)		Process 3 LNA Catapult setup process		Outputs (CTQs)		Customers
CI		Rubber band height on bracing arm		Select rubber band height on the bracing arm		Hit rate of 99.99966%		LNA
	>	Position of pin that stops the throwing arm Rubber band height on throwing arm	>	Select position of the pin that stops the throwing arm Select rubber band height on the throwing arm	>		>	

Completing Your Case Study

Prepare the Define phase and submit it for review to: Dr. Howard Gitlow at hgitlow@ miami.edu. Once the define phase passes the tollgate, you can proceed to the Measure phase, using the same critiquing procedure, and so on, until you complete the case. Once you successfully complete the case study, you will be awarded a Six Sigma Green Belt Certification of Achievement by the Executive Education Center of the School of Business Administration of the University of Miami. The cost for the critiquing process is $500 per hour. Please contact sixsigma@miami.edu to establish a critiquing process contract. Usually, Green Belts do not require more than 2 or 3 hours of consultation.

SUMMARY

This chapter describes the protocol for achieving Six Sigma Green Belt certification from the University of Miami. It ends with a fictitious case study that can be used instead of a "real-life" project to meet the University's Green Belt certification criteria. Good luck in your Six Sigma journey!

APPENDICES

REVIEW OF ARITHMETIC AND ALGEBRA

In writing this book, we realize that there are wide differences in the mathematical background of readers. Some readers may have taken various courses in calculus and matrix algebra, whereas others may not have taken any mathematics courses in a long, long time. Because the emphasis in this book is on statistical concepts and the interpretation of Minitab output, no prerequisite beyond elementary algebra is needed. To assess your arithmetic and algebraic skills, we suggest that you answer the following questions, then read the review that follows.

Part 1 Fill in the Correct Answer

1. $\dfrac{\frac{1}{2}}{\frac{2}{3}} =$

2. $(0.4)^2 =$

3. $1 + \dfrac{2}{3} =$

4. $\left(\dfrac{1}{3}\right)^{(4)} =$

5. $\dfrac{1}{5} =$ (in decimals)

6. $1 - (-0.3) =$

7. $4 \times 0.2 \times (-8) =$

8. $\left(\dfrac{1}{4} \times \dfrac{2}{3}\right) =$

9. $\left(\dfrac{1}{100}\right) + \left(\dfrac{1}{200}\right) =$

10. $\sqrt{16} =$

Part 2 Select the Correct Answer

1. If $a = bc$, then $c =$
    a. ab
    b. b/a
    c. a/b
    d. none of the above

2. If $x + y = z$, then y
    a. z/x
    b. $z + x$
    c. $z - x$
    d. none of the above

3. $(x^3)(x^2) =$
    a. x^5
    b. x^6
    c. x^1
    d. none of the above

4. $x^0 =$
    a. x
    b. 1
    c. 0
    d. none of the above

5. $x(y - z) =$
    a. $xy - xz$
    b. $xy - z$
    c. $(y - z)/x$
    d. none of the above

6. $(x + y)/z =$
    a. $(x/z) + y$
    b. $(x/z) + (y/z)$
    c. $x + (y/z)$
    d. none of the above

7. $x/(y + z) =$

    a. $(x/y) + (1/z)$

    b. $(x/y) + (x/z)$

    c. $(y + z)/x$

    d. none of the above

8. If $x = 10$, $y = 5$, $z = 2$, and $w = 20$, then $(xy - z^2)/w =$

    a. 5

    b. 2.3

    c. 46

    d. none of the above

9. $(8x^4)/(4x^2) =$

    a. $2x^2$

    b. 2

    c. $2x$

    d. none of the above

10. $\sqrt{\dfrac{X}{Y}} =$

    a. $\sqrt{Y}/\sqrt{X}$

    b. $\sqrt{1}/\sqrt{XY}$

    c. $\sqrt{X}/\sqrt{Y}$

    d. none of the above

The answers to both parts of the quiz appear at the end of this appendix.

Symbols

Each of the four basic arithmetic operations—addition, subtraction, multiplication, and division—is indicated by an appropriate symbol:

[+] add   [×] or [•] multiply   [−] subtract   [÷] or [/] divide

In addition to these operations, the following symbols are used to indicate equality or inequality:

= equals   ≠ not equal   ≅ approximately equal to   > greater than

< less than   ≥ greater than or equal to   ≤ less than or equal to

Addition

Addition refers to the summation of a set of numbers. In adding numbers, there are two basic laws, the commutative law and the associative law.

The *commutative law* of addition states that the order in which numbers are added is irrelevant. This can be seen in the following two examples.

$$1 + 2 = 3 \qquad 2 + 1 = 3$$
$$x + y = z \qquad y + x = z$$

In each example, it did not matter which number was listed first and which number was listed second.

The *associative law* of addition states that in adding several numbers, any subgrouping of the numbers can be added first, last, or in the middle. This is seen in the following examples:

1. $2 + 3 + 6 + 7 + 4 + 1 = 23$
2. $(5) + (6 + 7) + 4 + 1 = 23$
3. $5 + 13 + 5 = 23$
4. $5 + 6 + 7 + 4 + 1 = 23$

In each of these examples, the order in which the numbers have been added has no effect on the results.

Subtraction

The process of subtraction is the opposite, or inverse, of addition. The operation of subtracting 1 from 2 (i. e., $2 - 1$) means that one unit is to be taken away from two units, leaving a remainder of one unit. In contrast to addition, the commutative and associative laws do not hold for subtraction, as indicated in the following examples:

$8 - 4 = 4$	but	$4 - 8 = -4$
$3 - 6 = -3$	but	$6 - 3 = 3$
$8 - 3 - 2 = 3$	but	$3 - 2 - 8 = -7$
$9 - 4 - 2 = 3$	but	$2 - 4 - 9 = -11$

When subtracting negative numbers, remember that that same result occurs when subtracting a negative number as when adding a positive number. Thus:

$$4 - (-3) = +7 \qquad 4 + 3 = 7$$
$$8 - (-10) = +18 \qquad 8 + 10 = 18$$

Multiplication

The operation of multiplication is a shortcut method of addition when the same number is to be added several times. For example, if 7 is to be added three times $(7 + 7 + 7)$, you could multiply 7 by 3 to obtain the product of 21.

In multiplication, as in addition, the commutative laws and associative laws are in operation, so that:

$a \times b = b \times a$

$4 \times 5 = 5 \times 4 = 20$

$(2 \times 5) \times 6 = 10 \times 6 = 60$

A third law of multiplication, the *distributive law*, applies to the multiplication of one number by the sum of several numbers:

$a(b + c) = ab + ac$

$2(3 + 4) = 2(7) = 2(3) + 2(4) = 14$

The resulting product is the same, regardless of whether b and c are summed and multiplied by a, or a is multiplied by b and by c, then the two products are added together. You also need to remember that when multiplying negative numbers, a negative number multiplied by a negative number equals a positive number. Thus,

$(-a) \times (-b) = ab$

$(-5) \times (-4) = +20$

Division

Just as subtraction is the opposite of addition, division is the opposite, or inverse, of multiplication. Division can be viewed as a shortcut to subtraction. When 20 is divided by 4, you are actually determining the number of times that 4 can be subtracted from 20. In general, however, the number of times one number can be divided by another may not be an exact integer value, because there could be a remainder. For example, if 21 is divided by 4, the answer is $5\frac{1}{4}$ or 5 with a remainder of 1. In division the number on top is called the numerator and the number on the bottom is called the denominator.

As in the case of subtraction, neither the commutative nor the associative law of addition and multiplication holds for division:

$a \div b \neq b \div a$

$9 \div 3 \neq 3 \div 9$

$6 \div (3 \div 2) = 4$

$(6 \div 3) \div 2 = 1$

The distributive law will hold only when the numbers to be added are contained in the numerator, not the denominator. Thus:

$$\frac{a + b}{c} = \frac{a}{c} + \frac{b}{c} \qquad \text{but} \qquad \frac{a}{b + c} \neq \frac{a}{b} + \frac{a}{c}$$

For example:

$$\frac{6 + 9}{3} = \frac{6}{3} + \frac{9}{3} = 2 + 3 = 5$$

$$\frac{1}{2 + 3} = \frac{1}{5} \qquad \text{but} \qquad \frac{1}{2 + 3} \neq \frac{1}{2} + \frac{1}{3}$$

The last important property of division states that if the numerator and the denominator are both multiplied or divided by the same number, the resulting quotient will not be affected. Therefore:

$$\frac{80}{40} = 2$$

then

$$\frac{5(80)}{5(40)} = \frac{400}{200} = 2$$

and

$$\frac{80 \div 5}{40 \div 5} = \frac{16}{8} = 2$$

Fractions

A fraction is a number that consists of a combination of whole numbers and/or parts of whole numbers. For instance, the fraction 1/3 consists of only one portion of a number, whereas the fraction 7/6 consists of the whole number 1 plus the fraction 1/6. Each of the operations of addition, subtraction, multiplication, and division can be used with fractions. When adding and subtracting fractions, you must obtain the lowest common denominator for each fraction prior to adding or subtracting them. Thus, in adding $\frac{1}{3} + \frac{1}{5}$, the lowest common denominator is 15, so:

$$\frac{5}{15} + \frac{3}{15} = \frac{8}{15}$$

In subtracting $\dfrac{1}{4} - \dfrac{1}{6}$, the same principles applies, so that the lowest common denominator is 12, producing a result of:

$$\frac{3}{12} - \frac{2}{12} = \frac{1}{12}$$

Multiplying and dividing fractions do not have the lowest common denominator requirement associated with adding and subtracting fractions. Thus, if a/b is multiplied by c/d, the result is $\dfrac{ac}{bd}$.

The resulting numerator, ac, is the product of the numerators a and c, and the denominator, bd, is the product of the two denominators b and d. The resulting fraction can sometimes be reduced to a lower term by dividing the numerator and denominator by a common factor. For example, taking

$$\frac{2}{3} \times \frac{6}{7} = \frac{12}{21}$$

and dividing the numerator and denominator by 3 produces the result $\dfrac{4}{7}$.

Division of fractions can be thought of as the inverse of multiplication, so the divisor can be inverted and multiplied by the original fraction. Thus:

$$\frac{9}{5} \div \frac{1}{4} = \frac{9}{5} \times \frac{4}{1} = \frac{36}{5}$$

The division of a fraction can also be thought of as a way of converting the fraction to a decimal number. For example, the fraction 2/5 can be converted to a decimal number by dividing its numerator, 2, by its denominator, 5, to produce the decimal number 0.40.

Exponents and Square Roots

Exponentiation (raising a number to a power) provides a shortcut in writing numerous multiplications. For example, $2 \times 2 \times 2 \times 2 \times 2$ can be written as $2^5 = 32$. The 5 represents the exponent (or power) of the number 2, telling you that 2 is to multiplied by itself five times.

There are several rules that can be applied for multiplying or dividing numbers that contain exponents.

Rule 1. $x^a \cdot x^b = x^{(a+b)}$

If two numbers involving a power of the same number are multiplied, the product is the same number, raised to the sum of the powers.

$$4^2 \cdot 4^3 = (4 \cdot 4)(4 \cdot 4 \cdot 4 \cdot 4) = 4^5$$

Rule 2. $(x^a)^b = x^{ab}$

If you take the power of a number that is already taken to a power, the result will be a number that is raised to the product of the two powers. For example:

$$(4^2)^3 = (4^2)(4^2)(4^2) = 4^6$$

Rule 3. $\dfrac{x^a}{x^b} = x^{(a-b)}$

If a number raised to a power is divided by the same number raised to a power, the quotient will be the number raised to the difference of the powers. Thus:

$$\frac{3^5}{3^3} = \frac{3 \cdot 3 \cdot 3 \cdot 3 \cdot 3}{3 \cdot 3 \cdot 3} = 3^2$$

If the denominator has a higher power than the numerator, the resulting quotient will be a negative power. Thus:

$$\frac{3^3}{3^5} = \frac{3 \cdot 3 \cdot 3}{3 \cdot 3 \cdot 3 \cdot 3 \cdot 3} = \frac{1}{3^2} = 3^{-2} = \frac{1}{9}$$

If the difference between the powers of the numerator and denominator is 1, the result will be the number itself. In other words, $x^1 = x$. For example:

$$\frac{3^3}{3^2} = \frac{3 \cdot 3 \cdot 3}{3 \cdot 3} = 3^1 = 3$$

If, however, there is no difference in the power of the numbers in the numerator and denominator, the result will be 1. Thus:

$$\frac{x^a}{x^a} = x^{a-a} = x^0 = 1$$

Therefore, any number raised to the zero power equals 1. For example:

$$\frac{3^3}{3^3} = \frac{3 \cdot 3 \cdot 3}{3 \cdot 3 \cdot 3} = 3^0 = 1$$

The square root represented by the symbol $\sqrt{}$ is a special power of number, the 1/2 power. It indicates the value that, when multiplied by itself, will produce the original number.

Equations

In statistics, many formulas are expressed as equations where one unknown value is a function of another value. Thus, it is important to be able to know how to manipulate equations into various forms. The rules of addition, subtraction, multiplication, and division can be used to work with equations. For example, the equation $x - 2 = 5$ can be solved for x by adding 2 to each side of the equation. This results in $x - 2 + 2 = 5 + 2$. Therefore, $x = 7$.

If $x + y = z$, you could solve for x by subtracting y from both sides of the equation, $x + y - y = z - y$. Therefore, $x = z - y$.

If the product of two variables is equal to a third variable, such as $x \cdot y = z$, you can solve for x by dividing both sides of the equation by y. Thus:

$$\frac{x \cdot y}{y} = \frac{z}{y}$$

$$x = \frac{z}{y}$$

Conversely, if

$$\frac{x}{y} = z,$$

you can solve for x by multiplying both sides of the equation by y.

$$\frac{xy}{y} = zy$$

$$x = zy$$

In summary, the various operations of addition, subtraction, multiplication, and division can be applied to equations as long as the same operation is performed on each side of the equation, thereby maintaining the equality.

Answers to Quiz

Part 1

1. 3/2
2. 0.16
3. 5/3
4. 1/81
5. 0.20
6. 1.30
7. −6.4
8. +1/6
9. 3/200
10. 4

Part 2

1. c
2. c
3. a
4. b
5. a
6. b
7. d
8. b
9. a
10. c

SUMMATION NOTATION

Because the operation of addition occurs so frequently in statistics, the special symbol Σ is used to indicate "take the sum of." If there is a set of n values for a variable labeled X, the expression $\sum_{i=1}^{n} X_i$ indicates that these n values are to be added together from the first value to the last (n^{th}) value. Thus:

$$\sum_{i=1}^{n} X_i = X_1 + X_2 + X_3 + \cdots + X_n$$

To illustrate summation notation, suppose there are five values for a variable X:

$$X_1 = 2, X_2 = 0, X_3 = -1, X_4 = 5, \text{ and } X_5 = 7.$$

For these data,

$$\sum_{i=1}^{n} X_i = X_1 + X_2 + X_3 + X_4 + X_5$$
$$= 2 + 0 + (-1) + 5 + 7 = 13$$

In statistics, it is also often necessary to sum the squared values of a variable. Using summation notation, the sum of the squared Xs is written as:

$$\sum_{i=1}^{n} X_i^2 = X_1^2 + X_2^2 + X_3^2 + \cdots + X_n^2$$

and using the preceding data:

$$\sum_{i=1}^{n} X_i^2 = X_1^2 + X_2^2 + X_3^2 + X_4^2 + X_5^2$$

$$= 2^2 + 0^2 + (-1)^2 + 5^2 + 7^2$$
$$= 4 + 0 + 1 + 25 + 49$$
$$= 79$$

It is important to understand that $\sum_{i=1}^{n} X_i^2$, the sum of the squares, is *not* the same as $\left(\sum_{i=1}^{n} X_i \right)^2$, the square of the sum.

$$\sum_{i=1}^{n} X_i^2 \neq \left(\sum_{i=1}^{n} X_i \right)^2$$

In the preceding example, the sum of squares, $\sum_{i=1}^{n} X_i^2$, equals 79. That is not equal to the square of the sum, $\left(\sum_{i=1}^{n} X_i \right)^2$, which is $(13)^2 = 169$.

Another frequently used operation involves summing the product of two variables, called the *cross-product*. This operation involves two variables, X and Y, each having n values. Then,

$$\sum_{i=1}^{n} X_i Y_i = X_1 Y_1 + X_2 Y_2 + X_3 Y_3 + \cdots + X_5 Y_5$$

Continuing with the preceding data, suppose that a second variable, Y, has the following five values: $Y_1 = 1$, $Y_3 = 3$, $Y_3 = -2$, $X_4 = 4$, and $X_5 = 3$. Then,

$$\sum_{i=1}^{n} X_i Y_i = X_1 Y_1 + X_2 Y_2 + X_3 Y_3 + X_4 Y_4 + X_5 Y_5$$
$$= (2)(1) + (0)(3) + (-1)(-2) + (5)(4) + (7)(3)$$
$$= 2 + 0 + 2 + 20 + 21$$
$$= 45$$

In computing $\sum_{i=1}^{n} X_i Y_i$, the first value of X is multiplied by the first value of Y, the second value of X is multiplied by the second value of Y, and so on. These cross-products are then summed. Note that the sum of the cross-products is *not* equal to the product of the individual sums. That is:

$$\sum_{i=1}^{n} X_i Y_i \neq \left(\sum_{i=1}^{n} X_i \right) \left(\sum_{i=1}^{n} Y_i \right)$$

Using the preceding data, $\sum_{i=1}^{n} X_i = 13$ and $\sum_{i=1}^{n} Y_i = 1 + 3 + (-2) + 4 + 3 = 9$, so that:

$$\left(\sum_{i=1}^{n} X_i\right)\left(\sum_{i=1}^{n} Y_i\right) = (13)(9) = 117.$$

This is not the same as $\sum_{i=1}^{n} X_i Y_i$, which equals 45.

The four basic rules of summation notation are as follows:

Rule 1: The sum of the values of two different variables is equal to the sum of the values of each variable.

$$\sum_{i=1}^{n} (X_i + Y_i) = \sum_{i=1}^{n} X_i + \sum_{i=1}^{n} Y_i$$

Thus, for the preceding data,

$$\sum_{i=1}^{n} (X_i + Y_i) = (2 + 1) + (0 + 3) + (-1 + (-2)) + (5 + 4) + (7 + 3)$$
$$= 3 + 3 + (-3) + 9 + 10$$
$$= 22 = \sum_{i=1}^{5} X_i + \sum_{i=1}^{5} Y_i = 13 + 9 = 22$$

Rule 2: The sum of the difference between the values of two variables is equal to the difference between the sum of the two variables.

$$\sum_{i=1}^{n} (X_i - Y_i) = \sum_{i=1}^{n} X_i - \sum_{i=1}^{n} Y_i$$

Using the preceding data,

$$\sum_{i=1}^{n} (X_i - Y_i) = (2 - 1) + (0 - 3) + (-1 - (-2)) + (5 - 4) + (7 - 3)$$
$$= 1 + (-3) + 1 + 1 + 4$$
$$= 4 = \sum_{i=1}^{5} X_i - \sum_{i=1}^{5} Y_i = 13 - 9 = 4$$

Rule 3: The sum of a constant times a variable is equal to the constant times the sum of the values of the variable:

$$\sum_{i=1}^{n} cX_i = c\sum_{i=1}^{n} X_i$$

where c is a constant. Thus, if $c = 2$,

$$\sum_{i=1}^{5} cX_i = 2\sum_{i=1}^{5} X_i = (2)(2) + 2(0) + (2)(-1) + (2)(5) + (2)(7)$$

$$= 4 + 0 + (-2) + 10 + 14$$

$$= 26 = 2\sum_{i=1}^{5} X_i = (2)(13) = 26$$

Rule 4: A constant summed n times is equal to n multiplied by the value of the constant.

$$\sum_{i=1}^{n} c = nc$$

where c is a constant. Thus, if the constant $c = 2$ is summed five times,

$$\sum_{i=1}^{n} c = 2 + 2 + 2 + 2 + 2$$

$$= 10 = (5)(2) = 10$$

REFERENCES

1. Bashaw, W. L. *Mathematics for Statistics* (New York: Wiley, 1969).
2. Lanzer, P. *Video Review of Arithmetic* (Hickville, NY: Video Aided Instruction, 1999).
3. Levine, D. *The MBA Primer: Business Statistics* (Cincinnati, OH: Southwestern Publishing, 2000).
4. Levine, D. *Video Review of Statistics* (Hickville, NY: Video Aided Instruction, 1989).
5. Shane, H., *Video Review of Elementary Algebra* (Hickville, NY: Video Aided Instruction, 1996).

APPENDIX C

STATISTICAL TABLES

TABLE C.1

The Cumulative Standardized Normal Distribution

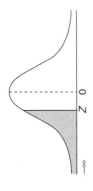

Entry represents area under the cumulative standardized normal distribution from −∞ to Z

Z	0.00	0.01	0.02	0.03	0.04	0.05	0.06	0.07	0.08	0.09
−3.9	0.00005	0.00005	0.00004	0.00004	0.00004	0.00004	0.00004	0.00004	0.00003	0.00003
−3.8	0.00007	0.00007	0.00007	0.00006	0.00006	0.00006	0.00006	0.00005	0.00005	0.00005
−3.7	0.00011	0.00010	0.00010	0.00010	0.00009	0.00009	0.00008	0.00008	0.00008	0.00008
−3.6	0.00016	0.00015	0.00015	0.00014	0.00014	0.00013	0.00013	0.00012	0.00012	0.00011
−3.5	0.00023	0.00022	0.00022	0.00021	0.00020	0.00019	0.00019	0.00018	0.00017	0.00017
−3.4	0.00034	0.00032	0.00031	0.00030	0.00029	0.00028	0.00027	0.00026	0.00025	0.00024
−3.3	0.00048	0.00047	0.00045	0.00043	0.00042	0.00040	0.00039	0.00038	0.00036	0.00035
−3.2	0.00069	0.00066	0.00064	0.00062	0.00060	0.00058	0.00056	0.00054	0.00052	0.00050
−3.1	0.00097	0.00094	0.00090	0.00087	0.00084	0.00082	0.00079	0.00076	0.00074	0.00071
−3.0	0.00135	0.00131	0.00126	0.00122	0.00118	0.00114	0.00111	0.00107	0.00103	0.00100
−2.9	0.0019	0.0018	0.0018	0.0017	0.0016	0.0016	0.0015	0.0015	0.0014	0.0014
−2.8	0.0026	0.0025	0.0024	0.0023	0.0023	0.0022	0.0021	0.0021	0.0020	0.0019
−2.7	0.0035	0.0034	0.0033	0.0032	0.0031	0.0030	0.0029	0.0028	0.0027	0.0026
−2.6	0.0047	0.0045	0.0044	0.0043	0.0041	0.0040	0.0039	0.0038	0.0037	0.0036
−2.5	0.0062	0.0060	0.0059	0.0057	0.0055	0.0054	0.0052	0.0051	0.0049	0.0048
−2.4	0.0082	0.0080	0.0078	0.0075	0.0073	0.0071	0.0069	0.0068	0.0066	0.0064
−2.3	0.0107	0.0104	0.0102	0.0099	0.0096	0.0094	0.0091	0.0089	0.0087	0.0084
−2.2	0.0139	0.0136	0.0132	0.0129	0.0125	0.0122	0.0119	0.0116	0.0113	0.0110

z	.00	.01	.02	.03	.04	.05	.06	.07	.08	.09
-2.1	0.0179	0.0174	0.0170	0.0166	0.0162	0.0158	0.0154	0.0150	0.0146	0.0143
-2.0	0.0228	0.0222	0.0217	0.0212	0.0207	0.0202	0.0197	0.0192	0.0188	0.0183
-1.9	0.0287	0.0281	0.0274	0.0268	0.0262	0.0256	0.0250	0.0244	0.0239	0.0233
-1.8	0.0359	0.0351	0.0344	0.0336	0.0329	0.0322	0.0314	0.0307	0.0301	0.0294
-1.7	0.0446	0.0436	0.0427	0.0418	0.0409	0.0401	0.0392	0.0384	0.0375	0.0367
-1.6	0.0548	0.0537	0.0526	0.0516	0.0505	0.0495	0.0485	0.0475	0.0465	0.0455
-1.5	0.0668	0.0655	0.0643	0.0630	0.0618	0.0606	0.0594	0.0582	0.0571	0.0559
-1.4	0.0808	0.0793	0.0778	0.0764	0.0749	0.0735	0.0721	0.0708	0.0694	0.0681
-1.3	0.0968	0.0951	0.0934	0.0918	0.0901	0.0885	0.0869	0.0853	0.0838	0.0823
-1.2	0.1151	0.1131	0.1112	0.1093	0.1075	0.1056	0.1038	0.1020	0.1003	0.0985
-1.1	0.1357	0.1335	0.1314	0.1292	0.1271	0.1251	0.1230	0.1210	0.1190	0.1170
-1.0	0.1587	0.1562	0.1539	0.1515	0.1492	0.1469	0.1446	0.1423	0.1401	0.1379
-0.9	0.1841	0.1814	0.1788	0.1762	0.1736	0.1711	0.1685	0.1660	0.1635	0.1611
-0.8	0.2119	0.2090	0.2061	0.2033	0.2005	0.1977	0.1949	0.1922	0.1894	0.1867
-0.7	0.2420	0.2388	0.2358	0.2327	0.2296	0.2266	0.2236	0.2206	0.2177	0.2148
-0.6	0.2743	0.2709	0.2676	0.2643	0.2611	0.2578	0.2546	0.2514	0.2482	0.2451
-0.5	0.3085	0.3050	0.3015	0.2981	0.2946	0.2912	0.2877	0.2843	0.2810	0.2776
-0.4	0.3446	0.3409	0.3372	0.3336	0.3300	0.3264	0.3228	0.3192	0.3156	0.3121
-0.3	0.3821	0.3783	0.3745	0.3707	0.3669	0.3632	0.3594	0.3557	0.3520	0.3483
-0.2	0.4207	0.4168	0.4129	0.4090	0.4052	0.4013	0.3974	0.3936	0.3897	0.3859
-0.1	0.4602	0.4562	0.4522	0.4483	0.4443	0.4404	0.4364	0.4325	0.4286	0.4247
-0.0	0.5000	0.4960	0.4920	0.4880	0.4840	0.4801	0.4761	0.4721	0.4681	0.4641

(continued)

TABLE C.1

The Cumulative Standardized Normal Distribution (Continued)

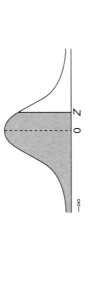

Z	0.00	0.01	0.02	0.03	0.04	0.05	0.06	0.07	0.08	0.09
0.0	0.5000	0.5040	0.5080	0.5120	0.5160	0.5199	0.5239	0.5279	0.5319	0.5359
0.1	0.5398	0.5438	0.5478	0.5517	0.5557	0.5596	0.5636	0.5675	0.5714	0.5753
0.2	0.5793	0.5832	0.5871	0.5910	0.5948	0.5987	0.6026	0.6064	0.6103	0.6141
0.3	0.6179	0.6217	0.6255	0.6293	0.6331	0.6368	0.6406	0.6443	0.6480	0.6517
0.4	0.6554	0.6591	0.6628	0.6664	0.6700	0.6736	0.6772	0.6808	0.6844	0.6879
0.5	0.6915	0.6950	0.6985	0.7019	0.7054	0.7088	0.7123	0.7157	0.7190	0.7224
0.6	0.7257	0.7291	0.7324	0.7357	0.7389	0.7422	0.7454	0.7486	0.7518	0.7549
0.7	0.7580	0.7612	0.7642	0.7673	0.7704	0.7734	0.7764	0.7794	0.7823	0.7852
0.8	0.7881	0.7910	0.7939	0.7967	0.7995	0.8023	0.8051	0.8078	0.8106	0.8133
0.9	0.8159	0.8186	0.8212	0.8238	0.8264	0.8289	0.8315	0.8340	0.8365	0.8389
1.0	0.8413	0.8438	0.8461	0.8485	0.8508	0.8531	0.8554	0.8577	0.8599	0.8621
1.1	0.8643	0.8665	0.8686	0.8708	0.8729	0.8749	0.8770	0.8790	0.8810	0.8830
1.2	0.8849	0.8869	0.8888	0.8907	0.8925	0.8944	0.8962	0.8980	0.8997	0.9015
1.3	0.9032	0.9049	0.9066	0.9082	0.9099	0.9115	0.9131	0.9147	0.9162	0.9177
1.4	0.9192	0.9207	0.9222	0.9236	0.9251	0.9265	0.9279	0.9292	0.9306	0.9319
1.5	0.9332	0.9345	0.9357	0.9370	0.9382	0.9394	0.9406	0.9418	0.9429	0.9441
1.6	0.9452	0.9463	0.9474	0.9484	0.9495	0.9505	0.9515	0.9525	0.9535	0.9545
1.7	0.9554	0.9564	0.9573	0.9582	0.9591	0.9599	0.9608	0.9616	0.9625	0.9633
1.8	0.9641	0.9649	0.9656	0.9664	0.9671	0.9678	0.9686	0.9693	0.9699	0.9706

z	.00	.01	.02	.03	.04	.05	.06	.07	.08	.09
1.9	0.9713	0.9719	0.9726	0.9732	0.9738	0.9744	0.9750	0.9756	0.9761	0.9767
2.0	0.9772	0.9778	0.9783	0.9788	0.9793	0.9798	0.9803	0.9808	0.9812	0.9817
2.1	0.9821	0.9826	0.9830	0.9834	0.9838	0.9842	0.9846	0.9850	0.9854	0.9857
2.2	0.9861	0.9864	0.9868	0.9871	0.9875	0.9878	0.9881	0.9884	0.9887	0.9890
2.3	0.9893	0.9896	0.9898	0.9901	0.9904	0.9906	0.9909	0.9911	0.9913	0.9916
2.4	0.9918	0.9920	0.9922	0.9925	0.9927	0.9929	0.9931	0.9932	0.9934	0.9936
2.5	0.9938	0.9940	0.9941	0.9943	0.9945	0.9946	0.9948	0.9949	0.9951	0.9952
2.6	0.9953	0.9955	0.9956	0.9957	0.9959	0.9960	0.9961	0.9962	0.9963	0.9964
2.7	0.9965	0.9966	0.9967	0.9968	0.9969	0.9970	0.9971	0.9972	0.9973	0.9974
2.8	0.9974	0.9975	0.9976	0.9977	0.9977	0.9978	0.9979	0.9979	0.9980	0.9981
2.9	0.9981	0.9982	0.9982	0.9983	0.9984	0.9984	0.9985	0.9985	0.9986	0.9986
3.0	0.99865	0.99869	0.99874	0.99878	0.99882	0.99886	0.99889	0.99893	0.99897	0.99900
3.1	0.99903	0.99906	0.99910	0.99913	0.99916	0.99918	0.99921	0.99924	0.99926	0.99929
3.2	0.99931	0.99934	0.99936	0.99938	0.99940	0.99942	0.99944	0.99946	0.99948	0.99950
3.3	0.99952	0.99953	0.99955	0.99957	0.99958	0.99960	0.99961	0.99962	0.99964	0.99965
3.4	0.99966	0.99968	0.99969	0.99970	0.99971	0.99972	0.99973	0.99974	0.99975	0.99976
3.5	0.99977	0.99978	0.99978	0.99979	0.99980	0.99981	0.99981	0.99982	0.99983	0.99983
3.6	0.99984	0.99985	0.99985	0.99986	0.99986	0.99987	0.99987	0.99988	0.99988	0.99989
3.7	0.99989	0.99990	0.99990	0.99990	0.99991	0.99991	0.99992	0.99992	0.99992	0.99992
3.8	0.99993	0.99993	0.99993	0.99994	0.99994	0.99994	0.99994	0.99995	0.99995	0.99995
3.9	0.99995	0.99995	0.99996	0.99996	0.99996	0.99996	0.99996	0.99996	0.99997	0.99997
4.0	0.99996832									
4.5	0.99999660									
5.0	0.99999971									
5.5	0.99999998									
6.0	0.99999999									

TABLE C.2

Critical Values of t

For a particular number of degree of freedom, entry represents the critical value of t corresponding to a specified upper-tail area (α)

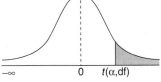

Upper-Tail Areas

Degrees of Freedom	0.25	0.10	0.05	0.025	0.01	0.005
1	1.0000	3.0777	6.3138	12.7062	31.8207	63.6574
2	0.8165	1.8856	2.9200	4.3027	6.9646	9.9248
3	0.7649	1.6377	2.3534	3.1824	4.5407	5.8409
4	0.7407	1.5332	2.1318	2.7764	3.7469	4.6041
5	0.7267	1.4759	2.0150	2.5706	3.3649	4.0322
6	0.7176	1.4398	1.9432	2.4469	3.1427	3.7074
7	0.7111	1.4149	1.8946	2.3646	2.9980	3.4995
8	0.7064	1.3968	1.8595	2.3060	2.8965	3.3554
9	0.7027	1.3830	1.8331	2.2622	2.8214	3.2498
10	0.6998	1.3722	1.8125	2.2281	2.7638	3.1693
11	0.6974	1.3634	1.7959	2.2010	2.7181	3.1058
12	0.6955	1.3562	1.7823	2.1788	2.6810	3.0545
13	0.6938	1.3502	1.7709	2.1604	2.6503	3.0123
14	0.6924	1.3450	1.7613	2.1448	2.6245	2.9768
15	0.6912	1.3406	1.7531	2.1315	2.6025	2.9467
16	0.6901	1.3368	1.7459	2.1199	2.5835	2.9208
17	0.6892	1.3334	1.7396	2.1098	2.5669	2.8982
18	0.6884	1.3304	1.7341	2.1009	2.5524	2.8784
19	0.6876	1.3277	1.7291	2.0930	2.5395	2.8609
20	0.6870	1.3253	1.7247	2.0860	2.5280	2.8453
21	0.6864	1.3232	1.7207	2.0796	2.5177	2.8314
22	0.6858	1.3212	1.7171	2.0739	2.5083	2.8188
23	0.6853	1.3195	1.7139	2.0687	2.4999	2.8073
24	0.6848	1.3178	1.7109	2.0639	2.4922	2.7969
25	0.6844	1.3163	1.7081	2.0595	2.4851	2.7874
26	0.6840	1.3150	1.7056	2.0555	2.4786	2.7787
27	0.6837	1.3137	1.7033	2.0518	2.4727	2.7707
28	0.6834	1.3125	1.7011	2.0484	2.4671	2.7633
29	0.6830	1.3114	1.6991	2.0452	2.4620	2.7564
30	0.6828	1.3104	1.6973	2.0423	2.4573	2.7500

(continued)

TABLE C.2

Critical Values of *t* (Continued)

For a particular number of degree of freedom, entry represents the critical value of t corresponding to a specified upper-tail area (α)

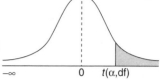

Upper-Tail Areas

Degrees of Freedom	0.25	0.10	0.05	0.025	0.01	0.005
31	0.6825	1.3095	1.6955	2.0395	2.4528	2.7440
32	0.6822	1.3086	1.6939	2.0369	2.4487	2.7385
33	0.6820	1.3077	1.6924	2.0345	2.4448	2.7333
34	0.6818	1.3070	1.6909	2.0322	2.4411	2.7284
35	0.6816	1.3062	1.6896	2.0301	2.4377	2.7238
36	0.6814	1.3055	1.6883	2.0281	2.4345	2.7195
37	0.6812	1.3049	1.6871	2.0262	2.4314	2.7154
38	0.6810	1.3042	1.6860	2.0244	2.4286	2.7116
39	0.6808	1.3036	1.6849	2.0227	2.4258	2.7079
40	0.6807	1.3031	1.6839	2.0211	2.4233	2.7045
41	0.6805	1.3025	1.6829	2.0195	2.4208	2.7012
42	0.6804	1.3020	1.6820	2.0181	2.4185	2.6981
43	0.6802	1.3016	1.6811	2.0167	2.4163	2.6951
44	0.6801	1.3011	1.6802	2.0154	2.4141	2.6923
45	0.6800	1.3006	1.6794	2.0141	2.4121	2.6896
46	0.6799	1.3022	1.6787	2.0129	2.4102	2.6870
47	0.6797	1.2998	1.6779	2.0117	2.4083	2.6846
48	0.6796	1.2994	1.6772	2.0106	2.4066	2.6822
49	0.6795	1.2991	1.6766	2.0096	2.4049	2.6800
50	0.6794	1.2987	1.6759	2.0086	2.4033	2.6778
51	0.6793	1.2984	1.6753	2.0076	2.4017	2.6757
52	0.6792	1.2980	1.6747	2.0066	2.4002	2.6737
53	0.6791	1.2977	1.6741	2.0057	2.3988	2.6718
54	0.6791	1.2974	1.6736	2.0049	2.3974	2.6700
55	0.6790	1.2971	1.6730	2.0040	2.3961	2.6682
56	0.6789	1.2969	1.6725	2.0032	2.3948	2.6665
57	0.6788	1.2966	1.6720	2.0025	2.3936	2.6649
58	0.6787	1.2963	1.6716	2.0017	2.3924	2.6633
59	0.6787	1.2961	1.6711	2.0010	2.3912	2.6618
60	0.6786	1.2958	1.6706	2.0003	2.3901	2.6603

(continued)

TABLE C.2

Critical Values of *t* (Continued)

For a particular number of degree of freedom, entry represents the critical value of t corresponding to a specified upper-tail area (α)

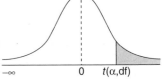

Upper-Tail Areas

Degrees of Freedom	0.25	0.10	0.05	0.025	0.01	0.005
61	0.6785	1.2956	1.6702	1.9996	2.3890	2.6589
62	0.6785	1.2954	1.6698	1.9990	2.3880	2.6575
63	0.6784	1.2951	1.6694	1.9983	2.3870	2.6561
64	0.6783	1.2949	1.6690	1.9977	2.3860	2.6549
65	0.6783	1.2947	1.6686	1.9971	2.3851	2.6536
66	0.6782	1.2945	1.6683	1.9966	2.3842	2.6524
67	0.6782	1.2943	1.6679	1.9960	2.3833	2.6512
68	0.6781	1.2941	1.6676	1.9955	2.3824	2.6501
69	0.6781	1.2939	1.6672	1.9949	2.3816	2.6490
70	0.6780	1.2938	1.6669	1.9944	2.3808	2.6479
71	0.6780	1.2936	1.6666	1.9939	2.3800	2.6469
72	0.6779	1.2934	1.6663	1.9935	2.3793	2.6459
73	0.6779	1.2933	1.6660	1.9930	2.3785	2.6449
74	0.6778	1.2931	1.6657	1.9925	2.3778	2.6439
75	0.6778	1.2929	1.6654	1.9921	2.3771	2.6430
76	0.6777	1.2928	1.6652	1.9917	2.3764	2.6421
77	0.6777	1.2926	1.6649	1.9913	2.3758	2.6412
78	0.6776	1.2925	1.6646	1.9908	2.3751	2.6403
79	0.6776	1.2924	1.6644	1.9905	2.3745	2.6395
80	0.6776	1.2922	1.6641	1.9901	2.3739	2.6387
81	0.6775	1.2921	1.6639	1.9897	2.3733	2.6379
82	0.6775	1.2920	1.6636	1.9893	2.3727	2.6371
83	0.6775	1.2918	1.6634	1.9890	2.3721	2.6364
84	0.6774	1.2917	1.6632	1.9886	2.3716	2.6356
85	0.6774	1.2916	1.6630	1.9883	2.3710	2.6349
86	0.6774	1.2915	1.6628	1.9879	2.3705	2.6342
87	0.6773	1.2914	1.6626	1.9876	2.3700	2.6335
88	0.6773	1.2912	1.6624	1.9873	2.3695	2.6329
89	0.6773	1.2911	1.6622	1.9870	2.3690	2.6322

(continued)

TABLE C.2

Critical Values of t (Continued)

For a particular number of degree of freedom, entry represents the critical value of t corresponding to a specified upper-tail area (α)

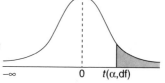

Degrees of Freedom	Upper-Tail Areas					
	0.25	0.10	0.05	0.025	0.01	0.005
90	0.6772	1.2910	1.6620	1.9867	2.3685	2.6316
91	0.6772	1.2909	1.6618	1.9864	2.3680	2.6309
92	0.6772	1.2908	1.6616	1.9861	2.3676	2.6303
93	0.6771	1.2907	1.6614	1.9858	2.3671	2.6297
94	0.6771	1.2906	1.6612	1.9855	2.3667	2.6291
95	0.6771	1.2905	1.6611	1.9853	2.3662	2.6286
96	0.6771	1.2904	1.6609	1.9850	2.3658	2.6280
97	0.6770	1.2903	1.6607	1.9847	2.3654	2.6275
98	0.6770	1.2902	1.6606	1.9845	2.3650	2.6269
99	0.6770	1.2902	1.6604	1.9842	2.3646	2.6264
100	0.6770	1.2901	1.6602	1.9840	2.3642	2.6259
110	0.6767	1.2893	1.6588	1.9818	2.3607	2.6213
120	0.6765	1.2886	1.6577	1.9799	2.3578	2.6174
∞	0.6745	1.2816	1.6449	1.9600	2.3263	2.5758

TABLE C.3

Critical Values of *F*

For a particular combination of numerator and denominator degrees of freedom, entry represents the critical values of F corresponding to a specified upper-tail area (α).

Denominator df_2	Numerator, df_1								
	1	2	3	4	5	6	7	8	9
1	161.40	199.50	215.70	224.60	230.20	234.00	236.80	238.90	240.50
2	18.51	19.00	19.16	19.25	19.30	19.33	19.35	19.37	19.38
3	10.13	9.55	9.28	9.12	9.01	8.94	8.89	8.85	8.81
4	7.71	6.94	6.59	6.39	6.26	6.16	6.09	6.04	6.00
5	6.61	5.79	5.41	5.19	5.05	4.95	4.88	4.82	4.77
6	5.99	5.14	4.76	4.53	4.39	4.28	4.21	4.15	4.10
7	5.59	4.74	4.35	4.12	3.97	3.87	3.79	3.73	3.68
8	5.32	4.46	4.07	3.84	3.69	3.58	3.50	3.44	3.39
9	5.12	4.26	3.86	3.63	3.48	3.37	3.29	3.23	3.18
10	4.96	4.10	3.71	3.48	3.33	3.22	3.14	3.07	3.02
11	4.84	3.98	3.59	3.36	3.20	3.09	3.01	2.95	2.90
12	4.75	3.89	3.49	3.26	3.11	3.00	2.91	2.85	2.80
13	4.67	3.81	3.41	3.18	3.03	2.92	2.83	2.77	2.71
14	4.60	3.74	3.34	3.11	2.96	2.85	2.76	2.70	2.65
15	4.54	3.68	3.29	3.06	2.90	2.79	2.71	2.64	2.59
16	4.49	3.63	3.24	3.01	2.85	2.74	2.66	2.59	2.54
17	4.45	3.59	3.20	2.96	2.81	2.70	2.61	2.55	2.49
18	4.41	3.55	3.16	2.93	2.77	2.66	2.58	2.51	2.46
19	4.38	3.52	3.13	2.90	2.74	2.63	2.54	2.48	2.42
20	4.35	3.49	3.10	2.87	2.71	2.60	2.51	2.45	2.39
21	4.32	3.47	3.07	2.84	2.68	2.57	2.49	2.42	2.37
22	4.30	3.44	3.05	2.82	2.66	2.55	2.46	2.40	2.34
23	4.28	3.42	3.03	2.80	2.64	2.53	2.44	2.37	2.32
24	4.26	3.40	3.01	2.78	2.62	2.51	2.42	2.36	2.30
25	4.24	3.39	2.99	2.76	2.60	2.49	2.40	2.34	2.28
26	4.23	3.37	2.98	2.74	2.59	2.47	2.39	2.32	2.27
27	4.21	3.35	2.96	2.73	2.57	2.46	2.37	2.31	2.25
28	4.20	3.34	2.95	2.71	2.56	2.45	2.36	2.29	2.24
29	4.18	3.33	2.93	2.70	2.55	2.43	2.35	2.28	2.22
30	4.17	3.32	2.92	2.69	2.53	2.42	2.33	2.27	2.21
40	4.08	3.23	2.84	2.61	2.45	2.34	2.25	2.18	2.12
60	4.00	3.15	2.76	2.53	2.37	2.25	2.17	2.10	2.04
120	3.92	3.07	2.68	2.45	2.29	2.17	2.09	2.02	1.96
∞	3.84	3.00	2.60	2.37	2.21	2.10	2.01	1.94	1.88

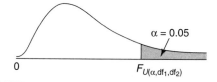

$\alpha = 0.05$

10	12	15	20	24	30	40	60	120	∞
241.90	243.90	245.90	248.00	249.10	250.10	251.10	252.20	253.30	254.30
19.40	19.41	19.43	19.45	19.45	19.46	19.47	19.48	19.49	19.50
8.79	8.74	8.70	8.66	8.64	8.62	8.59	8.57	8.55	8.53
5.96	5.91	5.86	5.80	5.77	5.75	5.72	5.69	5.66	5.63
4.74	4.68	4.62	4.56	4.53	4.50	4.46	4.43	4.40	4.36
4.06	4.00	3.94	3.87	3.84	3.81	3.77	3.74	3.70	3.67
3.64	3.57	3.51	3.44	3.41	3.38	3.34	3.30	3.27	3.23
3.35	3.28	3.22	3.15	3.12	3.08	3.04	3.01	2.97	2.93
3.14	3.07	3.01	2.94	2.90	2.86	2.83	2.79	2.75	2.71
2.98	2.91	2.85	2.77	2.74	2.70	2.66	2.62	2.58	2.54
2.85	2.79	2.72	2.65	2.61	2.57	2.53	2.49	2.45	2.40
2.75	2.69	2.62	2.54	2.51	2.47	2.43	2.38	2.34	2.30
2.67	2.60	2.53	2.46	2.42	2.38	2.34	2.30	2.25	2.21
2.60	2.53	2.46	2.39	2.35	2.31	2.27	2.22	2.18	2.13
2.54	2.48	2.40	2.33	2.29	2.25	2.20	2.16	2.11	2.07
2.49	2.42	2.35	2.28	2.24	2.19	2.15	2.11	2.06	2.01
2.45	2.38	2.31	2.23	2.19	2.15	2.10	2.06	2.01	1.96
2.41	2.34	2.27	2.19	2.15	2.11	2.06	2.02	1.97	1.92
2.38	2.31	2.23	2.16	2.11	2.07	2.03	1.98	1.93	1.88
2.35	2.28	2.20	2.12	2.08	2.04	1.99	1.95	1.90	1.84
2.32	2.25	2.18	2.10	2.05	2.01	1.96	1.92	1.87	1.81
2.30	2.23	2.15	2.07	2.03	1.98	1.91	1.89	1.84	1.78
2.27	2.20	2.13	2.05	2.01	1.96	1.91	1.86	1.81	1.76
2.25	2.18	2.11	2.03	1.98	1.94	1.89	1.84	1.79	1.73
2.24	2.16	2.09	2.01	1.96	1.92	1.87	1.82	1.77	1.71
2.22	2.15	2.07	1.99	1.95	1.90	1.85	1.80	1.75	1.69
2.20	2.13	2.06	1.97	1.93	1.88	1.84	1.79	1.73	1.67
2.19	2.12	2.04	1.96	1.91	1.87	1.82	1.77	1.71	1.65
2.18	2.10	2.03	1.94	1.90	1.85	1.81	1.75	1.70	1.64
2.16	2.09	2.01	1.93	1.89	1.84	1.79	1.74	1.68	1.62
2.08	2.00	1.92	1.84	1.79	1.74	1.69	1.64	1.58	1.51
1.99	1.92	1.84	1.75	1.70	1.65	1.59	1.53	1.47	1.39
1.91	1.83	1.75	1.66	1.61	1.55	1.50	1.43	1.35	1.25
1.83	1.75	1.67	1.57	1.52	1.46	1.39	1.32	1.22	1.00

(continued)

TABLE C.3

Critical Values of *F* (Continued)

Denominator df$_2$	Numerator, df$_1$								
	1	**2**	**3**	**4**	**5**	**6**	**7**	**8**	**9**
1	647.80	799.50	864.20	899.60	921.80	937.10	948.20	956.70	963.30
2	38.51	39.00	39.17	39.25	39.30	39.33	39.36	39.39	39.39
3	17.44	16.04	15.44	15.10	14.88	14.73	14.62	14.54	14.47
4	12.22	10.65	9.98	9.60	9.36	9.20	9.07	8.98	8.90
5	10.01	8.43	7.76	7.39	7.15	6.98	6.85	6.76	6.68
6	8.81	7.26	6.60	6.23	5.99	5.82	5.70	5.60	5.52
7	8.07	6.54	5.89	5.52	5.29	5.12	4.99	4.90	4.82
8	7.57	6.06	5.42	5.05	4.82	4.65	4.53	4.43	4.36
9	7.21	5.71	5.08	4.72	4.48	4.32	4.20	4.10	4.03
10	6.94	5.46	4.83	4.47	4.24	4.07	3.95	3.85	3.78
11	6.72	5.26	4.63	4.28	4.04	3.88	3.76	3.66	3.59
12	6.55	5.10	4.47	4.12	3.89	3.73	3.61	3.51	3.44
13	6.41	4.97	4.35	4.00	3.77	3.60	3.48	3.39	3.31
14	6.30	4.86	4.24	3.89	3.66	3.50	3.38	3.29	3.21
15	6.20	4.77	4.15	3.80	3.58	3.41	3.29	3.20	3.12
16	6.12	4.69	4.08	3.73	3.50	3.34	3.22	3.12	3.05
17	6.04	4.62	4.01	3.66	3.44	3.28	3.16	3.06	2.98
18	5.98	4.56	3.95	3.61	3.38	3.22	3.10	3.01	2.93
19	5.92	4.51	3.90	3.56	3.33	3.17	3.05	2.96	2.88
20	5.87	4.46	3.86	3.51	3.29	3.13	3.01	2.91	2.84
21	5.83	4.42	3.82	3.48	3.25	3.09	2.97	2.87	2.80
22	5.79	4.38	3.78	3.44	3.22	3.05	2.93	2.84	2.76
23	5.75	4.35	3.75	3.41	3.18	3.02	2.90	2.81	2.73
24	5.72	4.32	3.72	3.38	3.15	2.99	2.87	2.78	2.70
25	5.69	4.29	3.69	3.35	3.13	2.97	2.85	2.75	2.68
26	5.66	4.27	3.67	3.33	3.10	2.94	2.82	2.73	2.65
27	5.63	4.24	3.65	3.31	3.08	2.92	2.80	2.71	2.63
28	5.61	4.22	3.63	3.29	3.06	2.90	2.78	2.69	2.61
29	5.59	4.20	3.61	3.27	3.04	2.88	2.76	2.67	2.59
30	5.57	4.18	3.59	3.25	3.03	2.87	2.75	2.65	2.57
40	5.42	4.05	3.46	3.13	2.90	2.74	2.62	2.53	2.45
60	5.29	3.93	3.34	3.01	2.79	2.63	2.51	2.41	2.33
120	5.15	3.80	3.23	2.89	2.67	2.52	2.39	2.30	2.22
∞	5.02	3.69	3.12	2.79	2.57	2.41	2.29	2.19	2.11

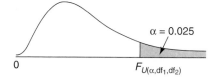

$\alpha = 0.025$

$F_{U(\alpha, df_1, df_2)}$

10	12	15	20	24	30	40	60	120	∞
968.60	976.70	984.90	993.10	997.20	1,001.00	1,006.00	1,010.00	1,014.00	1,018.00
39.40	39.41	39.43	39.45	39.46	39.46	39.47	39.48	39.49	39.50
14.42	14.34	14.25	14.17	14.12	14.08	14.04	13.99	13.95	13.90
8.84	8.75	8.66	8.56	8.51	8.46	8.41	8.36	8.31	8.26
6.62	6.52	6.43	6.33	6.28	6.23	6.18	6.12	6.07	6.02
5.46	5.37	5.27	5.17	5.12	5.07	5.01	4.96	4.90	4.85
4.76	4.67	4.57	4.47	4.42	4.36	4.31	4.25	4.20	4.14
4.30	4.20	4.10	4.00	3.95	3.89	3.84	3.78	3.73	3.67
3.96	3.87	3.77	3.67	3.61	3.56	3.51	3.45	3.39	3.33
3.72	3.62	3.52	3.42	3.37	3.31	3.26	3.20	3.14	3.08
3.53	3.43	3.33	3.23	3.17	3.12	3.06	3.00	2.94	2.88
3.37	3.28	3.18	3.07	3.02	2.96	2.91	2.85	2.79	2.72
3.25	3.15	3.05	2.95	2.89	2.84	2.78	2.72	2.66	2.60
3.15	3.05	2.95	2.84	2.79	2.73	2.67	2.61	2.55	2.49
3.06	2.96	2.86	2.76	2.70	2.64	2.59	2.52	2.46	2.40
2.99	2.89	2.79	2.68	2.63	2.57	2.51	2.45	2.38	2.32
2.92	2.82	2.72	2.62	2.56	2.50	2.44	2.38	2.32	2.25
2.87	2.77	2.67	2.56	2.50	2.44	2.38	2.32	2.26	2.19
2.82	2.72	2.62	2.51	2.45	2.39	2.33	2.27	2.20	2.13
2.77	2.68	2.57	2.46	2.41	2.35	2.29	2.22	2.16	2.09
2.73	2.64	2.53	2.42	2.37	2.31	2.25	2.18	2.11	2.04
2.70	2.60	2.50	2.39	2.33	2.27	2.21	2.14	2.08	2.00
2.67	2.57	2.47	2.36	2.30	2.24	2.18	2.11	2.04	1.97
2.64	2.54	2.44	2.33	2.27	2.21	2.15	2.08	2.01	1.94
2.61	2.51	2.41	2.30	2.24	2.18	2.12	2.05	1.98	1.91
2.59	2.49	2.39	2.28	2.22	2.16	2.09	2.03	1.95	1.88
2.57	2.47	2.36	2.25	2.19	2.13	2.07	2.00	1.93	1.85
2.55	2.45	2.34	2.23	2.17	2.11	2.05	1.98	1.91	1.83
2.53	2.43	2.32	2.21	2.15	2.09	2.03	1.96	1.89	1.81
2.51	2.41	2.31	2.20	2.14	2.07	2.01	1.94	1.87	1.79
2.39	2.29	2.18	2.07	2.01	1.94	1.88	1.80	1.72	1.64
2.27	2.17	2.06	1.94	1.88	1.82	1.74	1.67	1.58	1.48
2.16	2.05	1.94	1.82	1.76	1.69	1.61	1.53	1.43	1.31
2.05	1.94	1.83	1.71	1.64	1.57	1.48	1.39	1.27	1.00

(continued)

TABLE C.3

Critical Values of *F* (Continued)

For a particular combination of numerator and denominator degrees of freedom, entry represents the critical values of F corresponding to a specified upper-tail area (α).

	Numerator, df₁								
Denominator df₂	**1**	**2**	**3**	**4**	**5**	**6**	**7**	**8**	**9**
1	4,052.00	4,999.50	5,403.00	5,625.00	5,764.00	5,859.00	5,928.00	5,982.00	6,022.00
2	98.50	99.00	99.17	99.25	99.30	99.33	99.36	99.37	99.39
3	34.12	30.82	29.46	28.71	28.24	27.91	27.67	27.49	27.35
4	21.20	18.00	16.69	15.98	15.52	15.21	14.98	14.80	14.66
5	16.26	13.27	12.06	11.39	10.97	10.67	10.46	10.29	10.16
6	13.75	10.92	9.78	9.15	8.75	8.47	8.26	8.10	7.98
7	12.25	9.55	8.45	7.85	7.46	7.19	6.99	6.84	6.72
8	11.26	8.65	7.59	7.01	6.63	6.37	6.18	6.03	5.91
9	10.56	8.02	6.99	6.42	6.06	5.80	5.61	5.47	5.35
10	10.04	7.56	6.55	5.99	5.64	5.39	5.20	5.06	4.94
11	9.65	7.21	6.22	5.67	5.32	5.07	4.89	4.74	4.63
12	9.33	6.93	5.95	5.41	5.06	4.82	4.64	4.50	4.39
13	9.07	6.70	5.74	5.21	4.86	4.62	4.44	4.30	4.19
14	8.86	6.51	5.56	5.04	4.69	4.46	4.28	4.14	4.03
15	8.68	6.36	5.42	4.89	4.56	4.32	4.14	4.00	3.89
16	8.53	6.23	5.29	4.77	4.44	4.20	4.03	3.89	3.78
17	8.40	6.11	5.18	4.67	4.34	4.10	3.93	3.79	3.68
18	8.29	6.01	5.09	4.58	4.25	4.01	3.84	3.71	3.60
19	8.18	5.93	5.01	4.50	4.17	3.94	3.77	3.63	3.52
20	8.10	5.85	4.94	4.43	4.10	3.87	3.70	3.56	3.46
21	8.02	5.78	4.87	4.37	4.04	3.81	3.64	3.51	3.40
22	7.95	5.72	4.82	4.31	3.99	3.76	3.59	3.45	3.35
23	7.88	5.66	4.76	4.26	3.94	3.71	3.54	3.41	3.30
24	7.82	5.61	4.72	4.22	3.90	3.67	3.50	3.36	3.26
25	7.77	5.57	4.68	4.18	3.85	3.63	3.46	3.32	3.22
26	7.72	5.53	4.64	4.14	3.82	3.59	3.42	3.29	3.18
27	7.68	5.49	4.60	4.11	3.78	3.56	3.39	3.26	3.15
28	7.64	5.45	4.57	4.07	3.75	3.53	3.36	3.23	3.12
29	7.60	5.42	4.54	4.04	3.73	3.50	3.33	3.20	3.09
30	7.56	5.39	4.51	4.02	3.70	3.47	3.30	3.17	3.07
40	7.31	5.18	4.31	3.83	3.51	3.29	3.12	2.99	2.89
60	7.08	4.98	4.13	3.65	3.34	3.12	2.95	2.82	2.72
120	6.85	4.79	3.95	3.48	3.17	2.96	2.79	2.66	2.56
∞	6.63	4.61	3.78	3.32	3.02	2.80	2.64	2.51	2.41

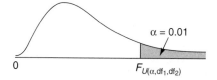

$\alpha = 0.01$

$F_{U(\alpha, df_1, df_2)}$

10	12	15	20	24	30	40	60	120	∞
6,056.00	6,106.00	6,157.00	6,209.00	6,235.00	6,261.00	6,287.00	6,313.00	6,339.00	6,366.00
99.40	99.42	99.43	94.45	99.46	99.47	99.47	99.48	99.49	99.50
27.23	27.05	26.87	26.69	26.60	26.50	26.41	26.32	26.22	26.13
14.55	14.37	14.20	14.02	13.93	13.84	13.75	13.65	13.56	13.46
10.05	9.89	9.72	9.55	9.47	9.38	9.29	9.20	9.11	9.02
7.87	7.72	7.56	7.40	7.31	7.23	7.14	7.06	6.97	6.88
6.62	6.47	6.31	6.16	6.07	5.99	5.91	5.82	5.74	5.65
5.81	5.67	5.52	5.36	5.28	5.20	5.12	5.03	4.95	4.86
5.26	5.11	4.96	4.81	4.73	4.65	4.57	4.48	4.40	4.31
4.85	4.71	4.56	4.41	4.33	4.25	4.17	4.08	4.00	3.91
4.54	4.40	4.25	4.10	4.02	3.94	3.86	3.78	3.69	3.60
4.30	4.16	4.01	3.86	3.78	3.70	3.62	3.54	3.45	3.36
4.10	3.96	3.82	3.66	3.59	3.51	3.43	3.34	3.25	3.17
3.94	3.80	3.66	3.51	3.43	3.35	3.27	3.18	3.09	3.00
3.80	3.67	3.52	3.37	3.29	3.21	3.13	3.05	2.96	2.87
3.69	3.55	3.41	3.26	3.18	3.10	3.02	2.93	2.81	2.75
3.59	3.46	3.31	3.16	3.08	3.00	2.92	2.83	2.75	2.65
3.51	3.37	3.23	3.08	3.00	2.92	2.84	2.75	2.66	2.57
3.43	3.30	3.15	3.00	2.92	2.84	2.76	2.67	2.58	2.49
3.37	3.23	3.09	2.94	2.86	2.78	2.69	2.61	2.52	2.42
3.31	3.17	3.03	2.88	2.80	2.72	2.64	2.55	2.46	2.36
3.26	3.12	2.98	2.83	2.75	2.67	2.58	2.50	2.40	2.31
3.21	3.07	2.93	2.78	2.70	2.62	2.54	2.45	2.35	2.26
3.17	3.03	2.89	2.74	2.66	2.58	2.49	2.40	2.31	2.21
3.13	2.99	2.85	2.70	2.62	2.54	2.45	2.36	2.27	2.17
3.09	2.96	2.81	2.66	2.58	2.50	2.42	2.33	2.23	2.13
3.06	2.93	2.78	2.63	2.55	2.47	2.38	2.29	2.20	2.10
3.03	2.90	2.75	2.60	2.52	2.44	2.35	2.26	2.17	2.06
3.00	2.87	2.73	2.57	2.49	2.41	2.33	2.23	2.14	2.03
2.98	2.84	2.70	2.55	2.47	2.39	2.30	2.21	2.11	2.01
2.80	2.66	2.52	2.37	2.29	2.20	2.11	2.02	1.92	1.80
2.63	2.50	2.35	2.20	2.12	2.03	1.94	1.84	1.73	1.60
2.47	2.34	2.19	2.03	1.95	1.86	1.76	1.66	1.53	1.38
2.32	2.18	2.04	1.88	1.79	1.70	1.59	1.47	1.32	1.00

(continued)

TABLE C.3

Critical Values of F (Continued)

Denominator df$_2$	Numerator, df$_1$								
	1	2	3	4	5	6	7	8	9
1	16,211.00	20,000.000	21,615.00	22,500.00	23,056.00	23,437.00	23,715.00	23,925.00	24,091.00
2	198.50	199.00	199.20	199.20	199.30	199.30	199.40	199.40	199.40
3	55.55	49.80	47.47	46.19	45.39	44.84	44.43	44.13	43.88
4	31.33	26.28	24.26	23.15	22.46	21.97	21.62	21.35	21.14
5	22.78	18.31	16.53	15.56	14.94	14.51	14.20	13.96	13.77
6	18.63	14.54	12.92	12.03	11.46	11.07	10.79	10.57	10.39
7	16.24	12.40	10.88	10.05	9.52	9.16	8.89	8.68	8.51
8	14.69	11.04	9.60	8.81	8.30	7.95	7.69	7.50	7.34
9	13.61	10.11	8.72	7.96	7.47	7.13	6.88	6.69	6.54
10	12.83	9.43	8.08	7.34	6.87	6.54	6.30	6.12	5.97
11	12.23	8.91	7.60	6.88	6.42	6.10	5.86	5.68	5.54
12	11.75	8.51	7.23	6.52	6.07	5.76	5.52	5.35	5.20
13	11.37	8.19	6.93	6.23	5.79	5.48	5.25	5.08	4.94
14	11.06	7.92	6.68	6.00	5.56	5.26	5.03	4.86	4.72
15	10.80	7.70	6.48	5.80	5.37	5.07	4.85	4.67	4.54
16	10.58	7.51	6.30	5.64	5.21	4.91	4.69	4.52	4.38
17	10.38	7.35	6.16	5.50	5.07	4.78	4.56	4.39	4.25
18	10.22	7.21	6.03	5.37	4.96	4.66	4.44	4.28	4.14
19	10.07	7.09	5.92	5.27	4.85	4.56	4.34	4.18	4.04
20	9.94	6.99	5.82	5.17	4.76	4.47	4.26	4.09	3.96
21	9.83	6.89	5.73	5.09	4.68	4.39	4.18	4.02	3.88
22	9.73	6.81	5.65	5.02	4.61	4.32	4.11	3.94	3.81
23	9.63	6.73	5.58	4.95	4.54	4.26	4.05	3.88	3.75
24	9.55	6.66	5.52	4.89	4.49	4.20	3.99	3.83	3.69
25	9.48	6.60	5.46	4.84	4.43	4.15	3.94	3.78	3.64
26	9.41	6.54	5.41	4.79	4.38	4.10	3.89	3.73	3.60
27	9.34	6.49	5.36	4.74	4.34	4.06	3.85	3.69	3.56
28	9.28	6.44	5.32	4.70	4.30	4.02	3.81	3.65	3.52
29	9.23	6.40	5.28	4.66	4.26	3.98	3.77	3.61	3.48
30	9.18	6.35	5.24	4.62	4.23	3.95	3.74	3.58	3.45
40	8.83	6.07	4.98	4.37	3.99	3.71	3.51	3.35	3.22
60	8.49	5.79	4.73	4.14	3.76	3.49	3.29	3.13	3.01
120	8.18	5.54	4.50	3.92	3.55	3.28	3.09	2.93	2.81
∞	7.88	5.30	4.28	3.72	3.35	3.09	2.90	2.74	2.62

Source: Reprinted from E. S. Pearson and H. O. Hartley, eds., Biometrika Tables for Statisticians, 3rd ed., 1966, by permission of the Biometrika Trustees.

α = 0.005

0    $F_{U(\alpha,df_1,df_2)}$

Numerator, df_1

10	12	15	20	24	30	40	60	120	∞
24,224.00	24,426.00	24,630.00	24,836.00	24,910.00	25,044.00	25,148.00	25,253.00	25,359.00	25,465.00
199.40	199.40	199.40	199.40	199.50	199.50	199.50	199.50	199.50	199.50
43.69	43.39	43.08	42.78	42.62	42.47	42.31	42.15	41.99	41.83
20.97	20.70	20.44	20.17	20.03	19.89	19.75	19.61	19.47	19.32
13.62	13.38	13.15	12.90	12.78	12.66	12.53	12.40	12.27	12.11
10.25	10.03	9.81	9.59	9.47	9.36	9.24	9.12	9.00	8.88
8.38	8.18	7.97	7.75	7.65	7.53	7.42	7.31	7.19	7.08
7.21	7.01	6.81	6.61	6.50	6.40	6.29	6.18	6.06	5.95
6.42	6.23	6.03	5.83	5.73	5.62	5.52	5.41	5.30	5.19
5.85	5.66	5.47	5.27	5.17	5.07	4.97	4.86	4.75	1.61
5.42	5.24	5.05	4.86	4.75	4.65	4.55	4.44	4.34	4.23
5.09	4.91	4.72	4.53	4.43	4.33	4.23	4.12	4.01	3.90
4.82	4.64	4.46	4.27	4.17	4.07	3.97	3.87	3.76	3.65
4.60	4.43	4.25	4.06	3.96	3.86	3.76	3.66	3.55	3.41
4.42	4.25	4.07	3.88	3.79	3.69	3.58	3.48	3.37	3.26
4.27	4.10	3.92	3.73	3.64	3.54	3.44	3.33	3.22	3.11
4.14	3.97	3.79	3.61	3.51	3.41	3.31	3.21	3.10	2.98
4.03	3.86	3.68	3.50	3.40	3.30	3.20	3.10	2.89	2.87
3.93	3.76	3.59	3.40	3.31	3.21	3.11	3.00	2.89	2.78
3.85	3.68	3.50	3.32	3.22	3.12	3.02	2.92	2.81	2.69
3.77	3.60	3.43	3.24	3.15	3.05	2.95	2.84	2.73	2.61
3.70	3.54	3.36	3.18	3.08	2.98	2.88	2.77	2.66	2.55
3.64	3.47	3.30	3.12	3.02	2.92	2.82	2.71	2.60	2.48
3.59	3.42	3.25	3.06	2.97	2.87	2.77	2.66	2.55	2.43
3.54	3.37	3.20	3.01	2.92	2.82	2.72	2.61	2.50	2.38
3.49	3.33	3.15	2.97	2.87	2.77	2.67	2.56	2.45	2.33
3.45	3.28	3.11	2.93	2.83	2.73	2.63	2.52	2.41	2.29
3.41	3.25	3.07	2.89	2.79	2.69	2.59	2.48	2.37	2.25
3.38	3.21	3.04	2.86	2.76	2.66	2.56	2.45	2.33	2.21
3.34	3.18	3.01	2.82	2.73	2.63	2.52	2.42	2.30	2.18
3.12	2.95	2.78	2.60	2.50	2.40	2.30	2.18	2.06	1.93
2.90	2.74	2.57	2.39	2.29	2.19	2.08	1.96	1.83	1.69
2.71	2.54	2.37	2.19	2.09	1.98	1.87	1.75	1.61	1.43
2.52	2.36	2.19	2.00	1.90	1.79	1.67	1.53	1.36	1.00

TABLE C.4

Control Chart Constants

Number of Observations in Subgroup, n	A_2	A_3	B_3	B_4	c_4	d_2	d_3	D_3	D_4	E_2
2	1.880	2.659	0.000	3.267	0.7979	1.128	0.853	0.000	3.267	2.660
3	1.023	1.954	0.000	2.568	0.8862	1.693	0.888	0.000	2.574	1.772
4	0.729	1.628	0.000	2.266	0.9213	2.059	0.880	0.000	2.282	1.457
5	0.577	1.427	0.000	2.089	0.9400	2.326	0.864	0.000	2.114	1.290
6	0.483	1.287	0.030	1.970	0.9515	2.534	0.848	0.000	2.004	1.184
7	0.419	1.182	0.118	1.882	0.9594	2.704	0.833	0.076	1.924	1.109
8	0.373	1.099	0.185	1.815	0.9650	2.847	0.820	0.136	1.864	1.054
9	0.337	1.032	0.239	1.761	0.9693	2.970	0.808	0.184	1.816	1.010
10	0.308	0.975	0.284	1.716	0.9727	3.078	0.797	0.223	1.777	0.975
11	0.285	0.927	0.321	1.679	0.9754	3.173	0.787	0.256	1.744	
12	0.266	0.886	0.354	1.646	0.9776	3.258	0.778	0.283	1.717	
13	0.249	0.850	0.382	1.618	0.9794	3.336	0.770	0.307	1.693	
14	0.235	0.817	0.406	1.594	0.9810	3.407	0.762	0.328	1.672	

15	0.223	0.789	0.428	1.572	0.9823	3.472	0.755	0.347	1.653
16	0.212	0.763	0.448	1.552	0.9835	3.532	0.749	0.363	1.637
17	0.203	0.739	0.466	1.534	0.9845	3.588	0.743	0.378	1.622
18	0.194	0.718	0.482	1.518	0.9854	3.640	0.738	0.391	1.608
19	0.187	0.698	0.497	1.503	0.9862	3.689	0.733	0.403	1.597
20	0.180	0.680	0.510	1.490	0.9869	3.735	0.729	0.415	1.585
21	0.173	0.663	0.523	1.477	0.9876	3.778	0.724	0.425	1.575
22	0.167	0.647	0.534	1.466	0.9882	3.819	0.720	0.434	1.566
23	0.162	0.633	0.545	1.455	0.9887	3.858	0.716	0.443	1.557
24	0.157	0.619	0.555	1.445	0.9892	3.895	0.712	0.451	1.548
25	0.153	0.606	0.565	1.435	0.9896	3.931	0.709	0.459	1.541
More than 25	$3/\sqrt{n}$		$1-3/\sqrt{2n}$	$1+3/\sqrt{2n}$					

Source: A_2, A_3, B_3, B_4, c_4, d_2, d_3, D_4, E_2 reprinted with permission from ASTM Manual on the Presentation of Data and Control Chart Analysis (Philadelphia, Penn.: ASTM, 1976), pp. 134–36. Copyright ASTM.

DOCUMENTATION OF DATA FILES

The following is an alphabetical listing and description of all the Minitab files found on the text web site located at **http://www.prenhall.com/gitlow/**. The icons that appear throughout the text identify these files.

ACCIDENT	Number of accidents
AUTOTHEFT	Time, Month, number of car thefts (before)
AUTOTHEFT1	Time, Month, number of car thefts (before and after)
BANK	Waiting time
BANKWAIT	Waiting time
BASELINE	Hour, durability, functionality, X_4 = RCT, X_5 = Discr., X_6 = Inv, X_7 = Shelf, X_8 = Usage
BEARINGS	Ring osculation, cage design, heat treatment, relative life
BEARINGS2	Balls, cage design, grease, amount of grease, average life
CAKE	Flour, shortening, egg powder, oven temperature, baking time, and rating score
CHEMICAL	Batch and Viscosity
CHOCOLATE	Weight of chocolate bars
CIRCUITS	Batch, position 1, position 2, position 18, position 19, position 28, thickness, position
COMPLAINTS	Week and number of complaints
CTQ	X_1, X_2, CTQ
CTQ2	Standard order, run order, center point, blocks, A, B, C, CTQ
CYCLETIME2	Time, transaction, cycle time

CYCLETIME	Time
DATAMINING	Sample number, day, hour, X_1, X_2, X_3, X_7, durability, functionality
DEFECTIVES	Number of defective entries
FACTORIAL	Standard order, run order, center point, blocks, vendor, size, ridges, durability, functionality
FIGURE15-1	Entries for cause-and-effect diagram of Figure 15.1
GAGE	Inspector, reading, and CTQ value
GAGER&R1	Random order, standard order, unit, inspector, measure
GAGER&R-FUNCTIONALITY	Box, inspector, count, functionality
GAGER&R-FUNCTIONALITY2	Box, inspector, count, functionality
GEAR	Tooth size, part positioning, distortion
GNOMES	Day, sample size, number cracked
HELICOPTER	Operator, helicopter 1, helicopter 21, helicopter 38, helicopter 59
HOSPITAL	Hospital supply
IBIX-LARGE	Vendor, size, ridges, durability
INSULATOR	Day, number inspected, nonconforming
INTAGLIO	Untreated, treated
KEYBOARD	Cause, frequency, percent
MULTIVARI	Row, X_1, X_2, X_3, and Y values
PAPER	Lots, square feet, defects
PEANUT	Carbon dioxide pressure, carbon dioxide temperature, peanut moisture, carbon dioxide flow rate, peanut particle size, and amount of oil dissolved
PILOT	Vendor, size, ridges, durability
PROCESSING1	Total time, record pull time
PROCESSING2	Total time, record pull time, before ($= 1$) and after ($= 2$)
PRODUCTIONCOST	Month, production cost in PSD, project ($1 =$ before Six Sigma, $2 =$ after Six Sigma), production cost
READY	Time
REVENUE	Month, revenue in millions of dollars
TENSILE	Strength
THICKNESS	Thickness
TRANSMIT	Day and number of errors in transmission
VIALS	Observation number, time, value 1, value 2, value 3, value 4, value 5, value 6

α **risk**—The α risk is the probability of committing a Type I error or the probability of rejecting the null hypothesis when it is true.

Additive flag system—An additive flag system is used to track corporate indicators that are the summation of departmental indicators; for example, the corporate indicator (Y) is a linear combination of the departmental indicators $(X_1 + X_2 + X_3 + X_4)$.

Affinity diagram—An affinity diagram is used to organize verbal and pictorial data consisting of facts, opinions, intuition, and experience into natural clusters that bring out the latent structure of the problem under study.

Aids for transformation—Top management studies the aids for a fruitful transformation to Six Sigma management at all levels within an organization and throughout the organization's interdependent system of stakeholders.

Army Air Corps (AAC)—The AAC is the air corps of the Lilliputian National Army.

Alternative hypothesis (H_1)—The alternative hypothesis is the opposite of the null hypothesis (H_0).

Analysis of Variance (ANOVA)—Analysis of Variance is a statistical method that tests the significance of different factors (Xs) on a CTQ.

Analytic study—An analytic study leads to actions on the cause-and-effect system of a process.

Analyze phase—The analyze phase involves identifying the upstream variables (Xs) for each CTQ using a flowchart. Upstream variables are the factors that affect the performance of a CTQ. Additionally, the analyze phase involves operationally defining each X, collecting baseline data for each X, performing studies to determine the veracity of the measurement system for each X, establishing baseline capabilities for each X, and understanding the effect of each X on each CTQ.

Arithmetic mean—Also called the *mean*, the arithmetic mean is the most commonly used measure of central tendency. It is calculated by summing the observed numerical values of a variable in a set of data, then dividing the total by the number of observations involved.

Attractive Kano category (A)—An attractive Kano cognitive image is one in which user satisfaction is not proportional to the performance of the feature; low levels of performance create feelings of indifference to the feature, but high levels of performance create feelings of delight to the feature.

Attribute check sheet—An attribute check sheet is used to collect baseline data about a CTQ or an X that is count attribute data.

Attribute data—Attribute data occurs when an item is either classified into two or more categories (e.g. defective or conforming) or is used as an area of opportunity to count occurrences of a phenomenon (e.g., number of defects per item).

Attribute key indicators—Attribute indicators are used when a key objective is being

683

monitored using attribute data (classification or count data) over time.

Attribute process capability—Attribute process capability studies determine a process's capability in terms of fraction of defective output or counts of defects for a unit of output.

β risk—The β risk is the probability of committing a Type II error or the probability of failing to reject the null hypothesis when it is false.

Bar chart—a pictorial device that presents each category as a bar whose length is the frequency or percentage of observations falling into a category.

Barriers against transformation—Top management studies the barriers against a fruitful transformation to Six Sigma management at all levels within an organization and throughout the organization's interdependent system of stakeholders.

Bias over domain—Bias over domain (accuracy) is the difference between the observed process average and a reference value over the domain of a gage.

Bias over time—Bias over time (also called *accuracy*) is the difference between the observed process average and a reference value over time.

Bimodal distribution—A bimodal distribution is a distribution with two concentrations of data.

Binary key indicators—Binary indicators (Yes/No by date) are used when a key indicator monitors whether an action has been accomplished by a given data.

Binomial distribution—The binomial distribution is a probability distribution that finds the probability of a given number of successes for a given probability of success and sample size.

Black Belt—A Black Belt is a full-time change agent and improvement leader who may not be an expert in the process under study. A Black Belt is an individual who possesses a deep understanding of statistical methods and has successfully led two or more Six Sigma projects that have led to dramatic quality improvements and cost reductions.

Blocking—Blocking is a method that allows team members to collect experimental data about a CTQ in such a way that it is possible to isolate the effect of a controllable nuisance variable on the CTQ.

Bottleneck—A bottleneck is any step in a process whose capacity is lower than the outputs produced by the previous process step and limits the amount of information or material that flows through a process.

Box-and-whisker plot—A box-and-whisker plot is a graphical representation of the five-number summary that consists of the smallest value, the first quartile (or 25th percentile), the median, the third quartile (or 75th percentile), and the largest value.

Brainstorming—Brainstorming is a technique used to elicit a large number of ideas from a team using its collective thinking power.

Brown Belt certification—A Brown Belt is an individual who has a deep understanding of statistical methods and can lead a team. She or he is a Green Belt, has passed the Black Belt certification examinations, but has not completed two Six Sigma projects.

Business Case—A business case identifies the financial and customer rationales for doing a Six Sigma project.

Business Objectives—Business objectives are the goals that must routinely be pursued within an organization if it is to function.

Calibration—Calibration is the adjustment of a measurement instrument to eliminate bias.

Cause-and-Effect (C&E) diagram—A C&E diagram is a tool used to organize the possible sources of variation (*X*s) in a CTQ and assist team members in the identification of the most probable causes (*X*s) of the variation. C&E diagrams are also known as *Ishikawa diagrams* or *fishbone diagrams.*

C&E matrix—A C&E matrix is a tool used to organize the possible sources of variation (*X*s) for several CTQs simultaneously and to assist team members in the identification of the most probable causes (*X*s) for each CTQ. A C&E matrix is a multivariate C&E diagram.

Champion—Champions take a very active sponsorship and leadership role in conducting and implementing Six Sigma projects. A Champion is an individual who is aware of the theory and practice of Six Sigma project teams while able to adequately review projects, remove impediments, and secure adequate resources and support.

Change-many-factors-at-once design—An experiment in which a researcher changes the levels of all of the factors, or *X*s, simultaneously.

Check sheets—Check sheets are used to collect data on *X*s and CTQs in a format that permits efficient and easy analysis by team members. There are three types of check sheets: attribute check sheets, measurement check sheets, and defect location check sheets.

Circumstantial data—Circumstantial data presents the emotions, images, and circumstances that come to mind for lead and heavy users when they think about a product, service, or process. Circumstantial data is useful for identifying major new features of existing products, services, or processes, or for creating entirely new products, services, or processes.

Classical approach for assigning probability—The classical approach for assigning probability is based on prior knowledge of the population involved.

Cluster sample—A Cluster sample is a probability sample in which the *N* individuals or

items in the frame are divided into many clusters.

Cognitive images—Cognitive images are the detailed, unambiguous, qualitative statements of needs and wants in the language of design engineers that are translations from focus point (user's underlying and unexpressed needs and wants).

Collectively exhaustive events—Collectively exhaustive events are a set of events in which one of the events must occur.

Common variation—Common variation is the variation in a process due to the process itself, for example, variation due to policies and procedures.

Completely randomized design—A completely randomized design is a design in which there is only a single factor (*X*) affecting a CTQ.

Confidence interval estimate—A confidence interval is an estimate of a population parameter given by an interval with a lower and upper limit.

Confounding—Confounding occurs when the effect of one factor or interaction is mixed up with the effect of another factor or interaction.

Contingency plan—A contingency plan provides the alternative actions immediately available to a process owner when a failure mode occurs in his or her process, despite process improvement actions.

Continuous improvement view of quality—The continuous improvement view of quality expresses the view that it is always economical to reduce variation and center a process on nominal, absent capital investment.

Control chart—A control chart is a tool for distinguishing between the common and special causes of variation for a CTQ or *X*.

Control phase—The control phase involves avoiding potential problems with the *X*s with risk management and mistake proofing, standardizing successful system revisions, controlling the critical Xs, documenting each control plan, and turning the revised system over to the system owner.

Control plan (quality control process chart)—The control plan specifies the documentation for the revised process, a data collection plan for the revised process, and procedures and training necessary to continuously turn the PDSA cycle for the revised process.

Controllable nuisance variable—A controllable nuisance variable is a factor (X) whose levels can be set by an experimenter but is not of direct interest to the experimenter. The principle of blocking is used to deal with controllable nuisance variables.

Cost avoidance—Cost avoidance includes those costs that can be reduced if management chooses to do so, but until action is taken, no real costs are saved.

Cost reduction—Cost reduction includes decreases in costs that fall to the bottom of the profit and loss statement.

Crisis—A crisis is a circumstance that endangers the life of an organization. It is frequently the stimulus that provokes top management to begin Six Sigma management.

Critical value—A critical value divides the nonrejection region from the rejection region in a hypothesis test.

CTQ—CTQ is an acronym for critical-to-quality characteristic for a product, service, or process. It is a measure of what is important to customers. Six Sigma projects are designed to improve one or more CTQs.

Customer satisfaction key objectives—Customer satisfaction key objectives are the set of objectives that focus on the needs of customers. They include: (1) customer's desired outcomes, (2) customer's undesired outcomes, (3) customer's desired product

and service attributes, and (4) customer's desired process characteristics.

Dashboard—A dashboard is a tool used by management to clarify and assign accountability for the "critical few" key objectives, key indicators, and projects/tasks needed to steer an organization toward its mission statement.

Data—Information collected about a product, service, process, individual person, item, or thing.

Decrease project or task—A decrease project or task is a Six Sigma project that tries to get the value of a CTQ to be X units or Y percentage points lower than the current value of the CTQ.

Defect—A defect is a nonconformance on one of many possible quality characteristics of a unit that causes customer dissatisfaction.

Defect location check sheet—A defect location check sheet is used to gather attribute data about one or more CTQs or Xs that are difficult to quantify. Usually, defect location check sheets include a picture of a product or service that allows a respondent to circle the part of the product or service that is causing trouble.

Defect opportunity—A defect opportunity is each circumstance in which a CTQ can fail to be met. There may be many opportunities for defects within a defined unit.

Defective—A defective unit is a unit that does not meet specification limits. It is a nonconforming unit.

Defects per million opportunities (DPMO)—DPMO equals DPO multiplied by 1 million.

Defects per opportunity (DPO)—Defects per opportunity refers to the number of defects divided by the number of defect opportunities.

Defects per unit (DPU)—Defects per unit refers to the average of all the defects for a given number of units, that is, the total number of defects for *n* units divided by *n,* the number of units.

Define phase—The define phase involves preparing a business charter (rationale for the project), understanding the relationships between Suppliers-Inputs-System-Outputs-Customers (called *SIPOC analysis*), and analyzing Voice of the Customer data to identify the CTQs characteristics important to customers and to developing a project objective.

Degrees of freedom—Degrees of Freedom are the number of data points that are free to vary once the statistic is known in a set of data.

Dependent variable—A dependent variable is the *Y,* or response variable, in a designed experiment.

Descriptive statistics—Descriptive Statistics focus on the collection, analysis, presentation, and description of a set of data.

Design of experiments (DOE)—Design of experiments is a collection of statistical methods for studying the relationships between independent variables or factors, the *X*s (also called *input variables* or *process variables*), and their interactions on a dependent variable, the CTQ, or *Y* (also called the *outcome variable* or *response variable*).

Detection scale—The detection scale shows the ability to detect the failure of a critical parameter of a product, service, or process.

Diffusion—Diffusion is the act of spreading an idea or change throughout an organization.

DMAIC Model—The DMAIC model has five phases: Define, Measure, Analyze, Improve, and Control. It is the model utilized in Six Sigma management to move from the existing system to the revised system. It is an alternative to the SDSA and PDSA models.

Dot plot—A dot plot is a graph of measurement data in which dots that represent data values are stacked vertically on the horizontal axis for each value of the variable of interest.

Early adopters—Early adopters are the individuals in an organization who are the embodiment of the successful, discrete use of ideas. They are the key to spreading process improvements.

Early majority—Early majority are the individuals in an organization who deliberate for some time before adopting new ideas and interact frequently with their peers. They are not opinion leaders.

Emperor Nova—Emperor Nova is the twenty-second emperor of Lilliputia.

Employee growth and development key objectives—Employee growth and development key objectives are the class of organizational objectives that focus on the needs of employees. They include improving leadership skills, providing training opportunities, providing educational opportunities, and creating the opportunity to work on stimulating special assignments.

Enumerative studies—Enumerative Studies are statistical investigations that have the purpose of drawing conclusions about a population.

Event—An event is the most basic unit for analysis in a statistical study.

Executive Committee—The members of the Executive Committee are the top management of an organization.

Expected value—The expected value is the mean (μ) of a probability distribution.

Experimental run—An experimental run is a test of a process with preset values of the *X*s.

F distribution—The F distribution is the probability distribution used for testing the ratio of two variances.

Factorial designs—A factorial design is an experimental design in which more than one factor (*X*) is examined simultaneously to determine the effect on a CTQ.

Failure modes and effects analysis (FMEA)—A tool used to identify, estimate, prioritize, and reduce the risk of failure in CTQs through the development of actions (process changes) and contingency plans based on Xs.

Feedback loop—A feedback loop is a key indicator that relates information about outputs from any stage or stages back to another stage or stages to make an analysis of the process.

Financial key objectives—Financial key objectives are the organizational objectives that focus on the financial health of an organization. They include management and stockholder's desire for more profit, market share, dominance, and growth, and the desire for less waste, turnover, financial loss, and customer defection.

Five-number summary—A five-number summary is a set of statistics that consists of the *smallest value, Q_1*, median, Q_3, and the largest value.

Flag diagram—A flag diagram is a tool used to track the contributions of subordinate key objectives to the pursuit of a superior key objective.

Flowchart—A flowchart is a pictorial representation of the decisions, steps and their interrelationships in a process.

Focus points—Focus points are the underlying themes for one or more circumstantial data points. Team members determine the focus point for each key circumstantial data point or group of key circumstantial data points using an affinity diagram. Focus points are the initial statements of the CTQs.

Fractional factorial designs—A fractional factorial design is an experimental design that is most often used when the number of Xs to be studied is large or when there is a moderate level of knowledge about the interactions between the key Xs needed to optimize the CTQ. Fractional factorial designs are used to decrease the number of trials, hence the cost, of an experiment by taking advantage of knowledge about interactions. They are a design in which only a subset of all possible treatment combinations is used.

Full factorial designs—A full factorial design is an experimental design used when researchers want to understand all of the interactions between the high-risk Xs necessary to optimizing the CTQ or when there are only a few Xs to be studied in the experiment.

Frame—A frame is the aggregate listing of all units, items, or people in a population using an enumerative statistical study.

Gage Repeatability and Reproducibility (R&R) study—A Gage R&R study is used to estimate the proportion of observed total variation due to unit-to-unit variation and R&R variation. R&R variation includes repeatability, reproducibility, and operator-part interaction (different people measure different units in different ways).

Gantt chart—A Gantt chart is a simple scheduling matrix that plots tasks and subtasks against time. It indicates which tasks are on or behind schedule.

Gantt chart key indicators—Gantt chart indicators are used when a key indicator is a record-keeping device for following the progression in time of the tasks required to complete a project.

Goalpost view of quality—An individual unit of product or service is considered to possess good quality if it is at or inside the upper and lower specification limits.

Goal statement—The goal statement describes the team's improvement objective. It begins with a verb, such as reduce, eliminate, control, or increase.

Graphic—A graphic is a visual representation of data.

Green Belt—A Green Belt is an individual who works on projects part time (25%), either as a team member for complex projects or as a project leader for simpler projects.

Green Belt certification—A Green Belt is an individual who understands statistical methods and is a member of one or more Six Sigma process improvement teams. She or he is not sufficiently trained to lead a complex Six Sigma process improvement team but is trained to lead a simple Six Sigma project. A Green Belt has passed the Green Belt and Champion examinations and has successfully led a Six Sigma Project.

Half-normal plot—A half-normal plot is a type of normal probability plot in which the estimated effects in rank order are plotted on normal probability paper.

Hard benefits—Hard (financial) benefits include but are not limited to increasing revenues or decreasing costs that affect the bottom-line of an organization.

Heavy users—Heavy users are consumers who purchase relatively large quantities of a product, service, or process.

Histogram—A histogram is a special bar chart for measurement data in which the X-axis shows adjacent numerical categories and the Y-axis shows the frequency or percentage of data values in each category.

Hypothesis—A hypothesis states a premise about a CTQ (for example, the mean value of CTQ > 25 units) or about a relationship between variables (for example, $CTQ = b_0 - b_1 X_1 + b_2 X_2$). $CTQ = b_0 - b_1 X_1 + b_2 X_2$ is a hypothetical statement of: "If I increase X_1, then CTQ will decrease, and if I increase X_2, then CTQ will increase," assuming there is no interaction between X_1 and X_2.

Hypothesis testing—Hypothesis testing consists of methods used to make inferences about the hypothesized values of population parameters using sample statistics.

Improve phase—The Improve phase of the DMAIC model involves designing experiments to understand the relationships between the CTQs and the Xs, determining the levels of the critical Xs that optimize the CTQs, developing action plans to formalize the level of the Xs that optimize the CTQs, and conducting a pilot test of the revised system.

Increase project or task—An increase project or task is a project or task in which the ideal value of the key indicator is X units or Y percentage points higher than the current value of the key indicator.

Independent events—Independent events are events in which the occurrence of one event in no way affects the probability of the second event.

Independent variables—Independent variables are the Xs, or factors, in a designed experiment that may or may not affect a CTQ.

Indifferent Kano category (I)—An indifferent Kano cognitive image is one in which a user does not care about the feature.

Inferential statistics—Inferential statistics are statistics that focus on making decisions about a large set of data, called the frame, from a subset of the set of data, called the sample.

Intangible costs—Intangible costs are costs that are difficult to measure.

Interaction effects—Interaction effects are the effects on a CTQ caused by one X variable depending on the level(s) or value(s) of other X variables.

Interaction plot—An interaction plot is used to identify interaction effects among a set of Xs on a CTQ. All combinations of levels of X variables are studied to produce an interaction plot.

Innovators—Innovators are the first people in an organization to utilize a new idea.

International Standards Organization (ISO)—The world's largest developer of technical standards. Its principal activity is the development of technical standards.

ISO 9000 and ISO 14000—The ISO 9000 and ISO 14000 families of standards are among ISO's most widely known and successful standards. ISO 9000 has become an international reference for quality requirements in business-to-business dealings, and ISO 14000 appears set to achieve at least as much, if not more, in helping organizations to meet their environmental challenges.

J-shaped Kano cost distribution—The J-shaped Kano cost distribution shows that 10% of a market segment will pay at least a 10% cost increase to obtain the product feature described by the cognitive image under study. Cognitive images exhibiting the J-shaped cost distribution can be used to improve existing products, services, or processes.

Kano questionnaire—A Kano questionnaire is a survey instrument used by team members to classify a CTQ into an appropriate Kano quality category.

Key indicators—A key indicator is a measurement that monitors the status of a key objective.

Key objectives—Key objectives are the "critical few" goals that an individual needs to focus on in performing his/her job.

Laggards—Laggards are the last people in an organization to adopt a new idea. They are suspicious of change, and their reference point is in the past.

Late majority—Late majority are the people in an organization that require peer pressure to adopt a new idea. They have limited economic resources that require the removal of uncertainty surrounding an innovation.

Lead users—Lead users are the consumers of a product, service, or process who are months or years ahead of regular users in their use of the item and will benefit greatly by an improvement or innovation of the item.

Lead and heavy user characteristics by market segment matrix—A lead and heavy user characteristics matrix aids management in identifying the characteristics of lead and heavy users, the market segments for regular users, and the names and addresses of lead and heavy users in each feasible cell of the matrix.

Level of significance—The level of significance for a hypothesis test is the probability of committing a Type I error.

Levene test—The Levene test is a hypothesis test for the difference between variances.

Likelihood of occurrence scale—The likelihood of occurrence scale shows the frequency of failure of a critical parameter of a product, service, or process.

Lilliputia—Lilliputia is one of the countries portrayed in *Gulliver's Travels* by Jonathan Swift and a member of the Small Countries Treaty Organization.

Lilliputian Freedom Fighters (LFF)—The LFF is a violent and hostile faction that is known and feared for its takeovers of cities, as well as its radical social and political doctrine in Lilliputia.

Lilliputian National Army (LNA)—The LNA is the royal army of Lilliputia.

Lilliputian National Dashboard Office—Lilliputian National Dashboard Office maintains the dashboard of Lilliputia.

Linearity—Linearity is the difference (bias) between the part reference value and the part average over the different values of the domain of a gage.

Line chart—A line is a chart graph of a CTQ or X plotted on the vertical axis and time plotted on the horizontal axis.

List Key Indicators—A list indicator is a key indicator that monitors a list of people or items for compliance to some deadline or standard.

Local Steering team—A local steering team is a team that coordinates the multiple Six

Sigma projects or tasks in an area of an organization.

Lower specification limit (LSL)—The lower specification limit is the smallest acceptable value for a CTQ or *X*.

Lurking variable—See *noise variable.*

Marketing mix—A marketing mix is a unique combination of a version of the product or service; a pricing structure; a promotional strategy; and a place or distribution strategy.

Market segmentation—Market segmentation is the division of a market into homogeneous subsets of customers where any subset may conceivably be selected as a target market to be reached with a distinct marketing mix.

Master Black Belt—A Master Black Belt is a Six Sigma professional who takes on a leadership role of keeper of the Six Sigma process and advisor to executives or business unit managers, and mentor to projects led by Black Belts and Green Belts. A Master Black Belt is an individual who has successfully supervised two or more Black Belts while leading at least two Six Sigma projects that led to dramatic revenue enhancements or cost reductions in their organizations.

Mean squares—A Mean Square is a variance in an analysis of variance table.

Measure phase—The Measure phase of the DMAIC model involves developing operational definitions for each CTQ, performing studies to determine the validity of the measurement procedure for each CTQ, and establishing baseline capabilities for each CTQ.

Measurement check sheet—A measurement check sheet is a tool used to gather measurement data about a product, service, or process, such as cycle time, temperature, size, length, weight, and diameter.

Measurement data—Measurement data is continuous data representing a characteristic of a product, process, or service. Results from a measurement taken on an item or person of interest.

Measurement key indicators—A measurement key indicator is a key indicator using measurement type data over time.

Measurement system analysis checklist—A measurement system analysis checklist involves determining whether the following tasks have been completed: (1) description of the ideal measurement system (flowchart the process); (2) description of the actual measurement system (flowchart the process); (3) identification of the causes of the differences between the ideal and actual measurement systems; and (4) identification of the accuracy (bias) and precision (repeatability) of the measurement system using a test-retest study.

Median—The median is the middle value in a set of data that has been ordered from the lowest to the highest value.

Metallic securing devices (MSDs)—MSDs are paper clips.

Mission statement—A mission statement presents the reason for an organization to exist.

Mistake proofing—Mistake proofing is a technique used to create "robustness" for the optimized settings of the *X*s; that is, the optimized settings of the *X*s are not susceptible to human error.

Mode—The mode is the value in a set of data that appears most frequently.

Multiple comparisons—A multiple comparison is a procedure used to determine which of the means are statistically significantly different from each other.

Multivari chart—A multivari chart is a tool that shows the effect of nuisance variables on a CTQ.

Must-be Kano category (M)—A must-be Kano cognitive image is one in which user satisfaction is not proportional to the performance of the feature; the lower the performance, the lower the user satisfaction, but high performance creates feelings of indifference to the feature.

Mutually exclusive events—Mutually exclusive events are events that *cannot* occur at the same time.

Natural limits—Natural limits are computed for stable processes by adding and subtracting three times the process's standard deviation to the process center line.

Noise variable—A noise variable (also called a lurking variable) is a factor (X) that is not included in an experiment and can affect the center, spread, and shape of a CTQ.

Nominal value—The nominal value for a quality characteristic (CTQ or X) is its target or desired value.

Nonadditive flag system—A nonadditive flag system is used to track corporate indicators that are not the summation of departmental indicators; for example, the corporate indicator (Y) is not a linear combination of the departmental indicators ($Y = f[X_{11}, X_{12}, X_{21}, X_{22}, X_{31}, X_{32}, X_{41}, X_{42}]$).

Nonprobability sample—A nonprobability sample is a nonrandom sample in which the items or individuals included are chosen without the benefit of a frame; hence, the individual units have an unknown probability of selection into the sample.

Normal distribution—The normal distribution is one possible shape for the output of a process. It is defined by its mean (μ) and standard deviation (σ) and is bell-shaped.

Normal probability plot—A normal probability plot is a graphical device used to evaluate whether a set of data follows a normal distribution.

Null hypothesis—The null hypothesisis is a statement about a parameter being equal to a specific value or a statement that there is no difference between the parameters for two or more populations.

One-factor-at-a-time experiments—Experiments in which the researcher simply changes one X at a time to determine its effect on Y while maintaining the other Xs at some specified fixed level.

One-way Kano category (O)—A cognitive image in which user satisfaction is proportional to the performance of the feature; the lower the performance, the lower the user satisfaction, and the higher the performance, the higher the user satisfaction.

Operational Definition—An operational definition promotes understanding between people by putting communicable meaning into words. An operational definition contains three parts: a criterion to be applied to an object or group, a test of the object or group, and a decision as to whether the object or group met the criterion.

Ordered array—An ordered array in a data set lists the values from smallest to largest.

Outliers—Outliers are extreme values in a data set.

_p_-value—A p-value is the probability of obtaining a test statistic equal to or more extreme than the result obtained from the sample data, given that the null hypothesis H_0 is true.

Paper Organizers International (POI)—POI is a company that offers a full range of filing, organizing, and paper-shuffling services.

Pareto diagram—A Pareto diagram is a special type of bar chart in which the categories of responses are listed on the X axis, the frequencies of responses (listed from largest to smallest frequency) are shown on the left side Y axis, and the cumulative percentage of responses are shown on the right side Y axis.

Part-to-part variation—Part-to-part variation is the variability created by the measurement of multiple parts under identical conditions (same operator, same lab).

PDSA model—The **PDSA** model is a method used by employees to improve and/or innovate a process by reducing the difference between customers' needs and process performance. It consists of four stages: Plan, Do, Study, and Act. Initially, a revised flowchart is developed to improve or innovate a standardized best practice method (plan). The revised flowchart (plan) is tested using an experiment on a small-scale or trial basis (do). The effects of the revised flowchart are studied using measurements from key indicators (study). Finally, if the study phase generated positive results, the revised flowchart is inserted into training manuals, and all relevant personnel are trained in the revised method (act). If the study phase generated negative results, the revised flowchart is abandoned, and a new plan is developed by employees. The PDSA cycle continues forever in an uphill progression of never-ending improvement.

Percent R&R—Percent R&R is the percentage of the process variation due to the repeatability and reproducibility of the measurement system.

Percent tolerance—Percent tolerance is the percentage of the part tolerance due to the repeatability and reproducibility of the measurement system.

Pilot Study—A pilot study is a small-scale test of a process. It can be in a limited number of locations for a trial period of time or in all locations for a limited period of time.

Poisson distribution—The Poisson distribution is a distribution to find the probability of the number of occurrences in an area of opportunity.

Power of a statistical test—The power of a statistical test is the conditional probability of rejecting the null hypothesis when it is false and should be rejected.

Prediction interval—A prediction interval is an interval estimate of the outcome of a future individual value.

Proactive intervention—A proactive intervention is a process change (X) that is planned and tested by an experimenter with the purpose of determining the effect of the process change on a CTQ. This kind of experiment does more than passively collect data from a functioning process; rather, it actively intervenes in the function of the process while collecting data to determine the impact of the interventions.

Probability—A probability is the numeric value representing the chance, likelihood, or possibility that a particular event will occur. Probabilities are between 0 and 1 inclusive.

Probability distribution for a discrete random variable—A probability distribution for a discrete random variable is a listing of all possible distinct outcomes and their likelihood of occuring.

Probability sample—A probability sample is a random sample in which the items or individuals are chosen from a frame; hence, the individual units in the frame have a known probability of selection.

Process—A process is a collection of interacting components that transform inputs into outputs toward a common aim, called a *mission statement.*

Process improvement key objectives—Process improvement key objectives include: (1) consistency and uniformity of output; (2) high productivity; (3) products, services, and processes that exceed the needs and wants of current and future stakeholders; (4) products, services, and processes that are easy to create and of low cost to provide; (5) products and services that meet technical specifications; (6) products and services that do not incur warranty costs; and (7) products that are easy to distribute throughout the channels of distribution.

Process Owner—A Process Owner is the manager of a process and has the authority to change the process.

Process sigma—Process sigma is a measure of the process performance determined by using DPMO and a stable normal distribution. Process sigma is a metric that allows for process performance comparisons across processes, assuming all comparisons are made from stable processes whose output follows the normal distribution.

Product-related data—Product-related data identifies the current expectations and perceptions of lead users and heavy users. Product-related data is useful for improving existing products, services, or processes.

Project objective—A project objective contains five key elements: (1) process, (2) CTQ measure, (3) CTQ target, (4) CTQ direction, and (5) a deadline. A project objective is SMART (Specific, Measurable, Attainable, Relevant, Time Bound). The Champion, team leader (Green or Black Belt), Process Owner, and team members develop the draft project objective.

Project—A project is a process improvement activity in which the necessary process change is unknown by the Process Owner. Generally, the Process Owner and Champion forms a Six Sigma project team to identify and test the necessary process change.

Project prioritization—A project prioritization matrix is a tool to rank order Six Sigma projects for attention by management in an organization.

Project scope—The project scope identifies the boundaries of a Six Sigma project.

Quality project tracking (QPT) system—A quality project tracking system is used by a Master Black Belt to spread improvements and innovations throughout an organization.

Quartiles—A quartile is a descriptive measure that splits the ordered data into four quarters.

Questionable Kano category (Q)—A questionable Kano cognitive image is one in which a user's response does not make sense.

Randomization—Randomization allows for the control and measurement of variation resulting from factors not considered in the experiment, called lurking variables.

Range—The range is the difference between the largest and smallest observations in a set of data.

Region of rejection—The region of rejection consists of the values of the test statistic that are unlikely to occur if the null hypothesis is true.

Repeatability—Repeatability (or precision) is the variability created by multiple measurements of the same unit under identical conditions (same operator, same lab). This is called *within-group variation* or *common variation.*

Replicate—A replicate is the sample size for a given combination of the factors (Xs) in an experiment on a CTQ.

Reproducibility—Reproducibility is the variability created by multiple conditions, such as multiple operators or labs.

Resolution—Resolution (discrimination or number of distinct categories) is the fineness of the measurement system (meters, centimeters, millimeters, etc.).

Resolution III designs—A Resolution III design is an experiment in which main effects are confounded with two-way interactions (such as A being confounded with BC).

Resolution IV designs—A Resolution IV design is an experiment in which a two-way interaction is confounded with another two-way interaction, or a main effect is confounded with a three-way interaction.

Resolution V designs—A Resolution V design is an experiment in which main effects are confounded with four-way interactions and two-factor interactions are confounded with three-way interactions.

Response surface methodology designs—Response surface methodology designs are experimental designs used to determine the settings of the Xs that will optimize the CTQs. Usually, a response surface design is used following the use of factorial design because there is will now be a higher level of knowledge about the key Xs, and their interactions, needed to optimize the CTQ.

Reverse Kano category (R)—A reverse Kano cognitive image is one in which a user offers responses opposite the responses expected by individuals conducting the Kano survey.

Risk elements—A risk element is a potential failure mode of an X or CTQ in a process, product, or service.

Risk management—Risk management is used to identify the risk elements of the proposed settings of the Xs.

Robust test—A robust test is a test that is not sensitive to departures from the assumptions.

Rolled throughput yield (RTY)—Rolled throughput yield is the product of the yields from each step in a process, if all the steps are independent of each other. It is the probability of a unit passing through all k steps of a process and incurring no defects.

RPN (risk priority number)—The RPN shows the relative risk of failure of a critical parameter of a product, service, or process.

Run—A run is a consecutive series of similar items that are preceded or followed by items of a different type.

Run chart—A run chart is a type of line chart in which all of the measurements at a particular time for a CTQ or X are plotted on the Y axis at that time period and time is plotted on the X axis.

Sample—A sample is a portion of the frame under investigation and is selected so that

information can be drawn from it about the frame.

Sampling distribution—A sampling distribution is the distribution of a sample statistic (such as the arithmetic mean) for all possible samples of a given size n.

Sampling error—Sampling error is the variation of the sample statistic from sample to sample.

Schedule—A Gantt chart is used to construct a schedule for the project and list out any milestones.

Screening designs—A screening design is an experimental design that provides information about which individual Xs impact a CTQ for a low number of experimental runs (low cost) at the expense of understanding the impact of the interactions between the Xs (for example, X_2X_3) on the CTQ (high cost).

SDSA Model—The SDSA (Standardize-Do-Study-Act) model is a method that helps employees standardize a process. It includes four steps: (1) Standardize: Employees study the process and develop best practice methods with key indicators of process performance. (2) Do: Employees conduct planned experiments using the best practice methods on a trial basis. (3) Study: Employees collect and analyze data on the key indicators to determine the effectiveness of the best practice methods. (4) Act: Managers establish standardized best practice methods and formalize them through training.

Senior Executive—The Senior Executive provides the impetus, the direction, and the alignment necessary for Six Sigma's ultimate success in an organization.

Severity scale—The severity scale shows the impact of failure of a critical parameter of a product, service, or process.

Shape—The shape of a distribution of data indicates how the data is distributed between its lowest value and its highest value.

Simple random sample—A simple random sample is a probability sample in which every sample of a fixed size (*n*) has the same chance of selection as every other sample of that size.

SIPOC analysis—SIPOC analysis is a simple tool for identifying the **S**uppliers and their **I**nputs into a **P**rocess, the high-level steps of a process, the **O**utputs of the process, and the **C**ustomer segments interested in the outputs.

Six Sigma database—The Six Sigma database is a vehicle to spread the newly discovered improvements and/or innovations from Six Sigma projects throughout the entire organization.

Six Sigma management(nontechnical definition)—Six Sigma management is the relentless and rigorous pursuit of the reduction of variation in all critical processes to achieve continuous and breakthrough improvements that impact the bottom and/or top line of the organization and increase customer satisfaction.

Six Sigma management (technical definition)—Six Sigma management creates processes that are twice as good as the customer demands so that if the process mean shifts by 1.5 standard deviations it will not generate more than 3.4 defects per million opportunities.

Skewness—Skewness is a statistic that measures the symmetry of a distribution.

Soft benefits—Soft benefits of a Six Sigma project include but are not limited to improving quality and morale, and decreasing cycle time.

Special variation—Special variation is the variation in a process due to external forces.

Stability—Stability (or drift) is a change in the accuracy (bias), repeatability (precision), or reproducibility of a measurement system when measuring the same part for a single characteristic over time. Addition-

ally, stability defines a process exhibiting only common causes of variation

Standard deviation—The standard deviation is a measure of variation around the arithmetic mean.

Standard order—The standard order for the trials in an experiment is a listing of the trials such that the first factor alternates between – and +, the second factor alternates between –,– and +,+, the third factor alternates between –,–,–,– and +,+,+,+, and so on.

Standard Unit—A standard unit is the reference value required to determine if the bias exists in a measurement system. Bias = (Reference value – mean value). Without a standard unit it is impossible to determine the accuracy of the measurement system.

Statistics—Statistics is the study of data to provide a basis for action on a population or process.

Stick-with-a-winner experiments—A stick-with-a-winner experiment is an experiment in which the researcher introduces and deletes factors one at a time in an attempt to optimize the center, spread, and shape of a CTQ. However, if a factor improves the CTQ, it is left in the experiment.

Stratification—Stratification is a procedure used to describe the systematic subdivision of a data set. It can be used to break down a problem to discover its root causes and set into motion appropriate corrective actions. Stratification is important to the proper functioning of the DMAIC model.

Stratified sample—A stratified sample is a probability sample in which the *N* items in the frame are divided into subpopulations, or strata, according to some common characteristic.

Strategic objectives—Strategic objectives are the goals that must be accomplished to pursue the presidential strategy of an organization. Its purpose is to use decreased within strata variation to reduce the sample size.

Sum of squares due to factor *A* or X_A (SSA)—Sum of squares due to factor *A* is the sum of squares of the deviations of the mean levels of factor *A* with the grand mean of the CTQ.

Sum of squares due to factor B or X_B (SSB)—Sum of squares due to factor *B* is the sum of squares of the deviations of the mean levels of factor *B* with the grand mean of the CTQ.

Sum of squares due to the interaction effect of *A* and *B* (SSAB)—Sum of squares due to the interaction effect of *A* and *B* is the effect of the joint combination of factor *A* and factor *B* on the CTQ.

Sum of squares error (SSE)—Sum of squares due to error is the sum of squares of deviations of the individual observations of the CTQ within each cell (i.e., each specific combination of one level of X_A and one level of X_B) with the corresponding cell mean.

Sum of squares total (SST)—Sum of squares total is the total squared deviation of all the observations around the grand mean of the CTQ.

Symmetry—Symmetry is a characteristic of a distribution in which each half of a distribution is a mirror image of the other half of the distribution.

Systematic sample—A systematic sample is a probability sample in which the *N* individuals or items in the frame are placed into *k* groups by dividing the size of the frame *N* by the desired sample size *n*.

***t* distribution**—The *t*-distribution is the sampling distribution of the sample mean when the population standard deviation is unknown.

Taguchi Loss Function—The Taguchi loss function that explains the relationship between cost and variation (deviation from nominal) within the specification limits for a characteristic of a product, service, or process.

Tampering—Tampering is the act of treating a common cause of variation as a special cause of variation.

Tangible costs—Tangible costs are easily identified costs, for example, the costs of rejects, warranty, inspection, scrap, and rework.

Task—A task is a process improvement activity in which the necessary process change is known by the Process Owner but he or she has not yet had an opportunity to effectuate the process change.

Test statistic—A test statistic is the statistic used to determine whether to reject the null hypothesis in a hypothesis test.

Tolerance—Tolerance is the allowable departure from a nominal value used to compute specification-limits.

Tollgate—A tollgate is a management review by a Process Owner and a Champion at the end of each phase of the DMAIC model.

Triangular Kano cost distribution—The triangular Kano cost distribution shows that 60% of a market segment will pay at least a 10% cost increase to obtain the feature described by the cognitive image under study. Cognitive images exhibiting the triangular cost distribution can be used to develop major new features of existing products, services, or processes.

Type I error—A Type I error occurs if the null hypothesis H_0 is rejected when in fact it is true and should not be rejected. The probability of a Type I error occurring is α.

Type II error—A Type II error occurs if the null hypothesis H_1 is not rejected when in fact it is false and should be rejected. The probability of a Type II error occurring is β.

Uncontrollable nuisance variable—An uncontrollable nuisance variable is a factor (X) that can be measured but not controlled in an experiment.

Uniform Kano cost distribution—A uniform Kano cost distribution shows that 80% of a market segment will pay at least a 10% cost increase to obtain the feature described by the cognitive image under study. Cognitive images exhibiting the uniform cost distribution can be used to develop ideas for completely new products, services, or processes.

Unit—A unit is the item (e.g., product or component, service or service step, or time period) to be studied with a Six Sigma project.

Upper specification limit (USL)—The upper specification limit is the largest acceptable value for the CTQ or X.

Value-added/non–value-added (VA/NVA) flowchart—A tool used to identify non–value-added steps in a process for possible elimination or modification, thereby reducing the complexity of a process.

Variable—A variable is a characteristic of interest that differs from item to item or person to person.

Variables check sheet—A variables check sheet is a data collection form used to collect baseline data about a CTQ or an X that consists of measurement data.

Variables process capability—A variables process capability study determines a process's ability to meet specifications that is measured using measurement type data.

Variation—Variation is the amount of dispersion, or spread, in a data set.

Vision—A vision is the desired future state of an organization. It is the reason an organization exists. Sometimes it is the stimulus that provokes top management to begin Six Sigma management.

Voice of the Customer (VoC)—The Voice of the Customer is the domain of a characteristic of a product, service, or process that is included within the lower specification limit and upper specification limit.

Voice of the Process (VoP)—The Voice of the Process is the distribution of measurements of the outputs from a process over time.

Yellow Belt—A Yellow Belt is an individual who is aware of the theory and practice of Six Sigma and can provide support to team members (for example, data collection), but is not sufficiently trained in statistical methods to perform the duties of a Six Sigma team member. A Yellow Belt has passed the Green Belt certification examination but has not yet completed a Six Sigma project.

Yield—Yield is the proportion of units within a specification divided by the total number of units.

Zero project or task—A zero project or task is a project or task in which the ideal value of a key indicator is zero or the optimal difference between the current value and the ideal value of a key indicator is zero.

INDEX

Leading Six Sigma

In *Leading Six Sigma*, two of the world's most experienced Six Sigma leaders offer a detailed, step-by-step strategy for leading Six Sigma initiatives in your company. Six Sigma consultant Dr. Ronald D. Snee and GE quality leader Dr. Roger W. Hoerl show how to deploy a Six Sigma plan that reflects your organization's unique needs and culture, while also leveraging key lessons learned by the world's most successful implementers. Snee and Hoerl share leadership techniques proven in companies both large and small, and in business functions ranging from R&D and manufacturing to finance. They also present a start-to-finish sample deployment plan encompassing strategy, goals, metrics, training, roles and responsibilities, reporting, rewards, and management review. Whether you're a CEO, line-of-business leader, or a project leader, *Leading Six Sigma* gives you the one thing other books on Six Sigma lack: a clear view from the top.

Coping with Toxic Managers, Subordinates... And Other Difficult People

Many managers engage in destructive behavior that does considerable harm to their subordinates, their organization, and eventually themselves. Whether they are narcissistic, unethical, rigid, or aggressive, working with them can be a nightmare. In *Coping with Toxic Managers,* psychiatrist and organizational consultant Dr. Roy H. Lubit shows you how to develop your emotional intelligence and protect yourself and your organization from the destructive impact of toxic managers. Drawing on his extensive experience as both a mental health professional and organizational consultant to Fortune 500 firms and large law firms, Dr. Lubit offers concrete advice as well as a way to better understand with whom you are dealing.